ROMANS 9–11

An Exegetical, Expositional, and Applicational Commentary

Steven P. Sullivan

STONE TOWER PRESS

ROMANS 9–11:
An Exegetical, Expositional, and Applicational Commentary

Stone Tower Press
7 Ellen Rd.
Middletown, RI 02842

ISBN: 979-8-9919831-2-9

Cover design by Amy Landheer, JPL Design Solutions

Cover image: *Apostle Paul* (1633?) by Rembrandt. Kunsthistorisches Museum, Vienna, Public domain

Printed in the United States of America

TABLE OF CONTENTS

PREFACE

The genesis of my interest in the book of Romans began in my college years where my father in the Faith, Russ McKnight, taught a Saturday morning Bible Study on the book of Romans in the Student Union of the University of Oklahoma. My interest continued as I obtained my Th.M. and D.Min. from Dallas Theological Seminary and had the privilege to have classes and listening to lectures under the teaching of Dr. S. Lewis Johnson, Jr. Besides preaching and teaching Bible studies and college classes on the book of Romans as a Pastor and Professor at the College of Biblical Studies–Houston, I had the privilege to study and write my Ph.D. thesis on the Isaianic New Exodus in Romans 9–11 at the University of Wales Trinity Saint David, in the United Kingdom. The content of this effort may be found in the 2nd edition of my book *The Isaianic New Exodus in Romans 9–11*.

I began working on this commentary when I was asked by the general editor Dr. Wayne House in July 2015 to write an exegetical commentary on Romans 9–16 for the Evangelical Exegetical Commentary series. I had completed chapters 9–12 when in 2022 Dr. House was replaced by another general editor and I was no longer under contract. Thus, having all this effort and writing already written and now nowhere to produced it, I thought it was worth the effort to seek to publish my thoughts in this commentary on Romans 9–11. This commentary is basically four commentaries in one. For every verse in Romans 9–11 there are four sections. These four sections deal with: (1) textual criticism on the Greek text of Romans, (2) exegetical comments on the Greek text with an explanation of the meaning of the verse, (3) a biblical theology explanation which gives a bigger picture of the verse in the section, and (4) a practical comment on the text. Therefore, there is food for thought for everyone no matter what level of study one may want.

I want to thank everyone who has encouraged, prayed, and helped me in this endeavor. I want to thank Dr. Jobe Martin and his wife, Jenna Dee, as well as their two daughters, Dr. Taryn Martin and Dr. Mirren Martin. As a family they all serve the Lord as a team in their Biblical Discipleship Ministries. I want to thank my life-long friend and colleague Dr. J. Randall Price of the World of the Bible Ministries and scholar in Judaic studies and archaeology, especially his digs and studies at Qumran. I am grateful for the encouragement and commitment of my friend Dr. Tim Demy, Professor at the Naval War College and owner and publisher of Stone Tower Press. I am also grateful for all my fellow colleagues at the College of Biblical Studies–Houston where God had me teach and minister for 30 years.

Finally, I want to thank God for the support and love of my parents Paul and Helen Sullivan (both home with the Lord). I am also grateful for my two grown sons, Samuel and Andrew and their families. I am especially grateful for the faithful, spiritual and loving support of my wife Vicki, who has faithfully supported me since our marriage in 1975. Most importantly, all praise, glory and honor go to the Lord Jesus who guided my studies and gave grace and perseverance to write this commentary. Soli Deo Gloria!

Steven P. Sullivan
Oklahoma City, Oklahoma
Summer 2024

ABBREVIATIONS

Gen	Genesis	Nah	Nahum
Ex	Exodus	Hab	Habakkuk
Lev	Leviticus	Zeph	Zephaniah
Num	Numbers	Hag	Haggai
Deut	Deuteronomy	Zech	Zechariah
Josh	Joshua	Mal	Malachi
Jud	Judges	Mt	Matthew
Ruth	Ruth	Mk	Mark
1 Sam	1 Samuel	Lk	Luke
2 Sam	2 Samuel	Jn	John
1 Kgs	1 Kings	Act	Acts
2 Kgs	2 Kings	Rom	Romans
1 Chron	1 Chronicles	1 Cor	1 Corinthians
2 Chron	2 Chronicles	2 Cor	2 Corinthians
Ez	Ezra	Gal	Galatians
Neh	Nehemiah	Eph	Ephesians
Esth	Esther	Phil	Philippians
Job	Job	Col	Colossians
Ps	Psalms	1 Th	1 Thessalonians
Prov	Proverbs	2 Th	2 Thessalonians
Eccl	Ecclesiastes	1 Tim	1 Timothy
Song Sol	Song of Solomon	2 Tim	2 Timothy
Isa	Isaiah	Tit	Titus
Jer	Jeremiah	Philem	Philemon
Lam	Lamentations	Heb	Hebrews
Ezk	Ezekiel	Jas	James
Dan	Daniel	1 Pet	1 Peter
Hos	Hosea	2 Pet	2 Peter
Joel	Joel	1 Jn	1 John
Am	Amos	2 Jn	2 John
Obad	Obadiah	3 Jn	3 John
Jon	Jonah	Jud	Jude
Mic	Micah	Rev	Revelation

B.C.E.	Before the Common Era
bis	twice
CD	Cairo Genizah copy of the *Damascus Document*
C.E.	Common Era
cf.	*confer*, compare

chp(s)	chapter(s)
contra	against
DBAG	William Arndt, Frederick W. Danker, and Walter Bauer, *A Greek-English Lexicon of the New Testament and Other Early Christian Literature* (Chicago: University of Chicago Press, 2000)
DCH	*Dictionary of Classic Hebrew*, David J. A. Clines, ed., 8 vols.
diss.	dissertation
ed(s).	editor(s), edited by, edition
EDBT	*Evangelical Dictionary of Biblical Theology*
EDNT	*Evangelical Dictionary of the New Testament*
e.g.	*exempli gratia*, for example
Eng	English
esp.	especially
ESV	English Standard Version
et. al.	*et alii*, and others
exp.	Expanded
f(f)	and the following one(s)
Gk	Greek
GEL	*Greek English Lexicon (Liddle & Scott)*
HALOT	*The Hebrew & Aramaic Lexicon of the Old Testament*
HCSB	Holman Christian Standard Bible
Ibid.	*ibidem*, in the same place
i.e.	*id est*, that is
INE	Isaianic New Exodus
JBL	*Journal of Biblical Literature*
JSNT	*Journal for the Study of the New Testament*
JSOT	*Journal for the Study of the Old Testament*
KJV	King James Version
LEB	Lexham English Bible
loc.	locative
LXX	Septuagint
MSS	manuscripts
MT	Masoretic Text
NA^{28}	Nestle-Aland, 28th ed. Greek New Testament
NASB	New American Standard Bible
n.d.	no date
NE	New Exodus
NET	New English Translation
NETS	New English Translation of the Septuagint
NIDNTTE	*New International Dictionary of New Testament Theology and Exegesis*
NIV	New International Version
NIVAC	New International Version Applicational Commentary
Note or n.	footnote
NKJV	New King James Version
NRSV	New Revised Standard Version
NT	New Testament

NT Gk Mss, Rom	*New Testament Greek Manuscripts Romans*
OG	Old Greek
OT	Old Testament
p(p).	page(s)
passim	here and there
Repr.	reprint
rev.	revised
SBLGNT	Society of Biblical Literature Greek New Testament
sic	*sic erat scriptum*, thus was it written
Sir	Sirach, Ecclestasticus
TDNT	*Theological Dictionary of the New Testament*
TLOT	*Theological Lexicon of the Old Testament*
trans.	translated by
UBS5	United Bible Society Greek New Testament 5th edition
v(v).	verse(s)
vol(s).	volume(s)

Symbols

𝔐 Majority Text (large majority represented)

Under Textual Criticism section for symbols and numbers see: *The Greek New Testament* 5th edition, pp.1–63; or Reuben Swanson, ed. *New Testament Greek Manuscripts, Romans* (Wheaton: Tyndale House Publishers, Inc., 2001), xvi–xxiii.

Introduction to Romans 9–11[1]

Peter Gorday summarizes the early Church fathers concerning the understanding of Romans 9–11. Origen recognized Romans 9–11 as the keystone and climax of the epistle. Chrysostom understood this section as a side argument of Romans 1–8. Augustine related this section not to Judaism but to a theological discussion of predestination and grace.[2] The influence of Chrysostom and Augustine on the understanding on Romans 9–11 lasted for centuries, even up to the nineteenth century.[3] The themes of predestination and grace do exist in Romans 9–11, but the question is whether these themes are the primary focus. Those who held to these past themes usually did not see a strong link between Romans 9–11 and Romans 1–8.

Ferdinand Baur seemed to be the first to challenge the traditional view that Romans 1–8 has no significant relationship with Romans 9–11.[4] In his day, Romans 9–11 was considered an appendix to Romans 1–8, where justification was the main topic. Baur considered Romans 9–11 "the gem and centre of the whole, from which the other parts sprang; and we should take our stand on these three chapters in order to enter into the Apostle's original conception, from which the whole organism of the Epistle was developed, as we have it especially in the first eight chapters."[5] Others followed Baur's understanding, connecting Romans 1–8 and 9–11 so that the latter section becomes the climax of the letter.[6] According to Karl Donfried, "there is today [1991] a wide-ranging agreement that these chapters [Rom 9–11] form an integral part of the main argument and that they are not simply a Pauline afterthought as has been argued."[7]

Krister Stendahl contends that all of Romans centers on the theme of Jews and Gentiles.[8] There is no doubt that Paul focuses his attention on Jewish and Gentile relationships in Romans 9–11; however, this argument is difficult to maintain as the central theme of the book. The topic of Jew and Gentile relationships in Romans 9–11 needs to be evaluated and placed into sharper focus. In these chapters, the discussion of Jews and Gentiles appear to be the secondary means by which God demonstrates his glory through his grace and mercy in salvation. Lung-Kwong Lo argues that Romans 1–8 provides a basis for building solidarity between Jewish and Gentile Christians. He also concludes that in Romans 9–11, the significance of the relationship between

---

[1] The majority of the information was taken from Sullivan, *The Isaianic New Exodus in Romans 9-11.*

[2] Peter Gorday, *Principles of Patristic Exegesis*, 231–35.

[3] Ibid., 243–45, note 1, 15–26. See also Sanday and Headlam, 269–75.

[4] See J. Christiaan Beker, *Paul the Apostle*, 59; Johnson, *The Function of Apocalyptic and Wisdom Traditions in Romans 9–11*, 112; Donfried, "Introduction 1977: The Romans Debate," xli.

[5] Baur, *Paul, the Apostle of Jesus Christ*, 315. Wright, "The Messiah and the People of God," 170 and Wright, *The Climax of the Covenant*, 234 agree that Rom 9–11 is the climax of the epistles. However, Wright, "Romans," 620 modifies this point by saying that Rom 9–11 is an important section but not the climax. Moo, 551 and Campbell, "Romans III as a Key," 255 agree with Wright's later position, though Campbell called Rom 9–11 a climax in his conclusion (p. 264).

[6] See Stendahl, *Paul among Jews and Gentiles*, 4, 85; Beker, *Paul the Apostle*, 87–93; Dahl, *Studies in Paul*, 138–58; Fitzmyer, *Romans*,76, 541; Dunn, "The Purpose of Romans," 248. Beker, "Romans 9–11," 44 agrees that Rom 9–11is a climax but he questions the cohesiveness of the section. Noack, "Current and Backwater," 156 also sees Rom 9–11 as central but goes to the other extreme by saying Rom 3–8 is more a "back water" (159) and "side–issue" (164).

[7] Donfried, "Introduction 1991," lxx. See also Munck, *Christ and Israel*, 33–34; Byrne, 282.

[8] Stendahl, *Paul among Jews and Gentiles*, 3–4. Dunn, 520 says the true theme of Rom 9–11 is God and Israel.

Jewish and Gentile Christian solidarity and the non-Christian Jew needs more explanation.[9] Lo's understanding fits well with Romans 14:1 –15:13,[10] but it appears to underplay the major theme of the gospel.

N. T. Wright's understanding of Romans 9–11 is the theological issue of God's covenant faithfulness that is worked out in the history of his people.[11] However, the inclusion of the Gentiles and the exclusion of the majority of the Israelites have created a problem. Thus, in this section of the letter, Paul decides to address Israel's unbelief, Gentile's salvation, and God's faithfulness. According to Wright, the Abrahamic promises are the hidden foundation or theology in these chapters by which Paul built his case, though the promises are not peripheral throughout the letter (Wright, 622). The certainty of God's faithfulness to his covenantal promises to Israel (and also to the Gentiles) illustrates the "root of the olive tree" (Rom 11:18). God's promises to the "fathers" (Rom 11:28) are stated by Paul as "gifts and the calling of God" and they are "irrevocable" (Rom 11:29). This is important, for while God's covenantal faithfulness has been mentioned in the scholarly discussion, the topic of the Abrahamic covenant has been a neglected dialogue in the "Romans debate" (Murray, 2:xiv–xv).[12]

Wright suggests that Paul retells Israel's story in Romans 9:6–10:21 to challenge the tension in Rome dealing with anti-Jewish sentiment (Wright, 623).[13] This is possible, but the anti-Jewish sentiment is difficult to confirm in the Roman church.[14] However, Paul did warn Gentile believers against the attitude of arrogance toward "the branches" (Rom 11:18). In addition, he seems to be addressing both Jews and Gentiles in this section.[15]

Douglas Moo argues that Paul has also a practical purpose in Romans 9–11: "[T]o unite the squabbling Roman Christians behind his vision of the gospel and its implication for the relationship of Jew and Gentiles" (Moo, 553). There is no specific indication of any squabbles in the context (except possibly Rom 11:18), but it is easy to understand how Paul could have anticipated problems, which he encountered in other places.[16] Looking at the letter as a whole, Paul may be addressing an undercurrent of misunderstandings as one examines Romans 3:1–8, which has some parallels with Romans 9–11.[17]

Righteousness is a major topic in Romans and some herald it as the theme or main topic of the book, which impacts the significance attributed to chapters 9–11.[18] However, there are

---

[9] Lo, "Paul's Purpose in Writing Romans," 488. In sum, Lo argues that Rom 9–11 is an important part of Paul's theology to persuade Jews and Gentile Christians to build up the church community (Rom 14–15).

[10] See Dahl, *Studies in Paul*, 139–41 who also brings out the epistolary framework and Moo, 553.

[11] Wright, *The Climax of the Covenant*, 236; Wright, "Romans," 622.

[12] See Wright, "The Messiah and the People of God," 76, 79–80 for a good discussion.

[13] See also Stanley, *Arguing with Scripture*, 137; Nanos, *The Mystery of Romans*, 64–68.

[14] Jervell, "The Letter to Jerusalem," 53–64 argues that Romans is a letter more for Paul's situation in Jerusalem. A more nuanced position is taken by Francis Watson who grants that Paul's letters may concern himself with Jerusalem but cannot exclude the situation at Rome as the primary location (*Paul, Judaism and the Gentiles*, 165).

[15] Moo, 552, note 17 indicates that most scholars identify Gentiles as part of the audience. *Contra* Räisänen, "Paul, God and Israel," 181 and Das, *Solving the Romans Debate*, *passim*.

[16] Of course, there are problems in the church, which are brought out in Romans 14–16. See Schreiner, 471. Also, see how this Jewish and Gentile issue is developed in Campbell, "Romans III as a Key," 260–62.

[17] See Johnson, "Romans 9–11," 218–19, who enumerates some pitfalls to avoid with this parallel.

[18] Käsemann, 253–56 and Käsemann, *New Testament Questions of Today,* 168–82. See Moo, 88–89 and Noack, "Current and Backwater," 158 for a critique of Käseman view of the righteousness of God. For others who view righteousness as the main theme, see Lenski, 583-84; Bornkamm, *Paul*, 149-51; Beasley-Murray, "The Righteousness of God," 437-50; Wright, "The Messiah and the People of God," 76; Bell, "The Origin and Purpose,"

different understandings of Paul's use of the term righteousness of God:[19] (1) Roman Catholics (from the Council of Trent) – claim that righteousness or justification may mean to be "declared righteous" but it must also include moral transformation.[20] (2) Käsemann says that God's eschatological righteousness in Jesus goes beyond the covenant people to all of creation and draws one into the sphere of power for service.[21] Therefore, Käsemann's understanding of righteousness seems to contain the "ideas of status given by God and exercised by God" (Moo, 27–30). (3) Historical Protestantism states that righteousness or justification is to be declared righteous (forensic) and to acquit the guilty of all sins.[22] (4) N. T. Wright defines the righteousness of God in Romans: "God is in the right, as the judge of all the earth, in his dealings with Israel, man and the world."[23] He agrees with Käsemann that righteousness is God's own and not merely reckoned to man. Wright sees righteousness more as an attribute than an activity.[24]

However, for Moo, the broader theme of the gospel better suits the epistle of Romans and Romans 9–11 in particular (Moo, 27–30).[25] Against the backdrop of the controversy between Judaism and the Church, Paul presented and defended the gospel.[26] The majority of Israel has become enemies of the gospel (Rom 11:28). However, the gospel was to the Jew first (Rom 1:16) and now the Gentiles are responding to it. In accordance with this understanding, Wright stated that the "gospel itself actually becomes a part of the appeal."[27] What Paul expounds in Romans 9–11 becomes the basis of his missionary plans in Romans 15 (Fitzmyer, 541).[28] Indeed, several writers have understood the proper way to interpret Romans 9–11 is to read it in the light of Paul's missionary endeavors.[29] This emphasis certainly highlights the framework of the epistle and some of its practical aspects, but it cannot encompass the theological discussion of the entire

---

48; Fitzmyer, 540. Beker, "The Faithfulness of God," 13–15 gives four issues that relate to the theme of Romans and also the righteousness of God is the dominant concentration.

[19] See Moo's brief survey in *Romans*, 79–90 and *Romans,* 2nd, 82–100.

[20] The Council of Trent, Session VI, Decree of Justification, chapter 7 and The Council of Trent, Session VI, Canons of Justification, canon 11.

[21] Käsemann, *New Testament Questions of* Today, 180–82. See the analysis of Watson, *Paul, Judaism and the Gentiles*, 36–38.

[22] Holland, *Contours of Pauline Theology*, 207–34 added that this forensic understanding is the condition of entrance into a covenant with God. See Hodge, *Systematic Theology*, 3:114–212; Morris, *The Apostolic Preaching of the Cross*, 224–74 and Grudem, *Systematic Theology*, 722–34 for detail information of justification. Campbell, *The Deliverance of God*, 76-77 denies the substitutional or Anselmic view of Christ atonement and thus, develops a different view. For more of a comprehensive and fuller discussion of justification, see Michael Horton, *New Studies in Dogmatics: Justification*, Vol. 1 & 2 (Grand Rapids: Zondervan, 2018).

[23] Wright, "The Messiah and the People of God," 57. See also Wright, "Romans and the Theology of Paul," 38–39.

[24] Wright, "The Messiah and the People of God," 57.

[25] See Moo, 89–90 for a brief comment on the centrality of justification in Romans and the current debate. For further comments, see Cranfield, 2:445–46; Davies, "Paul and People of Israel," 13; Stuhlmacher, "The Theme of Romans," 335.

[26] Moo, "The Theology of Romans 9–11," 247.

[27] Wright, "The Messiah and the People of God," 234.

[28] See Dahl, *Studies in Paul*, 70–88 for his study in missionary theology in Romans. See Jewett, 86 for a critique of Dahl.

[29] See Richardson, *Israel in the Apostolic Church,* 10:126,136,146–47; Munck, *Christ and Israel*, 6–8; Leenhardt, 12–23; Jewett, "Following the Argument of Romans," 266, 277. Jewett believes Romans is an ambassador letter. Getty, "Paul and the Salvation of Israel," 457, 468-69 includes the missionary emphasis but incorporates this emphasis into the idea that Gentiles are included in God's plan for universal salvation. See also Jewett, *Romans*, 74-91 for his review and critique.

letter. The best solution is to conclude that Jesus Christ is the demonstration of the righteousness of God in the gospel, which God planned to extend world-wide in his salvation.[30] This understanding merges the historical and the theological perspectives.[31] Jesus Christ is the demonstration of the righteousness of God in the gospel, which God planned to extend to the whole world (Jews and Gentiles).

In this connection, a crucial issue being worked out in Paul's letter to the Romans is that despite the privileges given to the nation of Israel (Rom 9:4–5), the nation is not experiencing the privileges and salvation (except for a remnant) offered in Jesus Christ (Rom 9:1–3).[32] This tension is what Paul attempted to resolve in Romans 9–11.[33] Not only is there a historical tension of the gospel being rejected, but Paul's development of his argument in Romans 1–8 has also produced theological tension (Moo, 549). In Romans 4, Paul argues that Gentiles who become Christians are Abraham's true heirs. In Romans 8, Paul claimed that Gentile believers become God's adopted sons. They possess righteousness and the Holy Spirit and are able to fulfil the requirements of the law and have the hope of the glory of God. On the other hand, Paul denied that Jews are guaranteed salvation through their deeds.[34] He has enumerated the privileges of the Jewish people in Romans 9:4–5, which has many parallels with the promises to the church in Romans 8, and he has exacerbated this theological problem by the way he argued in the previous chapters. Along the way, Paul briefly indicated that Israel is neither disinherited nor replaced (Rom 3:1–8),[35] but in Romans 9–11 he takes up Israel's rejection in full (Schreiner, 469).

Paul must demonstrate that the gospel of salvation, which is proclaimed to the Gentiles, is not inconsistent with God's promises to Israel. He anticipates this problem and weaves his response into his letter (e.g., Rom 1:1–2; 3:21). Moo concludes that this is why Paul in Romans 9–11 quoted from the Old Testament more than any other place in his letter (Moo, 550). Also, Paul must answer another question that casts a shadow over his gospel. If God's promises to Israel have not been accomplished, then how can the Church be sure that the promises given to it will be accomplished?[36] The issue in Romans 9–11 is not only the proper place of Israel and the fulfilment of the promises to them, but the question involves the trustworthiness and

---

[30] Wright, "The Messiah and the People of God," 234, 242–43.

[31] For a discussion of the sociology and theological methodology for Romans see Donfried, "False Presuppositions in the Study of Romans," 102–125; Karris, "The Occasion of Romans: A Response to Professor Donfried," 125–27 and Wuellner, "Paul's Rhetoric of Argumentation in Romans," 128–46. Wuellner offers observation from the "argumentative situation" (128–46). Keck, 223–26 explains it in two historical reasons and one theological reason.

[32] Some have alleged that Israel is not under God's condemnation for they enjoy salvation through their own covenant with God in the Old Testament Torah. See Gaston, "Israel's Enemies in Pauline Theology," 400-23; Gaston, "Israel's Misstep in the Eyes of Paul," 309–26; Gager, *The Origins of Anti-Semitism:* 197–212; and Buren, "Paul, The Church and Israel," 10–11.

[33] Wasserberg, "Romans 9–11 and Jewish–Christian Dialogue," 185–86 did not agree that Paul believed in the two covenants view (one for Israel and one for the church); however, Wasserberg disagreed with Paul – he does not believe Judaism is a deficient religion. For a sound critique of this view see Johnson, *The Function of Apocalyptic and Wisdom Traditions in Romans 9–11*, 176–205; Thielman, *From Plight to Solution*, 123–32; Segal, *Paul the Convert*, 126–33; Segal, "Paul's Experience and Romans 9-11," 61-67; and Moo, 549, note 5.

[34] Thielman, "Unexpected Mercy, 173–74; Moo, 135–48.

[35] Robinson, *Wrestling with Romans*, 108–09 contended that Rom 9–11 is a detail expansion of Rom 3:1–31.

[36] See Munck, *Christ and Israel*, 35; Davies, "Paul and People of Israel," 13; Byrne, *'Sons of God' – 'Seed of Abraham'*, 127–29; Cranfield, 2:447; Meek, "On Trusting an Unpredictable God," 108–09; Volf, *Paul and Perseverance*, 161–62.

righteousness of God.[37] The rejection and hardening of Israel (temporarily) seems to indicate the word of God has failed (9:6a).[38] Thus, Paul must address this issue.

The theological dimension of Romans 9–11 is at times overlooked. James W. Aageson argues that through stylistic features supported by verbal and thematic links in Romans 9–11 one can understand the series of interconnecting arguments that develop the larger discourse of Paul.[39] Thus, he claims that the literary structure and character of Romans 9–11 helps the reader to understand this section better than the theological composition. The literary analysis is important, but it should not occur at the expense of the theological dimension of Paul's argument. Aageson's analysis is helpful, but Schreiner's critique seems to be correct when he pointed out that Aageson failed to appreciate the theological dimension of Paul's argument.[40]

In the studies surveyed so far, Romans 9–11 has been understood as a cohesive unit. However, some see instead a conflict in Paul's argument within these chapters. Räisänen concludes that there are "considerable internal contradictions in Romans 9–11."[41] He pitted Romans 9, where God is sovereign and dispenses his mercy and judgment as he pleases, against Romans 11, where God promises salvation and mercy. Räisänen's explanation of Romans 9–11 is to be understood "in terms of Paul's own experience,"[42] that is, Paul is trying to explain this new experience in light of his old tradition. Francis Watson also stated that the main issue at stake in Romans 9–11 is the consistency of the Pauline view of God's activity in the Old Testament – the rejection of the majority of Israel and the acceptance of Gentiles and the remnant of Jews.[43] However, according to Watson, this understanding seems to lead to tensions and contradictions between different parts of Paul's letter. His proposed answer is derived from the viewpoint that Paul's argument originates from a social function.[44] Watson, like Lung-Kwong Lo, developed his argument by interpreting Romans 14–16 and applying it systematically to the argument of Romans 1–11.[45] However, against this interpretation, whether it be personal or social, it must be stated that Paul's letter is more than an argument to solve a social function or a clash in Paul's experience.

Let's draw together the various and diverging views that outline and analyzed this section of Romans. Among those scholars who recognize a unity to Romans 9–11 (who represent the majority), there is a focus on the theological purpose of the argument expressed within them. Within that theological concern, the teaching of the gospel itself (especially the concept of

---

[37] See E. Elizabeth Johnson, "Romans 9–11," 214–15; Davies, "Paul and People of Israel," 13–14; Aune, "Romans as a Logos Protreptikos," 294; Stuhlmacher, 144; Schreiner, 472; Wright, "The Messiah and the People of God," 172; Das, *Paul, the Law and the Covenant*, 96; Wright, "Romans," 622; Keck, 224. Räisänen, "Paul, God and Israel," 178 also concurred but cluttered the point with other questions. See Moo, "The Theology of Romans 9–11," 240–58 for his response to Elizabeth Johnson's view of Rom 9–11.

[38] See Dahl, *Studies in Paul*, 143; Cranfield, 473; Hafemann, "The Salvation of Israel in Romans 11:25–32," 43.

[39] Aageson, "Scripture and Structure," 267; Aageson, "Typology, Correspondence and the Application of Scripture in Romans 9–11," 51–72.

[40] See Schreiner, 471, note 6 for an observation on this point.

[41] Räisänen, "Paul, God and Israel," 192. See also Watson, *Paul, Judaism and the Gentiles: A Social Approach*, 170. Meek, "On Trusting an Unpredictable God," 110–11 called it a dialectic or paradox. Beker, "Romans 9–11 in the Context of the Early Church," 45–48 said Paul is inconsistent in his argument.

[42] Räisänen, "Paul, God and Israel," 195–96.

[43] Watson, *Paul, Judaism and the Gentiles: A Social Approach*, 162.

[44] Ibid., 173. See also Watson, *Paul, Judaism and the Gentiles: Beyond the New Perspective*, 192–94. *Contra* Räisänen, "Paul, God and Israel," 194–95.

[45] Watson, *Paul, Judaism and the Gentiles: Beyond the New Perspective*, 193, 345. However, he does not wholly extract out the "Lutheran" law/grace concept (346).

righteousness) is the most dominant and controlling thread. Paul explains that salvation history and God's covenantal faithfulness are expounded in the unfolding of the gospel, which calls Jews and Gentiles to salvation through a wise and unique plan.

The Exodus Theme and the New Exodus (NE) Motif in Romans 9-11

The events in the book of Exodus, as well as the events leading up to and following the event of the Exodus, formed the powerful images and epoch-making Exodus themes, which are used repeatedly in both the Old and New Testament. Some of the major Exodus themes include the following: God's election of and mercy for his people, the advent of a divinely appointed leader, warfare against evil and the victory of God's superiority, the deliverance and flight from Egypt, the crossing of the sea or water, deliverance by the hand of God, the judgment of the Egyptians and other neighboring nations, the establishing of the law and the nation of Israel, God's wisdom and guidance in the way through the desert, the construction and worship of God in his sanctuary, the tabernacle (and later the temple), and the entrance into the Promised Land.[46] The period of the Exodus is widely defined but most scholars consider it the history of the descendants of Jacob from their oppression in Egypt (Ex 1) to at least their arrival at the Transjordan (Josh 1).[47] However, the pre-Exodus influence of the Abrahamic promises in Genesis 12, 15, 17, 22, 26, and 28 has an important place in shaping the Exodus theme concerning God's relationship with Israel (cf. Ex 15:17–18; Deut 29:2–16).[48] Others, like Nixon, extend the period of the Exodus through the time of King David, when the rule of the land is clearly established.[49]

The recognition of the Exodus theme is found in quotations, allusions, and echoes.[50] In this section of Romans, a quotation from the Exodus is defined as sharing more than two words in a particular verse from the Exodus events. An allusion shares a common word or two and an echo has conceptual correspondence with an Exodus event rather than verbal commonality. The criteria for determining quotations, especially allusions and echoes from earlier biblical texts in later ones are: (1) availability of the source to the author and original readers, (2) volume (the degree of explicit repetition of words or syntactical patterns), (3) recurrence (how often the occurrence is found elsewhere), (4) thematic coherence (how the reference fits in the overall argument of the author), (5) historical plausibility (the historical setting allows for the possibility that the author could have intended the OT reference and the readers/hears could have comprehended it), (6) historical interpretation (other interpreters have discerned the possibility of the reference), and (7) satisfaction (the reference makes sense in the author's larger contextual argument).[51] These criteria may have a cumulative effect in determining the three categories, but

---

[46] See Cushman, "A Critique of Rikki E. Watts," 148–84; and Cozart, *The Present Triumph*, 27–28 for many of these Exodus phrases and motifs. Many of the events or motifs of the Exodus are summarized in Ex 6:6–8.

[47] For examples, see Fishbane, *Biblical Text and Texture*, 121–25.

[48] Nixon, *The Exodus in the New Testament*, 6.

[49] Ibid.

[50] Hays, *Echoes of Scripture*, 23.

[51] Ibid., 29–32. Hays elaborates further in *The Conversion of the Imagination*, 34–44. Shum, *Paul's Use of Isaiah in Romans*, 6–11 critiqued Hay's seven criteria drawing out the strengths and weaknesses. He concluded that some of the criteria were not always workable (availability and historical plausibility), others less useful (history of interpretation and satisfaction) and still others were helpful and reliable (volume, recurrence, and thematic

ultimately the uniqueness of the word, word combination, word order, or the unique theme is significant. Furthermore, the weighing of the evidence to categorize the Old Testament citation should be recognized not as an exact science, but as a skillful art.[52]

The Exodus theme in the Old Testament is widely accepted in scholarship today.[53] Michael Fishbane gives one example by briefly summarizing the theme of Exodus 1–15 as ingrained into the national life and theology of the people of Israel:

> The interweaving of a broad diversity of recollections of this event into a coherent and expanded saga of cumulative force resulted in a *mythos* of the origins of Israelite religious consciousness and nationhood. Accordingly, the exodus tradition was used, from the first, as a paradigmatic teaching for present and future generations. Its incorporation into the texts of the national origins served as permanent record of the beneficent acts of God for Israel.[54]

The Exodus and the journey to Sinai create the nation and give them self-identity. The Exodus is woven into the fiber of the social life of Israel.[55] For example, Deuteronomy 10:19 admonishes Israel to love the alien in the land because the nation was once in the foreign land of Egypt (cf. Deut 15:15). The world identifies and associates the God of the Exodus with the Hebrews of this period. This God uses his mighty power and provision through the journey from Egypt to display his witness to the world (Ex 9:16).

These past subplots of the Exodus became the pattern for the future of the nation, especially in the prophets where the motif of restoration is found in the terms of the NE.[56] Brunson defines the NE:

> The widespread and general hope of deliverance and restoration can be divided into three distinct yet interlinked categories which account for all of the expectations: the return from exile; the defeat of Israel's enemies; and the return of Yahweh to live and reign among his people. I will refer to this complex of restoration hope as the *New Exodus*, a phrase which although not specially found in the ancient texts yet adequately describes the eschatological program presented by the Prophets and also ties these longings to the paradigmatic deliverance in Israel's past.[57]

---

coherence). Jobes, "Jerusalem, our Mother," 299–320 and Keesmaat, "Exodus and the Intertextual Transformation," 29–56 accepted Hays' criteria.

[52] Beale, "Colossians," 841–42 and Sommer, "Exegesis, Allusion and Intertextuality," 486.

[53] For an introduction to this topic, see: Piper, "Unchanging Promises," 3–22; Balentine, "The Death of Jesus as the New Exodus," 27–41; Daube, *The Exodus Pattern in the Bible*, *passim*; Nixon, *The Exodus in the New Testament*, 5–32; Watts, "Consolation or Confrontation?," 31–59; Keesmaat, *Paul and His Story*, 34–48; Brunson, *Psalm 118 in the Gospel of John*, 153–79; Sullivan, *The Isaianic New Exodus in Romans 9–11*, 2nd ed., 13–45.

[54] Fishbane, *Biblical Text and Texture*, 121.

[55] Keesmaat, "Exodus and the Intertextual Transformation," 36.

[56] Ibid.; Brueggemann, *Hope within History*, 87; Morales, *The Spirit and the Restoration of Israel*, 13–29.

[57] Brunson, *Psalm 118 in the Gospel of John*, 154. See also Marshall, "The Development of the Concept of Redemption," 153–69 especially pp. 153–56 who refers to this NE pattern as a type. Dennis, *Jesus' Death and Gathering of True Israel*, 141, note 106 indicates that the NE is the "gathering of the exiles, the return of YHWH, Israel's deliverance from their enemies, and a new Temple" (see also pp. 153–60). Holland, *Contours of Pauline Theology*, 29 adds the following NE themes: The New Covenant, circumcision of the heart, gift of the Spirit, pilgrimage, the return to Eden, the eschatological temple, conversion of the nations, and the eschatological marriage.

Thus, the theme of the NE involves the bondage of God's people (God's judgment) because of their disobedience and God's deliverance.[58] This deliverance involves some or all of the following: redemption, restoration, regathering, forgiveness, presence of God, and other marvellous blessings and changes. This theme of restoration and redemption is also prominent in the provisions of the new covenant.[59]

The NE is depicted in the Babylonian return in such places as Isaiah 44–45. The people of God needed to trust God's wise plan in using Cyrus as his deliverer. However, the rebellious hard hearts seen in the blind eyes and deaf ears motif in Isaiah demonstrated that the post-Babylonian world was not the end or the ultimate manifestation of the NE.[60] God's deliverer, Cyrus, did not bring about the prophetic restoration of creation, redeem God's people, or restore the land and Mt. Zion as many of the prophets predicted.

This lack of prophetic fulfilment caused disappointment that became evident in the post-exilic period of the nation of Israel.[61] The people returned to the land and through much struggle rebuilt cities and the temple, but the glorious restoration of Isaiah 4:2–6; 11:10–12:6; 35:1–10 did not happen. Nevertheless, the post-exilic prophet Zechariah pronounced the same NE message of restoration and redemption of the people, land, and Zion (Zech 10:6–12).[62] This same eschatological NE, which Isaiah describes in many places as a glorious restoration (e.g. Isa 65–66) is now considered future during the post-exilic period.[63] The nation of Israel must trust in the wise God and his plan to fulfil his promise of the eschatological NE.[64]

The theme of the Exodus and the NE motif are key concepts in understanding Paul's argument in Romans 9-11. The evidence of this point will be discovered as the background,

---

A legitimate case can be made for each of these themes as being part of the NE. Thus, the NE draws from a period of Israel's history (at least Ex through Josh) and many concepts and patterns in this period, which are repeated and paralleled in the Jewish Scripture (especially the Prophets and Psalms) and first century Scripture. All of these concepts and patterns contribute to the overall definition of Brunson.

[58] Wright, *Paul and the Faithfulness of God*, 1053 states that "the complex of 'new-Exodus' themes fits together in different patterns, but with the same regular overall content: Israel's God will act to rescue his people, to overthrow their pagan oppressors, to enable them to keep his Torah at last, to fill the whole earth with his glory and to set up his kingdom of justice, peace and prosperity. Not all these themes are found in all texts, of course."

[59] See an example in Keesmaat, "Exodus and the Intertextual Transformation," 41. For other covenant recognition, see Anderson, "Exodus in Covenant," 339–60.

[60] Hamlin, "Deutero-Isaiah's Reinterpretation of the Exodus in the Babylonian Twilight," 75. See also Ninow, *Indicators of Typology within the Old Testament*, *passim* who argued for and called the ultimate NE the eschatological NE.

[61] See an example from Neh 9:36–37.

[62] Ninow, *Indicators of Typology within the Old Testament*, 230–38.

[63] Oropeza, "Echoes of Isaiah in the Rhetoric of Paul," 96; Strauss, *The Davidic Messiah in Luke-Acts*, 287–88. Waldow, "The Message of Deutero–Isaiah," *Interpretation* 22 (1968): 277 called it a "new eschatological age" and "a new period of salvation history (*Heilsgeschichte*)." Patrick, "Epiphanic Imagery," 125–41 said that the NE of Isaiah was epiphanic imagery and eschatological but he is not sure how the people who returned from Babylon responded to the Isaianic passages, but concluded they looked ultimately to a divine intervention. Pao, *Acts and Isaianic New Exodus*, 56–57 called the Exodus paradigm "eschatolgized" in Isaiah – the past action of God paradigmatically pointed to future acts of Yahweh using the Exodus. Beale, *A New Testament Biblical Theology*, 173 believes the fulfilment of the NE was delayed. Pao and Schnabel, "Luke," 276-77 indicated that the eschatological reading of Isa 40:3-5 was found in the apocalyptic literature, rabbinic literature, and Qumran documents.

[64] Strauss, *The Davidic Messiah in Luke-Acts*, 291–92. For eschatological interpretations in Judaism, see Snodgrass, "Streams of Tradition," 24–45.

context, and argument from the OT is investigated in the citations that Paul uses in the Jewish Scripture.[65]

The Wisdom Polemic in Romans 9-11

The opposition of human wisdom to God's wise plan of judgment, redemption, and restoration sets up what may be called a "wisdom polemic."[66] Thus, a wisdom polemic is where God, usually through the prophet, uses the genre of wisdom to construct a disputation against the people of God because of their lack of knowledge, understanding, and rebellion against the character and plan of God.

Paul uses Isaiah 29:16 and 45:9 in Romans 9:20 together with Romans 11:34, which draws upon Isaiah 40:13 (and the supplement text Job 41:[3a] 11a), thereby creating an *inclusio* in the argument of Romans 9–11.[67] The first part of the *inclusio* uses the wisdom polemic in the motif of the NE to warn the readers not to rebel against God's wise plan. The election of some and the hardening of others are part of a difficult plan to understand and accept. In this polemic, Paul draws upon the theological context of the Isaianic wisdom polemic in Isaiah 29:16 and Isaiah 45:9. Paul also chooses the Isaianic wisdom polemic of Isaiah 40 and the wisdom section of Job 41 because certain portions of their teachings are parallel. The wisdom polemic in the theology of the Isaianic New Exodus (INE) is the theme and context of Paul's argument. The more the reader understood the history of Israel and the theology of Isaiah in particular, the more powerful would be the force of Paul's quotations from Isaiah. Paul makes use of the wisdom polemic to express God's redemption of Jews and Gentiles, which is conveyed in the NE theme.[68]

God's plan includes judgments and seemingly unrighteous events that call into question the character and plan of God. Romans 9–11 is Paul's attempt to explain God's faithfulness to his covenantal plan expressed in the Old Testament, though in the present age, Israel has been hardened (at least in part) and the nation as a whole is in unbelief. At the end of Romans 9–11, the Isaianic wisdom polemic culminates in the wisdom doxology because God is presented as executing the NE redemption plan in wonderful mercy that magnifies his righteous character and vindicates his eternal plan.

Scholars have recognized what this author calls the wisdom polemic in Isaiah;[69] however, only occasionally has it been linked to the NE. What is being proposed here is the association of

---

[65] For a more comprehensive understanding of this point, see Steve P. Sullivan, *The Isaianic New Exodus in Romans 9-11.*

[66] Watts, "Consolation or Confrontation?," 37 uses the terminology "anti-wisdom polemic" to refer to Isa 40:13–14, 28.

[67] Kim, *God, Israel, and the Gentiles*, 141 and Johnson, *The Function of Apocalyptic and Wisdom*, 173 recognize an *inclusio* with Rom 9:1–5 and 11:33–36. Naselli, *From Typology to Doxology*, 25 recognizes an *inclusio* with Rom 9:5b and 11:36b. One main point that goes against this being an *inclusio* is Rom 9:1–5, which is christological in emphasis where Rom 11:33–36 is not.

[68] See a full development of this argument in Sullivan, *The Isaianic New Exodus in Romans 9-11*, chapter 6.

[69] For studies in Isaiah on wisdom see: Fichtner, "Isaiah Among the Wise," 429–38; Lindblom, "Wisdom in the Old Testament Prophets," 192–204; Getsbenberger, "The Woe Oracles of the Prophets," 249–63; McKane, *Prophets and Wise Men, passim*; Whedbee, *Isaiah and Wisdom, passim*; Jensen, *The Use of Tôrâ by Isaiah, passim*; Morgan, *Wisdom in the Old Testament Traditions, passim*; Williamson, "Isaiah and the Wise," 133–41; Estes,

the wisdom polemic and the NE as inherent to Paul's use of his chosen Isaianic quotations in Romans 9:20 and 11:34. This clarifies the significance of using the particular quotation from Isaiah in order to underline his point. Whether it is in the days of the first Exodus or a NE, God's wisdom is sufficient to bring his people to deliverance and restoration even though they themselves do not comprehend his plan. The importance of the wisdom polemic motif of the NE will need to be borne in mind as the study of Paul's Isaianic quotations in Romans 9–11 is investigated.

The application of the theological context of Isaiah 29 and 45 to the argument of Romans 9 supplies scriptural evidence and support for the wisdom polemic and its overall role in Paul's argument in Romans 9–11. Therefore, Paul conflates Isaiah 29:16 and 45:9 in Romans 9:20 to warn his interlocutor by highlighting and intertwining the Isaianic wisdom polemic. In addition, the conflation of Isaiah 29:16 and 45:9 in Romans 9:20 anticipates the final Isaianic quotation in Romans 11:34 (Isa 40:13), which shares the same theme of a wisdom polemic. The connection of this theme with the NE will be demonstrated in the exegesis of Roman 9-11. The significance of this *inclusio* in Romans 9 is to direct the reader to Paul's overarching point in Romans 9-11 that is expressed in the wisdom polemic doxology in Rom 11:33–36 where everyone is called to marvel over the wise God and his sovereign plan.

We may outline Romans 9–11 as follows:

I. The Wisdom Polemic: The Tension between God's Righteous Promises and Israel's Condition 9–11
    A. Introduction to the Tension (9:1–5)
    B. Vindication of the righteous God and His Wise Plan (9:6–29)
    C. Israel's Knowledge of the Gospel of Righteousness: Faith and Works (9:30–10:21)
    D. Israel's election and partial hardening and not total rejection (11:1-10)
    E. A Wisdom Polemic: God's Merciful Plan for Israel and Gentiles (11:11-33)
        1. Israel's hardening and the Gentiles Inclusion (11:11-15)
        2. A Warning against Gentile Believers (11:16-22)
        3. The Mystery of Israel's Salvation (11:23-27)
        4. The Mercy of God in Salvation (11:28-32)
        5. A Wisdom Polemic Doxology (11:33-36)

Selected Bibliography

Aageson, James W. "Scripture and Structure in the Development of Argument of Romans 9–11." *Catholic Biblical Quarterly* 48 (April 1986): 265–89.

Aageson, James W. "Typology, Correspondence and the Application of Scripture in Romans 9–11." *Journal for the Study of the New Testament* 31 (September 1987): 51–72.

Anderson, Bernhard W. "Exodus in Covenant in Second Isaiah and Prophetic Tradition." In *Magnalia Dei, the Mighty Acts of God: Essays on the Bible and Archaeology in Memory of G. Ernest Wright*, eds. George Ernest Wright, Patrick D. Miller, Jr., Frank Moore Cross, and Werner E. Lemke. (New York: Doubleday, 1976), 339–60.

"Wisdom and Biblical Theology," 853–58; Shields, "Wisdom and Prophecy," 876–84 and Wilson, "Wisdom in Isaiah," 145–67.

Aune, David E. "Romans as a Logos Protreptikos." In *The Romans Debate*, ed. Karl P. Donfired. revised and expanded, 278–96. (Peabody: Hendrickson, 1977, 1991).

Balentine, George L. "The Death of Jesus as the New Exodus." *Review and Expositor* 59 (January 1962): 27–41.

Baur, Ferdinand C. *Paul, the Apostle of Jesus Christ: His Life and Work, His Epistles and His Doctrine: A Contribution to a Critical History of Primitive Christianity*, 2nd ed., trans. Eduard Zeller. (London: Williams and Norgate, 1876).

Beale, Gregory K. *A New Testament Biblical Theology: The Unfolding of the Old Testament in the New*. Grand Rapids: Baker Academic, 2011.

Beale, Gregory K. "Colossians." In *Commentary on the New Testament Use of the Old Testament*, eds. G. K. Beale and D. A. Carson. (Grand Rapids: Baker, 2007), 841-870.

Beasley-Murray, G. R. "The Righteousness of God in the History of Israel and the Nations: Romans 9–11." *Review and Expositor* 73 (fall 1976): 437–50.

Beker, J. Christiaan. *Paul the Apostle: The Triumph of God in Life and Thought.* (Philadelphia: Fortress Press, 1980).

Beker, J. Christiaan. "Romans 9–11 in the Context of the Early Church," *Princeton Seminary Bulletin*. Supplementary, no. 1 (1990): 40–55.

Beker, J. Christiaan. "The Faithfulness of God and the Priority of Israel." In *Christians Among the Jews and Gentiles: Essays in Honor of Krister Stendahl on His 65th Birthday*, eds. G. W. Nickelsburg and G. W. MacRae. (Philadelphia: Fortress Press, 1986).

Bell, Richard H. "The Origin and Purpose of the Jealousy Motif in Romans 9–11 A Case Study in the Theology and Technique of Paul" (D. Theo. diss., Eberhard-Karls-Universtiät zu Tübingen, 1990).

Bornkamm, Günther. *Paul*, trans. D. M. G. Stalker. (London: Hodder and Stoughton, 1971).

Brueggemann, Walter. *Hope Within History*. (Atlanta: John Knox Press, 1987).

Brunson, Andrew C. *Psalm 118 in the Gospel of John: An Intertextual Study of the New Exodus Pattern in the Theology of John*. Wissenshaftliche Untersuchungen zum Neuen Testament 2, Reihe 158. (Tübingen: Mohr Siebeck, 2003).

Buren, Paul van. "Paul, The Church and Israel: Romans 9–11," *The Princeton Seminary Bulletin,* Supplemental issue 1 (1990): 5–18.

Byrne, Brendan. *'Sons of God' – 'Seed of Abraham': A Study of the Idea of the Sonship of God of All Christians in Paul Against the Jewish Background.* (Rome: Biblical Institute Press, 1979).

Campbell, Douglas A. *The Deliverance of God: An Apocalyptic Rereading of Justification in Paul* (Grand Rapids: Eerdmans, 2009).

Campbell, William S. "Romans III as a Key to the Structure and Thought of the Letter." In *Romans Debate*, ed. K. P. Donfried, revised and expanded edition. (Peabody, MA: Hendrickson, 1991), 251–64.

Cozart, Richard M. *The Present Triumph: An Investigation into the Significance of the Promise of the New Exodus of Israel in the Letter to the Ephesians*, WEST Theological Monograph Series (Eugene, OR: Wipf and Stock, 2013).

Cushman, Neal D. "A Critique of Rikki E. Watts' Isaianic New Exodus in the Markan Prologue." (Ph.D. diss., Baptist Bible Seminary, 2012).

Dahl, Nils. *Studies in Paul*. (Minneapolis: Augsburg Publishing House, 1977).

Das, A. Andrew. *Paul, the Law and the Covenant* (Peabody: Hendrickson, 2001).

Das, A. Andrew. *Solving the Romans Debate*. (Minneapolis: Fortress Press, 2007).

Davies, W. D. "Paul and People of Israel." *New Testament Studies* 24 (October 1977): 4–39.

Daube, David. *The Exodus Pattern in the Bible*. (London: Faber & Faber, 1963).

Dennis, John A. *Jesus' Death and Gathering of True Israel*. Wissenschaftliche Untersuchungen zum Neuen Testament 2. Reihe, 217. (Tübingen: Mohr Siebeck, 2006).

Donfried, Karl P. "False Presuppositions in the Study of Romans." In *The Romans Debate,* ed. Karl P. Donfried, revised and expanded edition, 102–25. Peabody: Hendrickson, 1977, 1991.

Donfried, Karl P. "Introduction 1977: The Romans Debate," in *The Romans Debate,* ed. Karl P. Donfried, rev. and exp. ed. (Peabody: Hendrickson, 1977, 1991), xli–xlvii.

Dunn, James G. D. "The Purpose of Romans." In *Romans Debate*, ed. K. P. Donfried, revised and expanded edition. (Peabody, MA: Hendrickson, 1991), 245–50.

Estes, Daniel J. "Wisdom and Biblical Theology." In *Dictionary of the Old Testament Wisdom, Poetry and Writings*, eds. Tremper Longman III and Peter Enns. (Downers Grove: InterVarsity Press, 2008), 853–858.

Fichtner, Johannes. "Jesaja unter den Weisen." *Theologische Literaturzeitung* 74 (1949) 75–80, ed. and trans. "Isaiah Among the Wise." In *Studies in Ancient Israelite Wisdom* ed. J. L. Crenshaw, 429–38. (New York: KTAV, 1976).

Fishbane, Michael *Biblical Text and Texture*. (Oxford: Oneworld Publication, 1998).

Gager, John G. *The Origins of Anti-Semitism: Attitudes toward Judaism in Pagan and Christian Antiquity* (New York: Oxford University Press, 1983).

Gaston, Lloyd. "Israel's Enemies in Pauline Theology," *New Testament Studies* 28 (1982), 400–23.

Gaston, Lloyd. "Israel's Misstep in the Eyes of Paul," in *The Romans Debate*, ed. Karl P. Donfried, rev. and exp. ed. (Minneapolis: Augsburg Press, 1977, 1991), 309–26.

Getsbenberger, E. R. "The Woe Oracles of the Prophets." *Journal of Biblical Literature* 81 (1962): 249–263.

Getty, Mary Ann. "Paul and the Salvation of Israel: A Perspective on Romans 9–11." *Catholic Biblical Quarterly* 50 (July 1988): 456–89.

Gorday, Peter. *Principles of Patristic Exegesis: Romans 9–11 in Origen, John Chrysostom, and Augustine*, Studies in the Bible and Early Christianity (New York: Edwin Mellen Press, 1983), 231–35.

Grudem, Wayne A. *Systematic Theology: An Introduction to Biblical Doctrine*. (Grand Rapids: Zondervan, 2004).

Hafemann, Scott. "The Salvation of Israel in Romans 11:25–32: A Response to Krister Stendahl." *Ex Auditu* 4 (1988): 38–58.

Hamlin, E. John. "Deutero-Isaiah's Reinterpretation of the Exodus in the Babylonian Twilight." *Proceedings: Eastern Great Lakes and Midwest Biblical Societies* 11 (1991): 75–80.

Hays, Richard B. *Echoes of Scripture in the Letters of Paul*. (New Haven: Yale University Press, 1989).

Hays, Richard B. *The Conversion of the Imagination: Paul as Interpreter of Israel's Scripture*. (Grand Rapids: Eerdmans, 2005).

Hodge, Charles. *Systematic Theology*, 3 vols. Grand Rapids: Eerdmans, repr. 1970.

Holland, Tom. *Contours of Pauline Theology: A Radical New Survey of the Influences on Paul's Biblical Writings*. (Fearn, Scotland: Christian Focus Publications, 2004).

Horton, Michael. *New Studies in Dogmatics: Justification*, vols. 1-2, eds. Michael Allen and Scott R. Swain. Grand Rapids: Zondervan, 2018.

Jensen, Joseph. *The Use of Tôrâ by Isaiah: His Debate with the Wisdom Tradition*. Catholic Biblical Quarterly Monograph Series 3. (Washington: Catholic Biblical Association, 1973).

Jervell, Jacob. "The Letter to Jerusalem." In *The Romans Debate*, ed. Karl P. Donfried, revised and expanded editions. (Peabody: Hendrickson, 1991), 53–64.

Jewett, Robert. "Following the Argument of Romans." In *The Romans Debate*, ed. Karl P. Donfried, revised and expanded editions. (Peabody: Hendrickson, 1991), 265–77.

Jobes, Karen H. "Jerusalem, our Mother: Metalepsis and Intertextuality in Gal. 4:21–31." *Westminster Theological Journal* 55 (1993), 299–320.

Johnson, E. Elizabeth. "Romans 9–11: The Faithfulness and Impartiality of God." In *Pauline Theology III Romans*, eds. David M. Hay and E. Elizabeth Johnson. Society of Biblical Literature Symposium Series, ed. Christopher R. Matthews, no. 23. (Atlanta: SBL, 2002), 211–39.

Johnson, E. Elizabeth. *The Function of Apocalyptic and Wisdom Traditions in Romans 9–11*. Society of Biblical Literature Dissertation Series, ed. Charles Talbert, vol. 109. (Atlanta: Scholars Press, 1989).

Karris, Robert J. "The Occasion of Romans: A Response to Professor Donfried." In *The Romans Debate,* ed. Karl P. Donfried, revised and expanded edition. (Peabody: Hendrickson, 1977, 1991), 125–27.

Käsemann, Ernest. *New Testament Questions of Today,* The New Testament Library. (London: SCM Press, 1969), 168–82.

Keesmaat, Sylvia C. "Exodus and the Intertextual Transformation of Tradition in Romans 8:14–30." *Journal for the Study of the New Testament* 54 (1994): 29–56.

Keesmaat, Sylvia C. *Paul and His Story: (Re)Interpreting the Exodus Tradition*. Journal for the Study of the New Testament Supplement, ed. Stanley E. Porter, 181. (Sheffield: Sheffield Academic Press, 1999).

Kim, Johann D. *God, Israel, and the Gentiles: Rhetoric and Situation in Romans 9–11*. Society of Biblical Literature Dissertation Series, vol. 176. (Atlanta: Society of Biblical Literature, 2000).

Lindblom, Johannes. *The Servant Songs in Deutero-Isaiah: A New Attempt to Solve an Old Problem*. (Lunds: C. W. K. Gleerup, 1951).

Lo, Lung–Kwong. "Paul's Purpose in Writing Romans: The Upbuilding of a Jewish and Gentile Christian Community in Rome." Ph.D. diss., University of Durham, 1988.

Marshall, I. Howard. "The Development of the Concept of Redemption in the New Testament." In *Reconciliation and Hope: New Testament Essays on Atonement and Eschatology Presented to L. L. Morris on his 60th Birthday*, ed. Robert J. Banks. (Grand Rapids: Eerdmans, 1974), 153–169.

McKane, Williams. *Prophets and Wise Men*. London: SCM Press, 1965.

Meek, Wayne A. "On Trusting an Unpredictable God: A Hermeneutical Meditation on Romans 9–11." In *Faith and History*, ed. J. T. Carroll, et al. (Atlanta: Scholars, 1990), 105–24.

Moo, Douglas J. "The Theology of Romans 9–11." In *Pauline Theology Volume III Romans*, eds. David M. Hay and E. Elizabeth Johnson. Society of Biblical Literature Symposium Series. ed. Christopher R. Matthews, No. 23. (Atlanta: SBL, 2002), 240–58.

Morales, Rodrigo J. *The Spirit and the Restoration of Israel: New Exodus and New Creation Motifs in Galatians*. Wissenshaftliche Untersuchungen zum Neuen Testament 2. Reihe 282. Tübingen: Mohr Siebeck, 2010.

Morgan, Donn F. *Wisdom in the Old Testament Traditions*. Louisville: John Knox Press, 1981.

Morris, Leon. *The Apostolic Preaching of the Cross* (Grand Rapids: Eerdmans, 1955).

Munck, Johannes. *Christ and Israel: An Interpretation of Romans 9–11*. Translated by Ingeborg Nixon. Philadelphia: Fortress Press, 1967.

Nanos, Mark D. *The Mystery of Romans: The Jewish Context of Paul's Letter*. Minneapolis: Fortress Press, 1996.

Naselli, Andrew D. *From Typology to Doxology: Paul's Use of Isaiah and Job in Romans 11:34–35*. Eugene, OR: Pickwick Publication, 2012.

Ninow, Friedbert. *Indicators of Typology within the Old Testament: The Exodus Motif.* (New York: Peter Lang Publication, 2001).

Nixon, R. E. *The Exodus in the New Testament*. Tyndale Monographs. (London: Tyndale Press, 1963).

Noack, Bent. "Current and Backwater in the Epistle to the Romans." *Studia Theologica* 19 (1965): 155–66.

Oropeza, B. J. "Echoes of Isaiah in the Rhetoric of Paul: New Exodus, Wisdom, and the Humility of the Cross in Utopian-Apocalyptic Expectations." In *The Intertexture of Apocalyptic Discourse in the New* Testament, ed. Duane F. Watson. Society of Biblical Literature Symposium Series, ed. Christopher R. Matthews, No. 14. (Atlanta: Society of Biblical Literature, 2002), 87–112.

Pao, David W. *Acts and Isaianic New Exodus*. Biblical Studies Library. (Grand Rapids: Baker, 2002).

Pao, David W. and Eckhard J. Schnabel. "Luke." In *Commentary on the New Testament Use of the Old Testament*, eds. G. K. Beale and D. A. Carson, 251–414. Grand Rapids: Baker, 2007.

Patrick, Dale. "Epiphanic Imagery in Second Isaiah's Portrayal of a New Exodus." *Hebrew Annual Review* 8 (1984): 125–41.

Piper, Otto A. "Unchanging Promises: Exodus in the New Testament." *Interpretation* 11 (1957): 3–22.

Räisänen, Heikki. "Paul, God and Israel: Romans 9–11 in Recent Research." In *The Social World of Formative Christianity and Judaism: Essays in Tribute to Howard Clark Kee*, eds. Jacob Neusner et al., 178–206. Philadelphia: Fortress Press, 1988.

Richardson, Peter. *Israel in the Apostolic Church,* Society for New Testament Studies Monograph Series, ed. Mathew Black (Cambridge: Cambridge University Press, 1969).

Segal, Alan F. *Paul the Convert: The Apostolate and Apostasy of Saul the Pharisee* (New Haven: Yale University, 1990).

Segal, Alan F. "Paul's Experience and Romans 9-11." *Princeton Seminary Bulletin,* Supplementary no. 1 (1990): 61-67.

Shields, Martin A. "Wisdom and Prophecy." In *Dictionary of the Old Testament Wisdom, Poetry and Writings*, eds. Tremper Longman III and Peter Enns. (Downers Grove: InterVarsity Press, 2008), 876–84.

Shum, Shiu-Lun. *Paul's Use of Isaiah in Romans: A Comparative Study of Paul's Letter to the Romans and the Sibylline and Qumran Sectarian Texts*. (Tübingen: Mohr Siebeck, 2002).

Snodgrass, Klyne R. "Streams of Tradition Emerging from Isaiah 40:1–5 and Their Adaptation in the New Testament." *Journal for the Study of the New Testament* 8 (1980): 24–45.

Sommer, Benjamin D. "Exegesis, Allusion and Intertextuality in the Hebrew Bible, a Response to Lyle Eslinger." *Vetus Testamentum* 46 (1996): 479–89.

Stanley, Christopher D. *Arguing with Scripture: The Rhetoric of Quotations in the Letters of Paul* (London: T & T Clark, 2004).

Stendahl, Krister. *Paul among Jews and Gentiles*. (London: SCM, 1977).

Strauss, Mark L. *The Davidic Messiah in Luke-Acts: The Promise and Its Fulfillment in Lukan Christology*. Journal for the Study of the New Testament Supplement Series 110, ed. Stanley E. Porter. (Sheffield: Sheffield Academic Press, 1995).

Stuhlmacher, Peter. "The Theme of Romans." In *The Romans Debate*, ed. Karl P. Donfried, revised and expanded editions. (Peabody: Hendrickson, 1991). 333–45.

Sullivan, Steven P. *The Isaianic New Exodus in Romans 9-11: A Biblical and Theological Study of Paul's Use of Isaiah in Romans* (Silverton, Oregon: Lampion Press, 2017).

Sullivan, Steven P. *The Isaianic New Exodus in Romans 9–11: A Biblical and Theological Study of Paul's Use of Isaiah in Romans*, 2nd ed. (Middleton, RI: Stone Tower Press, 2023).

Swanson, Reuben, ed. *New Testament Greek Manuscripts Romans: Variant Readings Arranged in Horizontal Lines Against Codex Vaticanus*. (Wheaton: Tyndale House, 2001).

Thielman, Frank. *From Plight to Solution: a Jewish Framework to Understanding Paul's View of the Law in Galatians and Romans, Novum Testamentum,* Supplements (Leiden: Brill, 1989).

Thielman, Frank. "Unexpected Mercy: Echoes of a Biblical Motif in Romans 9–11." *Scottish Journal of Theology* 47 (April-June 1994): 169–81.

Volf, Judith M. Gundry. *Paul and Perseverance: Stay in or Fall Away*. Wissenschaftliche Untersuchungen zum Neuen Testament, no. 2 vol. 37. (Tübingen: Mohr Siebeck, 1990).

Waldow, H. E. von. "The Message of Deutero-Isaiah." *Interpretation* 22 (1968): 259–87.

Wasserberg, Günter. "Romans 9–11 and Jewish-Christian Dialogue: Prospects and Provisos."In *Reading Israel in Romans: Legitimacy and Plausibility of Divergent Interpretations,* eds. Christina Grenholm and Daniel Patte. Romans Through History and Cultures Receptions and Critical Interpretations. (Harrisburg: Trinity Press International, 2000), 174–86.

Watson, Francis. *Paul, Judaism and the Gentiles: Beyond the New Perspective*. Revised and expanded edition. (Grand Rapids: Eerdmans, 2007).

Watson, Francis. *Paul, Judaism and the Gentiles: A Social Approach*. (Cambridge, Cambridge Press, 1989).

Watts, Rikki E. "Consolation or Confrontation? Isaiah 40–55 and the Delay of the New Exodus." *Tyndale Bulletin* 41 (May 1990): 31–59.

Whedbee, J. William. *Isaiah and Wisdom*. (Nashville: Abingdon Press, 1971).

Williamson, H. G. M. "The Isaiah and the Wise." In *Wisdom in Ancient Israel*, eds. John Day, Robert P. Gordon and H. G. M. Williamson. (Cambridge: Cambridge Press, 1995), 133–141.

Wilson, Lindsay. "Wisdom in Isaiah." In *Interpreting Isaiah: Issues and Approaches*, eds. David G. Firth and H. G. M. Williamson. (Downers Grove: InterVarsity Academic, 2009), 145–167.

Wright, N. T. *Paul and the Faithfulness of God*. Christian Origins and the Question of God, vol. 4. Minneapolis: Fortress Press, 2013.

Wright, N. T. "Romans and the Theology of Paul." In *Pauline Theology Volume III Romans*. eds. David M. Hay and E. Elizabeth Johnson. Society of Biblical Literature Symposium Series. ed. Christopher R. Matthews, No. 23. (Atlanta: Society of Biblical Literature, 2002), 30–67.

Wright, N. T. *The Climax of the Covenant*: *Christ and the Law in Pauline Theology*. (Edinburgh: Clark, 1991).

Wright, N. T. "The Messiah and the People of God: A Study in Pauline Theology with Particular Reference to the Argument of the Epistle to the Romans." (Ph.D. diss., University of Oxford, 1980).

Wuellner, Wilhelm. "Paul's Rhetoric of Argumentation in Romans: An Alternative to the Donfried-Karris Debate over Romans." In *The Romans Debate,* ed. Karl P. Donfried, revised and expanded edition. (Peabody: Hendrickson, 1977, 1991), 128–46.

ROMANS 9:1–5

Introduction

The transition from the climatic spiritual blessing at the end of Romans 8 to the dramatic emotional lamentation of Paul in Romans 9:1-5 is quite abrupt. He makes this transition without any conjunction or particle connection but with an appeal to his conscience and the Holy Spirit and contrasts this appeal with not lying but telling the truth. His sorrow and grief are centered on the eternal consequence of his fellow Israelites rejecting the truth of the gospel (v. 3). However, Paul's passionate concerns go beyond his concern as a fellow Jew and the gospel. The rehearsal of the privileges to Israel in verses 4-5 indicate that Paul wants to address the promises of God and His faithfulness in fulling His promises even among a people who have rejected Him and His promises. Has God rejected His people Israel, disinherited them, and forfeited their promises? Romans 9:1-5 sets the stage for him to show that this is not the case.

Outline

I. The Wisdom Polemic: The Tension between God's righteous promises and Israel's condition 9–11
   A. Introduction to the Tension 9:1–5

Original Text

9.1 Ἀλήθειαν λέγω ἐν Χριστῷ[a], οὐ ψεύδομαι, συμμαρτυρούσης[b] μοι τῆς συνειδήσεώς μου ἐν
πνεύματι ἁγίῳ, 2 ὅτι λύπη μοί ἐστιν μεγάλη καὶ ἀδιάλειπτος ὀδύνη τῇ καρδίᾳ μου· 3 ηὐχόμην[c]
γὰρ ἀνάθεμα εἶναι αὐτὸς ἐγὼ ἀπὸ τοῦ Χριστοῦ ὑπὲρ τῶν ἀδελφῶν μου[d] τῶν συγγενῶν μου κατὰ
σάρκα, 4 οἵτινές εἰσιν Ἰσραηλῖται, ὧν ἡ υἱοθεσία καὶ ἡ δόξα καὶ αἱ διαθῆκαι[e] καὶ ἡ νομοθεσία καὶ
ἡ λατρεία καὶ αἱ ἐπαγγελίαι[f], 5 ὧν οἱ πατέρες, καὶ ἐξ ὧν ὁ χριστὸς τὸ κατὰ σάρκα, ὁ ὢν ἐπὶ
πάντων, θεὸς εὐλογητὸς εἰς τοὺς αἰῶνας· ἀμήν.

Textual Notes

[a] **9:1** There is little evidence for **Ιησου** (D*FG ar vg^{s}) after Χριστῷ.
[b] **9:1** B^{*}ℵACD^{2} 326 p^{46} D*FG 2464 W has **συνμαρτυρούσης** with early and strong support and diverse geographic witnesses. The majority of the manuscripts have συμμαρτυρούσης (NA28 UBS5 SBLGNT B^{c}KLΨ 6 88 424 1175 1836 and many others). In the end, it seems to be a spelling difference.
[c] **9:3** Large majority of manuscripts have **εὐχόμην** while NA28 UBS5 SBLGNT B*B^{c}ℵAp^{46}C FGΨ 056 and few minuscules have **ηὐχόμην**.
[d] **9:3** The majority of the manuscripts support **τῶν ἀδελφῶν μου**; however, B* omits it all and p^{46} only has **ἀδελφῶν**.

[e] **9:4 αἱ διαθῆκαι** is supported by NA28 UBS5 SBLGNT ℵCKΨ 049 056 with the majority of the minuscules, Latin texts, vulgate texts, Syriac texts and some early church fathers. ἡ διαθῆκη is supported by B p^{46} D* D^2 G F* F^c L with two Latin texts and vg^{cl} and some early church fathers. Alexandrian and western witnesses support both the singular and the plural while the majority of the Byzantine witnesses and the majority of the lectionaries follow the plural. Metzger, *A Textual Commentary*, p. 459 concluded that the copyist would have assimilated the plural into singular number with the rest of series of words. Also, the plural covenants appear to have theological difficulties and thus would be more likely changed. On the other hand, Metzger seems to be right that no good reason can be formulated why the singular would be changed to a plural. A omits ὧν ἡ υἱοθεσία καὶ ἡ δόξα καὶ αἱ διαθῆκαι καὶ ἡ νομοθεσία καὶ ἡ λατρεία καὶ αἱ ἐπαγγελίαι. Probably a mistake in skipping to verse 5 that begins with ὧν.
[f] **9:4 αἱ ἐπαγγελίαι** has the major support of B ℵ p^{46} C K L Ψ and the majority of the minuscules while ἡ ἐπαγγελία has the weaker support of D* D^2 G and F* F^c (without the article) and a few minuscules.

Translation

9:1 I am speaking the truth in Christ, I am not lying, my conscience bearing witness to me by the Holy Spirit, **2** that I have great pain and unceasing anguish in my heart. **3** For I could request[70] that I myself were accursed, separated from the Messiah[71] for the sake of my brethren, my kinsmen according to the flesh, **4** who are Israelites, to whom belongs the adoptions as sons, and the glory, and the covenants, and the giving of the Law, and the service of worship and the promises, **5** to whom are the fathers, and from whom, according to the flesh, is the Messiah, who is over all, God blessed forever. Amen.

Commentary

9:1 Ἀλήθειαν λέγω ἐν Χριστῷ, οὐ ψεύδομαι, "I am speaking the truth in Christ, I am not lying." Paul does not use a conjunction to connect with the previous section in chapter eight. This point seems to signal a break in his argument. However, this observation does not mean there is no connection between chapter eight and nine. Certain vocabulary and subject matter among the chapters help in a broad connection.[72] Dunn also notices the lack of conjunctions with the two phrases in verse one and concludes that it stresses a "solemn emphasis" (Dunn, 523; cf. 1 Tim 2:7) Also, Ἀλήθειαν ("truth") is pushed forward in verbal order of the first phrase for emphasis. Paul evidently did not want his readers to pass by too quickly the first part of verse one and his following introductory remarks. The construction of ἐν Χριστῷ ("in Christ") is not directly connected with Ἀλήθειαν ("truth"), but with λέγω ("I speak") (Cranfield, 451; Schreiner, 2nd, 468). However, the phrase connects Paul and his understanding of truth with Jesus Christ; thus,

[70] Or "pray."

[71] Literally, τοῦ Χριστοῦ ("the Christ"). See also the same translation in Rom 9:5.

[72] Moo, 2nd, 576, note 31 correctly states that the subject of election is found in common (Rom 8:26-30 and 9:6-23), with the following words: πρόθεσις (8:28; 9:11), καλεω/κλητός (8:28, 30; 9:7, 11, 24, 26); the concept of sonship and adoption (υἱοθεσία in 8:15, 23; 9:4; υἱός in 8:14, 19; 9:9, 26, 27; τέκνον in 8:16, 17, 21; 9:7, 8); and the hope of eschatological glory (δοξάζω/δόξα in 8:18, 21, 30; 9:4, 23).

strengthening the truthfulness of the statement.[73] Cranfield seems correct when he says that truth is "in accordance with the standards which obtain for one who is in Christ, with a due sense of his accountability to Christ" (Cranfield, 451–52). Implicit in this statement is an appeal to Jesus Christ as the ultimate standard of truth to which Paul is about to testify. To fortify his statement the opposite is stated: "I am not lying."[74]
συμμαρτυρούσης μοι τῆς συνειδήσεώς μου ἐν πνεύματι ἁγίῳ, "my conscience bearing witness to me by the Holy Spirit." The translation of συμμαρτυρούσης μοι is debated.[75] Some appeal to the συν- prefix in the participle and translate it "bearing witness together with me" emphasizing more of a dative of association[76] (Schreiner, 479; Cranfield, 452). The better evidence seems to take the preparation συν- prefix in the participle as intensifying the verb and translate it "bearing witness to me" (Moo, 2nd, 576, note 35; Jewett, 558).[77]

Paul explains further that his conscience witnesses to the fact that he speaks the truth by the Holy Spirit. Moo (2nd, 576) defines conscience in Paul as "an inborn faculty that monitors a person's conformity to a moral standard."[78] Jewett (558) explains it, as "the irrepressible knowledge one has "with oneself" that an action is consistent or inconsistent with one's ethical norm."[79] The unique reference to the conscience in this verse is its connection with the Holy Spirit. The veracity of Paul's witness of conscience is the Holy Spirit. Murray is correct when he says, "It is only as we are indwelt by the Spirit and live in the Spirit, only as our minds are governed by the Spirit may we be assured that the voice of conscience is in conformity with truth and right" (2:2).

9:2 ὅτι λύπη μοί ἐστιν μεγάλη καὶ ἀδιάλειπτος ὀδύνη τῇ καρδίᾳ μου· "That I have great pain and unceasing anguish in my heart." The ὅτι ("that") in verse 2 introduces the content of Paul's grief. Why did Paul express the depth and the intensity of his pain concerning this subject? The text does not explicitly state the answer. Paul may be under suspicion by the Jews because he was the apostle to the Gentiles (Acts 21:20-26). Possibly, the weight of the theological discourse he is about to discuss in Romans 9-11 has caused his pain. Most likely, Paul is feeling this grief because the glory and the faithfulness of God concerning the future of Israel is brought into question (Schreiner, 2nd, 469; Ellison, 31). The solemn emphasizes of the doubled rhetorical expressions from verse 1 ("I am speaking the truth"/"I am not lying"; and "in Christ"/"by the

---

[73] Some connect the phrase "in Christ" with the membership of the mystical body of the Church (Sanday and Headlam, 226-26; Murray, 2:1; Moo, 2nd, 576; Cranfield, 452; Jewett, 557) and/or what Paul says here is authorized and authenticated by Christ (Cranfield, 452; Käsemann, 257; Dunn, 2:523; Jewett, 557). See other statements by Paul in 2 Cor 1:21; 11:10.

[74] See 2 Cor 11:31; Gal 1:20; 1 Tim 2:7.

[75] συμμαρτυρούσης (a genitive participle) connected with συνειδήσεως in a genitive absolute construction.

[76] See Wallace, *Greek Grammar Beyond the Basic*, 139-75 for different categories of dative case. Some have used the dative of association (cf. p. 159). Wallace acknowledges that lexically συμμαρτυρέω originally developed an associative idea, but later developed "in the direction of merely intensifying μαρτυρέω" (160).

[77] BDAG, 957 states that as early as the sixth or seventh century BC that "the prefix συν-has in the highest degree the effect of strengthening." Wallace, "Witness of the Spirit," 37-51 argues a compelling case for translating the phrase "bearing witness to me" though the article is primarily centered on Rom 8:16. See also Wallace's endnote 25, pp. 292-298 for evidence of texts from the sixth century BC through ninth century AD for support of his position. See also Balz and Schneider, *EDNT*, 3:287 (*contra* Strathman, *TDNT*, 4:508-510, though he does recognize "bear witness to" in Rom 8:16).

[78] See Rom 2:15; 13:5; 1 Cor 8:7, 10, 12; 10:25, 27, 28, 29 (2x); 2 Cor 1:12; 4:2; 5:11; 1 Tim 1:5, 19: 3:9; 4:2; 2 Tim 1:3; Tit 1:15. See also Moo's comments on Rom 2:15.

[79] See his further argument in Robert Jewett, *Paul's Anthropological Terms: A Study in their Use in Conflict Settings* (Leiden: Brill, 1971), 458-460. See comments under "Biblical Theology" in this section.

Holy Spirit) continue in verse 2: "great pain"/"unceasing anguish" (Moo, 2nd, 577). There seems to be no solid evidence to make an absolute distinction between λύπη ("pain")[80] as an inner feeling of grief and ὀδύνη ("anguish")[81] as an outward expression of grief (Cranfield, 453; Moo, 2nd, 577, note 40; *contra* Godet, 339). The doubled expression intensifies Paul's mental grief (Dunn, 523).[82] Paul's mental and spiritual pain and anguish are deep and great because it deals with the eternal soul of his countrymen. The center of all this reaction is found in the heart. Traditional Judaism refers to the heart as the center of one's "will, emotion, thoughts and affections" (Jewett, 559) and even at times the conscience.[83]

9:3 ηὐχόμην γὰρ ἀνάθεμα εἶναι αὐτὸς ἐγὼ ἀπὸ τοῦ Χριστοῦ ὑπὲρ τῶν ἀδελφῶν μου τῶν συγγενῶν μου κατὰ σάρκα, "For I could request[84] that I myself were accursed, separated from the Messiah[85] for the sake of my brethren, my kinsmen according to the flesh." Paul begins this verse with γὰρ ("for") to explain further, why he expressed such strong feelings in verse 2.[86] In other words, verse 3 explains further verse 2 and verses 4-5 are attached to verse 3 which explain further the emotional response of verse 2 (Murray, 2:8-9; Piper, 45, note 58). The word ἀνάθεμα ("accursed")[87] projects the thought of being separated from the Christ[88] and thus, receiving eternal damnation.[89] In actuality, Paul could not be separated from Christ and suffer eternal

---

[80] BDAG, 604-505 gives a range of meaning: "pain of mind or spirit, grief, sorrow, affliction." The word can refer to physical pain as well as sorrow of spirit (Bultmann, *TDNT*, 4:313; Balz, *EDNT*, 2:362). Silva, *NIDNTTE*, 3:177-178 indicates that physical pain is used in connection to the word but most often λύπη refers to mental pain in the NT.

[81] BDAG, 692 gives the following meaning: "physical suffering or misery, pain, woe; mental pain, distress." Hauck, *TDNT*, 5:115 declares that the predominant use of the word is "profound and violent grief of the soul."

[82] λύπη and ὀδύνη are found in Prov 31:6; Isa 35:10; 51:11 (Psalm of Solomon 4:15 has both words but not connected closely together with καὶ). Dunn (523) seem to believe that Paul borrows from Isaiah while Moo, 2nd (577, n. 40) thinks it is unlikely. Paul borrows from Isaiah many times in Romans 9-11, but it is difficult to determine in this case.

[83] See Jewett, *Paul's Anthropological Terms*, 448; Alexander Sand, EDNT 2 (1991) 250.

[84] Or "pray."

[85] Literally, τοῦ Χριστοῦ ("the Christ"). Dunn, 525 thinks it possible that Paul is referring to Deut 18:15,18 with the double reference in using this phrase (Rom 9:3, 5).

86 [86] For a full discussion, see Abasciano, 93-94 (also note 157 and 158).

[87] BDAG, 63 defines ἀνάθεμα as what is devoted to the divinity, which can be either consecrated or accursed. In the NT, the latter is used (1 Cor 12:3; 16:22; Gal 1:8, 9). Acts 23:14 describes a person who places himself under an oath, which if he fails places him under a curse. The NT texts vary between the spelling of ἀνάθεμα and ἀνάθημα. Behm, *TDNT*, 1:354 states that ἀνάθεμα is a Hellenistic construction for the Attic form of ἀνάθημα with no change of meaning. See Moulton and Milligan, *The Vocabulary of the Greek Testament*, 33; Blass, Debrunner, and Funk, *A Greek Grammar*, §109 (3); and H. W. Kuhn, *EDNT*, 1:81 for more discussion. See Piper, 44-45 for a biblical and theological discussion.

[88] Paul adds the article: τοῦ Χριστοῦ, the Messiah.

[89] Some have alleged that Israel is not under God's condemnation for they enjoy salvation through their own covenant with God in the Old Testament Torah. See Lloyd Gaston who has two articles on this subject ("Israel's Enemies in Pauline Theology," 400–23; and "Israel's Misstep in the Eyes of Paul," 309–26). Two other authors favor this view: Gager, *The Origins of Anti-Semitism*, 197–212; and Buren, "Paul, The Church and Israel: Romans 9–11," 10–11. On the other hand, Wasserberg, "Romans 9–11 and Jewish–Christian Dialogue," 185–86 did not agree that Paul believed in the two covenants view (one for Israel and one for the church); however, Wasserberg disagreed with Paul – he does not believe Judaism is a deficient religion. For a sound critique of this view, see Johnson, *The Function of Apocalyptic and Wisdom Traditions in Romans 9–11*, 176–205; Thielman, *From Plight to Solution:* 123–32; Segal, *Paul the Convert*, 126–33; Segal, "Paul's Experience and Romans 9-11," 61–67; and Moo, 578, note 44.

damnation for someone else.[90] He has already expressed the security of the believer in Rom 8:35-39. However, this heart felt desire is a rare and unusual expression of love for his fellow Israelites. Paul is identifying with his Jewish brethren (ἀδελφῶν) in a national way and in a personal way, however not as spiritual believers but kinsmen (συγγενῶν) in the flesh.[91]

All the NT occurrences of the word εὔχομαι (here expressed as the imperfect ηὔχοντο "wish" or "pray") denote a desired request expressed to God (Acts 26:29; 2 Cor. 13:7, 9; Jas. 5:16; 3 John 2) with the possible exception in Acts 27:29 (the only other imperfect tense occurrence and could possibly be translated "desired request" or a "wish"). Thus, most likely Paul is expressing a prayer (see Cranfield 454–455, note 7; Moo, 558). Wallace categorized this imperfect as a voluntative/tendential imperfect (see more below under "Additional Exegetical Comments"). This usage is used to indicate an "unreal present situation."[92] The unreal situation is not necessarily that Paul would pray such a prayer, but that God would answer such a prayer and send Paul to eternal damnation as a substitute[93] for his fellow Israelite. Cranfield seems to give a good paraphrase of the imperfect, "I would pray (were it permissible for me so to pray and if the fulfillment of such a prayer could benefit them)."[94] The example by which Paul seems to associate with his situation and prayer is Moses in Exodus 32:30-32.[95] The use of Moses and the Exodus motif in Romans 9–11 is a prominent theme (9:14–18; 10:19; 11:13–14). See extra comments on this verse below under "Additional Exegetical Comments."

9:4 οἵτινές εἰσιν Ἰσραηλῖται, ὧν ἡ υἱοθεσία καὶ ἡ δόξα καὶ αἱ διαθῆκαι καὶ ἡ νομοθεσία καὶ ἡ λατρεία καὶ αἱ ἐπαγγελίαι. "who are Israelites, to whom belongs the adoptions as sons, and the glory, and the covenants, and the giving of the Law, and the service of worship and the promises." Paul's love and God-centered request in verse 3 is now expressed in the privileges God has given Israel. The listing of these privileges for Israel prepares the way for the question in Rom 9:6 and the polemic of Paul to establish the faithfulness of God to His covenantal promises. The main clause is οἵτινές εἰσιν Ἰσραηλῖται ("who are Israelites") stands at the head of at least four clauses: (1) ὧν ἡ υἱοθεσία . . . ("to whom belongs the adoptions . . ." v.4b); (2) ὧν οἱ

---

[90] Abasciano, 100 takes a different position. He concludes that the situation with Rom 9:3 is not a substitution but Paul's willingness to take the Lord's curse with Israel if Paul refused to forgive Israel. However, the similarities of Ex 32 with Moses are not exactly the same. God has not said that he was wiping out all of Israel in Rom 9–11, which would jeopardize the covenantal promises like in the case of Ex 32. In Rom 9:6–10, Paul begins to explain the true Israelite and that God's promises have not failed.

[91] Cranfield, 458–459 claims that Paul's use of the word ἀδελφοί as unbelieving Jews means that he "recognizes them still, in spite of their unbelief, as fellow-members of the people of God" and "unbelieving Israel is within the elect community." Moo, 559, note 24 points out that lexically 130 of Paul's 133 uses of ἀδελφός refer to a Christian brother (exceptions are 1 Cor 9:5 and Gal 1:19). However, why would Paul desire to be separated from Christ and condemned for the brethren who are already saved? Thus, the context of Rom 9:3 indicates that ἀδελφοί with the phrase "my kinsman according to the flesh" refers to Paul's fellow Israelite that has not accepted Jesus as the Christ. Moo (Ibid.) is correct to distinguish individual salvific election of Rom 9:6–29 and 11:5–7 and the general nonsalvific corporate election of Israel – kinsman according to the flesh (Acts 2:29; 3:17, 22; 7:2, 23, 25–26). The latter is Paul's point here in Rom 9:3.

[92] Wallace, *Greek Grammar Beyond the Basic*, 551.

[93] ὑπέρ ("in the place of" or "for the sake of") often expresses the action of someone acting "on behalf of" someone by taking his or her place (BDAG, 1031; Moo, 559–560).

[94] See Additional Exegetical Comments.

[95] See Moo, 559, note 21 and Moo, 2nd, 579 (also n. 52); Cranfield, 454; Munck, *Christ and Israel*, 29; Wiles, *Paul's Intercessory Prayer*, 256; Abasciano, 45-89. Abasciano argues that the allusion to Ex 32-34 holds the key to Rom 9:1-5. He describes the Exodus allusion as a type (p. 96).

πατέρες . . . ("whose are the fathers . . ." v. 5a); (3) καὶ ἐξ ὧν ὁ χριστὸς . . . ("and from whom is the Christ . . ." v. 5b); and (4) ὁ ὢν ἐπὶ πάντων . . . ("who is over all . . ." v. 5c).

Campbell states, "One gets the impression that when Paul wants to stress ethnic affiliation, he uses the term Jew, but when he comes to reflect upon their spiritual heritage, Israel/Israelite alone can clearly designate this people as a religious entity."[96] First, Paul's distinction between Israel and Gentiles is constant throughout the letter (cf. 9:24).[97] When Paul uses the term "Israel,"[98] he is not using it merely as a general designation of those who are physical descent from Abraham. Rather he uses it to designate the people of the covenant, which was made with Abraham. However, Paul also says that not all of Israel are Israel (cf. Rom 2:28–29; 11:28), "but the discussion is centered within Israel and around Israel."[99] In other words, Israel cannot be exactly reduced to all the physical offspring of Abraham (through Isaac and Jacob), but Israel in this context includes those physical offspring who share his faith. On the other hand, the solidarity of Israel as a people is also not sacrificed despite Paul's statement in Rom 9:6. "Paul himself appears to operate with a fluid concept of Israel. This doubtless originates from ancient Semitic concepts of solidarity which modern individualism finds hard to understand because it is so far removed from much contemporary (Western) religious thought."[100] This distinction and tension is not Paul's invention. Within the nation of Israel, God has always chosen "children of the promise" (Rom 9:8) to carry out his purposes. Paul demonstrates this from the history of Israel in his argument in Rom 9:7–11.[101] Finally, Paul makes a distinction between Israel whether it is faithful Israel or "the rest" (Rom 11:7).

The Greek text suggests a structure of two series of three:

ἡ υἱοθεσία καὶ ἡ δόξα καὶ αἱ διαθῆκαι
ἡ νομοθεσία καὶ ἡ λατρεία καὶ αἱ ἐπαγγελίαι

Though most of the Israelites refused God's salvation in Jesus Christ, they are called Israelites (εἰσιν – durative present).[102] Strikingly, Paul also states that they have υἱοθεσία (adoption). Israel's corporate election as a nation is God choosing and giving covenantal provisions, which is different from Christian adoption (cf. Rom 8:15, 23; Gal 4:5; Eph 1:5).[103] One major difference is that most of the nation of Israel rejected Jesus Christ and His salvation while Christian adoption is part of the benefits when one believes in the salvation of Jesus Christ (Murray, 2:5; Hodge, 298–299). However, it is also possible that Paul looks forward to the future

---

[96] William S. Campbell, "Israel," in *Dictionary of Paul and His Letters* (Downers Grove: InterVarsity Press, 1993), 441; *contra* James D. G. Dunn, *The Theology of Paul the Apostle* (Grand Rapids: Eerdmans, 1998), 505–07.

[97] William S. Campbell, *Paul and the Creation of Christian Identity* (London: T & T Clark, 2008), 124.

[98] This paragraph comes from William S. Campbell's thoughts in Sullivan, *The Isaianic New Exodus in Romans 9-11*, 119, 178, n. 61.

[99] Campbell, *Paul and the Creation of Christian Identity*, 124. However, in Rom 1–8 Paul used the word "Jew(s)" (1:16; 2:9, 10, 17, 28, 29; 3:1, 9; 3:9, 29; 9:24; 10:12) is prominent and Rom 9–11 he uses "Israel" (9:6, [2x], 27 [2x], 9:31; 10:19; 10:21; 11:2, 7, 25, 26) and "Israelite" (9:4) (Moo, 2nd, 581).

[100] Campbell, "Israel," 442. Pablo T. Gadenz, *Called from the Jews and from the Gentiles: Pauline Ecclesiology in Romans 9-11*, Wissenschaftliche Untersuchungen zum Neun Testament 2. Reihe, 267 (Tübingen: Mohr Siebeck, 2009), 64-82 has the same thought.

[101] Campbell, *Paul and the Creation of Christian Identity*, 124.

[102] Wallace, *Greek Grammar Beyond the Basics*, 518.

[103] See Rom 8:15, 23.

when what is only corporate election among the majority of unbelief in his day, God will make sonship part of the corporate election of all Israelites because He will save them (Rom 11:26).[104]

The word δόξα (glory) is usually understood to refer to the theophanies of God in the OT, especially the manifestation of God in the wilderness experience (Ex 16:10; 24:16-17; 29:43; 33:18, 22; 40:34; Lev 9:23).[105] The glory of the Lord in Exodus 32-34 appears to provide the background for God's covenantal presence (Abasciano, 125). Paul uses δόξα over seventy times but he only uses it in one place to refer to an OT theophany (2 Cor 3:7–11).[106] Piper is correct in saying that this fact alone should cause us to pause in assigning this meaning to Rom 9:4.[107] However, the absolute use of δόξα is often used for the future eschatological glory (Rom 2:7, 10; 8:18; 9:23b; Col 1:27b; 3:4; 2 Tim 2:10).[108] Piper ties the context of "adoption" in Rom 8 (vv. 17–18, 21, 23, 30) with glory and argues that δόξα in Rom 9 looks to the future eschaton while rooted to the past as an eschatological expectation.[109] Moo, 2nd, 583 and Abasciano are not necessarily as convinced with Piper's position. The positions of the OT glory of God and the eschatological glory do not seem to be necessarily mutually exclusive or fundamentally distinct. Just like adoption, the glory of the past is culminated in the eschatological glory in the future (Abasciano. 126–127).

The next term αἱ διαθῆκαι (the covenants)[110] refers to covenants that God gave in the Jewish Scripture, but the consensus to which covenants is debated. Some refer διαθῆκαι to the covenants with Abraham, Moses, and David (Murray 2:5) while others indicate the covenants during the time from Abraham to Moses (Alford, 2:404; Sanday and Headlam, 230).[111] Or more generally, all the biblical covenants including the new covenant (Jer 31; Rom 11:26-27) (Moo, 2nd, 583–84; Abasciano, 127).[112] Piper and Schreiner suggests that the unusual plural here points to a possible assonance with ἐπαγγελίαι (promises) and probably means that the meaning resides in the "total general impact" more than the particular meaning of each word (Piper, 35; Schreiner, 485). Piper and Schreiner, 484 also contend that covenants and promises are basically synonymous in 9:4. However, it is probably best to explain that the covenants contained promises, and the two concepts are complimentary rather than synonymous (Abasciano, 128, n.

---

[104] Piper, 32. Piper follows Martin Rese, "Die Vozuege Israels in Roem 9,4–5 und Eph 2,12," *ThZ* 31, 1975): 211–22; Schlier, *Roemerbrief*, 286 and Luz, *Das Geschichtsverstaendnis des Paulus*, 271. Moo, 2nd, 583 is open to the possibility of Paul "may therefore hint" at the future salvation of Israel, which is stated in Romans 11. Byrne, 127–140.

[105] Barrett, 166; Sanday and Headlam, 230; Murray, 2:5; Käsemann, 258; Fitzmyer, 546; Dunn 526; Byrne, 287. Schreiner, 484 refers to it as the presence of God; Cranfield, 462 as the manifestation of the divine presence.

[106] Abasciano, 125–126 believes the context of Rom 9:4 is rooted in Ex 32–34 and connects this background to Paul's use in 2 Cor 3.

[107] Piper, 33. Contra Schreiner, 484, n. 9.

[108] Other places in Paul where δόξα is used for eschatological glory but not in the absolute state: Rom 5:2; 8:21; 9:23a; 1 Cor 2:7; Eph 1:18; Phil 3:21; 1 Th 2:12; 2 Th 2:14; Tit 2:13. Dunn, 526 and Moo, 2nd, 583, n. 72 consider Paul's use as stylistic. Jewett, 563 refers glory to the eschatological salvation.

[109] Piper, 34. For example, see the Isaianic glory of the Lord in Isa 40:5; 42:8; 46:13; 48:11; 58:8; 60:1, 2, 7; 66:11, 18. He also traces this theme in later Jewish eschatological writings and the Messianic expectation and glory in Lk 2:32.

[110] Calvin Roetzel, "Διαθήκη in Rom 9,4," *Biblica* 51 (1970): 377-390 suggestion that the term means "ordinances, commandments, or oaths" is unconvincing (Abasciano, 127, n.248; Dunn, 527; Jewett, 564, n. 107; Fitzmyer, 546).

[111] See also Munck, *Christ and Israel*, 31.

[112] Though in the end, Abasciano states that the Abrahamic covenant and its promises found in the Mosaic covenant is what Paul means by covenants (p. 128-30). However, on this point, he seems to be overly influenced by the Ex 32-34 motif in Rom 9:4.

255). Paul seems to use the plural to express in a broad way the covenants that God has given because through these covenants God has revealed Israel's future destiny. God's past covenants have continual blessings and future promises. Schriener (2nd, 475) is correct when he warns because the promises have not come to pass for Israel should not be concluded that such promises has been "passed on to the church badly misconstrues Paul's argument."

The word ἡ νομοθεσία has two basic meanings: (1) the divine act of giving the law;[113] or (2) a reference to the content and passion of the law.[114] A few scholars do not make a rigid distinction between the two definitions. They conclude that the law has the character of divine revelation that was given (Calvin, 195; Alford, 404; Piper, 36-37; Dunn, 527). Piper argues that Paul used νομοθεσία instead of νομος (law) because νομοθεσία provides a rhythm counterpart to υἱοθεσία just as αἱ διαθῆκαι (the covenants) does to αἱ ἐπαγγελίαι (the promises) (Piper, 36; Dunn, 527). He also provides places in the Hellenistic Jewish literature where νομοθεσία and νομος are synonymous.[115] However, the first meaning has also a strong case. The three occurrences of word νομοθετέω (law-giving) in the Greek Bible (in Heb. 7:11 and 8:6 and νομοθέτης in Ps. 9:21)[116] are a cognate to νομοθεσία, as are many of the occurrences in Jewish Greek literature at the time (e.g., Josephus, *Against Apon* 2.170; *Ant.* 3.287; 12.37; Philo, *On the Life of Moses* 2.2).[117] Abasciano connects the original context of the allusion to Exod 32-34 which is relevant and fits the context of the words Paul uses in Rom 9:4. However, his argument for an eschatological significance with this term is unconvincing (Abasciano, 131–132). It is difficult to determine the meaning Paul has in mind. What needs to be avoided is packing a lot of theological concepts into the meaning of the word in this verse.

The "service of worship" (ἡ λατρεία) is used nine times in the LXX (including four usages in the Apocrypha) and it corresponds to the Hebrew word עֲבֹדָה (work/service or service of worship).[118] All nine LXX usages and three out of the other four usages in the NT have the concept of sacrificial worship to the Lord. Even the reference to spiritual worship in Rom 12:1 is compared to the sacrificial worship of the OT.[119] Cranfield, 463 and Jewett, 565 infer the likelihood of Paul also including the non-sacrificial worship of synagogue with such things as prayer, reading of the Scriptures, and observation of other cultic law. The word usage may be general in nature, but it is often restricted more to the sacrificial system (Fitzmyer, 547). Through the ministry of λατρεία the nation of Israel had access to atonement for their sins, which brought forgiveness and acceptance with God. Piper points out that the inaugural λατρεία (Ex 12:25-27) was at Passover. This point expresses an Exodus and NE motif which finds its fulfillment in the death and resurrection of the Messiah (our Passover Lamb, 1 Cor 5:7) who is promised first to Israel and then to the Gentiles (Rom 1:16; 2:9,10) (Piper, 38).

"The promises" (αἱ ἐπαγγελίαι) did not have an initial history in the OT, but the idea of the promise of God was developed before the time of the apostle Paul.[120] Paul uses the word

---

[113] Murray, 2:6; Munck, Christ and Israel, 32, n. 15; Käsemann, 247; Moo, 2nd, 584; Meyer, 116.

[114] Hodge, 299; Cranfield, 463; Fitzmyer, 546; Gutbrod, *TDNT*, 4:1089; Jewett, 564.

[115] Piper, 36. Piper cites 2 Macc. 6:23; 4 Macc. 5:35; 17:16; *Ep. Arist.* 15; Philo, *On Abraham* 5; *On the Cherubim* 87.

[116] Louw and Nida, *Greek-English Lexicon of the NT*, 33.339–340.

[117] Moo, 2nd, 584, n. 77.

[118] Koehler et al., *HALOT*, 776; Clines, *DCH*, 6:226–227.

[119] See H. Strathmann, *TDNT* 4:59–65; Cranfield, 463, n. 5; Moo, 2nd, 584, n. 80; Piper, 37–38.

[120] Schniewind and Friedrich, *TDNT*, 2:579. They list Test. Jos., 20; Ps. Sol. 12:8; Josephus, *Ant.*, 2, 219 and 3, 77 among others. See brief discussion of Fitzmyer, 547 who agrees.

"promise(s)" twenty-five times in the NT and uses the plural form six times (Rom 9:4; 15:8; 2 Cor 1:20; 7:1; Gal 3:16; 3:21). Most commentators understand that ἐπαγγελίαι as the general promises of God, especially those promises dealing with the Messiah (Murray, 2:6; Sanday and Headlam, 231; Hodge, 299; Käsemann, 259; Jewett, 565). Others concentrate more on the promises to Abraham and the other patriarchs, which includes broad aspect of the Messiah (Cranfield, 464; Moo, 2nd, 584; Morris, 349; Hultgren, 358). Paul also uses the word for the prophetic promises (2 Cor 7:1) and generally to all the promises of God (2 Cor 1:20). In Gal 3:21, he uses the promises of God over against the Law, which is able to convey life and righteousness. Piper expresses the promises as a summation of "all the good that God can possibly offer his people."[121] In Romans, the stress is more the promises to Abraham and the patriarchs (Dunn, 212). This word and the connection of it with the covenants (διαθῆκαι) anticipate the promises and covenants of God, which speaks of the future for the nation of Israel and the blessings that are expressed by these two words, especially in Rom 11 where the promises are irrevocable (11:29).

9:5 ὧν οἱ πατέρες, καὶ ἐξ ὧν ὁ χριστὸς τὸ κατὰ σάρκα, ὁ ὢν ἐπὶ πάντων, θεὸς εὐλογητὸς εἰς τοὺς αἰῶνας· ἀμήν. "to whom are the fathers, and from whom, according to the flesh, is the Christ, who is over all, God blessed forever. Amen." Most interpreters take οἱ πατέρες (the fathers) to refer to Abraham, Isaac and Jacob (Schreiner, 2nd, 475; Moo, 2nd, 585; Fitzmyer, 547; Piper, 40). Several others also designate the three patriarchs but also add the twelve sons of Jacob (Cranfield, 464; Bruce, 185), the wilderness generation (Dunn, 528), David (Stuhlmacher, 145–146; Cranfield, 464), and the fathers in distinction from Abraham through redemption history (Murray, 2:6; Jewett, 566). However, the context in Rom 4 and more importantly, Rom 9:6–13 and 11:28–29 direct the interpretation to Abrahamic promises and the three patriarchs. The significance of the fathers is not that the fathers or their seed merit such a great blessing, but the fathers received the irrevocable promises by the grace and choice of God (Rom 9:10–11). Paul seems to be placing overlapping privileges in Rom 9:4-5 to point to the certainty of Israel's salvation, but in paradoxical way because of the nation's disobedient that bring condemnation (Rom 9:3) (Piper, 41–42).

The third and final relative clause that describes an Israelite in Rom 9:4-5 is different from the other two (ὧν in vv. 4, 5a) for it is preceded by the preposition ἐξ ὧν (from whom). Piper suggests that not only is Paul expressing the Christ will be from a Jewish origin, but the fathers give rise to the people of Israel and from Israel, specifically from Judah, the Christ will come. Thus, the privilege of Israel reaches a climax.[122] The Christ comes in human flesh but not sinful flesh (2 Cor 5:21). This phrase stresses the humanity of the person of Christ. The historic question debated down through Church history is whether the last part of v. 5 refers to the deity of Christ or is it a blessing to the personhood of God the Father. Some commentaries exclaim that Rom 9:5 probably has been discussed at greater length than any other verse in the NT (Sanday & Headlam, 233).[123]

---

[121] Piper, 39. Abasciano, 133–134 seems to fit this definition. He also tries to connect this thought to Exod 32.

[122] Piper, 42–43.

[123] Metzger, "The Punctuation of Rom 9:5," 95; Burkitt, "On Romans IX 5," 451.

Those who support that the last part of v. 5 refers to Christ[124] usually punctuate the text as follows:[125] (1) "to them belong the patriarchs, and from them, according to the flesh comes the Messiah, who is over all, God blessed forever. Amen" (NRSV; cf. also KJV; NASB).[126] This translation is preferred and seems to communicate the universal sovereignty of God over all things (Sanday and Headlam, 238; Murray, 2:248; Cranfield, 451, 469; Harris, *Jesus as "God,"* 166; Schreiner, 2nd, 478–79). (2) "To them belong the patriarchs, and from their race, according to the flesh, is the Christ, who is God over all, blessed forever. Amen" (ESV; cf. also NIV).[127] If the reference is to God the Father,[128] then the punctuation is usually: (1) "of their race, according to the flesh, is the Christ. God who is over all be blessed forever. Amen" (RSV); or (2) "from them, in natural descent, sprang the Messiah. May God, supreme over all, be blessed forever! Amen" (NEB).

The support for the latter part of v. 5 referring to God the Father are: (1) εὐλογητὸς (blessed) in the NT predominately refers to God (Mk 14:61; Lk 1:68; Rom 1:25; 2 Cor 1:3; 11:31; Eph 1:3; 1 Pet 1:3). (2) The unusual order of εὐλογητὸς (blessed) following θεὸς (God) seems to follow the Jewish theme and emphasizes God's lordship. (3) In Pauline texts, nowhere else does θεὸς (God) refer to Christ; thus, one would not necessarily expect it here. (4) In the undisputed Pauline letters, doxologies to Christ are not found. (5) The closest parallel to v. 5 expression is in Eph 4:6 and in this verse the Father is the referent – He is said to be ὁ ἐπὶ πάντων ("the one who is over all"). This Greek phrase is close to the Rom 9:5 phrase. (6) A closing reference to God is a typical Jewish reference and it would refer to God and not likely to Christ who is God. (7) The doxology of Rom 11:33-36 is a closing response of Paul just like Rom 9:5 is the closing verse of Rom 9:1-5. The parallel point is that both sections refer to God and not to Christ.

These major points have their strength, but there are formidable arguments that Paul refers to Christ here as God. (1) Though this is not a usual expression in referring Christ as God, the phrase τὸ κατὰ σάρκα ("according to the flesh") fits more smoothly if the contrasting phrase is included. He was born from a Jewish heritage according to the flesh and He also transcends this identity to share the divine nature as God. (2) The clearest and closest antecedent to the participle ὁ ὢν ("who is") is ὁ χριστὸς ("the Christ"),[129] which 2 Cor 11:31 is a close parallel.[130] In the blessing of 2 Cor 11:31, the same participle ὁ ὢν ("who is") refers back to a previous

---

[124] Calvin, 342–343; Sanday and Headlam, 233–238; Alford, 2:404–406; Haldane, 445; Harrison and Hagner, 141–142; Hodges, 472–475; Liddon, 151–154; Murray, 245–248; Bruce, 186–187; Cranfield, 456–470; Jewett, 567–568; Metzger; Morris, 350; Fitzmyer, 548–549; Mounce, 196-197; Moo, 2nd, 585–86; Schreiner, 2nd, 475–76; Shedd, 278–279. For an in-depth defence of this position, see Harris, *Jesus as "God,"* 143–172.

[125] For a summary of the detail punctuation in translations, see Moo, 2nd, 586–588. See Metzger, "The Punctuation of Rom 9:5," 95–96 for a summary of eight different possibilities in punctuation. He concludes that latter part of verse 5 should be as follows: καὶ ἐξ ὧν ὁ χριστὸς τὸ κατὰ σάρκα, ὁ ὢν ἐπὶ πάντων θεὸς εὐλογητὸς εἰς τοὺς αἰῶνας, ἀμήν. (p. 112).

[126] Most of the church fathers favored this translation (Metzger, "The Punctuation of Rom 9:5," 102–103). For a discussion of the punctuation of Rom 9:5, see Ibid., 97–98.

[127] This translation seems to imply that Christ is universally sovereign even over the Father. However, the translation is supported by Alford, 405; Fitzmyer, 539; Moo, 2nd, 586–87.

[128] Meyer, 2:119–122; Käsemann, 259–260; Wilckens, 2:189; Dunn, 528–529; Stuhlmacher, 145–46; Byrne, 288. For a history of interpretation, see Kuss, 3:679–696.

[129] Asyndetic doxologies in the NT are not found or rare (cf. Rom 1:25; 11:36; 2 Cor 11:31; 1 Pet 4:11; Gal 1:5; Eph 3:21; Phil 4:20; 1 Tim 1:17; 2 Tim 4:18; Heb 13:21; 1 Pet 4:11; 2 Pet 3:18).

[130] ὁ θεὸς καὶ πατὴρ τοῦ κυρίου Ἰησοῦ οἶδεν, ὁ ὢν εὐλογητὸς εἰς τοὺς αἰῶνας, ὅτι οὐ ψεύδομαι ("The God and Father of the Lord Jesus, He who is blessed forever, knows that I am not lying" NASB).

antecedent just like in Rom 9:5. (3) The independent blessings in the LXX and NT always place the word order of εὐλογητὸς ("blessed") in the first position in Greek.[131] However, in Rom 9:5 εὐλογητὸς ("blessed") is not in the first position but after θεὸς (God), which suggests that the blessing is tied to the previous context of ὁ χριστὸς ("the Christ"). (4) For Paul to express praise to God the Father sits awkwardly in the context in Rom 9:1-5 where Paul's grief over Israel is their separation from Christ. To ascribe blessedness to Christ by identifying him as God fits more the context and flow of the passage. Also, the deity of the Christ would help explain Paul's grief and accentuate Israel's error in misunderstanding their divine privileges that he has previously mentioned in the context. (5) For Paul to call Christ "God" is consistent with his teaching and theology in his writings.[132] Thus, the notion that Paul would ascribe "God" to Christ in a doxology is not incompatible with Pauline thought. Therefore, I agree with Moo, 2nd, 588 that connecting "God" to "Christ" is "exegetically preferable, theologically unobjectionable, and contextually appropriate."

Biblical Theological Comments

Though Paul has stated "to the Jew first and also to the Greek" (1:16; 2:9, 10), his rhetorical viewpoint seems to side with the Gentiles against the Jews. He even states that he is an apostle of the Gentiles, and he magnifies his ministry (11:13). Paul downplays the acclaim of circumcision and the knowledge of the law and points out that their breaking of the law blasphemes God (2:23–29). This argument would not endear himself to his countryman, though it is absolutely essential to understand and accept the gospel of Jesus Christ. His argument at the end of Rom 2 leads to the question in Rom 3:1, whether there is any advantage or benefit in being a Jew. However, Paul's answer of yes is accompanied with only one reason, and he ends the argument of Rom 3 condemning all men both Jews and Greeks.

In Rom 9:1–5, Paul no longer characterizes his fellow-Jews with the awful potent sinful terms of Rom 3:10–20, though this is still true about their spiritual condition. He wants his fellow-kinsmen to know that he is not lying but telling the truth for he is genuinely concerned about their eternal destiny. Even to the desire, if it were possible (and it is not possible), for Paul to be accursed in their place.

The question of Rom 3:1 concerning the advantage and value of being a Jew is answered in more of a comprehensive way in Rom 9:4-5, which includes personal, eternal salvation (9:2-3). In Rom 3, Paul was concerned with the sin of the nation and their need for the gospel. A spiritual condition that is no different from the Gentiles, except that Israel was privileged with receiving special revelation and privileges that were not given to the Gentiles. In Rom 9, Paul begins to address the problematic issue of God's faithfulness to His covenantal promises. If there is "no distinction between Jew and Gentile, then what does the Jews' covenant status with God matter in the big scheme of things?" (Runge, 162). However, the covenantal status and privileges

---

[131] See in LXX Gen 9:26; 14:20; 24:27; Ex 18:10; Ruth 4:14; 1 Sam 25:32; 2 Sam 6:21; 18:28; 1 Kings 1:48; 8:15, 56; 2 Chron 2:11; 6:4; Ps 17:47; 27:6; 30:22; 40:14; 65:20, 36; 71:18; 88:53; 105:48; 123:6; 143:1; Dan 3:95; Zech 11:5; Ezra 7:27; and in the NT Lk 1:68; 2 Cor 1:3; Eph 1:3; 1 Pet 1:3. The only possible exception is Ps 67:19-20 and even in this case some are doubtful that the exception is legitimate (See Harris, *Jesus as "God,"* 161–162 and Fitzmyer, 549).

[132] See Phil 2:6, 10-11; Col 1:15, 19; 2:9; 1 Cor 8:6; Tit 2:13.

God gave the nations are the very thing Paul now is elevating. These promises and privileges have not been fully and finally fulfilled or cancelled.

Application and Devotional Implications

The big idea of Rom 9:1–5 is the attitude of believers toward unbelievers should be a loving desire to win them to Christ. The outline of the section:

1. Paul's attitude toward the lost in Israel (9:1–3)
2. The privileges of God given to Israel (9:4–5)

How could Paul love the Jewish people when so many of them wanted to kill him because he preached that Jesus was the Christ, the Son of God? This is a great illustration of God's agape love demonstrated through a human instrument, Paul. If Paul could stand before us today, he would be the first one to say that God has produced this kind of love and not something he produced. The love for lost souls kept him going back to his people. Paul says in verse 2 that he had great sorrow and unceasing grief in his heart. He even goes to the extent in verse 3 to desire, if it were possible (and it is not possible), to be damned in hell forever instead of them. These Greek words (see explanation above) indicate an unattainable wish or prayer. Paul explained in Romans 8 the most impressive evidence for the eternal security of the believer and now he says if it were permissible (which it is not) he would give it up to save others. This wishful prayer is the same kind of heart that Moses had in Ex 32:30–33. This OT passage is exactly what our Lord did when he died on the cross. He died in the place of his sinful people. He died for their curse, wrath, and penalty for sin.

Here in Rom 9:4-5 is Jesus Christ for which all the other privileges mentioned culminate on and in which Israel as a nation rejected. The privileges of every Israelite are dependent on acceptance of Jesus Christ by faith. They were hanging on to Judaism and rejecting the Messiah Jesus and this brought the curse of God. They were born with the privilege of knowing God's Law. They were taught the promises of the covenants to the Fathers and the promises of the Messiah. They participated in the rituals of the temple and the regulation of the Law. All of these great privileges were all around them. They were so close but so far. How could they be so dull? How could they miss it? Maybe we should turn the tables and ask ourselves if we have done the same thing.

Maybe all your life you have been brought to church. Or maybe you have had the privilege of attending church for many years. You have heard about the stories of the OT and you heard preacher after preacher talk about Christ and him dying on the cross and rising again the third day. When preachers talk about all have sinned and deserve the wrath of God, you always say he is talking about someone else and not you. How could I be under God's wrath? I have always heard that Jesus was born, lived, died, and was resurrected. Surely, I am OK. Yet, year after year you have been deceptively blinded by your sin, and religious pride. As you examine yourself you find that your belief has been only an intellectual assent, a shallow ritual or a family tradition. You are just like many of the Jews of Paul's day. You know many of the privileges of Christianity; you have participated in the services, fellowships, and meetings; you know about Christ and the Scripture, but you have never truly trust Him as the Savior who saves sinners that deserve His wrath. May God give you conviction unto faith for salvation and burden the saved to share it with others!

Additional Exegetical Comments

9:3 Cranfield, 454-457 presents 4 possible ways to understand ηὔχοντο: (1) imperfect denoting action progressive in the past – Paul would pray this in the past but no longer does so (Jewett, 560; Sanday and Headlam, 228). The context and doctrinal implications of Paul's statement do not fit well with this expression (Cranfield, 455). (2) Conative imperfect denoting attempted action, however, not accomplished or accepted by Paul's mind. Cranfield, 455 is probably correct that this understanding is least likely for in this context it seems forced. (3) The understanding of 3 and 4 have a slight distinction. This third meaning expresses a present wishful prayer that is capable of fulfillment but expressed with a certain vagueness (like a classical optative with ἄν).[133] This understanding in Rom 9:3 would not be biblically or theological compatible with NT doctrine. This prayer could not be fulfilled. However, those who take this position point to the example of Moses in Ex 32:31-33.[134] However, the Moses' example could fit just as well with the fourth understanding (see Moo, 2nd, 579; Schreiner, 2nd, 470; Dunn, 532; Morris, 347). (4) An imperfect where a prayer (or wish) is recognized as unattainable or impermissible (like a classical imperfect with ἄν) – Paul would pray or wish if it was permissible, but he knew it was not. This view seems to fit best.[135] Calvin seems to bring the balance of doctrinal clarity with the deep emotion of Paul together in precise tension and balance:

> [I]f then we love in God and not without God's authority, our love can never be too much. And such was the love of Paul; for seeing his own nation endued with so many of God's benefits, he loved God's gifts in them, and them on account of God's gifts; and he deemed it a great evil that those gifts should perish, hence it was that his mind being overwhelmed, he burst forth into this extreme wish. Thus I consent not to the opinion of those who think that Paul spoke these words from regard to God only, and not to men; nor do I agree with others, who say, that without any thought of God, he was influenced only by love to men: but I connect the love of men with a zeal for God's glory.[136]

Excursus

The conscience is affected by the Fall of Adam's sin and the consequence of personal sin in the individual's life. However, the Law is written on the heart of each person either excusing or accusing the person who violates the law (Rom 2:15). Thus, the conscience of a person either blames, pains or bothers the weak and guilty person (1 Cor 8:7, 10, 12; 10:25, 27–29) or bears witness of a blameless and good conscience to those who follow the moral law of God (Acts 23:1; 24:16; 2 Cor 1:12; 1 Tim 1:5; 1 Pet 3:16, 21). Those who violate a good conscience and faith are in danger of suffering shipwreck concerning the faith (1 Tim 1:19; 3:9). Paul states that the defiled and unbelieving have both their mind and conscience defiled (1 Tim 4:2; Tit 1:15). The author to the book of Hebrews states that the OT sacrifices could not cleanse the conscience

---

[133] See Hays, *Echoes*, 206, note 56.

[134] Käseman, 258 and Jewett, 651 argue that Paul did not have Moses's example in mind, nor the Servant of the Lord or any comparison with Christ as mediator.

[135] See Cranfield, 455-57 (also p. 457, note 1); Fitzmyer, 544; Robertson, *Grammar of the Greek NT*, 886; BDF, *A Greek Grammar of the New Testament*, 359(2); and McKay, "Time and Aspect in NT Greek," 213.

[136] Calvin, 335–337.

(Heb 9:9). Only a sincere belief in what the blood of Jesus did can cleanse the conscience from the defilement of sin (Heb 9:14; 10:2, 22). The believer in Christ does not have a perfect conscience in his Christian life, but by God's grace he can have a testimony of a good and blameless conscience before men and God (2 Cor 1:12; 4:2; 5:11). The concept of conscience seems to have two major definitions. First, a more narrow definition, which views the conscience as mental pain that one experiences when the moral law is transgressed. Second concept involves "the whole person, viewed as a responsible moral being."[137]

Meadors, "Conscience," *EDBT*, summarizes his thoughts on the conscience: (1) it is a God-given capacity to exercise self-critique; (2) it witnesses to the value system of the person; and (3) it is a servant of the value system of the person. "Conscience is an aspect of self-awareness that produces the pain and/or pleasure we 'feel' as we reflect on the norms and values we recognize and apply. Conscience is not an outside voice. It is a [*sic*] inward capacity humans possess to critique themselves because the Creator provided this process as a means of moral restraint for his creation. The critique conscience exercises related to the value system which a person develops."[138] Rom 12:1–2 points the believer to the divine values and process for renewal of a godly conscience.

Selected Bibliography

Arndt, William, Frederick W. Danker, and Walter Bauer, *A Greek-English Lexicon of the New Testament and Other Early Christian Literature* (Chicago: University of Chicago Press, 2000).

Balz, Horst Robert and Gerhard Schneider, eds. *EDNT*, 3 vols. (Grand Rapids: Eerdmans, 1990).

Behm. "ἀνάθεμα," *TDNT*. Vol. 1 (Grand Rapids: Eerdmans, 1964).

Blass, Friedrich, Albert Debrunner, and Robert Walter Funk. *A Greek Grammar of the New Testament and Other Early Christian Literature* (Chicago: University of Chicago Press, 1961).

Bultmann, Rudolph. "λύπη," *TDNT*. Vol. 4 (Grand Rapids: Eerdmanns, 1964).

Buren, Paul van. "Paul, The Church and Israel: Romans 9–11." *The Princeton Seminary Bulletin,* Supplemental issue 1 (1990): 5–18.

Burkitt, F. C. "On Romans IX 5 and Mark XIV 61." *Journal of Theological Studies* 5 (1903-1904): 451-455.

Campbell, William S. "Israel," in *Dictionary of Paul and His Letters* (Downers Grove: InterVarsity Press, 1993).

Cline, David J. A., ed. *DCH*, 8 vols. (Sheffield: Sheffield Academic Press, 1993-2011).

Dunn, J. D. G. *The Theology of Paul the Apostle* (Grand Rapids: Eerdmans, 1998).

Gadenz, Pablo T. *Called from the Jews and from the Gentiles: Pauline Ecclesiology in Romans 9-11*. Wissenschaftliche Untersuchungen zum Neun Testament 2. Reihe, 267 (Tübingen: Mohr Siebeck, 2009).

Gager, John G. *The Origins of Anti-Semitism: Attitudes toward Judaism in Pagan and Christian Antiquity* (New York: Oxford University Press, 1983).

---

[137] Silva, *NIDNTTE*, 2nd ed., 4:406.

[138] Gary T. Meadors, "Conscience," eds. Walter A. Elwell and Walter A. Elwell, EDBT (Grand Rapids: Baker Book House, 1996), 115.

Gaston, Lloyd. "Israel's Enemies in Pauline Theology." *New Testament Studies* 28 (1982), 400–23.

Gaston, Lloyd. "Israel's Misstep in the Eyes of Paul," in *The Romans Debate*, ed. Karl P. Donfried, rev. and exp. ed. (Minneapolis: Augsburg Press, 1977, 1991), 309–26.

Hauck, "ὀδύνη," *TDNT*, vol. 5 (Grand Rapids: Eerdmans, 1964).

Harris, Murray J. *Jesus as "God": Theos as a Christological Term in the New Testament* (Grand Rapids: Baker, 1992).

Hays, Richard B. *Echoes of Scripture in the Letters of Paul* (New Haven: Yale University Press, 1989).

Holmes, Michael W. ed. *The Greek New Testament: SBL Edition*. (Lexham Press; Society of Biblical Literature, 2011–2013).

Jewett, Robert. *Paul's Anthropological Terms: A Study in their Use in Conflict Settings*. (Leiden: Brill, 1971).

Johnson, E. Elizabeth. *The Function of Apocalyptic and Wisdom Traditions in Romans 9–11*. Society of Biblical Literature Dissertation Series, ed. Charles Talbert, vol. 109 (Atlanta: Scholars Press, 1989).

Kuhn, H. W. "ἀνάθεμα," *EDNT*. Vol 1 (Grand Rapids: Eerdmans, 1990).

Louw, Johannes P. and Eugene Albert Nida. *Greek-English Lexicon of the New Testament: Based on Semantic Domains* (New York: United Bible Societies, 1996).

Luz, Ulrich. *Das Geschichtsverstaendnis des Paulus* (München: C. Kaiser, 1968).

McKay, K. L. "Time and Aspect in New Testament Greek." *Novum Testamentum* 24, 3 (1992): 209–228.

Meadors, Gary T. "Conscience," eds. Walter A. Elwell and Walter A. Elwell, *EDBT* (Grand Rapids: Baker Book House, 1996).

Metzger, Bruce M. *A Textual Commentary on the Greek New Testament*. 2nd ed. (Stuttgart: Deutsche Bibelgesellschaft, 1994).

Metzger, Bruce M. "The Punctuation of Rom, 9:5." In *Christ and Spirit in the New Testament: In Honour of Charles, Francis Digby Moule*, eds. B. Lindars and S. S. Smalley (Cambridge: Cambridge Press, 1973), 95–112.

Moulton, James Hope and George Milligan, *The Vocabulary of the Greek Testament* (London: Hodder and Stoughton, 1930).

Munck, Johannes. *Christ and Israel: An Interpretation of Romans 9–11*. Translated by Ingeborg Nixon. Philadelphia: Fortress Press, 1967.

Rese, Martin. "Die Vozuege Israels in Roem 9,4–5 und Eph 2,12," *Theologische Zeitschrift* 31 (1975): 211–22.

Roetzel, Calvin. "διαθήκη in Rom 9,4." *Biblica* 51 (1970): 377–390.

Schniewind, Julius and Gerhard Friedrich, "ἐπαγγελία," *TDNT*. Vol 2 (Grand Rapids: Eerdmans, 1964).

Segal, Alan F. *Paul the Convert: The Apostolate and Apostasy of Saul the Pharisee* (New Haven: Yale University, 1990).

Segal, Alan F. "Paul's Experience and Romans 9-11." *Princeton Seminary Bulletin,* Supplementary no. 1 (1990): 56–70.

Silva, Moisés, ed. "συνείδησις," *NIDNTTE*, 2nd ed. Vol. 4 (Grand Rapids: Zondervan, 2014).

Strathman, Hermann. "συνεπιμαρτυρέω," *TDNT*. Vol. 4. (Grand Rapids: Eerdmans,1967).

Strathmann, Hermann. "λατρεία," *TDNT*. Vol.4. (Grand rapids: Eerdmans, 1967).

Sullivan, Steven P. *The Isaianic New Exodus in Romans 9-11: A Biblical and Theological Study of Paul's Use of Isaiah in Romans* (Silverton, Oregon: Lampion Press, 2017).

Sullivan, Steven P. *The Isaianic New Exodus in Romans 9–11: A Biblical and Theological Study of Paul's Use of Isaiah in Romans*, 2nd ed. (Middletown, RI: Stone Tower Press, 2023).

Swanson, Reuben, ed. *New Testament Greek Manuscripts: Romans*. (Wheaton: Tyndale House and Pasadena: William Carey International University Press, 2001).

Thielman, Frank. *From Plight to Solution: a Jewish Framework to Understanding Paul's View of the Law in Galatians and Romans, Novum Testamentum,* Supplements (Leiden: Brill, 1989).

Wallace, Daniel B. *Greek Grammar Beyond the Basic: An Exegetical Syntax of the New Testament* (Grand Rapids: Zondervan, 1996).

Wallace, Daniel B. "The Witness of the Spirit in Romans 8:16: Interpretation and Implications." In *Who's Afraid of the Holy Spirit?: An Investigation into the Ministry of the Spirit of God Today*, eds. M. James Sawyer and Daniel B. Wallace (Dallas: Biblical Studies Press, 2005).

Wasserbert, Günter. "Romans 9–11 and Jewish–Christian Dialogue: Prospects and Provisos." In *Reading Israel in Romans: Legitimacy and Plausibility of Divergent Interpretations,* eds. Christina Grenholm and Daniel Patte (Harrisburg: Trinity Press International, 2000), 174–186.

Wiles, G. P. *Paul's Intercessory Prayers: The Significance of the Intercessory Prayer Passages in the Letters of St. Paul* (Cambridge: Cambridge University Press, 1974).

ROMANS 9:6-29

Introduction

The stories of Abraham, Ishmael and Isaac, and Esau and Jacob are used by Paul in conjunction with the thoughts of Rom 9:4–5 to express the great privileges God has promised His people. These stories are also used to demonstrate the reason why some were included, and others were not chosen. How Paul uses these stories demonstrate that physical descent is not the crucial qualification to be the true spiritual people of God. The primary reason depends upon God's free choice. Many scholars point out that the stories Paul used from the OT do not clearly refer to the eternal destiny of the individuals.

Thus, commentators take three basic positions on the OT passages that Paul uses in Rom 9. (1) Paul applies the original meaning to the historical-salvation roles. This view usually emphasizes corporate salvation over personal eternal salvation. Others understand the chapter as corporate salvation history and not about eternal salvation (Sanday & Headlam, 245; Cranfield, 479).[139] (2) Paul uses the original sense of the OT more as "types" of God's salvific methods (Käsemann, 264).[140] (3) Paul uses the principles taken from the OT texts concerning the formation of Israel to show how God called out true spiritual people (Moo, 2nd, 591–592; Schreiner, 2nd, 482–492; Piper, 64–73). We advocate the third view. Three main points help to make the conclusion that Paul is arguing for individual salvation. First, Paul's argument in Rom 9:1-5 concerning the eternal salvation and condemnation is completely severed from Rom 9:6-13 if a historical corporate election of two people is the interpretation. However, Paul's desire to be accursed on the behalf of his brethren and countrymen does not make sense if the argument did not involve the eternal salvation of others. The difficulty is to imagine that Paul would wish that his eternal salvation would be forfeited in behalf of temporary and earthly promises of his Jewish brethren. On the other hand, he expresses his desire for Israel's salvation in Rom 10:1. It is also difficult to harmonize the phrase "for all those from Israel, are thus not of Israel" with Rom 9:12–13 if one takes it as corporate election dealing with Israel and Edom (Piper, 58). Second (see Sullivan, 239–45), the words like υἱός, τέκνα τῆς ἐπαγγελίας ("son," "children of promise," Rom 9:8–9, 26, 27), καλέω ("call," Rom 9:7, 11, 24, 25, 26),[141] and σπέρμα ("seed or descendant," Rom 9:7 [twice], 8, 29)[142] are used by Paul to connect the first part of Rom 9 with last part. Σπέρμα ("seed or descendant") also parallels the word ὑπόλειμμα ("remnant") in Romans 9:27. These Pauline terms are most often connected with spiritual salvation, and since these terms parallel many of the same terms at the beginning of the Romans 9; the argument that

---

[139] W. W. Klein, *The New Chosen People*, 173, 197–98; R. T. Forster and V. P. Marston, *God's Strategy in Human History* (Wheaton: Tyndale, 1973), *passium*. Munck, *Christ and Israel*, 42; Ellison, *The Mystery of Israel*, 43; W. S. Campbell, "The Freedom and Faithfulness of god in Relation to Israel," *JSNT* 13 (1981): 29.

[140] Nwachukwu, *Creation-Covenant Scheme and Justification by Faith*, 190–96 believes that Paul uses a typology of election to demonstrate that not every physical seed of Abraham is included in the community of blessing (Rom 9:7–11). The true seed of Abraham is determined by God's promise (9:8) and election (9:11).

[141] See also some other examples: 1 Cor 1:9; Gal 1:6, 15; 5:8; 1 Thess 2:12; 4:7; 5:24. In Paul, works also have soteriological implications: Rom 3:20, 27–28; 4:2, 6; 9:32; 11:6; Gal 2:16; 3:2, 5, 10; Eph 2:9; 2 Tim 1:9; Tit 3:5 (Schreiner, "Corporate and Individual Election in Romans 9," 374–375).

[142] Dunn, *Romans 9–16*, 574. For more parallels in Pauline texts indicating eternal salvation, see Schreiner, "Corporate and Individual Election in Romans 9," 374–375.

Paul is discussing eternal salvation is strengthened.[143] Paul knows that during the present time there is a partial hardening and judgment (Rom 11:7–10, 25) upon the "sons of Israel" (Rom 9:27) and he wants to give eternal hope to the "remnant," God's "seed" (Rom 9:26, 27, 29).[144] Third, the continuation of Rom 9:6-13 in 9:24-29 demonstrates that Paul desires to apply individual salvation from among the Jews and the Gentiles. This important context should not be ignored with the discussion of Rom 9:14-23. Furthermore, the argument of Rom 9 is integrally part of the argument of Rom 10-11, which is how God's saving purposes for Israel are accomplished. Finally, the connection between Rom 8:29–39 and 9:1–11:36 favors that Paul has eternal salvation in mind.[145] Those who have been predestined to glory, where no charge will stand against them, and nothing can separate them from the love of Christ (Rom 8:28-39) express the security of God's salvation. However, if the saving promises to Israel are not fulfilled then the saving promises to the Church (Rom 8:28-39) are seemingly in jeopardy. The link between the latter part of Rom 8 and Rom 9-11 helps to cast the context to the saving promises of God.[146] For other specific arguments, see the commentary section.

Romans 9:6–9

Outline

I. The Wisdom Polemic: The Tension between God's righteous promises and Israel's condition 9–11
   - B. Vindication of the Righteous God and His Wise Plan (9:6-29)
     - 1. Israel within Israel: Children of Promise (9:6-9)

Original Text

9.6 Οὐχ οἷον δὲ ὅτι[a] ἐκπέπτωκεν ὁ λόγος τοῦ θεοῦ. οὐ γὰρ πάντες οἱ ἐξ Ἰσραήλ, οὗτοι Ἰσραήλ·[b]
7 οὐδ' ὅτι εἰσὶν σπέρμα Ἀβραάμ, πάντες τέκνα, ἀλλ'· Ἐν Ἰσαὰκ κληθήσεταί σοι σπέρμα. **8** τοῦτ'
ἔστιν,[c] οὐ τὰ τέκνα τῆς σαρκὸς ταῦτα τέκνα τοῦ θεοῦ, ἀλλὰ τὰ τέκνα τῆς ἐπαγγελίας λογίζεται
εἰς σπέρμα· **9** ἐπαγγελίας γὰρ ὁ λόγος οὗτος· Κατὰ τὸν καιρὸν τοῦτον ἐλεύσομαι καὶ ἔσται τῇ
Σάρρᾳ υἱός.

---

[143] See Piper, passim; Schreiner, "Does Romans 9 Teach Individual Election unto Salvation?" 25–40; Schreiner, "Corporate and Individual Election in Romans 9," 373-86; Schreiner, 2nd, 482–493; Moo, 2nd, 592–608; Moo, "The Theology of Romans 9-11," 253-58. Dunson, *Individual and Community in Paul's Letter to the Romans*, *passim* identifies four different types of individuals in Romans and four different category types of individuals in the community. Dunson advances the discussion in this area of study.

[144] Mounce, 27:203 extends the promises of salvation in Rom 9:29 also to the Gentiles.

[145] Schreiner, "Does Romans 9 Teach Individual Election unto Salvation?" 29–31.

[146] Ibid., 29–30 (also n. 15).

Textual Notes

[a] **9:6** P[46] omits the **ὅτι**, as well as most of the Old Latin witness, Syriac versions and Peshitta versions and Ambrosiaster (*Novum Testamentum Graece*, 28th edition critical apparatus). However, the great majority of the Gk. manuscripts retain the ὅτι including ℵA B D.
[b] **9:6** D D[2] F G, 88 614 629 999 2147 2412 1881[c] have **Ἰσραηλῖται**. However, the great majority of the Gk. manuscripts have Ἰσραήλ including P[46] A B K L.
[c] **9:8** ℵ[c] B[1] Ψ, 104 365 614 999 1319 1505 1506 1573 1982 2147 2412 add a **ὅτι** after ἔστιν. The meaning is not changed and many of the manuscripts omit it (P[46] ℵ* B* A D F G K L, 33 049 056 1241 1243) (Swanson, *NT GK Mss, Rom*, 137). Though the evidence is split, there seems to be a slight better support to omit the ὅτι.

Translation

9:6 But it is by no means that the word of God has failed. For all those who are from Israel, these are not Israel. **7** Neither is it the case that all of Abraham's children are his seed; but, "In Isaac your seed shall be called." **8** That is, the children of the flesh, these are not the children of God, but the children of promise are counted as seed. **9** For this is the word of promise: "About this time I will come and Sarah will have a son."

Commentary

9:6 Οὐχ οἷον δὲ ὅτι ἐκπέπτωκεν ὁ λόγος τοῦ θεοῦ. οὐ γὰρ πάντες οἱ ἐξ Ἰσραήλ, οὗτοι Ἰσραήλ· "But it is by no means that the word of God has failed[147]. For all those from Israel, these are not of Israel." Paul is making a distinction between a broader, ethnical Israel and a narrow spiritual ethnical Israel to define the proposition that God's word has not failed. The translation of the idiomatic phrase οὐχ οἷον δὲ ὅτι is a mixture of two constructions: οὐχ οἷον ("by no means") and οὐχ ὅτι (with the ellipsis of ἐστιν: "it is not as if").[148] Paul use δὲ ("but") with the idiomatic phrase, which precedes the conjunction to bring out the adverse impression that anyone may have concerning God's promise or plan has failed toward Israel (Longenecker, 814). The phrase ὁ λόγος τοῦ θεοῦ ("the word of God")[149] has the possibility of referring to the gospel (Jewett, 574). Thus, Paul would be defending that failure of the gospel to bring Israel to salvation at the present time does not invalidate the gospel (Moo, 2nd, 593). However, the context of verses 4–5 that lists the privileges for Israel is the best contextual reference to explain the phrase "the word of God" (Moo, 2nd, 593; Godet, 346; Murray, 2:9; Jewett, 573–574). Others refer it to the OT

[147] BDAG, 308 correctly indicates that ἐκπέπτωκεν in Rom 9:6 is a metaphoric use of "fail" or "weaken" ("become inadequate for some function"). It is used in the same way in 1 Cor 13:8 though in the present tense while Rom 9:6 is in the perfect tense.

[148] BDAG, 701; Blass and Debrunner, *A Greek Grammar*, §304, 480 (5); Turner, *A Grammar of the NT Greek*, 47, 298.

[149] Paul uses ὁ λόγος τοῦ θεοῦ ("the word of God") as the message of the gospel in 1 Cor. 14:36; 2 Cor. 2:17; 4:2; Col. 1:25; 1 Thess 2:13; 1 Tim. 4:5; 2 Tim. 2:9; Tit. 2:5. See also ὁ λόγος τοῦ Χριστοῦ ("the word of Christ") in Col. 3:16 and ὁ λόγος τοῦ κυρίου ("the word of the Lord") in 1 Thess. 1:8; 2 Thess. 3:1.

promises and did not necessarily refer it back to verses 4–5 (Dunn, 539). These promises of the word of God have not been cancelled or failed.

In the latter half of verse 6, Paul begins his discussion on who constitutes true Israel, which he briefly discussed in Romans 2:28–29. However, many in contemporary Judaism believed that Israel was made up of all those who were physical descendants of Jacob, except for those who may have refused their inheritance for whatever reason. Paul does recognize ethnic Israel as a whole remains, in some sense, part of God's people (Rom 9:4–5; 11:1–2, 28). However, he denies that the corporate election of the descendants of Jacob means that all Israelites receive eternal salvation. In other words, all those who belong to Israel in a physical sense do not belong to Israel in a spiritual sense. The definition of what Paul meant when he uses the word "Israel" in Romans 9-11 is greatly debated. The two major positions are: ethnic Israel[150] or spiritual Israel made up of both Jews and Gentiles. The latter view has some supporters in modern times.[151] The contextual support indicates that Paul has used "Israel" 11 times[152] in

[150] William S. Campbell says, "One gets the impression that when Paul wants to stress ethnic affiliation, he uses the term Jew, but when he comes to reflect upon their spiritual heritage, Israel/Israelite alone can clearly designate this people as a religious entity." When Paul uses the term "Israel," he is not using it merely as a general designation of those who are physical descent from Abraham. Rather he uses it to designate the people of the covenant, which was made with Abraham. (William S. Campbell, "Israel," in *Dictionary of Paul and His Letters* [Downers Grove: InterVarsity Press, 1993], 441; *contra* James D. G. Dunn, *The Theology of Paul the Apostle* [Grand Rapids: Eerdmans, 1998], 505–07). However, Paul's statement that not all of Israel are Israel (cf. Rom 2:28–29; 11:28), is a discussion "centered within Israel and around Israel" (William S. Campbell, *Paul and the Creation of Christian Identity* [London: T & T Clark, 2008], 124).

Israel cannot be exactly reduced to all the offspring of Abraham (through Isaac and Jacob), but Israel in this context includes those Israelites who share his faith. The solidarity of Israel as a people is not sacrificed despite Paul's statement in Rom 9:6. "Paul himself appears to operate with a fluid concept of Israel. (Pablo T. Gadenz, *Called from the Jews and from the Gentiles: Pauline Ecclesiology in Romans 9-11*, Wissenschaftliche Untersuchungen zum Neun Testament 2. Reihe, 267 [Tübingen: Mohr Siebeck, 2009], 64-82 has the same thought). This distinction and tension are not Paul's invention. Within the nation of Israel, God has always chosen "children of the promise" (Rom 9:8) to carry out his purposes (Campbell, "Israel," 442.). Paul makes a distinction between Israel whether it is faithful Israel or "the rest" (Rom 11:7), as well as making a distinction with the Christ-followers among the Gentiles. Though these Gentiles are not Abraham's physical descendants, they benefit from Abraham's lineage and covenant (Gen 12:3) by virtue of believing in Jesus Christ (Gal 3:29) (Campbell, *Paul and the Creation of Christian Identity*, 125). However, these Gentile believers are not called Israel. See Sullivan, *Isaianic New Exodus in Romans 9-11*, chapter 6.2.4 on page 178, n. 61 and 179, n. 63.

[151] Fitzmyer, 624 cites the following church Fathers who support spiritual Israel (both Jews and Gentiles): Irenaeus, Clement of Alexandria, Theodore of Mopsuestia and Theodoret of Cyrrhus. See also Calvin, 437. Scholars from the 20th century onward include: Barth, 416; Lenski, 725–27; Dunn, 539–540; Wright, 689; Wright, *The Climax of the Covenant*, 231–67, especially 249–50; and Wright, "Romans and the Theology of Paul," 56–62. For a good concise critique of Wright, see Vanlaningham, "An Evaluation of N. T. Wright's View of Israel in Romans 11," 179-93; as well as the critique by Das, *Solving the Romans Debate*, 235-45. Wagner, *Heralds of the Good News*, 278-79 is open to the possibility that "all Israel" may also include Gentiles in Rom 11:25-26. However, he holds "the view that in Romans 11 Paul anticipates a massive turning of Jews to Christ as a result of and subsequent to the entrance of the full number of the Gentiles" (Wagner, *Heralds of the Good News*, 279, note 194). In Rom 11:28, Paul describes "Israel" as an enemy. If Israel is the church, how does one explain this? Holland, *Romans*, 385-86 believes Paul's use of "Israel" is quiet fluid. It has two meanings: (1) All believing Jews and (2) all sons of Abraham, Jewish and Gentile believers. See Sullivan, 2nd, *Isaianic New Exodus in Romans 9-11*, chapter 10.2.3.

[152] Rom 9:6[bis], 27[bis], 31; 10:19, 21; 11:2, 7, 25, 26.

Romans 9–11 and each time it refers to ethnic Israel.[153] Moo (574)[154] brings out three reasons for supporting Israel as ethnic Israel in Rom 8–11: (1) In Rom 9:1–5, Paul established the parameters of his language as ethnic Israel for Rom 9–11. (2) Paul explains v. 6b in vv. 7–13 and he used examples from within ethnic Israel. (3) The close relation between vv. 27–29 and vv. 6–13 where the quotations focus on the remnant (a smaller group within ethnic Israel) again favors ethnic Israel. Paul also is careful to distinguish between Gentiles and ethnic Israel in these chapters. Thus, in Rom 9:6 the word Ἰσραήλ (Israel) refers to ethnic Israel (Sanday & Headlam, 240; Murray 2:9; Cranfield, 474; Käsemann, 263; Fitzmyer, 560; Mounce, 197; Schreiner, 2nd, 482-83; Jewett, 574–575).[155]

Many translations take οὐ ("not") with πάντες οἱ ἐξ Ἰσραήλ ("all of those from Israel"). However, the best translation, though there are those who disagree (Jewett, 574),[156] is to take οὐ ("not") grammatically with οὗτοι Ἰσραήλ ("these are not of Israel") (Moo, 2nd, 594, n. 124; Dunn, 539; Piper, 65–66; Schreiner, 2nd, 482, n. 9).[157] Thus, the implication of the definite group within the nation of Israel helps to support a definite election in the following verses. If all Israel was to benefit from the Messianic salvation, then the Word of God has failed because many Israelites have rejected the salvation of the Messiah, Jesus. However, Rom 9:6b is the beginning of Paul's argument where he uses the election of Isaac over Ishmael and Jacob over Esau to establish an ongoing principle that God elects unconditionally not only a physical nation, but also individual Israelites to spiritual salvation (true spiritual Israel) within the physical nation of Israel (Murray, 2:18; Piper, 66; Schlier, 291). This conclusion fits the previous vv. 3–5 where Paul expressed his heart-felt wish that some of his fellow-brethren would not be accursed and cut off from the salvation of the Christ.

9:7 οὐδ' ὅτι εἰσὶν σπέρμα Ἀβραάμ, πάντες τέκνα, ἀλλ'· Ἐν Ἰσαὰκ κληθήσεταί σοι σπέρμα. "Neither is it the case that all of Abraham's children are his seed; but, 'In Isaac your seed shall be called.'" To support the distinction between ethnic Israel and spiritual ethnic Israel, Paul uses vv. 7–9 and vv. 10–13. The structure of 9:6b–8 may be understood this way: v. 8a corresponds to vv. 6b and 7a; and v. 8b corresponds to v. 7b.

---

[153] Watson, *Paul, Judaism and the Gentiles*, 311; Schreiner, 622; Moo, 721. Some would say Rom 9:6 (cf. Gal 6:16) refers to both Jews and Gentiles. Moo, 574, 721 and Schreiner, 494, 622 accept this view in Gal 6:16 and Phil 3:3 (maybe in other places) but not in Rom 9–11. Childs, *The Church's Guide for Reading Paul*, 185, note 169 concludes that anyone who believes the promises to ethnic Israel in Rom 9:1–5 have been forfeited and fulfilled by the church has a serious misunderstanding. For further support for ethnic Israel, see also Fitzmyer, 560, 624 and Murray, 2:96; Fruchtenbaum, "Israel and the Church," 118–120; Johnson, "Evidence from Romans 9–11," 200–205; Johnson, "Paul and 'The Israel of God'," 181–195; Vlach, "What Does Christ as 'True Israel' Mean for the Nation Israel?" 43–54. See Sullivan, *Isaianic New Exodus in Romans 9-11*, 2nd, 10.2.3.

[154] Moo in his second edition of his Roman's commentary (p. 595) modifies his opinion: "Paul may be using 'Israel' in its second occurrence in this verse as a formal category that he has not yet defined… that spiritual Israel is not the same as biological Israel."

[155] Campbell, *Paul and the Creation of Christian Identity*, 129–133.

[156] See below under "Additional Exegetical Comments."

[157] Piper (65–66) gives two reasons for this exegetical decision: (1) οὐ taken with the demonstrative pronoun οὗτοι ("these are not") refers to a definite group while οὐ taken with πάντες ("not all these") is an indefinite group. If οὐ ("not") is taken with the indefinite πάντες ("all the ones") then you have the awkward expression, "For not all the ones from Israel, these are Israel." (2) The difficulty of placing οὐ so far from πάντες in the sentence is supported by a parallel Greek construction in Rom 7:15. Here οὐ must modify the verb πράσσω at the end of the phrase (5 words away) rather than the closer verb θέλω because of the contrast in the sentence (. . . οὐ γὰρ ὃ θέλω τοῦτο πράσσω, ἀλλ' ὃ μισῶ τοῦτο ποιῶ. ". . . for what I want, this I do not practice, but I am doing the thing I hate").

(-) 6b οὐ γὰρ πάντες οἱ ἐξ Ἰσραήλ, οὗτοι Ἰσραήλ·	For all those who are from Israel (inclusive), these are not Israel (exclusive).
(-) 7a οὐδ' ὅτι εἰσὶν σπέρμα Ἀβραάμ πάντες τέκνα,	Neither is it the case that all of Abraham's children (inclusive) are *his* seed (exclusive);
(+) 7b ἀλλ'· Ἐν Ἰσαὰκ κληθήσεταί σοι σπέρμα.	But in Isaac shall your seed be called
(-) 8a τοῦτ' ἔστιν, οὐ τὰ τέκνα τῆς σαρκὸς ταῦτα τέκνα τοῦ θεοῦ,	That is, the children of the flesh, these are not the children of God
(+) 8b ἀλλὰ τὰ τέκνα τῆς ἐπαγγελίας λογίζεται εἰς σπέρμα·	but the children of promise are counted as seed.

Notice the parallel construction of vv. 6b and 8a:

6b	οὐ γὰρ	πάντες οἱ ἐξ Ἰσραήλ,	οὗτοι Ἰσραήλ·
	For	all those who are from Israel,	these are not Israel.
8a	. . . οὐ	τὰ τέκνα τῆς σαρκὸς	ταῦτα τέκνα τοῦ θεοῦ,
		. . . the children of the flesh,	these are not the children of God

The implication of Paul's parallel in vv. 6b and 8a is the continuation of his concerns of v. 6b, which is the distinction spiritually within ethnic Israel (Piper, 67). The phrase τέκνα τοῦ θεοῦ ("children of God") [158] in v. 8 is not referring to privileges of God for being part of the chosen nation (*contra* Sanday and Headlam, 242), but Paul uses this phrase and the phrase υἱοὶ θεοῦ ("sons of God;" Rom 8:14,19; 9:26; 2 Cor 6:18; Gal 3:26; 4:5–6) to refer to believers (Piper, 67; Michel, 202). Thus, the seed of Abraham is not the physical children of Abraham or the children of the flesh, but they are children of Isaac and the children of promise (vv. 8–9) (Schreiner, 2nd, 483).

There are two ways to understand the ὅτι clause in v. 7a. Either the clause is taken as an object clause or a causal clause (οὐδ' ὅτι εἰσὶν σπέρμα Ἀβραάμ, πάντες τέκνα, ἀλλ'). If it is taken as an object clause then the sentence may be translated "It is not that all the children are the seed of Abraham" (Barrett, 169; Dunn, 540; Schreiner, 2nd, 483; Moo, 2nd, 595, n. 133). This reading would indicate that the "seed" in v. 7 parallels "children of God" and "the children of promise" in v. 8.[159] In addition, "children" in v. 7a matches "the children of the flesh" in v. 8. The majority of the translations take the ὅτι clause as causal, "neither are they all children because they are the seed of Abraham" (Sanday and Headlam, 240; Fitzmyer, 560; Byrne, 293). In this translation, "children" in v. 7 parallels "children of God" in v. 8 and "seed of Abraham" in v. 7 would match "children of the flesh" in v. 8. The object clause is the preferable view for two reasons (Schreiner, 2nd, 484; Moo, 2nd, 595, n. 133; Jewett, 575).[160] First, the word σπέρμα ("seed" or "descendant") is a positive term and fits the positive term in vv. 7–8. This understanding also fits Paul's positive use elsewhere in his writings (Rom 4:13, 16, 18; 9:29; Gal

---

158 Rom 8:16, 17, 21; Eph 5:1; Phil 2:15.

159 "Adoption" in Rom 9:4 refers to the general salvation-history privileges and "children of God" and other parallel terms refer to salvific relationship (Moo, 577, n. 36).

160 Schreiner, 2nd, 484 also raises the syntactical awkwardness with the causal option that necessitates a elliptical clause to be added because "'All' (πάντες, *pantes*) can't modify 'children' (τέκνα, *tekna*), since πάντες is masculine and τέκνα is neuter, and so the phrase cannot be translated 'neither is it that all children are the offspring of Abraham.'"

3:16, 19, 29; for a more physical focus, see Rom 11:1; 2 Cor 11:22). Second, the phrase "all the children" in v. 7 matches "all those of Israel" in v. 6b confirming that merely being a descendant from Abraham's lineage does not ensure a Jew that they are part of the saving promises and spiritual blessings of God. Third, ὅτι is translated "that" in the four other occurrences in the NT (Mt 16:28; Mk 9:1; Lk 18:9; 1 Cor 3:20) when it is immediately preceded by εἰσὶν (Abasciano, 189, n. 119).[161]

Paul is positively stating in Rom 9:7b–8 what Rom 9:6b–7a has stated negatively. He supports the distinction between physical and spiritual descendants from Abraham by quoting Gen 21:12.[162] The OT context is the separation of Hagar and Ishmael from Sarah and Isaac because God had chosen Isaac to establish His covenant with him. Isaac, the child of promise (Gen 21:10,12; Gal 4:23, 28), will your seed be called. The larger context of Genesis 21 is the contrast between God's promise of a physical seed from Abraham and Sarah and the rejection of Ishmael who is part of his physical seed. However, the promise here is more than just physical descendants for God promised Ishmael many physical descendants (Gen 17:19-21; 21:13, 18). God will call a covenant people through Isaac, and this involved the spiritual realm not just the physical descendants. Paul is stressing the spiritual blessings of the covenant by quoting Gen 21:12 (Moo, 2nd, 596, n. 137). God's calling and salvation is not merely a Jewish birthright or physical heritage. Paul illustrated this point by indicating that the natural seed from Abraham, Ishmael, is not the true seed. The individual Isaac was called to be the spiritual seed of promise (Hodge, 480–481; Liddon, 157; Wardlaw, 252–253; Meyer, 2:126). Only through the divine act of God was Isaac born as the promised and called individual. If σοι σπέρμα ("your seed") is taken to be collective (Sanday & Headlam, 241) then the phrase "your seed" (v. 7b) is in contrast to "Abraham's seed" (v. 7a) and in parallel to the true seed who are called and received the promise. In other words, the same principle of differentiation would apply to the seed of Isaac which was functioning in the case of Isaac himself so that the unconditional eternal election of God establishes the true people of God (Murray 2:10–11; Piper, 68). Like in Gal 4:21-31, Paul seems to employ Isaac and Ishmael typologically and relates their history to God's saving purposes (Schreiner, 497).

The context of Gen 21 is the encouragement of God to the grief of Abraham who is to reject his son Ishmael and to send Hagar and Ishmael out from the home. The main word of comfort is that Isaac is the promised seed for which the covenant seed will be called (Gen 17:19–20). Paul now quotes Gen 21:12 as means of comfort for his grief (Rom 9:1-5) and anyone else who is grieved over the state of unbelieving Israel. The quotation is also an affirmation to the reliability of God's promise (Abasciano, 192). Isaac, the child of promise, is heir to the Abrahamic promises and Ishmael, Abraham's physical seed is rejected from the covenant, but was granted temporal blessings. The believing ethnic Israelites are heirs to the eschatological Abrahamic covenantal blessings while the unbelieving ethnic Israelites are rejected from those blessings, but were granted physical advantages and privileges that should lead them to believe in the covenantal blessings.

The word κληθήσεταί ("to be called, named") could be translated "be named" and emphasized the meaning "to be," thus, meaning in Isaac you will have your descendants (BDAG,

---

[161] Abasciano, 189, n. 119, suggests that οὐδ' ὅτι in Rom 9:7 echoes Οὐχ οἷον δὲ ὅτι in Rom 9:6.

[162] The part that Paul quotes from Gen 21:12 is the exact literal translation in the LXX from the MT.

503; Cranfield, 474).[163] However, καλέω ("call") has theological significance in this section and it at least has overtones of God's sovereign, spiritual blessings: "through Isaac will God call individuals to participate in the benefits of the covenant" (Moo, 2nd, 596, n. 136; See also Dunn, 541; Schreiner, 2nd, 484).

9:8 τοῦτ' ἔστιν, οὐ τὰ τέκνα τῆς σαρκὸς ταῦτα τέκνα τοῦ θεοῦ, ἀλλὰ τὰ τέκνα τῆς ἐπαγγελίας λογίζεται εἰς σπέρμα·[164] "That is, the children of the flesh, these are not the children of God, but the children of promise are counted as seed." The phrase τοῦτ' ἔστιν ("that is") seems to sum up what is said in 9:6b–7 (Piper 67). For Paul to claim that through Isaac the covenant blessings are given to the nation is what Jews acknowledged. However, what distinguished Paul's view is his thought in 9:7b, which is supported by his assertion in 9:6b (Moo, 2nd, 597–98). It is important to keep the parallel in view:

6b οὐ γὰρ πάντες οἱ ἐξ Ἰσραήλ, οὗτοι Ἰσραήλ·	For all those who are from Israel (inclusive), these are not Israel (exclusive).
8a τοῦτ' ἔστιν, οὐ τὰ τέκνα τῆς σαρκὸς ταῦτα τέκνα τοῦ θεοῦ,	That is, the children of the flesh, these are not the children of God

The parallel of "all those who are from Israel" with "the children of the flesh" and "these are not Israel" with "these are not the children of God" is notable for it helps support Paul's point in 9:6b. Everywhere else Paul uses τέκνα τοῦ θεοῦ ("children of God") it refers to believers (Rom 8:16, 17, 21; Eph 5:1; Phil 2:15). That Paul is pointing beyond the physical descendants of Isaac to the spiritual believing Israel is indicated by Rom 9:8b and paralleled in Gal 3:26–29; 4:21–31 and Rom 2:25–29 (Piper, 68–71; Abasciano, 196–197; Schreiner, 2nd, 484–85). In Gal 3:26, Paul says that you are the sons of God through faith in Jesus Christ. He concludes by stating that if you are in Christ then you Abraham's seed and heirs according to the promise (Gal 3:29). In Gal 4:23, 28–29, Paul demonstrates that the "children of promise" are heirs of spiritual and eternal promises. Therefore, the "principle of unconditional election, evident in God's choice of Isaac to be heir of the covenant, is applied now to Paul's contemporaries" to explain how only "some" of the Israelites are saved (Piper 69–70). It is not the children of the flesh but the children of God who are children of promise. The word λογίζεται ("are reckoned, counted, regarded") directs our attention back to Rom 4 where Paul connects it to Abraham being justified by faith in Gen 15:6 (used 11 times).[165] This point also indicates that Paul's subject is not merely salvation history or physical covenantal blessings, but eternal salvation.[166]

---

[163] See Abascinio, 199-202 for a good critique of BDAG. He understands this calling as a "creative naming" and has the possible echo of Rom 4:17. Paul's naming or calling does concern true elect of God. However, Abascinio takes a corporate election. For an overview word study, see *NIDNTT&E* 2:601–607.

[164] The phrase "children of the flesh" and "children of promise" may be genitive of description (children characterized by the flesh/by promise) or genitive of possession (children who belong to the flesh/promise) (Moo, 2nd, 597, n. 140).

[165] Dunn, 541 points out the strong echo of Rom 4 with ἐπαγγελία (Rom 4:13, 14, 16, 20: 9:4, 8, 9), λογίζομαι (Rom 4:3–6, 8–11, 22–24; 9:8), and σπέρμα (Rom 4:13, 16, 18; 9:7–8).

[166] We agree with Schreiner, 2nd, 485–86 that Cranfield's understanding concerning Ishmael is unwarranted. Ishmael stands as a type of unbelievers in Gal 4:21–31 and he seems to be in Rom 9 also. Ishmael is promised temporal blessings, but he is not to inherit the blessings of Isaac and his seed. For a short defense of individual salvation and not corporate salvation in this section, see Schriener, 2nd, 486–87. For a more detailed defense, see Schreiner, "Does Romans 9 Teach Individual Election unto Salvation?" 25–40 and Schreiner, "Corporate and Individual Election in Romans 9," 373–386.

9:9 ἐπαγγελίας γὰρ ὁ λόγος οὗτος· Κατὰ τὸν καιρὸν τοῦτον ἐλεύσομαι καὶ ἔσται τῇ Σάρρᾳ υἱός. "For this is the word of promise: About this time I will come and Sarah will have a son." The γὰρ ("for") indicates that Paul is explaining further the concept of "promise" mentioned in v. 8 as the "children of promise" and the emphasis on ἐπαγγελίας ("promise") which in the Greek text is the first word in v. 9. The source of the promise is revealed in Gen 18:10 and 14 and expressed in Gen 21:12 in Rom 9:7–8. God promised Abraham, advanced in age, and Sarah, aged and now barren, that they will have a child. This promise child through God's supernatural choice pictures God's choice of eternal salvation according to God's elective choice (cf. Gal 4:21-31). This promise does not come from natural birth (9:6) but supernatural which is pictured in Isaac (9:9). Not all of Abraham's children, but the seed (9:7); not the children of the flesh, but the children of God – children of promise are seed (9:8).

Gen 18:10 … ἐπαναστρέφων ἥξω πρὸς σε κατὰ τὸν καιρὸν τοῦτον εἰς ὥρας, καὶ ἕξει υἱὸν Σάρρα ἡ γυνή σου . . . ("… I will return to you about this time next season and Sara your wife will have a son").
Gen 18:14 … εἰς τὸν καιρὸν τοῦτον ἀναστρέφω πρός σε εἰς ὥρας, καὶ ἔσται τῇ Σάρρᾳ υἱός ("at this time I will return to you next season and there shall be for Sara a son").
Rom 9:9 Κατὰ τὸν καιρὸν τοῦτον ἐλεύσομαι καὶ ἔσται τῇ Σάρρᾳ υἱός ("About this time I shall come and there shall be for Sarah a son").

The conflation of Gen 18:10 and 14 is in the context of Gen 18:18-19 where the Abrahamic promise is again restated from Gen 12:3. This contextual setting helps to place the understanding not just on the physical but spiritual eternal covenantal blessings (cf. Gal 3:6–9, 16, 29). The eliminating of the temporal element by Paul in Rom 9:9 (though not from the reader who knows the passage) centers in on the important stress of the assurance of God to fulfill his promise.[167]

Biblical Theological Comments

One of the theological debates in Rom 9 is what kind of election is to be understood in this chapter. Is the group elected as a corporate entity, and the individuals are elected by their inclusion into the elect group or is the individual elected and becomes a part of the elect group of individuals – they are a group only because they are associated with elect individuals?[168] It is the latter for which Paul is arguing in Rom 9-11. There is a clear concept of corporate election of the nation in the OT. However, there is also a concept of the individual among a group often called a remnant – the true Israel or spiritual ethnic Israel (Rom 9:6, 27; 11:5, 7). Thus, the "elect" and the "remnant" are those who are heirs of eternal salvation.[169] This concept helps to reveal that in

[167] Christopher D. Stanley, *Paul and the Language of Scripture: Citation Technique in the Pauline Epistles and Contemporary Literature*, Society for New Testament Studies Monograph Series, ed. Richard Bauckham, vol. 74 (Cambridge: Cambridge University Press, 1992), 104–105. Jewett, 577 considers the reading of Paul "I shall come" instead of "I will return" as "probably to avoid a functionless reference to an earlier visitation" instead of an allusion to some future epiphany (Dunn, 541–541). However, Dunn's point is worth noting whether Paul is thinking of this point or not.

[168] See Abasciano, "Corporate election in Romans 9, 351–371; Schreiner, "Does Romans 9 Teach Individual Election unto Salvation?," 25–40; Schreiner, "Corporate and Individual Election in Romans 9, 373–386.

[169] See Longenecker's (803–810) "Excursus" on the term remnant in the MT, LXX, and second temple Judaism. His summary does not indicate that he took into account the possible different perspective between pre-AD

Rom 9:11, "God's purpose according to election" is connected with the phrase "not because of works, but because of Him who calls" and expresses a correlative idea of effectual call of God's elect individuals of the group, which is at times called the remnant (Murray, 2:15-21). The individual election cannot be separated from the individual decision in Rom 10 where the singular person is dominant in the grammar and meaning. The unity of Rom 9-11 indicates that the individual aspect of election cannot be removed (Schreiner, 498).

Rom 9:6-9 demonstrates that not every descendant of Abraham is a member of "Israel," who are reckoned as descendants by the promise. Thus, Abraham's real descendants are reckoned by faith and not by race, ritual or ranking. Though the nation is chosen for physical covenantal blessings, not all of the physical race of Israel has believed with the faith of Abraham. All those who are boasting in the Law are not the heirs of the promise (Rom 4:14). Briefly stated: (1) "Israel" does not equal "all Israel" (Rom 9:6); (2) Abraham's children are not equal to all of Abraham's descendants ("seed") – e.g., Isaac not Ishmael (see Gen 21:12 in Rom 9:7); (3) children of God are children of promise, not children of the flesh (Rom 9:8); and (4) The word of promise is supported by Gen 18:10 and 14 (Rom 9:9).

Application and Devotional Implications

In Rom 9:6, Paul states that there are two circles of Israelites. The larger circle is the physical descendants of Abraham, Isaac, and Jacob. The second circle inside the larger circle is the true Israelite or spiritual Israel. In Gal 3:7, Paul says, "Therefore, be sure that it is those who are of faith who are sons of Abraham." In Rom 2:28–29, "For he is not a Jew who is one outwardly; neither is circumcision that which is outward in the flesh. But he is a Jew who is one inwardly; and circumcision is that which is of the heart, by the Spirit, not by the letter, and his praise is not from men, but from God." In other words, the promises were never for all of the physical seed but the spiritual seed of Abraham. Therefore, God's promises do not fail because of the sovereign electing purpose of God. This is Paul's point and he will demonstrate it in verses 7–13.

In verses 7–9, Paul demonstrates God's sovereignty in election by using Isaac. Part of the Jewish belief was that a descendent of Abraham was sure to be saved. Paul reminds his listeners that Gen 21:12 tells us that it was through Isaac and not Ishmael that the promise came. Yet, he explains further that it is not children of the flesh, which are God's children, but it deals with the promise. Then in verse 9 Paul cites Gen 18:10 and 14 dealing with God coming to Abraham and Sarah and giving them a promised son. Yet, what makes this illustration significant is that the fulfillment of this promise had to come by a miraculous birth, because of the medical and biological impossibility of Abraham and Sarah to have a child. Sarah was past the years for having children. Isaac was elected to be the promise child by a miraculous birth to demonstrate God's sovereign choice apart from works. Believers are elected to be spiritual seeds of Abraham by the miraculous new birth, which demonstrates God sovereign election apart from works. Yet, an objector may contend that Ishmael was reject because his mother was a Gentile bondservant while Isaac was from Abraham and Sarah. Therefore, Paul turns to Jacob and Esau in verse 10.

---

70 and post-AD 70 in Jewish literature. He also understands that Paul's use of σπέρμα in 9:7–8 and 9:29 suggests an *inclusio*, which alerts the reader that this theme unifies the subsection in the overall argument of Rom 9–11 (812).

Additional Exegetical Comments

9:6b Abasciano (183–189) objects to the 2 points of Piper's exegetical reasoning that says οὐ does not modify πάντες but it modifies οὗτοι Ἰσραήλ. First, in the verbless clause of Rom 9:6b, Abasciano takes οὗτοι as a copula and translates Rom 9:6b "For not all who are of Israel are actually Israel" (Abasciano, 185). This possibility would highlight the contrast between the two words Ἰσραήλ but not because of definiteness. This is grammatically possible, but Abasciano has not demonstrated οὗτοι as a copula is a familiar construction of Paul. The only 2 examples he gives are from the gospels (e.g., Mk 6:2 . . . πόθεν τούτῳ ταῦτα . . .; Mt 13:56 . . . πόθεν οὖν τούτῳ ταῦτα πάντα . . .). In these 2 examples, the double use of οὗτος, one right after the other, is used and this construction is found only once in Pauline literature (out of 267 times in 247 verses).[170] The construction is found in 2 Cor 13:10, Διὰ τοῦτο ταῦτα ἀπὼν γράφω . . . (For this reason I am writing these things . . . NASB). However, in this Greek construction οὗτος is not translated as a copula. A survey of the other places Paul uses οὗτος in the NT does not reveal he used οὗτος as a copula. Thus, the weakness of this point favors Piper's position.

Abasciano also challenges Piper's second point involving the parallel construction in Rom 7:15 (. . . οὐ γὰρ ὃ θέλω τοῦτο πράσσω, ἀλλ' ὃ μισῶ τοῦτο ποιῶ.) concerning what clause the negative particle οὐ modifies and how it supports Piper's understanding in Rom 9:6b. Abasciano agrees with Piper that οὐ in Rom 7:15 cannot modify θέλω for the next clause would repeat instead of contrast (ἀλλ') what Paul had just said (Abasciano, 384). However, Abasciano does not agree that οὐ modifies the verb πράσσω, which is 5 words later. His conclusion is that οὐ modifies the relative clause ὃ θέλω (Ibid.). However, this would negate the whole clause and would not be much different then modifying θέλω. Thus, Piper's arguments for Rom 9:6b seems to be the best conclusion.

Selected Bibliography

Abasciano, Brian J. "Corporate election in Romans 9: A Reply to Thomas Schreiner." *Journal of the Evangelical Theological Society* 49 (April-June 2006): 351–371.

Blass, F. and A. Debrunner, *A Greek Grammar of the New Testament and Other Early Christian Literature*, trans. R. W. Funk (Chicago, Ill.: University of Chicago Press, 1961).

Campbell, William S. *Paul and the Creation of Christian Identity* (London: T & T Clark, 2008).

Campbell, William S. "The Freedom and Faithfulness of God in Relation to Israel, *JSNT* 13 (1981): 27–45.

Childs, Brevard S. *The Church's Guide for Reading Paul: The Canonical Shaping of the Pauline Corpus* (Grand Rapids: Eerdmans, 2008).

Das, A. Andrew, *Solving the Romans Debate* (Minneapolis: Fortress Press, 2007).

Dunson, Ben C. *Individual and Community in Paul's Letter to the Romans*. Wissenschaftliche Untersuchungen zum Neuen Testament, 2/332 (Tübingen: Mohr Siebeck, 2012).

Ellison, Henry E. *The Mystery of Israel: An Exposition of Romans 9-11* (Milton Keynes, England: Patemoster, 1966).

[170] Logos 6 search in Na[28].

Forster, R. T. and V. P. Marston, *God's Strategy in Human History* (Wheaton: Tyndale, 1973).

Fruchtenbaum, Arnold, "Israel and the Church," in *Issues in Dispensationalism*, (Chicago: Moody Press, 1994), 118–120.

Johnson, S. Lewis, Jr., "Evidence from Romans 9–11," in *A Case for Premillennialism: A New Consensus*, ed. Donald Campbell and Jeffery Townsend (Chicago: Moody Press, 1992), 199–223.

Johnson, S. Lewis, Jr., "Paul and 'The Israel of God': An Exegetical and Eschatological Case-Study," in *Essays in Honor of J. Dwight Pentecost*, ed. Stanley D. Toussaint and Charlie Dyer (Chicago, Moody Press, 1986), 181–195.

Klein, W. W. Klein, *The New Chosen People: A Corporate View of Election* (Grand Rapids: Zondervan, 1990).

Moo, Douglas J. "The Theology of Romans 9-11." In *Pauline Theology Volume III Romans*, Society of Biblical Literature Symposium Series, No. 23 (Atlanta: SBL, 2002), 253-58.

Moulton, James Hope, Wilbert Francis Howard, and Nigel Turner. *A Grammar of New Testament Greek*. Vol. 3 (Edinburgh: T. & T. Clark, 1988).

Munck, Johannes. *Christ and Israel: An Interpretation of Romans 9–11*. Translated by Ingeborg Nixon (Philadelphia: Fortress Press, 1967).

Nwachukwu, Mary Sylvia Chinyere. *Creation-Covenant Scheme and Justification by Faith: A Canonical Study of the God-Human Drama in the Pentateuch and Letter to the Romans* (Rome: Gregorian University Press, 2002).

Schreiner, Thomas R. "Does Romans 9 Teach Individual Election unto Salvation? Some Exegetical and Theological Reflections." *Journal of Evangelical Theological Society* 36 (March 1993): 25–40.

Schreiner, Thomas R. "Corporate and Individual Election in Romans 9: A Response to Brian Abasciano," *Journal of the Evangelical Theological Society* 49 (April - June 2006): 373–386.

Silva, Moisés, rev.ed. "καλέω," *NIDNTTE*, 2nd ed. (Grand Rapids: Zondervan, 2014), 2:601–607.

Stanley, Christopher D. *Paul and the Language of Scripture: Citation Technique in the Pauline Epistles and Contemporary Literature.* Society for New Testament Studies Monograph Series, ed. Richard Bauckham, vol. 74 (Cambridge: Cambridge University Press, 1992).

Sullivan, Steven P. *The Isaianic New Exodus in Romans 9–11: A Biblical and Theological Study of Paul's Use of Isaiah in Romans* (Silverton, OR: Lampion Press, 2017).

Sullivan, Steven P. *The Isaianic New Exodus in Romans 9–11: A Biblical and Theological Study of Paul's Use of Isaiah in Romans*, 2nd ed. (Middletown, RI: Stone Tower Press, 2023).

Swanson, Reuben, ed. *New Testament Greek Manuscripts: Romans*. (Wheaton: Tyndale House and Pasadena: William Carey International University Press, 2001).

Vanlaningham, Michael G. "An Evaluation of N. T. Wright's View of Israel in Romans 11," *Bibliotheca Sacra* 170 (Apr-Jun 2013): 179–93.

Vlach, Michael, J. "What Does Christ as 'True Israel' Mean for the Nation Israel?: A Critique of the Non-dispensational Understanding," *The Master's Seminary Journal* 23 (Spring 2012): 43–54.

Wagner, J. Ross. *Heralds of the Good News: Isaiah and Paul in Concert in the Letter to the Romans*. Supplements to Novum Testamentum, eds. M. M. Mitchell and D. P. Moessner, vol. 101 (Leiden: Brill, 2002).

Watson, Francis, *Paul, Judaism and the Gentiles: Beyond the New Perspective*, rev. and exp. ed. (Grand Rapids: Eerdmans, 2007).

Wright, N. T. *The Climax of the Covenant: Christ and the Law in Pauline Theology*, (Minneapolis: Fortress Press, 1993).
Wright, N. T. "Romans and the Theology of Paul," in *Pauline Theology, Romans* (Atlanta: Society of Biblical Literature, 2002).

Romans 9:10–13

Outline

B. Vindication of the Righteous God and His Wise Plan (9:6-29)
   1. Israel within Israel: Children of Promise (9:6-9)
   2. The Divine Call according to Election (9:10-13)

Original Text

9.10 οὐ μόνον δέ, ἀλλὰ καὶ Ῥεβέκκα ἐξ ἑνὸς κοίτην ἔχουσα, Ἰσαὰκ τοῦ πατρὸς ἡμῶν· 11 μήπω γὰρ
γεννηθέντων μηδὲ πραξάντων τι ἀγαθὸν ἢ φαῦλον[a], ἵνα ἡ κατ' ἐκλογὴν πρόθεσις τοῦ θεοῦ
μένῃ[b], 12 οὐκ ἐξ ἔργων ἀλλ' ἐκ τοῦ καλοῦντος, ἐρρέθη αὐτῇ ὅτι Ὁ μείζων δουλεύσει τῷ
ἐλάσσονι· 13 καθὼς[c] γέγραπται· Τὸν Ἰακὼβ ἠγάπησα, τὸν δὲ Ἠσαῦ ἐμίσησα.

Textual Notes

[a] **9:11 φαῦλον** is supported by WH NA28 UBS5 B ℵ A,6 69 424[c] 365 630 945 1243 1506 1739 1881 Origen; **κακόν** is supported by Byz p[46] D[1.2] K L Ψ. The Greek words are somewhat similar in meaning (Longenecker, 797) and the support of p[46] causes one to pause and consider, but the other support gives a slight edge to the NA28 position of φαῦλον.
[b] **9:11 μένῃ** is supported by NA28 UBS5 WH B ℵ D[2] K L Ψ, 049 69 88 365 945 1506 1739 1739 1881, Byz; **μένει** P, 6 33 489 1241 1646 1735 1836 2125 2464. μείνῃ is supported by p[46] F G. The verb μένῃ has the best support of the mss.
[c] **9:13 καθὼς** is supported by NA28 UBS5 Byz p[46] ℵ A D G K L P Ψ; **καθάπερ** is supported by WH B. The best support is καθὼς.

Translation

9:10 And not only this, but also Rebecca, when she conceived *twins* from one sexual encounter with Isaac, our father – **11** for *the twins*, not yet were born nor had done anything good or evil, in order that the purpose of God according to election might remain, not out of works but out of the one who calls. **12** It was said to her, "The Older will serve the younger." **13** Just as it is written: "Jacob I loved and Esau I hated."

Commentary

9:10 οὐ μόνον δέ, ἀλλὰ καὶ Ῥεβέκκα ἐξ ἑνὸς κοίτην[171] ἔχουσα, Ἰσαὰκ τοῦ πατρὸς ἡμῶν· "And not only this, but also Rebecca, when she conceived *twins* from one act with Isaac, our father." The possibility that someone may say that Isaac was chosen because both of his parents were from the correct lineage and Ishmael had one parent that was a Gentile, seems to prompt Paul to his next point. On the other hand, Paul proceeds down the patriarchal lineage to further explain the distinction between spiritual Israel from physical and ethical Israel (9:10-13). Three important points are established in this section (Moo, 578): (1) Jacob was not chosen because of race. Both boys came from the same mother and father. (2) In verse 12, Paul indicates that God's choice was not according to the normal ancient tradition of the first born. The younger not the older was chosen. (3) God's choice of Jacob was not based on anything in his character, actions, or devotion but on God's will alone.

The phrase οὐ μόνον δέ ("and not only") is almost exclusively used by Paul in the NT (Acts 19:27; Rom 5:3,11; 8:23; 9:10; 2 Cor 7:7; 8:19; 1 Tim 5:13; 2 Tim 4:8). The general sense of this phrase in connection with ἀλλὰ ("but") is to add something else to the argument. Thus, vv. 10–13 is adding to the argument of vv. 7–9. The phrase καὶ Ῥεβέκκα ("also Rebecca") does not have a verb connected with it. Some like Godet take it as an ellipsis and supplies the word ἐπάθη τὸ αὐτο ("she was treated in the same manner, or had to undergo the same lot" [Godet, 348]). Others like Moo, 579 and Käsemann 263 consider Ῥεβέκκα ... ἔχουσα as a "pendant nominative and resumed by (ἐρρέθη) αὐτῇ v. 12."[172] Thus, the thought would be "Rebecca (v. 10) . . . it was said to her" (v. 12). Since both boys had the same father and mother and conceived at the same time, neither boy had any advantage over the other in the womb to receive the divine promise. This point is further developed in verse 11.

9:11-12a μήπω γὰρ γεννηθέντων μηδὲ πραξάντων τι ἀγαθὸν ἢ φαῦλον, ἵνα ἡ κατ' ἐκλογὴν πρόθεσις τοῦ θεοῦ μένῃ, οὐκ ἐξ ἔργων ἀλλ' ἐκ τοῦ καλοῦντος. "For *the twins*, not yet were born nor had done anything good or evil, in order that the purpose of God according to election might remain, not out of works but out of the one who calls." The γὰρ ("for") sets up the reason for the thought in v. 10. The articles μήπω . . . μηδὲ ("not yet" . . . "nor") add the negation to the temporal force. Rom 9:11 begins with two genitive absolutes γεννηθέντων μηδὲ πραξάντων ("having been born or done") with an implied genitive (αὐτῶν, "they" or υἱών, "sons"), which functions as the subject of the phrase (Moo, 2nd, 601, n. 156; Meyer, 2:130). The genitive absolute participle normally expresses a temporal force, as it does in this verse.[173] The sense of v. 10, though not in the syntax, is picked up in v. 12b (v. 12 in English).[174] Paul's additional comment in v. 11 beginning with the ἵνα ("in order that") through v. 12a (the rest of v. 11 in English) is important but is considered by some as a parenthetical thought (Moo, 2nd, 600). Paul's point is that God's choice of Jacob and not Esau was decided before they were born and before they did anything good or bad. The ἵνα ("in order that") expresses purpose. However,

---

[171] BDAG, 554 defines the word as "marriage bed," or "engagement in sexual relations" such as "sexual intercourse" or "seminal emission." Through one intimate encounter or through one expelling of the seed from Isaac the children originated (see Moo, 579, n. 46; Dunn, 542).

[172] Max Zerwick and Mary Grosvenor, *A Grammatical Analysis of the Greek New Testament* (Rome: Biblical Institute Press, 1974), 479.

[173] Daniel B. Wallace, *Greek Grammar Beyond the Basics*, (Grand Rapids: Zondervan, 1996), 655.

[174] See more detail in the comments on v. 10.

Paul also explicitly expresses purpose by using the phrase πρόθεσις[175] τοῦ θεοῦ ("purpose of God"). How Paul expresses the phrase ἡ κατ' ἐκλογὴν πρόθεσις τοῦ θεοῦ ("the purpose of God according to election") using the article ἡ ("the"), which goes with πρόθεσις ("purpose") but placing κατ' ἐκλογὴν ("according to election") in between the article and the noun, gives insight that "the purpose of election" is his unifying thought and emphasis.[176] God's purpose of election and calling is the reason He chose Jacob. This thought ("purpose," "election," and "calling") is supported by the stair-step argument found in Rom 8:28–30. This elective purpose is not by works but sourced in the calling of God (ἐκ τοῦ καλοῦντος), which "remains" (μένῃ) for it is an abiding condition[177] that is immutable because it is sourced in God. When Paul uses the word "call" in the matter of salvation then it refers to the effectual call[178] to salvation.[179] Since καλοῦντος ("call") is correlative to the elective purpose of God, it is not of works, and it fits the soteric context of Rom 8:28-39 and 9:1-3; thus, eternal salvation is the context of the "call" in Rom 9:11.

Therefore, Paul begins with the choice of the promised child Issac. This point would accentuate that God's choice was according to promise, but Abraham having two offsprings with two different women does not sharpen the illustration enough. Hence, he uses Issac and Rebekah and the twin boys. Jacob, the younger who is chosen over the older Esau, is elected before both of them were born and before either one did anything good or bad. Paul is expressing through the historical illustration the immutable elective purpose of God for eternal salvation (Murray, 2:14–15).

9:12b ἐρρέθη[180] αὐτῇ ὅτι Ὁ μείζων δουλεύσει τῷ ἐλάσσονι· "It was said to her, "The Older will serve the younger." The context Rom 9:12b is the OT quotation from Gen 25:23. Rebekah's struggle with the birth of the twin boys lead to the announcement from the Lord. God states that there are two nations in her womb, and they will be divided against each other. One group of people will be stronger than the other and the older will serve the younger. This last phrase "the older will serve the younger" is the phrase that Paul chose to use in Rom 9:12. It is true that the previous phrases in Gen 25:23 involve the representative people and nations from Jacob and Esau, but Paul chose the last phrase that specifically refers to individuals. Furthermore, the choosing of the younger over the older was counter cultural to the custom of that era. However, this elective pattern of individuals, specifically the younger being chosen and not the older son becomes the story in Genesis. Issac was chosen and not Ishmael, Jacob instead of Esau, the choice of Joseph among his older brothers, and the choice to bless Ephraim as first born instead of Manasseh. Finally, the choice of God through Jacob's announcement of blessings in Gen 49

---

[175] The Pauline use of πρόθεσις where it refers to God's purpose: Rom 8:28; 9:11; Eph 1:11; 3:11; 2 Tim 1:9.

[176] Murray, 2:15 seems to be correct that this phrase κατ' ἐκλογὴν ("according to election") indicates the "thought of priority" whether it be the order of time or a logical relationship (cf. Rom 8:28; Gal 1:4; Eph 1:5, 11; 2 Tim 1:9 Heb 2:4; 1 Pet 1:2. Thus, "the purpose would be that which springs from election and fulfils its design."

[177] The presence tense often has this action.

[178] Grudem, *Systematic Theology*, 693 states that "the effective calling of God that actually brings about a willing response from the person who hears it is sometimes called *internal calling*. The gospel call is general and external and often rejected, while the effective call is particular, internal, and *always* effective."

[179] See καλέω (Rom 8:30 (2x); 9:24, 1 Cor 1:9; Gal 1:6, 15; 5:8, 13; Eph 4:1, 4; Col 3:15; 1 Thess 2:12; 4:7; 5:24; 2 Thess 2:14; 1 Tim 6:12; 2 Tim 1:9. See also κλῆσις (1 Cor 1:26; Eph 1:18; 4:1, 4; Phil 3:14; 2 Thess 1:11; 2 Tim 1:9) and κλητός (Rom 1:6, 7; 8:28; 1 Cor 1:2, 24).

[180] The "divine passive" (ἐρρέθη) is used in place of Genesis's εἶπεν κύριος (Dunn, 544). For information on a divine passive see this commentary on 9:22, n. 276.

where Judah, the fourth son and not the first son, becomes the lineage by which the Messiah would come. These illustrations from the historical lineage of Abraham are not the main point for Paul. The elective patterns of God's sovereign choice, especially the sovereign and elective choice of Jacob over Esau before they were born and before they did good or bad,[181] illustrate Paul's point on election.

The issue whether Paul has two people (Sanday and Headlam, 244–45) or two types (Käsemann, 264) does not seem to be his main point, but rather the context of the birth of Esau and Jacob which is reinforced by the argument in vv. 9–11 (Dunn, 544).[182] Schriener, 502 states that Paul uses the "histories as a type, model or pattern that relates to salvation."[183] The author of Hebrews (12:15-17) uses the model of Esau as an eschatological salvation illustration of eternal judgment (Schreiner, 502). However, some have indicated that Esau was eternally saved because of the blessing of Isaac (Gen 27:39–40); he was reconciled to Jacob (Gen 33); his genealogy is included in Gen 36; and Israel was instructed not to abhor Esau, his brother in Deut 23:7 and Amos 2:1-3 (Cranfield, 480; Morris, 353–354). However, the blessing that Esau received from Jacob gives no spiritual participation in the promises (Gen 27:39–40). Esau's reconciliation to Jacob and his inclusion in genealogies are not conclusive evidence for his salvation; and the warning instructions concerning Edom from the Lord does not give authoritative indication of the spiritual condition of that nation (cf. Deut 23:7 and the Egyptians) (Schreiner, 503).

Those who hold to the corporate election of salvation in the context of Rom 9 often appeal to the OT quotation context and do not sufficiently regard the context of Paul's argument in Rom 9:6ff. Paul began in Rom 9:6 with a question, which he answers in the following verses. Have the promises of God (briefly sketch out in 9:4-5) to the corporate nation of Israel failed since the corporate nation (the majority of Israelites) remain in unbelief and fall short of the covenant promises? Paul's answer would be confusing and unconvincing if he appeals to the corporate election of the nation when the corporate nation is in unbelief. However, Paul's answer in 9:6 helps us to view the following OT texts. Not all of corporate Israel is the true Israel! There is a distinction between Israel and true Israel. There is a distinction between unbelieving elect corporate Israel and believing elect among corporate elect Israel. Murray states when Paul uses the phrase, "'the purpose of God according to election' he is speaking of the electing purpose of God in a discriminating, differentiating sense that cannot apply to all who were embraced in the theocratic election" (Murray, 2:18). This election in Rom 9 is a personal election among the corporate nation of Israel. Notice also the concentration on the individuality in Rom 9:10-11a with the mentioning of conception, birth and "works" – language not easily applied to nations (Moo, 585). Therefore, Paul is using the elective pattern of God in his choice of the Abrahamic historic line of Isaac and Jacob to demonstrate the personal sovereign purpose of God in election.

9:13 καθὼς γέγραπται· Τὸν Ἰακὼβ ἠγάπησα,[184] τὸν δὲ Ἠσαῦ ἐμίσησα. "Just as it is written: Jacob I loved and Esau I hated." Jacob's pre-eminence over Esau is the result of God's love for

---

[181] We agree with Moo (2nd, 602–603, also n. 162); the reference to good and bad works is a general reference to work and not to the "works of the law" (*contra* Dunn, 543).

[182] Abasciano, *Rom 9:10-18*, 4–15 presents a corporate view of election but he also agrees that the individuals of Esau and Jacob are in view (p. 5). See Abasciano "Corporate election in Romans 9" and Schreiner, "Corporate and Individual Election in Romans 9." See also Schreiner, 2nd, 492, n. 52.

[183] See Odeberg, *TDNT*, 2:953 (*contra* Cranfield, 479; Sanday and Headlam, 245).

[184] The reason for the change from the order of the LXX is not clear. Some give the possibility that Paul wanted to make two phrases parallel and make it a closer parallel with Rom 9:12 (Moo, 2nd, 604, n. 173; Jewett, 580; Stanley, *Paul and the Language of Scripture*, 106; Koch, *Die Schrift als Zeuge des Evangeliums*, 107).

Jacob and Esau's servitude is the result of God's "hate" for him.[185] Moo (2nd, 604) is correct that v. 13 restates v. 12b and the contrasting destinies of Jacob and Esau are caused by God and not merely seen in advance by Him (p. 604).[186] The verb ἀγαπάω ("love") does not center in on feelings and emotions, but is a self-sacrificing service that meets the need of another regardless whether the person deserves or is worthy of the action. The concept of μισέω ("hate") does not necessarily center on feelings and emotions. When God hates evil, it is not so much an emotion, but a decision of the will to reject the deed.[187] The Wisdom literature often uses love and hate in their instruction, but the concept is also found in other places (Prov 13:24; 14:20; 51:22; 512; Mich 3:2). Thus, it is probably best not to think that this use of "love" and "hate" as a Semitic use of direct opposites expressing a lesser degree comparison (i.e., hate as love less), but more as election (God loves Jacob) and rejection (God hates Esau) (Sanday & Headlam, 247; Cranfield, 480; Jewett, 580; Meyer, 134–135; Murray, 2:21–23).

The source of Paul's quotation from the Jewish Scripture is Malachi 1:1–5. The context of Mal 1:1-5 is the nations that spring forth from Jacob and Esau. However, this fact should not disregard the applicability concerning Jacob and Esau individually. Paul again, as he did in Gen 25:23 in Rom 9:12, quotes from the only verse (Mal 1:2–3a) that applies to the individual person of Jacob and Esau in Mal 1:1–5. In the context of v. 2, Malachi expresses the importance of the free grace of God in God's choice of the destinies of the twin sons by using a question: "Was not Esau Jacob's brother?" The implication of this question indicates that there are no human reasons or distinction for God to choose to love Jacob and hate Esau. God's choice was made solely upon the basis of free grace and the sovereign will of God.[188] This point is what Paul expresses in Rom 9:11–12a (Eng. v. 11) and becomes the basis for why Paul is using the two OT quotations in Rom 9:12b–13 (Eng. vv. 12–13). Thus, the basis for God's love and hate existed before the children were born and did anything good or bad. In other places in the NT, Paul states that God's election was decided by God from all eternity (i.e., Eph 1:4; 2 Tim 1:9).

There are effects and consequences for the lineage of each son, but the immediate application involved two individual sons of Isaac. Those who advocate for a corporate election point to the fact that God's election in the OT is primarily a corporate calling out of Israel. They will also point out the surrounding corporate context of Paul's OT quotations in Rom 9:12-13. If Paul actually quoted from one of the surrounding contexts of Gen 25:23 and Mal 1:2e–3a, their case would be stronger.[189] However, Paul does just the opposite. With great intentionality, Paul quotes from the only verse within each context that deals with the individuality of two sons. Furthermore, the corporate election of Israel is also not the context of Paul's argument (see above argument in Rom 9:12b).

---

[185] For the possibility of double predestination see Schreiner (501) and Käsemann, 265.

[186] Murray states that Jacob's pre-eminence is the result of God's love; Sanday & Headlam (247) state that Jacob's pre-eminence is seen in the history of Isarel while Cranfield (480) attributes it to the same thought in Genesis as a corroborate with what has been said in Gen 25:23.

[187] Michel, *TDNT*, 4:687.

[188] Piper, 63; Weiser, *Das Buch der zwoelf s kleinen Propheten*, II, 191.

[189] See Abasciano, Rom 9:10-18, 16–21 for the corporate view. He does recognize both the individual and the corporate in note 15. He also acknowledges that it seems that Mal 1:2–3 involves a historical and salvation role (p. 20). Abasciano states "Its significance was never that each individual member of the elect people was chosen as an individual to become part of the elect people in the same manner as the corporate head was chosen" (p. 60). However, it was the corporate head, individual election of Isaac and Jacob, which Paul chose to quote in Rom 9:12–13 from both Gen 25 and Mal 1. This point is also in the context where Paul in Rom 9 is making the distinction that not all of corporate Israel is true (saved) Israel – individual Israelites among physical corporate Israel.

Biblical Theological Comments

(-) 9:6b - For all those who are from Israel (inclusive), these are not Israel (exclusive).
(-) 9:7a - Neither is it the case that all of Abraham's children (inclusive) are *his* seed (exclusive);
(+) 9:7b - But in Isaac shall your seed be called
(-) 9:8a - That is, the children of the flesh, these are not the children of God
(+) 9:8b - but the children of promise (believing Israel) are counted as seed (remnant – true Israel).

The key verse in Rom 9:10–13 is v. 11 which points to the elective choice of God that is decided freely according to God's grace and will alone. God's loving election of Jacob was not depended on anything good or bad in Jacob for this choice was made before he was born – before the foundation of creation (Eph 1:4). The quotation by Paul from Gen 25:23 in v. 12 and Mal 1:2–3a in v. 13 are used to support his point "not because of works, but because of Him who calls" (9:11c). The use of the word "call" (see commentary above) strongly indicates that Paul is addressing eternal salvation. This point is buttressed by the introductory thought of Rom 9:2–3 and Paul's argument that not all Israel is true Israel, part of the seed, or children of God. Furthermore, because Paul is making a distinction between corporate Israel and true Israel (see commentary above) he is indicating God's choice of individuals (remnant) within corporate Israel.

Application and Devotional Implications

The big idea of Rom 9:6–13 is: The sovereign unconditional election of God explains the reason why God's promises have not failed. The thought of Rom 9:10–13 may be summarized as: The election of Jacob over Esau establishes God's sovereign unconditional election.

Jacob and Esau have the same father and mother and being twins, they were born on the same day. Notice the characteristic of this choice. It was done before they were born. Actually, in Eph 1:4 and 2 Tim 1:9, our election unto salvation was done before the foundation of the world in what we call eternity past. Secondly, this election was done before the twins did anything good or bad. In other words, it was not based upon works. This election was not based upon God's foresight of the future works of Jacob. Even if it was based upon God's foresight (which it was not), He would see that Jacob was just as wicked as Esau apart from divine grace (of course, God is omniscient and does not need or depend on this kind of foresight). Paul tells us that God's election is unconditional. It does not depend upon what a person is or is not, and what a person has done or not done. God elects a person to salvation according to His purpose, which is according to His determinative will.

Paul backs this up by two OT quotations. In v. 12 he quotes Gen 25:23. This OT passage was given to Rebekah before the twins were born. This point gives evidence that God's choice was not based upon works but God who calls. In v. 13, Paul quotes Mal 1:2–3a. There is a debate concerning the meaning of the word "hate." Some believe the word means to love less or to regard with less favor (cp. Matt 10:37; Luke 14:26; Gen 29:30–33; Deut 21:15; Matt 6:24; John 12:25). Yet, the context of Mal 1:1–5 indicates God's displeasure is judgment. We read in Ps 5:5; 11:5; Prov 8:13 and other places that God is angry with the wicked all day long. They are by nature children of wrath (Eph 2:3) and the wrath of God abides on them (John 3:36). This truth is not to negate the point that God loves all mankind in the sense of common grace. However, this hate is not malice, vindictiveness or bitterness, which we associate with man's hatred. The closest interpretation concerning the concept of hatred associated with God from man's viewpoint seems to be the righteous indignation expressed for God's honor and rightful place (Ps 26:5; 31:6; 139:21–22; Rev 2:6; etc.). Yet, in reality God's hatred is a hate that transcends human analogy, which is an expression of His sovereign justice and righteousness.

We learn from v. 13 that God has a distinguishing love for those who are chosen and a divine displeasure toward those who are not chosen. However, we must keep in mind that neither Jacob or Esau or anyone else merited God's love. We all deserve His wrath and His chosen receive His mercy.

A man gave his testimony one day and he made the statement, "when I was saved I did my part and God did His part. I did all the sinning and God did all the saving"! He explained, "I went my way and sin carried me as fast as I could go away from God. Yet God, 'the hound of heaven' sought me; pursued me; ran me down; caught me; and won me." The ultimate cause of our salvation is not because we chose God but because He first chose us. We are not saved because we always had an inclination toward God. No, Paul says in Rom 3 that our natures apart from divine grace never seeks God and His way. "There is none who understands. There is none who seeks for God" apart from divine grace. We chose and willed to come to God for salvation because He sought us according to His elective purpose, which was rooted in divine love (Eph 1:3-5; Jn 6:35, 44, 65).

It is my experience that the rejection of the doctrine of election is not because it is unclear. It is not because it is never stated in the Bible. It is usually rejected because it raises so many questions. Such questions as: Is God unfair? Is God unjust? How can God hold me responsible if He predestined it? Paul deals with these questions in Rom 9:14–21. Let us not get upset about this doctrine. Don't think someone has to understand it all this week. May God give us grace to accept the Word of God even though we cannot answer all of the questions and problems. May we humbly bow before God and let God be God and let us be His creatures. Whatever the Bible says is true. May we humbly submit though we may not understand it all.

If by God's grace we do submit to His Word then there are several things that this doctrine will do practically in our lives. First, the doctrine of election will undermine self-sufficiency. When God reveals to us our utter sinfulness; when He destroys any merit that we thought we had before Him; and when nothing in us or action from us inclines God to us (but should have repelled Him away from us), He chose us – when this sobering thought sinks in, our pride and self-sufficiency is uprooted! Second, a correct understanding of this doctrine will elicit praise to our God. Read and count how many times in Ephesian chapter one Paul mentions the phrase "to the praise of His glory." Too many dwell on why God did not chose all, but the greater question is why did God choose anyone? All deserve His wrath. Oh, that we may be able to see pass the questions and bring forth praise to God for His distinguishing grace and mercy to us! Thirdly, this doctrine should become an encouragement for ministry and evangelism. William Carey, the father of modern missions, was burdened by God with the souls of the people in India. Therefore, he brought his plans for evangelism to his elders. One of the elders told him to sit down for if God wanted to convert the heathen, then He will do it without your aid or mine. That man did not have the biblical understanding of the doctrine of election, but William Carey did. It is true that God has ordained the elect to salvation, but He has also ordained the means to the end, which is the proclamation of the gospel. Paul was encouraged and motived in his missionary tours by the doctrine of election. He says in 2 Tim 2:10, “For this reason I endure all things for the sake of those who are chosen that they also may obtain the salvation, which is in Christ Jesus and with it eternal glory.” In Acts 18:10 God spoke to Paul in a vision and told him to stay in Corinth because God had many people in this city. It was a motivation for our Lord who says in John 10:16, “other sheep which are not of this fold; I must bring them also” (cp. Jn 17:2-3).

This doctrine has been an encouragement and motivation for men like Augustine, Calvin, Luther, Knox, Beza, Owen, and the Puritans. Men like Whitefield, Edwards, Spurgeon, Hodge, Shedd, Warfield, Lewis Chafer, John Murray, Lloyd-Jones, James Boice, and D. James Kennedy supported this view. This is the view of men today such as J. I. Packer, R. C. Sproul, S. Lewis Johnson, Jr., John MacArthur, John Piper, J. Randall Price, and many others. I hope that this exhortation will be a motivation and encouragement to you, to spread the gospel with the full assurance that God will use us to bring His own to Himself. God’s promises will not fail because He sovereignly accomplishes His elective purposes. May all praise and glory be given to His holy Name!

Excursus[190]

NT terms for Election

1. "Elect, chosen, select" (ἐκλετός) It refers to God's election of:
   a. Christ - Luke 23:35; 1 Pet 2:4, 6; John 1:34 (?)
   b. Holy angels - 1 Tim 5:21
   c. Believers (to eternal life) - Matt 22:14, 22, 24, 31; Mark 13:20,22,27; Luke 18:7; Rom 8:33; 16:13; Col 3:12; 2 Tim 2:10; Titus 1:1; 1 Pet 1:1; 2:9; 2 John 1, 13; Rev 17:14

2. "Election, selection" (ἐκλογή) It refers to God's election of:
   a. Paul - Acts 9:15
   b. God’s choice - Rom 9:11
   c. Believers (to eternal life) - Rom 11:5, 7; 1 Thess 1:4; 2 Pet 1:10
   d. Elect Israelite - Rom 11:28

3. "Choose, choose someone for oneself, to make a choice" (ἐκλέγομαι)
   In the NT it is used of:
   a. Christ - Luke 9:35
   b. Christ's choice of disciples - Luke 16:13; John 6:70; 13:18; 15:16 (twice); 15:19; Acts 1:2
   c. Divine choice of:
      1) persons - Mark 13:20; Acts 1:24; 13:17; 15:7; Eph 1:4; Jas 2:5
      2) things - 1 Cor 1:27 (twice), 28
   d. A person or persons choose(s) something - Luke 10:42; 14:7; Act 6:5; 15:22, 25

[190] Information in the Excursus was taken from Steele & Thomas, *Five Points of Calvinism*, 30–38; Berkhof, *Systematic Theology*, 114-115; Gary Long, *Doctrine of Salvation, Part II*, 39–45; Boettner, *Reformed Doctrine of Predestination*, 83-104.

4. "Chosen together with" (συνεκλεκτός) - 1 Pet 5:13
5. "Choose" (αἱρέω) - 2 Thess 2:13; (Phil 1:22; Heb 11:25)
6. "Choose, appoint before hand" (προχειροτονέω) - Acts 10:41
7. "Choose for oneself, select, appoint"(προχειρίζομαι) - Acts 3:20; 22:14; 26:16
8. "Appointed" - Acts 13:48 (eternal life); Acts 22:10; Rom 13:1 (God's appointment); Mt 28:16; Lk 7:8; Acts 15:2; 28:23; 1 Cor 16:15 (people appoint)

Characteristics of Individual Election unto Salvation

1. God chose (Mark 13:20; 1 Thess 1:4; 2 Thess 2:13).
2. God chose before the creation of the world (eternal choice) (Eph 1:4; 2 Thess 2:13; 2 Tim 1:9; Rev 13:8; 17:8).
3. God's choice was not based upon foreseen good works or meritorious character of people (Rom 9:11-13; 9:16; 10:20; 1 Cor. 1:27-29; 2 Tim 1:9).
4. The sovereign will and mercy of God determines who receives mercy and salvation. (Ex 33:19; Deut 7:6-7; Rom 9:10-24; 11:4-6; Eph 1:4-5; Jas 1:18; Matt 11:27; Luke 10:22).
5. God's choice in salvation is certain (Rom 8.29-30; 11:28-29; John 6:37-39; Acts 13:48).
6. Election is just (Isa 59:16–21; Rom 11:25–29; Ex 33:12–19; Rom 9:11–15).
7. God chose particular individuals unto salvation (Rev 13:8; 17:8).
8. Those who God appoints will believe (Acts 13:48).
9. Faith and good works confirm one's calling and election (1 Pet 1:3–11; 2 Pet 1:5–11; Eph 2:8–10; John 15:16).
10. Two-fold purpose of election:
    a. To result in salvation (2 Thess 2:13; 2 Tim 2:10; 1 Pet 2:9–10)
    b. To result in the glory of God (Eph 1:5–6, 12–14)

Selected Bibliography

Abasciano, Brian J. "Corporate election in Romans 9: A Reply to Thomas Schreiner." *Journal of the Evangelical Theological Society* 49 (April-June 2006): 351–371.

Boettner, Loraine. *The Reformed Doctrine of Predestination* (Philadelphia: Presbyterian and Reformed, 1972).

Berkhof, Louis. *Systematic Theology* (Grand Rapids: Eerdmans, 1972).

Grudem, Wayne A. *Systematic Theology: An Introduction to Biblical Doctrine* (Leicester, England; Grand Rapids, MI: Inter-Varsity Press; Zondervan Pub. House, 2004).

Hodges, Zane C. and Arthur L. Farstad, ed. *The Greek New Testament According to the Majority Text* (Nashville: Nelson , 1982).

Koch, Dietrich-Alex. *Die Schrift als Zeuge des Evangeliums: Untersuchungen zur Verwendung und zum Verständnis der Schrift bei Paulus*. Beiträge zur historischen Theologie, vol. 69 (Tübingen: Mohr Siebeck, 1986).

Long, Gary D. *The Doctrine of Salvation* (Sterling VA: G.A.M. Printers, 1978).

Robinson, Maurice A. and William G. Pierpont. *The New Testament in the Original Greek: Byzantine Majority Textform Greek New Testament* (Roswell, GA: The Original Word Publishers, 1995).

Schreiner, Thomas R. “Corporate and Individual Election in Romans 9: A Response to Brian Abasciano,” *Journal of the Evangelical Theological Society* 49 (April - June 2006): 373–386.

Stanley, Christopher D. *Paul and the Language of Scripture: Citation Technique in the Pauline Epistles and Contemporary Literature.* Society for New Testament Studies Monograph Series, ed. Richard Bauckham, vol. 74 (Cambridge: Cambridge University Press, 1992).

Steele, David N. and Curtis C. Thomas. *The Five Points of Calvinism: Defined, Defended, Documented* (Philadephia: Presbyterian and Reformed, 1975).

Swanson, Reuben, ed. *New Testament Greek Manuscripts: Romans*. (Wheaton: Tyndale House and Pasadena: William Carey International University Press, 2001).

Wallace, Daniel B. *Greek Grammar Beyond the Basics*, (Grand Rapids: Zondervan, 1996).

Weiser, Artur, *Das Buch der zwoelf kleine Propheten*, II, Altes Testament Deutsh (Göettingen: Vandenhoeck und Ruprecht, 1967).

Zerwick, Max and Mary Grosvenor, *A Grammatical Analysis of the Greek New Testament* (Rome: Biblical Institute Press, 1974).

Romans 9:14–18

Outline

B. Vindication of the Righteous God and His Wise Plan (9:6-29)
   1. Israel within Israel: Children of Promise (9:6-9)
   2. The Divine Call according to Election (9:10-13)
   3. Polemic: Objects of Mercy and Hardening according to God’s Choice (9:14-18)

Original Text

9.14 Τί οὖν ἐροῦμεν; μὴ ἀδικία παρὰ τῷ θεῷ; μὴ γένοιτο· 15τῷ Μωϋσεῖ[a] γὰρ λέγει· Ἐλεήσω ὃν ἂν
ἐλεῶ, καὶ οἰκτιρήσω ὃν ἂν οἰκτίρω. 16 ἄρα οὖν οὐ τοῦ θέλοντος[b] οὐδὲ τοῦ τρέχοντος ἀλλὰ τοῦ
ἐλεῶντος θεοῦ. 17 λέγει γὰρ ἡ γραφὴ τῷ Φαραὼ ὅτι Εἰς αὐτὸ τοῦτο ἐξήγειρά σε ὅπως ἐνδείξωμαι
ἐν σοὶ τὴν δύναμίν μου, καὶ ὅπως διαγγελῇ τὸ ὄνομά μου ἐν πάσῃ τῇ γῇ. 18ἄρα οὖν ὃν θέλει
ἐλεεῖ, ὃν δὲ θέλει σκληρύνει.

Textual Notes

[a] **9:15** There is a variety of spellings of **Μωϋσεῖ** (Μωϋσῇ, Μωσῇ, Μωσεῖ) and arrangement of the phrase Τῷ [Τῷι] Μωϋσεῖ γὰρ λέγει (Τῷ [Τῷι] γὰρ Μωϋσῇ λέγει). However, it does not seem to effect the understanding of the translation. Ignoring the spelling difference, B*, B[c], p[46], D, F, G, P, 1881, NA[28], UBS5 has **Τῷ γὰρ Μωϋσῇ λέγει.**

[b] **9:16 οὐ τοῦ θέλοντος[b] οὐδὲ τοῦ τρέχοντος** – The mss. p[46], 406, 618, 1506, 1738 reverse the order to: τοῦ τρέχοντος οὐδὲ τοῦ θέλοντος.

Translation

9:14 What then shall we say? There is no unrighteousness with God, is there? May it never be! **15** For to Moses he says, "I will have mercy on whom I have mercy, and I will have compassion on whom I have compassion." **16** Therefore it is not a matter of the person who wills or the person who runs, but of the God who shows mercy. **17** For the Scripture says to Pharaoh, "For this very reason I have raised you up, so that I might demonstrate through you my power and so that my name might be proclaimed in all the earth." **18** Therefore he has mercy on whomever he wills, and he hardens whomever he wills.

Commentary

9:14 Τί οὖν ἐροῦμεν; μὴ ἀδικία παρὰ τῷ θεῷ; μὴ γένοιτο· "What then shall we say? There is no unrighteousness with God, is there? May it never be!" The opening question Τί οὖν ἐροῦμεν; (What then shall we say?) is used seven other times in Romans (4:1; 6:1; 7:7; 8:31; 9:14; 9:30; and 3:5 only τί ἐροῦμεν;)[191] and six out of the seven times is at the beginning of the sentence. Paul uses this phrase in Rom 3:5–6; 6:1; 7:7; 9:14 to point out a false conclusion that could be reached instead of a true one (Cranfield, 481–482). Thus, raising the question and giving a negative answer introduce clarity to the argument. If God's choice determines who will be saved (vv.11–12) and who is rejected (v. 13), and this choice was decided before they were born, then the question of God being unrighteous[192] is an accusation that Paul encountered. Thus, an objector would raise the question, but since Paul uses the negative μή ("not") which in a question indicates that the writer wants the reader to answer "no" to the question raised, then it is Paul's opinion that is being expressed by the implied answer. He rejects the charge of unrighteousness by his classic negation, μὴ γένοιτο ("may it never be"). The basic meaning of ἀδικία ("unrighteous") is expressed by Moo, 591 as acting according to what is right; thus, the question is God acting according to what is right? He also indicates that the word is referred to a few times in the OT in the context of faithfulness to God's promise and covenant (592, n. 14; Dunn, 551).[193] In the main, ἀδικία is both a "disposition and conduct which contradicts the truth" (Piper, 94). See Rom 1:18; 2:8; 3:5; 1 Cor 13:6; 2 Thess 2:10, 12; 2 Tim 2:19. The norm for understanding truth is whatever conforms to the character of God. Schrenk commenting on John 7:18 says, "ἀδικία is present when we do not seek God's glory but our own reputation. Truth on the other hand consists in desiring the glory of the One who sends. Paul, too, makes great use of this contrast."[194] Thus, the question in v. 14 raises the accusation that God is not doing what is right, or involved in injustice, which is an attack on His character and honor.

The reason for the emphatic denial in v. 14 is introduced by γὰρ ("for") in both v. 15 and v. 17 as Paul cites the book of Exodus for his support. After each OT citation, he makes an inference with the introductory phrase ἄρα οὖν ("so then") in v. 16 and v. 18.

---

[191] See a similar construction Τί οὖν; in Rom 3:9; 6:15; 11:7 and more extended question using Τί οὖν in Rom 3:1; 9:19(?), 1 Cor 3:5; 10:19; 14:15, 26; Gal 3:19. See Piper, 91, n.1; Moo, 2nd, 611, n. 197.

[192] BDAG, 20.

[193] See Deut 32:4; 2 Chron 19:7; Ps 91:16 [LXX].

[194] Schrenk, *TDNT*, 1:156.

9:15 τῷ Μωϋσεῖ γὰρ λέγει· Ἐλεήσω ὃν ἂν[195] ἐλεῶ, καὶ οἰκτιρήσω ὃν ἂν οἰκτίρω. "For to Moses he says, 'I will have mercy on whom I have mercy, and I will have compassion on whom I have compassion.'" The γὰρ ("for") in v. 15 at least joins Paul's thought with v. 14.[196] Historically, Paul's argument in v. 15 has different views.[197] The question is: What is Paul's argument when he says God is not unrighteous and then quotes the later part of Ex 33:19? The background of Exodus section in brief is the theme of Israel's disobedience, God's judgment, and Moses' intercession for Israel's sin in chp 32. The theme of chp 33 is God's presence and Moses' intercession. The theme of the Ex 34:1–9 is God's presence and forgiveness. In the theme of God's presence, Moses specifically asked to see God's glory (Ex 33:13–18), which is discussed and described in Ex 33:19–34:7. No telling what glories Moses saw when he spent 40 days on the mountain. Whatever he saw and understood on the mountain he seems to be asking for more. This probe into the being of God is most intriguing and revealing about the character of God. In the light of the stiff-necked and sinfulness of the people and Moses' request that God would pardon, lead, and still keep them as His people, we have at least the following attributes of God's character displayed: goodness, mercy, grace, compassion, slow to anger, lovingkindness, truth, just, and forgiving (Ex 33:19; 34:6–7). On the other hand, what seems to be the central point in Ex 32–34, which is brought out with Moses' request to see God's glory is God's sovereign choice. The essence of God's nature, which He expresses in His glory is mainly displayed by His decree/choice. This choice in this context is to dispense His mercy[198] and wrath[199] on whom He pleases apart from any constrains or influence originating outside of Himself.[200] Thus, Paul chooses Ex 33:19 because he is aware of the total context that speaks to the very point in Rom 9:14-18. In sum, Moses asks to see the essence of God's glory and God response by telling him that fundamentally God's sovereign choice is the answer. Murray is correct when he said, "Justice presupposes rightful claims, and mercy can be operative only where no claim of justice exist. Since mercy alone is the constraining consideration, the only explanation is God's free and sovereign determination" (2:26).

The quotation by Paul agrees with the LXX which reflects also the MT.[201] There is some discussion whether "mercy" and "compassion" are synonymous expression of the heart or is mercy the attitude of the heart and compassion an outward expression. This quotation from Ex 33:19 is the beginning of multiple quotations from the Exodus motif and the New Exodus motif in Rom 9–11 (see introduction to Rom 9–11).

9:16 ἄρα οὖν οὐ τοῦ θέλοντος οὐδὲ τοῦ τρέχοντος ἀλλὰ τοῦ ἐλεῶντος θεοῦ. "Now therefore, it is not of the person who wills or the person who runs, but from God who shows mercy." The

[195] The construction ὃν ἂν … ὃν ἂν …. is probably indicating a generic subject ("whomever") (Wallace, *Greek Grammar Beyond the Basics*, 478). Schreiner (2nd, 495, n. 9), Murray (2:25), and Morris (359, n. 67) indicate that this Greek construction stresses God's freedom and sovereignty in his choice.

[196] Piper, 99, n. 17 points out that Paul normally gives a reason why he denies an objection with μὴ γένοιτο (Rom 3:6; 6:2,15; 7:7,13; 11:1,11).

[197] See Piper, 99–100.

[198] For synonymous expressions, see Moo (2nd, 612, n. 205) and for a distinction between the two words, see Godet (352).

[199] Cranfield, 482–483 states that God only exercises His will in mercy. There is no confliction between what God's will or decree is and His will to show mercy.

[200] This is God's ultimate standard and not the penultimate standard of God's covenant with Israel (Rom 11) that God's righteousness should be measured (Moo, 2nd, 612). See Piper, 75–89 for the development of God's righteousness and His name and glory.

[201] Bultmann, *TDNT*, 2:477 says that ἐλεεῖν occurs mostly for חָנַן.

thought of v. 16 is an inference (ἄρα οὖν) from Ex 33:19 in v. 15, which is a reassertion of God's calling and election from v. 11 (Gk. vv. 11-12a). Thus, God's sovereign freedom and choice in v. 16 corresponds to His freedom in vv. 11-13 (Piper, 157).

The subject of v. 16 is not clearly stated in the construction of v. 16, but it is clear from the context that Paul is referring to the subject of God bestowing mercy from v.15 (Moo, 2nd, 613; Cranfield, 484; Sanday & Headlam, 254). The genitive participial phrases τοῦ θέλοντος … τοῦ τρέχοντος … τοῦ ἐλεῶντος θεοῦ ("of him who wills … of him who runs … of God who has mercy") are probably best understood as genitives of source (Moo, 2nd, 613, n. 214).[202] God's mercy in salvation[203] is not sourced in the person's willing or doing, but it is sourced in God. Piper using Noack[204] and Maier[205] gives a compelling argument against Hellenistic background of athletics[206] in favor of a Jewish concept of work for the background of the word "running" (Piper, 152–153).[207] Thus, all "willing" and "running" whether from what is often called "bad works" or "good works" had no influence at all on God's choice to show mercy to anyone. The closest parallel to Rom 9:16 is the positive counterpart in Phil 2:13, "for it is God who is at work in you, both to will and to work for His good pleasure." John 3:12-13 also is analogous to the thought of v. 16 (Sanday & Headlam, 254). Therefore, generally, the "willing" denotes the desire, purpose, and readiness, or possibly the cheerfulness and hearty consent and "running" conveys the outward doing of the person's desire (Piper, 154–155; Moo, 2nd, 613). Paul is not trying to pit "willing" against "running," but he is using both words together to sum up "the totality of man's capacity" (Dunn, 553; Jewett, 582-583).

Schreiner is correct that this verse is one of the clearest verses in Scripture that indicates in its context that God's will and free choice and not human choice is the ultimate cause of mankind's divine election for salvation (2nd, p. 508).[208] Or as Barrett concludes: since God deals with mankind by his mercy "they cannot be determined by man's will, or earnest striving towards a goal" (p. 173). On the other hand, in Rom 10 Paul will indicate that mankind is held responsible to God for their unbelief. The tension between divine sovereignty and mankind's responsibility to believe is always in tension from the human viewpoint (Schreiner, 2nd, 561). Though we cannot adequately solve the tension satisfactorily, we should not deny either God's sovereignty to choose or man's responsibility before God for his unbelief.

9:17 λέγει γὰρ ἡ γραφὴ τῷ Φαραὼ ὅτι Εἰς αὐτὸ τοῦτο ἐξήγειρά σε ὅπως ἐνδείξωμαι ἐν σοὶ τὴν δύναμίν μου, καὶ ὅπως διαγγελῇ τὸ ὄνομά μου ἐν πάσῃ τῇ γῇ. "For the Scripture says to Pharaoh, 'For this very reason I have raised you up, so that I might demonstrate through you my power

---

202 *Contra* Dunn, 552.

203 See Piper's compelling argument that God's freedom in giving mercy and withholding it encompasses eternal salvation (Piper, 155–158).

204 Bent Noack, "Celui qui court, Romans IX, 16," *Studia Theologica* 24, (1970), 113–116.

205 Gerhard Maier, *Mennsch und frier Wille nach den juedischen Religionsparteien zwischen Ben Sira und Paulus*, Wissenschaftliche Untersuchungen zum Neuen Testament 12 (Tuebingen, 1971), 368–370.

206 For the view that understands the running as an imagery of a race, see Cranfield, 485, n. 1; Käsemann, 267.

207 See also Otto Bauernfeind, "τρέχω κτλ.," *TDNT* 8 (1972) 229. BDAG, 1015 defines τρέχω as "exert oneself to the limit of one's powers in an attempt to go forward, strive to advance Ro 9:16 (the emphasis is entirely on the effort that the person makes…)."

208 See the works of Augustine, Luther, Calvin and Edwards for the bondage of man's will and the freedom and sovereignty of God's will. For an introductory chapter see Gerstner, "Augustine, Luther, Calvin, and Edwards on the Bondage of the Will," 279–295.

and so that my name might be proclaimed in all the earth.'" The outline of Rom 9:14–18 is as follows:

v. 14 Question: Is God unjust? May it never be!
v. 15 Reason #1 (γὰρ, "for") Moses says in Ex 33:19 – Depends solely upon God's mercy
v. 16 Conclusion #1 (ἄρα οὖν, "now therefore") - Does not depend on man's willing or doing, but on God
v. 17 Reason #2 (γὰρ, "for") Scripture says to Pharaoh in Ex 9:16 – Depends upon God's power and His name proclaimed
v. 18 Conclusion #2 (ἄρα οὖν, "now therefore") – God is sovereign in mercy and hardening

There are two basic possibilities that have been presented to understand the above catena of verses. First, is that γὰρ ("for") in v. 17 is parallel with γὰρ ("for") in v. 15 and both support the answer to the question of v.14 (Hodge, 493). The second option is vv. 15–16 supports the question of v. 14 and the γὰρ ("for") in the v. 17 is connected to v. 16 (Sanday & Headlam, 225; Dunn, 553). However, vv. 17–18 do not support just the thought of mercy but includes hardening (Moo, 2nd, 614). On the other hand, vv. 17–18 develop the other side of God's sovereign will in his choice of mercy in vv. 15–16. Thus, Piper (159) concludes that v. 17 relates to both 9:14 and 9:16. The symmetry of the conjunctions in vv. 15–18 supports the first view; however, the thought that vv. 17–18 support v. 16 as a secondary connection should not be surprising since it strengthens the overall flow of the argument. The concluding thought of v. 18 which includes mercy and hardening supports God's freedom and will (vv. 16, 18). Thus, Paul seems to be using Ex 9:16 in Rom 9:17 and Ex 33:19 in Rom 9:15 to support that God is not unrighteous in his unconditional election (Rom 9:14). Piper's solution seems to fit the grammatical construction and logical structure of vv. 14-18 (see also Moo, 2nd, 614–15).

The following comparison of Paul's citation of Ex 9:16 in Rom 9:17:

Biblia Hebraica Stuttgartensia	**Septuaginta** John William Wevers, ed., Exodus, vol. II, 1, Vetus Testamentum Graecum. Auctoritate Academiae Scientiarum Gottingensis Editum (Göttingen: Vandenhoeck & Ruprecht, 1991)	**The Greek New Testament: SBL Edition** (Lexham Press; Society of biblical Literature 2011–2013)	**NT Translation**
וְאוּלָם בַּעֲבוּר זֹאת הֶעֱמַדְתִּיךָ בַּעֲבוּר הַרְאֹתְךָ אֶת־כֹּחִי וּלְמַעַן סַפֵּר שְׁמִי בְּכָל־הָאָרֶץ׃	καὶ ἕνεκεν τούτου διετηρήθης, ἵνα ἐνδείξωμαι ἐν σοὶ τὴν ἰσχύν μου, καὶ ὅπως διαγγελῇ τὸ ὄνομά μου ἐν πάσῃ τῇ γῇ.	λέγει γὰρ ἡ γραφὴ τῷ Φαραὼ ὅτι Εἰς αὐτὸ τοῦτο ἐξήγειρά σε ὅπως ἐνδείξωμαι ἐν σοὶ τὴν δύναμίν μου, καὶ ὅπως διαγγελῇ τὸ ὄνομά μου ἐν πάσῃ τῇ γῇ.	"The Scripture says to Pharaoh, 'For this very reason I have raised you up, so that I might demonstrate through you my power and so that my name might be proclaimed in all the earth.'"

The first part of Paul's citation from Ex 9:16 is different for the LXX and seems to follow better the Hebrew text unless Paul had a copy of the Greek OT that is now extant. The MT stresses that the Lord will cause Pharaoh to stand, and he is the instrument by which the Lord will show his power to all the earth. The LXX uses καὶ ("and") for וְאוּלָם ("but, indeed") while Paul uses the telic phrase εἰς αὐτὸ τοῦτο ("for this very reason"). This purpose phrase is important for Paul's use and understanding of Ex 9:16 and how to understand Rom 9:18. Paul is closer to the Hebrew הֶעֱמַדְתִּיךָ ("I cause you to stand" or "I established you") than to the LXX διετηρήθης ("you were preserved") when he writes ἐξήγειρά ("I have raised you up").[209] Two minor differences when he introduces the second purpose clause with ὅπως ("so that") rather than ἵνα ("so that") and renders כֹּחִי as δύναμίν ("power") instead of ἰσχύν ("strength") in the LXX. Paul uses the concept of God raising up Pharaoh on the scene of history to demonstrate the Lord's power and to proclaim his name in all the earth. The implication of this raising up of Pharaoh indicates that he appears on the scene of history according to and determined by God's will (Schriener, 2nd, 498). Though in v. 17 hardening is not mentioned the context of Ex 9:16 involved the hardening of the heart of Pharaoh (Ex 9:7, 12, 34, 35) which becomes the means of displaying the Lord's power and the greatness of his Name. It is not too much to assert that this power refers to God's mercy and to his judgment, especially since the context of the Ex 9:16 is in the theme of hardening Pharaoh's heart (Schreiner, 2nd, 498).[210] Moo (2nd, 615) is correct that God's so-called negative action of hardening serves a positive purpose overall, as Paul will point out in vv. 22–23. All the signs and miracles in Ex 4–14 not only demonstrated Yahweh's lordship, glory, and power to his people (Ex 10:1–2), but it demonstrated the greatness of his power, glory, and name to the Egyptians as well as those "in all the earth" (Ex 7:3–5; 9:16; 11:9; 14:4, 17–18).

The word "heart" in the Jewish Scripture can be used for the intellectual, emotional, volitional, and spiritual activities of a person.[211] All these aspects of a person (his heart) are involved in making decisions in life which ultimately make up a person's personality and character. Beale concludes that the Egyptians' concept of the heart as the inner spiritual, volitional, decision-maker were emphasized more than the Hebrews.[212] The hardening of Pharaoh's heart was likely viewed as a polemic against Pharaoh as deity and the belief that Pharaoh's heart was the controlling factor in history and society.[213] Ex 12:12 and Num 33:4 state that the plagues were against the gods of Egypt. According to Egyptian belief, the gods Anubis and Thoth await the person to enter the judgment hall to weigh and record answers of the deceased in the event called "the weighing of the heart."[214] The deceased in the judgment hall must successfully declare and prove oneself pure through denying a long list of sins read against the person ("the negative confession") before he could enter what they would call eternity. In the "negative confession" of the judgment hall is a pair of scales. On one side of the Scale of

---

[209] For possible reason why the difference in Paul's use of Ex 9:16, see Piper, 165–168; Abasciano, *Rom 9:10-18*, 155-156, 162–167; Seifried, "Romans," 643; and Stanley, *Paul*, 106–109.

[210] See Cranfield, 487; Dunn, 554. On the other hand, Kăsemann, 268 restrict God's power here to judgment.

[211] Beale, "Pharaoh's Heart in Exodus 4–14 and Romans 9," 132.

[212] Ibid., 133. See also Morenz, *Egyptian Religion*, 57–65.

[213] Beale, "Pharaoh's Heart in Exodus 4–14 and Romans 9," 149–150, see especially n. 84.

[214] Sometimes called the "weighing of the conscience" or "weighing of words". See Cox, "The Hardening of Pharaoh's Heart," 305–306, especially n.39. Budge, *The Book of the Dead*, see the plate in the front of the book where the weighing of the heart is displayed and the discussion of it on pp. 234–239. Hornung, *The Ancient Egyptian Books of the Afterlife* has the same plate (p. 20) as Budge and refers to it as the "Negative Confession" (p. 19).

Judgment is the heart of the deceased and it is weighed on the other side against the standard of truth (symbolized by a feather). The problem for the deceased is that the heart will declare the truth (the person is a sinner) against the deceased person's own "negative confession" showing the negative confession to be a lie. Since all persons were sinners and the heart had the natural inclination to confess the truth, the Egyptians devised a scheme to keep the heart from contradicting the negative confession. They wrote magical incantations on a stone scarab in the form of the sacred dung beetle being about the size and shape of the heart. They would place this scarab during mummification in or on the chest cavity believing that the incantation on the scarab would harden the heart in the afterlife which would keep the heart silent, not contradicting the negative confession.[215] The result would be that a harden heart would result in salvation because the harden heart would not speak against his negative confession. However, when God harden Pharaoh's heart He reversed the theology of the Egyptians. Instead of bringing salvation the hardening of Pharaoh's heart brought destruction both physically and spiritually.[216] The hardening of Pharaoh's heart became a tremendous polemic against the deity of Pharaoh and the gods of Egypt and magnified the name of Yahweh.

God's power to save and his power to judge is displayed in the Exodus to bring the Lord glory. One of the three Hebrew words used in Ex 4–14 for the hardening of Pharaoh's heart is כבד (Ex 7:14; 8:11, 28; 9:7, 34; 10:1). The basic definition of כבד is "to weigh heavily on," or "be heavy or dull."[217] This word is used in Exodus "to be heavy" in the sense to glorify and honor or "to be heavy" in the sense to harden. This word is apparently used as a word play for the writer used the same Hebrew word but this time the concept of heavy should be understood as honor or glory.[218] This word play is brought out in Ex 14:4, 17, 18 by the backdrop of all the hardening passages in Ex 4–14. Beale concludes this concept of כבד (kābēd) by saying , "Yahweh caused the kābēd of Israel's bondage (Ps 105:25; Ex 5:9) and the kābēd of Pharaoh's heart, both of which culminate in his own ʾikkabēdâ (Ex 14:4, 17, 18)."[219]

The Lord used all of these events and circumstance to spread his glory and name in all the earth (Exod 9:16). The song of Moses indicates that the events in Egypt caused Edom, Moab and Canaan to see the greatness of God (Ex 15:15–16). These events became the object of praise as generations heard about them in their Scripture (Num 14:21–23; Pss 78:12–13; 105:26–28; 106:9–11; 136:10–15). Even the pagan nations during the time of Joshua all the way down to the time of King Saul connected the wonders of God in Egypt with the name of Yahweh (Josh 2:9–10; 9:9; 1 Sam 4:7–8; 6:5–6). In fact, the Exodus and the New Exodus becomes a motif by which both OT and NT writers used in the cannon of Scripture.[220]

Therefore, Paul used the telic phrase "for this purpose" the Lord raised up Pharaoh "so that (purpose conjunctive ὅπως) I might demonstrate through you my power and so that (purpose

---

[215] We are indebted to J. Randall Price, *The Stones Cry Out*, 128, 410 who pointed out these references: Hermann, "Das steinhartes Herz," 102–103; Harris and Weeks, *X-Raying the Pharaohs*, 49. See also Cox, "The Hardening of Pharaoh's Heart," 306. See Price and House, *Zondervan Handbook*, 85–87.

[216] For further explanation see Price, *The Stones Cry Out*, 127–129; Cox, "The Hardening of Pharaoh's Heart," 306; Gregory Beale, "The Exodus Motif of YHWH as a Polemic," 46–52; Titus Kennedy, *Unearthing the Bible*, 52-53.

[217] Ludwig Koehler et al., *The Hebrew and Aramaic Lexicon of the Old Testament* (Leiden: E.J. Brill, 1994–2000), 455.

[218] Ibid., 455–456.

[219] Beale, "Pharaoh's Heart in Exodus 4–14 and Romans 9," 149.

[220] Sullivan, *Isaianic New Exodus in Romans 9–11*, 2nd, especially chapter 2. See also Tom Holland, *Romans: The Divine Marriage, passim.*

conjunctive ὅπως) my name might be proclaimed in all the earth." This purpose statement was fulfilled through the hardening of Pharaoh's heart (Meyer, 2:139–140). Piper is correct that the two ὅπως clauses in v. 17 function in the same way that the ἵνα clause in 9:11 – not on the basis of anything good or evil was Pharaoh raised up and hardened, but rather it was to accomplish the Lord's purpose (174). This statement is explored further in v. 18.

9:18 ἄρα οὖν ὃν θέλει ἐλεεῖ, ὃν δὲ θέλει σκληρύνει. "Therefore now, he has mercy on whomever he wills, and he hardens whomever he wills." Paul extends God's will to both the mercy and hardening of God in v. 18 and brings to an emphatic conclusion (ἄρα οὖν, "therefore now") his thoughts on vv. 15–17. The interpretation of Rom 9:11–16 was applied to the salvation of individuals (see above). However, is the concept of hardening in Rom 9 applied to eternal salvation or salvation-history? The following points direct us to the conclusion that Paul is applying his thoughts to eternal salvation (Moo, 2nd, 616–19). First, the structural and linguistic comparison of 9:22–23 and 9:18 where the former verses contrast the vessels of mercy, destined to glory with the vessels of wrath, prepared for destruction refer to the eternal destiny of people. Mercy refers characteristically in Paul's thought to eschatological salvation rather than salvation-history benefits (Rom 9:23; 11:30,31,32; 15:9; 2 Cor 4:1; Eph 2:4; 1 Tim 1:13,16; 2 Tim 1:16,18) (Piper, 177).[221] Second, Rom 11:7 parallels the hardening in Rom 9 and 11:25–26 and indicate that the lifting of the hardening brings eternal salvation.[222] Third, the condition of hardening in other places often indicates the spiritual condition of a person. Outside of Ex 4–14 the word σκληρύνω ("hardening")[223] is used 23 times in the LXX. Eight usages are not relevant to our discussion (Gen 49:7; Judg 4:24; 2 Kgdms 19:44; 4 Kgdms 2:10; 2 Chron 10:4; Ps 89:6; 1 Macc 2:30; Sirach 30:12). The remaining 15 texts refer to a spiritual condition that goes against God (Deut 2:30; 10:16; 4 Kgdms 7:14; 2 Chron 30:8; 36:13; Ps 94:8; Isa 63:17; Jer. 7:26; 17:23; 19:15; Esdr A 1:46; Esdr B 19:16, 17, 29; Ps Solomon 8:29). Therefore, σκληρύνω is well established to refer to the spiritual condition of a person that is hardened, insensitive and if not reversed ends in eternal damnation (Moo, 597; Piper, 175–178; Schreiner, 2nd, 499–500; Abasciano, *Rom 9:10–18*, 211). Paul's parallel statements in 9:18 concerning hardening and mercy point to the conclusion that he is making the same parallel statement but only in two different and opposite spheres. It is clear that Paul understands that God bestows mercy according to his own will and this salvific mercy is apart from anything the person is or does (9:11, 16). Furthermore, the correspondence between mercy/hardening (9:18) and the love/hate (9:13) reveals that the hardening is not a divine reaction to sin since the decision to "hate" Esau was before he was born and before he had not done anything good or evil (Piper, 175). Thus, the parallelism in v. 18 directs the interpretation of Paul toward hardening to be also apart from anything the person is or does (Calvin, 362; Meyer 2:141–142). However, some scholars reject this point. They point to Ex 4–14 and claim that Pharaoh hardened his own self first before God hardened him. Thus, they would conclude that God's hardening is a response to the person's prior decision to sin.[224] They would liken God's hardening to giving the person over to his sin,

---

[221] Cranfield, 472, 488–489 incorrectly places hardening and mercy under the God's mercy.

[222] The Greek words in 11:7 (ωρόω) and 25 (ώρωσις) are different then the Greek word in 9:18 (σκληρύνω). However, the concept is the same. See Karl and Matin Schmidt, *TDNT*, 5:1026–1030.

[223] In the NT Paul only uses it in Rom 9:18 and he does not use the noun. The verb is also used in Acts 19:9 and then it is used in Hebrews to refer to the Exodus (Heb 3:8,13,15; 4:7). In Ex 4–14, see 4:21; 7:3, 22; 8:19 [Eng. v. 15]; 9:12, 35; 10:1, 20, 27; 11:10; 13:15; 14:4, 8, 17.

[224] Dunn, 554–555 forcefully states, "So to look for reasons for God's hardening in Pharaoh's "evil disposition" or previous self-hardening (Lagrange, Murray, Leenhardt) is a rationalizing expediency . . . . Such a

which is expressed in Rom 1:24, 26, 28.[225] Pharaoh indeed was a sinner being guilty of Adam's sin (Rom 5:12ff), having a sinful nature, and practiced sin. However, the question is if any of the above classifications of sins are designated as the reason why God hardened Pharaoh.[226] Before Pharaoh hardened his own heart, God predicted that He would harden Pharaoh's heart and under compulsion bring out his people (Ex 3:19–20; 4:21; 7:3–4. Five times (7:13,14, 22; 8:11, 15 in the MT) Exodus says that Pharaoh's heart was hardened with the additional phrase "just as the Lord had said," which points to the Lord as the one who hardened him. These statements are all said before Pharaoh hardened his own heart in Ex 8:32 (MT 8:28).[227] Furthermore, if the Lord's hardening is based upon Pharaoh's sinful actions, then the questions in 9:19 are puzzling or the answers to the questions are easily directed to Pharaoh. The same puzzling thought could also be charged with the statement in 9:20.

The objector has rejected the unconditional election of God in 9:6–13 and thus has argued if Paul is correct then God is unrighteous. Paul has responded by saying God is not unjust (9:14). He defends this point by quoting two OT passages (9:15, 17). God's freedom from human willing and working is part of the character and freedom of God which preserves and displays his glory. In 9:16 and 18, Paul restates God's sovereignty and freedom in his unconditional choice of mercy or hardening that is not unrighteous (Piper, 180–181). Therefore, Paul describes hardening as a sovereign act of God that is not attributed to anything that the individual has done.[228] However, the person is still held responsible for who and what he does. This point is addressed next in v. 19.

Biblical Theological Comments

God's promises (vv. 4–5) to Israel have not failed even though most of the nation of Israel does not believe in Jesus the Christ. Just because a person is from the physical line of Abraham, Isaac, and Jacob does not make that person a believing Israelite who is an heir of God's promises. The believing Israelite is the one who according to God's choice is called by Him according to His purpose and it does not depend on anything good or bad in the person

---

thought clearly has no place in Paul's exposition and in fact contradicts what Paul has been so careful to stress in vv. 11 and 16 (Michel; Schmidt; Blackman, 130; Luz, *Geschichtsverständnis*, 78 n.211; Käsemann; Piper [1983], 154–56)." However, Dunn, 555 does not believe Paul is speaking of eternal reprobation.

[225] Those who advocate a conditional hardening are: Abasciano, *Rom 9:10–18*, 216–219; Fizmyer, 568; Morris, 361–362; Hendriksen, 326; Murray 2:29; Mounce, 200.

[226] Piper, 174, n. 28 is correct when he states that Paul's argument is not built on the *time* when God revealed to Moses the hardening of Pharaoh but the *way* that he revealed it. Paul repeatedly in this section grounded Pharaoh's hardening in the purposes to glorify God and not in Pharaoh's sin. It is theologically possible that "God's *act* of hardening (opposed to his initial choice of whom to harden) could be described as a judicial abandonment of Pharaoh to his own sinful blindness, and thus a punitive measure in response to Pharaoh's sin (so Hodge, *Romans*, 316; Murray, *Romans* II, 29). This would not necessarily contradict *Paul's* angle of view here. But it is virtually certain that this is *not* the point Paul wants to make here, since it is foreign to his emphasis on God's doing whatever he will *apart* from being determined by human willing or running."

[227] For a more extensive investigation see, Beale, "Hardening of Pharaoh's Heart," 129–154; Piper, 159–171. For more of a conditional view of hardening of Pharaoh's heart, see Chisholm, "Divine Hardening in the OT," 292–311.

[228] This is the conclusion of Calvin, 361–363; Dunn, 554–555; Kăsemann, 268–269; Meyer, 2:140–143; Moo, 595–600; Piper, 159–178; Schriener, 510–512. This interpretation is also used to support double predestination (Calvin, *Institutes* 3.31.5, 22.11; 23.1-14; 24.12-17; Heppe, *Reformed Dogmatics*, 155–162; Moo, 599–600; Schreiner, 510; Warfield, *The Plan of Salvation*, 13–32, 87–104).

(Rom 9:11–13). God's sovereign and unconditional election raises the question, is God unjust to choose this way? Paul uses Ex 33:19 to indicate that one of the fundamental freedoms of God's character and glory is His sovereign choice. The logical conclusion from this point is that the giving of God's salvific mercy does not depend on a person's willing or a person's doing, but upon God's choice (9:16). People have trouble understanding and accepting the divine viewpoint when they learn how God sovereignly dispenses His mercy and hardens others. Yet, these things should not surprise us for how can the finite totally and completely understand the infinite and His ways (Rom 11:33–36)? (1) When we hear that God loves Jacob and hates Esau (9:13), (2) God raises up Pharaoh and hardens his heart to proclaim God's name throughout the earth (9:17), and (3) God has mercy and hardens whom He wills (9:18), then it is that we struggle with all the questions because we are finite, and we cannot fully grasp the greatness and depth of the sovereign God of glory (Isa 40:13–14)! How Paul answers the objection of how God can hold us responsible when no one can successfully resist His will is simple and profound: I am God and you, O man, are not. The more you know God, the more this becomes a satisfying answer and the less you know of God, the more difficult and less satisfying is this answer.

Application and Devotional Implications

If you have been following Paul's thought in Rom 9 and have understood that God's call by his elective purpose is the only way anyone will believe, then the natural question is, "Is this fair? Is God unjust?" This is the very question which Paul anticipates in v. 14. This question would never be raised if Paul taught that man's salvation depended ultimately on man's free choice. If Paul taught that God looked ahead to see who would believe and based on man's choice God elected them to salvation, then there would be no place for this question about the supposed injustice of God. The very fact that this question is raised places the choice with God's purpose and will as the ultimate reason why a person wills and believes.

We should not be surprised or unduly concerned if we have the question of God's injustice buzzing in our heads. It means you probably understand the basic concept of divine election. Paul used the OT passages from Exodus to defend God's absolute sovereign freedom to do what he wills. Paul uses Ex 33:19 in Rom 9:15 to summarize a great deal of theology about God. The context of this passage is that the children of Israel had made a golden calf and worshipped it while Moses went up the mountain to meet God to receive the 10 commandments. After God deals with the rebellious people, Moses asks God to be with the nation. God graciously accepts Moses' request. In Ex 33:18, Moses prays that he may see God's glory. Moses knew that who God is gives the assurance of how He will act (Piper, 81). Thus, Moses desires to see His glory or proclaim His name–the essence of God's character–as an assurance of His grace and mercy toward Israel. God's answer to Moses in Ex 33:19 shows that the very essence of God's character as God is His sovereign freedom to dispense mercy and grace on whomever he pleases apart from any constraint outside of His own will. In other words, one of the most foundational characteristics of God is His sovereign freedom to do what He wills. God is the sovereign king. He is not accountable to anyone. No one dictates to Him. He is absolutely free to dispense mercy as He sees fit. If God has to consider man's will or his works to guide His plan, He is not the God of the Bible.

Paul's inference from Ex 33:19 is found in Rom 9:16. Before we were saved we were totally and thoroughly affected by sin. Our mind, will, and emotions were all influenced and shaped by our own sinful way instead of God's way. Rom 9:16 tells us that God's salvific mercy does not find its ultimate source in person's willing or ability but in God's mercy. However, God is not under obligation to give anyone His mercy.

Let me try to illustrate this point with the event of President Ford's pardon of President Nixon. No illustration is a perfect illustration, but this one may help. In the light of what we know now Nixon was guilty of breaking the law, but Ford pardoned him. He did not do this because of the worth, works, or rights of Nixon. Ford pardoned Nixon, he said, for the sake and interest of the nation to heal and to move forward and not concentrate on the past. As President he had the right to do this. Notice that the reason for the pardoning rests in the President and not in the man who is pardoned. Ford pardoned Nixon though from all the evidence he was guilty. Ford expressed mercy by his own choice for his own purposes. He was not under obligation to do it or to tell why he did it. He is not accountable to anyone when he did it. He has this right because he is the President. Yet, Charles Colson, an aid to Nixon, was found guilty of breaking the law and had to go to jail for years, but Ford did not pardon him. However, there is no injustice on the part of President Ford. Colson was guilty and deserved punishment. Ford was not under obligation to show mercy. Therefore, Ford showed mercy to one and no mercy to the other, but there is no injustice. President Ford had the sovereign right to show mercy or not to show mercy according to our constitution.

God is free to act according to His will in showing mercy or not showing mercy. He is not unjust if He does not show mercy because all of us deserve His wrath being sinners. God is not under obligation to show mercy. He is not accountable to anyone. He has this right because He is God. We may wonder why God didn't show mercy to all, but a bigger amazement is why He showed mercy to anyone for no one deserves it!

When we turn to Rom 9:17–18 we turn to some of the most difficult verses to understand in the Scripture. Here in these verses we see God is sovereign in hardening as well as showing mercy. The context behind these verses are the hardening of Pharaoh's heart in Ex 4–14 (see above in commentary section). These verses teach us that God is the ultimate cause in hardening Pharaoh's heart. No doubt Pharaoh's volitional decision is involved (8:15,22; 9:34) but God's sovereign choice was first (Ex 3:19 [6:1; 11:1]; 4:21; 7:3; 10:1,20, 27; 11:9–10; 14:4,8,17). Why did God hardened Pharaoh's heart? This is where Paul's quotation from Ex 9:16 plays a part. The purpose was to demonstrate God's power and glory and to proclaim His name (His character) throughout the whole earth. The chief end or purpose of all things is to glorify God (1 Cor 10:31). Paul is declaring God's sovereign freedom in mercy and in hardening as the means by which he declares the glory of His name! This truth brings into question mankind's responsibility before God. The mystery and tension of holding both man's responsibility and God's sovereignty is addressed in Rom 9:19–20.

Paul has dispelled the charge that God is unjust. The OT demonstrates that God is free and sovereign to dispense mercy and to harden who He desires. As a little child not completely understanding all these things, I bow to my God and glorify His name as the sovereign King of the universe. I believe Spurgeon catches the attitude concerning God's sovereignty. He says: "There is nothing for which the children ought more earnestly to contend than the doctrine of their Master over all creation–the kingship of God overall the works of His own hands–the Throne of God and His right to sit upon that Throne. On the other hand, there is no doctrine more hated by worldings, no truth of which they have made such a football, as the great, stupendous, but yet most certain doctrine of the sovereignty of the Infinite Jehovah. Men will allow God to be everywhere except on His throne. They will allow Him to be in His workshop to fashion worlds and make stars. They will allow Him to be in His almonry to dispense His alms and bestow His bounties. They will allow Him to sustain the earth and bear up the pillars thereof or light the lamps of heaven, or rule the waves of the evermoving ocean; but when God ascends His throne, His creatures then gnash their teeth, and we proclaim an enthroned God, and His right to do as He wills with His own, to dispose of His creatures as He thinks well, without consulting them in the matter; then it is that we are hissed and execrated, and then it is that men turn a deaf ear to us, for God on His throne is not the God they love. But it is God upon the throne that we love to preach. It is God upon His throne whom we trust" (quoted by Pink, *Attributes of God*, 32–33).

Selected Bibliography

Bauernfeind, Otto. "τρέχω κτλ.," *TDNT*, vol. 8 (Grand Rapids: Eerdmans, 1972), 226–235.

Beale, Gregory K. "An Exegetical and Theological consideration of the Hardening of Pharaoh's Heart in Exodus 4–14 and Romans 9." *Trinity Journal* 5 (fall, 1984): 129–154.

Beale, Gregory K. "The Exodus Motif of YHWH as a Polemic." (Th.M. thesis, Dallas Theological Seminary, 1976).

Budge, E. A. Wallis. *The Book of the Dead: The Hierogllyphic Transcripts of the Papyrus of Ani* (New Hyde Park, NY: University Books, 1960).

Bultmann, Rudolf . ""Έλεος, Ἐλεέω, Ἐλεήμων, Ἐλεημοσύνη, Ἀνέλεος, Ἀνελεήμων," *TDNT*, vol. 2 (Grand Rapids, MI: Eerdmans, 1964), 477–487.

Chisholm, Robert B., Jr. "Divine Hardening in the Old Testament." *Bibliotheca Sacra* 153 (October-December 1996): 410–434.

Cox, Dorian G. Coover. "The Hardening of Pharaoh's Heart in Its Literary and Cultural Contexts." *Bibliotheca Sacra* 163 (July–September 2006): 292–311.

Gerstner, John H. "Augustine, Luther, Calvin, and Edwards on the Bondage of the Will," *The Grace of God, The Bondage of the Will: Historical and Theological Perspectives on Calvinism*, ed. Thomas R. Schreiner and Bruce A. Ware, vol.2 (Grand Rapids: Baker, 1995), 279–295.

Harris, James E. and Kent R. Weeks. *X-Raying the Pharaohs* (New York: Scribner's Sons, 1973).

Hermann, Alfred. "Das steinhartes Herz," *Jahrbuch für Antike und Christentum* 4 (Munster: Aschendorffsche Verlagsbuchandlung, 1961).

Hornung, Erik. *The Ancient Egyptian Books of the Afterlife*. Trans. David Lorton (Ithaca and London: Cornell University Press, 1999).

Kennedy, Titus. *Unearthing the Bible* (Eugene, OR: Harvest House, 2020).

Morenz, Siegfried. *Egyptian Religion*. Trans. Ann E. Keep (Ithaca: Cornell University Press, 1973).

Pink, Arthur W. *The Attributes of God* (Swengel, PA: Reiner Publication, n.d.).

Price, Randall with H. Wayne House. *Zondervan Handbook of Biblical Archaeology* (Grand Rapids: Zondervan, 2017).

Price, Randall. *The Stone Cry Out: What Archaeology Reveals about the Truth of the Bible* (Eugene, OR: Harvest House, 1997).

Schmidt, Karl L. and Matin A. Schmidt. "Πωρόω (πηρόω), Πώρωσις (πήρωσις), Σκληρύνω," *TDNT*, vol. 5 (Grand Rapids: Eerdmans, 1964), 1025–1030.

Schrenk, Gottlob. "Ἄδικος, Ἀδικία, Ἀδικέω, Ἀδίκημα," *TDNT*, vol. 1 (Grand Rapids: Eerdmans, 1964), 149–163.

Stanley, Christopher D. *Paul and the Language of Scripture: Citation Technique in the Pauline Epistles and Contemporary Literature.* Society for New Testament Studies Monograph Series, ed. Richard Bauckham, vol. 74 (Cambridge: Cambridge University Press, 1992).

Sullivan, Steven P. *The Isaianic New Exodus in Romans 9–11: A Biblical and Theological Study of Paul's Use of Isaiah in Romans* (Silverton: Lampion Press, 2017).

Sullivan, Steven P. *The Isaianic New Exodus in Romans 9–11: A Biblical and Theological Study of Paul's Use of Isaiah in Romans*, 2nd ed. (Middletown, RI: Stone Tower Press, 2023).

Swanson, Reuben, ed. *New Testament Greek Manuscripts: Romans*. (Wheaton: Tyndale House and Pasadena: William Carey International University Press, 2001).

Wallace, Daniel B. *Greek Grammar Beyond the Basics* (Grand Rapids: Zondervan, 1996).

Romans 9:19–20

Outline

- B. Vindication of the Righteous God and His Wise Plan (9:6-29)
  1. Israel within Israel: Children of Promise (9:6-9)
  2. The Divine Call according to Election (9:10-13)
  3. Polemic: Objects of Mercy and Hardening according to God's Choice (9:14-18)
  4. Polemic: Objections against God's Character and Plan (9:19-20)

Original Text

9.19 Ἐρεῖς μοι οὖν· Τί [οὖν[a]] ἔτι μέμφεται; τῷ γὰρ βουλήματι αὐτοῦ τίς ἀνθέστηκεν; **20** [b]ὦ
ἄνθρωπε, μενοῦνγε[b] σὺ τίς εἶ ὁ ἀνταποκρινόμενος τῷ θεῷ; μὴ ἐρεῖ τὸ πλάσμα τῷ πλάσαντι Τί με
ἐποίησας οὕτως;

Textual Notes

[a] **9:19 οὖν** is supported by ℵ A K L P Ψ 33 81 104 365 630 1175 1241 1505 1506 1739 1881 2464 𝔐 vg sy. SBLGNT, NA28 (in brackets) UBS5 (in brackets), P[46] B D F G it vg[mss] include it. The evidence for the inclusion of it is few but they are early mss. Cranfield supports the omission and argues that copyist added it to match the previous word (2:489, n. 4). Someone may argue that the scribe in copying the text mistakenly wrote the conjunction twice. It is just as possible that the copier seeing the conjunction just two words earlier thought a previous copier made a mistake and thus, he dropped the word seeing it two words earlier. Or it is equally probable that a copyist omitted an original οὖν being so close together in the verse. Probably best to included it

in brackets like NA28 and UBS5. (See Swanson, 144; Hodges and Farstad, ed. *The Greek New Testament According to the Majority Text* for textual evidence.)
b–b **9:20 ὦ ἄνθρωπε μενοῦνγε** is supported by NA28, UBS5, SBLGNT, WH, Treg, B (+ μενοῦν) ℵ* A 𝔐; **μενοῦνγε ὦ ἄνθρωπε** is supported by ℵc 1837 194 1319; **μενοῦνγε ὦ ανε** is supported by D2 K L P Ψ 6 049 056 33 88 131 205 209 226 323 326 365 434 489 517 614 618 796 910 927 945 999 1242 1270 1315 1352 1448 1505 157 3 1611 1734 1827 1982 2400 2412 2495 2815 (Swanson, 144). The earliest and best evidence agrees with NA28 and UBS5.

Translation

9:19 "You will then say to me, why [then] does He still find fault? For who resists His will? O Man, on the contrary, who are you to answer back to God? That which is molded will not *say* to the molder, 'Why did you make me in this way?'"

Commentary

9:19᾿Ερεῖς μοι οὖν· Τί [οὖν] ἔτι μέμφεται; τῷ γὰρ βουλήματι αὐτοῦ τίς ἀνθέστηκεν. "You will then say to me, why [then] does He still find fault? For who resists His will?" Paul engages his interlocutor by introducing the questions they often espouse. If the reader follows Paul's argument, especially in vv. 11-18 then the questions are the natural questions to ask.[229] The question about who can resist God's will assumes that mankind cannot successfully resist the will of God. This will[230] is God's decretive or sovereign will that determines whatever comes to pass either directly and causatively or permissively through the unrestrained agency of His rational creatures.[231] This will cannot be thwarted, diminished, or diluted by mankind or His creation (cf. Dan 4:35). According to Rom 9:11, 16, God's choice in salvation or hardening did not depend on secondary causes or upon anything good or bad in the person.[232] The questions in v. 19 would have scarcely been raised or relevant to the argument if God's election and hardening depended upon human choice, sin or works.

Paul uses the word μέμφεται ("find fault"). BDAG, 628 defines it as "find fault with, blame."[233] The first question assumes the thought of the second question, "Who resists His will?"

---

[229] Dunn, 555 and Moo, 2nd, 620, n. 248 suggest that Paul had in mind Jewish objections because early Judaism debated over divine sovereignty and human free will. Josephus brings out three schools of thought: (1) Pharisees had a mixture of both. Some events are a work of Fate and other events depends upon man. (2) Essenes believed that nothing happened to men except by the decree of Fate's hand. (3) Sadducees held that human actions are not controlled by the hand of Fate but it is within the man's hand and he is responsible for what befalls him (See Josephus, *Antiquities* 13.171-173; *Jewish War* 2.119–166).

[230] βούλημα is used in 2 Macc 15:5 and 4 Macc 8:18 in the LXX and is found only in Acts 27:43; Rom 9:19 and 1 Pet 4:3 in the NT. When the verb βούλομαι is used and God is the subject (7 out of 37) it always refers to the sovereign or decretive will of God (Matt 11:27; Luk 10:22; 22:42; 1 Cor 12:11; Heb 6:17; Jas 1:18 and 2 Pet 3:9). The idea of purpose is conveyed, especially the ending -μα which strengthen the implication of "enacted purpose" (Dunn, 556). See also Schrenk, *TDNT,* vol. 1, 636-637.

[231] Berkhof, *Systematic Theology*, 77. God's perceptive or revealed will is "the rule of life which God has laid down for His moral creatures, indicating the duties which He enjoins upon them" (p. 77). Mankind does rebell, resist and disobey God's perceptive will.

[232] See Wardlaw, *Lectures on the Epistle to the Romans*, vol. 2, 274–275.

[233] This word is found also in Hebrew 8:8. In the LXX it is found in Sir 11:7; 41:7 2 Macc. 2:7.

The perfect verb ἀνθέστηκεν ("resist") seems best translated with a present force (Cranfield, 490; Sanday and Headlam, 259; Fitzmyer, 568; Moo, 2nd, 620, n. 250).[234] Often the perfect tense in Greek refers to a past act that has a present result.[235] The thought in 9:19 seems to have little difference between the act and the result of the resistance. At this point in Paul's argument, it seems logical that he would launch into a dialogue which reconciles God's absolute sovereignty in election and hardening with man's full responsibility to believe. He does indicate the responsibility of man to believe in 9:30–10:21and attributes condemnation to their willful unbelief. Paul does give a response in v. 20, but he leaves the conundrum of God's sovereignty and man's responsibility in tension for each is a necessary and important biblical concept.

9:20 ὦ ἄνθρωπε, μενοῦνγε σὺ τίς εἶ ὁ ἀνταποκρινόμενος τῷ θεῷ; μὴ ἐρεῖ τὸ πλάσμα τῷ πλάσαντι Τί με ἐποίησας οὕτως. "O Man, on the contrary, who are you to answer back to God? That which is molded will not *say* to the molder, 'Why did you make me in this way?" Paul's address to ὦ ἄνθρωπε ("O man") is not necessarily a negative or derogatory tone (Moo, 2nd, 621). It is used in a positive light in 1 Tim 6:11 and Jas 2:20 and negatively in Rom 2:1, 3. However, in each place it is used there is a clear heightening or emphasis. Here in this context Paul wants to make a clear distinction between Creator God and creature man. The word μενοῦνγε may have an intensifying meaning ("indeed" in Phil 3:8) but the context directs the thought more to a well-established adversative meaning ("on the contrary" in Rom 9:20; 10:18; Luk 11:28 in a variant reading).[236] The word σὺ ("you") is in an emphatic position to accent its emphasis (Cranfield, 491; Moo, 601, n. 69). The potter/clay example is given to rebuke created beings from their presumption that God is responsible to man, and he can rightly judge the way of the Creator. This presumptuous complaint is brought out by phrases ὁ ἀνταποκρινόμενος τῷ θεῷ ("answer back to God"), σὺ τίς εἶ ("who are you"), and the startling introduction ὦ ἄνθρωπε ("O man"). God's sovereign right to create and govern his creation and creatures as he determines is what is communicated in the illustration of the potter/clay illustration.[237] Human responsibility and freedom is subsumed under the God of divine sovereignty.[238]

Everyone will at times question why or how God could do and allow certain things in life. As long as our questions are not in pride, rebellion, or in a sinful attitude, but sincere, respectful, ultimately submits to God's word and will then our questions are acceptable to God. However, in this context the question is from those who are in doubt about God's justice and His will, thus, impugning His character. Schriener captures the profound thought of the apostle Paul, "How can finite, frail, and weak human beings venture to dictate to God how the world should be run (cf. also Wis. 12:12)? Who do we think we are that we presume to call God to account and pass judgment on him?" (2nd, p. 503).

---

[234] For the perfect used as a present, see Blass, Debrunner, and Funk, *A Greek Grammar of the New Testament* , §341 and Wallace, *Greek Grammar Beyond the Basics*, 579–581. Jewett, 591 calls it a gnomic perfect.

[235] Wallace, *Greek Grammar Beyond the Basics*, 572–573.

[236] See BDAG, 630; Blass, Debrunner, Funk, *A Greek Grammar of the New Testament*, §450 (4); Moule, *Idiom Book*, 163; Moo, 2nd, 621, n. 253.

[237] Forster and Marston, *God's Strategy in Human History*, 80–81 basically says that 9:20 corrects the theology of 9:19 which the critics of Paul misunderstand. They insist that people do resist God's will and mankind may successfully go against the purpose of God (cf. Luke 7:30). Their argument does not follow well the previous context and argument of Paul. See Schriener, 2nd, 503-504; Piper, 190–191, especially n. 5.

[238] This view is often called a compatibilist view of determination (Schreiner, 2nd, 503–504). See Feinberg, "God Ordains All things," 19–43 for a good summary of this view. Feinberg states "if the acts are constrained, then they are not free and the agent is not morally responsible for them. But if the act is according to the agent's desires, then even though the act is causally determined, it is free and the agent is morally responsible" (p. 37).

Paul conflates two Isaianic passages together from Isa 29:16 and Isa 45:9 in the context of NE (New Exodus) wisdom polemic.[239] The blinding and hardening of Isa 29:9–12 finds its foundation in Isa 6:9–10 and provides the background for the wisdom polemic. The Isaianic blindness parallels the hardening theme of Pharaoh in Rom 9:17–19. This comparison helps to understand why Paul may have chosen this section to respond to the questions in Rom 9:19 and the INE (Isaianic New Exodus) theme of the wisdom polemic in 9:20. Isaiah 29:14 connects the Exodus motif [240] with the wisdom polemic[241]. Thus, the Exodus motif is connected with the context of Isaiah 29:15-16 and God's wonderful deeds are associated with the wisdom, plan, or counsel of God. God's judgment and merciful redemption in Isa 29 are introduced by the wisdom parable of the farmer at the end of Isa 28 to help prepare the reader for God's astonishing and wise plan.[242] The context of Isaiah 29 may be described in the New Testament phrase, God "has mercy on whomever he chooses and he hardens the heart of whomever he chooses" (Rom 9:18). It is not surprising that Paul would choose Isaiah 29:16 in the context of Romans 9:17–20 because God's judgment, hardening, and mercy are present in both contexts. However, the ultimate point of Paul comes from the NE motif of the wisdom polemic theme, which is found in Isaiah 29:14–16 and becomes part of the quotation in Romans 9:20.

It is easy to see why Paul used Isaiah 45:9 in his argument of Romans 9:20. The wisdom polemic NE theme seems to be the framework of the argument. The context of the argument of Paul in Romans 9:14–20 and the context of Isaiah 44:24–45:13 have coinciding parallels, which accentuate the wisdom polemic theme. The Lord's plan to choose his people is called into the question by challenging the righteous character of God in Romans 9:14–18. Then, in the second accusation of Romans 9:19, the Lord's righteousness is questioned in view of the fact that his wise plan involves dispensing mercy and hardening others. Paul responds to the accuser with the wisdom polemic of the potter/clay motif (9:20). In Isaiah 44:24–45:25, the Lord chose Cyrus as a Moses-like figure to be a "shepherd" and an "anointed one" to deliver his people and restore

---

[239] A wisdom polemic is where God, usually through the prophet, uses the genre of wisdom to construct a disputation against the people of God because of their lack of knowledge, understanding, and rebellion against the character and plan of God. The wisdom polemic NE theme is a wisdom polemic used in the framework of the NE motif. For a full explanation of Paul's conflation of the Isaianic passages in the NE wisdom polemic, see Sullivan, *The Isaianic NE in Romans 9–11*, chapter 6.

[240] The threefold repetition of the word פלא, in Isaiah 29:14 introduces the Exodus motif. Both Brueggemann and Childs acknowledge that פלא expresses the Exodus motif in Isaiah 29:14. Brueggemann, referring to פלא, says, "The term 'amazing deed' refers characteristically to Yahweh's mighty deeds of rescue and transformation in behalf of Israel, as in a birth to barren mother Sarah or the Exodus from Egypt" (Brueggemann, *Isaiah 1–39*, 235). Childs, commenting on פלא, states that "[o]rdinarily the deliverance of Israel from Egypt is the primary illustration of God's working a 'marvellous thing,' (Micah 7:15)" (Childs, *Isaiah*, 219. Wildberger, *Isaiah 28–39*, 61 states that פלא generally points "in the OT to actions of Yahweh to deliver his people." For other detail, see Conrad, "פלא," *TDOT*, vol. 11, 536–44, especially 540 and 544 and Albertz, "פלא," in *TLOT*, vol.2, 984.) Paul A. Kruger also concludes that פלא is frequently connected with God's act of salvation, such as Exodus events, the wonders he worked in the crossing of the Red Sea, and the wilderness journey (Kruger, "פלא," in *NIDOTTE*, vol. 3, 616.). For background material on the word, see also Bertran, "θαῦμα, θαυμάζω, θαυμάσιος, θαυμαστός," *TDNT*, 3:32–33, 35. פלא is used in connection with the Exodus as a pointer to a pattern that is used throughout the OT: Deut 28:59–60; Josh 3:5–7; Judg 6:13; Pss 77:12, 15; 78:4, 11, 12; 106:7, 22; 107:8, 15, 21, 24, 31; 111:4; Jer 32:17–20, 27; Mic 7:15; Neh 9:17 and 1 Chr 16:9, 12, 14–24 (Pss 105:2, 4; 96:3).

[241] In Isa 29:14, God's wisdom will render the leaders and people without understanding and foolish. The third woe introduces Isa 29:15–24 where the wisdom polemic reaches its pinnacle point.

[242] The great sin and rebellious heart of the people in Isa 29:9–16 is deserving of God's full judgment and wrath. However, Isa 29:17–24 brings forth a tremendous contrast which may be described as God's mercy of the New Exodus. Furthermore, Isa 29:22–24 describes the Lord as one who "redeemed Abraham." This imagery echoes the thought that the Lord is redeeming the house of Israel, which is the major part of the wise plan of the NE theme.

them back to the land (Isa 44:28; 45:1). Cyrus like Pharaoh is raised up by God to proclaim God's name by accomplishing God's plan for Israel. This wise plan is to demonstrate to Cyrus, Israel, and the nations that Yahweh is the only God (Isa 45:3-6). Furthermore, this plan is declared to be righteous[243] and a demonstration that Yahweh is a redeeming Savior of his people.[244] Therefore, In Isaiah 45:8 the Lord calls upon heaven and earth to demonstrate his righteousness and warns the accusers not to quarrel with their Maker's plan. The prophet has used the NE motif to express the wisdom polemic by the potter/clay motif (45:9).

The comparison of Isa 29:16 and 45:9 in Rom 9:20 is an interesting study.[245] Paul uses the conflation of these two Isaianic passages to warn his interlocutor by using a NE wisdom polemic motif. Isaiah 29:16 seems to be chosen by Paul because the NE wisdom polemic context concentrates more on the people's idolatrous rebellion and apostasy against God's *character*. On the other hand, Isaiah 45:9 seems to be chosen by Paul because the wisdom polemic context concentrates more on the rebellion against *God's plan* where God defends his righteous plan in the NE redemption. Therefore, in Rom 9:20, Paul wants to stress both God's wise character and his sapiential plan through a NE wisdom polemic for this fits the present context of Israel and his writing in Rom 9–11.[246]

Biblical Theological Comments

The wisdom polemic concerning God's sovereign plan seems to be the over-arching point Paul makes in Romans 9-11. Romans 9:20 uses Isaiah 29:16 and 45:9 together with Romans 11:34, which draws upon Isaiah 40:13 (and the supplement text Job 41:3a). These texts form the core of an *inclusio* in the argument of Romans 9-11.[247] An *inclusio* involves references to a

[243] Isa 45:13, 19, 21, 23, 24.

[244] Isa 44:22, 23, 24; 45:15, 17, 20, 21, 22.

[245] First, though LXX Isaiah 29:16 has many structural similarities to Romans 9:20–21, the shared vocabulary (μὴ ἐρεῖ, πηλός, κεραμεύς and ποιέω), especially interrogative τί, has an affinity with LXX Isaiah 45:9. The possibility may be proposed that Paul may have accessed a form of the LXX text, or another version, no longer extant. Alternatively, Wagner proposes that Paul modifies the statement in LXX Isaiah 29:16 by omitting οὐ συνετῶς and adding τί and οὕτως. He also suggested that the addition of the pronoun τί is an influence from LXX Isaiah 45:9 (Wagner, *Heralds of the Good News*, 62). Wagner observes that this different word choice alters τί from the sense of "what" to "why" in Romans 9:20, but he did not connect any significance to the change (Wagner, *Heralds of the Good News*, 59, n. 50). In fact, this shift from "what" to "why" directs attention more to the content and thoughts of Isaiah 45:9 than to Isaiah 29:16. Wagner did point out that the addition of οὕτως in Romans 9:20 suggests that the mere fact of being created is not being challenged as much as what form that the creation is taken (Wagner, *Heralds of the Good News*, 59). It can be further commented that τί plus οὕτως seems to challenge God's reason or purpose for why he chose to make his creatures vessels for destruction (cf. 9:21–22). Thus, Paul voices the protest against God's injustice in Romans 9:19. Then in Romans 9:20, Paul rebukes people for questioning God's wisdom. Similarly, in Isa 29:16, the creature's arrogance is revealed by his questioning God's creation of humankind and God's understanding in doing it (MT) or God's understanding in forming him as he did (LXX). Second, MT Isaiah 45:9 begins with a warning about Israel quarrelling with his Maker while the LXX begins with a question. Third, in the last two colas of Isaiah 45:9, the MT and LXX are basically the same. There is, however, a question over the middle cola, which fits closely with Paul's thought in Romans 9:20. (For more discussion on this subject, see Sullivan, *The INE in Rom 9–11*, 2nd, chap. 6).

[246] For more information about the INE, see the introduction to Rom 9–11 or Sullivan, *The INE in Romans 9–11*, 2nd., chap. 2.

[247] Kim, *God, Israel, and the Gentiles*, 141 and Johnson, *The Function of Apocalyptic and Wisdom Traditions in Romans 9-11*, 173 recognize an *inclusio* with Rom 9:1-5 and 11:33-36. Naselli, *From Typology to*

word, phrase or theme that occur both at the beginning and the end of a unit of literature. "Inclusio holds a passage together and indicates to listeners the end of a section. The meaning of the repeated phrase is often enriched by what comes in between."[248] Paul invokes an *inclusio* in Romans 9:33 and 10:11. The first part of the *inclusio* uses the wisdom polemic in the motif of the NE to warn the readers not to rebel against God's wise plan. This argument makes sense when one understands why Paul discusses the topic in Romans 9. In the section of Romans 9:11-29, Paul briefly introduces God's plan, which highlights his character of mercy in electing a remnant, and his mercy in salvation for the inclusion of the Gentiles. However, God's plan also includes the unbelief and hardening of Israel. The election of some and the hardening of others are part of a difficult plan to understand and accept. Thus, the interlocutor questions the righteousness of God (his character) and the justness of God's determinative will. This rebellion is an affront and challenge to the wisdom of God. In this wisdom polemic, Paul draws upon the Isaianic wisdom polemic in Isaiah 29:16, where Israel is rebelling against the character of God conveyed in the wisdom of the INE. Paul also conflates this Old Testament passage with the Isaianic wisdom polemic in Isaiah 45:9. The background of this text indicates that Israel rebels against the plan of God, which uses the Moses-like figure, Cyrus, to redeem Israel. The wisdom polemic in the context of the INE is the theme and context of Paul's argument. The more the reader would have understood the history of Israel and the argument of Isaiah in particular, the more powerful would be the force of Paul's citation from Isaiah.

Paul chooses the wisdom polemic to express God's plan of redemption. The redemption of Jews and Gentiles, which is expressed in the wisdom polemic, is revealed in the NE motif. Paul seems to choose the Isaianic wisdom polemic of Isaiah 40 and the wisdom section of Job 41 because certain portions of their teachings are parallel. God's plan includes judgments and seemingly unrighteous events that call into question the character and plan of God. Romans 9–11 is Paul's attempt to explain God's faithfulness to his covenantal plan expressed in the Old Testament, though in the present age, Israel has been hardened (at least in part) and the nation as a whole is in unbelief. At the end of Romans 9–11, the Isaianic wisdom polemic culminates in the wisdom doxology because God is executing the NE redemption plan in wonderful mercy that magnifies his righteous character and vindicates his eternal plan. This grand plan of wisdom is the overarching point of Romans 9–11. In addition, Romans 9:20 and 11:34–35 and their Isaianic contexts serve as an *inclusio* expressing the overarching point of God's grand plan.

Application and Devotional Implications

In this section Paul deals with the problem and charge that God is unjust in choosing some and not others. Behind Paul's argument in vv. 14-18 is Pharaoh. From the history of Pharaoh, one sees that God has mercy on whom he wills and he hardens whom he wills. I can hear the objector say, "Wait minute Paul let me get this straight. God is ultimately responsible for the hardening of Pharaoh. In other words, Pharaoh could not successfully resist God's will and God hardened his heart. Yet, on the other hand, God holds Pharaoh responsible for what he did!" Paul would say, "That's exactly right!"

Doxology, 25 recognizes an *inclusio* with Rom 9:5b and 11:36b. One main point that goes against this being an *inclusio* is Rom 9:1-5, which is Christological in emphasis where Rom 11:33-36 is not.

[248] Jensen, "Poetry in the Bible," 457. Wagner, *Heralds of the Good News*, 168 recognizes that Rom 9:33 and 10:11 is an *inclusio*.

When Paul taught this I'm sure he encountered stiff opposition. I can hear them say, "That's not just! Why does God still find fault?" Since it is God's will for Pharaoh to be harden, then why does God find fault? How could he resist God's will? How can God control all things and still hold man responsible? It is important to notice that the objector agrees that no one can resist God's will. The question is how can God hold man responsible if God is the ultimate one who chooses?

Paul's answer is given in Rom 9:20 and following. At first glance, this verse may not seem like a very satisfying answer, but it really is. One needs to realize what the objector is doing to know the seriousness of his questions. Paul in the first half of v. 20 is telling the objector that he does not know his rightful place as a finite creature before the infinite Creator. These questions in v. 19 are statements that make God accountable to man who becomes judge over God! So Paul is saying, "Who are you, a mere man, to call God into court to defend Himself" (Isa 40:13–14).

God's will is law and God's will is free to do his good pleasure. Whatever God does, no matter whether we understand it or not, is holy, righteous, and just. If this is not true then our god is not the God of the Bible. God is not obligated to tell us why. He is accountable to no one. He is responsible to no one. He is free to do His will and whatever He does is righteous. God's righteousness is committed to act always for His own name sake, that is, to preserve and display his Name and glory (Piper, 157). This was the very purpose for which Pharaoh was raised up to do. Dan 4:35 says, "And all the inhabitants of the earth are account as nothing, But He does according to His will in the host of heaven and among the inhabitants of earth; and no one can ward off His hand or say to Him, what have you done?" Yet, the objector in Romans 9 is saying, "What have You done, God?" Because this question places man as judge over God, it is a blasphemous statement. Thus, Paul puts the objectors in their place as a mere creature. Paul is making it absolutely clear that God is free to create and do with his creatures as He sees fit. Then in 9:20–21 Paul uses the illustration of a potter and clay to demonstrate that God has the absolute right to create and dispose of his creatures as He wills just like the potter does the clay pot.

The response of people who do not acknowledge the total sovereignty of God is to become angry. I quote again a portion of Spurgeon's description of God's sovereignty and man's misguided response. "But when God ascends His throne, His creatures then gnash their teeth, and we proclaim an enthroned God, and His right to do as He wills with His own, to dispose of His creatures as He thinks well, without consulting them in the matter; then it is that we are hissed and execrated, and then it is that men turn a deaf ear to us, for God on His throne is not the God they love. But it is God upon the throne that we love to preach. It is God upon His throne whom we trust" [249]

This is one of the lessons Job had to learn. God was ultimately responsible for all of Job's tragedy (Job 1–2). Job never cursed God, but he did want his day in court to prove that he did not deserve what he is receiving and that he had not sinned like a wicked man who would deserve what he experienced. Job was critical of the Creator. Therefore, beginning with Job 38 God begins to speak and puts on a showcase of His sovereign majesty. Here are only three verses out of the Job 38–41. "Who is this that darkens counsel by words without knowledge? Now gird up your loins like a man, and I will ask you, and you instruct Me! Where were you when I laid the foundation of the earth! Tell me, if you have understanding" (Job 38:2-4). Job had spoken out of turn. He had forgotten who he was and how high, sovereign, and majestic God is! And Job shut his mouth in silence and bowed humbly in repentance.

---

[249] Pink, *The Attributes of God*, 32-33.

Well then, what is the answer to the question, is man responsible? The answer is, yes, man is responsible before God and will be held accountable for what he says and does. Why? There are multiple books written on the different views of this question and some of them are helpful and others are not. The simple big picture answer which challenges us all to bow the knee in worshipful submission, is this: It is because God as God says we are responsible and accountable to Him! The more a person knows the character and attributes of God spiritually, intellectually and experientially through the Holy Spirit, the more this answer is acceptable! The less we know of God's character and attributes spiritually, intellectually, and experientially, the less this answer will be acceptable! In other words, the answer to mankind for why we are responsible to God in His absolute sovereignty is the same answer Job received in Job 38-41, which gives the explanation for why God allowed him to experience all his suffering. As we come more often face to face with God's sovereign will and glory – the answer to why we are responsible is: because I am God! The more we come to know the depth of God in the Scripture and in spiritual maturity, the more this becomes a satisfying answer!

Selected Bibliography

Albertz, R. "פלא," in *Theological Lexicon of the Old Testament*, vol. 2 (Peabody: Hendrickson, 1997, 984).

Berkhof, Louis. *Systematic Theology* (Grand Rapids: Eerdmans, 1972).

Bertran, Georg. "θαῦμα, θαυμάζω, θαυμάσιος, θαυμαστός," in *TDNT*, eds. Gerhard Kittel, Geoffery W. Bromiley and Gerhard Fredrick, vol. 3 (Grand Rapids: Eerdmans, 1964), 32–33, 35.

Blass, Friedrich, Albert Debrunner, and Robert Walter Funk. *A Greek Grammar of the New Testament and Other Early Christian Literature* (Chicago: University of Chicago Press, 1961).

Brueggemann, Walter. *Isaiah 40–66.* Westminster Bible Companion. eds. Patrick D. Miller and David L. Bartlett (Louisville: Westminster John Knox Press, 1998).

Childs, Brevard S. *Isaiah.* Old Testament Library (Louisville: Westminster John Knox, 2001).

Conrad, J. "פלא," in *TDOT*, vol. 11 (Grand Rapids: Eerdmans, 2001), 536–44.

Hodges, Zane C. and Arthur L. Farstad, ed. *The Greek New Testament According to the Majority Text* (Nashville: Nelson, 1982).

Feinberg, John S. "God Ordains All Things," in *Predestination and Free Will: Four Views of Divine Sovereignty and Human Freedom*, eds. David Basinger and Randal Basinger (Downers Grove: InterVarsity Press, 1986), 19–43.

Forster, Roger and V. Paul Marston, *Gods Strategy in Human History* (Minneapolis: Bethany House, 1973).

Jensen, Philip. "Poetry in the Bible," in *New Bible Commentary: 21st Century Edition* (Downers Grove: InterVarsity Press, 1994).

Johnson, E. Elizabeth. *The Function of Apocalyptic and Wisdom Traditions in Romans 9–11.* Society of Biblical Literature Dissertation Series, ed. Charles Talbert, vol. 109. (Atlanta: Scholars Press, 1989).

Kim, Johann D. *God, Israel, and the Gentiles: Rhetoric and Situation in Romans 9-11*, Society of Biblical Literature Dissertation Series (Atlanta: Society of Biblical Literature, 2000).

Kruger, Paul A. "פלא," in *New International Dictionary of Old Testament Theology & Exegesis*, ed. Willem A. VanGemeren, vol. 3 (Grand Rapids: Zondervan, 1997).

Moule, C. F. D. An *Idiom Book of New Testament Greek* (Cambridge: Cambridge University Press, 1959).

Naselli, Andrew D. *From Typology to Doxology: Paul's Use of Isaiah and Job in Romans 11:34–35* (Eugene, OR: Pickwick Publication, 2012).

Pink, Arthur W. *The Attributes of God* (Swengel, PA: Reiner Publication, n.d.).

Schrenk, Gottlob. "Βούλομαι, Βουλή, Βούλημα," *TDNT*, vol 1 (Grand Rapids, MI: Eerdmans, 1964).

Sullivan, Steve P. *The Isaianic New Exodus in Romans 9–11: A Biblical and Theological Study of Paul's Use of Isaiah in Romans* (Silverton, OR: Lampion Press, 2017).

Sullivan, Steven P. *The Isaianic New Exodus in Romans 9–11: A Biblical and Theological Study of Paul's Use of Isaiah in Romans*, 2nd ed. (Middletown, RI: Stone Tower Press, 2023).

Swanson, Reuben, ed. *New Testament Greek Manuscripts: Romans*. Wheaton: Tyndale House and Pasadena: William Carey International University Press, 2001.

Wagner, J. Ross. *Heralds of the Good News: Isaiah and Paul in Concert in the Letter to the Romans*. Supplements to Novum Testamentum, eds. M. M. Mitchell and D. P. Moessner, vol. 101 (Leiden: Brill, 2002).

Wallace, Daniel B. *Greek Grammar Beyond the Basic: An Exegetical Syntax of the New Testament* (Grand Rapids: Zondervan, 1996).

Wildberger, Hans. *Isaiah 28–39: A Commentary*. Continental Commentaries. Trans. Thomas H. Trapp (Minneapolis: Fortress Press, 2002).

Romans 9:21–23

Outline

B. Vindication of the Righteous God and His Wise Plan (9:6-29)
   1. Israel within Israel: Children of Promise (9:6-9)
   2. The Divine Call according to Election (9:10-13)
   3. Polemic: Objects of Mercy and Hardening according to God's Choice (9:14-18)
   4. Polemic: Objects against God's Character and Plan (9:19-20)
   5. God's Wise Purpose for Vessels of Wrath and Mercy (9:21-23)

Original Text

9.21 ἢ οὐκ ἔχει ἐξουσίαν ὁ κεραμεὺς τοῦ πηλοῦ ἐκ τοῦ αὐτοῦ φυράματος ποιῆσαι ὃ μὲν εἰς τιμὴν
σκεῦος ὃ δὲ εἰς ἀτιμίαν; 22 εἰ δὲ θέλων ὁ θεὸς ἐνδείξασθαι[a] τὴν ὀργὴν καὶ γνωρίσαι τὸ δυνατὸν
αὐτοῦ ἤνεγκεν ἐν πολλῇ μακροθυμίᾳ σκεύη ὀργῆς κατηρτισμένα εἰς ἀπώλειαν, 23 [b]καὶ ἵνα[b]
γνωρίσῃ τὸν πλοῦτον τῆς δόξης αὐτοῦ ἐπὶ σκεύη ἐλέους, ἃ προητοίμασεν εἰς δόξαν.

Textual Notes

[a] **9:22** The majority of the mss.as well as NA28, UBS5, 𝔐 have **ἐνδείξασθαι**, while ℵ A witness to **ἐνδείξασθε**. The witness of ἐνδείξασθαι has the best evidence.
[b–b] **9:23** The evidence of **καὶ ἵνα** is found in the majority of mss., such as ℵ D* D[2] A K, Ψ 049, 426, 𝔐, NA28, UBS5, SBLGNT. The evidence of only **ἵνα** is P[46], B WH, 6, 69, 326, 426[c], 1837, 1912. See UBS5 apparatus and Swanson, *Romans*, 146 for a more complete list. *UBS Commentary* 2nd ed., 462 gives καὶ ἵνα a rating of {A}and said the absence of καὶ is a result of simplifying the construction. They concluded by saying that the versions are of limited significance, "since translational freedom, and not a different underlying Greek text, may account for the absence of the conjunction" (p. 462).

Translation

21 Or does the potter not have right over the clay, to make from the same lump both a vessel for honor and *a vessel* for dishonor? **22** And *what* if God, because he is willing to demonstrate his wrath and to make known his power, endured with much patience vessels of wrath, having been prepared for destruction, **23** and in order to make known the riches of his glory to vessels of mercy, whom he prepared beforehand for glory?

Commentary

9:21 ἢ οὐκ ἔχει ἐξουσίαν ὁ κεραμεὺς τοῦ πηλοῦ ἐκ τοῦ αὐτοῦ φυράματος ποιῆσαι ὃ μὲν εἰς τιμὴν σκεῦος ὃ δὲ εἰς ἀτιμίαν. "Or does the potter not have the right over the clay, to make from the same lump both a vessel for honor and *a vessel* for dishonor?" The vessels for honor and dishonor are a matter of debate whether they refer to the historical destiny of nations (Cranfield, 492; Dunn, 557; Fitzmyer 569) or the eternal destiny of individuals (Piper, 202–204; Moo, 2nd, 622–23; Schreiner, 2nd, 504). Much of the debate is centered in how one understands the connection with v. 22. Piper, 193–199 gives six arguments why the OT quotations in 9:20–21 do not make a successful argument for corporate national view.[250] Moo, 2nd, 623 is correct that the OT and Jewish text Paul may have used in dealing with the potter/clay motif is uncertain. However, the overall point in this motif is God's sovereign right[251] over the lump of clay. He not only has the ability to do it, but he has a perfect sovereign right to do it (Hodge, 501).
To prove contextually the corporate national view of this section, there is an attempt to make a contrast between 9:21 and 9:22-23. Some have tried to make the connecting δὲ conjunctive between vv. 21 and 22 to be understood as adversative and not a connective that continues to identify the same people as the "vessels" for honor and dishonor (v. 21) and the "vessels" of wrath and mercy in vv. 22–23. However, Godet (359) correctly argues that vv. 19–21 is the figure and vv. 22–24 is the application (Jewett, 595). Thus, the figure of "*a vessel* for dishonor"

[250] Some of the OT passages that Paul may have alluded to are Isa 29:16; 45:9–11; Jer 18:1–6, as well as Wisdom of Solomon 15:7 and Sir 33:7–13. The parallel with 2 Tim 2:20 is also alluded to by some and the individual predestination tradition at Qumran (Piper, 198 who depends upon Gerhard Maier's work *Mensch und Freier Wille nach den juedishchen Religionsparteien zwischen Ben Sira und Paulus*).
[251] BDAG, 352; Dunn, 557. Some prefer "power" (Jewett, 594).

(v. 21) finds its application or corresponding expression in "vessels of wrath" (v. 22). Furthermore, the figure of "a vessel for honor" (v. 21) finds its application or corresponding expression in "vessels of mercy" (v. 23) (Alford, 2:411; Schreiner, 2nd, 503–504; Murray, 2:33). The continued sense is the most natural sense for the term σκεῦος ("vessel") is the common term used twice in v. 21 and once each in vv. 22–23 (Schreiner, 2nd, 504–505). Furthermore, this is also shown by "the attributes κατηρτισμένα ['prepare'] and ἃ προητοίμασεν ['prepare beforehand'] corresponding to the ποιῆσαι ['to make'] of ver. 21, just as εἰς ἀπώλειαν ['unto destruction'] aptly corresponds to the εἰς ἀτιμίαν ['for dishonor'], and εἰς δόξαν ['for glory'] to the εἰς τιμήν ['for honor'], ver. 21" (Meyer, 2:147). Cranfield (495, n. 4) insists that a definite article would be required if the same vessels were indicated in vv. 21–23. Cranfield's statement lacks support for at least three reasons: (1) there are other ways, not just one grammatical rule, that dictates how an author may refer back to a metaphor and its application.[252] (2) The parallels mentioned above, especially the repetition of the term σκεῦος ("vessel") strongly point to parallel continuity. (3) A noun in the NT Greek may be definite even when the article is missing and even when the anathrous noun is in a prepositional phrase.[253]

The evidence is strong that a vessel for dishonor and the vessels of wrath prepared for destruction are the same vessels. The place for these vessels is εἰς ἀπώλειαν ("for destruction") which refers to eternal perdition or destruction.[254] This understanding of eternal existence fits the very opposite people who are described as vessels of mercy who receive eternal glory.[255] The implication from 9:24 is that some of the Jews and Gentiles are part of the vessels of honor and mercy. Since Jewish individuals and Gentile individuals are part of the vessels of mercy and glory as well as part of vessels of wrath and destruction, then there is no basis to argue that Paul is making a contrast between corporate entities as nations. In other words, the vessels of mercy in v. 24 are not corporate entities but individuals "called . . . from (ἐξ) Jews and from (ἐξ) Gentiles" (Piper, 199).

Thus, when Paul declares in 9:21 that God has the right to make a "vessel for dishonor" this means that these vessels were for destruction (v. 22). Cranfield objects to this notion because he believes that the potter does not make vessels just to destroy them (492, n. 2). This subject is taken up by Paul in vv. 22–23. At this point in the argument, Paul in v. 21 states that the potter (God) has the right over the clay to take "from the same lump" (ἐκ τοῦ αὐτοῦ φυράματος) and make different pots out of the clay.[256] This phrase harkens back to 9:11 where the election of

---

[252] Wallace, *Greek Grammar Beyond the Basics*, 217–218 states that an anaphoric article (an article plus a substantive) refers back to a previous substantive (that is usually anathrous). This is one way the author could have used, but not the only way.

[253] Ibid., 247. See also Piper, 200–201.

[254] Opeke, *TDNT*, 1:396–397 indicates that eternal destruction is the meaning of ἀπώλεια in the Synoptics (Matt 7:13), Paul (Rom 9:22; Phil 1:28; 3:19; 1 Tim 6:9; 2 Thess 2:3), and John (John 17:12; Rev 17:8 11). He states, "What is meant here is not a simple extinction of existence . . . but an everlasting state of torment and death" (p. 397).

[255] Schreiner (518) uses the term eschatological glory or life (Rom 2:7, 10; 8:18, 21; 1 Cor 2:7; 15:41; 2 Cor 4:17; Eph 1:18; Phil 3:21; Col 1:27; 3:4; 1 Thess 2:12; 2 Thess 2:14; 2 Tim 2:10). He also points out that τιμή ("honor") refers to eternal life in Rom 2:7, 10 and parallels the word δόξα ("glory").

[256] Meyer 2:146 explains this well: "In the *application* of the simile, *the same lump* denotes human nature in and by itself, as it is alike in all with its opposite moral capabilities and dispositions, but not yet conceived of in its definite individual moral stamp. Out of this, like the potter out of the clay-dough which is susceptible of various moulding, God—who does not merely '*allow to come into being*' the different moral quality of individuals, in order *then* to fulfill on them the ἐλεεῖν or σκληρύνειν which He will (Hofmann), but effectively *produces* it—makes partly such as are destined to stand in honour (namely, as partakers of the Messianic glory), partly such as are to stand in

Jacob is done before the twins were born and did not take into account anything good or bad. Their birth came from the same father and mother in the same time and womb. God's choice depended upon himself who calls. Here in 9:21 the choice to make one vessel for honor and the other for dishonor came from the same lump. There was no special merit or distinctiveness in the potter's choice because of the lump of clay. The choice of the potter (God) was done on his free choice and his sovereign good pleasure.[257]

9:22 εἰ δὲ θέλων ὁ θεὸς ἐνδείξασθαι τὴν ὀργὴν καὶ γνωρίσαι τὸ δυνατὸν αὐτοῦ ἤνεγκεν ἐν πολλῇ μακροθυμίᾳ σκεύη ὀργῆς κατηρτισμένα εἰς ἀπώλειαν. "And *what* if God, because he is willing to demonstrate his wrath and to make known his power, endured with much patience vessels of wrath, having been prepared for destruction." Some take the δὲ as adversative force trying to indicate a distinction between images of vv. 20–21 and its application of God in vv. 22–23. See argument above in v. 21 for reasons to take it as a transitional force "and." There are several difficulties in this verse that makes the understanding and translation challenging. First, Paul begins with a conditional sentence in v. 22 without clearly indicating where the conditional aspect finishes (e.g. the apodosis of the sentence is in question). There are several solutions possible but most commentaries can be categorized into two basic solutions. First, some make v.22 the first part of the conditional clause (protasis) and the second half of the condition v. 23 (apodosis).[258] Second, some make vv. 22–23 the protasis with an unexpressed apodosis (Moo, 2nd, 623–23; Cranfield, 492–493; Dunn, 558; Jewett, 595).[259] The second position seems to be the better solution.

Dunn (558) understands θέλων as a "desired purpose" and translates it "wanting to." However, the context supports the sovereign will of God who makes and uses the lump of clay as He wills.[260] Thus, θέλων is best translated "willing." The next important difficulty is how to take the force of the participle θέλων and the clause this participle introduces with the relation to the purpose clause in v. 23 (καὶ ἵνα, "and in order to"). Commentators propose several options concerning the participle and the clause it introduces and two are the most worthy to be investigated. The first is to consider the participle θέλων as concessive (Meyer, 148–149; Sanday and Headlam, 261; Lenski, 623; Fitzmyer, 569; NASB).

---

dishonour (namely, through the eternal ἀπώλεια)." Wardlaw, 280; Hodge, 502; Shedd, 296–297 and Murray, 2:32 indicate that the "lump" is a mass of fallen mankind. For more systematic discussion on the topic see Hodge, *Systematic Theology*, vol. 2, 313–320; Shedd, *Dogmatic Theology*, vol. 1, 311–344; Bavinck, *Reformed Dogmatics*, vol. 2, 337–347, 361–366; Turretin, *Institutes of Elenctic Theology*, vol.1, 342–390. Gill, "Romans to Revelation," vol. 6, 81 indicates that the "lump" is not fallen or corrupt. Bavinck, *Reformed Dogmatics*, vol. 2:365, n.73 lists about 16 works that espoused the supralapsarian position which often take the "lump" in Rom 9:22 as unfallen lump. Reymond, *Perspectives on Election*, 150–194 has a different way to list the supralapsarian decree of God by placing the "election of some sinful men to salvation in Christ" first. Murray, 2:33 may have the best solution which is basically Calvin's view. It is true that the vessels of wrath deserve their wrath, but the vessels of mercy do not deserve God's mercy. Thus, it may be best to take the vessels "in the sense that can apply to both" vessels.

[257] For those who want to use 2 Tim 2:19–21 to refute Paul's illustration should notice the differences between the texts. See Schreiner 518, n. 14.

[258] It is unusual that καὶ would introduce the apodosis but examples are found in Greek (see Blass, Debrunner, Funk, *Greek Grammar of the NT*, 442 [7]). Stählin, *TDNT*, vol. 5, 426 supports this position.

[259] Schreiner, 519, n. 15 also gives reference to other views where the apodosis is v.24 or vv. 23–24. He accepts the anacoluthon of v. 22. Blass, Debrunner, Funk, *Greek Grammar of the NT*, §482 calls it aposiopesis and states that Paul and other NT writers do use anacolutha (Luke 19:42; John 6:62; Acts 23:9). See also Robertson, *A Grammar of the Greek NT*, 1203.

[260] See Rom 9:19 section for definition of the God's sovereign will. See also Jewett, 595, n. 82 and Murray, 2:34. For a fuller discussion, see Schrenk, *TDNT*, vol. 3, 47–62.

22 But (what) if God, Although wishing (1) to manifest his wrath and (2) to make know his power, Bore with much patience the vessels of wrath prepared for destruction 23 And [bore with them] in order to make known the riches of glory to vessels of mercy that he prepared beforehand for glory.	22 εἰ δὲ θέλων ὁ θεὸς ἐνδείξασθαι τὴν ὀργὴν καὶ γνωρίσαι τὸ δυνατὸν αὐτοῦ ἤνεγκεν ἐν πολλῇ μακροθυμίᾳ σκεύη ὀργῆς κατηρτισμένα εἰς ἀπώλειαν, 23 καὶ ἵνα γνωρίσῃ τὸν πλοῦτον τῆς δόξης αὐτοῦ ἐπὶ σκεύη ἐλέους, ἃ προητοίμασεν εἰς δόξαν.

This understanding usually considers the infinitives (ἐνδείξασθαι . . . γνωρίσαι) to be what God wanted to do, but did not do and v. 23 expresses what God ultimately purposed to do with vessels of wrath (Moo, 605). They believe the idea of causative action of God clashes with the thought that God is patient with the vessels of destruction (Schriener, 519; Fitzmyer, 569). The second position takes the participle θέλων as casual (Calvin, 368–370; Alford, 2:411; Murray, 33–35; Cranfield, 494; Käsemann, 271; Barrett, 176–177; Moo, 605–606; Schreiner, 2nd, 508–510; Piper, 206–207; KJV).[261]

22 But (what) if God, because he is willing (1) to manifest his wrath and (2) to make know his power, Bore with much patience the vessels of wrath prepared for destruction (3) v. 23 And because [he wills] to make known the riches of glory to vessels of mercy that he prepared beforehand for glory.	22 εἰ δὲ θέλων ὁ θεὸς (1) ἐνδείξασθαι τὴν ὀργὴν καὶ (2) γνωρίσαι τὸ δυνατὸν αὐτοῦ ἤνεγκεν ἐν πολλῇ μακροθυμίᾳ σκεύη ὀργῆς κατηρτισμένα εἰς ἀπώλειαν, (3) v. 23 καὶ ἵνα γνωρίσῃ τὸν πλοῦτον τῆς δόξης αὐτοῦ ἐπὶ σκεύη ἐλέους, ἃ προητοίμασεν εἰς δόξαν.

This position understands the infinitives (ἐνδείξασθαι . . . γνωρίσαι) as secondary purposes and v. 23 (καὶ ἵνα γνωρίσῃ) as the primary purpose that God willed to make known (Cranfield, 496; Piper, 206).[262] In vv. 20–21, Paul has expressed the sovereign freedom of God to do what he wills with what he has created. Now in vv. 22–23, he gives the reason why God made vessels of

---

[261] Moo, 605–606 paraphrases this understand this way: "What objection can you make if it is in fact the case that God has tolerated with great patience vessels of wrath prepared for destruction when you realize that his purpose in doing so has been to demonstrate his wrath, make known his power, and—especially —to make known the riches of his glory to vessels of mercy, prepared beforehand for glory?"

[262] The construction of vv. 22 –23 where the conditional clause εἰ . . . θέλω is connected with an infinitive and ἵνα clause as a purpose statement is found in 1 Cor 14:5; Matt 7:12 (no infinitive); Mark 10:35 (no infinitive); John 17:24 (no infinitive or εἰ clause) (Piper, 206). However, none of these verses have the same distance in the sentence between εἰ . . . θέλω and ἵνα clause like in 9: 22–23. Piper, 206, n. 23 points out (though he does not agree with this view) that it is quite possible the ἵνα clause in v. 23 is depended on the main verb ἤνεγκεν instead of the distant participle θέλων. If so, the καὶ ἵνα in v. 23 coordinates with the two causal infinitives in v. 22 and there is not much difference in meaning (Piper, 206, n. 24). This understanding has much to commend it (Schreiner, 522 agrees). Both constructions would coordinate the purpose statement: "God endured because he willed to make known his glory" or "God endured in order to make known his glory" (Ibid.). Jewett, 595 advocates a "purposive view of the participial clause. Hoover, "The Wealth of God's Glory," 49–50 does not take this point into consideration in his article.

destruction and how these fit with the vessels of mercy. God's patience with the vessels of wrath[263] in this context is not that they may come to repentance (Rom 2:4) (*Contra*. Cranfield, 495; Dunn, 559).[264] These vessels are heading for eschatological judgment and eternal destruction.[265] Since they are prepared for destruction the implication directs one to the conclusion that there is no change in their destiny. In v. 22 the purpose for God in patiently bearing the vessels of wrath is that he may display his wrath and make known his power. The close parallel of v. 22–23 with vv. 17–18 indicates evidence to favor a casual view of θέλων (Piper, 207; Murray, 2:34; Moo, 605; Schreiner, 520). Some of the parallelism involves similar wording and the other is similar concepts of mercy and hardening with vessels of wrath and vessels of mercy.

9:17 λέγει γὰρ ἡ γραφὴ τῷ Φαραὼ ὅτι Εἰς αὐτὸ τοῦτο ἐξήγειρά σε ὅπως **ἐνδείξωμαι** ἐν σοὶ τὴν **δύναμίν μου**	9:22 εἰ δὲ θέλων ὁ θεὸς **ἐνδείξασθαι** τὴν ὀργὴν καὶ γνωρίσαι τὸ **δυνατὸν αὐτοῦ** . . . .

In the case of Pharaoh, God raised him up and patiently endured his multi-fold rebellion and resistance. However, the patience of God displayed its power in the judgments (Exod 11:9) and magnified the greatness of His name (Ex 9:14–16). This parallel in v. 22–23 finds a similar correspondence (Murray, 2:34–35; Piper, 207–209). God is patiently deferring the immediate judgment due the vessels of wrath so that his power and wrath may be fully displayed in a judgment later (Rom 2:5). God's great patience (ἐν πολλῇ μακροθυμίᾳ, "with much patience") is displayed toward the vessels of wrath and this attribute demonstrates the greatness of God.[266]

The next difficulty is how to interpret the word κατηρτισμένα[267] ("prepared")? Some adopt the interpretative view that the participle is a middle voice and has the understanding that the people prepared themselves for destruction. Wallace calls this understanding a direct middle (or reflexive or direct reflexive).[268] Chrysostom was one of the first to take it this way.[269]

---

[263] The phrase σκεύη ὀργῆς has been understood various ways: "vessels which deserve God's anger" (Sanday and Headlam, 261), "vessels for the purpose of wrath" (Murray, 2:33), "vessels destined for wrath" (Schreiner, 518; Schreiner, 2nd, 509–510) and "vessels which are objects of God's wrath now" (Dunn, 559). Jewett (596) stresses the genitive of quality rather a genitive or origin.

[264] Horst, *TDNT*, vol. 4, 382–383, declares: "Here [Rom 9:22] the reason for μακροθυμία is not so much to allow time for repentance. The delay is simply to bring out more clearly what God already wills (θέλων) and knows, but what He allows to come to plain fulfilment in man. In no case, then, does μακροθυμία give the sinner a possibility of securing a claim on God's goodness."

[265] See v. 21 for the argument that ἀπώλειαν (destruction) refers to eschatological or eternal destruction.

[266] Piper, 208 is correct when he says: "If God's command to Pharaoh ["Let my people go"] can be thwarted by God's own decree to harden Pharaoh's heart, then in the same way God's command to men to repent and the time he gives to obey (Rom 2:4) can also be thwarted in the case of the vessels of wrath by God's decree to harden whom he wills and thus show his wrath on the day of judgment." Thus, God "in much patience" is not inconsistent with God willing "to demonstrate his wrath and to make known his power."

[267] BDAG, 526 gives the definition of "to prepare for a purpose, prepare, make, create outfit." Delling gives the definition "to foreordain (for destruction)" for Rom 9:22 (*TDNT* vol. 1, 476). Piper (211) and Schreiner (522) consider this definition "quiet uncertain" or "probably too precise." Piper would agree that positive definition of "repair, prepare, equip or complete."

[268] Wallace, *Greek Grammar*, 416–417 states that a direct middle is where the subject acts on himself or herself.

[269] Chrysostom, "Homilies on the Epistle of St. Paul to the Romans," 468. See also Meyer, 2:150.

Wallace has four arguments against this view:[270] (1) the direct middle is quite rare in the NT and "almost exclusively used with certain verbs whose lexical nuance included a reflexive notion (such as putting on clothes) or set idiom" (p. 416).[271] (2) The perfect tense, middle-passive form of καταρτίζω are all passive in the NT (Luke 6:10; 1 Cor 1:10; Heb 11:3). (3) the lexical nuance of καταρτίζω with the perfect tense suggest something already done and not something progressing or ready for destruction. (4) The context argues strongly for a passive and a completed action.

Cranfield (495–496) acknowledges the possibility of a divine passive but settles on the meaning that vessels have the condition for "readiness, ripeness for destruction"[272] and this actions is not attributed to God or themselves (cf. Sanday and Headlam, 261–262; Fitzmyer, 570). Hodge (505) refers to this as a verbal adjective, "fit for destruction." Dunn (559) defines καταρτίζω as "fit together" in the sense of "adjust, restore, make ready or complete."[273] Others are convinced the word is passive and is in direct parallel with προητοίμασεν ("prepared before hand") in 9:23 (contra Dunn, 559). The parallel is the closest support in Scripture for double predestination[274] which is also found in the writings of Qumran.[275] The participial force would be as a perfect passive (a divine passive)[276] and could be translated "had been prepared (by God) for destruction."[277] Hodge, (506) states that the majority of the Augustinians and some Lutherans hold to this view. The context of Rom 9:13–23 supports this interpretation of God's divine agency (Piper, 212): (1) "Jacob I loved and Esau I hated" (v.13); (2) "I will have mercy on whom I have mercy and I will have compassion on whom I have compassion" (v. 15); (3) "So then it does not depend on the man who wills or the man who runs, but on God has mercy" (v. 16); (4)"So then He has mercy on whom He wills, and He hardens whom He wills" (v. 18); (5) He

---

[270] Wallace, *Greek Grammar*, 418.

[271] Wallace (Ibid.) states that the thirteen places where καταρτίζω is used in the NT it is not used as a direct middle. Out of thirteens times the word is used seven times as a middle or passive. In four places (Luke 6:40; 1 Cor 1:10; 2 Cor 13:11; Heb 11:3), the voice seems clearly passive. The other two verses (Matt 21:16; Heb 10:5) being aorist are middles, but they are indirect middles not direct middles. Direct middles are where the "subject acts *on* himself or herself" and indirect middles are where the "subject acts *for* (or sometimes *by*) himself or herself, or in his or her *own interest*" (Ibid., 416, 418–419, especially 418, n. 28). For a different opinion, see Brindle, "Prepared by Whom?," 143–145.

[272] Delling, *TDNT*, vol. 1, 476, n. 2 asserts that this meaning has "no philogical justification."

[273] See Liddell, *GEL*, 910. Dunn, 559 proposes the implication of the action is performed on something already present and it needs to be put in proper order (1 Cor 1:10; 2 Cor 13:11; Gal 6:1; 1 Thess 3:10; 1 Pet 5:10). Thus, he argues that the perfect passive does not indicate "the *initial* act of creation but more probably the effect of action in the period since then (the perspective of the perfect is from the time of 'destruction')" (p. 559). However, he does acknowledge the passive is probably a "divine passive" (see footnote 276) though he applies the outworking of God's wrath to the concept of Rom 1:18–32 with a corporate sense. This conclusion ignores the divine parallel preparation argument (eternal destruction and eternal glory) in v. 22 and v. 23 and the context of Rom 9:11–23 which deals with unconditional election where God gives mercy and hardens others. This argument also does not make sense why Paul would raise the dilemma and questions concerning people's responsibility and God's sovereign predestination in 9:19, or why he made the rebuke in 9:20, and gave the illustration of the initial creation of the lump of clay illustration in 9:21.

[274] Calvin, 367–370; Alford, 2:412; Schreiner, 522; Moo, 608–609; Piper, 212; Käsemann, 271–272.

[275] See Piper, 193–196, 212–213; Dunn, 559; Jewett, 598.

[276] A divine passive or sometimes called a theological passive is when God is the agent of the action of the passive verb. "Such *expressions* are obviously not due to any reticence on the part of the author to utter the name of God. It might be better to say that this phenomenon is due to certain collocations that would render the repetition of the divine name superfluous, even obtrusive. . . . That God is behind the scenes is self-evidently part of the worldview of the NT writers" (Wallace, *Greek Grammar*, 438).

[277] Ibid. 418.

makes "from the same lump a vessel for honor and *a vessel* for dishonor" (v.21); and (6) Paul use the parallels between both v. 17 and v. 18 with v. 22 (see above). Now in vv. 22–23 Paul asserts the parallel that through God's sovereign control He demonstrates the contrast between "vessels of wrath prepared for destruction" and "vessels of mercy prepared for glory." This kind of sovereignty is in harmony with other passages of Scripture (Ex 4:21; Prov 16:4; 21:1 Isa 10:5–12; 46:10–11; Dan 4:34–35; Hab 1:5–11; 1 Thess 5:9; 1 Pet 2:8; Rev 13:8; 17:17). The context of this passage is emphasizing God's sovereignty and freedom more than human activity.
In vv. 22–23, the first usage of "prepared" (κατηρτισμένα) is a perfect passive participle (v. 22) and the second "prepared" (προητοίμασεν)[278] is an aorist active indicative (v.23). The implication of the passive voice in v. 22 is that God is the agent of preparation through what is often called a "divine passive."[279] This change from a passive voice (v. 22c) to an active voice (v. 23c) may express God's asymmetrical involvement (though still in control of both) in the preparation between the vessels of wrath and the vessels of mercy (Schreiner, 522).[280] The implication which may be drawn from Romans 9:22-23 is that God involves Himself differently with good and evil but He is in ultimate control of both (e.g., Prov. 16:4; Acts 2:22–23; 4:27–28; Rev. 17:16–17; Eph. 1:11, Job 1–2, etc.) without reducing His holiness or righteousness and still holding man responsible for his actions (see Rom 9:19–20).[281]

---

[278] Wallace interacts with Cranfield (495–496). Cranfield argues against the view that κατηρτισμένα in v. 22 refers to predestination by comparing it to προητοίμασεν in v. 23. He points out that in v. 23 Paul used an active verb with a προ- prefix to indicate divine preparations of the vessels of mercy but did not do so in v. 22. "Although true, the reason for the switch in verbs seems to be that the focus of the passage is on the benefit that accrues to the elect (note the ἵνα-clause at the beginning of v 23 ['in order to make known the riches of his glory on the vessels of mercy'], indicating the purpose of God's dealing with the vessels of wrath in v 22). Further, this view ignores the context in which God's predetermining will for both kinds of vessels is asserted (vv 20–23)" (Wallace, *Greek Grammar*, 418, n. 30).

[279] Ibid., 437–438.

[280] Piper, 196 makes the following comment on this matter: "Another possible explanation for the passive κατηρτισμένα [v. 22], if we assume a good bit more grammatical reflection on Paul's part, is that he really does want to make a statement about the way God works: though God does accomplish all things by the counsel of his will he does not bring about all things in the same way. In the accomplishment of some things he employs intermediary agents perhaps. Or to put it another way, his heart is engaged differently in different acts, loving some deeds in themselves and inclining to others only as they are preferable in relation to greater ends (cf. Lam 3:33). If this is the case Paul would be implying that not wrath but mercy is the greater, overarching goal for which God does all things."

[281] Jonathan Edwards, "The Decrees of God," 67 may shed a little light on how God may not decree evil as evil but He decrees evil to work for the good. He says: "That we should say that God has decreed every circumstance of those actions; that He predetermines that they shall be in every respect as they afterwards are; that He determines that there shall be such actions, and just so sinful as they are, and yet that God does not decree the actions that are sinful, as sin, but decrees them as good - all of this is really consistent. For we do not mean by decreeing an action as sinful, I mean decreeing it for the sake of the sinfulness of the action. God decrees that they shall be sinful for the sake of the good that He causes to arise from the sinfulness thereof, whereas man decrees them *for the sake* of the evil that is in them.

Nor do we say that God may *do evil* that good may come of it. I do not argue that God may *commit evil* that good may come of it, but that He may ***will that evil should come to pass, and permit that it may come to pass, that good may come of it*** (My italics and boldness)." This point may be illustrated by the answer to this question, "What is the worse and most heinous sin that was ever committed in the history of the world?" Since Jesus was/is the God-Man and man is held responsible for crucifying him, a case could be made that this sin was the worse sin ever committed. Man is responsible for putting the God-man to death! However, Acts 2:23 says, this sinful act was done by the predetermine plan and foreknowledge of God (see also Acts 4:27–28). Therefore, the worse sin in the world brought about the greatest good for mankind!

9:23 καὶ ἵνα γνωρίσῃ τὸν πλοῦτον τῆς δόξης αὐτοῦ ἐπὶ σκεύη ἐλέους, ἃ προητοίμασεν εἰς δόξαν. "and in order to make known the riches of his glory to vessels of mercy, whom he prepared beforehand for glory?" The structure and exegetical decisions of how Rom 9:22 and 9:23 are connected is discussed under the 9:22 section. Rom 9:23 expresses the third and primary purpose statement introduced by καὶ ἵνα ("and in order to"). Paul's main emphasis is not the destiny of the vessels of wrath, but to know the riches of God's glory on the vessels of mercy who are prepared for glory. Moo, 2nd, 627–28 gives several options in understanding the thought of τὸν πλοῦτον τῆς δόξης αὐτοῦ. The qualitative nuance of "glorious riches" does not seem to catch the correct emphasis of the context. His glory seems to be emphasised, especially since it is mentioned twice in the verse. Therefore, he suggests an epexegetic use ("riches, that is, glory") or possibly a better use of a partitive genitive ("riches, consisting especially in glory"). The phrase σκεύη ἐλέους is likely a qualitative genitive in a ἐπὶ prepositional phrase stressing the quality of God's mercy rest on these individuals ("vessels") because God willed beforehand that they would receive mercy. Thus, God's ultimate purpose in His decreed plan though it includes some who are hardened to eternal destruction is to display his mercy to those who will receive eternal glory. Cranfield (496–497), Fitzmyer, 570, and Dunn (559–561) argue that God's mercy is God's plan and they seemed to imply that some or all vessels of wrath in the end will ultimately receive God's mercy and be saved. Their implication, though not argued in detail, is that Paul promises at the end of Rom 9–11 that God will show mercy to all (11:32). However, see the section in Rom 11 for this is not a statement by Paul for universal salvation. The "vessels of wrath" who reject God's Word and the gospel do so because of their sinful heart (Eph 2:1) and they will be held responsible for it. However, on the other hand, God also states that He hardens those who had been prepared for destruction. Correspondently, the vessels of mercy undeservingly receive God's mercy and will believe because God in eternity past "prepared them beforehand for glory." The word προητοίμασεν ("prepared beforehand") parallels the thought of predestination which was found in Rom 8:29 (Moo, 608; Schreiner, 523; Fitzmyer, 570).[282] Calvin boldly and tactfully states, "Though in the second clause he asserts more expressly, that it is God who prepares the elect for glory, as he had simply said before that the reprobate are vessels prepared for destruction; there is yet no doubt but that the preparation of both is connected with the secret counsel of God. Paul might have otherwise said, that the reprobate give up or cast themselves into destruction; but he intimates here, that before they are born they are destined to their lot.[283]

Biblical Theological Comments

Paul in Rom 9:21–23 is concentrating on the divine viewpoint of how God determines what He does in lives of human beings. He acknowledges in the questions of 9:19 and His answer in 9:20 that man is responsible for his actions, and no one can successfully resist God's will or legitimately question God's determinative will (or completely understand it). Our God, who makes vessels of honorable use and vessels of dishonorable use (v. 21) willed to endure with much patience the vessels of wrath. This divine enduring patience demonstrated God's just wrath and infinite power toward those who had been prepared for eternal destruction. However,

---

[282] Dunn, 561 and Jewett, 597–599 acknowledge the term refers to predestination but deny or question the same divine predetermination of the parallel term in Rom 9:22.

[283] Calvin, 369–370.

the greatest display of the riches of His glory was upon the vessels of mercy who He prepared for eternal glory.

Thus, God's promises have not failed toward Israel (Rom 9:6) because the true Israelite is one who will believe in their Messiah Jesus demonstrating God's election of mercy and magnifying God's glory. God's plan to demonstrate the faithfulness of God to true Israel by divine election has glorified the name and character of God. Strange as it may seem to mankind, God also hardened others manifesting God's power and wrath (Jn 12:37–41; 17:12; 1 Pet 2:7–8; Jude 4). It is not surprising that people find in Rom 9:18-23 objections, questions, and unacceptable answers. Here human beings come to the clash between the lump of clay and the Potter's sovereign control, the finite not understanding the Infinite, the brilliant scholar's ignorance in comparison to the omniscient Lord, and the woeful lack of understanding of the well-educated, seasoned sage in the present of the all-wise Counselor and Judge of the universe. Ultimately, in God's sovereignty He willed to display a fuller range of His glory where He ordained the greatness of His mercy more prominently than His wrath. However, in order to show the greatness of His mercy He displayed it in the backdrop of His wrath.[284] At this point every man and woman must bow the knee in humble submission and exclaim: "Who has directed the Spirit of Yahweh, and *as* a man of his counsel has informed Him? With whom has he consulted and *who* gave Him understanding? And *who* taught Him in the path of judgment and taught Him knowledge, And made known to Him the way of understanding?"[285]

Application and Devotional Implications

God's will is law and God's will is free to do His good pleasure. Whatever God does, no matter whether we understand it or not, is holy, righteous, and just because He always acts according to His character. God is not obligated to tell us why He does anything. He is accountable to no one but Himself. Thus, He is responsible to no one. He is free to do His will and whatever He does is righteous. Furthermore, God's righteousness is committed to act always for His own name sake, that is, to preserve and display His own glory (Piper, 157). Pharaoh was raised up to display this purpose. In v. 21 Paul uses the illustration of a potter and the clay to demonstrate that God has the absolute right to create and dispose of his creatures as He wills. This potter/clay motif is found in the OT in such places as Isa 45:9, "Woe to the one who quarrels with his Maker–and earthenware vessel among the vessels of earth! Will the clay say to the potter what are you doing? Or the thing you are making say, 'He has no hands'" (NASB). Also, see in Isa 64:8 and Jer 18:1–12 among other verses. The potter takes a lump of clay, and he puts it on the potter's wheel and he spins it into a beautiful vase which is admired on the mantle in a house. Yet, he will take another lump of clay from the same batch and fashion a slop vase for a farmer to feed the hogs. Yet, no one will charge the potter with injustice! Why? Because his choice of creation is his sovereign right as a potter. God is absolutely free to reach down into the lump of humanity and make a beautiful vessel like Moses to glorify God through His mercy and He has the right to harden Pharaoh as an object of dishonor and use him for His glory.

In Rom 9:22–23 we see God's will is to be merciful or to demonstrate His wrath in reprobation. Rom 9:22 is best translated as casual (see commentary above), "what if God because He is willing. . ." The construction of vv. 22–23 conveys three purposes: (1) to

[284] The positive side of God's grace is also brought out in Eph 2:4–7 (Piper, 214–215).

[285] Isa 40:13–14 (author's translation from the MT).

demonstrate God's wrath; (2) to make His power known; and (3) to make known His riches through the vessels of mercy. It is likely that the 3rd purpose is the primary purpose and the other two support the 3rd purpose.

Therefore, God has willed to demonstrate his wrath and power by enduring with much patience the vessels of wrath. Yet, this decision was only to magnify God's glory in his preparing vessels of mercy to show his blessing upon them. A good jeweller will always show his beautiful diamond jewelry by way of contrast to accent the beauty and brilliance of his wares. He often places a black satin cloth for his background and has a brilliant overhead light shining down on the cloth. Then he places the diamond jewelry on the black satin cloth to bring out all of the glory of the jewelry. The glory of God's character and name is brought out by the vessels of mercy being contrasted to the black satin background of the vessels of wrath as God's light of revelation is revealed in his Word.

Rom 9:22–23 sheds some light on why God determined that evil should exist in his universe. Dr. S. L. Johnson comments, "The greatest good that man may have is the knowledge of God, and the revelation of Him would be incomplete, if we did not know Him in His justice and in His mercy. But we can never know Him in these attributes, if sin does not exist in the universe. Thus, evidently God determined that sin exists in His world in order that angels and men alone should know Him in His mercy by virtue of the saving ministry of the Lamb of God."[286]

God has made vessels of wrath which v. 22 says are prepared for destruction. There is a debate exactly what this means (see commentary section above). The illustration in v. 21 shows that the potter made honorable and dishonorable vessels and the parallel thought in v. 23 where God is the one who prepared the vessels of mercy for glory, seems to indicate that God is ultimately the one who prepares the vessels of wrath for eternal destruction. This is very difficult to accept but Paul seems to be saying this (see also John 12:37–40; Rom 11:7; 1 Thess 5:9; 1 Pet 2:8; Jude 4; Rev 13:8; 17:8). If God took the lump that was fallen (v. 22) and demonstrated his power and glory in electing some to mercy and others he passed by for his wrath, then the thought of v. 22 is easier to grasp.

What is Paul telling us in all these verses about man's responsibility in the light of God's absolute sovereignty in dispensing his mercy and wrath? First, we need to watch what we say and how we approach God. We are creatures and His will is ultimate. God says that we are responsible before Him. We may not know how to reconcile these truths together, but this is what God declares. People act freely according to their sinful nature if they are lost. Our wills are in bondage to our fallen nature and apart from divine grace Paul says in Rom 3:11 that "no one understands" (1 Cor 2:14) and "no one seeks for God" (Rom 9:16). Yet, our inability does not negate our obligation to obey God. Our inability is not physical inability. We are made in the image of God and have a mind and physical ears and we are able to physically hear and perceive the content of God's Word. However, apart from divine grace and mercy, humans do not believe because they do not want it. Their nature is against it. God does not have to make a person not believe. We are all born with a sinful nature and will make decision accordingly apart from divine grace.

If you are saved, then it is because God chose you to be a vessel of mercy for his glory. You are not responsible for believing–God receives all the glory for this. If you never believe unto salvation, you are a vessel of wrath prepared for destruction; however, you are lost and condemned because you are a sinner and you would not believe. You are responsible for your

---

[286] S. Lewis Johnson, "Sermon Notes on Romans 9:19–33," 4.

unbelief because you did exactly what you wanted to do. How can these seemingly irreconcilable statements be true! This mystery can be illustrated by the same problem in the definition of light. There is cogent evidence to show that light consists of waves and equally cogent evidence to show that it consists of particles. According to physics both are true, but neither view cancels out the other. The two seemingly incompatible positions must be held together, and both must be treated as true.

God says plainly in his Word that he sovereignly chooses vessels of mercy for his glory and vessels of wrath to demonstrate his power and justice in destruction. On the other hand, God says man is held responsible for his sin and unbelief. Two undeniable truths which must be held together without cancelling out the other. Calvin gives us some parting wisdom on this point: "For the will of God is the highest rule of justice, so that what he wills must be considered just, for this very reason, because he wills it. When it is inquired therefore why the Lord did so, the answer must be because he would. But if you go further and ask why he so determined, you are in search of something greater and higher than the will of God, which can never be found."[287]

Selected Bibliography

Bavinck, Herman. *Reformed Dogmatics*, trans. John Vriend, ed. John Bolt, 4 vols. (Grand Rapids: Baker, 2004).

Blass, Friedrich, Albert Debrunner, and Robert Walter Funk. *A Greek Grammar of the New Testament and Other Early Christian Literature* (Chicago: University of Chicago Press, 1961).

Brindle, Wayne, A. "Prepared by Whom? Reprobation and Non-Calvinist Interpretations of Romans 9:22," *Criswell Theological Review* 12 (Spring 2015): 135–146.

Calvin, John. *Institutes of the Christian Religion*, 4 vols. (Bellingham, WA: Logos Bible Software, 1997).

Delling, Gerhard. "Ἄρτιος, Ἐξαρτίζω, Καταρτίζω, Καταρτισμός, Κατάρτισις," *TDNT*, vol. 1 (Grand Rapids, MI: Eerdmans, 1964), 476.

Edwards, Jonathan. "The Decrees of God," in *Our Great and Glorious God*, sermons compiled and edited by Don Kistler (Morgan, PA: Soli Deo Gloria Publications, 2003).

Hodge, Charles. *Systematic Theology*, 3 vols (Grand Rapids: Eerdmans, repr. 1970).

Hoover, Joseph, "The Wealth of God's Glory: A Response to John' Piper's 'Four Problems in Romans 9:22–23." *Stone-Campbell Journal* 12 (Spring, 2009), 47–58.

Horst, Johannes, "Μακροθυμία, Μακροθυμέω, Μακρόθυμος, Μακροθύμως," in *TDNT*, vol. 4 (Grand Rapids, Eerdmans, 1967), 374–387.

Johnson, S. Lewis. "Sermon Notes on Romans 9:19–33," at Believers Chapel, Dallas, Texas.

Liddell, Henry George, et al., *A Greek-English Lexicon* (Oxford: Clarendon Press, 1996).

Metzger, Bruce M. with editorial committee. *A Textual Commentary on the Greek New Testament*, 2nd ed. (New York: American Bible Society, 1994).

Oepke, Albrecht. "Ἀπόλλυμι, Ἀπώλεια, Ἀπολλύων," in *TDNT*, vol. 1 (Grand Rapids: Eerdmans, 1964), 394–397.

Reymond, Robert L. "A Consistent Supralapsarian Perspective on Election." In *Perspectives on Election: Five Views*, ed. Chad O. Brand (Nashville: B&H, 2006), 150–194.

[287] Calvin, *Institute of Christian Religion*, 3.23.2.

Robertson, A. T. *A Grammar of the Greek New Testament in the Light of Historical Research* (Logos Bible Software, 2006).

Schrenk, Gottlob. "Θέλω, Θέλημα, Θέλησις," *TDNT*, vol. 3 (Grand Rapids, MI: Eerdmans, 1965).

Shedd, William G. T. *Dogmatic Theology*, ed. Alan W. Gomes, 3rd ed. (Phillipsburg: P&R Publishing, 1894, repr. 2003).

Stählin, Gustav. "Ὀργή, Ὀργίζομαι, Ὀργίλος, Παροργίζω, Παροργισμός," in *TDNT*, vol. 5 (Grand Rapids: Eerdmans, 1964), 419–447.

Swanson, Reuben, ed. *New Testament Greek Manuscripts: Romans*. (Wheaton: Tyndale House and Pasadena: William Carey International University Press, 2001).

Turretin, Francis. *Institutes of Elenctic Theology*, trans. George M Giger, ed. James T. Dennison, Jr., 3 vols. (Phillipsburg: P&R Publishing, 1992).

Wallace, Daniel B. *Greek Grammar Beyond the Basic: An Exegetical Syntax of the New Testament* (Grand Rapids: Zondervan, 1996).

Romans 9:27–29

Introduction

Rom 9:14–23 is not an excursus or a parenthetical thought but part of the flow of Paul's argument as he answers Rom 9:6 (contra. Moo, 2nd, 629).[288] The citation of Paul in Rom 9:6–29 follows a pattern in the Jewish Scriptures beginning with patriarchal (vv. 7–13) and Exodus narratives (vv. 14–18) in the Pentateuch and then to the time of the prophets (vv.20–29). Paul has used what scholars now call the Exodus pattern and the NE motif. In fact, the NE motif will dominate all of Paul's OT citations in Rom 9–11 (see introduction to Rom 9–11).[289] The thought of Paul in vv. 24–29 picks up the theme of vv. 6–13. The individual among the group of Jews and Gentiles is brought out by the phrases "from the Jews" and "from the Gentiles" (9:24) and the word "remnant" (9:27).

God's mercy is demonstrated by the elective call to the remnant of Israel (Rom 9:27-29; 10:11, 15). The mercy of God is stressed because the point of calling the remnant is stated in the context of their sinfulness. Paul utilized Isaiah 1:9 and 10:22-23 to specifically express this theme. He also broadly supports this point when he employs Isaiah 28:16 and 52:7 in the context of a universal call for both Jews and Gentiles to believe the gospel of salvation.

God's mercy involves the inclusion of Gentile salvation (Rom 9:33; 10:11, 15, 20) which was not as clearly discussed in the OT. Paul employs the conflation of Isaiah 28:16 and 8:14 by way of a contrast between Israel's unbelief and the Gentiles' belief. He also draws upon Isaiah 28:16 and 52:7 to announce the universal proclamation of salvation to anyone (both Jew and Gentile) who will believe. The inclusion of Gentiles in salvation demonstrates God's mercy. This point is supported by Paul in an unusual way when he uses Isaiah 65:1.

---

[288] See Sullivan, *The INE in Romans 9–11*, 2nd, section 5.2.

[289] For a comprehensive study see my book, *The INE in Romans 9–11: A Biblical and Theological Study of Paul's Use of Isaiah in Romans*, 2nd ed.

Outline

B. Vindication of the Righteous God and His Wise Plan (9:6–29)
   1. Israel within Israel: Children of Promise (9:6–9)
   2. The Divine Call according to Election (9:10–13)
   3. Polemic: Objects of Mercy and Hardening according to God's Choice (9:14–18)
   4. Polemic: Objects against God's Character and Plan (9:19–20)
   5. God's Wise Purpose for Vessels of Wrath and Mercy (9:21–23)
   6. The Divine Call according to Election among Israel and Gentiles (9:24–26)
   7. The Remnant within Israel: Mercy within Judgment (9:27–29)

Original Text

9.24 οὓς καὶ ἐκάλεσεν ἡμᾶς οὐ μόνον ἐξ Ἰουδαίων ἀλλὰ καὶ ἐξ ἐθνῶν;— 25 ὡς καὶ ἐν τῷ Ὡσηὲ
λέγει· Καλέσω τὸν οὐ λαόν μου λαόν μου καὶ τὴν οὐκ ἠγαπημένην ἠγαπημένην· 26 [a]καὶ ἔσται ἐν
τῷ τόπῳ οὗ ἐρρέθη αὐτοῖς· Οὐ λαός μου ὑμεῖς,[a] ἐκεῖ κληθήσονται υἱοὶ θεοῦ ζῶντος. 27 Ἠσαΐας
δὲ κράζει ὑπὲρ τοῦ Ἰσραήλ· Ἐὰν ᾖ ὁ ἀριθμὸς τῶν υἱῶν Ἰσραὴλ ὡς ἡ ἄμμος τῆς θαλάσσης, τὸ
ὑπόλειμμα[b] σωθήσεται· 28 λόγον γὰρ συντελῶν καὶ συντέμνων[c] ποιήσει κύριος ἐπὶ τῆς γῆς. 29 καὶ
καθὼς προείρηκεν Ἠσαΐας· Εἰ μὴ κύριος Σαβαὼθ ἐγκατέλιπεν ἡμῖν σπέρμα, ὡς Σόδομα ἂν
ἐγενήθημεν καὶ ὡς Γόμορρα ἂν ὡμοιώθημεν.

Textual Notes

[a–a] **9:26 καὶ ἔσται ἐν τῷ τόπῳ οὗ ἐρρέθη αὐτοῖς Οὐ λαός μου ὑμεῖς,**– Most mss. attest to this order. See WH NA28 UBS5 SBLGNT א^{c} A K P and many minuscules. B* B^{c} leave out αὐτοῖς and P^{46} leaves out ὑμεῖς and א* has ω instead of οὗ. Finally, **(ε)αν κληθησονται** is found in P^{46} F G and Old Latin: ar b d* and sy^{p} instead of **οὗ ἐρρέθη αὐτοῖς** (Swanson, *NT GK Mss Romans*, 148; NA^{28} apparatus).

[b] **9:27 ὑπόλειμμα** is supported by Treg NA28 UBS5, A B^{c} 8. **ὑπόλιμμα** is supported by WH B* א*. **καταλιμμα** is supported by P^{46} א^{c} F G 88 1735 1837 and **καταλειμμα** by D K L P Ψ 33 104 365 630 1175 1241 1319 1505 1506 1739* 1881 2464 𝔐 (Swanson, *NT GK Mss Romans*, 149). The early mss. attest to ὑπόλειμμα (or the different spelling of it) except for P^{46}. Thus, a slight advantage to ὑπόλειμμα though the meaning does not change if one accepts καταλ(ε)ιμ(μ)α.

[c] **9:28 συντέμνων** is supported by WH Treg NA28 UBS5 P^{46} א*A B 6 1506 1739 1881 m* sy^{p} co. **ἐν δικαιοσύνῃ ὅτι λόγον συντετμημένον** is supported by א^{c} D F G K P Ψ 33 104 256 263 365 424* 459 630 1175 1241 1505 1573 1912 1962 2127 2200 2464 𝔐 lat sy^{h}. A number of mss. add the phrase from Isa 10:23. It is possible that the longer text was omitted by haplography (between συτέμνων and συντετμήμενον) but more likely a scribe assimilated Paul's quotation from the LXX (Moo, 2nd, 629, n. 291; Metzger, *A Textual Commentary*, 462).

Translation

24 Those whom He also called, namely us, not only from among Jews but also from among Gentiles. **25** As it says also in Hosea: "I will call *those who are* not my people, 'my people,' and *those who are* not loved, 'loved'; **26** and it will be that in the place where it was said to them, 'You are not my people,' there they shall be called sons of the living God." **27** But Isaiah cries out concerning Israel: "If the number of the sons of Israel should be as the sand of the sea, the remnant will be saved. **28** For the Lord will perform his word on the earth, completely and decisively." **29** And it is just as Isaiah foretold: "If the Lord of hosts had not left for us a seed, we would have become like Sodom and been made like Gomorrah."

Commentary

9:24 οὓς καὶ ἐκάλεσεν ἡμᾶς οὐ μόνον ἐξ Ἰουδαίων ἀλλὰ καὶ ἐξ ἐθνῶν. "Those whom He also called, namely us, not only from among Jews but also from among Gentiles." The syntax of 9:24 is a subject of much discussion. First, some consider v. 24 is a continuation of the sentence that began in vv. 22–23.[290] Under this option there are at least two ways to understand the sentence: (a) the antecedent of οὓς (masculine, plural; "whom") in v. 24 seems to refer to σκεύη ἐλέους (neuter, plural; "vessels of mercy") in v. 23, and ἡμᾶς (1st person, plural; "us") in v. 24 is in apposition to οὓς because of assimilation. Thus, it is translated, ". . . vessels of mercy prepared beforehand for glory whom He has also called, namely us [called] not only from among Jews but also from among Gentiles" (Hodge, 507; Cranfield, 497–498; Morris 369; Schreiner, 2nd, 512; Moo, 2nd, 630, n. 292; Jewett, 599). The difficulty with understanding the neuter σκεύη ἐλέους as the antecedent to οὓς is that it usually requires a neuter pronoun and not a masculine.[291] (b) the pronoun ἡμᾶς (v. 24) seems to be in apposition to σκεύη (v. 23) and οὓς (at the beginning of v. 24) introduces a relative clause dependent on ἡμᾶς: ". . . vessels of mercy prepared beforehand for glory, namely us, whom He has also called not only from among Jews but also from among Gentiles" (Moule, *Idiom Book,* 168; Barrett, 176). This construction is awkward if ἡμᾶς (later in the sentence and in apposition to neuter σκεύη ἐλέους in v. 23) is the antecedent to οὓς when οὓς is at the beginning of the sentence (Moo, 2nd, 630, n. 293). Second, Rom 9:24 is a new sentence that is continued with v. 25 and those who are called are the "vessels of mercy" (v. 23) (Piper, 184–185). Thus, the double object οὓς and ἡμᾶς are connected to the verb ἐκάλεσεν ("called")[292] in v. 24: ". . . vessels of mercy prepared beforehand for glory. He has also called us as those not only from among Jews but also from among Gentiles" or ". . . vessels of mercy prepared before hand for glory. Those whom He also called, namely us, not only from among Jews but also from among Gentiles." The syntactical parallel in Paul's writings is found in 1 Cor 12:28 (Moo, 2nd, 630, n. 293).

---

[290] See NIV, NRSV and NASB.

[291] Lenski, 625 suggests that the change to masculine is because the vessels (neuter) in v. 23 are people.

[292] See Rom 9:11 for a discussion on "called."

οὓς καὶ ἐκάλεσεν ἡμᾶς οὐ μόνον ἐξ Ἰουδαίων ἀλλὰ καὶ ἐξ ἐθνῶν; (Rom 9:24)	Καὶ οὓς μὲν ἔθετο ὁ θεὸς ἐν τῇ ἐκκλησίᾳ πρῶτον ἀποστόλους, δεύτερον προφήτας, τρίτον διδασκάλους, ἔπειτα δυνάμεις, ἔπειτα χαρίσματα ἰαμάτων, ἀντιλήμψεις, κυβερνήσεις, γένη γλωσσῶν (1 Cor 12:28)

It seems best to choose the second syntactical construction. Dunn (570) also agrees and believes the construction of the sentence would make an impact on the reader.[293] The καὶ ("and") builds on the predestination of προητοίμασεν ("prepared beforehand") in v. 23 and the overall sequence of predestination/election and calling refer back to Rom 8:30 (Ibid., Moo, 2nd, 631; Käsemann, 273). Paul is directing his attention to his brethren, the Jews, but he does not want them to think they alone were chosen but also from among the Gentiles. He also makes clear that it is a remnant that are chosen out from (ἐξ) among the Jews and out from (ἐξ) among the Gentiles. Paul is now transitioning to a discussion of the call of the Gentiles to faith. This manifestation of God's mercy to the Gentiles displays the wonder of his glory.

9:25–26 ὡς καὶ ἐν τῷ Ὡσηὲ λέγει· Καλέσω τὸν οὐ λαόν μου λαόν μου καὶ τὴν οὐκ ἠγαπημένην ἠγαπημένην· [26] καὶ ἔσται ἐν τῷ τόπῳ οὗ ἐρρέθη αὐτοῖς· Οὐ λαός μου ὑμεῖς, ἐκεῖ κληθήσονται υἱοὶ θεοῦ ζῶντος. [25] **"**As it says also in Hosea: "I will call *those who are* not my people, 'my people,' and *those who are* not loved, 'loved'; [26] and it will be that in the place where it was said to them, 'You are not my people,' there they shall be called sons of the living God." The OT background is important to understand how Paul used the prophet Hosea to support the calling of the Gentiles.[294]

Hos 2:23 (2:25 MT/LXX) – I will sow her for Myself in the land and **I will also have compassion on no-compassion,** And I will say those who were not My people, "You are my people!" And he will say, "You are the Lord my God!" **Hos 1:10** (2:1 LXX) – And the number of the sons of Israel was like the sand of the sea, which cannot be measured out or numbered; And it will be in the place where it was said to them, "You are not my people, there they shall be called sons of the living God."	**Rom 9:25** – As He says Also in Hosea, "I will call those who were not My people, My people, **and her who was not beloved, beloved.**" (NASB) **Rom 9:26** – "And it shall be that in the place where it was said to them, you are not my people, there they shall be called sons of the living God." (NASB)

What is unusual about the citation of Hosea 2:25 (MT/LXX) in Romans 9:25 is that Paul reverses the order of the verse in Hosea. He begins with the second half of the OT verse first because it apparently allows him to begin with a verb and topic he wants to stress (Cranfield,

---

[293] The unexpected οὓς follows ἃ (in v. 23) and the reinforced impact and identification with ἡμᾶς (Dunn, 570).

[294] The information in these two verses came from Sullivan, *The INE in Rom 9–11*, 2nd, chp. 7.

499, n. 4).[295] Paul reaches back to the word and concept of "call" in Romans 9:7 and 11 and connects 9:24 with 9:25-26 by using the verb form καλέω ("call") (Cranfield, 499). He appears to substitute the future form of λέγω ("say," a word used in LXX Hos 2:25), by replacing the word with the future form of καλέω (Rom 9:25).[296] Paul indicates that becoming part of the people of God is not by natural descent but by God's call.[297] The number of Jews who have responded to the gospel demonstrates the point that only a remnant will be saved. In Paul's argument, he draws upon Romans 9:14-23 to prepare people not to rebel against the wise plan of God who freely gives mercy to those who he calls. In Romans 9:24-26, Paul briefly introduces the inclusion of the Gentiles as the object of God's call, which the Old Testament and the Abrahamic promise (Gen 12:3) outline, but he does not develop this thought in great detail. Hosea 2:23 (LXX 2:25) is the closing verse in the NE section of 2:14-23 (MT/LXX 2:16-25). Hosea pictures sinful Israel back in Egypt. McKenzie states that "the most important theme in Hosea is that of covenant"[298] and Israel has broken the covenant. This concept is the historical setting of the book which is dramatized in the family life of Hosea.[299] Gomer is pictured as the wife of harlotry who broke the covenant marriage vows and deserved judgment.[300] In this section of Hosea, the author uses the Exodus motif of the deliverance and blessings in the wilderness. "Thus the many references to the Exodus indicate that in order for Israel to become again God's covenant people a NE had to take place."[301] The connection with the Exodus motif is found in Hosea 2:14-15 (LXX 2:16-17): "Therefore, I will now allure her, and bring her into the wilderness, and speak tenderly to her. From there I will give her vineyards, and make the Valley of Achor a door of hope. There she shall respond as in the days of her youth, as at the time when she came out of the land of Egypt" (NRSV). According to these verses, Israel will inherit her

---

[295] Schreiner (2nd, 514) suggests that the clauses are moved to highlight the inclusion of the Gentiles in the people of God. See chart in the Excursus.

[296] There is no manuscript evidence at this time to indicate the change. Paul also seems to change the LXX verb ἐλεέω and used the verb ἀγαπάω in Rom 9:25 (see chart in the Excursus). This is difficult to understand since Paul focuses so much on the concept of mercy in previous context. Some have concluded that he may have received ἀγαπάω from the LXX manuscript B or another text (V, 407). However, there is also a possibility that Paul may have translated the verb from the Hebrew text (Moo, 2nd, 632, n. 298; Schreiner, 2nd, 514; Stanley, *Paul and the Language of Scripture*, 112). Dunn, (571) believes that Paul inserts the change himself. Wagner, *Heralds of the Good News*, 81-82 agrees with Dunn and adds that the change recalls the earlier discussion of Jacob and Esau where "ἀγαπάω belongs to a cluster of terms (including καλέω) within the semantic field of election (Rom 9:11-12; cf. 11:28). By echoing the earlier allusion to the Jacob/Esau story in this way, Hosea's words intimate a reversal of the divine exclusion of Esau (= the Gentiles) from God's mercy" (See also Jewett, 600). Seifrid (647) states that the Lord's mercy is perhaps omitted because of its connection with the promise of "re-sowing" in the land in Hos 2:23a (Eng). He continued by contending that Paul's addition "summarizes the following context, in which Hosea is called to embody the redeeming love of the Lord in again taking to himself his adulterous wife. In this reference to the adulterous wife Paul elaborates what it means to be called God's people: it is to be a harlot embraced and restored by God's love." Seifrid's background explanation helps to support Dunn and Wagner's explanation, which seems to be the best justification for the change.

[297] Many believe that this change is intentional by Paul (Schreiner, 527; Aageson, "Scripture and Structure in the Development of Argument of Romans 9-11," 272, n. 30; Koch, *Die Schrift als Zeuge des Evangelium*,105; Stanley, *Paul and the Language of Scripture*, 109-10). However, this is not a distortion by Paul, but a good understanding of the prophet's argument (Belli, *Argumentation and Use of Scripture in Romans 9-11*, 112).

[298] Steve McKenzie, "Exodus Typology in Hosea," 100.

[299] Yair Hoffman, "A North Israelite Typological Myth and a Judaean Historical Tradition," 171 advocates that the Hosea considers the Exodus not merely a unique historical event but also a typological event.

[300] For the different views concerning God's command to marry "an adulterous wife" and to take "children of unfaithfulness," see Ninow, *Indicators of Typology within the Old Testament: The Exodus Motif*, 207-09.

[301] Ibid., 207.

land ("vineyards"); and the valley of Achor, which historically brought judgment on Achan in Joshua 7, will become a "door of hope" [302] and "a symbol of a new beginning."[303] This NE will be marked by faithfulness.

Paul connects Romans 9:25 with 9:26-27 by quoting Hosea 1:10b (LXX 2:1b) in Romans 9:26[304] and then Hosea 1:10a (LXX 2:1a) and Isaiah 10:22-23 in Romans 9:27-28. Paul takes up the latter part of LXX Hosea 2:1 and uses the words of the LXX. The immediate context of Hosea is the birth of the third child who is named "Lo-ammi": "for you are not my people and I am not your God" (1:9b). This last phrase is a reversal of God's declaration in Exodus 6:7: "I will take you as my people, and I will be your God, who has freed you from the burdens of the Egyptians." Literally, the last phrase of Hosea 1:9 in Hebrew is translated "I (am) not I am to you" (וְאָנֹכִי לֹא־אֶהְיֶה לָכֶם). This is a wordplay with Exodus 3:14 where God displays his name to Moses: "God said to Moses, 'I am who I am.'" God's name in Rom 9 is an important concept (cf. 9:17, 23).

The combination of Hosea 2:23 (LXX 2:25) and 1:10 (LXX 2:1) is used by Paul to convey the larger context of Hosea 1-2, which presents the promise of judgment and future redemption for Israel.[305] The fulfilment of the promises that are stated in Hosea 1:11 (LXX 2:2) and 2:21-23 (LXX 2:23-25) is through eschatological redemption. Paul seems to choose this text because it again demonstrates that the "sons of the living God" are called by the living God for redemption. Because of the disobedience and unbelief of Israel, they have been reduced to the status of the nations (the Gentiles). On the other hand, this new rejected status (liken to the pagan nations) sets up the condition where God can express his merciful call. Paul's emphatic use of "place" in LXX Hosea 2:1b recalls the judgment and exile of Israel, which the Lord will follow with mercy (Seifrid, 648).[306] These patterns of God's dealings with Israel in Hosea, such as considering their disobedience to the status of Gentiles followed by God giving some of them mercy, are understood by Paul. Thus, when Paul uses Hosea he is aware of these contextual patterns. He uses these OT contextually patterns by means of analogy[307] in this present age for

---

[302] Rooker, "The Use of the Old Testament in the Book of Hosea," 58.

[303] Ninow, *Indicators of Typology within the Old Testament*, 212.

[304] Wagner, *Herald the Good News*, 84-85 (see also note 126 and 127 and figure 2.5) states that P^{46} and some of the Western texts have preserved the original text: καὶ ἔσται ἐν τῷ τόπῳ οὗ ἐὰν κληθήσονται οὐ λαός μου [ὑμεῖς – F, G and Old Latin MSS], ἐκεῖ κληθήσονται υἱοὶ θεοῦ ζῶντος. See Swanson, ed. *New Testament Greek Manuscripts: Romans*, 148 for a list of Greek manuscript evidence. Stanley, *Paul and the Language of Scripture*, 113, n. 86 disagrees with Wagner. See Wagner's response to Stanley on pp. 84-85, n. 127. The external evidence is not strong, and the Western texts are mixed. Seifrid, 646 gives four good reasons why Wagner's reading is not correct: (1) temporal sense is unlikely indicated with τόπῳ and ἐκεῖ; (2) the use of οὗ ἐὰν with the indicative mood is very rare (6 times in the LXX and none in the NT); (3) καλέω in Pauline usage is consistently used in effectual calling in salvation but it would not mean this here; and (4) ἐὰν κληθήσονται could have been easily miscopied from the following ἐκεῖ κληθήσονται.

[305] Jewett, 600-601 and Käsemann, 273-74 join these two verses from Hosea. They are probably correct that the origin of this combination is Pauline and not tradition.

[306] See the examples: Hos 2:16-18 (LXX; 14-15 Eng); 5:8-15; 11:8-11; 14:1-7. See also Belli, *Argumentation and Use of Scripture in Romans 9-11*, 116-17 (*Contra* Fitzmyer, [573] who thinks the place needs not to be specified for it is only part of the quotation. Cranfield [500–501] does not think Paul has a particular place in mind. Jewett [601] and Dunn [571] state that "the very place" is a theological reference instead of a spatial one).

[307] See Johnson, Jr., "Evidence from Romans 9-11," 206-11; Hodge (326-27); Godet (365). Sanday and Headlam (264) state that applying this OT principle in Hosea to Gentiles are found in similar interpretations by Rabbis. Others describe the usage as a "type". See Shedd (301); Murray (2:38); Seifrid (648). Campbell, *Paul and the Creation of Christian Identity*, 130 says "citation from Hosea following in 9:25 has its primary reference to the

the calling of Gentiles (e.g. Rom 9:25-26).[308] However, Israel still has a future ethnic national calling and salvation (Schreiner, 2nd, 514–16). The fulfillment of Hosea's prophecy is not in the calling of the Gentiles and the church is not the renewed Israel (contra Schreiner, 2nd, 515).[309]

Dr. S. Lewis Johnson, Jr. explains the analogy as an emphasis of the "manner" of the analogy: "... the manner of the calling of the Gentiles and the manner of the future calling of Israel that forms the analogy. Paul thus lays stress from Hosea on the electing grace of the calling of both the Gentiles in the present time and the mass of ethnic Israel in the future."[310] Wagner considers these patterns "Paul's hermeneutic of reversal": "Israel's scriptures are read as testimony to the surprising reversal wrought by God's grace, in which those apparently outside the scope of God's mercy are included among the people God has redeemed for himself."[311] Moo states that the argument Paul uses is a "universalizing hermeneutic" by applying the universal principle of the Abrahamic promises as key lens through which he reads the Old Testament.[312] One of those universal principles is "in you all the families of the earth shall be blessed" (Gen 12:3c; cf. Gen 18:18; 22:18; 26:4; 28:14). Thus, Moo argues that Paul applies Hosea 1:10b (MT/LXX 2:1b) to the Gentiles in Romans 9:26 because the citation echoes the Abrahamic promises.[313] He also concludes that Abraham is the central figure in the argument about the "nature and extent of the people of God in Romans 9-11."[314] This theological pattern of Abraham helps to support the analogical interpretation of Romans 9:25-26 (Hos 2:23 and 1:10b) and helps to understand why Paul used the Hosea passage to refer to the Gentiles. The inclusion of the Gentiles into salvation history is seen in the Old Testament (cf. Isa 2:2-4; 56:6-7; 60:1-7; 66:18-20, 23) as well as Romans 9-11.[315] Thus, the contextual pattern arguments from the context of Hosea and the theological pattern from the Abrahamic promises provide a hermeneutical axiom for this analogy. In addition, Hosea 1:10a has the same context of the remnant and the Abrahamic promises as Romans 9:27 (Isa 10:22). Hosea 1:10a says, "Yet the number of the

---

restoration of Israel and only in a secondary sense by analogy can include the gentiles." Moo, (2nd, 632); Schreiner (2nd, 515) and Seifrid (648) state that an analogy is not adequate to explain what Paul is doing. See Battle, "Paul's Use of the Old Testament in Romans 9:25-26," 115-29 for a different view of Hos 1:10 (Eng) in Rom 9:25-28, as well as his view that Paul's quotation refers to Israel.

[308] Ellis, *Paul's Use of the Old Testament*, 138; Strathmann, *TDNT*, vol. 4, 54; Käsemann (274) and Hays, *Echoes of Scripture in the Letters of Paul*, 67 refer to "not my people" in Rom 9:25 as Gentiles. Belli, *Argumentation and Use of Scripture in Romans 9-11*, 118-19 argues that LXX Hos 2:25 in Rom 9:25 is not an analogy but literally refers to Gentiles. Stanley, *Arguing with Scripture*, 155-60 states that "not my people" refers to both Jews and Gentiles. Beale, *A New Testament Biblical Theology*, 705-06 takes the ὡς in Rom 9:25 as "a comparison of a NT situation to an OT prophecy that is [a]beginning fulfillment" (p. 706). He applies it to both believing Jews and Gentiles (see Barrett, 178 and Dunn, 571). Jewett (600) seems to argue correctly that a potential double reference (unbelieving Jews and Gentiles) is unsound and creates too much theological ambiguity, which the text does not suggest. However, he seems to critique himself when he concludes that the reference "my people" in Rom 9:25 refers to a "mixed community of the church." He points to Rom 9:6, 24 as reasons to interpret the phrase this way.

[309] See Campbell, *Paul and the Creation of Christian Identity*, *passim*.

[310] Johnson, Jr., "Evidence from Romans 9-11," 209.

[311] Wagner, *Heralds of the Good News*, 83. See examples in Rom 9:30; 10:19, 20; 15:21.

[312] Moo, "Paul's Universalizing Hermeneutic in Romans," 75.

[313] Ibid., 76.

[314] Ibid., 75.

[315] Ibid., 74-78.

people of Israel shall be like the sand of the sea, which can be neither measured nor numbered."[316] This section also displays a theological pattern from the Abrahamic promise.

9:27–28 Ἠσαΐας δὲ κράζει ὑπὲρ τοῦ Ἰσραήλ· Ἐὰν ᾖ ὁ ἀριθμὸς τῶν υἱῶν Ἰσραὴλ ὡς ἡ ἄμμος τῆς θαλάσσης, τὸ ὑπόλειμμα σωθήσεται· [28] λόγον γὰρ συντελῶν καὶ συντέμνων ποιήσει κύριος ἐπὶ τῆς γῆς. "Now Isaiah cries out concerning Israel: 'If the number of the sons of Israel should be as the sand of the sea, the remnant will be saved. [28]For the Lord will perform his word on the earth, completely and decisively.'" Some takes δὲ in v. 27 as an adversative making a contrast with the Gentiles in vv. 25–26 (Cranfield, 501; Schreiner, 2nd, 516; Jewett, 601). However, this understanding is not a clear conclusion among translators of the different versions. This conjunction is often used as a transition to a new topic.[317] Dunn (572) comments that κράζει ("cry out") denotes intensity and urgency to the threatening citation to follow. This verb was used by Paul earlier in an intense way (Rom 8:15). There is some debate over the preposition ὑπὲρ. Hays (*Echoes*, 68) supports the usual meaning of "on behalf of" while others settle on the lesser usage "concerning."[318] In v. 28, the participle συντελῶν has the idea of completion, however the participle συντέμνων is more difficult since it is used only once in the NT and four times in the LXX (Isa .10:22, 23; 28:22; Dan 5:17).[319] Both participles are connected with καὶ ("and") and are objects of the word λόγον ("word"). BDAG, 975 defines συντέμνων as "cut short, shorten, limit."[320] In the context of Israel as a remnant it may be best to understand that God is cutting down or trimming a remnant in salvation. Thus, λόγον as the object of participles refer to the "cutting the word" in the sense that God will thoroughly and decisively execute the word declared to Israel (Moo, 2nd, 635, n. 316; Cranfield, 502; Fitzmyer, 574; Meyer, 2:159). Thus, v. 28 explains how God will bring about the salvation of the remnant in v. 27. However, on the other hand, the statement cuts both ways though the remnant receives the promise of God, the others are judged. Judgment is brought out more specifically in 9:29 though again the remnant is mentioned in the word "posterity." Thus, Paul is continuing to support his argument in 9:6b–13 that God has chosen only some among the national Israel to be the true spiritual Israel–the saved remnant. Paul's OT citations in vv. 27–28 is a masterful use of contextual and theological arguments to make an important point.

Paul appropriates a NE motif of redemption from Hosea to express the call of Lo-ammi to be the sons of the living God. Having established the last half of Hosea 1:10 (LXX 2:1) in Romans 9:26 as the NE motif of redemption, Paul is able to easily transition into Romans 9:27–28 with these thoughts fresh on the reader's mind.[321] He accomplishes this transition by conflating the first half of LXX Hosea 2:1 and Isaiah 10:22-23 (see chart in the Excursus).

---

[316] How the remnant and the Abrahamic promises are connected to the NE, see Sullivan, *The INE in Rom 9–11*, 2nd, chp. 7.

[317] Wallace, *Greek Grammar*, 674.

[318] Moule, *Book of Idioms*, 65 and BDAG, 1031. This use invades the linguistic meaning of περί (Cranfield, 501; BDAG, 1031).

[319] Once in Dan 9:24 (Theod.) and once in 2 Macc 10:10.

[320] BDAG, 975 comments by saying, "*the Lord will act by accomplishing* (συντελέω 2) *his word and by shortening or cutting off*; in this case the shortening is thought of as referring either to God's promise to Israel, which will be fulfilled only to a limited degree (RLipsius, BWeiss), or to the Israelite nation, which is to enter into salvation trimmed and cut down, as a (vs. 27) 'remnant' (Jülicher, Sickenberger). Others take it to mean: *The Lord will act by closing the account and shortening (the time),* i.e. God will not prolong indefinitely the period of divine patience." See also Cranfield, 502 who takes it as "decisive."

[321] The information and source for these two verses, see Sullivan, *The INE in Rom 9–11*, 2nd, chp. 7.

Isa 10:22–23 (LXX) And if the people of Israel become like the sand of the sea, the remnant of them will be saved; for it is completing and cutting short in righteousness. [23] **For God will make a curtailed account with the whole inhabited land.**	**Hos 1:10** (2:1 LXX) – And the number of the sons of Israel was like the sand of the sea, which cannot be measured out or numbered; And it will be in the place where it was said to them, "You are not my people, there they shall be called sons of the living God."	**Rom 9:27–28** Isaiah cries out concerning Israel, Thought the number of the sons of Israel be like the sand of the sea, it is the remnant that will be saved; [28] **for the Lord will execute His word on the earth, thoroughly and quickly**.

In Romans 9:27, Paul quotes from either LXX Hosea 2:1a or LXX Isaiah 10:22, except for the word καί ("and"). He follows Isaiah in using ἐάν ("if") but accepts the fuller phrase ὁ ἀριθμὸς τῶν υἱῶν Ισραηλ ("the number of the sons of Israel") from Hosea.[322] The most plausible explanation for Paul using the latter phrase is his desire to "forge a link with the words of the preceding quotation, υἱοὶ θεοῦ ζῶντος (["sons of the living God"], LXX Hos 2:1b/Rom 9:26)."[323] Paul appears to draw upon LXX Hosea 2:1a because he wants to use υἱῶν Ισραηλ ("sons of Israel"), which connects with υἱοὶ θεοῦ ζῶντος ("sons of the living God") at the latter part of LXX Hosea 2:1.[324] However, he also wants to use Isaiah 10:22 because this verse places the number of Israelites in the concept of a smaller group – the remnant. Wilk asserts at that this point the importance of the term ὑπόλειμμα[325] ("remnant"): "Pointing back to Hosea's prophecy

---

[322] Stanley, *Paul and the Language of Scripture*, 114–115 postulated the possibility that Paul had memory lapse with the change of ὁ ἀριθμὸς τῶν υἱῶν Ισραηλ (Hos 2:1a) for the similar language of ὁ λαὸς Ισραηλ (Isa 10:22). However, he thinks the change is more likely an example of Paul mixing his citations. Koch, *Die Schrift als Zeuge des Evangeliums*, 167–168 favors the explanation that Paul is avoiding ὁ λαὸς Ισραηλ for this applies to the Gentiles in verses 25-26. Wagner, *Heralds of the Good News*, 90, n. 146 states that Koch's view "falters on the fact that Paul elsewhere refers to disobedient Israel as λαὸς (10:21; 11:2). Paul leaves out five words in LXX Isa 10:22c-23a, which seems to be fairly insignificant, but he uses κύριος for ὁ θεὸς and ἐπὶ τῆς γῆς for ἐν τῇ οἰκουμένῃ ὅλῃ in Rom 9:28 (Isa 10:23). The last two variants convinced Wagner to suggest that Isa 28:22b is also part of Paul's conflation (Wagner, *Heralds of the Good News*, 97-99). He also raises the possibility of a few verses later (Rom 9:33; 10:11) that Paul uses Isa 28:16, which may have played a role in shaping Paul's thoughts in Rom 9:27-28 (Ibid., 99, 104-05). Stanley concludes that the possibility of the influence of Isa 28:22 cannot be proven (Stanley, *Paul and the Language of Scripture*, 118-19). Koch also mentions the possibility but dismissed the idea (Koch, *Die Schrift als Zeuge des Evangeliums*, 149, note 46). Shum's final conclusion concerning influence of Isa 28:22 upon Rom 9:28 "is at best some kind of linguistic inspiration" (*Paul's Use of Isaiah in Romans*, 210–211). Isa 28:22b has a remote possibility of an echo in Rom 9:28, but it is difficult to prove. Furthermore, if ἐπὶ τῆς γῆς (Rom 9:28) is sourced in Hos 2:23 (LXX Hos 2:25) instead of Isa 28:22b then there is not much left to commend the Isa 28:22b as part of the conflation of the OT citation.

[323] Wagner, *Heralds of the Good News*, 90, note 146. It is interesting that the phrase υἱοὶ θεοῦ ζῶντος is found nowhere else in the LXX.

[324] The "sons of the living God" are the elective remnant of the "sons of Israel."

[325] Wilk, "Between Scripture and History, 205, 206, 208 makes an unwarranted change in Isa 10:22 by replacing κατάλειμμα with ὑπόλειμμα. He refers to Ziegler, *Isaias*, 14:167 which supports שְׁאָר with the translation of ὑπόλοιπος in Isa 11:11. Ziegler does not show a textual dispute in Isa 10:22 (Zielger, *Isaias*, 162-63). Jewett (602) indicates that κατάλειμμα and ὑπόλειμμα are synonyms. He draws upon Moulton and Howard, *A Grammar of New Testament Greek*, 2:316–317, 327–328) and suggests that the latter Greek word "may have lacked the antithetical, judgmental quality of the former." (See also Herntrich, *TDNT*, vol. 4, 196). Wagner, *Heralds of the Good News*, 96 (who follows Ziegler) states that a variation with initial preposition on compound words in the LXX

of the calling of the sons of God cited in Romans 9:26, it underlines Paul's positive notion of the remnant of Israel and stresses the connection between the quotations in verses 25-28."[326] Wagner states how Paul is using these two OT texts and explains how crucial it is to grasp what he is doing if one is to fully understand the argument: Paul's move to limit the scope of Hosea 1:10 LXX [2:1] to a portion of Israel would have been facilitated by his reading of Hosea's words in light of the similar oracle in Isaiah 10:22, where Isaiah draws a striking contrast between the present multitude of Israelites, "like the sand of the sea," and the far smaller remnant that will be saved through the judgment that is coming. Paul's conflation of these texts in Romans 9:27b suggests that he has indeed interpreted Hosea 1:10; 2:23 and Isaiah 10:22-23 in tandem. Isaiah's oracle concerning the remnant provides the lens through which Paul refracts the words of Hosea as he projects them onto the screen of his contemporary situation and sees that Hosea's promise of restoration and blessing is vouchsafed not to "all from Israel" (9:6), but rather to "us, whom God has called, not only from among the Jews, but also from among the Gentiles" (9:24).[327]

Both contexts of Hosea 1:10 (LXX 2:1) and Isaiah 10:22-23 have the backdrop of God's judgment on Israel, the NE motif of redemption, the faithfulness of God in the Abrahamic covenant, and the language of the "number of Israel will be like the sand of the sea." However, Paul seems to choose these two specific Old Testament texts to draw out at least two important points for his argument in Romans 9. LXX Hosea 2:1 is against the backdrop of the three children, which in the previous context (Hos 1:4-9) spoke about the disobedience of the people (Jezreel, Lo-ammi and Lo-ruhamah) and the rejection of the people by God ("I am not your God"). In this condition, God will show his mercy in calling sons of Israel to be among the sons of the living God (LXX Hos 2:1b). Even though the thought of "calling them sons of the living God" is in the second half of LXX Hosea 2:1, the phrase is quoted in Romans 9:26. Those saints who recognized the writing of Hosea the prophet in v. 26 would see that Paul is using the same context (since the phrase is in the same verse) when Paul cites the first half of LXX Hosea 2:1 in Romans 9:27. The following context of Hosea 1:10–2:1 (LXX 2:2–3) reverses the symbolism of the children's names (great day of Jezreel, Ammi and Ruhamah).[328] Thus, Hosea appropriates the theme of judgment to demonstrate God's mercy to Israel and does this also through the naming of the prophet's children. Paul understands the argument of Hosea and he uses this argument by stressing the mercy of God in his call to the sons of Israel.[329]

Wagner is correct when he states that "Isaiah's oracle concerning the remnant provides the lens through which Paul refracts the words of Hosea."[330] The backdrop of Isaiah 10 is that God uses Assyria to judge disobedient Israel and concurrently God promises to judge Assyria by leaving them few in number (Isa 10:12–19). In the midst of this declaration of God's righteous decree of judgment, God also proclaims his intention to save a remnant. This action demonstrates God's faithfulness to the Abrahamic covenant and would stir up a reminder of the Abrahamic covenant in the mind of the Israelites when they heard the phrase "the people of Israel will be like the sand of the sea" (Isa 10:22; cf. Gen 22:17; 32:12). The LXX Isaiah 10:22 translates יָשׁוּב

is a fairly common occurrence and often entails no significant meaning change. In sum, the reason for the change is not apparent.

[326] Wilk, "Between Scripture and History," 208.

[327] Wagner, *Heralds of the Good News*, 91–92.

[328] The same pattern of judgment redemption/salvation and reversal of the children's names is used in Hos 2:2-23 (Eng) and Paul used Hos 2:23 (Eng) in Rom 9:25.

[329] Fitzmyer,574.

[330] Wagner, *Heralds of the Good News*, 92.

("will return") with σωθήσεται ("will be saved") and contrasts the sons of Israel with the remnant that would be saved. This promise is found in Isaiah 10:24-27 where more detail concerning the theme of the INE is given. This NE redemption of the remnant in Isaiah 10 gives a hope and a future picture of the remnant's eschatological redemption declared in Isaiah 11. Therefore, by the conflation of Hosea 1:10a (LXX 2:1a) with Isaiah 10:22-23 in Romans 9:27-28, Paul is stressing the mercy of God's call to the remnant of Israel. Paul utilizes this conflation citation from these two prophets because the nation is in the same type of situation of judgment in Paul's day as when the prophets addressed their people. "The prophet's words in Romans function as they do in their context in Isaiah – as a message of *hope* in the midst of disaster, as a *promise* that Israel yet has a future."[331]

9:29 καὶ καθὼς προείρηκεν Ἠσαΐας· Εἰ μὴ κύριος Σαβαὼθ ἐγκατέλιπεν ἡμῖν σπέρμα, ὡς Σόδομα ἂν ἐγενήθημεν καὶ ὡς Γόμορρα ἂν ὡμοιώθημεν. "And it is just as Isaiah foretold: "Unless the Lord of hosts had not left for us a seed, we would have become like Sodom and would be made like Gomorrah." Again, the biblical context and theological patterns are important to fully understand Paul's argument.[332] The use of the cities "Sodom and Gomorrah" in Isaiah 1:9 are paralleled in Deuteronomy 32:32: "The vine comes from the vinestock of Sodom, from the vineyards of Gomorrah; their grapes are grapes of poison, their clusters are bitter." This figure of speech using the combination of a vineyard and Sodom and Gomorrah vividly expresses the source of the pagan gods. The false worship of gods reaps deadly and fatal consequences just like the sins of Sodom and Gomorrah. If anyone is spared from judgment when these conditions are present, it is only by the mercy of God and his commitment to fulfill his covenantal promises. At the end of the destruction of Sodom and Gomorrah, as Abraham was standing before the Lord, this summary statement is made: "So it was that, when God destroyed the cities of the Plain, God remembered Abraham, and sent Lot out of the midst of the overthrow, when he overthrew the cities in which Lot had settled" (Gen 19:29). In the time of the Exodus, God remembered Abraham and the promise he made to him and to his seed. During the time of Isaiah, the pattern continues: the people of God deserve his judgment, but in mercy, God remembers Abraham and spared a remnant.[333] Paul draws upon the background of the Abrahamic promise and the Exodus motifs of disobedience, judgment, and mercy to the remnant in his use of Isaiah 1:9 in Romans 9:29.[334]

In Isaiah 1:9, the writer uses the pre-Exodus event of Genesis 18-19 where God destroyed the cities of Sodom and Gomorrah for their gross ungodly actions. Secondly, the writer employs

---

[331] Ibid., 107. Seifrid, 649 says that Paul's use of Isa 10:22 is typological. "The pattern of divine judgment in the past has been repeated in the eschatological present. Just as past judgment portended salvation, so now God's rejection of Israel anticipates its salvation."

[332] See Sullivan, *The INE in Rom 9–11*, 2nd, chp 7:3.1 and 7.3.2.

[333] Isa 1:9 is the first contribution of Isaiah's doctrine of the remnant (Watts, *Isaiah 1-33*, 19).

[334] The imagery of Sodom and Gomorrah in Isaiah 1:9 reflects the Exodus motif. After their destruction in Genesis 19, the cities of Sodom and Gomorrah are not mentioned again in the Pentateuch, nor in the rest of the historical books, nor the wisdom literature in the Old Testament, except for the 2 times in Deuteronomy (29:23 and 32:32). The vast majority of the imagery of the two cities turns out to be a description or figure of speech connected with the disobedience or judgment on Israel and Judah. The Sodom and Gomorrah imagery, when it is found in an Exodus motif, is restricted in its use in the Old Testament to the Jewish people (cf. Deut 29:23; 32:32; Isa 1:9-10; Amos 4:10-11). In sum, the INE motif and the influence of a wisdom polemic setting is found in Isaiah one. For a detail argument on this point, see Sullivan, *The INE in Rom 9–11*, 2nd, chp 7.3.1.

the concept of "survivors" (שָׂרִיד)[335] and later the LXX translators used the word "seed" or "descendant" (σπέρμα) for the Hebrew word. Paul utilizes the word σπέρμα in Romans 9:29, which would easily bring to mind the concept of the seed in the Abrahamic promise. One example of many uses of σπέρμα in the context of the Abrahamic promises is Genesis 22:17. God speaks to Abraham: "I will surely bless you, and I will surely multiply your offspring (LXX, σπέρμα) as the stars of heaven and as the sand that is on the seashore."[336] The promise to Abraham would be fresh upon the readers mind in Romans 9:29, for Paul has already used the phrase "though the number of the children of Israel were like the sand of the sea, only a remnant of them will be saved" (Isa 10:22 and Hosea 1:10a in Rom 9:27). Wagner states that the idea of the preservation of a seed, which would guarantee the nation's survival and future growth, is widespread in the Second Temple Period.[337] Thus, the word σπέρμα carries with it an expectation of hope for the nation of Israel.

Because of the important emphasis on σπέρμα in the covenant purpose of Israel, helpful information is obtain in tracing where the author of Isaiah may have obtained the first part of Isaiah 1:9. Exodus 32:13 and 33:1 are the only two places in the Old Testament that σπέρμα[338] appears and also has the following context: (1) the topic of the Abrahamic promise,[339] (2) the setting of judgment, and (3) where the mercy of God spares a remnant.[340] Isaiah 1:9 has been established as being in the framework of the INE section of Isaiah 1:2–9.[341] The first and last part of Isaiah 1:9 appear to have their roots in Exodus 32:13; 33:1 and Deuteronomy 32:32. Paul seems to select this Isaianic citation, for its background fits his argument of a saved remnant, which deserved judgment but they received the mercy of God's promise to the seed of

---

[335] This Hebrew word is found 28 times in the OT, but it is only translated σπέρμα in the LXX in Deut 3:3 and Isa 1:9. This point has led Delitzsch to conclude that the LXX translators inaccurately translated the Hebrew word (Delitzsch, *Isaiah*, 7:88). Hatch and Redpath, *A Concordance to the Septuagint*, vol. 2, 1282 listed Deut. 3:3 and Isa 1:9 as doubtful in identifying the Greek and Hebrew; however, Muraoka, *Hebrew/Aramaic Index to the Septuagint*, 144 is correct to identify σπέρμα with שָׂרִיד in Deut 3:3 and Isa 1:9 (Wagner, *Heralds of the Good News*, 110-11, note 213 agrees).

[336] Passages in Genesis which refer to the Abrahamic promise and also have the word σπέρμα are: 12:7; 13:15-16; 15:5, 18; 16:10; 17:7-10; 17:19; 21:12; 22:17-18; 24:7; 26:3-4, 24; 28:4, 13-14; 32:12; 35:12.

[337] Wagner, *Heralds of the Good News*, 114-15. See Wisdom 14:6; 1 Esdras 8 and the prayer in *4QWords of the Luminaries*[a] (4Q504) frgs. 1-2, 5.6-14.

[338] According to Logos Alfred Rahlfs LXX, σπέρμα appears 280 results in 248 verses (this includes some of the Apocrypha). See also Wagner, *Heralds of the Good News*, 112, note 216.

[339] According to the Logos Alfred Rahlfs LXX and my count of the context of the Abrahamic promise with σπέρμα, there are approximately 48 verses.

[340] The context of both Ex 32:13 and 33:1 is the judgment of God for the sin of the people in making a golden calf at Sinai. When Moses was on the holy mountain receiving the commandments of God, the people were already blatantly violating the commandments. This disobedience of the people deserved the anger and judgment of God, but God was also testing Moses. God proposed that he would destroy the people and raise up from Moses a great nation. Moses was the means of pleading mercy for the people by establishing his petition before God. This petition was based on the Abrahamic promise in Exodus 32:13: "Remember Abraham, Isaac, and Israel, your servants, how you swore to them by your own self, saying to them, 'I will multiply your descendants (σπέρμα) like the stars of heaven, and all this land that I have promised I will give your descendants (σπέρμα), and they shall inherit it forever.'" God in mercy accepted Moses' petition and did not destroy all of the people. Exodus 33:1 appears to follow the same context of Exodus 32 (Durham, *Exodus*, 435–436). In spite of God's judgment on Israel, his mercy is demonstrated by the Abrahamic promise.

[341] See Sullivan, *INE in Rom 9–11*, 2nd, chp 7.3.1.

Abraham.[342] This promise would give those in the nation who believe God a hope for the future.[343]

It appears from the argument in Romans 9 that one of the reasons Paul chooses Isaiah 1:9 is for the LXX word σπέρμα, which is a rare translation for the Hebrew word שָׂרִיד ("survivors").[344] Just like the words υἱός ("son(s)" Rom 9:9, 26, 27), τέκνα τῆς ἐπαγγελίας ("children of promise"; Rom 9:8-9, 26, 27), and καλέω ("call;" Rom 9:7, 11, 24, 25, 26), the word σπέρμα (Rom 9:7 [twice], 8, 29) [345] is used by Paul to connect with his previous arguments at the beginning of Romans 9. Σπέρμα also parallels the word "remnant" (ὑπόλειμμα) in Romans 9:27.[346] These Pauline terms are most often connected with spiritual salvation, and since these terms parallel many of the same terms at the begin of the Romans 9, the argument that Paul is discussing eternal salvation is strengthened.[347] Paul knows that during the present time there is a partial hardening and judgment (Rom 11:7-10, 25) upon the "sons of Israel" (Rom 9:27) and he wants to give eternal hope to the "remnant," God's "seed" (Rom 9:26, 27, 29).[348] "Paul intends the second quotation from Isaiah [1:9 in Rom 9:29] to support the first" [Isa 10:22-23 in Rom 9:27-28].[349]

Biblical Theological Comments[350]

Paul uses the quotations from Hosea 1:10 (LXX 2:1) and 2:23 (LXX 2:25) as precursors to the Isaiah quotations. Both of these precursor quotations are embedded in the NE framework of the judgment/redemption motif. Paul uses the two Hosea quotations to fit his argument and maintains the thought of the verses in their original context.[351] He reverses the order of the phrases of LXX Hosea 2:25 in Romans 9:25 and substitutes καλέσω for the LXX ἐρῶ. Thus, by

---

[342] Murray, vol. 2, 41; Barrett, 178; Dunn, 574; Schreiner, 2nd, 517; Seifrid, 650; and Matera, 230. *Contra* Cranfield, 503.

[343] Johnson, "Romans 9-11," 226–27.

[344] שָׂרִיד is translated σπέρμα in Deut 3:3 and Isa 1:9.

[345] Dunn, 574.

[346] Ibid., 576 argues that σπέρμα is more of a positive term than ὑπόλειμμα (Rom 9:27). He reasons that σπέρμα is the seed of promise and from this "seed" "many nations" are promised to Abraham. Thus, a "remnant" expresses a few and the word "seed" embraces all nations. It is true that these words are used this way, but the context is not clear that Paul is trying to argue this way in Rom 9:29. Jewett, 605 follows Dunn. Cranfield, 502 Meyer, 2:161, and Nicoll, vol. 2, 666 seem to have a better case. They argue that σπέρμα is the same as the ὑπόλειμμα in the context of Rom 9:29.

[347] See Piper, *passim*; Schreiner, "Does Romans 9 Teach Individual Election unto Salvation?, 25–40; Schreiner, "Corporate and Individual Election in Romans 9," 373–386; Schreiner, 2nd, 482–93; Moo, 2nd, 589–608; and Moo, "The Theology of Romans 9-11," 253-58. Nwachukwu, *Creation-Covenant Scheme and Justification by Faith*, 190-96 believes that Paul uses a typology of election to demonstrate that not every physical seed of Abraham is included in the community of blessing (Rom 9:7-11). The true seed of Abraham is determined by God's promise (9:8) and election (9:11). Dunson, *Individual and Community in Paul's Letter to the Romans*, *passim* identifies four different types of individuals in Romans and four different category types of individuals in the community. Dunson advances the discussion in this area of study.

[348] Mounce, 27:203 extends the promises of salvation in Rom 9:29 also to the Gentiles.

[349] Wagner, *Heralds of the Good News*, 110.

[350] The information in this section was taken from Sullivan, *The INE in Rom 9–11*, 2nd, chp 7.4.

[351] Paul does apply these citations to the Gentiles at least by way of analogy.

these modifications, Paul emphasizes in the NE motif the importance of God's merciful, elective call.

Paul again reverses the order of the phrases in Hosea 1:10 (LXX 2:1). Reversing this order allows Paul to begin with God's calling (κληθήσονται) and connects the calling to the phrase "sons of the living God." Paul seems to use the Hosea quotations at least by way of an analogy to refer to the merciful, elective call of the Gentiles in Romans 9:25-26. The context and background of the NE in Hosea provide a framework for Paul to argue his case in Romans 9.

Having just used LXX Hosea 2:1b in Romans 9:26, Paul then conflates LXX Hosea 2:1a with Isaiah 10:22-23 in Romans 9:27-28.[352] Paul appropriates Hosea's phrase "sons of Israel" (instead of the "people of Israel" in Isaiah 10:22 LXX & MT) to connect by way of contrast with the phrase "sons of the living God" in LXX Hosea 2:1b, which is quoted in Romans 9:26. He utilizes the phrase "will be saved" (σωθήσεται, the LXX translation of יָשׁוּב) in Isaiah 10:22 to bring out the redemption of the remnant. Both the context of LXX Hosea 2:1 and Isaiah 10:22-23 have the background of God's judgment on Israel, the NE motif of redemption, and the faithfulness of God in the Abrahamic promise. Both Isaiah 10:22 and LXX Hosea 2:1a contain the phrase "Israel as the sand of the sea," which is used in Roman 9:27. This phrase brings the Abrahamic promise to the forefront.

Yet, Paul chooses to conflate LXX Hosea 2:1a and Isaiah 10:22-23 to portray at least two important points in his argument in Romans 9. Paul draws upon the LXX Hosea 2:1a to display God's mercy in salvation to the sons of Israel. However, to hone the focus of this truth, Paul uses the oracle of the remnant from Isaiah 10:22-23. The Hosea passage is reshaped through the lens of Isaiah so that the stress would fall upon the redemption of the remnant. Therefore, in the conflation of LXX Hosea 2:1a and Isaiah 10:22-23 in Romans 9:27-28, Paul is stressing the mercy of God's call in salvation to the remnant of Israel.

One additional point on reshaping, which may have been in the thinking of Paul, involves the replacement of the Isaianic phrase ἐν τῇ οἰκουμένῃ ὅλῃ ("with the whole inhabited land;" LXX Isa 10:23) with ἐπὶ τῆς γῆς ("on the earth") in Romans 9:28. It is possible that Paul adapted the phrase ἐπὶ τῆς γῆς from Hosea 2:23a (LXX 2:25a), which is the context of the quotation in Romans 9:25. If this is so, Paul possibly referred to this context because of the verb σπείρω ("seed") which is found in LXX Hosea 2:25a and its possible connection with the σπέρμα of Israel in Romans 9:29. In addition, the context of LXX Hosea 2:25 is the NE motif. All these factors point to Hosea 2:25 as a good possibility for the source of ἐπὶ τῆς γῆς in Romans 9:28. If this is the case, then Paul's overall argument of Romans 9:25-29 is strengthened.

Finally, Paul ends his four quotations in a row with Isaiah 1:9. This Old Testament quotation refers to the destruction of Sodom and Gomorrah in Genesis 18-19 and the σπέρμα of the Abrahamic promise. The continuity of the two Isaiah quotations in Romans 9:27-29 uses the Abrahamic promise; and the setting of the salvation of the remnant or the seed is placed in the context of the deserved judgment of God. The context of Isaiah 1:9 is positioned in an INE and the wisdom polemic. The background setting of Sodom and Gomorrah accentuates the devastating judgment (Rom 9:29b) and in a secondary way highlights only a small number (a remnant) that would escape. The context of Exodus 32:13 and 33:1 accents the mercy of God in continuing God's unconditional promises to a sinful, stiff-neck people that do not deserve it (Rom 9:29a). These two Exodus motifs provide the framework and contextual milieu for Paul to make his argument when he chose Isaiah 1:9 in Romans 9:29.

---

[352] Some would say that Isa 28:22b was also conflated with Hos 1:10a (LXX 2:1a) and Isa 10:22-23 (Wagner, *Heralds of the Good News*, 95-100).

One of the reasons Paul chose Isaiah 1:9 is for the LXX word σπέρμα ("seed"). The word σπέρμα also parallels the word "remnant" (ὑπόλειμμα) in Romans 9:27. Paul knows that during the present time there is a partial hardening and judgment (Rom 11:7-10, 25) upon the "sons of Israel" (Rom 9:27) and he wants to give eternal hope to those who he calls the "remnant," and the "seed" (Rom 9:27, 29). However, Paul desires Israel to sense that their overwhelming sinfulness deserves to be judged like Sodom and Gomorrah. Because of God's promise to Abraham, God will express, in a NE way, his mercy by calling out a remnant-seed to be saved. Paul uses the precursor quotations of Hosea to refer to the Gentiles being called God's people. Finally, he applies the two Isaianic quotations with the conflation of Hosea 1:10a (LXX 2:1a) to answer the question about a true Israelite. His answer is that God has called, in marvellous mercy, his elective seed (the remnant) from Israel. Just as God promised to Abraham a seed, he is fulfilling that promise (Rom 9:6). God is also fulfilling his promise to the families of the earth (Gen 12:3c) by calling Gentiles to be his people (Rom 9:24). The NE motif provides the framework by which Paul may use Hosea and Isaiah to validate his argument to the Romans. This indeed would give his people hope to believe God's sapiential sovereign plan in the midst of God's judgment in the present age.

Application and Devotional Implications

In Rom 9:24–29 Paul returns to his thought in Rom 9:6, "For all those who are from Israel, these are not Israel." In Rom 9:25–26 Paul quotes from Hosea 2:23 and 1:10. The context of Hosea is the ten northern tribes of Israel, but Paul applies it to the Gentiles. There is much debate on this point, but it seems best to understand Paul's use as analogy (some call it typology). The contextual pattern arguments from the context of Hosea and the theological pattern from the Abrahamic promises provide an interpretative basis for the analogy (see above on the commentary section). Once they were not a people of God and now by God's grace there is an elective group of Gentiles that now through God's gracious call are brought to salvation. In 9:27–29, Paul stresses God's election of a Jewish remnant by using Isa 10:22–23 and Isa 1:9. If God did not interfere in Israel's history and save a remnant, the nation would have received the same condemnation as Sodom and Gomorrah. It is God's mercy in election which saved the remnant.

The proper response to the sovereign election of God in mercy and hardening is the humble submission of bowing the knee to the incomprehensible God with praise and glory. The rhetorical questions of Isa 40:13–14 brings this out: "Who has directed the Spirit of the LORD, or as His counsellor has informed Him? With whom did He consult and who gave Him understanding and who taught Him in the path of justice and taught Him knowledge?" (NASB). After Job listens to God's display of His majesty, Job responses by saying, "I know that You can do all things, and that no purpose of Yours can be thwarted. 'Who is this that hides counsel without knowledge?'" "Therefore, I have declared that which I did not understand, Things too wonderful for me, which I did not know." 'Hear, now, and I will speak; I will ask You, and You instruct me'" (Job 42:2–4). John in Rev 1:12–17 sees a vision of the majesty of the sovereign LORD and he says, "When I saw Him I fell at His feet as a dead man." May this be our response to the understanding of the sovereign LORD of glory! As a piece of clay may we humbly bow to the Potter in worship, glory, awe, and fear!

Selected Bibliography

Aageson, James W. Aageson, "Scripture and Structure in the Development of Argument of Romans 9-11," *Catholic Biblical Quarterly* 48 (April 1986): 265–289.

Battle, John A. "Paul's Use of the Old Testament in Romans 9:25-26," *Grace Theological Journal* 2 (Spring 1981): 115-29.

Beale, Gregory K. *A New Testament Biblical Theology: The Unfolding of the Old Testament in the New* (Grand Rapids: Baker Academic, 2011).

Belli, Filippo. *Argumentation and Use of Scripture in Romans 9-11* (Roma: Gregorian & Biblical Press, 2010).

Campbell, William S. *Paul and the Creation of Christian Identity* (London: T & T Clark, 2008).

Delitzsch, Franz. *Isaiah.* Biblical Commentary on the Old Testament. Translated by J. Martin, vol. 7, 2 vols in 1 (Edinburgh: T & T Clark; New York: Scribner and Welford [distributor], 1890. Reprint, Grand Rapids: Eerdmans, 1973).

Dunson, Ben C. *Individual and Community in Paul's Letter to the Romans*, Wissenschaftliche Untersuchungen zum Neuen Testament, 2/332 (Tübingen: Mohr Siebeck, 2012).

Durham, John. *Exodus*, Word Biblical Commentary (Dallas: Word Books, 1987).

Ellis, E. Earle. *Paul's Use of the Old Testament* (Grand Rapids: Eerdmans, 1957).

Hatch, Edwin and Henry A. Redpath. *A Concordance to the Septuagint and the Other Greek Versions of the Old Testament (Including the Apocryphal books)* (Akademische Druck- u. Verlagsanstalt, 1975).

Hays, Richard B. *Echoes of Scripture in the Letters of Paul* (New Haven, CT: Yale University Press, 1989).

Herntrich, Vokmar. "Λεῖμμα, ὑπόλειμμα, καταλείπω [κατά-, περί-, διάλειμμα]," in *TDNT*, vol. 4 (Grand Rapids: Eerdmans, 1967), 196–209.

Hoffman, Yair. "A North Israelite Typological Myth and a Judaean Historical Tradition: The Exodus in Hosea and Amos." *Vetus Testamentum* 39 (1989): 171.

Johnson, Elizabeth E. "Romans 9-11: The Faithfulness and Impartiality of God," in *Pauline Theology III Romans*, Society of Biblical Literature Symposium Series (Atlanta: SBL, 2002).

Johnson, Jr., S. Lewis. "Evidence from Romans 9-11," in *A Case for Premillennalism: A New Consensus* (Chicago: Moody Press, 1992), 199–223.

Koch, Dietrich-Alex. *Die Schrift als Zeuge des Evangeliums: Untersuchungen zur Verwendung und zum Verständnis der Schrift bei Paulus*. Beiträge zur historischen Theologie, vol. 69 (Tübingen: Mohr Siebeck, 1986).

McKenzie, Steve. "Exodus Typology in Hosea." *Restoration Quarterly* 22 (1979): 100–108.

Metzger, Bruce M. *A Textual Commentary on the Greek New Testament.* 2nd ed. (Stuttgart: Deutsche Bibelgesellschaft, 1994).

Moo, Douglas J. "Paul's Universalizing Hermeneutic in Romans," *The Southern Baptist Journal of Theology* 11 (Fall 2007): 62–90.

Moo, Douglas J. "The Theology of Romans 9-11," in *Pauline Theology Volume III Romans*, Society of Biblical Literature Symposium Series, No. 23 (Atlanta: SBL, 2002), 240–258.

Moulton and Howard. *A Grammar of New Testament Greek* (Edinburgh: T & T Clark, 1976).

Muraoka, Takamitsu. *Hebrew/Aramaic Index to the Septuagint: Keyed to the Hatch-Redpath Concordance* (Grand Rapids: Baker, 1998).

Ninow, Friedbert. *Indicators of Typology within the Old Testament: The Exodus Motif* (New York: Peter Lang Publication, 2001).

Nwachukwu, Mary Sylvia Chinyere. *Creation-Covenant Scheme and Justification by Faith: A Canonical Study of the God-Human Drama in the Pentateuch and Letter to the Romans* (Rome: Gregorian University Press, 2002).

Rooker, Mark F. "The Use of the Old Testament in the Book of Hosea." *Criswell Theological Review* 7 (1993): 51–66.

Schreiner, Thomas R. "Does Romans 9 Teach Individual Election unto Salvation? Some Exegetical and Theological Reflections." *Journal of Evangelical Theological Society* 36 (March 1993): 25-40.

Schreiner, Thomas R. "Corporate and Individual Election in Romans 9: A Response to Brian Abasciano." *Journal of the Evangelical Theological Society* 49 (April - June 2006): 373-86.

Shum, Shiu-Lun. *Paul's Use of Isaiah in Romans: A Comparative Study of Paul's Letter to the Romans and the Sibylline and Qumran Sectarian Texts* (Tübingen: Mohr Siebeck, 2002).

Stanley, Christopher D. *Arguing with Scripture: The Rhetoric of Quotations in the Letters of Paul* (London: T & T Clark, 2004).

Stanley, Christopher D. *Paul and the Language of Scripture: Citation Technique in the Pauline Epistles and Contemporary Literature*. Society for New Testament Studies Monograph Series (Cambridge: Cambridge University Press, 1992).

Strathmann, Hermann. "Λάος," in *TDNT*, vol. 4 (Grand Rapids: Eerdmans, 1967), 29–39.

Sullivan, Steven P. *The Isaianic New Exodus in Romans 9–11: A Biblical and Theological Study of Paul's Use of Isaiah in Romans*, 2nd ed. (Middletown, RI: Stone Tower Press, 2023).

Swanson, Reuben, ed. *New Testament Greek Manuscripts: Romans* (Wheaton: Tyndale House and Pasadena: William Carey International University Press, 2001).

Wagner, J. Ross. *Heralds of the Good News: Isaiah and Paul in Concert in the Letter to the Romans*. Supplements to Novum Testamentum, eds. M. M. Mitchell and D. P. Moessner, vol. 101 (Leiden: Brill, 2002).

Wallace, Daniel B. *Greek Grammar Beyond the Basic: An Exegetical Syntax of the New Testament* (Grand Rapids: Zondervan, 1996).

Watts, John D. W. *Isaiah 1–33*. Word Biblical Commentary, ed. John D. W. Watts, vol. 24. Logos 5 Electronic version (Waco: Word Books, 1985).

Wilk, Florian. "Between Scripture and History: Technique and Hermeneutics of Interpreting Biblical Prophets in the Septuagint of Isaiah and Letters of Paul," in *The Old Greek of Isaiah: Issues and Perspective* (Leuven: Peeters, 2010), 189–209.

Ziegler, Joseph. *Isaias*, Septuaginta: Vetus Testamentum Graecum, 3rd ed. (Göttingen: Vandenhoeck & Ruprecht, 1939, 1983).

Excursus

Isaiah 10:22–23, 28:22b and Hosea 2:1, 25 in LXX and Romans 9:25–28

Septuagint Isaiah 10:22–23	Septuagint Isaiah 28:22b	Septuagint Hosea 2:1; 2:25 (1:10; 2:23 Eng)	Nestle-Aland Greek NT, 28th Rom 9:25–28
		2:25 καὶ σπερῶ αὐτὴν ἐμαυτῷ ἐπὶ τῆς γῆς καὶ ἐλεήσω τὴν Οὐκ-ηλεημένην καὶ ἐρῶ τῷ Οὐ-λαῷ-μου Λαός μου εἶ σύ, καὶ αὐτὸς ἐρεῖ Κύριος ὁ θεός μου εἶ σύ.	**25** ὡς καὶ ἐν τῷ Ὡσηὲ λέγει· **καλέσω** τὸν οὐ λαόν μου λαόν μου καὶ τὴν οὐκ ἠγαπημένην ἠγαπημένην
22 καὶ ἐὰν γένηται ὁ λαὸς Ισραηλ ὡς ἡ ἄμμος τῆς θαλάσσης, τὸ κατάλειμμα αὐτῶν σωθήσεται, λόγον γὰρ συντελῶν καὶ συντέμνων ἐν δικαιοσύνῃ,		**2:1** Καὶ ἦν ὁ ἀριθμὸς τῶν υἱῶν Ισραηλ ὡς ἡ ἄμμος τῆς θαλάσσης, ἣ οὐκ ἐκμετρηθήσεται οὐδὲ ἐξαριθμηθήσεται, καὶ ἔσται ἐν τῷ τόπῳ, οὗ ἐρρέθη αὐτοῖς οὐ λαός μου ὑμεῖς, ἐκεῖ **κληθήσονται** υἱοὶ θεοῦ ζῶντος.	**26** καὶ ἔσται ἐν τῷ τόπῳ οὗ ἐρρέθη αὐτοῖς· οὐ λαός μου ὑμεῖς, ἐκεῖ **κληθήσονται** υἱοὶ θεοῦ ζῶντος. **27** Ἠσαΐας δὲ κράζει ὑπὲρ τοῦ Ἰσραήλ· ἐὰν ᾖ ὁ ἀριθμὸς τῶν υἱῶν Ἰσραὴλ ὡς ἡ ἄμμος τῆς θαλάσσης, τὸ ὑπόλειμμα σωθήσεται.
23 ὅτι λόγον συντετμημένον ποιήσει ὁ θεὸς ἐν τῇ οἰκουμένῃ ὅλῃ.	διότι συντετελεσμένα καὶ συντετμημένα πράγματα ἤκουσα παρὰ κυρίου σαβαωθ, ἃ ποιήσει ἐπὶ πᾶσαν τὴν γῆν.		**28** λόγον γὰρ συντελῶν καὶ συντέμνων ποιήσει κύριος ἐπὶ τῆς γῆς.

Romans 9:30–10:21

Outline

C. Israel's Knowledge of the Gospel of Righteousness: Faith and Works (9:30–10:21)

   1. Righteousness by faith and a "Law Righteousness" (9:30-33)

Original Text

9.30 Τί οὖν ἐροῦμεν; ὅτι ἔθνη τὰ μὴ διώκοντα δικαιοσύνην κατέλαβεν δικαιοσύνην, δικαιοσύνην
δὲ τὴν ἐκ πίστεως· 31 Ἰσραὴλ δὲ διώκων νόμον δικαιοσύνης εἰς νόμον[a] οὐκ ἔφθασεν. 32 διὰ τί; ὅτι
οὐκ ἐκ πίστεως ἀλλ' ὡς ἐξ ἔργων[b]· προσέκοψαν[c] τῷ λίθῳ τοῦ προσκόμματος, 33 καθὼς
γέγραπται· Ἰδοὺ τίθημι ἐν Σιὼν λίθον προσκόμματος καὶ πέτραν σκανδάλου, καὶ[d] ὁ πιστεύων ἐπ'
αὐτῷ οὐ καταισχυνθήσεται.

Textual Notes

[a] **9:31 νόμον** is supported by WH Treg NA28 UBS5 P^{46vid} ℵ* B A D G 6 81 945 1506 1739 2464. **νόμον δικαιοσύνης** is supported by ℵ^{c} F K L Ψ 056 104 365 630 1175 1241 1505 1881 𝔐. The shorter reading is probably correct. The addition likely came from a scribal assimilation from previous part of the verse (See Swanson, *NT GK Mss Romans*, 151; NA28).

[b] **9:32 ἔργων** is supported by WH Treg NA28 UBS5 P^{46vid} ℵ* A B F G 6 629 630 1739 1881 2200. **ἔργων νόμου** is supported by ℵ^{c} D Ψ 33 81 104 256 263 365 424* 436 459 1175 1241 1319 1506 1573 1852 1912 1962 2127 2464 2815 𝔐 (See Swanson, *NT GK Mss Romans*, 152; NA28; UBS5). UBS5 leaves νόμου out and rates this as almost certain to be correct. Metzger, *A Textual Commentary*, 462–463 supports this conclusion by indicating the short reading has strong support. The Pauline antithesis of "faith" and "works of the law" may have led to the addition of νόμου (Moo, 2nd, 639, n. 334).

[c] **9:32 προσέκοψαν** is supported by WH Treg NA28 UBS5 P^{46} ℵ* A B D* F G 1506 1739 1881. **προσέκοψαν γὰρ** is supported by D^{c} K L P Ψ 049^{c} 056 1 6 33 69 88 𝔐. (Swanson *NT GK Mss Romans*, 152; Hodges and Farstad, *Gk NT*). The omission of γὰρ seems to be early and strongly supported.

[d] **9:33 καὶ** is supported by WH Treg NA28 UBS5 ℵ A B D F G 81 1506 1881. **καὶ πᾶς** is supported by K L P Ψ 049 056 33 104 365 630 1175 1241 1505 1739 2464 𝔐. There is early and strong support for omission of πᾶς. UBS5 indicates that this position as certain. Longenecker (829) states that this variation is likely a scribal assimilations to the same citation (Isa 28:16) in Rom 10:11 (πᾶς ὁ πιστεύων). However, πᾶς is not found in the LXX Isa 28:16.

Translation

30 What then shall we say? That Gentiles who did not pursue righteousness attained righteousness, that is, a righteousness that is based on faith. **31** But Israel pursuing a law for righteousness, did not attain the law *for righteousness*. **32** Why? *It was* because *Israel pursued it* not on the basis of faith, but as though *it were* on the basis of works. They *(Israel)* stumbled over the stone of stumbling. **33** As it is written, Behold, I am placing in Zion a stone of stumbling and a rock of offense; and the one who believes on him will not be put to shame.

Commentary

9:30 Τί οὖν ἐροῦμεν; ὅτι ἔθνη τὰ μὴ διώκοντα δικαιοσύνην κατέλαβεν δικαιοσύνην, δικαιοσύνην δὲ[353] τὴν ἐκ πίστεως. **"**What then shall we say? That Gentiles[354] who did not pursue righteousness attained righteousness, that is, a righteousness that is based on faith." Schreiner (2nd, 524) is correct when he summarizes Rom 9:6–29 as God's sovereign will which upholds His character and His word while 9:30–10:21 demonstrates man's failure, specifically Israel's failure, to believe God and His word. The Gentiles are forgiven and have received a righteous status with God by faith alone (9:30). On the other hand, Israel pursued the law rather than to whom the law pointed. Thus, Israel's lack of faith in their Messiah has demonstrated their failure to obtain forgiveness and the righteous status before God (9:31–32). This theme is addressed and expanded in Rom 10 (Cranfield 504–505; Käsemann, 276, Moo, 2nd, 640). Moo (2nd, 640, n. 338) points out that on several occasions Paul introduces a question to respond to an objection that he had previously stated (3:5– 6; 6:1, 15; 7:7; 9:14).[355] On three other occasions he introduces a summary or enlarges on his teaching (8:31; 9:30; 11:7).[356] Paul is not speaking of the moral righteousness of the Gentiles but the forensic righteousness[357] before God (Moo, 2nd, 641).[358] There may have been some Gentiles by God's common grace who desired moral lives,

---

[353] The connective δὲ links a narrative segment and in this context, it inserts an explanation (BDAG, 213).

[354] "Gentiles" without an article gives a qualitative sense and not the emphasis on the number of Gentiles but their identity as Gentiles, opposite of Israelites (Moo, 2nd, 640, n. 341). Dunn (580), Cranfield (506), and Sanday and Headlam, 279 take it as not referring to Gentiles generally, but "some" Gentiles who believed.

[355] Τί οὖν ἐροῦμεν is used in Rom 4:1; 6:1; 7:7; 8:31; 9:14 and 9:30. Τί οὖν is used in Rom 3:1, 9; 6:15; 11:7. Τί γάρ is used in 3:3; 4:3; 8:26. Paul also uses τί ἐροῦμεν (3:5), τί ἔτι (3:7), and τί 'οὖν ἔτι (9:19).

[356] Fitzmyer (577) states that often a question follows the previous question like τί οὖν ἐροῦμεν so he takes 9:30b–31 as a question (see previous footnote). However, this would make the question cumbersome and long. The question in 9:32 also makes more sense if the preceding is a statement and not a question (Schreiner, 2nd, 523; Moo, 2nd, 640, n. 339; Dunn, 580).

[357] Hodge (517–518) makes a good summary of righteousness in this context: "*Righteousness*, δικαιοσύνη, uniformly in Paul's writings, means either an attribute, as when we ascribe righteousness to God; or, what constitutes righteousness, i.e., that which satisfies the demands of justice or of the law, as when God is said to impute righteousness. That is, he ascribes to men, or sets to their account, that which constitutes them righteous in the sight of the law. Sometimes, however, the word includes by implication, the consequences of possessing this righteousness. This is the case in this passage. Those who sought after righteousness, sought to be regarded and treated as righteous in the sight of God; that is, they sought after justification. This, however, does not imply that δικαιοσύνη signifies justification. It means *righteousness*, the possession of which secures justification. Justification is a declarative act of God; righteousness is the ground on which that declaration is made."

[358] Cranfield (506–507) refers it to a righteous status before God. Dunn (580) refers it to covenant righteousness: "righteousness defined by the covenant between God and Israel, or a righteousness which can be pursued only with the covenant and from which those outside the covenant, *ipso facto*, are excluded."

but even in their moral pursuit of excellence they were not seeking the one true God by faith (Phil 3:9). How did some of the Gentiles obtain this righteous standing before God when they did not pursue[359] it? The nearest thought in the context of Romans concerning this point is Rom 9:16. The pursuit of this righteousness which comes by faith has its origin in God's elective mercy (Schreiner, 2nd, 524).

9:31–32a Ἰσραὴλ δὲ διώκων νόμον δικαιοσύνης εἰς νόμον οὐκ ἔφθασεν. διὰ τί; ὅτι οὐκ ἐκ πίστεως ἀλλ' ὡς ἐξ ἔργων. "But Israel pursuing a law for righteousness did not attain the law *for righteousness*. Why? *It was* because *Israel pursued it* not on the basis of faith, but as though *it was* on the basis of works."[360] The major debate in v. 31 which flows into v. 32 and beyond is the understanding of νόμον δικαιοσύνης ("law of righteousness"). Some have attempted to translate the phrase "righteousness of the law."[361] Grammatically, the word νόμον ("law") is the accusative noun and δικαιοσύνης is the genitive modifier (or accusative predicate).[362] Before we determine the relationship between these two words in this phrase what does Paul mean by the word νόμον in this context? There are two basic understanding that are usually put forth. First, the word νόμον means a "principle," rule, order" (Sanday and Headlam, 279; Murray, 2:43). This understanding places the emphasis on the concept of righteousness ("the principle of righteousness"). Thus, they pursued the correct and worthy goal of righteousness, but they did it the wrong way – by works. This view has in its favor the emphasis of the subject of righteousness in vv. 30–32a. Paul has also used the word νόμον as a principle or rule in Rom 3:27b; 7:21, 23, 25c; 8:2. However, the concept of the νόμον δικαιοσύνης is further explained in Rom 10:3–5 and the concept of law in this context is not a "principle."

The second understanding of νόμον is that it refers to the OT Scripture. Two views emerge from this understanding. The first view sees the OT in its revelatory dimension taught by Paul in Rom 3:21–righteousness that is a witness to the law and the prophets. Thus, Paul would laud them for their worthy goal of the law which testifies of righteousness, but Israel's demise was the wrong means. Their attempted obedience to the Mosaic Law could not secure their righteousness (Cranfield, 508). However, the phrase "law of righteousness" in 9:31 parallels the phrase "righteousness based on the law" in Rom 10:5 and this verse does not refer to the revelatory dimension of the law but refers to the laws and commands of the Mosaic Law

---

[359] Fitzmyer (577) defines διώκω as "hasten, run (after), press on (to a goal)" and pictures a runner trying to reach his goal. Dunn (580) looks at the combination of διώκω/καταλαμβάνω in 9:30 and defines it as "pursuit and catching up or overtaking." However, Dunn and Schreiner (2nd, 523–24) think that the imagery of the race may be Paul's thought. Moo (2nd, 343, n. 343) acknowledges this possibility but concludes that the word is used too broadly to conclude this meaning. Furthermore, Moo raises the possibility that the phrase "pursue righteousness" may be derived from Isa 51:1 (see also vv. 2–7). Since Paul often uses Isaiah in Romans 9–11, some have concluded that Paul was borrowing from this OT passage. Moo is less inclined to accept this but the influence of this section of Isaiah 51–52 and its citing by Paul in Rom 10 increases its possibilities.

[360] Godet (369) places a comma after ἔργων so that ὅτι is dependent on προσέκοψαν. However, most agree that there should be a full stop after ἔργων and begin a new sentence with προσέκοψαν as an asyndeton (Sanday and Headlam, 280; Schreiner, 2nd, 527).

[361] Calvin (378); Shedd (306). Moo (2nd, 643-44) gives three reasons one may give for this translation in this context which he does not accept: (1) it is grammatically possible, and this would make the two groups (Jews and Gentiles) pursing the same goal "righteousness." (2) The overall context (9:30–31; 10:3, 5–6) has three successive and parallel contrasts with two kinds of righteousness. (3) Verse 32 gives two different contrasts (by works and by faith) and seems to relate it to righteousness.

[362] Cranfield (507, n. 4) is correct concerning this phrase: "an instance of hypallage, surely Paul would either have repeated the phrase in the main clause or else have put δικαιοσύνης there alone rather than νόμον." See also Meyer (2:163).

(Longenecker, 841).[363] Therefore, the best view is to take the "law of righteousness" as the laws of Moses.

Understanding νόμον as the law of Moses, how should the phrase νόμον δικαιοσύνης be understood?[364] It could be a qualitative genitive (Meyer [2:164] "justifying law"; Barrett [180] "the law purporting to give righteousness"), subjective genitive ("law that involves righteous"), adjectival use ("righteous law"), or a genitive of result or purpose ("law resulting in or which causes righteousness"). Schreiner (2nd, 525) is probably correct that the simplest meaning of an objective genitive (law "for righteousness") is likely the best answer. Israel was seeking a right relationship with God by the law.

This "law for righteousness" seems to be carried over to be the implied object of the verb ἔφθασεν ("attained") in v. 31 and the verb διώκων ("pursue") seems to be implied at the beginning of v. 32 (Sanday and Headlam, 280, Cranfield, 509; Moo, 2nd, 644–455; Schreiner , 2nd, 525; Dunn, 582). Then the translation would be: "But Israel pursuing a law for righteousness did not attain the law (for righteousness). Why? (It was) because (she pursued it) not on the basis of faith, but as[365] though on the basis of works."[366] Notice that the admonishment is not that they pursued the Mosaic Law but they did not pursue the law ἐκ πίστεως (on the basis of faith). What this means is also subject of discussion. First, Paul has no problem with Israel seeking to fulfill the law for God gave it to them as a covenant. Why then does he now fault them for seeking the "law of righteousness"? At least two issues are prominent: the manner and goal which they pursued the law (Moo, 2nd, 645). In v. 32, Paul states that they did not pursue the law for righteousness by faith. On the other hand, they had not fully understood their inability to obtain righteousness through the law and they had not connected correctly the understanding how the Christ would fulfill the law and be the only source of righteousness (Rom 9:33; 10:4). The Christological key was missing in their understanding of the law. Jesus Christ fully meets the demands of the law of righteousness and only by faith in Him will anyone receive the righteousness which the law promised. Paul made it clear in the earlier part of this letter that righteousness could not be obtain by works that could meet the demands of the law (Rom 3:20; 4:13–21; cf. Gal 2:21). Thus, those who correctly pursued the law in faith would believe in Jesus Christ because they were given an understanding that the law points to Christ.

Dunn (581–583) centers in on the problem of works (ἔργων) and defines them too narrowly as works that distinguish between Jews and Gentiles.[367] Jews were erecting boundary

---

[363] See Moo (2nd, 642–45) for a more detail critique. For a good summary of the study of law in Paul, see Moo, "'Law,' 'Works of the Law,' and Legalism in Paul," 73–100.

[364] The words νόμος and δικαιοσύνη occur in Rom 3:21 and 10:4, 5; Gal 3:21; Phil 3:6, 9 but they are not connected grammatically by case. The phrase νόμος δικαιοσύνης occurs once in the LXX in Wisdom of Solomon 2:11 and Moo takes it as a genitive of description, "righteous law" (Moo, 2nd, 644, n. 359). In Rom 2:13 you have νόμου δίκαιοι παρὰ ⸀τῷ θεῷ, ἀλλ' οἱ ποιηταὶ ⸀νόμου δικαιωθήσονται. Rom 3:20, Gal 2:16; 3:11; 3:24; 5:4 do not help in the grammatical case construction.

[365] The ὡς before ἐξ ἔργων gives the thought of subjectivity in the last phrase (Sanday and Headlam, 280; Moo, 2nd, 645, n. 364; Blass, DeBrunner, Funk, *A Greek Grammar*, § 452[3]). The subjectivity arises from the false conception that the law could truly promises righteousness.

[366] See the discussion from Sanday and Headlam, 280 and Cranfield, 508–509.

[367] Dunn's (581) distinction between Israel and Jews here is not established. Das, *Paul, the Law, and the Covenant*, 237–242 expands upon the problem of a too narrow view of Paul's concept of work and law. "The key word ἔργα refers to human activity throughout Rom 9–11 (as was the case in Galatians and Rom 2–4). Whenever ἔργα is used with νόμου or in relation to the law, there is nothing to indicate that Paul has only ethnic boundary markers in mind" (Ibid., 238).

markers (covenantal barriers)–circumcision, food laws, Sabbaths, etc.–that separated Jews and Gentiles. It involves the nationalistic righteousness which excludes Gentiles. The weakness of this view is that it wrongly restricts "works" (v. 31) too narrowly. There is nothing in the context that Paul is narrowing his thoughts to nationalism or those rites which separate Jews and Gentiles.[368] Israel is criticized for a law works (legalism) toward the OT law. On the other hand, it does not mean that all Jews were legalistic in this way in second temple period.[369] Some scholars espouse that Israel is being corrected only for not believing in Christ.[370] This point is true, but it cuts off the rest of Paul's thought in v. 32 and is guilty of only looking through the lens of salvation history (Schreiner, 2nd, 527; Moo, 2nd, 638–39).

9:32b–33 προσέκοψαν τῷ λίθῳ τοῦ προσκόμματος,·καθὼς γέγραπται· Ἰδοὺ τίθημι ἐν Σιὼν λίθον προσκόμματος καὶ πέτραν σκανδάλου, καὶ ὁ πιστεύων ἐπ' αὐτῷ οὐ καταισχυνθήσεται.[371] "Israel stumbled over the stone of stumbling. As it is written, Behold, I am placing in Zion a stone of stumbling and a rock of offense; and the one who believes on it will not be put to shame." The OT background and imagery of the conflation of Isaiah 8:14 and 28:16 is important to understand why Paul uses the combination in Rom 9:33 and also the solo use in Rom 10:11. The preceding verse (Isa 8:13) identifies the "rock" as "the Lord of host." This title accentuates the military background of the chapter and Isaiah brings to the fore the theme of judgment with the phrases "stone of striking" נֶגֶף (לְאֶבֶן) and "rock of stumbling" (מִכְשׁוֹל לְצוּר).[372] On the other hand, God declares Himself in Isa 8:14 as the people's "sanctuary" (מִקְדָּשׁ), if they will regard him as holy and fear him. Ortlund and other scholars affirm that the combination of "sanctuary" and "stone" enhances the picture of the temple imagery in the text.[373]

The people in Isa 8:14 are called upon to make God their sanctuary by calling upon Him to be their rock of salvation. Failure in this area will make God "become a rock one stumbles over–a trap and a snare for the inhabitants of Jerusalem" (Isa 8:14b). This metaphor involves the "falling, or missing of eternal salvation."[374] The understanding of the stone and cornerstone in Isa 28:16 is not as clear. Maybe this is one of the reasons that Paul used Isa 8:14 and conflated it with 28:16. Oswalt gives his understanding of the cornerstone: it "may be the whole complex of ideas relating to the Lord's revelation of his faithfulness and the call to reciprocate with the same kind of faithfulness toward him."[375] Thus, declaring the stone as the Messiah or something connected with Messiah is the central idea of many commentators.[376] However, there seems to be

---

368 Schreiner, "Israel's Failure," 216–217.

369 Das, *Paul, the Law, and the Covenant*, *passim*; Elliott, *The Survivors of Israel*, *passim*; and Gathercole, *Where Is Boasting*, *passim*.

370 Sanders, *Paul, the Law and the Jewish People*, 42; Räisänen, *Paul and the Law*, 174–175.

371 Dunn (585) is likely correct that BDAG's (517) understanding of καταισχυνθήσεται as "disappointed" is not strong enough. This word is used in Rom 5:5 where it has the context of future judgment (Käsemann, 279). See also Jeremias, *TDNT*, vol. 4, 275–276 who states that "Whether Christ as the stone is for salvation or perdition is decided by faith" (276).

372 Brueggemann, *Isaiah 1–39*, 78.

373 Ortlund, "The Insanity of Faith," 272, 275–76, 288. Watts, *Isaiah 1–33*, 370; Roberts, "Yahweh's Foundation in Zion," 44–45; Wildberger, *Isaiah 28–39*, 41; Beale, *The Temple and Church's Mission*, 181–82; and Bavinck, *Reformed Dogmatics,* vol. 4, 650–51 support a temple imagery. For textual interaction on Isaiah 8:14 and 8:26 see Roberts, "Yahweh's Foundation in Zion," 27–45 and Wagner, "Identifying 'Updated' Prophecies in Old Greek (OG) Isaiah, 251–69. For more detailed argument see Sullivan, *The INE in Rom 9–11*, 2nd, chp. 8.

374 Jeremias, *TDNT*, vol. 4, 276.

375 Oswalt, *Isaiah 1–39*, 518.

376 Some try to make the "stone" the law (Barrett, 181).

a relationship with the temple or a temple concept or type, which pictures the laying of a new foundation of salvation and judgment.[377] Childs concludes, "The symbolism of the stone encompasses the reality of the new community, a faithful remnant, which is a foretaste of the coming righteous reign of God and which is ushered in by the promised messianic rule of Zion."[378] Oswalt's definition with more emphasis on the Messiah (like in Childs' definition, as well as others) seems to best encompass the concept and background of the stone/cornerstone. God expresses in the metaphors of Isaiah 28:16 the importance of laying this truth in Zion through His Messiah.

For an Israelite, the portrayal of God's presence in the temple is a fundamental imagery. God was using familiar imagery of the temple foundation that conveys one of the most secure and stable physical elements in the Jewish world. In the spiritual realm, this imagery would powerfully communicate to the people an unwavering belief and confidence in God who is their sanctuary when the difficult and confusing times of judgment come.

The cornerstone foundation imagery would communicate to the mind of an Israelite the sanctuary where God dwelled first in the tabernacle and then in the temple. This imagery is also appropriated by Paul to express Israel's stark and grievous stumbling in unbelief, which deserves God's judgment. At the same time, the temple imagery conveys the most secure, sure, and foundational promise in which the people should place their trust – a trust in God's merciful salvation that is found in Jesus Christ, the "stumbling stone."

The previous context of Roman 9:32a launches Paul off to his statement in Romans 9:32b-33.[379] The Jews are pursuing νόμον δικαιοσύνης, not by faith but by works, and this failure becomes evident when God places in Zion the "stone that will make people stumble, a rock that will make them fall." In Isaiah 8:14, the stone/rock is easily identified as the Lord of hosts (Isa 8:13). At this point, Paul's metaphor is rooted in "his theological and Christological convictions."[380]

The irony is that the Gentiles who did not seek righteousness received it by faith. For the Jews, the law, which according to Galatians 3:24, was to be the nation's παιδαγωγός ("tutor, guardian, disciplinarian") until Christ came so that they may be justified by faith, has become an end in itself. This misuse of the law has become a hindrance and they have stumbled over the stone/rock. Moo summarizes Paul's thought by stating that "Israel has chosen to keep her focus on the law, seeking to find righteousness through it, when Christ, the culmination of that law and the only source of righteousness, has already come (see 10:4). For it is only in Christ that the demand of the law is fully met; and only, therefore, by accepting him in faith that a person can find the righteousness that the law promises (Rom 3:31; 8:4)."[381]

---

[377] Cheyne, *The Prophecies of Isaiah*, 166 says that "the foundation-stone of the temple in the solid rock of Zion . . . might well be regarded as a type of the unchangeableness of that temple's God." See also Brueggemann, *Isaiah 1–39*, 226 and Roberts, "Yahweh's Foundation in Zion [Isa 28:16]," 41–45 for more background on the temple concept in Isa 28:16.

[378] Childs, *Isaiah*, 209. Terrien, "The Metaphor of the Rock in Biblical Theology," 164 states it this way: "The rock, which at the end of time will be laid in the Zion of a new earth by Yahweh himself, will be a temple 'not made by human hands.' It represents not the foundation of human faith but the reality of a divine presence in the midst of a new humanity."

[379] Ortlund, "The Insanity of Faith," 286; and Seifrid (650).

[380] Wagner, *Heralds of the Good News*, 157. See also Cranfield (511–512). Campbell, *The Deliverance of God*, 1136, note 80 states only a minority believe the stone is something other than Christ and he agrees that the minority view is unlikely.

[381] Moo (2nd, 646) (see also his critique on pages 222–37) and Moo, "Israel and the Law in Romans 5–11, 185–216. For similar understanding, see also Thielman, *From Plight to Solution*, 111-115; Schreiner (2nd, 522–534);

The two most sacred objects during Paul's day in the nation of Israel were the law and the temple, the sanctuary of God. From the salvation history viewpoint, both the law and the temple were given to Israel so that God could dwell with mankind, especially Israel, and the law would instruct them about God and life (2 Chron 6:18-21; Acts 7:46-47; Deut 4:1-14). Furthermore, the law was given to lead them to God through instructing (Gal 3:24) and picturing (Lk 24:27; Heb 9–10) the work of Christ. Paul uses two highly important points, the law and the imagery of the temple, to demonstrate how severe and appalling Israel's stumbling over Christ really is.[382] The common point to both the law and the temple in this argument is the stumbling over the stone/rock which is Christ, who provides redemption to those who believe–a NE theme.

Biblical Theological Comments

The two most sacred and highly regarded items in the nation of Israel were the law and the temple. The rare and unique words of Isaiah 28:16 and 8:14 in combination with the building and architectural language of the temple (Isa 28:16-17) help to define the stone in a tabernacle/temple imagery and verify the NE motif. God uses the law to instruct Israel and to give them types and shadows to lead them to Christ (Gal 3:24; Col 2:16–17; Heb 10:1). The sanctuary of God (the temple) was the center of this instruction. In this place, God dwelled in a unique way; and in the temple, the people were able to have their sins atoned and approach God for worship. The temple and its function pictured and pointed to Christ. Thus, the temple and the law were embedded in the story of the NE and became the foundation and cornerstone of the life of the nation. Paul draws on these two major and fundamental points in the life of Israel to express two important and opposing points. First, how heinous and abysmal it was for the nation to stumble over the true meaning and function of the law and the temple. Israel has failed and stumbled because they have not believed and confessed Jesus as Lord for their righteousness, but pursued righteousness through works (law of righteousness). The nation deserved the righteous judgment of God. Second, even though the nation did not deserve God's mercy, God has provided redemption just as he promised in the Old Testament. However, this redemption is now offered to all (Jews and Gentiles) who will believe the rock and stone, which depicts Jesus Christ.

Application and Devotional Implications

The number one misconception on how a person secures a way to heaven is by works. If you take a poll on the streets of America, you would receive a variety of answers on this subject. People most often say that the way to get to heaven is to keep the 10 commandments, the sermon on the Mount, or my good works to outweigh my bad works. Others set up the golden rule as the way: do unto others as you would want them to do to you. Still others postulate that sincerity to one's beliefs are the ones who will be accepted. Is it possible that people in church that speak

---

Shum, *Paul's Use of Isaiah in Roman*, 217–219; Meyer, *The End of the Law*, *passim*, especially 177–229; Ortlund, "Zeal Without Knowledge," 23–37.

[382] For Paul's view of the temple imagery in the Corinthians letters see Lim, "Paul's Use of Temple Imagery in the Corinthian Correspondence," 189–205.

about Jesus Christ could be deceived by trusting in their religious activities as a way to heaven? Is it possible that you have stumbled over Jesus Christ and are trusting in what you know or what you are doing to be righteous before God? This is where Paul finds the nation of Israel in Rom 9:30–10:4. In Rom 9:30–33, Paul discusses Israel's stumbling over Jesus Christ and Gentiles accepting Him by faith.

Paul, in Rom 9:1–29 has laid out the sovereignty of God in election. His main point is that God is absolutely free to bring about His eternal purpose with His creation. God is obligated to no one, and He is accountable to no one. Now in Rom 9:20–10:21 Paul directs our attention to our human responsibility and to Israel's rejection.

Paul in verse 30 begins with a question, "What shall we say then?" This question refers back to Paul's statement about the Gentiles in vv. 24–26. The Gentiles who did not pursue God's righteousness are now receptive to it. This point is again a great illustration of the sovereign electing grace of God. Jews were zealous for the law, but the Gentiles did not have the law or care about it. Paul says it this way in Eph 2:11–13, "Therefore, remember, that formerly you, the Gentiles in the flesh, who are called 'Uncircumcision' by the so-called 'Circumcision,' *which* is performed in the flesh by human hands–*remember* that you were at that time separate from Christ excluded from the commonwealth of Israel, and strangers to the covenants of promise having no hope and without God in the world. But now in Christ Jesus you who formerly were far off have been brought near by the blood of Christ" (NASB). The Gentiles received salvation by faith and not through the law. In fact, no one, Jew or Gentile, is saved through keeping the law.

In v. 31 Paul contrasts the Gentile's faith with the Jewish pursuit of law for righteousness (see commentary section). In other words, they tried to obtain the righteousness of God by religious law keeping. However, they could not attain to God's righteousness. Doesn't the Mosaic Law display the righteousness of God? Yes, it does. Yet, notice the problem at the very beginning when God gave the covenantal law to Israel. In Ex 19:8, it says, "And all the people answered together and said, 'All that the Lord has spoken we will do!' And Moses brought back the words of the people to the Lord." In a fuller account Deut 5:27–29 says, "'Go near and hear all that the LORD our God says; then speak to us all that the LORD our God will speak to you and we will hear and do it.' 'And the LORD heard the voice of your words when you spoke to me, and the LORD said to me, I have heard the voice of the words of this people which they have spoken to you. They have done well in all that they have spoken. Oh, that they had such a heart in them, that they would fear Me, and keep all My commandments always, that it may be well with them and their sons forever!'" (NASB). The people's desire to obey the Lord's law was good, but they had not recognized their inability to do it. They had not realized their utter sinfulness and inability to obey God's law perfectly. In Rom 10:5 Paul says, "For Moses writes that the man who practices the righteousness which is based on law shall live by that righteousness" (NASB). This means that a person who wants to obtain the righteousness of God by keeping the law must obey the law in each and every command all of his life. This included a multitude more commands then just the ten commandments. James 2:10 catches this understanding when he says, "For whoever keeps the whole law and yet stumbles in one point, he has become guilty of all" (NASB).

Paul asked the question, "Why didn't Israel obtain this legal righteousness?" The answer comes forth loud and clear. It is because they pursued it by works and not by faith! What was the purpose of the law? The main purpose was to reveal the righteousness of God and to point out that man is a sinner. In James the author uses the illustration of a mirror. When we read and study God's Word it becomes like a mirror to show where our face is dirty with sin. Yet, no one in his right mind will take down the mirror and ty to wash his face with the mirror. The same thing can be said about the law. The moral law points out that our face is dirty, but the law is helpless to cleanse us from sin. The law is good and perfect, but the law only condemns us because we cannot perfectly keep the law.

The Jews have the fullest revelation of God's Word about salvation but they stumbled over the most crucial and critical point. They turn to the law and law keeping instead of being convicted by the law and turn to the seed of the Abrahamic covenant which is Jesus Christ and place their trust in Him (Gal 3:13–29). He alone can impute to us God's righteous status and He does this only to those who believe upon Jesus' saving work on the cross. Israel more than any other people had the advantage. The law at nearly every point pictured and pointed to Christ. The very stone which was given to them as THE step to raise them to heaven is the very stone which they stumbled over and now will crush them in judgment if they do not believe.

My beloved, we can look with shame and wag our heads at Israel, but Christendom is no different! One preacher and another evangelist estimated that only 25–50% of their congregations were truly saved on a given Sunday! The rest are religious and talk a good "game," but they are lost! Many have testified that they thought they were saved because they grew up in the church and knew a few Bible stories but they were deceived and lost. My friend, you may have grown up in Sunday school and gone to church regularly, sang in the choir, served on committees and even taught a Bible class, but it is also possible that you are lost in your sins. It is even possible to confess Christ as your Savior, but in reality, it is only an intellectual assent and not a heart saving faith! I believe one of the most horrifying verses in Scripture is found in Mat 7:22–23 when Jesus says, "Many will say to Me on that day, Lord, Lord, did we not prophesy in Your name, and in your name cast out demons, and in Your name perform many miracles? And then I will declare to them, I never knew you; depart from Me, you who practice lawlessness." Reader, examine your heart this day! Do not be deceived! Are you religious or are you saved? Have you stumbled over THE ROCK?

Selected Bibliography

Bavinck, Herman. *Reformed Dogmatics, Holy Spirit, Church, and New Creation.* Translated by John Bolt and John Vriend, vol. 4 (Grand Rapids, Baker Academic, 2008).

Beale, Gregory K. *The Temple and Church's Mission: A Biblical Theology of the Dwelling Place of God.* New Studies in Biblical Theology, ed. D. A. Carson, 17 (Downers Grover: InterVarsity Press, 2004).

Blass, Friedrich, Albert Debrunner, and Robert Walter Funk. *A Greek Grammar of the New Testament and Other Early Christian Literature* (Chicago: University of Chicago Press, 1961).

Brueggemann, Walter. *Isaiah 1–39.* Westminster Bible Companion, eds. Patrick D. Miller and David L. Bartlett (Louisville: Westminster John Knox Press, 1998).

Campbell, Douglas A. *The Deliverance of God: An Apocalyptic Rereading of Justification in Paul* (Grand Rapids: Eerdmans, 2009).

Cheyne, T. K. *The Prophecies of Isaiah.* 5th ed. revised, in 2 vols. (New York: Thomas Whitaker, 1895).

Childs, Brevard S. *Isaiah.* Old Testament Library (Louisville: Westminster John Knox, 2001).

Das, A. Andrew. *Paul, the Law, and the Covenant* (Peabody, MA: Hendrickson, 2001).

Elliott, Mark A. *The Survivors of Israel: A Reconsideration of the Theology of Pre-Christian Judaism* (Grand Rapids: Eerdmans, 2000).

Gathercole, Simon J. *Where Is Boasting? Early Jewish Soteriology and Paul's Response in Romans 1–5* (Grand Rapids: Eerdmans, 2003).

Hodges, Zane C. and Arthur L. Farstad, ed. *The Greek New Testament According to the Majority Text* (Nashville: Nelson, 1982).

Jeremias, Joachim. "Λίθος, Λίθινος," ed. Gerhard Kittel, Geoffrey W. Bromiley, and Gerhard Friedrich, *TDNT* Grand Rapids, MI: Eerdmans, 1959), 268–280.

Lim, Kar Yong. "Paul's Use of Temple Imagery in the Corinthian Correspondence: The Creation of Christian Identity." In *Reading Paul in Context: Explorations in Identity Formation Essays in Honour of William S. Campbell*, eds. Kathy Ehrensperger and J. Brian Tucker. Library of New Testament Studies, ed. Mark Goodacre, 428, 189–205 (London: T & T Clark, 2010).

Metzger, Bruce M. *A Textual Commentary on the Greek New Testament.* 2nd ed. (Stuttgart: Deutsche Bibelgesellschaft, 1994).

Meyer, Jason C. *The End of the Law: Mosaic Covenant in Pauline Theology*. NAC Studies in Bible and Theology, ed. E. Ray Clendenen (Nashville: B & H Academic, 2009).

Moo, Douglas J. "Israel and the Law in Romans 5–11: Interaction with the New Perspective." In *Justification and Variegated Nomism: Paradoxes of Paul*, eds. D. A. Carson, Peter T. O'Brien, and Mark A. Seifrid. Vol. 2, 185–216 (Grand Rapids: Baker Academic, 2004).

Moo, Douglas J. "'Law,' 'Works of the Law,' and Legalism in Paul." *Westminster Journal* 45 (Spring, 1983), 73–100.

Ortlund, Dane C. "The Insanity of Faith: Paul's Theological Use of Isaiah in Romans 9:33." *Trinity Journal* 30 (Fall 2009): 269–288.

Ortlund, Dane C. "'Zeal Without Knowledge': For What Did Paul Criticize His Fellow Jews in Romans 10:2–3?" *Westminster Theological Journal* 73 (Spring 2011): 23–37.

Räisänen, Heikki. *Paul and the Law*, 2nd ed. (Eugene, OR: Wpif and Stock, 2010).

Roberts, J. J. M. "Yahweh's Foundation in Zion," *Journal of Biblical Literature* 106 (1987): 27–45.

Sanders, E. P. *Paul, the Law, and the Jewish People* (Minneapolis: Fortress Press, 1983).

Swanson, Reuben, ed. *New Testament Greek Manuscripts: Romans* (Wheaton: Tyndale House and Pasadena: William Carey International University Press, 2001).

Schreiner, Thomas R. "Israel's Failure to Attain Righteousness in Romans 9:30–10:3." *Trinity Journal* 12 (1991): 209–220.

Shum, Shiu-Lun. *Paul's Use of Isaiah in Romans: A Comparative Study of Paul's Letter to the Romans and the Sibylline and Qumran Sectarian Texts* (Tübingen: Mohr Siebeck, 2002).

Terrien, Samuel. "The Metaphor of the Rock in Biblical Theology." In *God in the Fray: A Tribute to Walter Brueggemann*. eds. T. Linafelt and T. K. Beal, 157–71 (Minneapolis: Fortress Press, 1998).

Thielman, Frank. *From Plight to Solution: A Jewish Framework for Understanding Paul's View of the Law in Galatians and Romans*. Novum Testamentum Supplements, 61 (Leiden: Brill, 1989).

Wagner, J. Ross. "Identifying 'Updated' Prophecies in the Old Greek (OG) Isaiah: Isaiah 8:11–16 as a Test Case." *Journal of Biblical Literature* 126 (2007): 251–69.

Wagner, J. Ross. *Heralds of the Good News: Isaiah and Paul in Concert in the Letter to the Romans*. Supplements to Novum Testamentum, eds. M. M. Mitchell and D. P. Moessner, vol. 101 (Leiden: Brill, 2002).
Watts, John D. W. *Isaiah 1–33*. Word Biblical Commentary, ed. John D. W. Watts, vol. 24. Logos 5 Electronic version (Waco: Word Books, 1985).
Wildberger, Hans. *Isaiah 28–39: A Commentary*. Continental Commentaries. Translated by Thomas H. Trapp (Minneapolis: Fortress Press, 2002).

Romans 10:1–4

Outline

C. Israel's Knowledge of the Gospel of Righteousness: Faith and Works (9:30–10:21)
  1. Righteousness by faith and a "Law Righteousness" (9:30-33)
  2. Israel's Lack of Understanding Concerning Righteousness (10:1-4)

Original Text

10.1 Ἀδελφοί, ἡ μὲν εὐδοκία τῆς ἐμῆς καρδίας καὶ ἡ δέησις[a] πρὸς τὸν θεὸν ὑπὲρ αὐτῶν[b] εἰς
σωτηρίαν. 2 μαρτυρῶ γὰρ αὐτοῖς ὅτι ζῆλον θεοῦ ἔχουσιν· ἀλλ' οὐ κατ' ἐπίγνωσιν, 3 ἀγνοοῦντες
γὰρ τὴν τοῦ θεοῦ δικαιοσύνην, καὶ τὴν ἰδίαν[c] ζητοῦντες στῆσαι, τῇ δικαιοσύνῃ τοῦ θεοῦ οὐχ
ὑπετάγησαν· 4 τέλος γὰρ νόμου Χριστὸς εἰς δικαιοσύνην παντὶ τῷ πιστεύοντι.

Textual Notes

[a] **10:1 δέησις** is supported by WH Treg NA28 UBS5 SBLGNT P[46] ℵ A (δέηεσις) B D Ψ 139* 1573 1739. **δέησις ἡ** is supported by K L 049 056 1 33 69, 𝔐. The early strong support for δέησις alone is amply supported (Swanson, *NT GK Mss*, 153).
[b] **10:1 αὐτῶν** is supported by WH Treg NA28 UBS5 SBLGNT P[46] ℵ A B D F G 6 365 1506 1739 1881 1962. It is the shortest reading and attested by early witnesses. **τοῦ Ἰσραήλ ἐστιν** is supported by K L 049 056 81 104 629 630 1175 1241 2464 𝔐 (**αὐτῶν ἐστιν** ℵ[c] P Ψ 33 88 1505 2344): the addition of ἐστιν may have been added to clarify the grammar and the addition of τοῦ Ἰσραήλ is postulated that it "may have occurred when this verse was made the beginning of a lesson read in church service." Also, the restatement from 9:31 that it is "the people of God" may have been asserted to stress Paul's concern (Metzger, *A Textual Commentary*, 463; Swanson, *NT GK Mss*, 154; Longenecker, 829–830).
[c] **10:3 ἰδίαν** is supported by WH Treg SBLGNT A B D* P 81 365 629 630 1506 1573 1739 1881. **ἰδίαν δικαιοσύνην** is supported by NA28 & UBS5 place δικαιοσύνην in brackets in the text; P[46] ℵ D[c] F G K L Ψ 049 1 6 33 104 1175 1241 1505 2464 𝔐 (Swanson, *NT GK Mss*, 154). It is difficult to determine whether to include or not to include δικαιοσύνην. However, if the

word is to be left out the idea of "righteousness" is strongly implied in the context (Longenecker, 830). Käsemann (281) concludes that a scribe most likely added the word to clarify ἰδίαν. Moo (630, n. 2) points out that the Alexander witness with the Western witness together probably gives the best evidence for ἰδίαν. However, the addition of δικαιοσύνην has the Alexandrian (P^{46} ℵ), Western and Byzantine witnesses. It seems best to put it in brackets like NA28 and UBS5.

Translation

1 Brothers and sisters, indeed, the desire of my heart and the prayer to God on their behalf is for their salvation. **2** For I testify about them that they have zeal for God, but it is not according to knowledge. **3** For, not knowing about the righteousness of God and seeking to establish their own *righteousness*, they have not subjected themselves to the righteousness of God. **4** For Christ is the goal and end of the law, with reference to righteousness to everyone who believes.

Commentary

10:1 Ἀδελφοί, ἡ μὲν εὐδοκία τῆς[383] ἐμῆς καρδίας καὶ ἡ δέησις πρὸς τὸν θεὸν ὑπὲρ [b]αὐτῶν εἰς σωτηρίαν. "Brothers and sisters, indeed, the desire of my heart and the prayer to God on their behalf is for their salvation." Paul uses γὰρ ("for") four times in vv. 2–5. In verses 2–3, he explains further the condition of his Jewish brethren that was stated in 9:30–33. However, in 10:1 Paul begins with his heart felt burden for their lost condition just like he began in Rom 9. He begins with the vocative expression Ἀδελφοί ("brethren") which kindly addresses the family of believers both brothers and sisters, but also functioned as a signal that he is about to convey some important and serious information (Longenecker, 845).[384] He accents his introduction with the postpositive particle μὲν ("indeed") that emphasizes the desire of his heart.[385] Thus, Paul's desire expresses his will[386] and he does this through prayer[387] that his Jewish kinsmen might be saved. This verse gives us an important lesson concerning God's sovereign viewpoint and the viewpoint of man's responsibility. In Rom 9, Paul gave us the viewpoint on how God understands salvation. God knows and has determined man's viewpoint and responsibility in salvation but God's divine viewpoint is profoundly different. God sovereignly determines by His own will whom He will elect and call (9:11). God's choice is not based on what people do or don't do, or what they will do or will not do, but by God's will He gives mercy and hardens

---

[383] Robertson, *A Grammar of the Greek*, 685 states, "The possessives in the N. T. usually have the article save when predicate. Thus ἡ ἐμή (Jo. 5:30), τῆς ἐμῆς (Ro. 10:1), τὸ ἐμόν (Mt. 18:20), τῷ σῷ (Mt. 7:3), etc."

[384] Blass, Debrunner, Funk, *A Greek Grammar*, §463 indicates that this asyndeton springs from Paul's emotional appeal (Fitzmyer, 582; Morris, 377).

[385] Robertson, *A Grammar of the Greek*, 1151; Longenecker 845. Blass, Debrunner, Funk, *A Greek Grammar*, §447[4] translates this phrase "so far as it depends on my desire."

[386] Some have adopted the translation "good will" (Sanday and Headlam, 282; Murray, 2:47; Meyer, 2:171). Barrett (182) has "heart's will". The word can also mean "favor" (Eph 1:5, 9) or "will" (2 Thess 1:11). BDAG (404) has "desire of the heart"; Schrenk, *TDNT*, vol. 2, 746 has "heart desire"; Cranfield (513) "desire" (Hodge, 524; Dunn, 585; Fitzmyer, 582; Schreiner, 2nd, 529). This use seems best here.

[387] The phrase ὑπὲρ αὐτῶν ("on their behalf") is best connected to δέησις ("prayer") (Godet, 374; Dunn, 586; Moo, 631). It is possible to take it as a predicate (Cranfield, 513; Barrett, 182 "my prayer to God is in their favor").

others (9:16–18). However, man does not know the secret counsel of God's will concerning who God has chosen. God has charged believers to share the gospel with everyone (Mt 28:18–20; Lk 24:46–47). God is well able to use the proclamation of the gospel to bring His own to salvation (Jn 6:37, 44, 65). Murray's warning is appropriate: "We violate the order of human thought and trespass the boundary between God's prerogative and man's when the truth of God's sovereign counsel constrains despair or abandonment of concern for the eternal interests of men" (2:47). Paul will admonish everyone to believe the gospel in Rom 10:8–13. However, in 10:1 he gives us the example and the desire of the heart that a believer should have toward the lost–pray for their salvation. Again, the wrong conclusion which one may draw from Rom 9 is: why should someone pray when God has already determined the outcome. Calvin and the reformers gave at least two reasons a believer should pray for the salvation of the lost. First, it is true that God does not need us to be involved in bringing people to salvation, but He has chosen to use us. He has ordained not only the end (the salvation of people) but also the means to that end (prayers, proclamation of the gospel and other things He may use). We have the great privilege to be used as part of the divine plan of God. Second, our prayers bring us in contact with our Lord who brings about manifold changes to mold us into His image and glory (Rom 8:29; 2 Cor 4:18).[388]

10:2 μαρτυρῶ γὰρ αὐτοῖς ὅτι ζῆλον θεοῦ ἔχουσιν· ἀλλ' οὐ κατ' ἐπίγνωσιν. "For I testify about them that they have zeal for God, but it is not according to knowledge." The γὰρ ("for") is used to give the reason for Paul's earnest prayer in v. 1. Paul's Jewish brethren were so close to the truth in one sense and so far from it in the true spiritual sense. Paul could testify about this kind of zeal which he also had for his ancestral traditions[389] before his Christian conversion (Acts 22:3–5; Gal 1:13–14; Phil 3:4–6). It is possible to say that Paul had the broad subject of the law and the temple in mind (Fitzmyer, 583). These two topics are in view in his comments and citation in Rom 9:30–33. The word ἐπίγνωσιν ("knowledge") is most often associated with God and the truth of God.[390] They did not know God or have the righteousness of God which only comes through faith in Jesus Christ (9:3–4, 9–10). Dunn (587) states, "Paul now judges his fellow Jews' and his own former zeal as misdirected—that is, not based on a recognition of how God's righteousness is bestowed (the point he elaborates in v 3), nor issuing in commendable living (defending prerogative by killing, rather than fulfilling the law by loving one's neighbor—13:8)." Calvin reminds us, "For it is better, as *Augustine* says, even to go limping in the right way than to run with all our might out of the way" (Calvin, 382).

10:3 ἀγνοοῦντες γὰρ τὴν τοῦ θεοῦ δικαιοσύνην, καὶ τὴν ἰδίαν ζητοῦντες στῆσαι, τῇ δικαιοσύνῃ τοῦ θεοῦ οὐχ ὑπετάγησαν. "For, not knowing about the righteousness of God and seeking to establish their own *righteousness*, they have not subjected themselves to the righteousness of

---

[388] See Woznicki, "Is Prayer Redundant?" 333–348; Packer, *Evangelism and Sovereignty of God*, *passim*; Schreiner, 543. *Contra* Dunn (586); Leenhardt (264).

[389] This zeal for the Jewish ancestral tradition may include some nationalistic zeal but it is not stated that this is the center of his thought (*contra* Dunn, 586–587). See Schreiner (2nd, 530), Dunn (586), and Jewett (616–617) for examples in the OT, Apocryphal, Qumran, and other sources.

[390] Bultmann, *TDNT*, vol. 1, 707 states that "the compound ἐπίγνωσις has become almost a technical term for the decisive knowledge of God which is implied in conversion to the Christian faith." Hackenberg, *EDNT*, vol. 2, 25 states it is a knowledge that recognizes God and the will of God, and it has an effect upon those who know God. At times, the context indicates that it is a technical term that describes "conversion to the Christian faith" (1 Tim 2:4; 2 Tim 2:24; 3:7; Tit 1:1). In this context (v. 3), many Jewish people did not know God; thus, not having the righteousness of God that would bring them in right (saving) relationship with God.

God." The γὰρ ("for") explains the lack of knowledge at the end of v. 2 as not knowing the righteousness of God. The two participles ἀγνοοῦντες[391] ("not knowing") and ζητοῦντες ("seeking") modify the main verb ὑπετάγησαν[392] ("have subjected") and help to explain why they did subject themselves to God (Schreiner, 2nd, 531; Moo, 2nd, 654, n. 401). Paul began this epistle by centering it on the gospel of God which focuses on Jesus Christ's saving work because in the gospel the righteousness of God is revealed (Rom 1:2–4, 16–17). This righteousness as explained in 9:31 is the righteous work of God by means of the cross whereby God declares righteous those who believe in Christ. This status of righteousness is given to those who believe in Christ and not by anyone's efforts (Rom 3:21) (Cranfield, 515). The possession of God's righteousness secures for us God's justification which is obtained as God's gift by faith alone. "Justification is a declarative act of God; righteousness is the ground on which that declaration is made" (Hodge, 518; see also Moo, 633). Paul states that Israel sought to establish their own righteousness and did not submit to the righteousness of God. The verb ὑπετάγησαν ("have submitted") is a constative aorist which describes the summary statement of how the people of Israel have responded (viewing the action as a whole).[393] Paul's understanding of their lack of submission to God's righteousness in this context is closely related to their lack of faith. Notice in 9:32–33 and 10:6 the emphasis on faith or their lack of faith. Moo (634) also suggests that the phrases "seeking to establish their own righteousness" and "their own" (righteousness) have a "general possessive sense" giving a "notion of status." Thus, the opposite (which is "the righteousness of God") would "include the idea of a status of righteousness conferred by God." There are two different ways to take the phrase "their own righteousness." First is a distributive sense ("each of their own righteousness") which would refer to each of the individual Israelite trying to establish their own righteousness (Calvin, 383; Murray, 2:48; Barrett, 183; Cranfield, 515; Kasemann, Moo, 634; Schreiner, 544). Second view is to take this phrase as a corporal sense concerning national Israel ("their [Israel's] own righteousness").[394] Those who espouse a corporate sense often state that this verse is against the Jewish nationalism that excluded Gentiles by erecting boundary markers (like circumcision, Sabbaths, food laws, etc.). There is no doubt that this kind of superiority may be present among Judaism, but the text does not indicate that this is the specific problem or the only problem. The Torah and all its commands seem to be more central to Paul's thought (Schreiner, 544; Fitzmyer, 583). Moo argues that "their own (righteousness)" and the contrasting parallel phrase "the righteousness of God" are not simply possessive but have a source nuance (634). Thus, the individual position is favored more than a corporate interpretation.[395] We should not conclude that all Jews sought their own righteousness from the law, but those who did seek law righteousness rejected the gospel in Jesus Christ. Thus,

---

[391] Dunn (587) citing BDAG, 13 suggests the translation of ἀγνοοῦντες as "disregarding." Jewett, 617 seems to be correct that Paul's earlier sense in Rom 1:13; 2:4; 6:3 and 7:1 has more of a neutral sense of "not knowing."

[392] Many declare that this is an aorist passive but has a middle sense (Blass, Debrunner, Funk, *A Greek Grammar*, §76.2; Godet, 376; Fitzmyer, 584; Murray, 2:49, n. 3; Morris, 379; Bergmeier, *EDNT*, vol. 3, 408; Delling, *TDNT*, vol. 8, 42). Moo (2nd, 652, n. 394) says it is not necessary to make it a middle and translates it "they have not submitted" (Lenski, 644).

[393] Wallace, *Greek Grammar*, 557. Some take this use as a historical rejection of the Messiah (Cranfield, 515). However, it is probably more of continual historical rejection of Israel but considered as a whole (Moo, 634, n. 19).

[394] Sanders, *Paul, the Law and the Jewish People*, 44–45; Dunn (587–588); Jewett (618).

[395] Rom 9:31–32 and 10:5 seems to have the same context of individual righteousness and not corporate. See Silva, *Philippians,* 160–162; O'Brien, *The Epistle to the Philippians*, 380, 394–400, 415–417 and their argument for individual righteousness in Phil 3:6–9.

many Jews did not submit to God's righteousness because they did not recognize the righteousness of God in Jesus Christ which is witnessed by the prophets (Rom 3:21). Furthermore, they mistakenly focused on seeking righteousness in connection to their obedience to the law.

10:4 τέλος γὰρ νόμου Χριστὸς εἰς δικαιοσύνην παντὶ τῷ πιστεύοντι. "For Christ is the goal and end of the law, with reference to righteousness to everyone who believes." For the third time Paul uses the conjunction γὰρ ("for") to explain that the righteousness of God is connected with the belief in Jesus Christ and not by obtaining it through the law. Matter of fact, the works and effort of people were never the way that human beings could establish righteousness before God. One of the crucial decisions in understanding this verse is how to understand the word τέλος. There are three basic understandings of the meaning of τέλος with some variants among the positions. Grammatically, τέλος is a predicate nominative and it seems to be placed at the beginning of the sentence for emphasis (Schreiner, 2nd, 531–32, n. 44). The word τέλος may be understood as: (1) termination or end (1 Cor 15:24);[396] (2) goal or purpose (1 Tim 1:5)[397] and (3) some have concluded it is both end and goal.[398] The word τέλος has a broad span depending on the context where it is used.[399] The meaning "end/termination" and "goal/purpose" for τέλος have been attested in Paul's writings. If we accept τέλος as termination/end then Paul is saying since Christ has come, the law in some way has ended. If we accept the meaning as goal/purpose then the relationship of the law is "in some sense directed toward, or pointing forward to Christ."[400] The view that understands τέλος as a goal has much to commend itself. For example,

---

[396] Dunn (590–591, 596–597); Hodge (527–528); Godet (376); Lenski (645); Meyer (172–173); Morris (380–381); Murray (2:49–50); Sanday and Headlam (284); Schreiner (2nd, 531–32); Schreiner, "Paul's View of the Law in Romans 10:4–5," 55–113. It must be noted that scholars differ on exactly what Christ has ended.

[397] Cranfield (519–520); Fitzmyer (584); Jewett (619–620); Fuller, *Gospel and Law*, 84–85. Some also give the translation "result" (cf. Rom 6:21) while others use "summation," "completion," or "fulfillment" (see Cranfield, 516–517, n. 2 for those who chose this view). Badenas, *Christ is the End of the Law,* 38–80 indicates that in nonbiblical Greek the meaning of "goal" (teleological sense) dominates and in the LXX and NT the meaning of "end/termination" is usually the meaning (see Moo, 639–640, n. 41 for his analysis of LXX and NT). However, Badenas points out that the historical church almost universally understood τέλος as goal in Rom 10:4 (Ibid., 7–37). He points out that the racing illustration in Rom 9:30–33 fits the thought that Christ is the goal of the race where the Jews stumble over him, but the Gentiles reached the goal (Ibid., 114–115). Schreiner, 545 is convinced that the racing illustration is dropped in 10:1–4.

[398] Barrett (184); Bruce (190); Dunn (589); Leenhardt (266); Moo (637–641); Bandstra, *The Law and the Elements of the World*, 105–106; Seifrid, "Paul's Approach to the Old Testament in Rom 10:6–8," 9–10; Strickland, "The Inauguration of the Law of Christ with the Gospel of Christ," 266–270; Meyer, *The End of the Law*, 212.

[399] See Henry George Liddell et al., *GEL* (Oxford: Clarendon Press, 1996), 1773. BDAG, 998–999 gives five definitions: (1) "a point of time marking the end of a duration, end, termination, cessation;" (2) "the last part of a process, close, conclusion, finally; in the end;" (3) "the goal toward which a movement is being directed, end, goal outcome;" (4) "last in a series, rest, remainder;" (5)" revenue obligation, (indirect) tax, tool-tax, customs duties." BDAG places Rom 10:4 under both (1) and (3). Moo (640, n. 41), Sanday and Headlam (285), and Schreiner (545) find only one indisputable verse (1 Tim 1:5) where the definition of "goal" is teleological. Moo (640, n. 41) concludes that Badenas (*Christ the End of the Law*, 71–76) finds more teleological occurrences which should be understood as "result" or "outcome". Here is where one has to make a decision concerning a broad or narrow view of teleological category.

[400] Moo (638). In this view, the relationship of the law to Christ seems to have at least three possible purposes: (1) Christ is the fulfillment or goal of the law (see Cranfield, 516–518 who indicates that many of the Fathers interpreted it this way). (2) Christ is the true essence or content of the law (Cranfield, 519). This view assumes that Israel should have understood that Christ is "in" the law (Moo, 638, n. 39). (3) Christ is the goal or aim

the context of Rom 9:31–32 has the content of pursuing and obtaining righteous according to the law. Thus, 10:4 speaks to the true goal of the law which is Christ. Secondly, Paul argues from the OT law when he references to Christ and righteousness (Rom 10:6–8, 11, 13). Therefore, Paul has in mind the true goal of the law which is Christ. (Moo, 639–640). On the other hand, there are plenty of indicators that Paul is arguing a discontinuity of the law and Christ (Rom 9:30–32; 10:3, 5–8) and in favor of a temporal termination of the law (Schreiner, 545–546; Moo, 640). Therefore, both emphases of goal and end are present in the context. Just as the law can be viewed by two perspectives in Rom 9:31–32, so a dual perspective seems to be used with τέλος in Rom 10:4.[401] Moo's (641) illustration of the race course is helpful. "The finish line is both the 'termination' of the race (the race is over when it is reached"–Christ brings the era of the law to a close) and "the 'goal' of the race (the race is run for the sake of reaching the finish line"–the law anticipated and pointed toward Christ). Most of the Jews had missed the righteousness of God because they have missed Jesus Christ. Christ's death and resurrection brought the righteousness of God not only to Jews but also Gentiles, to everyone who believed. Christ's coming brought the end of the era of the law where God dealt mainly with Israel, but now He deals with Jews and Gentiles in the church.

Commentators have defined νόμου ("law") in different ways. Some define it: (1) as law in general (Sanday and Headlam, 284); (2) OT revelation broadly speaking (Murray, 2:50); (3) law understood as legalism; and (4) the Mosaic law. The first two definitions are not clearly indicated in the context. The third use is possible but is not without debate if Paul used this concept as law.[402] Paul usual understanding for law is the Mosaic law and this seems best to use in this case (Hodge, 529; Moo, 636; Fitzmyer, 585; Morris, 380). However, what does this mean? It means that Christ and the new covenant is the basis of our relationship with God and not the Mosaic Law covenant. However, just because we are no longer under the Mosaic law does not mean we are without any "laws." First, part of the provisions of the new covenant is the indwelling Spirit (Rom 8:9) which gives the believer the ability to obey the law of Christ (Rom 8:3–4; 1 Cor 9:20–21; Gal 6:2).[403] Second, the Mosaic law is still profitable to the NT believer (2 Tim 3:16; 1 Cor 10:6–11), but the law must be used with a skillful and consistent hermeneutic (1 Tim 1:8; Mt 22:36–40; Rom 13:8–10; Gal 5:14; 6:2). What Paul states here in Rom 10:4 is like what Jesus says in Matt 5:17 (Moo, 642).[404]

Finally, how does the prepositional phrases εἰς δικαιοσύνην ("εἰς righteousness") connect in 10:4? Some scholars connect this phrase with νόμου ("law") as a general reference. This understanding would mean that Christ is the τέλος of the law according to righteousness or as a

---

of the law (Fitzmyer, 584; Jewett, 619–620). This view has more of a historical focus where Israel should have recognized in Christ the goal to which the law pointed (Moo, 638, n. 39).

[401] Das, *Paul, the Law, and the Covenant*, 251.

[402] See Moo (145–146, n. 7 and 388–391) for a good review of Paul and law. See also Moo, "The Law of Moses or The Law of Christ," 201–218 and "'Law,' 'Works of the Law,' and Legalism in Paul," 73–100.

[403] See Strickland, "the Inauguration of the Law of Christ with the Gospel of Christ," 229–279; Moo, "The Law of Christ as the fulfillment of the Law of Moses," 319–376. See also Schreiner, *The Law and Its Fulfillment: A Pauline Theology of Law*, *passim* and *Forty Questions about Christians and Biblical Law*, *passim*. For a variety of views of the law, see *The Law, the Gospel, And the Modern Christian Five Views*.

[404] Moo, "The Law of Moses or the Law of Christ," 217 summarizes the thought of Jesus fulfilling the law this way: "In that 'fulfillment' of the law, however, some of the Mosaic commandments are taken up and reapplied to the New Covenant people of God. Thus, while the Mosaic Law does not stand as an indifferentiated authority for the Christan, some of its individual commandments remain authoritative as integrated into the law of Christ." "In practical terms, this means that the Christian must always view the whole law only under the condition of its fulfillment."

means to righteousness (Dunn, 590; Hodge, 529; Morris, 381; Murray, 2:50; Schreiner, 547).[405] Most who understand τέλος as termination take it this way (see KJV, NASB, ESV). The second view takes the prepositional phrase as a purpose or result clause attached to the verse as a whole: "Christ is the τέλος of the law with a result that there is or with the purpose that there is righteousness to everyone who believes" (NIV, NRSV, NLT).[406] Both positions express the truth of sound theology, but the context is Jews who are trying to establish their own righteousness by the law. We could paraphrase the verse: "Christ is the goal/end of the law to establish one's righteousness for everyone who believes." It is true that εἰς δικαιοσύνην is closer to Χριστὸς than νόμου ("law") in the text but τέλος γὰρ νόμου (for the goal/end of the law") is moved up in the sentence for emphasis (Cranfield, 515; Schreiner, 548).[407]

In Rom 9:31–32 Israel pursued a "law of righteousness" and they failed to live up to that standard. Verse 32 says the reason why they failed was because they did not pursue the law righteousness by faith.[408] Then in Rom 10:4 Paul states the goal/end of the law is Christ. If Israel had pursued a "law of righteousness" by faith this would have led them to the Christ in the law and the "righteousness of faith"–as the law testifies (Lk 24:25–27; Deut 30:11–14). Meyer brings out the contrast as follows:[409]

The law falsely understood based on works:

1. Pursue the law by works (9:32)
2. Attempt to establish their own righteousness (10:3)
3. The righteousness of the law by works testimony = Lev 18:5 (10:5)

The law rightly understood based on belief:

1. Pursue the law by faith (9:32)
2. Submit to God's righteousness in Christ (the τέλος of the law) by faith (10:3–4)
3. Righteousness based upon faith testimony = Deut 30:12–14 (10:6–8)

Biblical Theological Comments

Paul in this section is expressing his thoughts concerning Gentiles having not the law and receiving righteousness and many Israelites who have the law and did not receive the righteousness of God. The central point of all of this discussion is "Christ is the goal/end of the

---

[405] Seifrid, "Paul's Approach to the Old Testament in Rom 10:6–8," 8–9, especially n. 29 indicates that the telic or result sense of εἰς or the function like dative of advantage (to or for) is more likely the view of εἰς rather than a restrictive sense of "with reference to." Moo (637, n. 34) concludes that there are no examples of εἰς being dependent on a noun (like νόμου) which is separated from the subject of the sentence (like Χριστὸς). Schreiner's rebuttal is that Paul's construction in Greek is relatively rare in the NT; thus, the exact parallel is not surprising. The construction of τέλος γὰρ νόμου is moved up in the sentence for emphasis (548, n. 41).

[406] Moo (636–638); Barrett (381).

[407] Das, *Paul, the Law, and the Covenant*, 252–253 gives a good summary of all the arguments concerning the different views of the syntactical connection for εἰς δικαιοσύνην.

[408] Moo, "Israel and the Law in Romans 5–11," 214–216 does not think that the Mosaic law demands faith since Paul in Gal 3:12 using Lev 18:5 argues that "the law is not of faith." However, he concedes that the OT demands faith as the "fundamental response that Israel is to make to God" (p. 215). It seems quite possible that this type of response is what Paul is doing since in Rom 10:4 he connects the law to Christ and then refers to Deut 30:11–14 and applies it to Christ.

[409] Meyers, *The End of the Law*, 213.

law with reference to righteousness to everyone who believes." The Gentiles who did not pursue righteousness in the law, have obtain the righteousness by faith in Jesus Christ. Whereas the nation of Israel (as a whole) pursued a law righteousness and did not obtain the righteousness in the law because they did not pursue the righteous one (Jesus Christ) for which the law revealed (Rom 1:1–4, 16–17; 3:21–22; 9:31–32). Paul connects Israel's failure to ignorance of God's righteousness though they had the knowledge of it in the law. They pursued the righteousness of God by the works of the law. The goal of the law pointed to Jesus Christ and when Jesus Christ came, He brought an end of the law. It is not possible to explain all the views and different aspects about the Mosaic law and its relevance to the new covenant believer.[410] The understanding of Sanders, Dunn, and Wright concerning covenantal nomism is overly simplistic. The Jews in Paul's day also emphasized the role of obedience to obtaining eternal salvation.

If someone asks if we, NT believers, are under the authority and rule of the OT as a code of conduct, we must say, "no and a qualified yes." In many ways we are not bound by the OT commands. The NT believer is not under the ceremonial laws or many of the social or civil laws of the OT. However, one of the main goals of the Mosaic law was to point to Jesus Christ. If one reads through Exodus, Leviticus, Numbers and Deuteronomy, one will see that all the feasts, sacrifices, and other things pictured, pointed, and prepared the Jewish people for their Messiah. The OT has many instructive points for the NT believer (Rom 15:4; 1 Cor 10:11). Thus, the OT should not be abandoned, and it should be taught in the church. But the OT in many places is no longer the ultimate standard for God's people. The OT is to be understood and applied in the light of its fulfillment in Christ.[411] Paul instructs us that we are under the law of Christ (1 Cor 9:20–21). James called it the "law of liberty" or the "royal law" (Jas 2:8–12). What is the law of Christ? It is those commands which are found in Christ, His teaching and the teaching of His apostles. It is basically the commands found in the NT under the new covenant. For example, nine out of the ten commandments are reinstated under the new covenant. However, before you place yourself under some kind of burden of rules lets hasten to say that there is a new dimension in the law of Christ. This new dimension makes it radically different from the old system. The new takes us to a higher level. It is the level of love: (1) If you obey the love command (love God and love your neighbor) then you are obeying the law of Christ (Gal 5:13–14; 6:2; Rom 13:8–10; Jas 2:8–12). (2) We should look at the love command (love God and love your neighbor) as something we cannot do from our own power. For this reason, God provided under the new covenant not only a new focus of love, but the ability to love and obey God through the power of the Holy Spirit (Rom 8:3–4, 12–13; Gal 5:16, 25). Therefore, our focus should be on Jesus Christ and not merely the commands. Our motivation to obey should be out of faith and love for Christ. The ability to obey will come from the Holy Spirit. When we lose our focus and we fail in our commitment then the Holy Spirit uses the law of Christ to convict us and cause us not merely to turn back to the commands, but strengthens and renews the heart to continue to love Christ and our neighbor.

---

[410] See the different views in *The Law, the Gospel, and the Modern Christian, Five Views*.

[411] Moo, "The Law of Moses or the Law of Christ, 206, 218; Moo, "The Law of Christ as the Fulfillment of the Law of Moses: A Modified Lutheran View," 376.

Application and Devotional Implications

In Rom 10:1–4 we see Paul praying for the salvation of his kinsman, Israel. Now, many people may be surprised that Paul would pray for others to come to salvation in the light of his view of the absolute sovereignty of God discussed in Rom 9. Paul, why do you pray if God has mercy on whom He desires and He hardens whom He desires? What's the use? The same kind of objection could be hurled at Paul when he talks about the necessity of proclaiming the gospel here in this chapter. Why preach the gospel if God chooses certain ones to be saved and guaranteed that they will come. If this is your thinking, then you have a misconception of the sovereignty of God and human responsibility. Paul has no problem praying for the lost, proclaiming the gospel, and believing in the absolute sovereignty of God because he believes that God decrees the means of salvation as well as the ends. It is through the means of prayer and proclaiming the gospel (as well as other factors) that God accomplishes His purpose. It is our privilege and responsibility as a Christian to pray and proclaim the gospel. When we do this, we become part of God's ordain purpose to accomplish His purpose. God can very easily do it without us, but it is our privilege that God allows us to participate in His eternal plan. Therefore, we like Paul should earnestly and sincerely pray for lost souls. It may be your prayer or your proclamation of the gospel that God uses to bring about His plan of salvation in other people's lives.

In Rom 10:2 Paul testifies that his Jewish kinsman have a great deal of zeal but little knowledge; so, it benefits them nothing in the spiritual realm in the sight of God. One of the most deceptive things which impress immature believers, and the worldlings is someone who is sincere in their belief and zealously acting out their belief. These people should be a rebuke for us as Christians if we are not living a devoted life for Christ. However, sincere beliefs are not the key. You may be very sincere in your beliefs but sincerely wrong! The key is whether your beliefs are true. Paul sees these sincere, highly devoted Jews clinging to the letter of the law as their means of salvation and refusing to submit to the righteousness of God in Jesus Christ. This devotion grieves Paul because all their sincerity, zeal, and devotion to the law will send them to hell if they do not abandon their own effort and trust in Christ alone for their salvation. Belief in Christ is the key for salvation.

In Rom 10:4 Paul buttresses his argument by declaring that Christ is the goal/end of the law for those who believe with reference to righteousness. The Mosaic law and the older order has an important key as its goal and end. The key is not the law of righteousness but faith in Christ who give us righteousness.

Three men, John, Louis, and Samuel were out to find the best time of their life. Willing to try anything, they were now on their way to New York City to "paint the town red." With a whole week ahead of them, they were anticipating some high times. They had money, position, and culture. The only thing they wanted was action and they were now ready to get it. They found the 29 story Ambassador Hotel and went in to obtain a room. At the main desk the clerk asked them what type of room they wanted and the three replied, "Give us the best you have! "The clerk looked at the register and then told the men that the only one of this type left was on the top floor (29 floors up). It had a TV, two cushioned chairs, and four beds. They took it. They went to the room and arranged their belongings and put on their tweed suit and went out on the town. Hours went by and the three began to get weary, so they headed back to the hotel. At the lobby desk they were told the elevator had developed some complications and would not be available to take them to the 29th floor. They could either take the stairs or sleep on the second-floor room that was much smaller and less luxurious. Though they were really tired they all agreed to take the stairs to the comfortable luxurious room on the 29th floor. The first few flights of stairs went quickly and easily, and the three companions were joking and having fun. Each flight seemed a little bit longer, but the men kept pressing on. Halfway up the journey they began really slowing down. On the 20th floor Sam sat down and said he could not go on. After resting a few moments, the others finally persuaded him to try it, after all only nine floors left and then those nice, soft mattresses and comfort would be theirs. At this point each flight seemed like a mile and it seemed as if it took an eternity to get there. All three men were now on their knees, crawling step by step in hopes of reaching the 29th floor–just one more to go. Slowly they proceeded until John shouted out that he could see the room, only eight more steps and then about 15 feet down the hall. With this added inspiration each fellow put all the energy into it that he had and to their relief they were all on the last floor. They had reached their goal and their mission ends as soon as the door is opened. They would enjoy all the luxuries which had spurred them on during their climb. Sam was the first to come to the door, so he reached down into his pocket for the key. To Sam's amazement the key wasn't there. He asked John if he had it, but John said that Louis must have it. They both looked a Louis but all he had was several empty pockets! Here they were on the 29th floor just inches from what they considered at this point heaven and yet they could not get in! They had forgotten to get the key![412]

My friend, this is an awesome illustration of a religious person. He is doing his best in life and possibly in the church, laboring in his work and for God's work, thinking they are inches away from heaven. But when they die and if they reach the door of heaven they will hear in great horror our Lord's voice, "I never knew you, depart from Me, you who practice lawlessness." It will be all because you forgot the key. The key is not my works and labor. The key is faith in Christ's death that paid for my sins and gave me the righteousness of God. The most important question that you need to answer is this: Do you have the key or have you been deceived?

Selected Bibliography

Arndt, William, Frederick W. Danker, and Walter Bauer. *A Greek-English Lexicon of the New Testament and Other Early Christian Literature* (Chicago: University of Chicago Press, 2000).

Badenas, Robert. *Christ Is the End of the Law: Romans 10:4 in Pauline Perspective* (Sheffield: JSOT Press, 1985).

Bandstra, Andrew J. *The Law and the Elements of the World: An Exegetical Study in Aspects of Paul's Teaching* (Kampen: Kok, 1964).

Bergmeier, R. "ὑποτάσσω." *EDNT*, vol. 3 (Grand Rapids: Eerdmans, 1990).

Blass, Friedrich, Albert Debrunner, and Robert Walter Funk. *A Greek Grammar of the New Testament and Other Early Christian Literature* (Chicago: University of Chicago Press, 1961).

Bultmann, Rudolf. "Γινώσκω, Γνῶσις, Ἐπιγινώσκω, Ἐπίγνωσις, Καταγινώσκω, Ἀκατάγνωστος, Προγινώσκω, Πρόγνωσις, Συγγνώμη, Γνώμη, Γνωρίζω, Γνωστός," *TDNT*, vol. 1 (Grand Rapids, MI: Eerdmans, 1964), 689–719.

Delling, Gerhard. "Ὑποτάσσω." *TDNT*, vol. 8 (Grand Rapids, MI: Eerdmans, 1969), 39–46.

[412] Tan, *Encyclopedia of 7,700 Illustration*, #5411.

Fuller, Daniel P. *Gospel and Law: Contrast or Continuum?* (Grand Rapids: Eerdmans, 1980).
Hackenberg, W. "Ἐπίγνωσις," *EDNT*, vol. 2 (Grand Rapids: Eerdmans, 1991), 25.
Henry George Liddell, Robert Scott and Stuart Jones. *GEL* (Oxford: Clarendon Press, 1996).
Meyer, Jason C. *The End of the Law: Mosaic Covenant in Pauline Theology* (Nashville: B&H, 2009).
Moo, Douglas J. "Israel and the Law in Romans 5–11: Interaction with the New Perspective." In *Justification and Variegated Nomism*, eds. D. A. Carson, Peter T. O'Brien, and mark A. Seifrid, vol. 2, 185–216 (Grand Rapids: Baker, 2004).
Moo, Douglas J. "'Law,' 'Works of the Law,' and Legalism in Paul." *Westminster Journal* 45 (Spring 1983): 73–100.
Moo, Douglas, J. "The Law of Christ as the Fulfillment of the Law of Moses: A Modified Lutheran View." In *The Law, the Gospel, and the Modern Christian Five Views* (Grand Rapids: Zondervan, 1993).
Moo, Douglas J. "The Law of Moses or the Law of Christ." In *Continuity and Discontinuity: Perspectives on the Relationship between the Old and New Testaments Essays in Honor of S. Lewis Johnson, Jr. ed. John S. Feinberg* (Wheaton: Crossway, 1988).
O'Brien, Peter Thomas. *The Epistle to the Philippians: A Commentary on the Greek Text*. New International Greek Testament Commentary (Grand Rapids: Eerdmans, 1991).
Packer, J. I. *Evangelism and the Sovereignty of God* (Downers Grove: InterVarsity, 1961).
Robertson, A. T. *A Grammar of the Greek New Testament in the Light of Historical Research* (Logos Bible Software, 2006).
Sanders, E. P. *Paul, the Law and the Jewish People* (Minneapolis: Fortress Press, 1983).
Schrenk, Gottlob. "Εὐδοκέω, Εὐδοκία," ed. Gerhard Kittel, Geoffrey W. Bromiley, and Gerhard Friedrich, *TDNT*, vol. 2 (Grand Rapids, MI: Eerdmans, 1964), 738–751.
Schreiner, Thomas R. *Forty Questions about Christians and Biblical Law* (Grand Rapids: Kregel, 2010).
Schreiner, Thomas R. "Paul's View of the Law in Romans 10:4–5. *Westminster theological Journal* 55 (Spring 1997): 55–113.
Schreiner, Thomas R. *The Law and Its Fulfillment: A Pauline Theology of Law*. Grands Rapids: Baker, 1993.
Seifrid, Mark A. "Paul's Approach to the Old Testament in Rom 10:6–8." *Trinity Journal* 6 (Spring 1985): 3–37.
Silva, Moisés. *Philippians,* 2nd ed., Baker Exegetical Commentary on the New Testament (Grand Rapids, MI: Baker Academic, 2005).
Strickland, Wayne G. "The Inauguration of the Law of Christ with the Gospel of Christ: A Dispensational View." In *The Law, the Gospel, and the Modern Christian Five Views* Grand Rapids: Zondervan, 1993.
Swanson, Reuben, ed. *New Testament Greek Manuscripts: Romans*. (Wheaton: Tyndale House and Pasadena: William Carey International University Press, 2001).
Tan, Paul Lee. *Encyclopaedia of 7,700 Illustrations* (Rockville, MA: Assurance Publisher, 1979).
Wallace, Daniel B. *Greek Grammar Beyond the Basic: An Exegetical Syntax of the New Testament* (Grand Rapids: Zondervan, 1996).
Woznicki, Christopher. "Is Prayer Redundant? Calvin and the Early Reformers on the Problem of Petitionary Prayer." *Journal of the Evangelical Theological Society* 60 (June–August 2017): 333–348.

Romans 10:5–13

Outline

C. Israel's Knowledge of the Gospel of Righteousness: Faith and Works (9:30–10:21)
   1. Righteousness by faith and a "Law Righteousness" (9:30–33)
   2. Israel's Lack of Understanding Concerning Righteousness (10:1–4)
   3. The Gospel of Righteousness and Law (10:5-13)

Original Text

10.5 Μωϋσῆς γὰρ γράφει[a] [b]τὴν δικαιοσύνην τὴν ἐκ τοῦ νόμου ὅτι[b] [c]ὁ ποιήσας αὐτὰ[c] ἄνθρωπος
ζήσεται ἐν αὐτοῖς[d]. 6 ἡ δὲ ἐκ πίστεως δικαιοσύνη οὕτως λέγει· Μὴ εἴπῃς ἐν τῇ καρδίᾳ σου· Τίς
ἀναβήσεται εἰς τὸν οὐρανόν; τοῦτ' ἔστιν Χριστὸν καταγαγεῖν· 7 ἤ· Τίς καταβήσεται εἰς τὴν
ἄβυσσον; τοῦτ' ἔστιν Χριστὸν ἐκ νεκρῶν ἀναγαγεῖν. 8 ἀλλὰ [e]τί λέγει[e]; Ἐγγύς σου τὸ ῥῆμά ἐστιν,
ἐν τῷ στόματί σου καὶ ἐν τῇ καρδίᾳ σου, τοῦτ' ἔστιν τὸ ῥῆμα τῆς πίστεως ὃ κηρύσσομεν. 9 ὅτι
ἐὰν ὁμολογήσῃς ἐν τῷ στόματί σου κύριον Ἰησοῦν, καὶ πιστεύσῃς ἐν τῇ καρδίᾳ σου ὅτι ὁ θεὸς
αὐτὸν ἤγειρεν ἐκ νεκρῶν, σωθήσῃ· 10 καρδίᾳ γὰρ πιστεύεται εἰς δικαιοσύνην, στόματι δὲ
ὁμολογεῖται εἰς σωτηρίαν· 11 λέγει γὰρ ἡ γραφή· Πᾶς ὁ πιστεύων ἐπ' αὐτῷ οὐ καταισχυνθήσεται.
12 οὐ γάρ ἐστιν διαστολὴ Ἰουδαίου τε καὶ Ἕλληνος, ὁ γὰρ αὐτὸς κύριος πάντων, πλουτῶν εἰς
πάντας τοὺς ἐπικαλουμένους αὐτόν· 13 Πᾶς γὰρ ὃς ἂν ἐπικαλέσηται τὸ ὄνομα κυρίου σωθήσεται.

Textual Notes

[a] **10:5 ὅτι** is supported by WH SBLGNT NA25 ℵ* A D* 6 33* 1506 1739 1881 2344. **Absent ὅτι** NA28 UBS5 ℵ[c] B P[46] D[2] Ψ P F G K L 049 056 𝔐 (Swanson, *NT GK Mss*, 155). The evidence for the ὅτι is mixed and it seems to be an early variant. Moo (2nd, 661, n. 424) points out that the presence of the ὅτι in this location makes τὴν δικαιοσύνην . . . the object of ὁ ποιήσας in the Lev 18:5 quotation (NASB, RSV). Sanday and Headlam (286); Murray (2:46); Käsemann (285) and Cranfield (520–521) support this variant. Those who do not accept ὅτι here (Meyer, 2:170; Godet 376–377; Dunn, 599; Morris, 381; Fitzmyer, 589; Moo 643, n. 1; Longenecker, 830) usually accept the ὅτι after νόμου (τὴν δικαιοσύνην τὴν ἐκ [τοῦ] νόμου ὅτι). See below in the textual critical notes in this section on Rom 10:5. Those who accept this variant most often accept also αὐτὰ after ποιήσας and accept αὐτοῖς at the end on v. 5 instead of αὐτῇ. External evidence is stronger for absent of ὅτι here and accept the ὅτι after νόμου. See below in the next three notes.

[b-b] **10:5 τὴν δικαιοσύνην τὴν ἐκ νόμου** ℵ* WH. A has την εκ πιστεως and SBLGNT has ἐκ **τοῦ** νόμου but no ὅτι after νόμου (see D* 6 1739 1506 1827 1881). τὴν δικαιοσύνην τὴν ἐκ νόμου **ὅτι** ℵ[c] B Ψ 945. **τὴν δικαιοσύνην τὴν ἐκ τοῦ νόμου ὅτι** is supported by P[46] D[c] F G K L P 049 056 33 1735, 𝔐. NA28 UBS5 place **τοῦ** in brackets. The ὅτι here is better supported and

whether the article τοῦ is before νόμου does not change the meaning of the text. The decision of NA28 and UBS5 is probably the best decision: τὴν δικαιοσύνην τὴν ἐκ [τοῦ] νόμου ὅτι.

[c–c] **10:5 ὁ ποιήσας** is supported by SBLGNT WH ℵ* A D 6 81 424[c] 630 1506 1739. **ὁ ποιήσας αὐτὰ** is supported by NA28 UBS5 P[46] ℵ[c] B F G K L P Ψ 796 1245 1319 1352 1448 1881 049 056 𝔐. The support from manuscripts from Alexanderian, Western, and Byzantine give evidence for αὐτὰ. However, it is not found in the LXX Lev 18:5. Paul does include it in his citation of Lev 18:5 in Gal 3:12.

[d] **10:5 ἐν αὐτῇ** is supported by SBLGNT WH B ℵ* A 33 1506 1739 1881. **ἐν αὐτοῖς** is supported by NA28 UBS5 P[46] ℵ[c] D F G K L P Ψ 049 056 1 88 104 365 1175 1241 1505 𝔐. The textual evidence is split and singular is often supported by context for it does not contain a plural reference (Longenecker, 831). However, it seems clear Paul is referring to the law which has many commands. Again the support from Alexandrian, Western, and Byzantine is strong external evidence. The LXX Lev 18:5 includes ἐν αὐτοῖς and Paul uses αὐτοῖς in Gal 3:12 when he cites Lev 18:5.

[e–e] **10:8** F and G supports **τί η γραφη λεγει** and D 33 88 104 326 365 1245 1319 1573 1611 1735 1837 have **τί λέγει η γραφη** (Swanson, *NT GK Mss*, 157). NA28, UBS5 SBLGNT and P[46] ℵ B A K L P and many others have **τί λέγει**. The previous variant is an explanation to τί and is a secondary variant (Longenecker, 831), Therefore, the earliest MSS of **τί λέγει** seems to be correct.

Translation

5 For Moses writes concerning the righteousness that is based on the law: "The man who does these things will live by them." **6** But the righteousness from faith speaks in this way: "Do not say in your heart, 'Who will ascend into heaven?'" (That is, to bring Christ down). **7** Or "Who will descend into the abyss?" (That is, to bring Christ up from the dead). **8** But what does it say? The word is near you, in your mouth and in your heart; that is, the word of faith that we are preaching. **9** For if you confess with your mouth that Jesus is Lord and believe in your heart that God raised him from the dead, you will be saved. **10** For with the heart one believes for righteousness, and with the mouth one confesses for salvation. **11** For the Scripture says, "No one who believes on him will be put to shame." **12** For there is no distinction between the Jew and the Greek, for the same Lord *is Lord* of all, bestowing riches to all who call upon him. **13** For "everyone who calls on the name of the Lord will be saved."

Commentary

10:5 Μωϋσῆς γὰρ γράφει τὴν δικαιοσύνην τὴν ἐκ τοῦ νόμου ὅτι ὁ ποιήσας αὐτὰ ἄνθρωπος ζήσεται ἐν αὐτοῖς. "For Moses writes concerning the righteousness that is based on the law: 'The man who does these things will live by them.'" The γὰρ ("for") in v. 5 indicates that v. 4 is supported by vv. 5–8. The righteousness of the law demands that a person must keep the law. However, no one is able to keep the law. There are at least three basic views on how v. 4 is related with v. 5. (1) Verse 5 is in positive relationship with v. 4 and in complement with v. 6.[413] The τὴν δικαιοσύνην τὴν ἐκ τοῦ νόμου ("righteousness that is by the law") in v. 5 is positive for the phrase conveys a person that does the law by faith and trusts the Lord. Usually advocates of this view take τέλος to mean "goal." They understand that vv. 5–8 is a demonstration of the goal of the law. However, the complementary view is not likely since in Rom 9:30–31 and 10:3 both bring forth a contrast: "righteousness that is based on faith" with "law of righteousness" (9:30–31) and "the righteousness of God" with "seeking to establish their own [righteousness]" (10:3). This contrast is also confirmed for v. 5 stresses "practice" and v. 6 "faith." Moo (2nd, 664) points out that the only other passage where "righteousness based on the law" and "righteousness based on faith" are found is in Phil 3:6–9 and in this context these phrases are in direct contrast to each other.

(2) The second view places a mild contrast between δικαιοσύνην τὴν ἐκ τοῦ νόμου ("righteousness that is by the law") and ἡ δὲ ἐκ πίστεως δικαιοσύνη (righteousness based on faith"). They identify the one who does righteousness is Christ. By doing the law perfectly, Christ has lived up to the law in Lev 18:5 and makes righteousness available to those who believe (Cranfield, 521–522).[414] Thus, again Christ becomes the aim and goal of the law. However, accepting this interpretation places Paul's application of Lev 18:5 (Rom 10:5) in conflict with the application in Gal 3:12. Though this view is possible, much of the context of both passages have much in common; thus, it is likely that the application of Lev 18:5 is the same (Moo, 2nd, 665). The generic references to ὁ ποιήσας ("one who does") and ἄνθρωπος ("man") to support this view is possible but not likely.

(3) The final view is that the δικαιοσύνην τὴν ἐκ τοῦ νόμου ("righteousness that is by the law") is in contrast to ἡ δὲ ἐκ πίστεως δικαιοσύνη ("righteousness based on faith") (Moo, 2nd, 664–65). The γὰρ ("for") in v. 5 introduces the section of vv. 5–8 or vv. 5–13. Rom 10:5 gives a negative argument concerning righteousness and works and v. 6 is a positive argument concerning faith and righteousness. The context of Lev 18:5 is a unit where God gives laws and exhortations concerning sexual relationships (18:1–30). In 18:1–5 the Lord gives a general introduction about obeying his statues and judgments so that the people of Israel may live. The same kind of statement is found in several places in the OT (Deut 4:1–2, 40; 5:33; 6:1–3; 7:12–16; 8:1; Ezk 20:11, 13, 21). At the end of Lev 18, Israel is again admonished to be obedient and warned that judgment would follow if they disobeyed (vv. 24–30; cf. Deut 28–29). Deut 30:15 and 19 are a good example how the Pentateuch understands life in this context as the reward that God gives his people for obedience to the law. Moo (2nd, 665, n. 435) states, "This life consists in material prosperity, deliverance from enemies and peace and longevity in the land that the Lord is giving the people (Lev. 26:3–13; Deut. 28:15, 19)." Therefore, the context of Lev 18:5 is not centered on eternal life but the reward or blessing of God based on obedience to the law. On the other hand, Paul principally and potentially understands if one could obey the law perfectly without breaking it they could obtain eternal life (Rom 2:13; 7:10). However, Paul is clear that no one is able to do this (Rom 3:9–20). Paul's argument is more of a nuanced one since in Rom 10:6–8 he brings in the context of Duet 30. Here Paul brings the obedience of the commands and the obedience of the heart by the provision of the new covenant. Obedience to the commands cannot give you eternal life, but those to whom have eternal life the Lord "will circumcise your

---

[413] Fuller, *Gospel and Law*, 66–68; Badenas, *Christ the End of the Law*, 120–125; Bandstra, *Law and the Elements, 102–110.*

[414] Bandstra, *Law and the Elements*, 103–105.

heart and the heart of your descendants, to love the LORD your God with all your heart and with all your soul, in order that you may live" (Deut 30:6).[415]

"This commandment" (הַמִּצְוָה הַזֹּאת) in Deuteronomy 30:11 refers back to the two כִּי clauses in 30:10.[416] The first כִּי ("if") clause in 30:10 concentrates on the commandments and statutes in the law and the second כִּי ("if") clause focuses on the internal source of the heart and soul, which must be either changed or strengthened to obey the law. Deuteronomy 30:11 sets up the continuity with the Mosaic law in one sense, which is the broader context of the prophetic portion in Deuteronomy 30:1-14, but there is also an element of contrast formulated in Deuteronomy 30:12–13.[417] Deuteronomy 30:12 says, "It is not in heaven, that you should say, 'Who will go up to heaven for us, and get it for us so that we may hear it and observe it?'" This verse has great similarity to the new covenant law in Jeremiah 31:31–34 and Ezekiel 36:26–27, which will not be given on tablets of stone by Moses who went up on the mountain before God, but the new law will be written on the circumcised heart. Deuteronomy 30:13 states that this commandment is not like Moses leading the people across the Red Sea to Sinai to obtain the law. In contrast, Deuteronomy 30:14 declares, "No, the word is very near to you; it is in your mouth and in your heart for you to observe." This statement is again similar to the new covenant in Jeremiah 31.[418] The summation is that Deuteronomy 30:11–14 should be considered an integral part of Deuteronomy 30:1-10 and functions as an eschatological NE restoration for Israel.[419]

The chapters preceding Deuteronomy 30 exhort Israel concerning the blessing and cursing of obedience or disobedience to the Lord's covenantal provisions.[420] At this point in time, the Israelites have not entered into the promised land and Moses is warning them about their future unfaithfulness and God's judgment resulting in exile from the land. However, Moses

---

[415] In Deut 30:14, it says "For the word is very near you, in your mouth and in your heart that you may observe it." Sometimes the word in the mouth refers to the Old Testament prophecy (Deut 18:18; 1 Kgs 17:24), but here in verse 14 God's word refers to God's law or commandments. God's word in the mouth is an idiom that refers to a thorough knowledge of God's law to a point that the person knows it extensively, intimately and can repeat it to others (Ex 13:9; Deut 6:5-8; 11:18-20; Josh 1:8) (Coxhead, "Deuteronomy 30:11–14 as a Prophecy," 308-09). The concept of God's word/law in the heart is parallel with the word in the mouth. This concept is an idiom which is connected with the person who has a willing obedience to the word (Deut 8:2; Ps 40:8). This concept also points to the new covenant in Jeremiah 31:33. In Jeremiah, God will write the law on the hearts of the people so that eschatological Israel will be obedient to God (cf. Ezk 36:26–27). If Israel has the word in their mouth and heart, then they would have a thorough knowledge of the word/law and would be living in obedience to it. However, at this point in the history of Israel, no such understanding or obedience existed (for this would be the implication of Deut 30:11–14 if it is translated in the present tense) (Ibid., 309). There is no question that Israel had the law, but their obedience was lacking (Deut 31:16, 20–21, 27). Consequently, Deuteronomy 30:14 argues for a future orientation for Deuteronomy 30:11-14. See Sullivan, *The INE in Rom 9–11*, 264–278.

[416] מִצְוָה (singular) is often accompanied with כָּל (Deut 5:31; 6:25; 8:1; 11:8,22; 15:5; 19:9; 27:1; 31:5). מִצְוָה is also found with words like "statues and judgments" (Deut 5:31; 6:1; 7:11). In Ex 24:12, the word seems to refer to the ten commandments and in Num 15:31, the reference is to the commandment of blasphemy. Finally, this construction is also connected with loving God in Deut 7:9, 11; 11:22 and 19:9.

[417] Sailhammer, *The Pentateuch as Narrative*, 473–74.

[418] Ibid., 474. Coxhead, "Deuteronomy 30:11–14 as a Prophecy," 310 states: "It seems that a deliberate contrast is being drawn between the situation of the law as described in [Deut 30] vv. 11–14 with Moses' reception of the law at Mount Sinai previously. Moses had to go over the sea and up to heaven (on Mount Sinai as it were), in order to receive the Sinaitic revelation on behalf of Israel (Ex 24:10–18); but the content of [Deut 30] vv. 12–13 speaks as if the mediation of Moses either was no longer necessary in the present or else would not be necessary at some time in the future."

[419] For a review of the broad scope of the Exodus motif and definition of the concept of the NE, see Sullivan, *INE in Rom 9–11*, 5–6 and 12–28.

[420] See Rock, "Another Reason for Romans," 74–89 for an overview of Deut 32 in Rom 9–11.

also declares that God promises that he would restore the nation when they turn back to the Lord. Therefore, the broader context of Deuteronomy 30 is the Mosaic law and the covenant blessing or cursing, even to the point of Israel's exile from the land. In Deuteronomy 30:19, Moses calls "heaven and earth to witness against" them just like he did at the beginning of the Song of Moses in Deuteronomy 32. Moses admonishes them to "choose life" (30:19) by loving and obeying God's word so that they would be able to live in the land. In the midst of this context, the Lord proclaims the prophetic promise of restoration and the circumcision of the heart in the NE language in Deuteronomy 30:1–14.

The Old Testament circumcision was essential for every person to be identified with the covenant community and to participate in Passover (Gen 17:9–14; Ex 12:43–44; Josh 5:8–11), which is the classic picture of redemption (Ex 12; 1 Cor 5:7). Paul denies the requirement of physical circumcision for membership in the new covenant community (Gal 6:14-15). However, he does argue that membership in the new covenant community is conditioned on the circumcision of the heart (Rom 2:28–29; 4:9-11; Gal 6:15), which Jesus Christ accomplished on the cross (Col 2:11–15).[421] Thus, the circumcision of the heart is a NE motif.[422] The key to the restoration to blessing back in the land is the return of the people to obey the Lord with all their heart and soul (Deut 30:2–3, 10). This kind of obedience necessitates that the Lord would "circumcise your heart and the heart of your descendants, so that you will love the Lord your God with all your heart and with all your soul, in order that you may live" (30:6). The declaration of Deuteronomy 30:12–13 is in the context of receiving the law, but it is making a contrast concerning the obedience to the law. The ability to obey the law and love God comes by the NE redemption – the circumcision of the heart.[423] There is a big difference between a law righteousness which demands a person to live by the law (which no one can) and a righteousness based upon faith in Jesus Christ which Paul describes as the "obedience of faith" (Rom 1:5) that the Holy Spirit produces through us (Rom 8:3–4) by the "circumcision of the heart" (Rom 2:28–29; Gal 6:15) from the new covenant (Heb 8).

10:6-7 ἡ δὲ ἐκ πίστεως δικαιοσύνη οὕτως λέγει· Μὴ εἴπῃς ἐν τῇ καρδίᾳ σου· Τίς ἀναβήσεται εἰς τὸν οὐρανόν; τοῦτ' ἔστιν Χριστὸν καταγαγεῖν· 7 ἤ· Τίς καταβήσεται εἰς τὴν ἄβυσσον; τοῦτ' ἔστιν Χριστὸν ἐκ νεκρῶν ἀναγαγεῖν. 6 "But the righteousness from faith speaks this way: Do not say in your heart, who will ascend into heaven? (that is, to bring Christ down). 7 Or Who will descend into the abyss? (That is, to bring Christ up from the dead)." Verse 6 is connected with v. 5 through the adversive δὲ ("but").[424] Thus, there is a contrast between the righteousness based on law and the righteousness based upon faith, which Paul personifies as speaking in vv. 6b–8 in the quotation of Deut 30. Some commentators concluded that Paul is not quoting Deut 30, but is using similar language as Deut 30 (Sanday & Headlam, 286–287; Fitzmyer, 590–91). However,

---

421 Holland, *Contours of Pauline Theology*, 213, 285–86.

422 Ibid.

423 Rom 2:29; 2 Cor 3:6; Phil 3:3; Col 2:11–12.

424 Badenas, *Christ the End of the Law*, 123 takes δὲ as a connective and not as an adversative. He argues that Paul does not use γάρ . . . δὲ in an adversative but in a connective way (Rom 7:8; 10:10; 11:15–16). However, Rom 11:15–16 is complicated for it is in εἰ clauses. Moo (650) is likely correct that γάρ . . . δὲ is not a correlative pair in Greek and it is "artificial" to place any consistent meaning to the combination. In Romans, this sequence occurs about 24 times when it is not complicated with other facts: in seven, δέ is continuative (4:3, 15; 7:8c–9; 8:7–8; 10:10; 12:4; 13:1; possibly also in 8:24; 9:9–10; 15:8–9); in three other places it is explanatory ("that is," "now"; 1:11–12; 2:1b–2; 6:7–8; possibly also in 5:13; 15:8–9); and in 10 contrastive (5:7–8, 16; 6:10, 23; 7:14, 18b, 22–23; 8:5, 6; 11:30; possibly also in 5:13).

the verbal similarities and the repeated phrase τοῦτ' ἔστιν ("that is") suggest that Paul is making reference to Deut 30:12–14 (Moo, 652; Schreiner, 554–556). Thus, Paul is applying Lev 18:5 in Rom 10:5 to the Law covenant and Deut 9: 4 and 30:11–14 to the application of the New Covenant in Rom 10:6-8 (Schreiner, 557; contra Moo, 652).[425] Many commentators prefer the understanding that Paul is substituting the commandment of Deut 30:11–14 with Christ though it is not a classic straightforward exegesis.

Paul appears to bring the context of Deuteronomy 30:11–14 into Romans 10:6–8 because Deuteronomy fits the theological framework of the NE salvation reflected in the new covenant language of the law written on the heart and the circumcision of the heart.[426] This new heart is a work of God and it gives the people the ability to love and obey God. In Romans 10:6, Paul places Deuteronomy 30:12 into a NE setting by using the phrase "that is, to bring Christ down." Jesus Christ has already come, and through his death and resurrection provided this NE redemption. Just as Jesus promised in the upper room discourse, he has sent another comforter (the Holy Spirit) to believers,[427] whom Paul calls the "Spirit of Christ" in Romans 8:9. Therefore, no one needs to ascend to heaven to bring Christ down for he is already with his people by the Spirit of Christ.[428] Paul appears to have read "back through redemption history and, as he looks back, the most recent event was the ascension and gift (or outpouring) of the Spirit (Rom 10:6), preceded by the death and resurrection of Christ (Rom 10:7)."[429] This reading of historical events retrospectively is done again by Paul in Romans 10:14–15.[430] If indeed, Paul is reading back through the events of salvation history, then the difficulty of the ascension-outpouring and death-resurrection order in Romans 10:6–7 is resolved. Most scholars interpret Romans 10:6 as referring to Christ's incarnation.[431] However, this view seems to be often assumed and not carefully argued.[432]

Paul's NE setting of Deuteronomy 30:12–13 in Romans 10:6–7 and the particular form of the verse Paul quotes[433] accentuate the resurrection of Jesus Christ. The resurrection of Jesus Christ is used by Paul as the central point of the quotation because Deuteronomy 30:12–14 is the part that is stressed in Romans 10:6–10. Instead of the Deuteronomy reading of "who will cross the sea to get it" [the book of the law] Paul reads "who will descend into the abyss?"[434]

Some hold that Paul conflates Deuteronomy 30:13 with LXX Psalm 106:26 (MT Ps 107:26).[435] The commonality in the two verses is the phrase that says, "They mounted up to the

---

[425] See comments on Rom 10:5 and detailed comments in Sullivan, *The INE in Rom 9–11*, 264–278. Other scholars posit Christ with the figure of wisdom and draw on the intertestamental Judaism. See Sullivan's critique Ibid., 269–271.

[426] This paragraph is taken from Sullivan, *The INE in Rom 9–11*, 271–272.

[427] Cf. Jn 7:38–39; 14:16–17; 15:26–27.

[428] Holland, 345–50. Dunn, 616 considers Romans 10:6 to be about the ascension and Holland refers the verse to the ascension, glorification, and the outpouring of the Spirit. The major objection is the order of ascension (10:6) and then resurrection (10:7). See Holland and Dunn for a sound defence of the ascension before resurrection order.

[429] Holland, 348.

[430] Ibid.

[431] Seifrid, "Romans," 657; Schreiner, 558; Moo, 655; Fitzmyer, 590; Barrett, 185; Cranfield, 2:525; and Murray, 2:53.

[432] Dunn, *Romans 9–16*, 605.

[433] Jewett, 627 suggests that Paul uses the translation of the Targums, an idea that is refuted by Seifrid, "Paul's Approach to the Old Testament in Rom 10:6–8," 23–25; Schreiner, 557; and Fitzmyer, 591.

[434] This paragraph is taken from Sullivan, *The INE in Rom 9–11*, 273.

[435] Schreiner, 559; Fitzmyer, 590, and Moo, 655 disagree.

heavens, they went down to the depths" (MT/LXX Ps 107[106]: 26). This Psalm has the motif of the Exodus concerning the return of the exile.[436] The Exodus theme of LXX Psalm 106 is easily recognized and it has some commonality with Deuteronomy 30:13. For example, in LXX Psalm 106, four groups of people are in danger, each group cries out to the Lord,[437] he hears their cry, and rescues them.[438] This context of crying out to God to deliver fits the context of Romans 10:6–13, where the theme of calling on the Lord brings deliverance of salvation. Only the resurrected Jesus Christ is able to save the one who calls upon his name. This deliverance is accomplished by God and thus, the response should be believing and not doing.[439]

Thus, Deuteronomy 30:12–13 and Psalm 107 in Romans 10:6–7 direct the church at Rome to the one who replaced David and Moses. It is no longer about receiving the law of Moses but receiving the point or substance of the law: Jesus Christ's redemption and the Spirit's ministry in the new covenant. Paul uses the NE motif to express these truths in Romans 10:6–7.[440]

10:8 ἀλλὰ τί λέγει; Ἐγγύς σου τὸ ῥῆμά ἐστιν, ἐν τῷ στόματί σου καὶ ἐν τῇ καρδίᾳ σου, τοῦτ' ἔστιν τὸ ῥῆμα τῆς πίστεως ὃ κηρύσσομεν. "But what does it say? The word is near you, in your mouth and in your heart; that is, the word of faith that we are preaching." The introductory phrases ἀλλὰ τί λέγει ("But what does it say?") refers the reader back to the Deuteronomy citations in Rom 10:6-7 where Paul is advocating a righteousness from faith in contrast to 10:5; thus, he uses the adversative ἀλλὰ ("but"). Again, Deut 30:14 is used by Paul to make his point. He proclaims that the message of the righteousness of God is brought near to the people – "in your mouth and in your heart." In Moses' day the law was brought near to Israel because Moses brought it down to the people and proclaim it to them. Paul uses this OT concept because he wants to parallel the thought that the gospel of righteousness is brought near to the people through "the word (τὸ ῥῆμα) of faith" preached (v. 8) – the gospel. The "confession with your mouth" and "believe in your heart" (v. 9) indicates the benefit of the circumcision of the heart to love God (Deut 30:6), which is the promise of the new covenant in Jer 31:31-34 (cf. 2 Cor 3:3). Indeed, if they will accept the message of the gospel, it brings eternal salvation when one response in faith.[441] Schreiner (2nd, 546) and Dunn (606) are probably right to conclude that both the content of faith (Käsemann, 290; Fitzmyer, 591) and the act of trusting (Sanday and

---

436 Allen, *Psalm 101–150*, 88–89. Hill, "Reading Isaiah," 147 recognizes the general nature of the following description, however, the accumulation of them is descriptive of the Exodus background: gathering from the lands (v. 3); the wandering in the wilderness (v. 4), hunger and thirst (v. 5); the way in the wilderness (v. 7) the prison motif (vv. 10–14) and the water in the desert (vv. 33–35).

437 LXX Ps 106:6, 13, 19, 28.

438 See Holland, 342, who gives more detail on this argument.

439 This paragraph is taken from Sullivan, *The INE in Rom 9–11*, 273–274. He also states that the NE motif in this Psalm is the use of פלא (5 times) in the context of God's "wonderful" deliverance to humankind, an aspect of the NE that was identified and discussed in *The INE in Rom 9–11*, 161–169. Four times in the Psalm the word is used in the same refrain: "Let them thank the LORD for his steadfast love, for his wonderful (פלא) works to humankind" (Ps 107:8, 15, 21, 24, 31). This refrain is the response to God's deliverance when the people called out to him (Ibid., 274).

440 This paragraph is taken from Sullivan, *The INE in Rom 9–11*, 274.

441 Objective genitive, which refers to the gospel word, that calls forth for a person to believe the gospel (Moo, 657, Meyers, 181, Sanday and Headlam, 288; Murray, 2:54; Fitzmyer, 591).

Headlam, 288; Cranfield, 536) are involved in vv. 9–13. Jewett (629) points out that ῥῆμα (word) is basically the synonym of λόγος (word).[442]

10:9 ὅτι ἐὰν ὁμολογήσῃς ἐν τῷ στόματί σου κύριον Ἰησοῦν, καὶ πιστεύσῃς ἐν τῇ καρδίᾳ σου ὅτι ὁ θεὸς αὐτὸν ἤγειρεν ἐκ νεκρῶν, σωθήσῃ· "For if you confess with your mouth that Jesus is Lord and believe in your heart that God raised him from the dead, you will be saved." The connective word ὅτι may be translated as explanatory ("that") or causal ("for/because"). If it is translated "that" then v. 9 is indicating the content of the "word of faith" which is being preached (Schreiner, 2nd, 546; Murray, 2:55; Käsemann, 291; Barrett, 186). However, Moo (2nd, 675) is correct when he points out that this would be awkward for Paul putting two "content" clauses in a row. However, Paul does at times seem to write in ways that may seem awkward. On the other hand, the second option taking ὅτι as causative should probably be adopted (Cranfield, 526; Jewett, 629). Dunn (607) and Middendorf (974) think both functions are present. Thus, Paul is saying if someone has faith in the "nearness" of the word (v. 8), the preaching of the "word of faith" (v. 8), the gospel, then he is saved. Paul expresses this exercising of faith with the two phrases: "if you confess with your mouth" and if "you believe in your heart." These two phrases correspond to the Deut 30:14 passage in Rom 10:8 referring to the word brought near the Israelites. "The word is near you, in your mouth and in your heart." Paul has been using the context of Deuteronomy 30 in Rom 10:6–10. He is not making an internal and external requirement to be saved. This expression is the "two sides of the one coin kind" of expression (Dunn, 609). He is rhetorically using the authority of the OT and its wording to express that the outward confession manifests the inner ward belief in the gospel. Paul has made this clear in his argument in Rom 9:30, 32, 33; 10:4, 6a, 11.

Paul expresses the confession with the phrase κύριον Ἰησοῦν ("Jesus is Lord").[443] This confession is one major way that the NT expresses a person's salvation (2 Cor 9:13; 1 Tim 6:12–13; Tit 1:16).[444] Furthermore, this confession is considered the common held teaching of the early Church and a pre-Pauline confessional tradition (Schreiner, 2nd, 546; Cranfield, 527; Dunn, 607; Fitzmyer, 591). The confession of the lordship of Jesus and His resurrection are inseparable since He was appointed as Lord at His resurrection (Acts 2:36; Rom 1:4) (Schreiner, 559). The confession of "Jesus is Lord" is publicly declared in Acts 2:36, confirmed throughout the NT, and is necessary for salvation (Rom 4:23–25).[445] This confession is expressing that Jesus is the only God and He alone can save. It is the objective lordship, which is the cornerstone of our faith, and without which one could not be saved (Harrison and Hagner, 162–163). Cranfield (529) states "Jesus is Lord meant the acknowledgment that Jesus shares the name and the nature, the holiness, the authority, power, majesty and eternity of the one and only true God." Thus, Jesus demands the same respect, allegiance, and commitment as Yahweh in the OT (Ex 3:14; Jn 8:58). Paul's use of Joel in Rom 10:13 helps to identify Jesus with the Yahweh of the OT (Middendorf, 996–997). One day every person will acknowledge, "Jesus Christ is Lord" (Phil

---

[442] Albert Debrunner et al., "λέγω κτλ.," *TDNT* 4 (1967) 109–19; Walter Radl, "ῥῆμα," *EDNT* 3 (1993), 210–11.

[443] A double accusative (κύριον Ἰησοῦν) after ὁμολογέω is found in 1 Jn 4:2 and 2 Jn 7 (*BDF* 157[2]).

[444] See Johannian literature: 1 Jn 2:23; 4:2, 3, 15; 2 Jn 7; Rev 3:5.

[445] The abundance of evidence of this declaration of lordship is trace through Acts (2:26; 3:20; 4:26 [Ps 2:2], 4:33, 7:59; 8:12, 16; 9:5, 17, 34–35, 42; 10:36; 11:17, 20–21, 24; 15:11; 16:31–32; 19:4–5; 20:21, 24; 26:15; 28:31). The reference to Jesus is Lord in various ways in Paul's writings is overwhelming. See just in Romans (1:4, 7; 4:24; 5:1, 11, 21; 7:25; 8:39; 10:9; 14:14; 15:6, 30; 16:20, 24).

2:10–11) whether on earth (probably a mixture of some joyful and others in dismay), in heaven (in joy) or under the earth (in dismay).

Paul declares "Therefore I make known to you, that no one speaking by the Spirit of God says, 'Jesus is accursed'; and no one can say, 'Jesus is Lord,' except by the Holy Spirit" (1 Cor 12:3). It is obvious anyone may merely say those words, "Jesus is Lord" (Mt 7:21), but they cannot do this with saving conviction apart from the Spirit's saving work. James also addresses this point when he says, "You believe that God is one, you do well; the demons also believe, and shudder" (Jas 2:19). Thus, "the righteousness based on faith speaks thus . . ." (10:6) by confessing with your mouth Jesus is Lord and believing with the heart that God raised Him from the dead (10:9).

Paul expresses salvation in the future tense (σωθήσῃ). Some understand the future tense of salvation to be the deliverance from sin and death in the final judgment (Barrett, 188; Cranfield, 530; Dunn, 609). Moo (2nd, 676, n. 491) is probably correct to take this as a "relative or logical future" where salvation is look upon as a "result of and future to" the time one confessed and believed Jesus as Lord who was raised from the dead. This is not to deny one is also delivered from eschatological judgment. Thus, present belief and confession of the past event of Christ's death and resurrection results in future salvation (Dunn, 609).

10:10 καρδίᾳ γὰρ πιστεύεται εἰς δικαιοσύνην, στόματι δὲ ὁμολογεῖται εἰς σωτηρίαν· "For with the heart one believes for righteousness, and with the mouth one confesses for salvation." A chiastic arrangement (confess–believe and believe–confess) in vv. 9–10 is observed. The word order of v. 9 seems to be taken from the Deuteronomy 30:14 quotation in v. 8 while the order of v. 10 conveys the logical order of belief in the heart then confession with the mouth. The only addition is the believing resulting in righteousness in v. 10. Schriener (2nd, 547) is correct to point out that the parallel results of "righteousness" and "salvation" (cf. 10:9) is not a significant difference (see 1:16–17; 4:5) in this context (Dunn, 609; Cranfield, 530).[446] Dunn (609) states that "righteousness" and "salvation" is often parallel in the Psalms and Isaiah. In most cases σωτηρίαν ("salvation") is used in an eschatological hope for the future deliverance from destruction; however, salvation is also presented as a salvation-history concept that one is saved in this life (Dunn, 40; Moo, 67). Paul has already addressed righteousness in Rom 3-5 and in the recent context of Rom 9:30–32 and 10:3–6.

10:11 λέγει γὰρ ἡ γραφή· Πᾶς ὁ πιστεύων ἐπ' αὐτῷ οὐ καταισχυνθήσεται. "For the Scripture says, 'No one who believes on him will be put to shame.'" Paul uses γὰρ ("for") five times in four verses (10:10, 11, 12 [2x], 13). In v. 10, Paul explains further and completes the chiastic structure beginning in v. 9. Verse 11 presents scriptural support from Isa 28:16 (cf. Rom 9:33). The two usages of γὰρ in v. 12 express the universality of the gospel and again in v. 13 Paul presents scriptural support from Joel 2:32.

Paul reads the Greek word πᾶς ("all" or "anyone"), which is not literally found in Isaiah 28:16b nor is it in the quotation of Romans 9:33 and 1 Peter 2:6. Some have claimed that Paul's textual modification technique shaped the text toward a theological end, and compared it to the common method of exegesis found at Qumran, though he admitted that this type of technique

[446] However, both Cranfield (530) and Dunn (609) refer to salvation and righteous in the eschatological future. Murray (2:56) makes more of a difference between the two terms.

was not like those found in rabbinic literature.[447] J. Ross Wagner explained the addition of πᾶς in Romans 10:4 by claiming that it gave the text a Christological focus.[448] Others see that Paul used πᾶς to bring out a more universalistic sense.[449] Oss called the addition of πᾶς in Romans 10:11 an *ad hoc* rendering but not an arbitrary feature, which shaped Paul's theological end.[450] However, the use of πᾶς (nominative singular) in Romans 10:11 corresponds well with the hiphil masculine singular participle (MT הַמַּאֲמִין) and the present active masculine singular participle (LXX ὁ πιστεύων) in Isaiah 28:16b. Paul seemed to use a singular collective πᾶς ("anyone") to emphasize the masculine singular participle ("one who believes"). Therefore, Paul's adaption is established as part of the context and theology of Isaiah and is not as *ad hoc* as some claim.[451]

Paul invokes an *inclusio* in Romans 9:33 and 10:11 by means of the repeated quotation of Isaiah 28:16. An *inclusio* involves references to a word, phrase, or theme that occur at both the beginning and the end of a unit of literature. "Inclusio holds a passage together and indicates to listeners the end of a section. The meaning of the repeated phrase is often enriched by what comes in between."[452] This point is certainly accurate in this case. The enrichment that is displayed in Romans 9:33–10:11 is the framework of the NE using the analogy and contrast of the law and temple/stone language to picture Jesus Christ. The figure of laying the stone/rock in Zion and the analogy with the law ascending and descending as Christ (Rom 10:4) became the word Paul preaches so that the changed heart would believe and confession the resurrected Lord Jesus Christ who is available to all, both Jews and Gentiles.[453]

10:12 οὐ γάρ ἐστιν διαστολὴ Ἰουδαίου τε καὶ Ἕλληνος, ὁ γὰρ αὐτὸς κύριος πάντων, πλουτῶν εἰς πάντας τοὺς ἐπικαλουμένους αὐτόν· "For there is no distinction between the Jew and the Greek, for the same[454] Lord *is Lord* of all, bestowing riches to all who call upon him." See v. 11 for comments about γὰρ. The central theme of Romans 10:8–10 is that whoever believes and confesses the resurrected Lord will be saved.[455] To substantiate this central theme, Paul quotes part of Isaiah 28:16 in Romans 10:11. Paul's reading of πᾶς ("all", "everyone") in this Old Testament quotation is not found in the MT or the extant manuscripts of the LXX. Romans

---

[447] Oss, "Paul's Use of Isaiah," 62–63; and Ellis, *Paul's Use of the Old Testament*, 140–41. For a more informed discussion, see Fitzmyer in chapter 3.3 in Sullivan, 2nd, *The INE in Rom 9-11*.

[448] Wagner, *Heralds of the Good News*, 169.

[449] Shum, *Paul's Use of Isaiah in Romans*, 220–21; and Stanley, *Paul and the Language of Scripture*, 133.

[450] Oss, "Paul's Use of Isaiah," 63. Wagner, "Isaiah in Romans and Galatians," 123 and Stanley, *Paul and the Language of Scripture*, 133–34 claimed that Paul added πᾶς to connect it more closely with Joel 2:32 in Rom 10:13. *Contra* Shreiner (561) Moo, "Paul's Universalizing Hermeneutic in Romans," 66 and others who says there is no textual basis for πᾶς.

[451] There is a modification but with a contextual basis. Furthermore, Paul does not use the plural (πάντων, πάντας) like he does in Rom 10:12. He returns to the πᾶς in Rom 10:13, which reflects the context of the singular כֹּל and πᾶς (LXX) in Joel 2:32 (3:5 LXX and MT) and his parallel use of πᾶς in Rom 10:11. See Sullivan, *The INE in Rom 9–11*, 95-96.

[452] Jensen, "Poetry in the Bible," 457. Wagner, *Heralds of the Good News*, 168 recognizes that Rom 9:33 and 10:11 is an *inclusio*.

[453] This paragraph was taken from Sullivan, *The INE in Rom 9–11*, 276–277.

[454] Wallace states: "When modifying an articular substantive in the *attributive* position, αὐτός is used as an identifying adjective. As such it is translated *same*" (*Greek Grammar*, 349).

[455] The phrase ἐπ' αὐτῷ in Rom 10:11 and in the context of Isa 28:16 is the rock and the rock refers to Jesus Christ in Rom 10:11. See Shum, *Paul's Use of Isaiah in Romans*, 220–22.

10:12–13 focuses on the word πᾶς (used twice in the plural form in v. 12 and once in the singular as πᾶς in v. 13) and summarizes the concept of "believe" (πιστεύω) and "confess" (ὁμολογέω) with the word "call" (ἐπικαλέω, used in vv. 12 and 13). The presence of πᾶς stresses the universality of the gospel to both Jews and Gentiles.[456] The word πᾶς with Isaiah 28:16 includes "Jews and Greeks" (10:12). The prophet does not say, "the one born into God's covenant of law will not be put to shame," but instead Paul, using the prophet, says "One who trusts will not panic." "Since anyone can believe, anyone can partake of the Isaianic promises."[457] The riches that Paul mentions is often used by Paul to express the spiritual blessings of God's glory, mercy, and grace (2 Cor 8:9; Rom 2:4; 9:23; Eph 1:7, 18; 2:7; 3:8, 16). He points out that there is "no distinction" (cf. Rom 3:22) between Jews and Gentiles who call upon the Lord Jesus for salvation (Rom 10:9; 3:29–30).[458] This calling is the result of the effectual calling of God (Rom 8:29–30; Jas 2:7) where the individual in faith calls upon the Lord for salvation (Acts 2:21; 9:14, 21; 22:16; Rom 10:13, 14; 1 Cor. 1:2).[459]

10:13 Πᾶς γὰρ ὃς ἂν ἐπικαλέσηται τὸ ὄνομα κυρίου σωθήσεται. "For everyone who calls on the name of the Lord will be saved." See v. 11 for comments about γὰρ. The subjective mood of ἐπικαλέσηται ("call") is in an indefinite relative clause (ὃς ἂν ἐπικαλέσηται) and is roughly considered to be a third or fifth class condition where "the element of contingency is not that of time but of person."[460] Thus, the subjunctive is often translated like an indicative because the potentiality is in the subject rather than the verb. The preceding comments of Paul are again stressed by the quotation from Joel 2:32 (MT/LXX 3:5) in Romans 10:13: "For, 'everyone (πᾶς) who calls (ἐπικαλέω) on the name of the Lord shall be saved.'"[461] The context of Joel 2:32 is the eschatological judgment, but the verse also stresses the salvation for every Israelite who calls upon the Lord.[462] The immediate context of Joel 2:32 is the outpouring of the Spirit of God upon all flesh,[463] which is the same theme as Deuteronomy 30:1–14. Though Moses does not mention the Spirit in Deuteronomy 30, the circumcised heart that changes to love and obedience toward God is the result of the Spirit's work. Joel 2:28–29 says, "I will pour out my spirit on all flesh; your sons and your daughters shall prophesy, your old men shall dream dreams, and your young men shall see visions. Even on the male and female slaves, in those days, I will pour out my

---

[456] The thought that God did not make a distinction between Jews and Gentiles began in Rom 3:22–23, 29–30. Bekken, *The Word is Near You*, 228; Shum, *Paul's Use of Isaiah in Romans*, 221; Koch, *Die Schrift als Zeuge des Evangelium*, 133; and Stanley, *Paul and the Language of Scripture*, 133–34 point out the universality of using πᾶς.

[457] Ortlund, "The Insanity of Faith," 285.

[458] Most commentators refer the Lord in v. 12 to Jesus (Moo, 2nd, 677–78; Schreiner, 2nd, 548–49; Murray, 2:57; Fitzmyer, 592; Hodge 543).

[459] Some commentators (e.g., Cranfield, 532) point out that this word can also mean to call on Christ in prayer and espouse that this calling is what Paul means here. However, that is unlikely here in v. 12 for the context of how ἐπικαλέω is used in vv. 13 and 14 support the calling upon the Lord to save them. However, if someone considers calling out to the Lord Jesus for salvation as a prayer, then indeed this is a prayer. See Dunn, 611 who makes a distinction between a prayer of entreaty and a prayer that appeals to covenant obligation.

[460] Wallace, *Greek Grammar*, 478.

[461] Most of the comments on v. 13 were taken from Sullivan, *The INE in Rom 9–11*, 275.

[462] Steve Moyise, *Paul and Scripture*, 75 points out that Joel 2:32 "is not as universal as it sounds, for it refers specifically to the 'fortunes of Judah and Jerusalem.'"

[463] LXX/MT Joel 3:1 (Eng Joel 2:28).

spirit." The framework of Joel 2:28–32 is the eschatological NE for these verses bring forth the themes of the future salvation and the giving of the Spirit.[464]

The connection of the Spirit with the Exodus is found in Ezra's prayer in Nehemiah 9, where the prophet outlines salvation history and connects the Spirit's ministry to the Exodus (Neh 9:19–20).[465] The concept of the Spirit is also found in the NE context of Isaiah 63:10–14.[466] The immediate context of Joel 2:28–32 helps to support the background of the changed heart (Deut 30:6, 12–14) and the implication that the Spirit is involved in the calling out for salvation (Joel 2:32; Rom 10:13). Paul uses Deuteronomy 30:12–14 and Joel 2:32 and applies them typologically to his day. Peter uses Joel 2:28–29 typologically or analogically to explain the pouring out of the Spirit in Acts 2, which suggests widespread recognition of the textual relationship.[467]

Biblical Theological Comments[468]

In Isaiah 8:14, the combination of "sanctuary" (מִקְדָּשׁ), "stone" (אֶבֶן or λίθος LXX), and "rock" (צוּר or πέτρα LXX) points to Exodus temple imagery, which focuses on God who dwelt there. The distinctive and unique words of Isaiah 8:14 and 28:16 help to define the stone/rock in a tabernacle/temple imagery. Furthermore, the combination of the building and architectural language in Isaiah 28:16–17 helps build the NE framework. This framework helps to support Paul's argument of judgment and salvation in Romans 9–10.

The Jews were pursuing νόμον δικαιοσύνης ("law righteousness") not by faith but by works, and this failure becomes evident when God places in Zion the stone/rock. Consequently, instead of the law being a παιδαγωγός ("tutor, guardian, disciplinarian") to bring them to Christ (Gal 3:24), the misuse of the law has become a hindrance and they have stumbled over the stone/rock. Paul uses these two important points in Israel to express how serious and abysmal their stumbling has become. What is missing, for the most part, in the discussion is that the NE theme provides Paul the theological pattern (judgment/salvation) to make these compelling arguments from the important objects in the life of Israel.

The NE motif is prominent in the context of Deuteronomy 30 and Paul's utilization of it in Romans 10:6–10. First, Paul appropriates the setting of Deuteronomy 30:11–14 into Romans 10:6–8 because this passage matches well the motif of the NE salvation that is revealed in the new covenant language of the law written on the heart, the circumcision of the heart, and the ability to love and obey God. Second, Paul appears to conflate Deuteronomy 30:12–13 with

---

[464] See Isa 32:15; 44:1–5; 59:21; Ezk 11:17–20; 36:24–28; Zech 12:10.

[465] See also Pao, *Acts and Isaianic New Exodus*, 129–34.

[466] See also Hag 2:5.

[467] Seifrid, 660. Moo, 653 and "Paul's Universalizing Hermeneutic in Romans," 67 conclude that Paul uses Deut 30:11–14 and Joel 2:32 by way of application. This is a good possibility. Bekken, *The Word is Near You*, 224 calls Paul's christological exposition of Deut 30:12–14 an exegetical paraphrase. This conclusion seems to be too generic. Coxhead, "Deuteronomy 30:11–14," 219 calls Rom 10:6–8 a christological midrash. Aageson, "Scripture and Structure in the Development of Argument of Romans 9–11," 275–76 notes that Rom 10:6–8 is similar in some degree to Qumran pesher though the phrase "that is" does not signal a Qumran pesher technique. Grieb, *The Story of Romans*, 100 thinks that Paul, in Rom 10:6–8, adopts a pesher style of interpretation. Heil, "Christ, the Termination of the Law (Romans 9:30–10:8)," 496 agrees with Seifrid, ("Paul's Approach to the Old Testament in Rom 10:6–8, 27–34) and Moo that this is not Qumran pesher.

[468] These comments are taken from Sullivan, *The INE in Rom 9–11*, 277–278.

Psalm 107:26.[469] The NE theme of Psalm 107 is the cry of the people's trouble and the response of the salvation of God. This four-fold theme in Psalm 107 fits the context of Romans 10:6–13 where the theme is calling on the Lord for salvation.

Third, Deuteronomy 30:14 draws upon a NE motif and Paul cites this text in Romans 10:8 and further explains his point in Romans 10:9–13. The central theme is that whoever believes and confesses the resurrected Lord, will be saved. Paul ties together the Old Testament texts in Romans 9:33–10:13 by using the different motifs of the NE theme. Though there are good discussions among scholars concerning the passages from the Old Testament in Romans 9:33–10:13, there has been a neglect in the understanding of the Exodus imagery and the NE motifs, which provides a systematic foundation for Paul's argument.

Thus, Paul's framework in using all of these Old Testament texts in this Romans section is the NE theme. The framework of the NE uses the figure of laying the stone/rock in Zion and the analogy of the law ascending and descending as pointing to Christ and the Spirit of Christ. Without this common framework of the NE motif, Paul's argument is disjointed and loses continuity.

Application and Devotional Implications

Paul draws upon Lev 18:5 to show that the prerequisite for a righteous standing before God was to obey the Law perfectly. If a person according to God's standards would never sin in thought, word, or deed his/her entire life then that person would be righteous in God's sight. However, no one can do this! Therefore, doing the law can never give us eternal life. Gal 3:21 says, "Is the Law then contrary to the promises of God? May it never be! For if a law had been given which was able to impart life, then righteousness would indeed have been based on law." Furthermore, Gal 3:10 states "For as many as are of the works of the Law are under the curse; for it is written, 'Cursed is everyone who does not abide by all things written in the book of the law to perform them.'" Therefore, the law presents a hypothetical way of righteousness, yet it is impossible for anyone to obtain. You say to me, "why would anyone attempt to obtain eternal life by works? It is impossible." I don't know why but people do! Ask people why they think they are going to heaven. They often respond: because I try to keep the 10 commandments (Ex 20:3–17). Are you saying that you never broke any of the 10 commandments? Most people reply, "Oh yes, I have broken them, but I keep most of them most of the time." They explain that they are a good person and live by the golden rule (Mat 7:12) and do good charitable things. Surely, God will accept me? My friend, God will not accept you! If you choose the way of law keeping for salvation, then from the moment you draw your first breath until you breathe your last breath you must obey all of God's laws and your standard obedience must meet God's standards – 100% perfection. No mere mortal man will storm the gates of heaven claiming he has earned righteousness by keeping the law. We are all lawbreakers.

Then how does one get to heaven? Paul presents the second and only way in Rom 10:6–13. In Rom 10:9–10 Paul explains further in detail how one obtains this righteousness. It is amazing that something so simple becomes so confused, clouded, and complicated by many who

---

[469] The Jewish believers and leaders would help the largely Gentile congregation in understanding the Abrahamic/Davidic NE themes in the letter of Romans (see the background of Lampe, "The Roman Christians of Romans 16," 224–25). See the general background material of Wiefel, "The Jewish Community in Ancient Rome and the Origins of Roman Christianity," 85–101.

say they proclaim the gospel. Paul says a person must confess Jesus as Lord. He must believe in his heart that God raised Jesus Christ from the dead. These two points are really cause and effect in their relationship one to the other. A person believes from his heart then he will confess with his mouth. Jesus says out of the mouth the heart speaks. A person who confesses salvation and does not believe it is a hypocrite, deceiver or possibly confused. He will be condemned in this state. A person who believes and does not confess it is a coward, which God will discipline, or it is a spurious belief. Notice Paul says we are to confess that Jesus is Lord or Jesus as Lord. The word Lord (*kurios*) is used more than 6,000 times in the Greek OT translation for the Hebrew word Yahweh (the tetragrammaton). Cranfield (529) in his commentary concludes that confessing Jesus as Lord in Romans 10 is to acknowledge "that Jesus shares the name and the nature, the holiness, the authority, power, majesty and eternity of the one and only true God." Next Paul says we must believe that God raised Jesus from the dead. This implies one believes Jesus died and the reason why He died–to pay the penalty for our sins. By His resurrection from the dead, Jesus secures our salvation and demonstrates that the Father was and is satisfied with the payment. The key for each person is: Have you placed your faith in Christ alone for the payment of your sins as the resurrected Lord over your life?

Selected Bibliography

Aageson, James W. "Scripture and Structure in the Development of Argument of Romans 9–11," *Catholic Biblical Quarterly* 48 (April 1986), 265–289.

Allen, Leslie C. *Psalm 101–150 Revised.* Word Biblical Commentary, ed. John D. W. Watts, revised, vol. 21 (Dallas: Word and Thomas Nelson, 2002).

Badenas, Robert. *Christ Is the End of the Law: Romans 10:4 in Pauline Perspective* (Sheffield: JSOT Press, 1985).

Bandstra, Andrew J. *The Law and the Elements of the World: An Exegetical Study in Aspects of Paul's Teaching* (Kampen: Kok, 1964).

Bekken, Per Jarle. *The Word is Near You: A Study of Deuteronomy 30:12–14 in Paul's Letter to the Romans in a Jewish Context.* Berlin: Deutsche Nationalbibliografie, 2007.

Blass, Friedrich, Albert Debrunner, and Robert Walter Funk. *A Greek Grammar of the New Testament and Other Early Christian Literature* (Chicago: University of Chicago Press, 1961).

Coxhead, Steven R. "Deuteronomy 30:11–14 as a Prophecy of the New Covenant in Christ." *Westminster Theological Journal* 68 (2006): 305–20.

Fuller, Daniel P. *Gospel and Law: Contrast or Continuum?* (Grand Rapids: Eerdmans, 1980).

Grieb, A. Katherine Grieb. *The Story of Romans: A Narrative Defense of God's Righteousness* (Louisville: Westminster John Knox Press, 2002).

Heil, John P. "Christ, the Termination of the Law (Romans 9:30–10:8)," *The Catholic Biblical Quarterly* 63 (2001): 484–498.

Hill, Linzy H., Jr. "Reading Isaiah as a Theological Unity Based on an Exegetical Investigation of the Exodus Motif" (Ph.D. diss., Southwestern Baptist Theological Seminary, 1993).

Holland, Tom. *Contours of Pauline Theology: A Radical New Survey of the Influences on Paul's Biblical Writings* (Scotland: Christian Focus Publications, 2004).

Jensen, Philip. "Poetry in the Bible," in *New Bible Commentary: 21st Century Edition* (Downers Grove: InterVarsity Press, 1994).

Koch, Dietrich-Alex. *Die Schrift als Zeuge des Evangeliums: Untersuchungen zur Verwendung und zum Verständnis der Schrift bei Paulus*. Beiträge zur historischen Theologie, vol. 69. (Tübingen: Mohr Siebeck, 1986).

Lampe, Peter. "The Roman Christians of Romans 16," in *The Romans Debate*, rev. and exp. ed. (Peabody: Hendrickson, 1991).

Moo, Douglas J. "Paul's Universalizing Hermeneutic in Romans," *The Southern Baptist Journal of Theology* 11 (Fall 2007): 62–90.

Moyise, Steve. *Paul and Scripture: Studying the New Testament Use of the Old Testament* (Grand Rapids: Baker Academic, 2010).

Ortlund, Dane C. "The Insanity of Faith: Paul's Theological Use of Isaiah in Romans 9:33." *Trinity Journal* 30 (Fall 2009): 269–288.

Oss, Douglas A. "Paul's Use of Isaiah in Its Place in His Theology with Special Reference to Romans 9–11" (Ph.D. diss., Westminster Theological Seminary, 1992).

Pao, David W. *Acts and Isaianic New Exodus*, Biblical Studies Library (Grand Rapids: Baker, 2002).

Rock, Ian E. "Another Reason for Romans – A Pastoral Response to Augustan Imperial Theology: Paul's Use of the Song of Moses in Romans 9–11 and 14–15." In *Reading Paul in Context: Explorations in Identity Formation Essays in Honour of William S. Campbell*, eds. Kathy Ehrensperger and J. Brian Tucker. Library of New Testament Studies, ed. Mark Goodacre, 428, 74–89 (London: T & T Clark, 2010).

Seifrid, Mark A. "Paul's Approach to the Old Testament in Rom 10:6–8." *Trinity Journal* 6 (spring 1985): 3–37.

Shum, Shiu-Lun. *Paul's Use of Isaiah in Romans: A Comparative Study of Paul's Letter to the Romans and the Sibylline and Qumran Sectarian Texts* (Tübingen: Mohr Siebeck, 2002).

Stanley, Christopher D. *Paul and the Language of Scripture: Citation Technique in the Pauline Epistles and Contemporary Literature* (Cambridge: Cambridge University Press, 1992).

Sullivan, Steven P. *The Isaianic New Exodus in Romans 9–11: A Biblical and Theological Study of Paul's Use of Isaiah in Romans* (Silverton, OR: Lampion Press, 2017).

Sullivan, Steven P. *The Isaianic New Exodus in Romans 9–11: A Biblical and Theological Study of Paul's Use of Isaiah in Romans*, 2nd ed. (Middletown, RI: Stone Tower Press, 2023).

Swanson, Reuben, ed. *New Testament Greek Manuscripts: Romans*. (Wheaton: Tyndale House and Pasadena: William Carey International University Press, 2001).

Wagner, J. Ross *Heralds of the Good News: Isaiah and Paul "In Concert" in the Letter to the Romans*, Supplements to Novum Testamentum, ed. M. M. Mitchell and D. P. Moessner (Leiden: Brill, 2002).

Wiefel, Wolfgang. "The Jewish Community in Ancient Rome and the Origins of Roman Christianity," in *The Romans Debate*, rev. and exp. ed. (Peabody: Hendrickson, 1991), 85–101.

Wright, N. T. "Romans 9–11 and the 'New Perspective.'" In *Between Gospel and Election: Explorations in the Interpretation of Romans 9–11*, eds. Florian Wilk and J. Ross Wagner with Frank Schleritt. Wissenschaftliche Untersuchungen zum Neuen Testament, 257, 37–54 (Tübingen: Mohr Siebeck, 2010)

Romans 10:14–21

Outline

C. Israel's Knowledge of the Gospel of Righteousness: Faith and Works (9:30–10:21)
   1. Righteousness by faith and a "Law Righteousness" (9:30–33)
   2. Israel's Lack of Understanding Concerning Righteousness (10:1–4)
   3. The Gospel of Righteousness and Law (10:5–13)
   4. The Proclamation of the Gospel and the Lack of Response (10:14–21)

Original Text

10.14 Πῶς οὖν ἐπικαλέσωνται[a] εἰς ὃν οὐκ ἐπίστευσαν; πῶς δὲ πιστεύσωσιν[b] οὗ οὐκ ἤκουσαν; πῶς
δὲ ἀκούσωσιν[c] χωρὶς κηρύσσοντος; 15 πῶς δὲ κηρύξωσιν[d] ἐὰν μὴ ἀποσταλῶσιν; καθὼς[e]
γέγραπται· Ὡς ὡραῖοι οἱ πόδες τῶν εὐαγγελιζομένων[f] [τὰ][g] ἀγαθά. 16 ἀλλ’ οὐ πάντες ὑπήκουσαν
τῷ εὐαγγελίῳ· Ἠσαΐας γὰρ λέγει· Κύριε, τίς ἐπίστευσεν τῇ ἀκοῇ ἡμῶν; 17 ἄρα ἡ πίστις ἐξ ἀκοῆς,
ἡ δὲ ἀκοὴ διὰ ῥήματος Χριστοῦ[h]. 18 Ἀλλὰ λέγω, μὴ οὐκ ἤκουσαν; μενοῦνγε· Εἰς πᾶσαν τὴν γῆν
ἐξῆλθεν ὁ φθόγγος αὐτῶν, καὶ εἰς τὰ πέρατα τῆς οἰκουμένης τὰ ῥήματα αὐτῶν. 19 ἀλλὰ λέγω, μὴ
Ἰσραὴλ οὐκ ἔγνω; πρῶτος Μωϋσῆς λέγει· Ἐγὼ παραζηλώσω ὑμᾶς ἐπ’ οὐκ ἔθνει, ἐπ’ ἔθνει
ἀσυνέτῳ παροργιῶ ὑμᾶς. 20 Ἠσαΐας δὲ ἀποτολμᾷ καὶ λέγει· Εὑρέθην ἐν τοῖς ἐμὲ μὴ ζητοῦσιν,
ἐμφανὴς ἐγενόμην τοῖς ἐμὲ μὴ ἐπερωτῶσιν. 21 πρὸς δὲ τὸν Ἰσραὴλ λέγει· Ὅλην τὴν ἡμέραν
ἐξεπέτασα τὰς χεῖράς μου πρὸς λαὸν ἀπειθοῦντα καὶ ἀντιλέγοντα.

Textual Notes

[a] **10:14 ἐπικαλέσωνται** is supported by WH Tregelles NA28 SBLGNT UBS5 B ℵ A D F G. **ἐπικαλέσονται** is supported by 𝔐 P^{46} K L P Ψ. (Swanson, *NT GK Mss*, 160). The earlier manuscripts except for P^{46} reflect that Paul used the subjective mood probably derived from the quotation in Joel from v. 13.

[b] **10:14 πιστεύσωσιν** is supported by WH Tregelles NA28 SBLGNT UBS5 B $ℵ^c$ ℵ D K P Ψ P^{46} 1 460 618 1245 1424 1611 1735 1738 1739. **πιστεύσουσιν** is supported by A 𝔐. (Swanson, *NT GK Mss*, 160). Paul seems to continue with the pattern of subjunctive and then an indicative (Sanday & Headlam, 295–296).

[c] **10:14 ἀκούσωσιν** is supported by WH Treg NA28 SBLGNT UBS5 B $ℵ^c$ A 33 88 460 1241 1424 1735 1836 1874 2464. **ἀκούσωνται** is supported by P^{46}. **ἀκούσουσι(ν)** is supported by L 049 205 209 226 323 440 489 517 547 618 769 910 927 945 1175 1242 1352 1448 1738 1854 1891 2125 2147 2344 2815. **Ακουσονται** is supported by ℵ D K P F G 6 104, 365, 424 1243 1270 1319 1505 1506 1739 1881 2495. See Swanson, *NT GK Mss*, 160. The external evidence is mixed for ἀκούσωσιν and ακουσονται. The internal parallel of subjective mood first in the previous clauses makes it likely that the original was subjective.

[d] **10:15 κηρύξωσιν** is supported by WH Treg NA28 SBLGNT UBS5 ℵ A B C D K L P Ψ 33 88 326 796 1245 1270 1424 1573 1611 1735 1836 1837 1874 2344 2412 2464; P^{46} has **κηρύξωσι**

(Swanson, *NT GK Mss*, 161). **κηρύξουσιν** is supported by 049 𝔐. Early and some late external evidence favors **κηρύξωσιν**.
[e] **10:15 καθὼς** is supported by Treg NA28 SBLGNT UBS5 P[46] ℵ A B D F G K L P Ψ 𝔐. **καθάπερ** is supported by WH and B. External evidence strongly supports καθὼς. (Swanson, *NT GK Mss*, 161).
[f] **10:15 εὐαγγελιζομένων** is supported by WH Treg NA28 SBLGNT UBS5 B ℵ P[46] A C 056 460 1270 1506 1739 1836 1881. **εὐαγγελιζομένων plus εἰρήνην τῶν εὐαγγελιζομένων** is supported by K L P Ψ 049 D 𝔐 (Swanson, *NT GK Mss*, 161). The shorter reading could possibly be due to an accidental skipping over to the same word in the line. However, it is likely the addition was used to conform more closely to the LXX. The stronger evidence for the shorter reading seems best (Sanday & Headlam, 297; Longenecker, 831–832; Bruce M. Metzger, M. *A Textual Commentary on the Greek New Testament* [New York: United Bible Society, 1994], 463).
[g] **10:15 τὰ** is supported by SBLGNT P[46] ℵ D[1.2] K L Ψ 049 056 𝔐. NA28 UBS5 put it in the text with brackets. **Omit article**: This reading is supported by WH Treg ℵ[c] A B C D F G P 618 1505 1506 1738 1739 1881 2495. (Swanson, *NT GK Mss*, 161). Evidence is mixed and LXX Isa 52:7 does not have the article, thus, I put it in brackets in the text because the evidence is not strong.
[h] **10:17 Χριστοῦ** is supported by WH Treg NA28 SBLGNT UBS5 P[46] ℵ B C D 6 81 1243 1270 1506 1739 1852. **θεοῦ** is supported by ℵ[c] A D K L P Ψ 049 056 33 88 104 326 424 1175 1836 𝔐. It was omitted by F and G (Swanson, *NT GK Mss*, 162). The manuscript evidence is split but there seems to be a little stronger case for **Χριστοῦ**.

Translation

14 "How can they call upon Him in whom they have not believed. And how can they believe in whom they have not heard? And how can they hear without a proclaimer? **15** And how can they proclaim unless they are sent? Just as it is written, 'How timely are the feet of those who bring good news of good things!' **16** But not all have obeyed the gospel. For Isaiah says, 'Lord, who has believed our report?' **17** Therefore, faith *comes* from hearing, and hearing is through the word of Christ. **18** But I say, did they fail to hear? On the contrary; their voice has gone out into all the earth, and their words to the ends of the inhabited world. **19** But I say, has not Israel known? Moses first says, I will make you jealous with what is not a nation, with a nation that is without understanding, I will make you angry. **20** And Isaiah also boldly says, I have been found by those who did not seek me, I became known to those who did not ask for me. **21** But with reference to Israel he says, All the day long I have held out my hands to a people who are disobedient and obstinate."

Commentary

10:14 Πῶς οὖν ἐπικαλέσωνται εἰς ὃν οὐκ ἐπίστευσαν; πῶς δὲ πιστεύσωσιν οὗ οὐκ ἤκουσαν; πῶς δὲ ἀκούσωσιν χωρὶς κηρύσσοντος. "How then can they call upon Him in whom they have not believed. And how can they believe in whom they have not heard? And how can they hear without a proclaimer?" Paul uses οὖν ("then") as a deductive conjunctive to introduce questions that involve a chain of repetition through a stair-step argument, which takes up a key word in each preceding phrase ending with a climax in v. 15.[470] In v. 13, Paul has concluded the universal principle that everyone who calls upon the Lord will be saved. In v. 14, Paul beginnings with his series of four rhetorical questions (vv. 14–15a). He uses the pattern of the subjective mood in the first part of the question and the indicative mood in the second part of the questions. The exception is with the third question where the latter part of the phrase uses a participle (κηρύσσοντος, "a proclaimer"[471]) and the latter part of the fourth question he uses a conditional and a negative particle (ἐὰν μὴ, "except"), which most often uses a subjective verb. The significance of the deliberative rhetorical subjunctive in the first part of the four questions is to draw the listener into the text to do what he is asking. The question is not a question of fact but a question of obligation. "It is supremely a question of 'oughtness.'"[472] Thus, it is appropriate to translate it with a verb of "oughtness" ("can").

Paul begins his chain of thought with the ἐπικαλέσωνται ("can they call"), which is drawn from v. 13, which is a citation from Joel 2:32. The message of the gospel has been proclaimed according to Paul in v. 8 where he called it the "word of faith which we are preaching." This good news (v. 16) has been heard throughout the inhabited earth (v. 18). Secondly, to some extent this gospel has been understood (vv.19–20). However, Paul is concerned in v. 16 about their unbelief. Thus, the question is who are the "they"? It seems fairly clear that Romans 10:14-15 is referring to all peoples, both Jews and Gentiles.[473] Paul's argument in Romans 10:12-13 deals with the phrase "no distinction between Jew and Greek" and three Greek words for "all" (πᾶς twice in the plural form in 10:12 and once in the singular in 10:13).[474] Therefore, the "they" in verses 14-15 can be easily explained by the universal context of the previous verses.[475] Generally, Paul seems to address in Romans 10:14-18 all people in general while at the same time he seems, at times, to place emphasis on Israel (v.16)[476] or the Gentiles (v.18).

Paul is working backwards from the ultimate goal of calling on the Lord in belief. This belief requires someone to hear the gospel. The genitive οὗ ("whom") οὐκ ἤκουσαν ("have not heard") is usually identified with a person who is heard, and the accusative pronoun is normally used with a thing. However, the exact construction οὗ οὐκ ἤκουσαν is found in Rom 15:20, which is a quotation from Isa 52:15. Though some suggest that Paul is the preacher (Käsemann,

---

[470] Blass, Debrunner, and Funk, *A Greek Grammar*, §493 (3). He states that Rom 10:14 "is decidedly rhetorical." BDAG, 737 propose that οὖν "may be slightly adversative" ("but, however"). This is a debatable category (Beale, Brendsel, and Ross, *NT Gk Analysis of prepositions*, 77, n. 22).

[471] BDAG. 544.

[472] Wallace, *Greek Grammar Beyond the Basic*, 467.

[473] The rest of the paragraph was taken from Sullivan, *The INE in Rom 9–11*, 307–308.

[474] See Bell, *Provoked to Jealousy*, 83-84.

[475] Scholars who believe that Rom 10:14-15 (and perhaps vv.14-18, except many think v. 16 is to Israel) refer to people in general: Käsemann, 294; Dunn, 620; Moo, 2nd, 680–81; Schreiner, 2nd, 552–53. Others think that Paul is addressing Gentiles: Haldane, 512; Hodge, 346-47. Still others who believe that Paul is addressing Israel: Godet, 385; Sanday and Headlam, 295; Barrett, 203–205; Cranfield, 2:533; Fitzmyer, 595. Bell, *Provoked to Jealousy*, 83-87 gives four solid reasons why Israel is not the main people, but Jews and Gentiles are addressed in Rom 10:14-15, 17-18 (see also Jewett, 637–638). Bell, *Provoked to Jealousy*, 90-93 and Murray, 2:60 argue correctly that the subject changes to the Jews at Romans 10:16.

[476] Scholars that support Israel as the addressee in Rom 10:16 are Bell, *Provoked to Jealousy*, 90-92; Morris, 391; Moo, 2nd, 682–83; Schreiner, 2nd, 556–57. Wright, 10:668 stated that it "is far more likely to be a comment on the Gentile mission. . . ." Bell points out that Paul uses the context of Isa 52:15 in Rom 15:21 to speak of the Gentiles and the context of Isa 53:1 in Rom 10:16 as well as in Jn 12:38 to speak to the Jews (Bell, *Provoked to Jealousy*, 92).

293) or Christ as preached (Godet, 212)[477] the context seems to refer to the word of the gospel (Moo, 663, n. 11) in Rom 10 and if Paul was thinking of Isa 52:15 the context in this OT text is the content proclaimed. However, in v. 17 Paul does use an interesting phrase "word of Christ" (Jewett, 638). The message of the gospel is centered in who Jesus Christ is and what He did on our behalf. Thus, we are all admonished to proclaim the message of this person!

10:15 πῶς δὲ κηρύξωσιν ἐὰν μὴ ἀποσταλῶσιν; καθὼς γέγραπται· Ὡς ὡραῖοι οἱ πόδες τῶν εὐαγγελιζομένων [τὰ] ἀγαθά. "And how can[478] they proclaim unless they are sent? Just as it is written, 'How timely are the feet of those who bring good news of good things!'" Paul uses a citation from Isa 52:7 to supplement his admonishment to proclaim the gospel. The stress on redemption (Isa 52:3, 9), the declaration of the name of "Yahweh," (Isa 52:6), the implication of captivity and deliverance in Egypt, Assyria, and most likely Babylon (Isa 52:4–5), and the parallels of Isa 52:7–12 with Isa 40:1–11 all reflect a NE motif as the background for Paul's citation.[479] The background of this section entails the Babylonian deliverance, which pictures, in a typico-prophetic way,[480] the eschatological future.[481] The future is indicated with the phrase in Isa 52:6 "in that day," which is often used "when prophecies are fulfilled, in the nearer or more distant future."[482] The poetic setting of 52:7-8 is in typical historical surroundings of the Old Testament where the runner/messenger is anticipated to bring important news to awaiting people. The messenger indeed has good news, peace, and the message of salvation. However, this victory does not come by ordinary means; it is a victory won by the Lord who reigns (Isa 52:7; cf. Ex 15:18).[483] This victory is called a restoration (Isa 52:8), redemption (Isa 52:3, 9; cf. Ex 15:13, 16), and salvation (Isa 52:7, 10; cf. Ex 14:13, 30; 15:2). The people see with their own eyes the restoration of Zion (Isa 52:8; cf. Deut 30:3-5) and the redemption of Jerusalem (Isa 52:9). There is the announcement of the good news of salvation in the sight of all the nations for the Lord will lay bare his holy arm (cf. Ex 15:16) that all the ends of the earth may see his salvation (Isa 52:7, 10; cf. Ex 9:16).[484] Shum summarizes three important points concerning the context of Isaiah 52:7: (1) the triumph of the God of Israel is that he will become the King over the whole earth in Zion; (2) before God's triumphant reigning, messengers will be sent out to

---

[477] Others suggest that the genitive refers to Christ as the one who is heard in the message of the gospel (Sanday and Headlam, 296; Murray, 2:58; Cranfield, 534; Dunn, 620).

[478] See comments on v. 14 concerning the translation "can."

[479] Sullivan, *The INE in Rom 9–11*, 281. See also chapters 6.2.3 and 6.5.

[480] Douglas J. Moo, "The Problem of *Sensus Plenior*," 196 defines this aspect of typology: "The 'anticipatory' element in these typological experiences may sometimes have been more or less dimly perceived by the participants and human authors; but it is to be ascribed finally to God, who ordered these events in such a way that they would possess a 'prophetic' function." Delitzsch, *Psalms*, 1:69–70 describes typico-prophetically messianic as a Davidic statement (for example) that goes beyond David and is historically true about Christ. Beale, *Handbook on the New Testament Use of the Old Testament*, 16–18, 58–59 calls this concept "indirect typological fulfillment." This indirect typology "fulfills what was implicitly foreshadowed by historical events, which have been narrated" (p.18). See Sullivan, *The INE in Rom 9–11*, 281–286.

[481] There is agreement with some parts, even word for word agreement, when Isa 52:7–8 is compared to Nah 2:1–3 (Eng 1:15–2:2). However, the Nahum quotation does not have the prophetic connotation like Isa 52:7–10 (Blenkinsopp, *Isaiah 40–55*, 342).

[482] Goldingay, *The Message of Isaiah 40–55*, 450. בַּיּוֹם הַהוּא is found 41 times in Isa 1–31 and once (52:6) in Isa 32–66.

[483] Goldingay and Payne, *A Critical and Exegetical Commentary on Isaiah 40-55*, 2:264-65 give the debate on the verb מָלַךְ and states that either way one takes the verb "the prophet is declaring that Yhwh is now asserting sovereignty in the community's life."

[484] Sullivan, *The INE in Rom 9–11*, 282–283.

declare his victory; and (3) God's triumphant reign will bring about the salvation of Israel as well as affecting the nations of the earth (Isa 52:10).[485] This summary is the context of the passage in Isa 52:7, which Paul cites in Romans.

Behind Paul's thought of a herald who proclaims good news, there seems to reside a broader contextual theology than just Isaiah 52:7. This broader context is the good news of salvation, restoration, and the reign of God, which points to an Exodus motif that forms the framework of Paul's use and modification of Isaiah 52:7. The proclamation of good news is brought out by the Hebrew word בָּשַׂר ("bring good news"),[486] which is rendered by the LXX word εὐαγγελίζω ("bring good news") and is part of the broader contextual theology that Paul is drawing on in Isaiah.[487] Significance is found not only in the words Paul uses from Isaiah 52:7 in Romans 10:15, but also in the words that are absent or different.[488] First, the phrase "on the mountains" referring most likely to the area surrounding Jerusalem, is not read in Paul's form of the quotation. This omission, whether a deliberate alteration or from a no longer extant variant LXX text broadens the scope geographically so that the application of the quotation may refer to Gentiles as well as Jews.[489] Second, Paul does not include the phrase "of one bringing glad tidings of a report of peace" (εὐαγγελιζομένου ἀκοὴν εἰρήνης), for Paul appears to express his message of peace (ἀκοή, Rom 10:16, 17[*bis*]) as the "word of faith" (Rom 10:8–10) or the "word of Christ" (Rom 10:17), which causes the focus to be on the gospel of Christ. Third, in place of the singular participle form of εὐαγγελίζω, Paul uses a plural participle. This reading helps to reveal how Paul sees his ministry and the Church's ministry typologically prefigured in Isaiah 52:7. The good news is now the responsibility of every believer to proclaim it to both Jews and Gentiles.

The biblical background of the NE proclamations, which is found in Isaiah, sets the framework so that Paul may use the quotation from Isaiah 52 (cf. Isa 40:9; 52:7; 60:6; 61:1–2). The historical background is the proclamation of God's redemption of Israel from the Babylonian captivity. However, some of the language in Isaiah 52:7, as well as some of its immediate context, directs the reader to the eschatological redemption. This eschatological redemption not only includes spiritual redemption, but also a physical restoration of the people, Jerusalem, and the land; a restoration where God will reign as king and the nations will see the salvation of God (Isa 52:3–12; cf. Isa 40:1–11). This typico-prophetic eschatological NE redemption provides the prophetic proclamation Paul needs to demonstrate to the Jewish people that God has indeed provided salvation in the gospel (Rom 10:8–10). This "gospel finds its conceptual home within the context of God's ancient promises to deliver his people."[490] Paul knows that the completion of the eschatological redemption is not yet here, so he does not use the phrase "your God reigns." However, the Lord God who will reign, has come, provided salvation, and has been raised from the dead and one day will come again. In the INE motif of heralding the good news, Paul has chosen or adapted a form of Isaiah 52:7 that allows him to

---

[485] Shum, *Paul's Use of Isaiah in Romans*, 224; Wagner, *Heralds of the Good News*, 170.

[486] See Isa 40:9(*bis*); 41:27; 52:7(*bis*); 60:6; 61:1; Nah 1:15 (MT 2:1). Isa 41:27 and the connection with Isa 42 may associate this verse with the NE motif. See Sullivan, *The INE in Rom 9–11*, 288–291 for a development of the good news proclamation and the Exodus theme.

[487] See Isa 40:9(*bis*); 52:7(*bis*); 60:6; 61:1; Nah 1:15 (LXX 2:1); Joel 2:32 (LXX 3:5). Watts, *Isaianic New Exodus and Mark,* 96 recognizes that in the "Hebrew Scriptures and the LXX, the theological use of the verbal form (בָּשַׂר, εὐαγγελίζω) occurs almost twice as often in Isaianic NE contexts as in the rest of the OT."

[488] The rest of paragraph and the next paragraph were taken from Sullivan, *The INE in Rom 9–11*, 291–292.

[489] Wagner, *Heralds of the Good News*, 173.

[490] Wagner, *Heralds of the Good News*, 175. See also Seifrid, "Romans," 662.

present the pattern of the ancient good news proclamation as a NE motif, which was established in the OT prophets to communicate the universal mandate and message of spreading the good news. The good news proclamation understood in the INE motif would communicate like an amplified loudspeaker to his Jewish audience for it is grounded in the patterns, promises, and history of the Old Testament. Furthermore, his proclamation argument would, at the same time, confront the Jewish present situation, comfort those who believe the message, and challenge them to proclaim the gospel to both Jews and Gentiles. The good news in the context of Rom 10 is the gospel that is expressed as the "the word of faith" (vv. 8-10) or "the word of Christ" (v. 17).

Moo points out that the word ὡραῖοι in Rom 10:15 may be translated "timely," rather than "beautiful," giving "support to the eschatological focus" on this proclamation (Moo, *The Epistle to the Romans*, 664. See the same point in Jewett, *Romans*, 640; and Dunn, *Romans 9–16*, 621–22).[491] The evidence points to the meaning of "timely." The gospel message and its proclamation came at the opportune time. This translation supports the eschatological focus on the gospel.

10:16 ἀλλ' οὐ πάντες ὑπήκουσαν[492] τῷ εὐαγγελίῳ· Ἠσαΐας γὰρ λέγει· Κύριε, τίς ἐπίστευσεν τῇ ἀκοῇ ἡμῶν. "But not all have obeyed the gospel. For Isaiah says, 'Lord, who has believed our report?'" Though the mission of Paul and the Church is to send out heralds to proclaim the gospel of Jesus Christ, not everyone accepts the message. Paul uses the words of Isaiah to ask the question, "Lord who has believed our message (ἀκοή)?" This witness from Isaiah seems to designate the pattern of disobedience and unbelief that characterizes the nation of Israel. The unbelief in the "message" (ἀκοή) that Isaiah 53:1 addresses corresponds to the unbelief that Paul faced in his day. The word ἀκοή also appears in Isaiah 52:7 ("good news of a report [ἀκοή] of peace") and connects the concept of the NE proclamation theology with the "message," as well as Israel's pattern of unbelief to this message.[493] The message of Isaiah 53:1 relates to the servant (Isa 52:13), whose identity is possibly best characterized as the greater Moses (Deut 18:15–22; 34:10–12). The message of this servant is described with the NE theme, the "arm of the Lord"[494] (Isa 53:1b; 52:10), and the servant's actions. The servant's actions become an important part of the message and are further described in Isaiah 53:2-12. This entire NE framework is the background that surrounds the work of the Servant. This NE framework exerts its force when Paul cites the first part of Isaiah 53:1 in Romans 10:16.[495]

---

[491] Louw and Nida, *Greek-English Lexicon of the New Testament*, 67.3 translated it "timely, or happened at the right time." BDAG, 1103 translated Rom 10:15 "opportune point of time or timely." Liddell, and Scott, *A Greek-English Lexicon*, 2036 is dominated by the meaning of "timely," or "produced, happen or done at the right season." The parallel Hebrew word נָאווּ is translated by Brown, Driver, and Briggs, *A Hebrew and English Lexicon*, 610 as "becomely" or "befitting." However, Koehler, Baumgartner, Richardson and Stamm, *The Hebrew and Aramaic Lexicon*, 657 give the meaning as "be pleasing, delightful."

[492] Shedd (322) defines it as a willing subjection and not merely the assent of the understanding. BDAG, 1029 defines the term as "to follow instructions, obey, follow, be subject to" and places Rom 10:16 under the definition "to which one is obedient" or "of which one embraces in full surrender" (Act 6:7; 2 Th 1:8; 2 Th 3:14). Blass, Debrunner, and Funk, *A Greek Grammar*, §186 (6) states that with the dative it has the meaning of "trust or obey".

[493] Seifrid, 662.

[494] See Sullivan, *The INE in Rom 9–11*, 202–205 for a development of the concept of God's "arm" as a NE motif.

[495] This section was taken from Ibid., 304–305.

Verse 16 emphasizes that faith is missing in the very people who God physically chose to be his people (Moo, 2nd, 682–83; Cranfield, 535–536).[496] The adversive ἀλλ' ("but") accents this point. Dunn (622) argues for more of a general failure in the chain of events vv. 14–15a. The phrase οὐ πάντες ("not all") is to be understood as a litotes[497] (others use the term meiosis – Schreiner, 2nd, 556; Cranfield, 536; Dunn, 622; Jewett, 640–41), which indicates that the majority of the Jews had not believed the proclaimed gospel. This point is brought out in Paul's lament (Rom 9:1-3 and 10:1) and his declaration in Rom 9:6. Cranfield (536) is correct to point out that 10:16 again brings out the connection of faith and obedience (cf. Rom 1:5 with the phrase "obedience of faith") for obedience to the gospel "is to believe it and to believe in Him who is its content. . . ." This obedience is not faith plus works, but a faith through the power of the Holy Spirit that expresses itself in the life of the believer (Eph 2:10; 1 Pet 1:3–5) (Fitzmyer, 598; Jewett, 641).

10:17 ἄρα ἡ πίστις ἐξ ἀκοῆς, ἡ δὲ ἀκοὴ διὰ ῥήματος Χριστοῦ. "Therefore, faith *comes* from hearing, and hearing is through the word of Christ." The use of ἀκοή ("hearing" or "message") has an important force in Rom 10:17 to bring out the background of Paul's thought from Isaiah 53:1, which he cites in 10:16. Some scholars think this verse is out of place or possibly added by later additions.[498] However, Rom 10:17 is an appropriate conclusion to at least Rom 10:14–17 for it is picking up the context of the kind of hearing that leads to faith (Moo, 2nd, 684). The word ἀκοή can mean: (1) The act of hearing (listening), or (2) that which is heard (e.g., report, message).[499] In Rom 10:16, the latter is indicated, but in Rom 10:17, the former definition is best, especially if 10:17 sums up the preceding thought: "How are they to believe in one of whom they have never heard?" (Rom 10:14).[500] If the word is translated "message," then the connection with the idea of μὴ οὐκ ἤκουσαν ("have they not heard") in Romans 10:18 is obscured and sits awkwardly with the phrase διὰ ῥήματος Χριστοῦ ("by the word of Christ") in Romans 10:17.[501]

The message (ἀκοή) of Rom 10:16 must have content. The content of the message is called the ῥῆμα τῆς πίστεως ("word of faith") in Rom 10:8 and the ῥήματος Χριστοῦ ("word of Christ") in Rom 10:17.[502] The former underscores "the call to faith that is inherent to God's work in Christ" and the latter emphasizes "the unchanging content of that address."[503] These two phrases complement each other, and at the same time, are interwoven into an inverted pattern.[504] Paul first speaks of the "word of faith" and describes the content of the gospel in Rom 10:8–10, which is also described in some detail in Isa 53:2–12. Then he uses the phrase "the word of

---

[496] See v. 15 discussion on who Paul is addressing in this section.

[497] Litotes or meiosis refers to "one thing is diminished in order to increase *another* thing" (E. W. Bullinger, *Figures of Speech Used in the Bible*, Explained and Illustrated [Grand Rapids: Baker reprint, 1968], 155).

[498] There does not seem to be any textual evidence for this (see Swanson, ed. *NT Gk Mss, Rom*, 162). See the solid discussion to retain the verse by Cranfield, 2:536–37; and Bell, *Provoked to Jealousy*, 92–93.

[499] BDAG, 36.

[500] Barrett, 205; Murray, 2:60–61; Dunn, *Romans 9–16*, 623; Schreiner, 566–67.

[501] Sanday and Headlam, 197–98; Schreiner, 567.

[502] See Bekken, *The Word is Near You*, 200 for three different views for understanding the phrase "word of Christ": (1) the objective genitive – message about Christ; (2) the genitive of origin – Christ as the bearer of the message and (3) Christ's word of commission to his apostles. He thinks the first two positions are possible but settles on the second. However, there is good reason for preferring the objective genitive (Moo, 2nd, 684, n. 534; Sanday and Headlam, 298).

[503] Seifrid, 663.

[504] This insight derives from Ibid., 663.

Christ" to describe the proclamation of the gospel, which is declared in Isa 52:7–10. Interestingly, Paul's quotation of Isa 53:1 in Rom 10:16 is found in between the two Isaianic thoughts (Isa 52:7–10; 53:2–12) and is connected with both. Whether one is speaking about the act of faith or the content of faith, both concepts are centered in the suffering servant, the new Moses – Jesus Christ. His death and resurrection provide redemption for everyone who believes and will provide the promised eschatological salvation in the future.[505]

10:18 Ἀλλὰ λέγω, μὴ οὐκ[506] ἤκουσαν; μενοῦνγε· Εἰς πᾶσαν τὴν γῆν ἐξῆλθεν ὁ φθόγγος αὐτῶν, καὶ εἰς τὰ πέρατα τῆς οἰκουμένης τὰ ῥήματα αὐτῶν. "But I say, did they fail to hear? On the contrary; their voice has gone out into all the earth, and their words to the ends of the inhabited world." In the remainder of Rom 10:18-21, Paul considers and answers objections to his conclusion in Rom 10:17. In Rom 10:18, the objection is raised with the following question: "Have they not heard?" Paul answers the question with "indeed they have" and then cites Ps 19:4 (MT 19:5 and LXX 18:5). Generally, Paul seems to address in Rom 10:14–18 all people in general while at the other times he seems to place emphasis on Israel (v. 16)[507] or the Gentiles (v.18). Much may be said about why Paul uses Ps 19:4 in the context of Rom 10. The context of Ps 19 deals with general revelation in nature (19:1–6), special revelation (19:7–10), the application concerning the revelation (19:11–13), and ends with a benediction to God as rock and redeemer (19:14).[508] The final prayer of the psalmist "serves as the focal point and climax of the entire psalm."[509] The prayer says, "Let the words of my mouth and the meditation of my heart be acceptable to you, O Lord, my rock and my redeemer." The word rock (צוּר) and redeemer (גאל) are used in the Old Testament as NE motifs.[510] Wagner concludes that the entire composition and weight of Ps 19 comes to focus in the psalmist's address in the last verse, because there is a "progressive narrowing of focus from the heavens' praise of El as creator to the petition of the human heart to Yhwh as rock and redeemer."[511] Wagner recognizes the

---

[505] Most of the information of this section was taken from Sullivan, *The INE in Rom 9–11*, 305–306.

[506] Blass, Debrunner, and Funk, *A Greek Grammar*, §365 indicates this negative construction μὴ οὐκ with an aorist subjunctive or future indicative is the most definite form of negation regarding the future. However, this negative construction is connected with an aorist indicative verb. Robertson, *A Grammar of the Greek New Testament*, 1174 states that μὴ is the interrogative particle and οὐκ is the negative of the verb. Robertson translates it "did they fail to hear" expecting a negative answer. See also Rom 10:19.

[507] Scholars who support Israel as the addressee in Rom 10:16 are Bell, *Provoked to Jealousy*, 90–92; Morris, 391; Moo, 2nd, 682–83; Schreiner, 2nd, 556. Wright, 10:668 stated that it "is far more likely to be a comment on the Gentile mission. . . ." Bell points out that Paul uses the context of Isa 52:15 in Rom 15:21 to speak of the Gentiles and the context of Isa 53:1 in Rom 10:16 as well as in Jn 12:38 to speak to the Jews (*Provoked to Jealousy*, 92).

[508] Wagner, "From the Heavens to the Heart," 245–61. See also Dunn, 624 who suggests that Rom 10:18 could be prophetic or looking at the total context of the psalm.

[509] Wagner, "From the Heavens to the Heart," 259.

[510] Sullivan, *The INE in Rom 9–11*, 248–260. Wagner, "From the Heavens to the Heart," 260, makes a solid argument to connect both "rock" and "redeemer," to the Exodus: (1) the characterization of God as rock in Deut 32:4 (see also more support in chapter 8.1 of Sullivan's book); (2) Yahweh acts as a redeemer (Ex 6:6; 15:13; Isa 41:14; 43:1,14); and (3) the compound לְרָצוֹן is used as a technical term, which describes an acceptable offering to God (Ex 28:38; Lev 1:3; 19:5; 22:19–21; 22:29; 23:11; cf. Isa 56:7; Jer 6:20). The creator of the universe, the giver of the perfect Torah, and the one who accepts sacrifice of praise and forgives him is also a rock and a redeemer. "He understood the whole psalm as the 'the words of my mouth and meditation of my heart.' Thus, the entire composition, which has embraced the majesty of the universe and the perfection of Torah, comes to focus on the psalmist and his prayer" (p. 260).

[511] Ibid., 246.

progressive narrowing, but he misses the importance of the NE motif, though he recognizes the Exodus connection. The context of Ps 19:4 is influenced by the NE phrase "O LORD, my rock and my redeemer" at the end of the psalm. Ps 19 keeps the NE climatic end in focus throughout the psalm. The concept of redemption is refracted throughout Psalm 19. Thus, the context of the NE narrowing to the climax of redemption needs to bring its weight to bear when Ps 19:4 is used in Rom 10:18.[512]

The progressive narrowing is the shift in Ps 19 from general revelation in creation as a testimony to the God of creation, to special revelation where God is addressed as redeemer. The progressive narrowing points out how Paul uses Ps 19:4 in Rom 10:18. Natural revelation portrays and anticipates the spreading of the gospel message to the end of the earth.[513] It is quite possible that the reader would associate the words like ἤκουσαν ("they heard") and ῥήματα ("words") in Ps 19:4, which are cited in Rom 10:18 with the preceding argument in Rom 10:14–17. In the preceding argument, Paul used the verb ἀκούω ("hear") twice (Rom 10:14) as a reference to hearing the gospel.[514] In addition, the word ἀκοή ("message, hear") is used three times (Rom 10:16–17) in relationship to the gospel. Finally, the word ῥῆμα ("word") is used three times (Rom 10:8, 17) to refer to the gospel message. As a result, Paul seemed to draw on Ps 19:4 to demonstrate that all people have heard the Creator's word in creation (Rom 1:19–20). However, Paul appropriated Psalm 19:4 with the anticipation and understanding that the redemption message at the end of the psalm is refracted back throughout the psalm. Thus, this influence is flavoring all the psalm that the Redeemer God has done all these things. Understanding this contextual point, Paul is using the way of analogy in the context of a NE motif to utilize the image of the universal proclamation of the word in general revelation as the anticipatory picture of the gospel spreading throughout the world. Therefore, Paul draws the following themes together to make his point: (1) the testimony of the word in creation going throughout the earth in Psalm 19:4; (2) the broader context of Ps 19:4 with its progressive narrowing, which focuses on the NE address in prayer to the rock and redeemer, which should be refracted back through all of Psalm 19; and (3) the preceding argument in Rom 10:14–18 where Paul stresses the proclamation of the word or message, hearing the message, and believing or having faith in the word of Christ. Therefore, in the framework of the argument concerning the message, proclamation, and Redeemer, is the NE background.[515] This point will also be strengthened when Paul quotes Moses in Rom 10:19. In this present age, the Redeemer God (Rom 10:14–15; cf. Ps 19:14) commissions and sends out heralds to proclaim the message of the gospel to the ends of the inhabited earth,[516] just as he ordains the creation to proclaim his message to all the earth.[517]

Moo (2nd, 684–85) suggests Paul may be using the term "earth" and "inhabited earth" to refer to the Roman empire or possibly corporately. However, he settles on Paul's use as a hyperbole. Paul's use of Ps 19:4 as an analogy indicates Paul is not using this to mean

---

512 Most of the paragraph was taken from Sullivan, *The INE in Rom 9–11*, 308–309.

513 Johnson, *The Function of Apocalyptic and Wisdom Traditions in Romans 9–11*, 159; Schreiner, 2nd, 557–59. *Contra* Hahne, "Paul's Use of the Old Testament in Romans 10:16–11:10," 2–3 who applies the argument with Israel as the addressees. Seifrid, 663 applies the argument to the nations.

514 The word ὑπακούω is also used in Rom 10:16, which is related to ἀκούω (Keck, 259).

515 Wagner is correct that the larger framework was established by Paul's quotation from Isa 52:7; 53:1 and allusion to Isa 40:21, 28 (Ibid., 185).

516 Wagner, *Heralds of the Good News*, 186. He also believes Paul is addressing Israel. Israel, being one of the nations of the earth, would be included in this statement.

517 This paragraph came from Sullivan, *The INE in Rom 9–11*, 309–310.

individualistic.[518] Generally, Murray (2:61) seems correct that Paul is referring to "all without distinction" or possibly all kinds of people geographically in the inhabited world.

Thus, the following summarizes the difficult text of Ps 19:4 and how it seems to be interpreted in the context of Romans 10:16–18. The total context of the psalm is an important key. There is a progressive narrowing of the subject of psalm 19: from general revelation, to special revelation, to application, and finally the benediction, which is the climax and focal point. This progressive narrowing ends with the Lord being "my rock and my redeemer." This climax and focal point is the most important part of the psalm and should be refracted back through all the verses, making the NE statement that God is "my rock and my redeemer" the focus of the psalm. By way of analogy, Paul applies the universal proclamation of the word through general revelation of creation as a picture of the gospel of redemption that is being spread to Jews and Gentiles throughout the inhabited earth. One may suspect that Paul is using this OT verse as an analogy, but commentators' explanations as to why Paul may have used this verse are numerous and diverse. The explanation of the framework of the NE motif that draws on the climatic ending that refracts back through the psalm gives a solid base for Paul's analogy. Without this explanation, one is puzzled how and why Paul used this text.[519]

10:19 ἀλλὰ λέγω, μὴ Ἰσραὴλ οὐκ ἔγνω; πρῶτος Μωϋσῆς λέγει· Ἐγὼ παραζηλώσω ὑμᾶς ἐπ' οὐκ ἔθνει, ἐπ' ἔθνει ἀσυνέτῳ παροργιῶ ὑμᾶς. "But I say, has not Israel known? Moses first says, I myself will make you jealous with what is not a nation, with a nation that is without understanding, I will make you angry." The repetition of ἀλλὰ λέγω ("but I say") in vv. 18 and 19 seem to indicate a second point in Paul's argument that began in v. 18. In v. 18, Paul addresses the possibility that Israel was prevented from hearing the message and in v. 19, he investigates that their hearing may be hindered or merely superficial hearing. This concern harkens back to Paul's point in vv. 14–17. Shocking as it may seem, Israel did know, and Paul uses the Song of Moses in Deut 32 to demonstrate his point. The use of πρῶτος may be comparative and translated "formerly." However, it is most likely referring to time ("first") where Moses is the first witness in a long line of witness to the truth of Paul's argument (Murray, 2:62, n.23 ; Dunn, 625; Jewett, ; Longenecker, 857, n.54).[520] The Jewish people could not level a legitimate accusation that they did not know because God made it known in the OT. Cranfield (538) is correct when he says that in one sense Israel knew and, in another sense, they did not know. The thought of "not a nation" in the Duet 32 citation was already used by Paul in Hos 2:23 and 1:10 citations in Rom 9:25–26.

There are verbal connections that help to validate the Song of Moses, which is connected not just with Deut 32:21 in Rom 10:19, but with Isa 65:1–2 in the quotation of Rom 10:20–21.[521]

---

[518] Schreiner (2nd, 558) and Cranfield (537) have similar opinions.

[519] This paragraph came from Sullivan, *The INE in Rom 9–11*, 380.

[520] See Cranfield (539) for a discussion of the punctuation of the first part of v. 19. His conclusion seems to be sound. Robertson, *A Grammar of the Greek New Testament*, 657 understands the word adjectivally and translates it "Moses is the first who says." See also Matt 5:24; 10:2; Jn 1:41.

[521] See Sullivan, *The INE in Rom 9–11*, 315–316. For more connection of Deut 32 with Rom 9–11, see Bell, *Provoked to Jealousy*, 279–81. Bell states that the broad influence of the Song of Moses on Rom 9–11 is: the "faithfulness of God"; the "inscrutable nature of God's purposes"; the tension between God's judgment and love for Israel; and the portrayal of the Song in the history of Israel (i.e., her election, fall, judgment, and salvation). Bell also indicates that Sifre Deuteronomy 32 may have similar understanding with Paul concerning Israel. Yahweh will intervene to save Israel despite their disobedience. However, Bell recognizes Paul and Sifre Deuteronomy 32 differ on at least two points: how many will be saved, and salvation is only through faith in Christ (Ibid., 243). For more information on Deuteronomy 32 and the Jewish and Christian traditions, see Ibid., 209–50.

Wagner briefly outlines Deut 32: (1) the address to the heavens and earth (vv. 1–3); (2) Israel's unfaithfulness and the astonishing faithfulness of Israel's God (vv. 4–6); (3) God's election and redemption through the events of the Exodus (vv. 7–14); (4) Israel's fall into idolatry (vv. 15–18); (5) God's jealous response by bringing the curses of the covenant (vv. 19–25); (6) God has mercy upon Israel because of his name and delivers them (vv. 26–42); and (7) doxology of praise from Israel and the nations to the faithful and righteous God.[522] In section 5, Paul draws out his quotation in Rom 10:19. In this section, the concept of God being called Father in regard to the nation of Israel is important. This motif of God being Father seems to find its roots in Deut 32:6.[523] This motif is reinforced by the theme of "sons" in Deut 32:5. Moses says of God, "Yet his degenerate children (בָּנָיו, "his sons") have dealt falsely with him, a perverse and crooked generation." The same context of a father/son motif is also found in Paul's quotation of Deut 32:21, though the word "father" is not used. This motif is brought out by the phrase "his sons (בָּנָיו) and daughters" in 32:19 and the clause "for they are a perverse generation, children (בָּנִים, "sons") in whom there is no faithfulness" in 32:20. If all the evidence on the concept of father/sons is accepted, then both quotations in Rom 10:19–21 (Deut 32:21 and Isa 65:1–2) have an Exodus father/son motif[524] and a context in which a disobedient nation experiences the consequences of rebelling against God and his covenant.[525] The context of Deut 32:19–25 is from God's perspective through Moses and Isa 63:7–64:12 (MT/LXX 63:7–64:11) is from the nation's perspective concerning God as expressed by the writer until God speaks in Isaiah 65:1–7.[526]

In all of Israel's unfaithfulness, the Lord stands unswervingly faithful to fullfil his promises to Israel. In Deut 32:19, God saw their idolatry and sin and "was jealous; he spurned his sons and daughters." God decides to hide his face from the unfaithful sons (Deut 32:20) and he brings terrible judgments upon them (Deut 32:23–25). Though God judges them, he will not destroy them, but he will use the Gentile nations to provoke them to jealousy (Deut 32:21). The implication in the text is that God will use his relationship with the Gentiles to provoke to jealousy his sons so that they return to him (cf. 32:36, 43). This point is strongly indicated in the latter part of the Song of Moses where God arose, defended his people, and defeated Israel's enemies.

Though Deut 32:43 in the MT and LXX is different, they both address the Gentiles concerning what God will accomplish for his people.[527] Paul has a tendency to adopt negative

---

522 Wagner, "Moses and Isaiah in Concert," 91–93. Wagner, *Heralds of the Good News*, 193 gives a brief outline of Deut 32 from the LXX.

523 For a detail discussion of this point see Sullivan, *The INE in Rom 9–11*, 310–315.

524 Notice the four points concerning the Exodus and the NE in Isa 63–64: (1) the Exodus motif is used to express redemption in Isa 63:7–14); (2) a NE appeal of the Lord as Father and Redeemer is used though the nation acts like the Gentile nations (Isa 63:15–64); (3) in Isa 64:1–7, there is a confession that includes an appeal from the NE motif and a declaration of trust in the midst of Israel's rebellion and sin; (4) a renewed appeal to the Creator Father that draws on earlier themes (Isa 64:8–12). For a detail discussion on these points, see Ibid., 311–315.

525 See Wagner, *Heralds of the Good News*, 195, note 224 for vocabulary connections with the covenantal curses. It is clear from Deut 28 that the nation will experience these covenantal curses when they disobey God.

526 This paragraph and the following two paragraphs came from Sullivan, *The INE in Rom 9–11*, 316–318.

527 The translation of Deut 32:43 (LXX) says, "Be glad, O skies, with him, and let all the divine sons do obeisance to him. Be glad, O nations, with his people, and let all the angels of God prevail for him. For he will avenge the blood of his sons and take revenge and repay the enemies with a sentence, and he will repay those who hate, and the Lord shall cleanse the land of his people." The translation of the MT says, "Rejoice, O Gentiles, with His people; For He will avenge the blood of his Servants, And render vengeance to His adversaries; He will provide atonement for his land and His people" (NKJV). The NRSV accepts some of the LXX. It says, "Praise, O heavens,

descriptions from Scripture to refer to Gentiles "in order to highlight the reversal wrought by God's grace. The similarity of description, 'no-nation,' to the appellation, 'not my people,' quoted by Paul from Hosea in Rom 9:25–26, may well have contributed to his selection of Deut 32:21."[528] The Exodus motif of Deut 32:21 uses a father/son motif and introduces the concept of provoking Israel to jealousy by the Gentiles who are addressed at the end of the Song of Moses. The implication is that God will use the Gentiles as part of his plan to bring atonement to the land and the people (32:43). Part of this eschatological future of the Gentiles is God's use of them in Paul's own day. He will take up this thought in Rom 11:11–14. Paul introduces Deut 32:21 from the Exodus motif of the Song of Moses in Rom 10:19 to alert the reader to a Gentile orientation, which he will applied to Isa 65:1 in Rom 10:20. In other words, Paul seems to interpret Deut 32:21 and Isa 65:1 in concert with each other[529] by way of analogy drawing upon NE theme as the connection (see further comments in v. 20).

10:20 Ἠσαΐας δὲ ἀποτολμᾷ καὶ λέγει· Εὑρέθην ἐν τοῖς ἐμὲ μὴ ζητοῦσιν, ἐμφανὴς ἐγενόμην τοῖς ἐμὲ μὴ ἐπερωτῶσιν. "And Isaiah also boldly says, I have been found by those who did not seek me, I became known to those who did not ask for me." Paul begins with a declaration of the boldness of the prophet Isaiah's writing in Isaiah 65:1 (Cranfield, 540; Dunn, 625). The decisive reason that Gentiles who did not seek righteousness, receive righteousness is because God manifested Himself to them (Rom 9:30; 10:20) (Schreiner, 2nd, 561).

Deut 32 reinforces the Exodus motif of the immediate context of Isa 65:1–2, as well as the broader context of Isa 63:7–64:12 (MT/LXX 63:7–64:11). Wagner appears to be correct when he states that Paul interprets Deut 32 and Isa 65 in the light of one another in Rom 10:19-21.[530] Deut 32 reinforces the Exodus motif of the immediate context of Isa 65:1-2, as well as the broader context of Isa 63:7-64:12. This claim is demonstrated in the verbal and thematic connections between the two passages.[531]

---

his people, worship him, all you gods! For he will avenge the blood of his children, and take vengeance on his adversaries; he will repay those who hate him, and cleanse the land for his people." The ESV is close to the NRSV.

[528] Wagner, *Heralds of the Good News*, 197. Wagner, "'Not from the Jews Only, But Also from the Gentiles,'" 423 reinforces the same point. For example, see: "not my people . . . not beloved" in Rom 9:25–26 (Hos 2:23/1:10); "Gentiles, who did not strive for righteousness" in Rom 9:30 (Isa 51:1); "who are not a nation . . . a foolish nation" in Rom 10:19 (Deut 32:21); "those who have never been told . . . those who have never heard" in Rom 15:21 (Isa 52:15) (Wagner, *Heralds of the Good News*, 212, note 275).

[529] Wagner, *Heralds of the Good News*, 190.

[530] Ibid.

[531] This paragraph was taken from Sullivan, *The INE in Rom 9–11*, 319.

The contemporary debate concerning the interpretation of Isa 65:1[532] is: whom did God address in the passage? Most commentators consider that Isa 65:1-2 refers to Jewish people[533] while others believe that verse 1 refers to Gentiles and verse 2 to the Jewish people, which parallel the way Paul uses it in Rom 10:20-21.[534] There are good arguments on both sides of the issue, which have led to a third view that makes modifications to both sides and relies upon arguments on both sides.[535] The third view correctly states that the context before and after Isa 65:1-2 is a Jewish context. However, there are also Gentile connections before and after Isa 65:1-2. Isa 64:1-3 (Isa 64:2-4 LXX/MT) is an INE motif, which is used not only to communicate to the Jewish people but also to cause the nations to tremble at God's presence and make his name known (64:2). The Gentiles are part of the subject of this address, at least through Isa 64:4. What surrounds and spirals out from this NE motif of Isa 63:1b–64:5 are verbal themes and images, which are laden with Gentile-type rebellious and disobedient conduct that is applied to Jewish people.[536] This is key to the understanding of the correct interpretation of this passage in Romans 10:20. Isaiah uses this INE in a Gentile motif, and Paul understanding this motif chose Isa 65:1 for the Isaianic context fits his argument in Rom 10:19-21.[537]

Though Paul did not use the word ἔθνος ("nation") in Rom 10:20, which is found in Isa 65:1b, the word ἔθνος is used in Rom 10:19 from the quotation of Deut 32:21 (LXX). Paul seems to play off the phrases ἐπ' οὐκ ἔθνει ("*what* is not a nation") and ἐπ' ἔθνει ἀσυνέτῳ ("against a foolish nation") in Deut 32:21, which is quoted in Rom 10:19 so that he might take the quotation from Isa 65:1 as a description of the Gentiles.[538] This interplay with Deut 32:21 would be easy

---

[532] In the two phrases that Paul cites from Isa 65:1, each began with a "God-related verb" and ends with a "man-related verb." In the first phrase, the LXX is in a chiastic arrangement when compared to the MT. Paul chooses the God-related verb "I was ready to be sought out" (NRSV) or "I permitted myself to be sought" (NASB) from the MT and translated "I became visible" in NETS or "I have been found" in Rom 10:20, thus, nullifying the MT permissive force from the Niphal verb (often referred to as a tolerative Niphal; see Gesenius, *Gesenius' Hebrew Grammar*, 2nd, §51c; Waltke and O'Connor, *An Introduction to Biblical Hebrew Syntax*, §23.4f-g and Joüon and Muraoka, *A Grammar of Biblical Hebrew,* §51.c). Seifrid, 666 suggests that the irony in Isa 65:1 makes the permissive sense unlikely and supports an effective sense that expresses an invitation. MacRae, "Paul's Use of Isaiah 65:1," 369-74 argues that the N*iphal tolerativum* is "highly questionable." MacRae's arguments are compelling, but the debate remains.

In the man-related verbs, the LXX and Paul's NT citation are identical, and both are in chiastic arrangement when compared to the MT. When one compares Paul's citation in both the God-related verbs and the man-related verbs with the MT, both phrases of Paul's NT citation are in chiastic arrangement with the MT. Dunn, 626 attributes these changes to either an inversion from a quotation from memory or Paul has the original Hebrew in mind, which the LXX altered in word order and sense. Dunn's last point is difficult to see because Paul's citation is in chiastic relationship in both the God-related verbs and man-related verbs when both phrases are compared to the MT.

[533] Delitzsch, *Isaiah*, 2:474-76; Cheyne, *The Prophecies of Isaiah*, 2:114-15; Leupold, *Exposition of Isaiah*, 2:359-60; Whybray, *Isaiah 40-66*, 268; Oss, "Paul's Use of Isaiah," 93-94; and Shum, *Paul's Use of Isaiah in Romans*, 226-28.

[534] Alexander, *Isaiah*, 2: 436-38; Young, *The Book of Isaiah*, 3:501-02; Grogan, "Isaiah," 349; Motyer, *The Prophecy of Isaiah*, 523; and Kidner, "Isaiah," in loc. 65:1. Delitzsch, *Isaiah*, 2:474-75 states that only one Jewish expositor (Gecatilia) refers this passage to the Gentiles.

[535] Shum, *Paul's Use of Isaiah in Romans*, 229-30 and Pinto, "The Contribution of the Isaiah Quotations to Paul's Argument in Romans 9-11," 154-58.

[536] These Gentile-type themes and images are sewn together by the repeated use of the word קרא ("call") and the phrase "on" (or "by") "your (or 'my') name." For a detailed argument for this point see Sullivan, *The INE in Rom 9–11*, 321–323.

[537] This paragraph was taken from Sullivan, *The INE in Rom 9–11*, 320–321.

[538] Wagner, "Moses and Isaiah in Concert," 88–89 agrees that Paul frequently "conflates or juxtaposes material from Isaiah with other texts from Israel's Scripture." It would be fair to say with Wagner, *Heralds of the*

for Paul to use knowing the extensive network connection between the two passages and the Isaianic context of Isa 65, which has a Gentile-type of motif.[539] According to the prologue in Deut 31:19–22 and the postlude to the Song of Moses in 32:44–47, Israel is to learn the Song and teach it to their children throughout the generations to come. The witness of the Song of Moses testified that they were told about God's plan. From Isa 65:1, the nation of Israel is told that the Gentiles will receive the good news because God will give it to them. Paul takes the Old Testament texts of Hos 1:10 and 2:23 in Rom 9:24–26, which speak about Israel, and applies them "on the principle of analogy, to the Gentiles."[540] The believing Gentiles are accepted and included while the unbelieving Israelites are rejected and excluded, at least in part. Israel could have discerned this point from the Old Testament. If Paul's argument is placed in the background of the NE theme, then this background argument could be likened to the ocean coral reef. The coral reef does not appear above the surface of the water, but it beautifully supports everything around it. Placing Paul's argument in the coral reef of the NE, helps to understand the framework for his appropriations of the Old Testament quotations.[541]

10:21 πρὸς δὲ τὸν Ἰσραὴλ λέγει· Ὅλην τὴν ἡμέραν ἐξεπέτασα τὰς χεῖράς μου πρὸς λαὸν ἀπειθοῦντα καὶ ἀντιλέγοντα. "But with reference to Israel he says, All the day long I have held out my hands to a people who are disobedient and obstinate." The expression of gesturing with the hands by God to Israel is an appeal to them for welcome and fellowship (Jewett, 649). The expression of "all day long" is a semiticism to convey the thought of "uninterruptedly" (Jewett, 649).

God's daily hand of mercy is not received by Israel because they are rebellious and disobedient (Isa 65:2).[542] Cranfield gave two major functions of Isa 65:2 in Rom 10:21[543]: (1) it looks back at Israel's disobedience as an enormous comprehensive statement of their rejection of God's steadfast grace and mercy and (2) it looks forward to the future hope for Israel because of God's steadfast patience and divine grace in the face of Israel's continuous sin.[544] "The quotation points firmly to the point that the last word is not with Israel's disobedience but with God's mercy and patience."[545] In light of the NE father/son motif found in Isa 63–65, Rom 10:21 pictures God the Father in mercy and grace continuing to extend his hand to the rebellious nation (his sons). The NE theme is Paul's framework that allows him to use these texts and apply them

---

Good News, 216–17 that Paul hears Deut 32 and Isa 65 in concert. However, we do not insist that Paul made a "radical interpretation" of Isa 65:1. Mann, *The Bible as Read and Preached in the Old Synagogue*, *passim*; Perrot, "The Reading of the Bible in the Ancient Synagogue," 137–59 do not indicate that Deut 32:21 and Isa 65:1 were connected in the synagogue liturgy. (Wagner, Ibid., 91, note 18 indicates that Deut 32:1 and Isa 1:2 were associated together in the liturgy.)

[539] Wagner, *Heralds of the Good News*, 212.

[540] Moo, 2nd, 687; Moo, *NIV Romans*, 348. Seifrid, 666 says "Paul cites the text typologically in precisely this sense: God's dealings with Israel in the past have been recapitulated in the present."

[541] This paragraph was taken from Sullivan, *The INE in Rom 9–11*, 325–326.

[542] In Rom 11, Paul makes it clear that the rejection of the nation involves the majority of the people but not a complete rejection of everyone in Israel (See Wagner, *Heralds of the Good News*, 215–16).

[543] The quotation of Isa 65:2 in Rom 10:21 is the same as the LXX, except the order of ὅλην τὴν ἡμέραν in relation to ἐξεπέτασα. As Johnson, "Romans 9–11: The Faithfulness and Impartiality of God," 231 points out the shifting of the order in Rom 10:21 highlights "God's *continual* reaching out to Israel," an effect achieved by moving the temporal phrase before the verb.

[544] Cranfield, 541.

[545] Ibid., 541–42.

to Gentiles (Rom 10:20) and Israel (Rom 10:21). The former appears to be used by analogy or possibly typology (see 10:20 for more comments).[546]

Biblical Theological Comments

Paul's thoughts in Rom 10:14-21 deals with the hardness of many in Israel which is approached from the divine side in Rom 9 and now from man's responsibility in Rom 10. In this section Paul transitions from the message of the gospel to the messenger of the gospel (10:14–15). This message of the gospel has gone to Israel and it should be taken to the Gentiles (Ps 19:4 in 10:19). The universal proclamation of the gospel is beautifully unfolded with the admonishment that we who are believers in Jesus should be part of this proclamation. Furthermore, he demonstrates that Israel has heard the message, but most did not heed the message. Many have pointed out that Rom 9:30–10:21 builds upon what Paul began to discuss in Rom 2:17–29 (Longenecker, 860). The plan of God is to use the believing Gentiles as an instrument to make the nation of Israel jealous in the sense that they would believe in their Messiah Jesus.

Paul used Isa 65:1 by way of analogy in Rom 10:20. Several important themes are present in Isa 63–64, but the sinful Gentile-type of description in these two chapters that portrays Israel's sin and rebellion is crucial to the understanding of the argument. In other words, Isaiah describes the sin of Israel in many cases with descriptions that are usually described as the sins of the Gentiles. Therefore, Paul introduced Deut 32:21 from the Exodus motif of the Song of Moses in Rom 10:19 to help alert the reader to a Gentile orientation that he wants to use next in Rom 10:20 from Isaiah 65:1. Now since he has alerted the reader to his intentions to appropriate Isa 65:1 with the understanding of the larger context of the sin of Israel in the description of sinful Gentile-type, he applies Isaiah 65:1 to the Gentiles and then applied Isa 65:2 to Israel. Paul appears to have interpreted the Gentile-oriented Deut 32:21 and Isa 65:1 in concert with each other. The common background of both Old Testament texts is the NE theme, which helps to provide the network of connection for Paul to play these two texts in concert by way of analogy. A thorough examination of the Isaianic total context is crucial, for it resulted in the discovery of the Gentile-type sin and rebellion theme, as well as the NE motif.[547] These themes are crucial to understand Paul's argument as he uses several OT texts.

The various NE motifs provide a biblical theology in Isaiah 63–66 concerning Gentiles and provide in the Isaianic context a legitimate application of Isaiah 65:1 to the Gentiles.[548] Paul highlights this interpretation by saying in Romans 10:19, "First Moses says." This statement helps the reader to see that both Romans 10:19 and 20 are used to express Moses's thoughts about the Gentiles. Paul first draws on the Exodus motif in the Song of Moses (Deut 32:21) and

---

[546] This paragraph was taken from Sullivan, *The INE in Rom 9–11*, 326–327.

[547] Ibid., 378

[548] Pinto, "The Contribution of the Isaiah Quotations to Paul's Argument in Romans 9–11," 157 believes Yahweh is speaking in terms of irony and sarcasm making it easier for Paul to apply Isa 65:1 to Gentiles and Isa 65:2 to Israel. Wagner, *Heralds of the Good News*, 213–14 also see irony in Paul's quotation of Isa 65:1. It is the irony of the "lament over Israel's obduracy into a positive celebration of Gentile inclusion in the people of God." It is possible to construct an argument from irony and sarcasm, but a more substantial and compelling argument is the argument from the broader context and the NE, which is the argument of my book, *The Isaianic New Exodus in Romans 9–11*, 2nd ed.

then he follows it up with the INE theme from Isaiah 64–65 that bears the weight of a Gentile-type of motif.

Though Paul did not use the word ἔθνος ("nation") in Romans 10:20, which is found in Isaiah 65:1b (LXX), the word ἔθνος is used in Romans 10:19 from the quotation of Deuteronomy 32:21 (LXX). Paul seems to play off the phrases ἐπ' οὐκ ἔθνει ("*what* is not a nation") and ἐπ' ἔθνει ἀσυνέτῳ ("against a foolish nation") in Deuteronomy 32:21, which is quoted in Romans 10:19 so that he might take the quotation from Isaiah 65:1 as a description of the Gentiles.[549] This interplay with Deuteronomy 32:21 would be easy for Paul to use knowing the extensive network connection between the two passages and the Isaianic context of Isaiah 65, which has a Gentile-type of motif as has been discussed in my book, *The Isaianic New Exodus in Romans 9–11* (9.3.2).[550]

Application and Devotional Implications

Paul's thought in Rom 10:14–17 centers on the universal proclamation of the gospel and every believer's responsibility to proclaim it. Paul launches in to a four-linked chain using four questions. Paul starts with the 4th link of the chain in v. 14 and works backwards to the first link. He does this because he really wants to stress the importance of the believers being sent to proclaim the gospel. Rarely do you find among believers someone who does not know that they are responsible to proclaim the gospel. It is not that we don't know; it is that we often fail to do this. Here are some of the excuses we hide behind: too busy, afraid of losing a friend or business, they won't like me, fear of men, don't know how to approach them, someone else would be better suited to witness to them, and they would not be interest in the gospel. Every excuse we have is exploded away as we hear our Lord commission us into His service in Matt 28:18–20. God has made us adequate servants by the indwelling Spirit and we have been given the gracious privilege of being ambassadors of the King of Kings (2 Cor 3:4–6; 5:20). Oh, that we would plead with men to believe upon Him!

Notice Paul in Rom 10:15 supports his point by quoting Isa 52:7, "How timely are the feet of those who bring good news of good things!" How much attention do feet receive? How many times when you meet someone that you gaze at their feet? We notice the hair or the eyes and other features but seldom the feet. Yet the feet become one of the most hard-working part of our body. Maybe God used "feet" to demonstrate that our commission will be hard work and something that must be done regularly. It will be something we take to people and not just sit back and wait for them to come to us. I'm afraid that Christendom has a lot of ugly feet because we are sitting and enjoying our salvation to the neglect of laboring to bring the good news to others.

In verse 16, Paul warns us by using the example of Israel that all do not heed the gospel. He supports this by using the prediction of Isa 53:1, which was prophesied hundreds of years before it happened. We must not be dejected or discouraged if men reject the message. We must

---

[549] Wagner, "Moses and Isaiah in Concert," 88–89 agrees that Paul frequently "conflates or juxtaposes material from Isaiah with other texts from Israel's Scripture." It would be fair to say with Wagner, *Heralds of the Good News*, 216–17 that Paul hears Deut 32 and Isa 65 in concert. However, we do not insist that Paul made a "radical interpretation" of Isa 65:1.

[550] This last paragraph was taken from Sullivan, *The Isaianic New Exodus in Romans 9–11*, 2nd ed., section 9.3.2 and 9.3.3. See also Wagner, *Heralds of the Good News*, 212.

expect that this kind of response is part of the mission that God has given us. They said to Moses, "You have gone far enough" (Num 16:3); to Ezekiel, "Is he not just speaking parables?"; to Amos, ". . . the land is unable to endure all his words . . . . Go you seer, flee away . . . ." (7:10–13); to Jeremiah, "As for the message that you have spoken to us in the name of the Lord, we are not going to listen to you!" (Jer 44:16). Paul declares in 1 Cor 1:21, "For since in the wisdom of God the world through its wisdom did not come to know God, God was well-pleased through the foolishness of the message preached to save those who believe." Faith is a gift of God, but it is produced in the context of the Word of God (Rom 10:17).

In Rom 10:18-21 Paul turns to some objections about Israel's rejection of the gospel of Christ. The first is found in v. 18. Surely Israel had never heard. But Paul comes back with a forceful "Indeed they have." To support this point, he quotes from Ps. 19:4. The second objection is stated in v. 19 and answered by three OT citations in vv. 19–21. Paul's point is if the Gentile nations who were ignorant of God have come to believe the gospel certainly it cannot be supposed that Israel has not known about the gospel. Why then did they not believe? Hearing and knowing the gospel (though important) is not enough to save anyone. Ultimately, the problem is not intellectual but a spiritual heart problem. This problem is not unique with Israel. This is the state of everyone born into this world.

I can vividly see a man who I shared the gospel with acknowledge that he was a sinner and he knew the gospel of Jesus Christ for salvation, but he refused to trust in it because his wife was against it. His decision was influenced by his sinful heart (or sinful nature) and his excuse came through the influence of his wife. Today, mankind's freedom is grounded to his nature. Before the Fall of Adam, he had the freedom to do evil or good (in the sight of God). After the Fall, everyone before salvation has the freedom to do evil but not good (good in sight of God) because of their sinful nature. In heaven we will have the freedom to do good but not evil. It is important to know this as we go out to share the gospel because it will not frustrate us so much as we labor and see little fruit. We will not turn in critical condemnation on ourselves, thinking the problem is always us–our ignorance, our lack of techniques or knowledge in evangelism or apologetics, our personality, our lack of spirituality, our lack of knowledge in the Word. What it should do is to cause us to rely on God to open the heart as we proclaim the gospel. There is not one word I can say to convince anyone about the gospel unless God's Spirit moves them. Therefore, God is sending us out to speak to spiritually dead men and women (Eph 2:1). They are physically alive and can physically hear your proclamation, but their spiritual ears are deaf (Rom 3:10–12). They can know or understand on a surface level, but they have a rebellious heart. They are spiritually dead in their sin (1 Cor 2:14). However, as we proclaim the gospel to these spiritually dead people, God is pleased to use our voice to open many hearts and make them alive so that they can truly hear and believe (Acts 16:14–15).

Selected Bibliography

Alexander, Joseph A. *Commentary on the Prophecies of Isaiah* (New York: Scribner's, 1846, repr. ed., Grand Rapids: Zondervan, 1953).

Arndt, William, Frederick W. Danker, and Walter Bauer, *A Greek-English Lexicon of the New Testament and Other Early Christian Literature*, 3rd ed. electronic version (Chicago: University of Chicago Press, 2000).

Beale, Gregory K. *Handbook on the New Testament Use of the Old Testament: Exegesis and Interpretation*. (Grand Rapids: Baker, 2012).

Beale, G. K., Daniel J. Brendsel, William A. Ross, *An Interpretive Lexicon of New Testament Greek: Analysis of Prepositions, Adverbs, Particles, Relative Pronouns, and Conjunctions* (Grand Rapids: Zondervan, 2014).

Bekken, Per Jarle. *The Word is Near You: A Study of Deuteronomy 30:12–14 in Paul's Letter to the Romans in a Jewish Context* (Berlin: Deutsche Nationalbibliografie, 2007).

Bell, Richard H. *Provoked to Jealousy: The Origin and Purpose of the Jealousy Motif in Romans 9–11*. Wissenshaftliche Untersuchungen zum Neuen Testament, vol. 263 (Tübingen: Mohr Siebeck, 1994).

Blass, Friedrich, Albert Debrunner, and Robert Walter Funk, *A Greek Grammar of the New Testament and Other Early Christian Literature* (Chicago: University of Chicago Press, 1961).

Blenkinsopp, Joseph. *Isaiah 40–55: A New Translation with Introduction and Commentary*. The Anchor Bible, vol. 19A. (New York: Doubleday, 2002).

Brown, Francis, Samuel R. Driver, and Charles A. Briggs, *A Hebrew and English Lexicon of the Old Testament: With an Appendix Containing the Biblical Aramaic* (Oxford: Clarendon Press, 1907).

Bullinger, E. W. *Figures of Speech Used in the Bible*, Explained and Illustrated. (Grand Rapids: Baker reprint, 1968).

Cheyene, T. K. *The Prophecies of Isaiah*. 5th ed. rev. (New York: Thomas Whitaker, 1895).

Delitzsch, Franz. *Isaiah*. Biblical Commentary on the Old Testament. Translated by J. Martin, vol. 7, 2 vols in 1. (Edinburgh: T & T Clark; New York: Scribner and Welford [distributor], 1890. Reprint, Grand Rapids: Eerdmans, 1973).

Delitzsch, Franz. *Psalms*, Biblical Commentary on the Old Testament, vol. 5 (3 vols. in 1) (Reprint, Grand Rapids: Eerdmans, 1973).

Gesenius, Fredrich W. *Gesenius' Hebrew Grammar*, 2nd English ed. (Bellingham, WA: Logos Research Systems, Inc., 2003), §51c.

Goldingay, John. *The Message of Isaiah 40–55: A Literary-Theological Commentary* (London: T & T Clark, 2005).

Goldingay, John and David Payne, *A Critical and Exegetical Commentary on Isaiah 40-55*, The International Critical Commentary (London: T & T Clark, 2006).

Grogan, Geoffrey W. "Isaiah." In *Expositor's Bible Commentary*, ed. Frank Gaebelein, vol. 6, 1–354. (Grand Rapids: Zondervan, 1986).

Hahne, Harry A. "Paul's Use of the Old Testament in Romans 10:16–11:10 to Explain Israel's Unbelief in Jesus," presented at the Evangelical Theological Society Annual Meeting (Unpublished paper, November 16, 2000), 2–3.

Johnson, E. Elizabeth. "Romans 9–11: The Faithfulness and Impartiality of God," in *Pauline Theology III Romans*, Society of Biblical Literature Symposium Series (Atlanta: SBL, 2002).

Johnson, E. Elizabeth. *The Function of Apocalyptic and Wisdom Traditions in Romans 9–11*, Society of Biblical Literature Dissertation Series (Atlanta: Scholars Press, 1989).

Joüon, Paul and Takamitsu Muraoka, *A Grammar of Biblical Hebrew,* electronic ed. (Editrice Pontificio Istituto Biblico, 2003, 2005), §51c.

Kidner, Derek. "Isaiah," *New Bible Commentary: 21st Century Edition*, 4th ed. Electronic (Downers Grove: InterVarsity Press, 1994).

Koehler, Ludwig, Walter Baumgartner, M. E. J. Richardson and Johann Jakob Stamm. *The Hebrew and Aramaic Lexicon of the Old Testament*, electronic ed. (Leiden: Brill, 1999).

Liddell, Henry G. and Robert Scott. *A Greek-English Lexicon*, rev. and augmented by Sir Henry S. Jones with Roderick McKenzie, et. al. (Oxford: Clarendon Press, 1996).

Leupold, H. C. *Exposition of Isaiah* (Grand Rapids: Baker, 1971).

Louw, Johannes P. and Eugen A. Nida. *Greek-English Lexicon of the New Testament Based on Semantic Domains*, ed. Ronald Smith, 2nd ed. (New York: United Bible Society, 1988–89).

MacRae, Allan A. "Paul's Use of Isaiah 65:1," in *The Law and the Prophets: Studies Prepared in Honor of Oswald T. Allis*, ed. John H. Skliton (Philadelphia: Presbyterian and Reformed, 1974).

Mann, Jacob. *The Bible as Read and Preached in the Old Synagogue*, The Library of Biblical Studies, vol. 1 (New York: Ktav Publishing House, 1971).

Moo, Douglas J. "The Problem of *Sensus Plenior*." In *Hermeneutics, Authority and Canon*, eds. D. A. Carson and John Woodbridge, 179–211 (Grand Rapids: Zondervan, 1986).

Alec J. Motyer, *The Prophecy of Isaiah: An Introduction and Commentary* (Downers Grove: InterVarsity Press, 1993).

Oss, Douglas A. "Paul's Use of Isaiah and Its place in His Theology with Special Reference to Romans 9-11" (Ph.D. diss., Westminster Theological Seminary, 1992).

Perrot, Charles. "The Reading of the Bible in the Ancient Synagogue," in *Mikra: Text, Translation, Reading and Interpretation of the Hebrew Bible in Ancient Judaism and Early Christianity*, ed. Martin Jan Mulder (Minneapolis: Fortress Press, 1990).

Pinto, Carlos O. C. "The Contribution of the Isaiah Quotations to Paul's Argument in Romans 9-11" (Ph.D. diss., Dallas Theological Seminary, 2003).

Robertson, A. T. *A Grammar of the Greek New Testament in the Light of Historical Research* (Logos Bible Software, 2006).

Shum, Shiu-Lun. *Paul's Use of Isaiah in Romans: A Comparative Study of Paul's Letter to the Romans and the Sibylline and Qumran Sectarian Texts* (Tübingen: Mohr Siebeck, 2002).

Sullivan, Steven P. *The Isaianic New Exodus in Romans 9–11: A Biblical and Theological Study of Paul's Use of Isaiah in Romans* (Silverton, OR: Lampion Press, 2017).

Sullivan, Steven P. *The Isaianic New Exodus in Romans 9–11: A Biblical and Theological Study of Paul's Use of Isaiah in Romans*, 2nd ed. (Middletown, RI: Stone Tower Press, 2023).

Swanson, Reuben, ed. *New Testament Greek Manuscripts: Romans*. (Wheaton: Tyndale House and Pasadena: William Carey International University Press, 2001).

Wagner, J. Ross. "From the Heavens to the Heart: The Dynamics of Psalm 19 as Prayer," *The Catholic Biblical Quarterly* 61 (1999): 245–61.

Wagner, J. Ross. *Heralds of the Good News: Isaiah and Paul in Concert in the Letter to the Romans*. Supplements to Novum Testamentum, eds. M. M. Mitchell and D. P. Moessner, vol. 101 (Leiden: Brill, 2002).

Wagner, J. Ross Wagner. "Moses and Isaiah in Concert: Paul's Reading of Isaiah and Deuteronomy in the Letter to the Romans," in *"As Those Who Are Taught" The Interpretation of Isaiah from the LXX to the SBL*, Society of Biblical Literature Symposium Series (Atlanta: Society of Biblical Literature, 2006).

Wagner, J. Ross. "'Not from the Jews Only, But Also from the Gentiles': Mercy to the Nations in Romans 9–11," in *Between Gospel and Election: Explorations in Interpretation of*

Romans 9–11, Wissenschaftliche Untersuchungen zum Neuen Testament (Tübingen: Mohr Siebeck, 2010).

Waltke, Bruce K. and Michael Patrick O'Connor, *An Introduction to Biblical Hebrew Syntax*, (Winona Lake.: Eisenbrauns, 1990).

Wallace, Daniel B. *Greek Grammar Beyond the Basic: An Exegetical Syntax of the New Testament* (Grand Rapids: Zondervan, 1996).

Watts, Rikki E. *Isaianic New Exodus and Mark,* Wissenshaftliche Untersuchungen zum Neuen Testament 88 (Tübingen: Mohr Siebeck, 1997).

Whybray, Roger N. *Isaiah 40–66*. New Century Bible, ed. Ronald E. Clements (Greenwood, SC: Attic Press, Inc., 1975).

Young, Edward J. *The Book of Isaiah*. 3 vols. New International Commentary on the Old Testament, ed. Edward J. Young. (Grand Rapids: Eerdmans, 1965–72).

Romans 11:1–10

Introduction

Romans 11:1–32 have a single basic theme centered around Israel and whether they have been rejected, but an argument can be made that under this umbrella theme is another thought division in 11:1–10 and 11–32. Each section begins with "therefore, I say" (Λέγω οὖν) which leads into a question where the Paul wants the reader to answer "no" (μὴ with a question). Then, Paul also reinforces this negative with an emphatic negative, "may it never be!" (μὴ γένοιτο). In Rom 11:1–10 Paul discusses the question, has God rejected His people, Israel? After a personal testimony, Paul responds in 11:2 that God has not rejected His people. However, he says this declaration in the context of those whom God foreknew (11:2a) and chose while the "rest were hardened" (11:7). Thus, Paul indicates that God's redemption of Israel involves more than Abraham's physical descendants.

Outline

I. The Wisdom Polemic: The Tension between God's Righteous Promises and Israel's Condition 9–11
   A. Introduction to the Tension (9:1–5)
   B. Vindication of the righteous God and His Wise Plan (9:6–29)
   C. Israel's Knowledge of the Gospel of Righteousness: Faith and Works (9:30–10:21)
   D. Israel's election and partial hardening and not total rejection (11:1-10)

Original Text

11.1 Λέγω οὖν, μὴ ἀπώσατο ὁ θεὸς τὸν λαὸν[a] αὐτοῦ;[b] μὴ γένοιτο· καὶ γὰρ ἐγὼ Ἰσραηλίτης εἰμί, ἐκ
σπέρματος Ἀβραάμ, φυλῆς Βενιαμίν. 2 οὐκ ἀπώσατο ὁ θεὸς τὸν λαὸν αὐτοῦ ὃν προέγνω. ἢ οὐκ
οἴδατε ἐν Ἠλίᾳ τί λέγει ἡ γραφή, ὡς ἐντυγχάνει τῷ θεῷ κατὰ τοῦ Ἰσραήλ;[c] 3 Κύριε, τοὺς
προφήτας σου ἀπέκτειναν, τὰ θυσιαστήριά σου κατέσκαψαν, κἀγὼ ὑπελείφθην μόνος, καὶ
ζητοῦσιν τὴν ψυχήν μου. 4 ἀλλὰ τί λέγει αὐτῷ ὁ χρηματισμός; Κατέλιπον ἐμαυτῷ ἑπτακισχιλίους
ἄνδρας, οἵτινες οὐκ ἔκαμψαν γόνυ τῇ Βάαλ. 5 οὕτως οὖν καὶ ἐν τῷ νῦν καιρῷ λεῖμμα κατ'
ἐκλογὴν χάριτος γέγονεν· 6 εἰ δὲ χάριτι, οὐκέτι ἐξ ἔργων, ἐπεὶ ἡ χάρις οὐκέτι γίνεται χάρις[d]. 7 τί
οὖν; ὃ ἐπιζητεῖ Ἰσραήλ, τοῦτο οὐκ ἐπέτυχεν, ἡ δὲ ἐκλογὴ ἐπέτυχεν· οἱ δὲ λοιποὶ ἐπωρώθησαν, 8
καθὼς[e] γέγραπται· Ἔδωκεν αὐτοῖς ὁ θεὸς πνεῦμα κατανύξεως, ὀφθαλμοὺς τοῦ μὴ βλέπειν καὶ
ὦτα τοῦ μὴ ἀκούειν, ἕως τῆς σήμερον ἡμέρας. 9 καὶ Δαυὶδ λέγει· Γενηθήτω ἡ τράπεζα αὐτῶν εἰς
παγίδα καὶ εἰς θήραν καὶ εἰς σκάνδαλον καὶ εἰς ἀνταπόδομα αὐτοῖς, 10 σκοτισθήτωσαν οἱ
ὀφθαλμοὶ αὐτῶν τοῦ μὴ βλέπειν, καὶ τὸν νῶτον αὐτῶν διὰ παντὸς σύγκαμψον.

Textual Notes

[a] **11:1 τὸν λαὸν** is supported by NA28 SBLGNT UBS5 WH B ℵ A C D Ψ L P 049 056 𝔐 6 33 69 81 88 104 256 365 424 436 440 459 618 1175 1241 1319 1506 1573 1646 1735 1738 1739 1852 1874 1881 1891 2125 2400 2495. **τὸν λαὸν την κληρονομιαν** is supported by P[46] F G. (Swanson, *NT GK Mss*, 165; UBS5, 530). The mss. evidence is decisively against the addition to the text. However, it is interesting that P[46] supports this addition. The longer reading appears to be a Western assimilation from Ps 94:13 (LXX 93:14).[551] See Given, "Restoring the Inheritance in Romans 11:1," 89–96 for an argument for τὸν λαὸν την κληρονομιαν.

[b] **11:1 αὐτοῦ** is supported by NA28 SBLGNT UBS5 WH B ℵ C D[c] Ψ L P 056 𝔐 6 33 69 88 104 205 209 226 323 326 365 424 460 489 517 547 614 1175 1241 1319 1506 1573 1611 1734 1739 1827 1836 1881 1962 2127 2200 2464. **αὐτοῦ ον (ην P[46vid]) προεγνω** is supported by ℵ[c] A D (Swanson, *NT GK Mss*, 165; NA28, 503). The mss. evidence is decisively against the addition to the text.

[c] **11:2 Ἰσραήλ** is supported by NA28 SBLGNT UBS5 WH Treg B ℵ[c] A C D Ψ F G P 6 81 365 1243 1319 1505 1506 1573 1739 1881 2495. **Ἰσραήλ λεγων** is supported by ℵ L 049 056 𝔐 1 69 88 104 131 205 209 226 323 440 517 614 796 927 1175 1241 1315 1424 1611 1735 1827 2125 2400 2815 and others (Swanson, *NT GK Mss*, 167; NA28, 503). The addition may have been added to make it clear that the following was a biblical quotation (Longenecker, 868).

[d] **11:6 χάρις** is supported by NA28 SBLGNT UBS5 WH Treg P[46] ℵ A F G C D P 263 1739 1852 1881 2200. **χάρις. ει δε εξ εργων ουκετι χαρις επι το εργον ουκετι εστιν χαρις** B. **χάρις. ει δε εξ εργων ουκετι εστι(ν) χαρις, επει το εργον ουκετι εστιν εργον** is supported by ℵ[c] L Ψ 056 𝔐 1 6 69 88 205 209 226 323 326 330 365 424 460 517 547 614 618 910 927 945 999 1241 1243 1270 1352 1424 1448 1505 1611 1734 1737 1827 2125 2400 2815. (Swanson, *NT GK Mss*, 169–170; UBS5, 531). The long version adds "But if it be of works, then is it no more grace; otherwise work is no more work" (AV). B has a little shorter version. What is stated in the long version is true and an expansion to what is already stated. The difficulty with the long version is why would someone delete the longer version to make it shorter. Thus, it seems best to accept the shorter version as original.[552]

[e] **11:8 καθὼς** is supported by NA28 SBLGNT UBS5 P[46] A C D F G L P Ψ 049 056 𝔐 1 6 33 88 104 131 205 209 226 323 326 330 365 424 440 460 489 517 547 614 618 796 910 927 999 1175 1241 1242 1245 1270 1319 1352 1424 1448 1505 1573 1611 1734 1735 1738 1827 1854 1874 1881 1891 2125 2400 2412 2495 2815. **καθάπερ** is supported by WH Treg B ℵ 81. (Swanson, *NT GK Mss*, 170). The early support for both variants is evident and there is little difference in meaning between the two adverbs. However, the expression καθὼς γέγραπται is a common expression by Paul in introducing an OT passage (Longenecker, 869). For example, in Romans see: 2:24; 3:4, 10; 8:36; 9:13, 33; 10:15; 11:26; 15:3, 9, 21 (88 times καθὼς is used in Paul's epistles counting Rom 11:8). In Romans, καθάπερ is used in 4:6 and 12:4 (13 times in the NT).

---

[551] Metzger, *A Textual Commentary*, 2nd ed., 464; Cranfield, 543, n. 1; Longenecker, 867–868.

[552] Metzger, *A Textual Commentary*, 2nd ed., 464; Moo, 2nd, 688, n. 561; Schreiner, 584; Longenecker, 868–869.

Translation

1 Therefore, I say, God has not rejected his people, has he? By no means! For even I am an Israelite, from the seed of Abraham, of the tribe of Benjamin. **2** God has not rejected his people, whom he foreknew. Or do you not know what the Scripture says about Elijah, how he appeals to God against Israel? **3** "Lord, they have killed your prophets, they have torn down your altars, and I was left alone, and they are seeking my life." **4** But what does the divine answer say to him? "I have left for Myself seven thousand men who have not bowed the knee to Baal." **5** Therefore, then, at the present time there has also come to be a remnant because of the election of grace. **6** And if by grace, *it is* not on the basis of works; for otherwise, grace is no longer manifested as grace. **7** What then *is the outcome*? What Israel is seeking, this she has not attained; but the chosen has attained it. But the rest have been hardened. **8** Just as it is written, "God has given them a spirit of stupor, so that eyes do not see and ears that do not hear, until the present day." **9** And David says, "Let their table become for *them* a snare and a trap and a stumbling block and a retribution. **10** Let their eyes be darkened so that they do not see and cause their backs to be bent continually."

Commentary

11:1 Λέγω οὖν, μὴ ἀπώσατο ὁ θεὸς τὸν λαὸν αὐτοῦ; μὴ γένοιτο· καὶ γὰρ ἐγὼ Ἰσραηλίτης εἰμί, ἐκ σπέρματος Ἀβραάμ, φυλῆς Βενιαμίν. "Therefore, I say, God has not rejected His people, has He? By no means! For even I am an Israelite, from the seed of Abraham, of the tribe of Benjamin." After Paul's explanation of the failure of Israel as whole (though God has a remnant of Israel that He chose and will believe) and the inclusion of the Gentiles (Rom 9:3–10:21), he explores the promises to Israel and what this means in Romans 11. Romans 11 may be divided into two related units: 11:1–10 and 11:11–32 with a closing wisdom polemic doxology in vv. 33–36 that makes a climatic end to the larger section of Romans 1–11.[553] Thus, broadly speaking Romans 9:6-29 considers the history of Israel and God's promises, 11:1–10 centers on the present, and 11:11–32 directs our attention to the future. Here is the construction that begins each section in Romans 11:

Romans 11:1	**Romans 11:11**
Λέγω οὖν, **μὴ** ἀπώσατο ὁ θεὸς τὸν λαὸν αὐτοῦ; **μὴ γένοιτο·** καὶ γὰρ ἐγὼ Ἰσραηλίτης εἰμί, ἐκ σπέρματος Ἀβραάμ, φυλῆς Βενιαμίν.	**Λέγω οὖν,** **μὴ** ἔπταισαν ἵνα πέσωσιν; **μὴ γένοιτο·** ἀλλὰ τῷ αὐτῶν παραπτώματι ἡ σωτηρία τοῖς ἔθνεσιν, εἰς τὸ παραζηλῶσαι αὐτούς.
Therefore, I say, God has not rejected his people, has he?	Therefore, I say, they did not stumble so as to fall, *did they*?

[553] The basic division of Rom 11:1–10 and 11:11–32 is seen in Moo 2nd, 689; Hafemann, "Salvation of Israel," 45–46; Godet, 391; Käsemann, 298. Cranfield, 542 also makes another division in v. 25. An argument could also be made for the division of the wisdom doxology of vv. 33–36 which is the closing section.

By no means! For even I am an Israelite, from the seed of Abraham, of the tribe of Benjamin.	By no means! But by their transgression salvation *has come* to the Gentiles, in order to make them jealous.

Each section in Romans 11 begins with the same connective particle and verb followed by a question expecting a negative answer, and then fortified by an emphatic negative phrase. Finally, each section ends the literary unit with a mixture of quotation from the OT (cf. 9:25–29; 10:19–21; 11:9–10; 11:26–27, 34–35). Paul in chapter 11 returns to the thought he raised in Romans 9:6–29 where again he writes about the remnant (the chosen) and "the rest" of Israel who are hardened by God in their spiritual disobedience (11:7–10; cf. 9:18–23). He directs his attention to the situation of first century Israelites and compares this time with Elijah and the remnant that had not bow the knee to Baal. The unbelief of Israel in Elijah's day was the majority, but God by his gracious choice had a believing remnant. Such was the case in Paul's day.

Paul understands the state and condition of the corporate nation of Israel–it is in unbelief. The οὖν ("therefore") connects this section with the latter part of Romans 10 where Paul states that Israel did hear and did know; thus, they are without excuse. So, he begins with the rhetorical question using the negative particle μη which indicates that Paul wanted the reader to answer the question with a negative answer. Furthermore, he accented the negative answer with the emphatic negative phrase μὴ γένοιτο ("by no means!").[554] The use of the word λαός ("people") in the LXX occurs about 1670 times with only 140 times in the plural and the word is predominantly used for Israel.[555] Paul uses the term almost exclusively in citations from the OT and uses it most of the time for ethnic Israel (citations from the OT: Rom 9:25, 26; 10:21; 15:10, 11; 1 Cor 10:7; 14:21; 2 Cor 6:16; others: Rom 11:1, 2; Tit 2:14).

The possibility that God has rejected (ἀπώσατο)[556] the nation is a logical and important question to ask. This question has been brought up in different ways already in Romans 9:1–3, 27, 29, 31–32; 10:2, 3, 21 (Murray, 2:66). The leadership and most of the nation rejected Jesus Christ who was their sole means of being justified before God (Rom 9:30–10:3). He was the one that the Jewish Scriptures pointed and pictured and for whom the nation of Israel long to see. However, the vast majority not only missed Him, but they were either indifferent or agreed with the Roman and Jewish leadership to put Him to death. Many may wrongly conclude that Israel is now no longer God's people. However, Paul rejects this conclusion. Paul will expound upon this subject in the rest of Romans 11. Here in this verse, he briefly explains, using γὰρ ("for"), his first reason to reject this false conclusion. He identifies himself as an "Israelite" (Rom 4:16; 9:4; 2 Cor 11:22; Phil 3:5) from the tribe of Benjamin (see 9:3–5), to whom God has not rejected.[557] Some Israelites like Paul had trusted the Messiah Jesus and were saved; thus, being the true Israel of God (Rom 9:6) to which belongs the riches of God briefly stated in Rom 9:4–5. At this time in the church age these believing Israelites are the remnant and, in the future, the full number of the nation of Israel will come to believe (11:26). Many commentators suggest or

---

[554] See Rom 3:4, 6, 31; 6:2, 15; 7:7, 13; 9:14; 11:1, 11; 1 Cor 6:15; Gal 2:17; 3:21; 6:14.

[555] Strathmann, *TDNT*, 4:32–35. Logos Bible Software 8.0 indicated 1670 usages in the OT and 142 usages in the NT.

[556] "Reject" or "repudiate" see Acts 29; 13:46; Rom 11:1, 2; 1 Tim 1:19. Acts 7:27 is translated "pushed aside" (BDAG, 126).

[557] Cranfield (544) stresses also that Paul was an apostle to the Gentle as part of the emphasis. This is possible, but this is not explicitly stated. Sanday and Headlam (309) state that Paul is giving "the motive for his deprecation, not a proof of his denial" (see also Meyer, 2:200)

argue that Paul mentions his tribe because it was almost exterminated (Judg 20–21) or it was the tribe of Saul who was rejected or the Rabbinic tradition that this tribe was first to enter the Red Sea (Käsemann, 299). All this maybe interesting but does not seem to be Paul's argument. However, he seems to mention his lineage to emphasize his descendance from ethnic Israel (Moo, 2nd ed., 691, n. 570; Schreiner, 2nd ed., 564; Dunn, 635).[558] He more than most exemplified Israel's unbelief and God's mercy in not forsaking Israel (Murray, 2:66). Next, in v. 2b and following he turns to the concept of the remnant by using the OT illustration of Elijah.

11:2a οὐκ ἀπώσατο ὁ θεὸς τὸν λαὸν αὐτοῦ ὃν προέγνω. 2a "God has not rejected His people, whom he foreknew." What Paul questioned in v. 1 he now answers clearly in v.2. Whether Paul intentionally borrowed the phrase οὐκ ἀπώσατο ὁ θεὸς τὸν λαὸν αὐτοῦ ("God has not rejected his people") from Ps 94:14 or 1 Sam 12:22 is a possibility. Both OT contexts fit the Romans 11 context of God not rejecting His people, Israel.[559] However, there are some differences in the quotations:

Psalm 94:14 (LXX Ps 93:14)	Romans 11:2
ὅτι οὐκ ἀπώσεται (future) κύριος τὸν λαὸν αὐτοῦ καὶ τὴν κληρονομίαν αὐτοῦ οὐκ ἐγκαταλείψει	οὐκ ἀπώσατο[560] (aorist) ὁ θεὸς τὸν λαὸν αὐτοῦ
For the Lord will not reject his people and he will not forsake his inheritance.	God has not rejected his people

1 Samuel 12:22 (LXX 1 Kingdoms 12:22)
ὅτι οὐκ ἀπώσεται (future) κύριος τὸν λαὸν αὐτοῦ
For the Lord will not reject his people

Some scholars suggest that Paul changes ἀπώσεται ("will reject") to the aorist tense for he is applying the thought to Israel rejecting Jesus Christ and the change from κύριος ("Lord") to θεός ("God") because he generally prefers to use κύριος for Jesus (Moo, 2nd, 692, n. 574; Dunn, 636).[561]

Psalm 94 pictures the nation as God's people and inheritance though some have been unfaithful (94:1-8). The psalmist calls upon the righteous judge to arise (v. 1) for the wicked among them are crushing (vv. 2-5) God's people and his inheritance or heritage (94:5, 14). This covenantal truth of Israel being God's people and inheritance is a foundational doctrine that is

---

[558] Three possible meanings have been given: (1) as an Israelite himself he cannot accept that God has rejected Israel (Sanday & Headlam, 309; Dunn, 635); (2) this point would signal to the reader that God continued his concern for Israel because Paul, being a Israelite was chosen to be the apostle to the Gentiles (Cranfield, 544–45); or (3) Paul first turns to himself as the obvious point of God's faithfulness to Israel for he is a Israelite who God did not abandon (Godet, 391–92; Käsemann, 299; Moo, NIVAC, 354). The third position is the easiest position to support from the immediate context.

[559] J. Ross Wagner, *Heralds of the Good News*, 224 comes to the same conclusion. Longenecker (879–880) refers to it as a possible contextual echo or more likely a Jewish and/or Christian aphorism originally from either 1 Sam 12:22 or Ps 94:14 (or both).

[560] ἀπωθέω is used 6 times in the NT. Each use is in the aorist except for Acts 13:46. Paul uses it 3 times (Rom 11:1, 2; 1 Tim 1:19).

[561] Wagner, *Heralds of the Good News*, 223.

repeated here from the narrative of the Exodus motif in Duet 32:8–9, as well as other places.[562] Once again Paul uses the wider context of Ps 94 which expresses the Exodus motif in the Moses' Song to accentuate the unchallengeable commitment and fidelity to redeem and preserve Israel.[563] Ps 94 stresses that the Lord will not abandon His people (inheritance) and He will ultimately be their "stronghold" and their "rock" of "refuge" (v. 22). Most of the people rejected God's plan to be his inheritance. However, 1 Samuel 12:12 has the context of Israel rejecting God as King for they wanted an earthly king (cf. 8:7). Here in both time periods (1 Sam 12 and Rom 9–11) the majority of Israel have rejected the personhood of God as their King. In one sense if they rebel and reject the One who is King, they have also rejected God's plan to be his inheritance and people. Though most of Israel had rejected the Lord's person (kingship) and plan in Paul's day, the Lord will not allow his plan and promise to fail. Thus, both OT passages (1 Sam 12:22 and Ps 94:14) seem to play apart in undergirding the point that God has not rejected His people whom He foreknew.

The word "foreknow" is closely associate with God's sovereign love and his predestination.[564] The word προγινώσκω ("foreknow") is used 5 times as a verb (Acts 26:5; Rom 8:29; 11:2; 1 Pet 1:20; 2 Pet 3:17) and twice as a noun πρόγνωσις (Acts 2:23; 1 Pet 1:2). In Acts 26:5 the word is used in an everyday sense, such as knowing someone previously. Also, in 2 Peter 3:17 it refers to advance knowledge of end time dangers. However, when God is the subject of foreknowing or is the one who has foreknowledge this knowledge is not referring to a cognitive perception ahead of time, but rather, it refers to a established relation between God and his elect people prior to the creation of the world.[565] Grudem states that the word foreknow or foreknowledge in the NT is not used in the context of knowing facts about a person but a personal relational knowledge of people.[566] Indeed, by God's omniscience he knows all things past, present, and future intuitively and all at once. At times in the discussion of foreknowledge the comprehensive knowledge of God is discussed, but the use of the word "foreknowledge" in the context of the NT is the subject of this definition. Therefore, foreknowledge refers to God's elective, loving knowledge that chose the people of Israel without any consideration of their action, status, and even before the nation existed. God's foreknowledge guarantees that Israel will not be cast off (Amos 3:2a). This "foreknew" (v. 2a) functions as an antonym for "has rejected" (v. 1a) (Murray, 2:67; Käsemann, 299; Schriener, 2nd, 556).

Even now when most of the nation rejected Jesus, the Messiah/King, and their sinful ways disqualified so many from their promised inheritance, God will not reject his people (Rom 3:3). The thought of Romans 9:6 helps us to see that not all of Israel is Israel. Through the election of God in Romans 9 God demonstrates his faithfulness to his promise (Hodge, 557). This point is demonstrated in Paul's argument in Romans 9:6–29. However, Paul directs the

---

[562] Ibid., 225. See Ex 19:5; 33:16; Lev 20:26; Deut 7:6,14; 10:15; 14:2; 26:19; 28:1. Especially notice Deut 9:16-29; 1 Kings 8:53.

[563] Ibid., 226–228.

[564] Casper W. Hodge defines foreknowledge: "Foreknowledge, therefore, in the NT is more than mere prescience. It is practically identical with the Divine decree in two instances, and in the other places where the term occurs it denotes the sovereign loving regard out of which springs God's predestination or election of men to salvation" ("Foreknow, Foreknowledge," 1130-1131). See also John Murray, "Foreknow, Foreknowledge," 590–593; Murray, 1:317; Moo 2nd, 554–555. In Rom 11:1-2a the context is not eternal salvation but a special loving corporate relationship with Israel.

[565] Silva, Moisés, rev. ed. *NIDNTTE*, 2nd ed., 4:139.

[566] Grudem, *Systematic Theology*, 676–677. See S. M. Baugh, "The Meaning of Foreknowledge," 1:183–200, but *contra* Jack W. Cottrell, "Conditional Election," 62 and Richard Rice, "Divine Foreknowledge and Free-Will Theism," 134–137.

reader to another argument. This argument encompasses the future election of the nation as a corporate group in Romans 11 (Murray, 2:67–68, Cranfield, 545; Godet, 223; Moo, 2nd, 692–693). The phrase τὸν λαὸν αὐτοῦ ("His people") in v. 1 directs the context to a corporate understanding in the immediate context and the argument of Romans 9:30–10:21 calls into question the national status (Moo, 2nd, 692; Cranfield, 545). In this context, God's foreknowledge and choosing the nation of Israel brings with it the guaranteed blessings and benefits to the nation as a whole, but it does not secure the spiritual salvation for every Israelite. Furthermore, corporate Israel will be confirmed in the olive tree illustration (11:16–24), his statement about all Israel in Romans 11:25–26, and his argument in Romans 11:28–32.

11:2b–4 ἢ οὐκ οἴδατε ἐν Ἠλίᾳ τί λέγει ἡ γραφή, ὡς ἐντυγχάνει τῷ θεῷ κατὰ τοῦ Ἰσραήλ; [3]Κύριε, τοὺς προφήτας σου ἀπέκτειναν, τὰ θυσιαστήριά σου κατέσκαψαν, κἀγὼ ὑπελείφθην μόνος, καὶ ζητοῦσιν τὴν ψυχήν μου. [4] ἀλλὰ τί λέγει αὐτῷ ὁ χρηματισμός; Κατέλιπον ἐμαυτῷ ἑπτακισχιλίους ἄνδρας, οἵτινες οὐκ ἔκαμψαν γόνυ τῇ Βάαλ.[567] 2b "Or do you not know what the Scripture says about Elijah, how he appeals to God against Israel? 3 Lord, they have killed your prophets, they have torn down your altars, and I was left alone, and they are seeking my life. 4 But what does the divine answer say to him? I have left for Myself seven thousand men who have not bowed the knee to Baal." In v. 3 Paul reverses the order of the LXX and writes "they killed the prophets, they have torn down your altars."[568] Some have surmised that Paul may have done this to contemporize the text (Moo, 2nd, 694, n. 584; Jewett, 655–56). There is no biographical reason to connect Elijah and Paul by trying to argue that both of their lives were often threatened (Sanday and Headlam, 311; Dunn, 637; Käsemann, 299). Elijah did not have the correct perspective in the OT context while Paul does have the correct perspective and is using the text in vv. 3–4 to demonstrate his point about a remnant in v. 5 (Schreiner, 2nd, 567).[569]

To refute those who think that Paul (11:1) may be the only one or that there are only a few of Israel left as God's chosen people, Paul turns to the event of Elijah in 1 Kg 19:10-18. Elijah accuses Israel of heinous deeds, but he also affirms that God has not cast off his people. At first Elijah thought he was the only faithful one left, but God unbeknownst to the prophet has kept seven thousand[570] Israelites from bowing the knee to Baal (1 Kg 19:18). The implication left by Paul is that just like in the time of Elijah there are more of the remnant of Israel at the present time then many people think. Paul's use of Elijah to express the remnant in 11:2b–4 should remind them of the "remnant" and "seed" in 9:27–29 and a fuller expression in 11:26. Here in 11:2b-4 the remnant functions more as an anticipatory way where preservation of the remnant indicates that God is not finished with the nation. The anticipation is that God will save Israel in a more dramatic way in the future (11:26) (Schreiner, 2nd, 566-68).[571] The phrase Κατέλιπον ἐμαυτῷ ("I have kept for Myself") indicates God's decisive action that will preserve a remnant (Murray, 2:69; Schriener, 582; Wagner, 236). Paul's day is like Elijah's day in that God has not

---

[567] The comparison of Paul's citation from 1 Kg 19:10 and 19:18 with the Greek OT reveals that the Lucianic texts have many identical wording (Stanley, *Scripture*, 147–158; Jewett, 655–58).

[568] This assumes that Paul was not looking at extant manuscript or quoting from memory (Cranfield, 546; Dunn, 637; Schreiner, 2nd, 567). Schreiner, 2nd, 567 thinks that Paul probably adapted the verse from the MT.

[569] Wagner, *Heralds of the Good News*, 234.

[570] Schreiner, 2nd, 567, n. 13, Dunn (638–639), Cranfield (546–47), and Jewett (657) entertain the possibility of this number as an open number indicating "the open-endedness of God's covenant promise." It is possible that this was an approximate number of men but there are no clear indications in the OT context that it was an open-ended number.

[571] Scott Hafeman, "Romans 11:25–32," 49–50; Wagner, *Heralds of the Good News*, 237.

abandon Israel even though the majority have rejected Jesus Christ and the gospel. God has kept a remnant of Israelite believers through His electing grace.

11:5 οὕτως οὖν καὶ ἐν τῷ νῦν καιρῷ λεῖμμα κατ' ἐκλογὴν χάριτος γέγονεν. "Therefore, then, at the present time there has also come to be a remnant because of the election of grace." Paul has penned an interesting combination of familiar Greek connecting words in v. 5. The words οὕτως, οὖν, and καὶ used somewhere in the same verse can be found in 9 verses in the NT but only here in 11:5 are all three words found one after the other and used together. Furthermore, the words οὕτως and οὖν used somewhere in the same verse can be found in 14 verses in the NT, but both words found one after the other and used together to express one thought is only found in 3 places in the NT (Mt 6:9; Lk 14:33; Rom 11:5). After the unique expression of οὕτως οὖν, Paul uses the connection word καὶ ("and" or "also") and then uses another interesting phrase ἐν τῷ νῦν καιρῷ ("at the present time"). The words νῦν and some form of καιρός in the same verse is found 7 times in the NT. However, the words used together as a phrase (νῦν καιρῷ) is used only 5 times and all them used by Paul.[572] Therefore, these infrequent Greek constructions would catch the attention of the listener or reader. Paul wants his audience to see the parallel of Elijah's day and their time period. The rejection and unbelief of the people in Elijah's time did not cancel the faithfulness and unconditional promises to Israel. Thus, the same truth can be counted on in Paul's day. The promise of the remnant flows from God's election of grace which he developed in great detail in 9:6–29. The Greek perfect verb γέγονεν ("come to be") conveys the thought of an action completed in the past resulting in a present action.[573] In this context, the action of God's election in eternity is now resulting in the salvation of the remnant. The prepositional phrase κατ' ἐκλογὴν χάριτος has the thought of casual or purpose and may be translated "because of the election of grace."[574] Thus, the election of the remnant of Israel in this present age is not due to their wisdom, spiritual perception, or free will,[575] but to God's sovereign grace in election. By definition grace is the undeserved and unmerited work of God.

11:6 εἰ δὲ χάριτι, οὐκέτι ἐξ ἔργων, ἐπεὶ ἡ χάρις οὐκέτι γίνεται χάρις. "And if by grace, *it is* not on the basis of works; for otherwise, grace is no longer manifested as grace." The polemical power of Paul is stressing that works are antithetical to grace when it comes to God's election of a remnant for salvation. The basic definition of grace is the unmerited and undeserve favor and blessing of God. The word χάριτι ("by means of grace") is dative of means.[576] Thus, there is nothing a human being could do to earn God's grace.[577] The word ἔργων ("works") would include the works of the law, but it is not restricted to the works Jews do for national identity (contra Dunn, 639). In this context ἔργων includes human works of any kind (Moo, 2nd, 696; Schreiner, 2nd, 569). The last half of the verse begins with ἐπεὶ ("for otherwise," Moo, 696) which is a causal marker.[578] While the two usages of οὐκέτι ("not the case," "no longer") are not

[572] The exact dative phrase ἐν τῷ νῦν καιρῷ is found in Rom 3:26; 11:5 and 2 Cor 8:14. The genitive phrase is found in Rom 8:18 and the nominative phrase is found in 2 Cor 6:2. Moo (2nd, 695, n. 590) indicates that these 4 passages denote the "eschatological age of fulfillment."

[573] Wallace, *Greek Grammar*, 573–74; Blass, Debrunner, Funk, *A Greek Grammar*, §340.

[574] Ibid., 377; BDAG, 512; Moo, 2nd, 695, n. 593.

[575] See Martin Luther, *The Bondage of the Will* and John Calvin, *The Bondage and Liberation of the Will.*

[576] Wallace, *Greek Grammar*, 162.

[577] Jewett, 660 briefly discussed that the Greco-Roman and Jewish cultures granted grace to the honorable and deserving. However, this is not how Paul uses it.

[578] BDAG, 360; Wallace, *Greek Grammar*, 674; Blass, Debrunner, Funk, *A Greek Grammar*, §456 (3).

temporal for this would mean that salvation in the OT was by works. Salvation in both the OT and NT is by grace through faith. Thus, the two usages of οὐκέτι are logical (Godet, 227; Dunn, 639; Jewett, 660; Moo, 2nd, 696, n. 599; Schreiner, 2nd, 583). Most commentators equate γίνεται ("to become") in this context as equivalent to a "to be" verb (ἐστί). However, Meyer (206) and Jewett (660) bring out the meaning of γίνεται as not "showing itself as" or "manifesting as" grace.[579] The sinful depravity of every person born into this world necessitates the supremacy and purity of God's grace in election to be saved and not the work of human beings. Paul specifically affirms that a remnant of Jews will receive saving grace because of God's sovereign election of His will (11:5-6).[580]

11:7 τί οὖν; ὃ ἐπιζητεῖ Ἰσραήλ, τοῦτο οὐκ ἐπέτυχεν, ἡ δὲ ἐκλογὴ ἐπέτυχεν· οἱ δὲ λοιποὶ ἐπωρώθησαν. "What then *is the outcome*? What Israel is seeking, this she has not attained; but the chosen has attained it. But the rest have been hardened." There is a question about the function of the rhetorical question τί οὖν ("What then"). Most commentators (Sanday & Headlam, 313; Murray, 2:70; Cranfield, 548) think that verse 7 and what follows take up the implication of vv. 1–6. Moo (2nd, 697, n. 601) connects the subject with the remnant in vv. 2b–6 while Schreiner (2nd, 570) understands that vv. 7–10 sum up 9:30–11:6. It is interesting that Paul used the concept of the remnant (9:27; 11:5) though he does not always use the word (9:29; 11:26). He also brings out the election theme (9:11-15, 18, 21, 23; 11:7) and hardening theme (9:18, 21, 22; 11:7-10, 25) throughout Romans 9–11. Paul refers to Israel as the corporate whole and then by those who were elect and those who are hardened. Some have understood the word elect in this verse to mean both Gentiles and Jews (Schreiner, 2nd, 570–571; Dunn, 640), but the context favors the restriction to Jews (Moo, 2nd, 698; Jewett, 661; Fitzmyer, 606). Paul chose the present tense ἐπιζητεῖ ("is seeking")[581] with the aorist tense ἐπέτυχεν ("has obtained") to express the contrast in the first part of this verse. The present tense ἐπιζητεῖ may be an iterative present describing an event that repeatedly happens. However, this present verb may be a candidate for extending-from-past present which describes the action that begun in the past continues in the present and emphasizes the present time.[582] Either way the thought is that the majority of Israel is presently and progressively seeking a right standing with God but as a whole they did not obtain it (Rom 9:30–33; 10:2–3). However, the elected Israelites by grace (11:5) received it and the "rest were hardened" (cf. Rom 9:18-23). The word ἐκλογὴ ("chosen," 9:11; 11:5, 7, 28) is usually used in the active sense, but here it is used in the passive sense emphasizing the nature of the group chosen from a larger group by the divine initiative (Theilman, 518; Jewett, 661; Moo, 2nd, 698, n. 606; Murray, 2:71).[583] The election in 11:7 is paralleled to vv. 4–5. This election is nothing less than a grace gift (11:6) of God's righteousness which promises eternal life.[584] The word σκληρύνω ("harden") is used in Romans 9:18 and the word πωρόω ("harden") in Romans 11:7. These two verbs are basically synonymous in their contextual meaning (Moo, 2nd, 698, n.

---

[579] See BDAG, 196–199.

[580] See Calvin, 414–415 for his critique of trying to blend foreknowledge of works with election.

[581] Horst Balz and Gerhard Schneider, "ἐπιζητέω," *EDNT* 2 (1991) 27 emphasizes the intensive form "strive for; (eagerly) seek after." BDAG (2000) 371 (2) give the following definition "be seriously interested in or have a strong desire for." Moo, 2nd, 697, n. 604 and Jewett, 661, n. 104 doubt that the intensive meaning conveyed in earlier classical Greek by the prefix ἐπί.

[582] Wallace, Greek Grammar, 519–521. If this view is taken then Wallace recommends to translated it with an English present perfect, "has sought."

[583] BDAG, 306.

[584] Murray, 2:71 gives four reason why the election here is eternal salvation.

609). The verb πωρόω is used in Mk 6:52; 8:17; Jn 12:40 and 2 Cor 3:14, and all of the usages are metaphorical referring to spiritual harden of the heart or mind.[585] The passive form ἐπωρώθησαν ("were hardened") is likely a divine passive referring to God being the agent of the hardening (Barrett, 210; Cranfield, 549; Schreiner, 2nd, 571–572; Dunn, 640; contra Sanday and Headlam, 313–314). Since the subject of the choosing involved grace unto eternal salvation, then the opposite use of "hardened" should be understood with the opposite meaning, eternal judgment like in Romans 9:18 (Murray, 2:72). There is much debate on who or what caused the hardening. However, Moo (2nd, 698, n. 610) is correct that it is stretching this text and counter to Romans 9:17–23 to say that human sin is the cause of God's hardening.[586] Everyone is born into the world as a sinner (Rom 5:12ff; 6:23). Calvin (416–417) understood this hardening as a pretemporal decree of God to eternal damnation and some Reformed theologians have followed Calvin's thought. This is possible but at least we can say that Paul keeps in tension, or it is an antinomy[587] that God hardened Israel and Israel is responsible for choosing the wrong path to righteousness before God (Moo, 2nd, 699, especially n. 613). Barrett (195) states that it is impossible to distinguish between "hardened because of disobedience" and "disobedience because hardened" for both processes are concurrent. Furthermore, this hardening is not a permanent condition for the nation in the future. Paul indicates that one day in the future God will lift the hardening from Israel (Rom 11:25–26). Those Israelites who were hardened are the subject of Paul's discussion in vv. 7–10. Moo (2nd, 699) is correct that 11:11–32 addresses Israel from a corporate perspective, but 11:7–11 makes distinction among the people within the corporate entity of Israel.

11:8 καθὼς γέγραπται· Ἔδωκεν αὐτοῖς ὁ θεὸς πνεῦμα κατανύξεως, ὀφθαλμοὺς τοῦ μὴ βλέπειν καὶ ὦτα τοῦ μὴ ἀκούειν, ἕως τῆς σήμερον ἡμέρας. "Just as it is written, 'God has given them a spirit of stupor, so that eyes do not see and ears that do not hear, until the present day.'" Paul introduces his ground of proof from the OT by the conjunction καθὼς ("just as"). The blinding and hardening in Isaiah 29:9–12 and Deuteronomy 29:4 (MT/LXX 29:3) have their foundation in Isaiah 6:9–10. The theme of Israel's blindness and deafness extends as far as Isaiah 64 and it relates to Israel's redemption, which is described as the opening of the eyes and ears.[588] Paul's use of Isaiah 6:9–10 provides an intertextual connection with the conflation of Isaiah 29:19 and Deuteronomy 29:4 (MT/LXX 29:3). Thus, these intertextual connections are present in the citation of Romans 11:8. The hardening, deafening, and blinding of Israel in Isaiah 6:9–13 find its seed of hope in God leaving the stump of the fallen tree because "the holy seed is its stump" (6:13). Isaiah 29 also has the movement from blindness and judgment (vv. 9–16) to restoration and redemption (vv. 17–24), which is a NE redemption motif. Wagner calls this an eschatological reversal.[589] This eschatological reversal becomes a background pattern for all the

---

[585] Cranfield, 549 defuses the confusion between πωροῦν, πώρωσις and πηροῦν, πήρωσις. He correctly states that πωροῦν should be translated "harden" and not "blind." See also K. L. and M. A. Schmidt, *TDNT*, 5:1025–1028. Contra Jewett's (661) who translates it "made obtuse."

[586] See Rom 9:22 comments on the "divine passive" and hardening.

[587] See J. I. Packer's book *Evangelism and the Sovereignty of God*," 18–25. Briefly, an antinomy in theology is "an apparent incompatibility between two apparent truths. . . seemingly irreconcilable, yet both undeniable."

[588] See Isa 6:9–10; 29:10, 18; 32:3–4; 35:5; 42:7, 16, 18–20, 23; 43:8; 44:18–20; 48:8; 56:10; 59:10; 63:17; 64:4. Williamson, *The Book Called Isaiah*, 46–51 states that Isa 6:9–10 exerts influence in many parts of the book of Isaiah.

[589] Wagner, *Heralds of the Good News*, 253.

Old Testament passages, which Paul chose to use in Romans 11:7–10. However, what also needs to be brought to light is that these background patterns (eschatological reversal) in these Old Testament passages are the framework of the NE motif.[590] Thus, the failure of Israel in the heart-eyes-ears motif is Paul's point in Isaiah 29:10, but the extended context of Isaiah 29:18–24 brings out the reversal in a NE motif.[591]

Paul also conflates Deuteronomy 29:4 with Isaiah 29:10.[592] Moses spoke of the memory of the Exodus in Deuteronomy 29:2-4 (MT/LXX 29:1–3). Three times Moses uses the keyword "eye" in vv. 2–4 (once in each verse) and adds the phrase "ears to hear" in v. 4. Israel saw all that the Lord did in the delivery from Egypt and the journey in the wilderness, but the Lord did not give them a "heart to know, nor eyes to see, nor ears to hear" (v. 4). The Deuteronomic quotation attributes the dullness of Israel to the Lord and exhorts them to be faithful to the covenant (29:9). Isaiah 29:10 expresses a judgmental tone based upon the condition of the nation. The message of Deuteronomy 29 is rooted in the context of the first Exodus, which occurred about 40 years beforehand and incorporates the NE theme by using the message of the Abrahamic promises, the eschatological restoration of the land, and the people in Deuteronomy 30. Therefore, Paul's choice of the context of Deuteronomy 29–30 is a rich NE message where God will be faithful to His people even in the midst of judgment for their unbelief.

Deut 29:3 καὶ οὐκ ἔδωκεν κύριος ὁ θεὸς ὑμῖν καρδίαν εἰδέναι καὶ ὀφθαλμοὺς βλέπειν καὶ ὦτα ἀκούειν ἕως τῆς ἡμέρας ταύτης ("and the Lord God did not give you a heart to know and eyes to see and ears to hear until this day")
Isa 29:10 ὅτι πεπότικεν ὑμᾶς κύριος πνεύματι κατανύξεως καὶ καμμύσει τοὺς ὀφθαλμοὺς αὐτῶν καὶ τῶν προφητῶν αὐτῶν καὶ τῶν ἀρχόντων αὐτῶν, οἱ ὁρῶντες τὰ κρυπτά ("because the Lord has made you drunk with a spirit of stupor and he shall shut their eyes and [the eyes] of their prophets and their rulers, who see the secrets")
Rom 11:8 Ἔδωκεν αὐτοῖς ὁ θεὸς πνεῦμα κατανύξεως, ὀφθαλμοὺς τοῦ μὴ βλέπειν καὶ ὦτα τοῦ μὴ ἀκούειν, ἕως τῆς σήμερον ἡμέρας ("God gave them a spirit of stupor, so that eyes do not see and ears do not hear, until the present day.")

Paul utilized the NE framework in Isaiah 29 and borrows three words from verse 10 (LXX): πνεύματι ("spirit"), κατανύξεως ("A spirit of deep sleep"), and ὀφθαλμούς ("eyes"). The word κατανύξεως is only used twice in the Old Testament[593] and once in the New Testament (Moo, 2nd, 700, n. 616; Dunn, 641). The phrase πνεῦμα κατανύξεως ("spirit of stupor") seems to give the indication that this slumber is not death but a deep spiritual slumber that one day in the future God will awaken the nation.[594] In Isaiah 29:18 it says, "On that day the deaf shall hear words of a book, and out of their gloom and darkness the eyes of the blind will see" (NASB). This event brings about the change stated in 29:19–24 which describes the eschatological reversal in the motif of the NE.

---

590 See in this commentary on Rom 9:20 and the Biblical Theological section after the comments on this verse.

591 For more detail, see Sullivan, *The INE in Rom 9–11*, 327–332.

592 Some scholars also support the conflation of Ps 35:8 as part of the citation (Dunn, 642, 649; Wagner, *Heralds of the Good News*, 259–261.

593 Isa 29:10 and Ps 60:3 (60:5 MT; 59:5 LXX).

594 Seifrid, 670. See also Stanley, *Paul and the Language of Scripture*, 161; Wilk, *Die Bedeutung des Jesajabuches für Paulus*, 54, 145; Wagner, *Heralds of the Good News*, 265; Jewett, 663.

Jewett (663) takes the phrase τοῦ μὴ βλέπειν καὶ ὦτα τοῦ μὴ ἀκούειν as articular infinitives in the genitive case that convey purpose.[595] The two infinitives conveying purpose fit Paul's argument better in Rom 11 ("so that eyes do not see and ears do not hear"). Paul appears to conflate Deuteronomy 29:3 and Isaiah 29:10 and then he ends with reference to Psalms 69:22–23 in Rom 11:9–10.

11:9–10 [9]καὶ Δαυὶδ λέγει· Γενηθήτω ἡ τράπεζα αὐτῶν εἰς παγίδα καὶ εἰς θήραν καὶ εἰς σκάνδαλον καὶ εἰς ἀνταπόδομα αὐτοῖς, [10]σκοτισθήτωσαν οἱ ὀφθαλμοὶ αὐτῶν τοῦ μὴ βλέπειν, καὶ τὸν νῶτον αὐτῶν διὰ παντὸς σύγκαμψον. 9 "And David says, Let their table become for *them* a snare and a trap and a stumbling block and a retribution. 10 Let their eyes be darkened so that they do not see and cause their backs to be bent continually." The imprecation of Psalm 69 makes clear the overall interpretation of judgment and physical downfall for this citation in Romans. However, the difficulty of understanding the particulars is noted as many interpreters have commented. The sum of the understandings of how Paul used the word "table" from Psalm 69:22 in Romans 11:9 are: (1) an allusion to cult sacrifices (Käsemann, 302; Godet, 231; Dunn, 650; Jewett, 664); (2) a general sense concerning divine judgment (Cranfield, 551–552; Moo, 2nd, 701 ; Schreiner, 2nd, 574; Longenecker, 883); (3) a general sense that relate to God's providence intending for their joy but becomes the judgment of God (Murray, 2:74); (4) a feast that relates to trust in the law that becomes their fall (Sanday and Headlam, 315; Barrett, 195; Goppelt, *TDNT* 8:212; Seifrid, 671); (5) falling over a table set up on the ground to illustrate Israel stumbling (Fitzmyer, 606). What is clear in v. 9 involves the results: it has become a trap, snare, stumbling block, and retribution. The interpretation of the "bending of the back" may refer to slavery or some kind of grief (Moo, 2nd, 701, n. 623; Schreiner, 2nd, 574). The phrases διὰ παντὸς in v. 10 should not be translated "forever" but the idea of "continually" (Moo, 2nd, 700, n. 620; Jewett, 665; Cranfield, 552).[596] Wagner is correct that Paul found in his kinsmen a prefiguration of those who rejected the gospel of the Lord Jesus Christ, and they stand in hostile insensibility of David's imprecation.[597]
Ps 68:23–24 (LXX) γενηθήτω ἡ τράπεζα αὐτῶν ἐνώπιον αὐτῶν εἰς παγίδα καὶ εἰς ἀνταπόδοσιν καὶ εἰς σκάνδαλον· σκοτισθήτωσαν οἱ ὀφθαλμοὶ αὐτῶν τοῦ μὴ βλέπειν, καὶ τὸν νῶτον αὐτῶν διὰ παντὸς σύγκαμψον· ("Let their table before them become a snare, and for retribution a stumbling block. Let their eyes be darkened so they cannot see and bend their backs continually.")

The verbal connection of ὀφθαλμός ("eye") in these three quotations in Romans 11:8–10 is significant. In v. 10 Paul uses ὀφθαλμοὶ ("eyes") in Ps 69:23 (LXX 68:24), which parallels Isaiah 6:10, Deuteronomy 29:4, and Isaiah 29:10. Secondly, Deuteronomy 29:4 (LXX 29:3) is used by Paul concerning the time period of Israel's blindness, "to this day," and Psalm 69:23 (LXX 68:24) is used from David's prayer against his enemies to suffer judgment "continually." Finally, in Ps 69:23 (LXX 68:24) it states "let their eyes be darkened that they cannot see" which parallels the thought of Romans 11:8 (LXX Deut 29:3).[598] The overall movement of Psalm 69 is from judgment on Israel's enemies (imprecatory lament vv. 1–28) to eschatological salvation

---

[595] For support, see Blass, DeBrunner, Funk, *A Greek Grammar*, § 400 and Stanley, *Paul and the Language of Scripture*, 162. LXX-A has one articulate infinitives τοῦ βλέπειν in Deut 29:3 (Ziegler, *Isaias*, 316). Moo (2nd, 699, n. 615) takes the articulate infinitives in Rom 11:8 as "probably adjectival." Blass, DeBrunner, Funk, § 400[2] explain the infinitives as consecutive: "such eyes that they" see.

[596] The Hebrew word is תָּמִיד and is best translated "continually" (*HALOT*, 1748–1749).

[597] Wagner, *Heralds of the Good News*, 261, 265; Jewett, 665.

[598] Sullivan, *The INE in Rom 9-11*, 337.

(vv. 29–36) which is a NE pattern.[599] Notice the earnest desire to be saved in Psalm 69:1, 29, 35 and the redemptive language of verse 18. Finally, the psalm reaches a climax in the eschatological deliverance in verses 35–36. Paul draws from the imprecatory section in Psalm 69:22–23 in Romans 11:9–10, but the whole context of Psalm 69 helps the reader who knew the psalm to anticipate restoration of Israel discussed in Romans 11:11–32. What brings Paul to call upon these three witnesses (Moses [Torah], Isaiah [the Prophets], and David [the Writings]) is the NE motif background that moves from judgment to eschatological salvation. God's faithfulness to his covenant word extends to the time of Moses (Deut 29:14–15), to the exilic period (Isa 29:17–24), and now by Paul's extension to his very day (σήμερον ἡμέρας); thus, paving his way to discuss Israel's national destiny in verses 11–32. However, the divine blinding is not the final state or last word to his covenant people.[600]

Biblical Theological Comments

Paul introduces Romans 11:1-10 with the question whether God has rejected his people (11:1a) and then answers the question in 11:1b–6 with a firm negative. Finally, he ends the section with a logical conclusion (v. 7) which he supports with the OT in vv. 8–10. Paul needed to come back to the question of Israel's status before God because of the strong statements in Romans 10:16–21. The textual pattern of the OT citations in Rom 11:8-10 may be explained as an eschatological reversal. This reversal in the context of the OT citations involves judgment concerning blind eyes to the truth that ultimately are changed to the blessings of eschatological salvation from God. This theological shift from judgment to salvation is a classic expression of the NE motif. Each of the three OT citations that Paul uses express this pattern. Moses in Deuteronomy 29–30 exposes the failure of the heart-eyes-ears of the people to perceive the truth. Furthermore, the primary goal of Moses was to admonish the present generation and the future generations to be faithful to the Abrahamic promises and God's future restoration and redemption (Deut 29:13; 30:1–16). In Isaiah 29:17-24, the author moves from the people's state of blindness that deserves the judgment of God to the blessing of God's physical and spiritual restoration. Finally, Psalm 69:29–36 moves from judgment to praise and thanksgiving for God's physical and eschatological deliverance, which is foreshadowed in Psalm 69:13–18. Therefore, Moses (the Law), Isaiah (the Prophets) and David (the Writings) witness together through a verbal connection and similar contextual background from the Exodus motif to provide a powerful trio for Paul to use in his argument. In the context of Romans 11:8–10, the hardening and judgment is prominent. However, the NE reversal contexts of deliverance in the three OT passages (Deut 29; Isa 29 and Ps 69) anticipates the salvation of Israel which Paul will detail in Romans 11:11–32.[601]

Just like in the days of Elijah it may appear that God has abandon Israel because of their disobedience and unbelief. However, things are not as they appear. Just like in the days of Elijah, God has selected on the bases of grace a remnant according to His own sovereign election (11:5–6). In Romans 11:7, Paul returns to his thought of God's gracious election in the latter half of v. 5 and Israel's failure mentioned in Romans 9:30–33, which was broadly expanded by him in

---

[599] See Ibid., 338–341. Ps 69 is quoted or alluded to in the life of Jesus Christ: Matt 27:34, 48; Mark 3:21; 15:23, 36; Lk 13:35; 23:36; Jn 2:17; 15:25; 19:29; Acts 1:20; Rom 15:3; Heb 11:26; Phil 4:3; Rev 3:5; 16:1.

[600] Wagner, *The Herald of the Good News*, 264–265.

[601] Sullivan, *The INE in Rom 9–11*, 327–345.

Romans 10. He also brings the concept of election and hardening from Rom 9:11–23 and applies it to Israel and the remnant in Israel. The failure of Israel as a whole was the failure to pursue the righteousness of God by faith. However, the remnant of Israelites who obtain righteousness by faith did so because of God's sovereign election of grace! Therefore, in a broad sense Rom 11:7–10 summarizes Romans 9:30–11:6.

Application and Devotional Implications

God has not completely rejected Israel whom He foreknew (11:2). The word foreknowledge is a word used in the context of an intimate relationship between God and Israel. It has to do with God's love to choose the nation of Israel as His people. It was a decision based upon His sovereign will (Deut 7:6–8). Paul supports his point in Romans 11:2–6 with a quotation from 1 Kings 19:10. Elijah looks around at all the apostasy of Israel and he believes he is the only one left who has not abandon God. However, there are 7,000 Israelites that had not bowed to Baal. Just like in the day of Elijah God had kept a remnant. This remnant did not exist because of their works, but only because of God's elective grace. Salvation is a gift of God (Eph 2:8–9) given to those who deserve the Lake of Fire! Dr. Lewis S. Chafer gave at least three principles which cannot co-exist with grace.[602] First, God's grace does not recognize human guilt. If God considered man's guilt, then no one would be saved. We are all guilty of sin. Second, God's grace does not recognize human obligation. If God is obligated to give man salvation because of something human beings are or have done, then salvation is not by grace. In other words, if God is to be free to act in unlimited divine grace toward sinners, then human work and obligation must be set aside. Thirdly, God's grace does not recognize human merit. Divine grace is the undeserved, unmerited gift from God.

The phrase "the rest were hardened" (v. 7) is describing the same spiritual hardening of Romans 9:18 that prevents people from responding to God and His message of salvation. The tension of God's hardening of people and their own disobedience that hardens them in unbelief seems to happen concurrently (Moo, 2nd, 699, n. 613; Barrett, 195). This theological point is a great mystery. Our responsibility as believers is to call out to the rebellious and disobedient sinners to come to Jesus Christ and His salvation through believing the gospel and leave the rest in the hand of the sovereign God (Rom 11:33–36).

Selected Bibliography

Arndt, William, Frederick W. Danker, and Walter Bauer, *A Greek-English Lexicon of the New Testament and Other Early Christian Literature*, 3rd ed. electronic version (Chicago: University of Chicago Press, 2000).

Balz, Horst and Gerhard Schneider, "ἐπιζητέω," in *EDNT* 2 (Edinburg: T & T Clark, 1991) 27.

Baugh, S. M. "The Meaning of Foreknowledge," in *The Grace of God: The Bondage of the Will*, ed. Thomas R. Schriener and Bruce A. Ware (Grand Rapids: Baker, 1995).

[602] Chafer, *Grace*, 37–46.

Blass, Friedrich, Albert Debrunner, and Robert Walter Funk, *A Greek Grammar of the New Testament and Other Early Christian Literature* (Chicago: University of Chicago Press, 1961).

Calvin, John. *The Bondage and Liberation of the Will: A Defence of the Orthodox Doctrine of Human Choice Against Pighius*, ed. A. N. S. Lane and trans. G. I. Davies (Grand Rapids: Baker, 1996).

Chafer, Lewis S. *Grace: The Glorious Theme*. Grand Rapids: Zondervan, 1922.

Cottrell, Jack W. "Conditional Election," in *Grace Unlimited*, ed. Clark H. Pinnock (Minneapolis: Bethany House, 1975), 51–73.

Grudem, Wayne. *Systematic Theology: An Introduction to Biblical Doctrine* (Grand Rapids: Zondervan, 1994).

Given, Mark D. "Restoring the Inheritance in Romans 11:1," *Journal of Biblical Literature* 118/1 (1999): 89–96.

Hafemann, Scott. "The Salvation of Israel in Romans 11:25–32: A Response to Krister Stendahl," *Ex Auditu* 4 (1988): 38–58.

Metzger, Bruce M. *A Textual Commentary on the Greek New Testament*. 2nd ed. (Stuttgart: Deutsche Bibelgesellschaft, 1994).

Hodge, Casper W. "Foreknow, Foreknowledge," in *International Standard Bible Encyclopaedia*, gen. ed. James Orr (Chicago: The Howard-Severance Co., 1915), 1128-1131.

Murray, John. "Foreknow, Foreknowledge," in *The Zondervan Pictorial Encyclopaedia of the Bible*, vol. 2, gen. ed. Merrill C. Tenny (Grand Rapids: Zondervan, 1980), 590–593.

Packer, J. I. and O. R. Johnston, eds. *Martin Luther on the bondage of the Will: A New Translation of De Servo Arbitrio (1525) Martin Luther's Reply to Erasmus of Rotterdam* (Grand Rapids: Fleming H. Revell Co., 1957).

Packer, J. I. *Evangelism and the Sovereignty of God* (England: InterVarsity Fellowship, 1967).

Rice, Richard. "Divine Foreknowledge and Free-Will Theism," in *The Grace of God, The Will of Man*, ed. Clark H. Pinnock (Grand Rapids: Zondervan), 121–139.

Schmidt, K. L. and M. A. Schmidt, "πωρόω," *TDNT*, 5:1022–1028.

Silva, Moisés. rev.ed. "προγινώσκω," *NIDNTTE*, 2nd ed. Vol. 2. (Grand Rapids: Zondervan, 2014), 4:139.

Stanley, Christopher. *Paul and the Language of Scripture: Citation Technique in the Pauline Epistles and Contemporary Literature* (Cambridge: Cambridge University Press, 1992).

Strathmann, Hermann. "λαός," in *TDNT* (Grand Rapids: Eerdmans, 1964), 4:32–35.

Sullivan, Steven P. *The Isaianic New Exodus in Romans 9–11: A Biblical and Theological Study of Paul's Use of Isaiah in Romans* (Silverton, OR: Lampion Press, 2017).

Sullivan, Steven P. *The Isaianic New Exodus in Romans 9–11*, 2nd ed. (Middletown, RI: Stone Tower Press, 2023).

Swanson, Reuben, ed. *New Testament Greek Manuscripts: Romans*. (Wheaton: Tyndale House and Pasadena: William Carey International University Press, 2001).

Wagner, J. Ross. *Heralds of the Good News: Isaiah and Paul in Concert in the Letter to the Romans*. Supplements to Novum Testamentum, eds. M. M. Mitchell and D. P. Moessner, vol. 101. (Leiden: Brill, 2002).

Wagner, J. Ross. "'Not from the Jews Only, But Also from the Gentiles': Mercy to the Nations in Romans 9–11," in *Between Gospel and Election: Explorations in Interpretation of Romans 9–11*, Wissenschaftliche Untersuchungen zum Neuen Testament (Tübingen: Mohr Siebeck, 2010).

Wallace, Daniel B. *Greek Grammar Beyond the Basic: An Exegetical Syntax of the New Testament* (Grand Rapids: Zondervan, 1996).
Wilk, Florian. *Die Bedeutung des Jesajabuches für Paulus*, in Forschungen zur Religon und Literatur des Alten und Neuen Testaments (Göttingen: Hubert & Co., 1998).
Williamson, H. G. M. *The Book Called Isaiah: Deutero-Isaiah's Role in Composition and Redaction* (Oxford: Clarendon Press, 1994).
Ziegler, Joseph. *Isaias*, Septuaginta: Vetus Testamentum Graecum, 3rd ed. (Göttingen: Vandenhoeck & Ruprecht, 1939, 1983).

Romans 11:11–15

Introduction

Paul's argument in Rom 11:7–10 again (see 11:1) leaves the possibility in the mind of the reader that Israel's future is a failure and a permanent loss. Paul endeavors to correct this misunderstanding and show how the failure of Israel at the present time allows for the blessings of God to come to the Gentiles. The third person plural pronouns in verses 11–12 refer not to λοιποὶ ("the rest") in v. 7b–10, but to Israel as a whole (v. 7a) (Moo, 2nd, 704; Thielman, 534).[603] Romans 11:7a summarizes what Paul has already expounded upon in Rom 9:31–32 and 10:3. Thus, he addresses mainly corporate groups and not in terms of individuals within the corporate bodies. There is no question that Israel as a whole (but not every individual) is in unbelief and is hardened, but Paul wants to demonstrate how the Gentiles fit into God's plan and in the future how God will save Israel. Romans 11:11–15 alternates between Israel and the Gentiles:

ISRAEL	GENTILES
But by their (Israel's) transgression (11b)	Gentiles salvation to make Israel jealous (11b)
Israel's transgression and failure (12) How much more will their fullness be? (12)	Be spiritual riches for the world of the Gentiles (12)
	Paul, as an apostle to the Gentiles speaking to Gentiles – He magnifies his ministry to the Gentiles (v. 13)
To move to jealousy some of his fellow Israelites to salvation (14)	
For if their (Israel) rejection (15) What will the acceptance *of Israel* be except life from the dead? (15)	Be the reconciliation of the world (15)

Outline

I. The Wisdom Polemic: The Tension between God's Righteous Promises and Israel's Condition 9–11
   A. Introduction to the Tension (9:1–5)
   B. Vindication of the righteous God and His Wise Plan (9:6–29)
   C. Israel's Knowledge of the Gospel of Righteousness: Faith and Works (9:30–10:21)
   D. Israel's election and partial hardening and not total rejection (11:1-10)
   E. A Wisdom Polemic: God's Merciful Plan for Israel and Gentiles (11:11-33)
      1. Israel's hardening and the Gentiles Inclusion (11:11-15)

[603] Hafemann, "The Salvation of Israel," 50.

Original Text

11.11 Λέγω οὖν, μὴ ἔπταισαν ἵνα πέσωσιν; μὴ γένοιτο· ἀλλὰ τῷ αὐτῶν παραπτώματι ἡ σωτηρία
τοῖς ἔθνεσιν, εἰς τὸ παραζηλῶσαι αὐτούς. 12 εἰ δὲ τὸ παράπτωμα αὐτῶν πλοῦτος κόσμου καὶ τὸ
ἥττημα αὐτῶν πλοῦτος ἐθνῶν, πόσῳ μᾶλλον τὸ πλήρωμα αὐτῶν.[a] 13 Ὑμῖν δὲ[b] λέγω τοῖς ἔθνεσιν.
ἐφ' ὅσον μὲν οὖν[c] εἰμι ἐγὼ ἐθνῶν ἀπόστολος, τὴν διακονίαν μου δοξάζω,[d] 14 εἴ πως παραζηλώσω
μου τὴν σάρκα καὶ σώσω τινὰς ἐξ αὐτῶν. 15 εἰ γὰρ ἡ ἀποβολὴ αὐτῶν καταλλαγὴ κόσμου, τίς ἡ
πρόσλημψις εἰ μὴ ζωὴ ἐκ νεκρῶν.

Textual Notes

[a] **11:12** The overwhelming majority of mss. includes v. 12 with minor changes by a few mss. Codex A omits v. 12 (Swanson, *NT Gk Mss*, *Rom*, 173). Since early mss. like P^{46} ℵ B contain the verse, the omission seems to happen in the fifth century. Longenecker, 869, postulates the following possibilities: (1) the scribe considered the word πλοῦτος (used twice and implied once) too repetitive; (2) the scribe viewed the expression "riches of the world and "riches for the Gentiles to have no difference or the verse is elliptical statement and was too difficult to translate; (3) he considered this statement to be redundant in comparison to the more explicit statement in v. 15; thus, omitted it. Of course, no one knows for sure why the scribe omitted it. However, the text of v. 12 is abundantly attested and should be considered as original. Jewett, 666, states that some suspect the deletion was for theological reasons, but it is more likely an accidental omission.

[b] **11:13 δὲ** is supported by WH Treg NA28 SBLGNT UBS5 ℵ B A P 81 104 630 1243 1506 1735 1739 1874 1881. **γὰρ** is supported by D F G L Ψ 049 056 1 6 33 69 88 131 205 209 330 323 326 330 365 424 440 489 614 910 927 945 999 1175 1241 1242 1245 1270 1319 1424 1505 1611 1734 1836 1854 1891 2344 2464 2495 𝔐. C has οὖν. (Swanson, *NT Gk Mss, Rom*, 173). The variant reading of γὰρ strengthens the connection between vv. 12–13, but the textual history of δὲ is the stronger reading (Longenecker, 870; Cranfield, 558).

[c] **11:13 μὲν οὖν** is supported by WH Treg NA28 SBLGNT UBS5 P^{46} ℵ B A C P 81 104 1506. Only **μὲν (no οὖν)** is supported by D F G L Ψ 049 056 1 6 33 69 88 131 205 209 330 323 326 330 365 424 440 489 614 910 927 945 999 1175 1241 1242 1245 1270 1319 1424 1505 1611 1734 1836 1854 1891 2125 2147 2400 2412 2344 2464 2495 2815 𝔐 (Swanson, *NT Gk Mss, Rom,* 174). The stronger reading is to include οὖν (Cranfield, 559, n. 2). The reading μὲν οὖν was the more difficult reading being an "early oral, vernacular, and poetic idiom" (Longenecker, 870).

[d] **11:13 δοξάζω** is supported by WH NA28 SBLGNT UBS5 ℵ B A C D L P 049 056 1 6 69 131 205 209 330 323 326 365 424 440 489 614 618 796 910 927 945 999 1241 1242 1243 1245 1270 1315 1319 1352 1424 1448 1505 1506 1573 1611 1734 1735 1738 1739 1827 1837 1854 1891 2125 2147 2400 2412 2464 2495 2464 2495 2815. **δοξάσω** is supported by P^{46} F G Ψ 33 88 460 1175 1646 1836 1874 2344. (Swanson, *NT Gk Mss, Rom*, 174). Jewett, 666 believes that δοξάσω is a dictation error for the letter σ is close in sound to ζ. Most of the earliest mss. and the majority of the other mss. read δοξάζω. The only evidence that gives one pause is P^{46} with a few uncials

and other minuscules. Longenecker, 870 is convinced to accept the future δοξάσω, but agrees that the variant probably came with the similar letter sounds.

Translation

11 I say therefore, they did not stumble so as to fall, *did they*? By no means! But by their transgression salvation *has come* to the Gentiles, in order to make them jealous. **12** Now if their transgression *means* riches for the world and their loss *means* riches for the Gentiles, how much more *will* their fullness *mean*? **13** Now to you Gentiles I am speaking. In so far, then as I am an apostle to the Gentiles, I glorify my ministry. **14** If somehow, I might provoke to jealousy my *countryman in* the flesh and might save some of them. **15** For if their rejection *of God* means the reconciliation of the world, what will their acceptance mean, except life from the dead?

Commentary

11:11 Λέγω οὖν, μὴ ἔπταισαν ἵνα πέσωσιν; μὴ γένοιτο· ἀλλὰ τῷ αὐτῶν παραπτώματι ἡ σωτηρία τοῖς ἔθνεσιν, εἰς τὸ παραζηλῶσαι αὐτούς. "I say therefore, they did not stumble so as to fall, *did they*? By no means! But by their transgression salvation *has come* to the Gentiles, in order to make them jealous." This verse begins with the same three Greek words as 11:1, Λέγω οὖν ("therefore, I say") and the negative particle μὴ plus an aorist verb. The οὖν relates to vv. 1–10 (Moo, 2nd, 704) and possibly 9:30–11:10 (Schriener, 2nd, 576). The negative particle μὴ indicates the author expects the reader to answer the question in the negative. The negative is then followed up with the emphatic negative phrase μὴ γένοιτο ("by no means") just like in 11:1. The aorist verb ἔπταισαν (πταίω) has the idea of "stumbling to make a mistake or go astray" or to "be ruined or be lost."[604] The usage in James refers to stumbling into sin and 2 Pet 1:10 refers to being ruined or lost. The next verb πέσωσιν (πίπτω) has the meaning "to fall down, fall down (violently or break into pieces), to be destroyed, be completely ruined, or perish."[605] This word is a strong word for it conveys the sense of a final state of Israel–fall to rise no more (Jewett, 673).[606] Thus, the use of both words in Paul's question is accentuating the stumbling to a ruin and broken state that they will not be restored or experience salvation. The use of ἵνα in this context seems best taken as consecutive (ecbatic) use which expresses the result of the action and may be translated "so as" (Sanday and Headlam, 320; Cranfield, 554; Moo, 2nd, 704–705; Thielman, 534).[607] In this strong expression, Paul is asking whether Israel's rejection of Jesus Christ, his salvation, and promises are permanent and irrevocably lost. Paul's strong negative constructions are the correct answer to the question. Israel's fall and rejection is neither total (11:1–10) nor final (11:11–32) (Moo, 2nd, 701). The ἀλλὰ is a strong adversive and best

---

604 BDAG, 894; Karl L. Schmidt, *TDNT*, 6:883. The other NT usages are Jas 2:10; 3:2 (2x), 2 Pet 1:10.

605 BDAG, 815–16; Wilhelm Michaelis, *TDNT*, 6:161–63.

606 Godet, 234 expresses it this way: "Have they stumbled so as to leave forever their position as God's people, and to remain, as it were, lying on the ground (plunged in perdition)?"

607 Robertson, *A Grammar of the Greek New Testament,* 997–98; Wallace, *Greek Grammar*, 473. See also the discussion of Moulton, *New Testament Greek: Prolegomena*, 206–209; Turner, *Syntax*, 100–105; Moule, *Idiom Book*, 142–46. Schreiner, 2nd, 577 and Käsemann, 304 believe it should be taken as purpose. If so, then Paul is asking whether it was God's purpose for Israel to stumble that leads to her fall. Most commentators confess that it is often difficult to determine whether ἵνα is purpose or result.

translated "but." The dative phrase τῷ αὐτῶν παραπτώματι ("by their transgression") is likely causal ("by" or "because of," Moo 2nd, 705; Cranfield, 555).[608] The word παραπτώματι ("transgression")[609] is singular and it is modified by the plural "their" (αὐτῶν) referring to Israel's (as a whole) rejection of Jesus Christ in the gospel message (Cranfield, 556).[610] Moo 2nd, 705, n. 642 takes this transgression to be the way Paul and others turned to the Gentiles after Jewish rejection (Acts 8:1ff; 13:45–48; 18:4–6; 19:8–10; 28:24–28). The phrase ἡ σωτηρία τοῖς ἔθνεσιν ("the salvation to the Gentiles" or possibly a dative of benefit, "for the Gentiles" [Jewett, 673, n. 66]) lacks a verb and most commentaries add a past tense phrase "has come" (γέγονεν) to smooth out the sentence (Moo, 2nd, 705, n. 641; Cranfield, 555). However, Dunn, 653 and Jewett, 674 favor a future perspective and add "is come."[611] Moo, 2nd, 705 seems to be correct that the logic of verse prefers a past reference. The Jewish rejection became the benefit for the Gentiles to hear and believe the gospel. Four times Paul states that the stumbling of Israel is used by God to bless Gentiles in this age (11:11c, 12, 15, 30).[612] In turn, the Gentiles' salvation also has the benefit of prompting Israel jealousy which would stimulate some Israelites back to the Lord of salvation. At least in part, this was part of Paul's argument in Rom 10:19 when he uses Deut 32:21. The exact thought of Paul is not expressed in this text. However, the last phrase of v. 11 expresses purpose by a preposition plus an article plus an infinitive (εἰς τὸ παραζηλῶσαι).[613] Thus, the thought of Paul is that Gentile salvation has the purpose of making Israel jealous.[614]

The concept of God being called Father in regard to the nation of Israel is established in the OT and finds its roots in this context in Deuteronomy 32:6.[615] This motif is reinforced by the theme of "sons" in Deuteronomy 32:5. Moses says of God, "They are not His children (בָּנָיו, "his sons") because of their defect; but are a perverse and crooked generation" (NASB). The same context of a father/son motif is also found in Paul's quotation of Deuteronomy 32:21, though the word "father" is not used. This motif is brought out by the phrase "His sons (בָּנָיו) and daughters" in 32:19 and the clause "for they are a perverse generation, sons (בָּנִים) in whom there is no faithfulness" in 32:20 (NASB). Both quotations in Romans 10:19–21 (Deut 32:21 and Isa 65:1–2) have an Exodus father/son motif and a context in which a disobedient nation experiences the consequences of rebelling against God and his covenant. The implication in the text is that God will use his relationship with the Gentiles to provoke to jealousy his sons so that they return to him (cf. 32:36, 43). This point is strongly indicated in the latter part of the Song of Moses where

---

[608] Wallace, *Greek Grammar*, 162, 167 indicates that at times it is difficult to distinguish between a dative of means and a dative of cause. Both indications may be translated "by." The causal use indicates the cause or basis of an action, and the dative of means is the means or instrument of the action.

[609] BDAG, 770 defines it as making a false step, thus, "a violation of moral standards, offense, wrongdoing, sin" (see Wilhelm Michaelis, *TDNT*, 6:171–72; Cranfield, 555; Dunn, 653; Schreiner, 2nd, 578; Dunn, 653). Michaelis specifically states that it refers to Israel's rejection of the Gospel (172). The neutral meaning of "fall aside" (Sanday and Headlam, 321; Barrett, 197) is not the best choice here.

[610] Cranfield, 556 entertains the possibility that the rejection could be the Jews' rejection of Jesus Himself and their delivering Jesus to the Gentiles.

[611] Schreiner, 2nd, 577, n. 4 does not believe that the present possession of salvation contradicts the future-oriented character of salvation. His view is that Paul's eschaton is inaugurated in this age though we wait the consummation.

[612] Vlach, "A Non-Typological Future-Mass-Conversion View," 40.

[613] Dunn, 653; Moule, *Idiom-Book*, 140; Moulton, *New Testament Greek: Prolegomena*, 218–19; Turner, *Syntax*, 143; Wallace, *Greek Grammar*, 611; Robertson, *A Grammar of the Greek New Testament*, 1088.

[614] Jewett, 675 gives a good discussion on the possible meaning of παραζηλῶσαι, but in the end, it is puzzling how religious "jealousy" may lead to Jewish salvation. Jewett's example of Paul's conversion may be the zealousness that may shed some light on the meaning.

[615] For more support see Sullivan, *The INE in Rom 9–16*, 310–15.

God will arise, defend his people, and defeat Israel's enemies. This NE redemption motif that is brought out by the Father/son motif seems to be Paul's thought that bridged the OT and NT usages together.[616]

Though Deuteronomy 32:43 in the MT and LXX is different, they both address the Gentiles concerning what God will accomplish for his people. Paul has a tendency to adopt negative descriptions from Scripture to refer to Gentiles "in order to highlight the reversal wrought by God's grace. The similarity of description, 'no-nation,' to the appellation, 'not my people,' quoted by Paul from Hosea in Romans 9:25–26, may well have contributed to his selection of Deuteronomy 32:21."[617] The Exodus motif of Deuteronomy 32:21 uses a father/son motif and introduces the concept of provoking Israel to jealousy by the Gentiles who are addressed at the end of the Song. The implication is that God will use the Gentiles as part of his plan to bring atonement to the land and the people (32:43). Part of this future of the Gentiles is God's use of them in Paul's own day and in the eschatological future.

11:12 εἰ δὲ τὸ παράπτωμα αὐτῶν πλοῦτος κόσμου καὶ τὸ ἥττημα αὐτῶν πλοῦτος ἐθνῶν, πόσῳ μᾶλλον τὸ πλήρωμα αὐτῶν. "Now if their transgression *means* riches for the world and their loss *means* riches for the Gentiles, how much more *will* their fullness *mean*?" Paul uses the phrase εἰ δὲ ("now if") 5 times (vv. 12, 16, 17, 18 and 23 δέ, ἐὰν μὴ) in vv. 11–24 where εἰ is used 11 times. Paul seems to use the conditional phrase εἰ δὲ in continuity with the previous verse, except for v. 18. Verse 12 and v. 15 have parallel thought. Here in v. 12 Paul uses the "how much more" logic (5:9, 10, 15, 17) which is a lesser to a greater argument (*a minore ad maius*). If the lesser is true, then how much more is the greater to be. Thus, the argument is stressing the final stage of the "fullness" which is the greater. The "lesser" is Israel's (corporate) transgression (παράπτωμα, see comments on v. 11) concerning their rejection of Jesus Christ and their ἥττημα ("loss");[618] thus, their transgression and loss brought the πλοῦτος ("riches")[619] of spiritual salvation to the Gentiles. In Paul's parallel he equates the κόσμου ("world") with the ἐθνῶν ("Gentiles"). The three αὐτῶν ("their") in v. 12 refer to Israel.[620] The parallel thought in v. 15 indicates that the τὸ πλήρωμα αὐτῶν ("their fullness" v. 12) involves ζωὴ ἐκ νεκρῶν ("life from the dead," v. 15). The two basic meanings of πλήρωμα is qualitative and quantitative.[621] The implication of the

---

[616] Thus, I would not agree with Wagner, *Heralds of the Good News*, 271 that Paul is making a radical rereading of Moses' Song. See Sullivan, *The INE in Rom 9–16*, 2nd ed., chapter 9.

[617] Wagner, *Heralds of the Good News*, 197.

[618] BDAG, 441 has "loss" and Liddle and Scott, 780 has "loss, discomfiture." It is used in 1 Cor 6:7 as the only other use in the NT and Isa 31:8 in the LXX. Moulton and Milligan, 283 settled on "defeat" "without any special ethical tinge." The qualitative sense ("defeat" or "loss") fits well with the context (Sanday and Headlam, 322; Dunn, 654; Jewett, 676; Fitzmyer, 611; Moo, 2nd, 706; Thielman, 535). Some settle on the quantitative nuance ("diminished number") for it provides a contrast with πλήρωμα.

[619] Moulton and Milligan, 521 indicates that Paul's use is generally a figurative sense. The NT uses πλοῦτος 22 times. Paul uses it 13 times and with only one exception (1 Tim 6:17) he uses it in a spiritual context. The word πλούσιος ("rich") is used 3 times by Paul. Twice he applies πλούσιος in a spiritual sense (2 Cor 8:9; Eph 2:5) and once (1Tim 6:17) he uses it literally. Finally, πλουσίως ("richly") is used 3 times by Paul where in Col 3:16 and Tit 3:6 the word refers to spiritual things and 1 Tim 6:17 seems to refer to both physical and spiritual things. Thus, Godet (400), Murray, (2:77), Cranfield (557), and Moo (2nd, 676) all refer to πλοῦτος as salvation, while Kasemann, (305) Schreiner (2nd, 580), and Dunn (654) refer it to eschatological blessings.

[620] See Cranfield, 558 for discussion of other options for αὐτῶν with different definition of πλήρωμα.

[621] BDAG, 829–30 gives five different usages in the NT: (1) that which fills: fill up, that which makes something full/complete; (2) that which is full of something; (3) that which is brought to fullness or completion: full number, sum total; (4) act of fulfilling, fulfillment; (5) the state of being full, fullness. BDAG indicates that definition number 3 (quantitative) and number 4 (qualitative) are two possible definitions of πλήρωμα in Rom

quantitative meaning is that the full and complete number of Jewish believers will take place after the full number of Gentiles believers is completed during this present age (Cranfield, 558; Käsemann, 305, Thielman, 536). This quantitative meaning is found in the parallel occurrence of πλήρωμα ("fullness, full number") in v. 25 (Moo, 2nd, 707; Dunn, 655; Jewett, 678). Moo, 2nd, 708 suggests that the definition of qualitative and quantitative could both be represented here. The qualitative denotation is brought about through the quantitative number suggested in v. 25. This seems to be the best option. Therefore, the reduction of the numerical count of Israel at the present time will be reversed to a far greater number of Jewish believers–full and complete number (Cranfield, 558). Murray, 2:79 is correct that the argument at this point in v. 12 is not centered so much on the restoration of Israel (though he mentions this point in the phrase "fullness"), but the blessing on the Gentiles which comes from Israel's future "fullness." Thus, the future fullness of Israel will provide a greater blessing for the Gentiles than the gospel blessing the Gentiles now are experience during Israel's (corporate) present unbelief. In the future when the conversion of national Israel happens on the scale corresponding to her present disobedience and unbelief, the Gentiles will receive a magnificent blessing (Moo, 2nd, 706–707; Schreiner, 2nd, 581; Fitzmyer, 611). Though this Gentile blessing is not mentioned in this context, it is compared to "life from the dead" in v. 15 which points to the blessing of the kingdom of God at Jesus Christ's second coming (Mt 19:28; Acts 3:19–21).

11:13 Ὑμῖν δὲ λέγω τοῖς ἔθνεσιν. ἐφ' ὅσον μὲν οὖν εἰμι ἐγὼ ἐθνῶν ἀπόστολος, τὴν διακονίαν μου δοξάζω "Now to you Gentiles I am speaking. In so far, then as I am an apostle to the Gentiles, I glorify my ministry." Paul begins by addressing the Gentile Christians in the church.[622] The δὲ is more transitional here ("now") and not contrastive; however, Ὑμῖν ("to you")[623] is placed in an emphatic position (Sanday and Headlam, 324; Cranfield, 558; Dunn, 655; Jewett, 678) to emphasize that the addresses are the Gentiles. This emphasis does not mean the congregation of the Romans were exclusively Gentile, but at this point Paul wanted to address the Gentiles in the congregation. However, the majority of the church in Rome were likely Gentiles.

The next four Greek words ἐφ' ὅσον μὲν οὖν ("in so far, then as") are only found here together in the NT. However, the phrase ἐφ' ὅσον is used eight times[624] and the phrase μὲν οὖν is used 39 times[625] in the NT. Cranfield, 559 states that Paul is about to say something expected about the Gentiles. Schreiner, 2nd, 578 is probably correct that this emphasis would be more convincing if μενοῦνγε ("on the contrary") had been used as in 9:20; 10:18 (Dunn, 655). Fitzmyer, 612 takes οὖν as inferential and μὲν as an anacoluthon (abrupt change). Dunn, 655 understand μὲν οὖν as a summary of the preceding verses. However, BDAG, 630 is probably best in translating these four words as a contrast but not as an adversive with "in so far, then as I am an apostle to the nations." Cranfield, 559 also accepts this translation.

The phrase ἐθνῶν ἀπόστολος ("apostle to the Gentiles") is an anarthrous predicate nominative ("an apostle of the Gentiles") following the copulative verb εἰμι ("I am") and this

---

11:12. The word πλήρωμα is used 17 times in the NT and 10 times by Paul (Rom 11:12, 25; 13:10; 15:29; 1 Cor 10:26; Gal 4:4; Eph 1:10, 23; 3:19; 4:13; Eph 1:19; 2:9) (Logos 8.7 version).

[622] Wagner, *Herald of the Good News*, 35–36, 268. He directs his attention to the Gentiles but understanding the Jews would be listening or hearing wherever the letter is read or discussed.

[623] Dunn, 655 points out that Gentiles are directly address in the second person and Jews in third person.

[624] Mt 9:15; 25:40,46; Rom 7:1; 11:3; 1 Cor 7:39; Gal 4:1; 2 Pet 1:13 (Logos 8.7 version).

[625] Four times in the Gospels; 27 times in Acts; 5 times in Paul (Rom 11:13; 1 Cor 6:4, 7; 9:25; Phil 2:23); and 3 in Hebrews.

construction is usually qualitative or indefinite.[626] On the other hand, ἐθνῶν ἀπόστολος may be considered a "proper noun" and lacks the article because it is understood to be articulate being a proper title for Paul. Thus, it may be best to translate the phrase "apostle of the Gentiles" (Moo, 2nd, 709, n. 661).[627] The word ἀπόστολος ("apostle") is used in the technical sense as an apostle of Jesus Christ (1 Cor 9:1-2; 15:6–9). Paul magnifies his διακονίαν ("ministry")[628] not only for the blessing of salvation which comes to the Gentiles, but also according to v. 11 the salvation of Gentiles is also part of how God will make Israel jealous and bring them back to their salvation (Moo, 2nd, 709; Cranfield, 560; Sanday and Headlam, 324; Barrett, 199). Thus, he δοξάζω ("glories") in this ministry for it glorifies God and His plan not the instrument of His plan which was Paul's basic ministry (Jewett, 679). Such boasting or glorying is biblical (Rom 2:17; 5:2, 11; 1 Cor 1:31; 2 Cor 10:17).

11:14 εἴ πως παραζηλώσω μου τὴν σάρκα καὶ σώσω τινὰς ἐξ αὐτῶν. "If somehow, I might provoke to jealousy my *countryman in* the flesh and might save some of them." The phrase εἴ πως is used three other places in the NT (Acts 27:12; Rom 1:10 and Phil 3:11). BDAG, 279 give two translational options: "if perhaps" or "if somehow."[629] This phrase expresses the expectation and the indefiniteness of how this purpose will be fulfilled (Schreiner, 2nd, 579; Dunn, 656).[630] Paul's contingent hope is the "jealousy" that the preaching of the gospel to the Gentiles might bring to his Jewish brethren which is first mentioned in v. 11. He is concerned for μου τὴν σάρκα (lit. "the flesh of mine") which Paul means his fellow countrymen, the Jews (cf. Rom 9:3). His concern is that God may use his ministry as apostleship to the Gentiles in such a way that he would be the instrument of God to win not just Gentiles but some of his fellow Jews to salvation. Some relate Paul's statement of τινὰς ἐξ αὐτῶν ("some of them") back to the "fullness" of the eschatological salvation in v. 12. However, this comparison of the τινὰς ἐξ αὐτῶν ("some of them" in v. 14) and τὸ πλήρωμα αὐτῶν ("their fullness" in v. 12) have more of a contrasting context. The word τινὰς ("some") in v. 14 should not be quantified by comparing it to the meaning of "some" in Rom 3:3 or 11:17 where τινὰς refers to the majority. Thus, in the context of v. 14 the "some" is an indefinite group that is not the majority. There is no indication that Paul is trying to relate v. 14 either "causally or temporally to the 'fulness' of Israel" (Murray, 2:80). Both παραζηλώσω ("might provoke to jealousy") and σώσω ("might save") are in the subjunctive mood and in a conditional construction (εἴ πως).[631] This construction conveys the thought that v. 14 is likely to occur in the future. Paul's ministry to the Gentiles is not because he believes that God has chosen Gentiles in the place of Israel, but because he is convinced that his Gentile mission is part of God's ultimate plan to restore Israel back to God. (see also the discussion on v. 11).

---

[626] Wallace, Greek Grammar, 256. There is a lot of confusion concerning Colwell's Rule and an important discussion concerning this rule is found pp. 256–70.

[627] Turner, *Syntax*, 183.

[628] Cranfield, 622 discusses the different senses of διακονία. He classifies this instance as a general theological-technical use which the context indicates Paul's ministry as apostle of the Gentiles. Weiser, *EDNT*, 1:303 indicates that διακονία designates the apostolic service of proclamation.

[629] BDAG, 279 classify the two verbs (παραζηλώσω and σώσω) as futures, but they are most likely subjunctives (Moo, 2nd, 710, n. 667; Jewett, 679).

[630] Blass, Debrunner, Funk, *Greek Grammar*, §375.

[631] Cranfield, 560, n. 6; Moo, 2nd, 709, n. 667; Jewett, 680 points out that some have taken these two verbs as future indicatives, but they favor the subjunctive.

11:15 εἰ γὰρ ἡ ἀποβολὴ αὐτῶν καταλλαγὴ κόσμου, τίς ἡ πρόσλημψις εἰ μὴ ζωὴ ἐκ νεκρῶν. "For if their rejection *of God* means the reconciliation of the world, what will their acceptance mean, except life from the dead?" Verse 15 takes up the thought of v. 12 and further develops the thought of vv. 13–14 (Sanday and Headlam, 325; Cranfield, 651–52). Thus, Paul begins with εἰ γὰρ ("for if").[632] He is continuing the conditional aspect while at the same time developing further the thought from vv. 12–14. Paul shifts from a "if … how much more" structure in v. 12 to a "if … what" in v. 15 (Moo, 2nd, 700). The question in these two verses is whether Paul shifts to God's viewpoint in v.15 or is he reflecting the action of Israel response to God. The answer centers around the grammatical and theological debate on whether ἡ ἀποβολὴ αὐτῶν is a subjective or an objective genitive. Most commentaries take the phrase as an objective genitive, "the rejection of them (Israel) *by God.*" Many would also conclude that this understanding does not contradict Rom 11:1 because the casting off of Israel in v. 15 is a temporary hardening of Israel until it is removed in the future time (Rom 11:25–26).[633] Their first support for the objective genitive is to compare the contrast from the latter half of v. 15 as referring to the acceptance (ἡ πρόσλημψις) of God and conclude that the former part of the verse would be likely speaking about God's rejection. Though the exact word πρόσλημψις is not used anywhere else in the NT, some turn to a related verb in Rom 14:3 (προσλαμβάνω "accept") and 15:7 (προσλαμβάνω used twice). Moo, 2nd, 711 concludes that Paul's choice of these verbs is used to refer to God's and Christ's accepting of believers. However, the same verb (προσλαμβάνω) is used in Rom 14:1 and 15:7a to refer to man's action. Thus, it is difficult to see how this helps the argument for the objective genitive.[634] The second argument for the objective genitive is the stress on the broader context of God being the one who is responsible for the spiritual hardening (11:8) and many in the nation being cut off (11:17). However, the tension of God's sovereignty and Israel's responsibility is seen throughout the section. The responsibility side in this context is found in vv. 11–12 ("their transgression"). Sibley may be correct that God's blinding should not necessarily mean that God has rejected Israel and His promises to them. A good illustration seems to be Duet 29:1–6.[635] One may say that God has rejected some Israelites that have not believed but he has not rejected the nation (11:28–29). Some of the branches were broken off but the olive tree was not cut down (11:17–21). Therefore, the subjective genitive seems more supportive of the context – "their rejection (of God)".[636] The rejection of Israel was specifically settled in Rom 11:1–2. God has not rejected His people. Secondly, some Israelites are rejecting God, hardened, and in unbelief, but Paul would say not all who are of Israel are Israel (9:6) for at the present time God has a remnant according to the election of grace (11:5, 25). Thirdly, many commentators bring out the parallelism of v. 12 and v. 15. The genitives in v. 12 are subjective genitives ("they have transgressed;" "they have failed") and this would make it natural for them to be subjective genitives in v. 15. Finally, the γὰρ ("for") in v. 15 draws on vv. 13–14 to further the argument and the viewpoint is manward and not Godward. In v. 13 the Gentiles are the subject and in v. 14 the subject is Paul's "fellow countrymen." Thus, the previous context is the Israelites salvation through the Gentiles moving Israel to jealousy. For this reason, Paul's

---

[632] Paul uses εἰ γὰρ often in Romans (12 times) and three times in chapter 11 (vv. 15, 21, 24). It is used 37 times in the NT with Paul using it 29 times. This conjunction seems to be an incomplete first class condition for the "to be" verb is implied but not written.

[633] Thielman, 537–38; Moo, 2nd, 700; Schreiner, 2nd, 581; Cranfield, 562; Godet, 403; Dunn, 657; Murray, 2:81; Sanday and Headlam, 325.

[634] Jim Sibley, "Has the Church Put Israel on the Shelf?" 574.

[635] Ibid., 575.

[636] Ibid., 571–81; Fitzmyer, 612; Jewett, 680; Matera, 267; Middendorf, 1113–1114.

ministry is directed to the Gentiles, but it also involves saving some of his brethren because of their rejection of God.

The word ἀποβολὴ is defined by BDAG, 108 as "rejection" or "loss" (Moo, 2nd, 711, n. 673). Israel's rejection of God is used in a lesser to a greater argument (*a minore ad maius*) just like in v. 12. If the rejection by Israel brings reconciliation to the world what will their acceptance of Christ be but "life from the dead." The meaning of the phrase εἰ μὴ[637] ζωὴ ἐκ νεκρῶν ("except life from the dead") is debated. The logic of the argument from v. 12 and v.15 points to a greater climactic event then the "fulfillment" (v.12) and the "reconciliation of the world" (v. 15). Moo, 2nd, 712 rightly divides the debate into two general categories: (1) "Life from the dead" refers to the enjoyment of eternal life provided by Jesus Christ's death and resurrection, to humans generally or to Israel particularly.[638] (2) "Life from the dead" refers to the end of history, either at the general resurrection of the dead or to the blessing that follows the resurrection.[639] The phrase ζωὴ ἐκ νεκρῶν is not used anywhere else in the NT. The phrase ἐκ νεκρῶν ("from the dead") is used 44 times in the NT.[640] This phrase refers exclusively to resurrection. However, the word ζωὴ may refer to physical life, the promise of eternal life, the new life of the believer or the final consummation out of death (resurrection).[641] Though it is possible to take the first view, we believe the second view is best. The second view would anticipate Paul's words in Rom 11:25–27 which deal with the Christ's second coming. This final state of eschatological salvation is expressed by Paul in Rom 5:17, 18, 21; 11:25–27. Thus, the vocabulary and structure of Paul's argument likely points to eschatological salvation (Moo, 2nd, 713; Schriener, 2nd, 583). An eschatological salvation that includes the covenant promises in the OT.[642]

Therefore, Israel's transgression (vv. 11b, 12) by their rejection of God (v. 15) is the present state of history since the first century. The sad state for the nation of Israel has become a blessing of salvation to the Gentiles. God is using the blessings of salvation to Gentiles as a goad to make Israel jealous to come back to God by accepting Jesus Christ. The acceptance of Jesus Christ by Israel will cause the climatic events to the eschatological plan of God (cf. Acts 3:19–21).

Biblical Theology

Paul returns to his thoughts at the beginning of Rom 11. He wants to develop further the thought that God has not rejected Israel (11:1-6) though the nation corporately has been hardened because of their unbelief (11:7–10). He begins to apply his doctrine of election (11:5–7) and hardening (11:7–10) which he articulated in Rom 9. In Rom 11:14, Paul also returns to his thought on "provoking to jealousy" (10:19) which has its roots in Deut 32:21. This pericope is found in the broader argument of how the transgression and unbelief of Israel was part of the

---

[637] The phrase εἰ μὴ may be translated "if not, but, or except" (BDAG, 278).

[638] Middendorf, 1116–1117; Murray, 2: 82–84; Hodge, 575–76; Godet, 243; Morris, 411; Lenski, 701; Fitzmyer, 613; Mounce, 219; Leenhardt, 285.

[639] Thielman, 538; Moo, 2nd, 712–13; Schreiner, 2nd, 582; Jewett, 681; Dunn, 658; Meyer, 424–25; Sanday and Headlam, 325–26; Barrett, 199–200; Black, 199–200; Cranfield, 562–63; Käsemann, 307; Matera, 267.

[640] According to Logos 8.7.

[641] BDAG, 430–31. BDAG, 430 places Rom 11:15 in the final consummation out of death.

[642] See Saucy, "Does the Apostle Paul Reverse the Prophetic Tradition of Salavtion of Israel and the Nations?" 66–90.

sovereign plan of salvation which now has come to the Gentiles (11:11-15). Israel's affection for other gods brought God's jealousy; thus, God will make them jealous to cause other people to rule over them. In the Song of Moses (Deut 32) the nations punished Israel, and the nations do not put their trust in the God of Israel. Also, in Deut 32:34-43 God reaffirms His faithfulness and choice of Israel by defeating the nations. However, in all of this Paul demonstrates that God is graciously accepting many of those of the nations to stir up His people Israel to come back to Him (Deut 32:21). Paul understands and uses the concept of the NE motif in the OT and connects this passage in Deuteronomy with his thoughts in Rom 11.[643]

This Gentile plan was part of the overall plan of God that was stated in summary form to Abraham in Gen 12:3, "… And in you all the families of the earth shall be blessed" (NASB). But Israel desired to form their own righteousness which would exclude the Gentiles (Rom 9:30–10:3). God in His graciousness has chosen a remnant among Israel (11:5, 7). Paul's ministry as the apostle to the Gentiles has a two-fold prong to it. The more Gentiles that come to faith in Jesus the Messiah, the more the potential that they will be used by God to provoke Israel to jealousy and bring them to faith in their own Messiah. Thus, Paul can pursue with a clear motive the mission to the Gentiles and even magnify his ministry without abandoning his countrymen. Paul will expand the theology of this thought by using the illustration of the Olive tree.

Application and Devotional Implications

Notice one of the reasons why the Lord allowed salvation to come to the Gentiles according to Deut 32:21. It was to provoke Israel to jealous and turn some back to their Messiah, Jesus. How are we doing in our role as an instrument in the hand of God to win Jewish people back to their Jesus Christ? How many Jewish people have you befriended and sought to establish a relationship with them? Using our gifts and talents is an easy and natural way to establish relationships and in due time to explain the gospel in our actions and then with words. E. Stanley Jones was said to ask Mahatma Gandhi what Christian should do to win Indians to Christ. He replied with four things: (1) Christians should live like Jesus Christ; (2) do not compromise your faith; (3) learn about other religions; and (4) let everything you do be characterized by love (Boice, 3:1325).

Gandhi's advice is important especially in the light of the centuries of persecution of the Jewish people. In the Middle Ages the Jews often had to wear a "badge of shame" and put in ghettoes. In most European countries they were prohibited from owning property, taxed outrageously, plundered, and excluded from schools and universities. In 1298 the great persecution swept across Europe and multitude of Jews were killed. In 1349-50 the Black Plague engulfed Europe and thousands of people died, and many people blamed the Jews and the Jewish people in Europe were murdered by the thousands. In 1411 the Roman Catholic Church instituted the Inquisition and tens of thousands of Jews in Europe were murdered. In World War I, hundreds of thousands of Jews died in the battles on both sides of the war. After World War I the Jews suffered false accusation, displacement and hardship. For example, about one million Jews became refugees because of the Czar. In World War II Hitler aimed to exterminate all Jews. His reign of terror exterminated about six million Jewish people leaving only about 6 out of every 10 Jews in Europe. So much more could be written about the tragedy of the Jewish people.

---

[643] See introduction to Romans 9-11 and Sullivan, *The INE in Rom 9–11*, 2nd ed., 264–278.

Thus, when your attempts to share Jesus with them is rebuffed may we be kind, loving, and understanding for so much has been wrongly done to them in the name of so-called Christianity. May we be the kind of Gentiles believers whose life and actions cause the Jewish people to consider their Messiah, Jesus.

Selected Bibliography

Arndt, William, Frederick W. Danker, and Walter Bauer, *A Greek-English Lexicon of the New Testament and Other Early Christian Literature*, 3rd ed. electronic version (Chicago: University of Chicago Press, 2000).

Balz, Horst Robert and Gerhard Schneider, *Exegetical Dictionary of the New Testament* (Grand Rapids, Mich.: Eerdmans, 1990).

Blass, Friedrich, Albert Debrunner, and Robert Walter Funk, *A Greek Grammar of the New Testament and Other Early Christian Literature* (Chicago: University of Chicago Press, 1961).

Liddell, Henry G. and Robert Scott. *GEL*, rev. and augmented by Sir Henry S. Jones with Roderick McKenzie, et. al. (Oxford: Clarendon Press, 1996).

Michaelis, Wilhem, *TDNT*, 6:161–63.

Moule, C. F. D. *An Idiom-Book of New Testament Greek*, 2nd ed. (Cambridge: Cambridge Press, 1975).

Moulton, J. H. *New Testament Greek: Prolegomena*, vol. 1 of *A Grammar of New Testament Greek*, 3rd ed. (Edinburgh: T & T Clark, 1967).

Moulton, James Hope and George Milligan, *The Vocabulary of the Greek Testament* (London: Hodder and Stoughton, 1930).

Saucy, Robert L. "Does the Apostle Paul Reverse the Prophetic Tradition of the Salvation of Israel and the Nations?" in *Building on the Foundations of Evangelical Theology: Essays in Honor of John S. Feinberg*, eds. Gregg R. Allison and Stephen J. Wellum (Wheaton: Crossway, 2015), 66–90.

Sibley, Jim R. "Has the Church Put Israel on the Shelf? The evidence from Romans 11:15," *Journal of the Evangelical Theological Society* 58/3 (2015): 571–81.

Schmidt, Karl L. *TDNT*, ed. 6:883.

Sullivan, Steven P. The Isaianic New Exodus in Romans 9–11 (Silverton, OR: Lampion Press, 2017).

Sullivan, Steven P. The Isaianic New Exodus in Romans 9–11, 2nd ed. (Middletown, RI: Stone Tower Press, 2023).

Swanson, Reuben, ed. *New Testament Greek Manuscripts: Romans*. (Wheaton: Tyndale House and Pasadena: William Carey International University Press, 2001).

Turner, Nigel, *Syntax*, vol. 3 of *A Grammar of New Testament Greek* (Edinburgh: T & T Clark, 1963).

Robertson, A. T. *A Grammar of the Greek New Testament in the Light of Historical Research* (Logos Bible Software, 2006).

Vlach, Michael J. "A Non-Typological Future-Mass-Conversion View," in *Three Views on Israel and the Church: Perspectives on Romans 9–11*, eds. Jared Compton and Andrew D. Naselli (Grand Rapids: Kregel, 2018).

Wagner, J. Ross. *Heralds of the Good News: Isaiah and Paul in Concert in the Letter to the Romans*. Supplements to Novum Testamentum, eds. M. M. Mitchell and D. P. Moessner, vol. 101 (Leiden: Brill, 2002).

Wallace, Daniel B. *Greek Grammar Beyond the Basic: An Exegetical Syntax of the New Testament* (Grand Rapids: Zondervan, 1996).

Weiser, Alfons. "διακονέω κτλ.," *EDNT* 1 (Edinburgh: T & T Clark, 1990) 302–3.

Romans 11:16–22

Introduction

In Rom 11:16-22 Paul turns his attention to the Gentiles (the unnatural branches) in light of the breaking off of some of the natural branches (Israelites) who are in unbelief (vv. 17, 19–20). The blessing on the Gentiles comes through the root and trunk of the olive tree which represents the promises given to Abraham and the patriarchies (Gen 12:3; Rom 11:28-29). The blessings to the Gentiles who are grafted into the promises comes because of their faith. The Israelites who are broken off from the blessings of the tree are those who are in unbelief. Therefore, the Gentile believers should not become arrogant but fear the Lord. If the Lord does not spare the natural branches because of their unbelief, He surely will not spare the unnatural Gentile branches if they do not persevere in their faith. This salvation plan by the Lord demonstrates at least two attributes of God: His severity in judgment and His goodness in salvation of undeserved sinners.

One must also be aware that the primary argument by Paul is a national purpose and not an individual purpose. Of course, we cannot have national purpose ultimately without individual participation. However, Paul is primarily declaring the relationship between the nation of Israel and the Gentiles.[644]

Outline

E. A Wisdom Polemic: God's Merciful Plan for Israel and Gentiles (11:11-33)
   1. Israel's hardening and the Gentiles Inclusion (11:11-15)
   2. A Warning against Gentile Believers (11:16-22)

Original Text

11.16 εἰ δὲ ἡ ἀπαρχὴ ἁγία, καὶ τὸ φύραμα· καὶ εἰ ἡ ῥίζα ἁγία, καὶ οἱ κλάδοι. 17 Εἰ δέ τινες τῶν
κλάδων ἐξεκλάσθησαν, σὺ δὲ ἀγριέλαιος ὢν ἐνεκεντρίσθης ἐν αὐτοῖς καὶ συγκοινωνὸς τῆς
ῥίζης[a] τῆς πιότητος τῆς ἐλαίας ἐγένου, 18 μὴ κατακαυχῶ τῶν κλάδων· εἰ δὲ κατακαυχᾶσαι[b], οὐ
σὺ τὴν ῥίζαν βαστάζεις ἀλλὰ ἡ ῥίζα σέ. 19 ἐρεῖς οὖν· Ἐξεκλάσθησαν κλάδοι ἵνα ἐγὼ
ἐγκεντρισθῶ. 20 καλῶς· τῇ ἀπιστίᾳ ἐξεκλάσθησαν, σὺ δὲ τῇ πίστει ἕστηκας. μὴ ὑψηλὰ φρόνει,
ἀλλὰ φοβοῦ· 21 εἰ γὰρ ὁ θεὸς τῶν κατὰ φύσιν κλάδων οὐκ ἐφείσατο, [μή πως] [c] οὐδὲ σοῦ
φείσεται. 22 ἴδε οὖν χρηστότητα καὶ ἀποτομίαν θεοῦ· ἐπὶ μὲν τοὺς πεσόντας ἀποτομία, ἐπὶ δὲ σὲ
χρηστότης[d] θεοῦ, ἐὰν ἐπιμένῃς τῇ χρηστότητι, ἐπεὶ καὶ σὺ ἐκκοπήσῃ.

---

[644] S. Lewis Johnson, Jr., "Parable of the Olive Tree, Romans 11:11–24," Sermon at Believers Chapel, Dallas, Texas, 2008, p. 5.

Textual Notes

[a] **11:17 (1) τῆς ῥίζης τῆς πιότητος** is supported by NA28 SBLGNT UBS5 WH ℵ* B[c] C[c] C 1175[c] 1506 1912 2464; B* (τῆς ῥίζης τῆς πειότητος); Ψ 1646 (τῆς ῥίζης τῆς πιότητος καὶ) **(2) τῆς ῥίζης καὶ τῆς πιότητος** ℵ[c] is supported by A D[1] L P 049 056 1 6 33 81 88 104 131 205 209 226 323 326 330 365 424 440 460 517 547 618 796 910 945 1219 1241 1242 1243 1245 1270 1315 1352 1434 1448 1505 1573 1611 1734 1735 1738 1739 1827 1836 1854 1873 1881 1891 1962 2125 2127 2147 2200 2344 2400 2464 2495 2815 𝔐 **(3) τῆς πιότητος** is supported by P[46] D* F G (UBS5, 532 and Swanson, *NT Greek Mss. Rom*, 176). The UBS, 2nd committee accepted the number (1) textual phrase above and rates it "B" in their UBS5 text. The committee seems to be correct that the number (1) textual phrase above seems to explain best the other readings. This textual problem is difficult because of a few early majuscules and P[46] testify a different text.

[b] **11:18 κατακαυχᾶσαι** is supported by NA28 UBS5 SBLGNT WH ℵ B C Ψ 049 056 1 6 69 81 88 104 131 205 209 226 323 326 365 424 440 460 489 517 547 614 796 910 927 945 999 1175 1241 1242 1243 1245 1270 1319 1352 1424 1448 1505 1506 1573 1611 1646 1734 1735 1738 1739 1827 1836 1837 1854 1874 1881 1891 2125 2147 2344 2412 2464 2495 2815 𝔐 (A L P 618 1315 has **κατακαυχᾶσε**). **σὺ καυχᾶσαι** is supported by P[46] D* F G. (NA28, 504; Swanson, *NT Greek Mss. Rom*, 176). The textual evidence is weighted to κατακαυχᾶσαι as original.

[c] **11:21 οὐδὲ** is supported by SBLGNT WH Treg ℵ B A C P 6 81 365 630 1319 1506 1573 1739 1881 2127 2200. **μή πως οὐδέ** is supported by P[46] D F G L Ψ 049 056 1 6 33 69 88 104 205 209 226 323 326 330 424* 440 460 459 489 517 547 614 796 618 910 927 999 1175 1241 1242 1243 1245 1270 1315 1352 1424 1448 1505 1611 1646 1734 1735 1738 1827 1836 1837 1854 1874 1891 1912 1962 2125 2147 2344 2400 2412 2464 2495 2815 𝔐. NA28 and UBS5 place [μή πως] in brackets with οὐδὲ which indicates that it is a disputed text (UBS5, 532; NA28, 504; and Swanson, *NT Greek Mss*, 177). The strong support of ℵ B A C with some significant minuscules for the short reading is usually preferred but as the UBS committee 2nd ed. points out: (1) **μή πως** is a familiar combination for it used together nine times in the NT, all in Paul (1 Cor 8:9; 9:27; 2 Cor 2:7; 9:4; 11:3; 12:20 (2X); Gal 2:2; 4:11; 1 Thess 3:5). However, nowhere else is μή πως used in combination together with οὐδὲ like in Rom 11:21. (2) The committee states that copyists may have been troubled by the "unrelatedness" of the phrase or thought the phrase unnecessary or struggled with the phrased used with a future verb and possibly **omit it** (Meyer, 2:198; Godet, 250). Often the rule is to go with the shorter reading, but the shorter reading can possibly be explained by the copyists' struggle in the previous statement above. Moo, 2nd, 714, n. 691, Schreiner, 2nd, 592; Longenecker, 871; Sanday and Headlam, 329, Murray, 2:88; Cranfield, 569, n. 6 support the shorter reading. UBS 2nd ed. committee, 465 retain the reading with brackets. This textual problem is very difficult, but UBS committee 2nd is probably correct to keep the phrase μή πως in brackets. They rated their decision a "C". See UBS5 pp. 7–8 for explanation of this indication.

[d] **11:22 χρηστότης θεοῦ** is supported by NA28 UBS5 SBLGNT WH P[46] B A C D 1243 1573 1739 1881 (**χρήστότος θεοῦ** ℵ). **χρηστότητα** is supported by D[1] D[2] Ψ F G L 049 056 1 33 69 88 104 131 205 209 226 323 326 424 440 460 489 517 547 614 618 796 910 927 945 999 1175 1241 1242 1245 1270 1315 1319 1352 1424 1448 1505 1611 1646 1734 1827 1836 1837 1854 1874 1891 2125 2147 2344 2464 2495 2815 𝔐 (Swanson, *NT Greek Mss*, *Rom,* 178). The Western witnesses and Majority Text omit the θεοῦ. Schreiner, 592 is probably correct that the

copyists likely omitted it to preserve the parallelism with ἀποτομία. The earlier witnesses keep θεοῦ and this strong evidence seems to be the best support.

Translation

16 Now if the first fruits *of dough* is holy, also *is* the lump; and if the root is holy, also *are* the branches. **17** Now if some of the branches have been cut off, and you being a wild olive branch, have been grafted in among them and become partakers of the rich root of the olive tree, **18** do not boast over the branches. But if you are to boast, it is not you who supports the root, but the root *that supports* you. **19** You will say then, 'Branches have been broken off in order that I might be grafted in.' **20** Quite right. They have been broken off because of *their* lack of faith, but you stand because of *your* faith. Do not think proudful, but fear. **21** For if God did not spare the natural branches, [perhaps] he will not spare you. **22** Notice therefore the goodness and the severity of God. For those who have fallen, *there is* severity, but for you, the goodness of God, if you continue in that goodness; for otherwise you also will be cut off."

Commentary

11:16 εἰ δὲ ἡ ἀπαρχὴ ἁγία, καὶ τὸ φύραμα· καὶ εἰ ἡ ῥίζα ἁγία, καὶ οἱ κλάδοι. "Now if the first fruits *of dough* are holy, also *is* the lump; and if the root is holy, also *are* the branches." The δὲ ("now") has a loose connection with vv. 11–15.[645] Paul makes his argument using horticulture to make his case for the future restoration of Israel. He begins with two metaphors that express the part with the whole. The background of Paul's use of "first fruits of dough" and "lump" are expressed in Num 15:17–21. The first part of the grain from the harvest was to be made into a lump of dough and the first cake from it was to be lifted to the Lord representing a holy offering as a part of the grain for the whole harvest of grain. This concept of the part for the whole is also seen in Rom 8:23 and 16:5 where something now represents a future more comprehensive or full representation will happen (cf. 1 Cor 15:20; 16:15; Jas 1:18; Rev 14:4).[646] Paul does not tell the meaning of the illustration. Some advocate that "first fruit" is Adam,[647] or Christ[648] (1 Cor 15:20, 23), while a number support that it refers to Christian Jews (the remnant).[649] If the Christian Jewish remnant is the case, then it is possible to take v. 16a as referring back to 11:1–10 and 11:16b as a transition to 11:17ff.[650] But Moo (2nd, 717) seems to be correct that the second

---

[645] Paul uses εἰ δὲ in vv. 16, 17, and 18. Verse 23 has δέ, ἐὰν μὴ. Verse 16 seems to be an incomplete first class conditional sentence since the "to be" verb is implied.

[646] See Horst R. Balz and Gerhard Schneider, *EDNT*, vol. 1 (Grand Rapids: Eerdmans 1990), 116–117 and Gerhard Delling, *TDNT* ed. Gerhard Kittel, Geoffrey W. Bromiley, and Gerhard Friedrich (Grand Rapids, MI: Eerdmans, 1964–), 1:484–486.

[647] See Dunn, 659 for those who support this position.

[648] See Cranfield, 564; Moo, 2nd, 717, n. 706 and Schreiner, 2nd, 583, n. 32 who list supporters.

[649] Cranfield, 564; Fitzmyer, 614; Hafemann, "Salvation of Israel," 51. Jewett, 682–83 refers it to Israel in general while Dunn, 659 argues that it includes Gentiles and takes the "lump" as all of the seed of Abraham. Others refer "first fruits" as the Jewish Christian remnant and the "root" as the patriarchs (Cranfield, 564; Fizmyer, 614; Matera, 267–68). For other views see Schreiner, 2nd, 583-84. Longenecker, 890–91 connects it with the relation between the remnant of Israel and the remnant among the Gentiles.

[650] Moo, 2nd, 718 gives this argument as a possibility but does not chose it as his own.

metaphor in the verse (root/branches) appears to parallel the first (i.e. first fruits of the dough/lump). Thus, v. 16 is a transition from vv. 11–15 to vv. 17–24 (Barrett, 200; Käsemann, 307; Dunn, 652; Schreiner, 2nd, 583). The "branches" in vv. 17–18 are Israelites, and this helps the understanding that "branches" represent Israel in v. 16. Paul does not identify the "root," but most commentators refer the root to Abraham and his descendants or both, specifically the promises given to them (Godet, 244; Meyer, 220–21; Sanday and Headlam, 326; Hodge, 576–77; Cranfield, 565; Murray, 2:85; Käsemann, 308; Moo 2nd 717; Schreiner, 2nd, 584). This understanding is also supported by the near contextual statements of Rom 9:5 and 11:28–29. Schreiner (2nd, 584–85) argues that Paul in 1 Cor 3:9 parallels the metaphorical type of argument here in Rom 11:16. Paul again uses two metaphors to describe the same point in 1 Cor 3. The shift from the agricultural metaphor to an architectural metaphor is used for Paul desired to expand on the latter metaphor in 1 Cor 3:10–17. Likewise, from the two metaphors in Rom 11:16 the final metaphor of the root/branches is used and further expanded in vv. 17–24. Furthermore, the Greek construction of v. 16 also fits this interpretation of two metaphors but one major thought better for the Greek phrases in the text have parallel construction:[651]

εἰ δὲ ἡ ἀπαρχὴ ἁγία, καὶ τὸ φύραμα
καὶ
εἰ ἡ ῥίζα ἁγία, καὶ οἱ κλάδοι.

Thus, it seems best to consider both metaphors in v. 16 representing the holiness of the patriarchs that is conveyed to their descendants. The theology of Rom 4 and Gal 3 make it clear that the spiritual benefits are only conveyed to those descendants that received the promises of God and passed it down to the next generation (Moo, 2nd, 718). Thus, Israel is holy[652] in the sense that God has set apart the nation as the conduit, instrument, and messenger of the Messiah and the salvation message. Paul is not conveying that every Israelite will accept salvation. Thus, he is not contradicting his earlier argument in 9:6–13 where ethnic Israel and ethnic spiritual Israel are distinguished. No individual Israelite can assume he is spiritually a part of God's elect except those who have believed in Jesus as their Messiah. God has chosen some Israelites and allow the others to go their own way. On the other hand, God has not rejected corporate Israel as His people because He promised to save (11:12, 15) what is left of the nation at the end-times (Schreiner, 2nd, 585)[653] and give to the nation of Israel what he has promised (Rom 9:4–5, 11:28–29). See the statement of "all Israel will be saved" discussed under the comments of the 11:26.

11:17 Εἰ δέ τινες τῶν κλάδων ἐξεκλάσθησαν, σὺ δὲ ἀγριέλαιος ὢν ἐνεκεντρίσθης ἐν αὐτοῖς καὶ συγκοινωνὸς τῆς ῥίζης τῆς πιότητος τῆς ἐλαίας ἐγένου. "Now if some of the branches have been cut off, and you being a wild olive branch, have been grafted in among them and become partakers of the rich root of the olive tree." Paul introduces the olive tree illustration in v. 16 and now he continues his thought with a first class conditional clause as he did in v. 16. The protasis clause of εἰ δὲ ("now if") is concluded with the last part of the apodosis clause in the first part of v. 18 ("do not be … branches"). Is the conditional clause true? The context is the most important

[651] It is not impossible to fit the construct with the other views; however, the interesting way Paul crafted the text seems to me to favor my stated position.

[652] Like the generic use of holy in 1 Cor 7:14. See Benjamin D. Gordon, "On the Sanctity of Mixtures and Branches: Two Halakic Sayings in Romans 11:16–24," JBL 135 (2016): 355–68 for some background to Jewish practice.

[653] Thielman, 539–40 takes "first fruits" as the time when unbelieving Israel accepts the gospel in the final day and the "dough" as the wealth and life of the whole world on the final day when the Gentiles enter the number (Rom 11:25–26). He refers the root to the rich heritage of Israel (Rom 9:4–5).

indicator whether it is true or false.[654] Paul's argument indicates that he believes the statement is true (Moo, 2nd, 718). Some classify vv. 17–24 as an allegory (Jewett, 684, 685) while others prefer to call it a figure (metaphor)[655] using a commonly known olive tree in the land. The natural branches of the olive tree are ethnic Israel. Some of the olive branches in this figure represents the unbelieving Israelites–ethnic Jews who are called by Paul in his olive tree illustration, "natural branches" (κατὰ φύσιν v. 21) and refer to them as having "their own olive tree" (τῇ ἰδίᾳ ἐλαίᾳ v. 24). The olive tree is used as an illustration in the OT for Israel (Jer 11:16; Hos 14:6).[656] However, Paul's illustration of the olive tree in Romans 11 cannot be equivalent to just the ethnic Israelite in the age in which Paul is now living. In this age there are natural branches (Israelites) and unnatural branches (Gentiles) and some of the branches are attached to or detached from the olive tree in this illustration (Sanday and Headlam, 327; Fitzmyer, 610; Schreiner, 2nd, 588). The olive tree is Paul's illustration to show the relationship of Israel and Gentiles to the Abrahamic promises. The branches that are not grafted in or the branches broken off represent their unbelief and disconnection to the Abrahamic promises.[657]

Putting both the divine and human sides together the branches were cut off because of the hardening by God (11:7–11) and their own unbelief (11:20). The aorist passive ἐξεκλάσθησαν ("have been cut off") is a divine passive indicating that God is the cause of the action to cut them off (Moo, 2nd, 719, n. 714; Jewett, 683). The parallel statement about the "wild olive branch has been grafted in" (ἐνεκεντρίσθης) is also a divine passive (Jewett, 685).[658] Thus, some of the Israelites in their unbelief were cut off from the blessings that were promised to the patriarchs. This by no means refers to all of them, but the word τινες ("some") is easily estimated as the majority of them. On the other hand, Gentile believers (vv. 13, 17 σὺ δὲ ἀγριέλαιος ὢν "and you being a wild olive branch") are described by Paul corporately with a second person singular ("you") in vv. 17–24 (except one time in v. 19 he refers to them in the first person singular, "I might be grafted in" ἐγὼ ἐγκεντρισθῶ).[659] These Gentile believers ("you") "have been grafted in among them" (ἐνεκεντρίσθης ἐν αὐτοῖς), the Israelites, and "become fellow participants in the richness of the root of the olive tree" (καὶ συγκοινωνὸς τῆς ῥίζης τῆς πιότητος τῆς ἐλαίας ἐγένου)[660] (Gen 12:3; Gal 3:6–9). Israel is described by Paul with a 3rd person plural in vv. 17–24 (either by "some" or "branches" or "they").

---

[654] Wallace, *Greek Grammar*, 692 states among many things that if the logic in the conditional clause is coherent in both the protasis and apodosis then the statement is true. Of course, the context will be your guide.

[655] Philip F. Esler, "Ancient Oleiculture and Ethnic Differentiation: The Meaning of the Olive-Tree Image in Romans 11," JSNT 26 (2003): 104–107 indicates he could take it either way. William Campbell, *Paul and the Creation of Christian Identity* (London: T & T Clark, A Continuum Imprint, 2008), 101, Sanday and Headlam, 326, and Cranfield, 586 take it as a metaphor. See also Mark D. Nanos, "'Broken Branches': A Pauline Metaphor Gone Awry?" in *Between Gospel and Election*, 357–58, n. 44.

[656] For other reference of the olive tree referring to Israel in extra-biblical text see Moo, 2nd, 720, n. 720 and Schriener, 2nd, 588.

[657] Michael J. Vlach, "A Non-Typical Future–Mass–Conversion View," in *Three Views on Israel and the Church: Perspectives on Romans 9–11*, eds, Jared Compton and Andrew D. Naselli (Grand Rapids: Kregel, 2018), 46–47.

[658] See Romans 9:22 in this commentary for more explanation of a divine passive.

[659] Robertson, *Grammar of the Greek NT*, 678; Jewett, 683-84.

[660] συγκοινωνὸς requires a genitive τῆς ῥίζης, while τῆς πιότητος may be epexegetic, "the root that is the richness of the olive tree" or qualitative "the root that belongs to the olive tree;" τῆς ἐλαίας ἐγένου is either possession or source (tree having olives or olive tree) (Moo, 2nd, 719, n. 719; Dunn, 661; Cranfield, 567; Murray, 2:86, n. 34).

This richness to the Gentiles is only because of the kindness and mercy of the Lord (vv. 22, 30–31). The prepositional phrase ἐν αὐτοῖς in v. 17 should be translated "among them" (Moo, 2nd, 719; Cranfield, 567; Dunn, 661; Murray, 2:86; Fitzmyer, 615) and not "in them" or "in place of them" or "in their place (contra Käsemann, 308; Dunn, 661; Godet, 246). The Gentiles were grafted into the same olive tree which is supported by the root of Abraham and the patriarchies with the promises and was anticipated in Gen 12:3 (18:18; 22:18; 26:4; 28:14). Campbell is correct when he states that the olive tree image supports a relationship between Gentile Christ-followers and Israel Christ-followers, but one should not deny the existence of one at the expense of the other or allow one to swallow up the other and displace the other. The church of believing Israelites and Gentiles have no real warrant for claiming the title of Israel or the new Israel.[661] The believing remnant of Israel who is part of the Church of Jews and Gentiles in this age is part of the future hopeful promises that one day "all Israel" will be saved (see v. 26).

Nothing in Rom 11:16–24 seems to suggest that the tree including its roots depends on the wild olive branch grafted into the tree. On the contrary, the movement is from root to branches (11:16); the ingrafted olive scion depends on the richness of the root (11:17).[662] The key to Paul's illustration is the root and the tree which supports the branches, which are wild olive branches (Gentile believers) and natural branches (believing Israelites). In oleiculture, the wild olive branch does not bear good fruit and would not be grafted into the cultivated olive tree (v. 24); thus, Paul is making a statement that would be unflattering to the Gentiles but demonstrates the mercy and grace of God which will be stated in the latter part of Romans 11. We should be cautious that we don't make a biblical or theological interpretation based only upon arboricultural practice (Godet, 247–48; Murray, 2:85–86; Käsemann, 308; Cranfield, 565–66; Schreiner, 2nd, 587; Moo, 2nd, 721). Even if the practice of grafting of wild olive branches into a cultivated olive tree was never done in the culture, Paul's theological point is still valid.

11:18 μὴ κατακαυχῶ τῶν κλάδων· εἰ δὲ κατακαυχᾶσαι, οὐ σὺ τὴν ῥίζαν βαστάζεις ἀλλὰ ἡ ῥίζα σέ. "Do not boast over the branches. But if you are to boast, it is not you who supports the root, but the root *that supports* you." The prohibition μὴ κατακαυχῶ τῶν κλάδων ("do not boast over the branches") is the completion of the conditional sentence that began in v. 17 (see comments on v. 17). The verb used twice in the verse (κατακαυχῶ and κατακαυχᾶσαι) has a strong emphasis on boasting in triumphant over others with a comparison superiority.[663] The debatable question is who are the branches? Is it the unbelieving Israelites who have been cut off (Murray, 2:86) or the Israelite believers in Jesus that remain attached to the tree or is it both (Godet, 248; Cranfield, 567–68; Dunn, 662; Jewett, 686; Moo, 2nd, 721; Schreiner, 2nd, 588, n. 9)? Jewett, 685 and others point out that in v. 17 the branches imply all of Israel – the branches cut off and the branches still attached. However, the context in v. 17 is not the "branches" but "some of the branches broken off" (unbelieving Israelites) and in vv. 19–22 the context is the Israelites who

---

[661] Campbell, *Paul and the Creation of Christian Identity*, 101–102, 125–139. See comments on Rom 11:26 in this commentary.

[662] The possibility that a rejuvenating of an olive tree by a "wild olive branch grafting" is credited to the Roman author Columella (purported by A. G. Baxter and J. A. Ziesler, "Paul and Arboriculture: Romans 11:17–24," JSNT 24 [1985]: 25–32) seems to be refuted by the investigation of Esler, "Ancient Oleiculture and Ethnic Differentiation," 103–124. Jewett, 685 agrees.

[663] Bultmann, *TDNT*, 3:653. BDAG, 518 defines the word as "to boast at the expense of another" or "boast against" or "exult over." Only other use in the NT is Jas 2:13 and 3:14. Dunn, 661–62 states that the κατά accents the competitive superiority in the boasting.

are cut off from the tree (unbelieving Israelite). Thus, the immediate context seems to point to the unbelieving Israelite (the branches broken off from the tree). Paul warns the Gentile believer not to be arrogant toward the Israelite's cutting off in unbelief thinking they are now the center and source of the Lord's favor and blessing. Paul reminds the Gentile believers that the root continually supports both Israelite and Gentile. The negative article οὐ ("not") is placed in an emphatic position (Dunn, 662) to stress that the branches do not support the root of the tree. There is one tree and one root which continually supports (present tense βαστάζεις) both Israelite and Gentile branches and represents salvation that comes only through Abrahamic promises (Gen 12:3; Gal 3:16, 29). Dunn's (662) suggestion that βαστάζεις carries the idea of fruit bearing is helpful in this tree illustration by Paul.[664] Paul is stressing that mere physical descent from the patriarchs does not in itself bring salvation (Rom 2:25–29; 9:6b–29) (Moo, 2nd, 722). Also, Gentiles seemed to have the temptation to boast because God has grafted them into the olive tree and cut off the unbelieving Israelites. Thus, Paul reminds these Gentiles that the root of the promises supports them and do not be arrogant to the branches who were broken off. Dunn, 662 seems to be correct that the letter of Romans was not written to combat anti-Semitism though Paul would be against this activity. However, Paul is warning the Gentiles not to use the fact that God has broken some of the branches off to graft the believing Gentiles into the blessing of God as a means of division and superiority.

11:19–20 ἐρεῖς οὖν· Ἐξεκλάσθησαν κλάδοι ἵνα ἐγὼ ἐγκεντρισθῶ. [20] καλῶς· τῇ ἀπιστίᾳ ἐξεκλάσθησαν, σὺ δὲ τῇ πίστει ἕστηκας. μὴ ὑψηλὰ φρόνει, ἀλλὰ φοβοῦ· 19 "You will say then, 'Branches have been broken off in order that I might be grafted in.' 20 Quite right. They have been broken off because of *their* lack of faith, but you stand because of *your* faith. Do not think proudful, but fear." After Paul's admonishment in v. 18 he anticipates a possible reply and rebuttal, so he raises the following hypothetical argument in v. 19. Paul stresses the subject of ἐγκεντρισθῶ ("I might be grafted in") by adding the nominative pronoun ἐγὼ ("I, myself,") to likely bring emphasis to their proudful attitude (Moo, 2nd, 722, n. 733). The ἵνα clause in v. 19 expresses purpose. The unbelieving Israelites (natural branches) were broken off for the purpose of grafting in the believing Gentile (unnatural branches). Both of these verbs Ἐξεκλάσθησαν ("have been broken off") and ἐγκεντρισθῶ ("I might be grafted in") are in the passive voice and are likely expressing the divine passive – a sovereign work of God.[665] One other interesting point, Paul uses a plural noun (κλάδοι) to express the unbelieving Israelite branches and a singular first person pronoun and verb (ἐγὼ ἐγκεντρισθῶ) to represent the believing Gentiles. The use of the word καλῶς ("quite right") in v. 20 introduces a statement that the writer agrees with a degree of qualification (Moo, 2nd, 722, n. 734; Cranfield, 568; Dunn, 663). The breaking off of the Jewish branches and grafting in of the Gentile branches is indeed because of the unbelief of the Israelites. However, this is not the full story. This event and divine design declare that the Israelites would be moved to jealousy and be spiritually restored back to the Lord and grafted back into the olive tree. Again, Paul uses a causal form for his argument as he did in v. 19 but in a different way. He uses two causal datives phrases in contrast with each other: τῇ

---

[664] Henry George Liddell et al., *GEL* (Oxford: Clarendon Press, 1996), 310. Jewett, 686 says that this word is used in an allegorical sense where the root bears the weight of the branches (see Werner Stenger, "βαστάζω," *EDNT* 1:208–9).

[665] See Romans 9:22 in this commentary for more explanation of the divine passive.

ἀπιστίᾳ (causal dative:[666] "because of *their* lack of faith") ἐξεκλάσθησαν, σὺ δὲ (contrast: "but") τῇ πίστει[667] (causal dative: "because of *your* faith") ἕστηκας.[668] Both of these causal dative phrases are emphasized in the Greek text by placing them before the verb. The perfect ἕστηκας ("you stand") describe the standing of the Gentile Christian within the people of God. However, the response to the standing that God has given to the Gentile believers should not be boasting or conceited, but fear (φοβοῦ). This godly fear should be the prime response to God according to the wisdom literature of the OT. This response is the correct response to the grace and mercy that God has poured upon undeserving sinners. The NT also indicates that fearing God is the correct response in working out our salvation to the glory of God (Phil 2:12–13; 2 Cor 7:1; Col 3:22). The fear of the LORD is the awe and holy caution that arises from the realization of the greatness of God. Because we know that God is a God of splendor, majesty, power, justice, righteousness, holiness, mercy, grace, etc., we want to obey Him. Zuck defines the fear of the Lord: "to acknowledge His superiority over man, to recognize His deity and thus respond in awe, humility, worship, love, trust and obedience."[669]

11:21-22 εἰ γὰρ ὁ θεὸς τῶν κατὰ φύσιν κλάδων οὐκ ἐφείσατο, [μή πως] οὐδὲ σοῦ φείσεται. 22 ἴδε οὖν χρηστότητα καὶ ἀποτομίαν θεοῦ· ἐπὶ μὲν τοὺς πεσόντας ἀποτομία, ἐπὶ δὲ σὲ χρηστότης θεοῦ, ἐὰν ἐπιμένῃς τῇ χρηστότητι, ἐπεὶ καὶ σὺ ἐκκοπήσῃ. 21 "For if God did not spare the natural branches, [perhaps][670] he will not spare you. 22 Notice therefore the goodness and the severity of God. For those who have fallen, *there is* severity, but for you, the goodness of God, if you continue in that goodness; for otherwise you also will be cut off." The connective εἰ γὰρ ("for if") is the second use of this combination in vv. 11–24 (see note on v. 15). This connective phrase refers back and supports further v. 20b and is a first class condition which assumes for the sake of argument that the statement is true.[671] In short, the message is that believing Gentiles ("unnatural branches") should fear instead of being proud (Schreiner, 2nd, 590). The phrase τῶν κατὰ φύσιν κλάδων ("the natural branches") refers to the Israelites. The failure of the natural branches though not literally stated by the word "judgment," results in judgment. The verbs οὐκ ἐφείσατο ("did not spare") and οὐδὲ σοῦ φείσεται ("he will not spare you") indicate judgment for both the natural broken off branches (unbelieving Israelites – vv. 17, 20a), as well as the possibility of broken off unnatural branches (unbelieving professing Gentiles – v. 21, 22c). Furthermore, v. 22 does make judgment explicit with the phrases ἀποτομίαν θεοῦ ("the severity of God") and the phrase ἐπὶ μὲν τοὺς πεσόντας ἀποτομία[672] ("for those who have fallen, *there is* severity"). The word πεσόντας ("those who have fallen") was also used in 11:11 and has the

---

[666] Blass, Debrunner, Funk, *A Greek Grammar*, §196(1); Käsemann, 310; Dunn, 663; Cranfield, 569, n. 1; Fitzmyer, 615.

[667] Some classify this dative phrase as instrumental (Moo, 2nd, 722, n. 736; Dunn, 663).

[668] The perfect verb may refer to a status of the person based upon result of a prior act (Dunn, 663). Wallace, *Greek Grammar*, 577 calls this a consummative perfect. The emphasis is on the past action and not so much the present state. Moo, 2nd, 772, n. 737 prefers that the verb accentuates present state one is in. Wallace, *Greek Grammar*, 575–76 calls this an intensive perfect. This action is probably the best choice.

[669] Zuck, "Theology of the Wisdom Books and Song of Songs," 251.

[670] See BDAG, 901. See above in textual criticism section. Thielman, 543, n. 50 responds to those who resist accepting the fuller text of μή πως because this would soften Paul's point. He suggests that Paul's use of "perhaps" is irony. Therefore, no softening idea is intended. This is a possibility.

[671] Wallace, *Greek Grammar*, 690.

[672] The word ἀποτομίαν is only found in 11:22 (twice). In the LXX it is used for the "unbending 'severity' of God in His judgment of the wicked" or the "'unrelenting severity' of the divine judgment" (Helmut Köster, *TDNT*, 8:107, 108). The adverb ἀποτόμως, "severely, rigorously" (BDAG, 124) is found in Tit 1:13; 2 Cor 13:10.

meaning “to fall down, fall down (violently or break into pieces), to be destroyed, be completely ruined, or perish.”[673] Also, to add to these two phrases on judgment comprise the ending of the verse: ἐπεὶ[674] καὶ σὺ ἐκκοπήσῃ (“for otherwise you also will be cut off”). This description pictures a very serious spiritual condition of judgment in the past and now is presented to those in the present. On the other hand, the judgment of God is coupled and contrasted with the kindness of God[675] (used 3 times in v. 22) given to the unnatural branches (believing Gentiles). Paul uses the third class condition ἐὰν ἐπιμένῃς[676] (“if you continue”) expressing some uncertainty of their perseverance but still believing they likely will[677] though he warns them of judgment if they prove that they do not continue in the faith (Acts 13:43). Paul refers to the believing Gentiles with the singular 2nd person, “you” (once in v. 21 and three times in v. 22). Romans 11:19-22 has been used by some to promote the insecurity of the believer, that is, a genuine believer may lose his salvation. The possibility of this view could be inferred from these verses but when Paul’s argument is considered in the broader context this position is not compelling. Paul has argued in Rom 5:9–10; 8:29–30, 31–39 a strong case for the eternal security of the believer. Thus, Paul is not arguing for the insecurity of the believer, but the perseverance of a true believer (Rom 15:4–5; Eph 1:13–14; 2:9–10; 1 Pet 1:3–5; Jude 24–25) because the Holy Spirit who lives in every true believer will not allow the true believer to fully or finally fall away from the faith (Col 1:22–23; Heb 3:6, 14).[678] As Murray states, “God’s saving embrace and endurance are correlative” (2:88). Every profession of faith in Jesus Christ and Christianity may not be a true belief in Jesus Christ for salvation (1 Cor 15:1-2; Gal 4:8-11; Tit 1:15–16). As one examines the argument of the illustration of the olive tree it becomes apparent that the true spiritually saved people of God are the branches belonging to the root and trunk of the olive tree through their faith. Also, some of the branches who appear to be a part of the tree are seemingly part of the tree for a season–being associated with the nation of Israel but are in unbelief–not truly having saving faith. Rom 11:17 speaks about “some” of the natural branches (Israelites) were cut off because of “their unbelief” (v.20). The nation of Israel as whole but not necessarily each particular Israelite was part of the illustration of the blessings of being part of the olive tree. These “broken off branches” were part of the outward physical make-up of the nation but not all of the individuals of the nation of Israel are part of believing Israel (Rom 9:6). Thus, Paul presents the concept of perseverance in the metaphor of the olive tree by indicating that all the branches were part of the tree (Moo, 2nd, 724, n. 747) until the time where God breaks off the unbelieving branches who were only part of corporate Israel, but not believing Israel. In like manner, Paul argues the same way with the Gentiles in Rome when it

---

[673] BDAG, 815–16; Wilhem Michaelis, *TDNT*, 6:161–63.

[674] The conjunction ἐπεὶ is a marker of cause or reason – “because, since” (BDAG, 360). See Blass, Debrunner, and Funk, *A Greek Grammar*, §456.3; Fitzmyer, 661; Jewett, 691.

[675] The Greek word χρηστότης is used 10 times in the NT (5 times in Romans) and all the uses are by Paul. BDAG, 1090 defines it as “the quality of being helpful or beneficial: goodness, kindness, generosity.” “It denotes here salvation for the Gentiles as this is accomplished by Paul’s apostolic commission. It has a special reference, then, to God’s act of grace effected in and through Christ” (Wesis, *TDNT*, 9:488). The phrase τῇ χρηστότητι (“in that goodness”) is either a dative of respect/reference or sphere and the article preceding it is an anaphoric use (“that”) pointing out the two previous uses of the noun χρηστότης in the same verse (Wallace, *Greek Grammar*, 153–55; 217–20; see also Thielman, 544, n. 56).

[676] BDAG, 375 defines ἐπιμένῃς: “to continue in an activity or state, continue, persist (in), persevere.” The Lexicon translates the phrase “continue in the sphere of (God’s) goodness” (375). See Dunn, 665. Middendorf, 1106 points to the subjunctive mood and prefers the passive use of “to remain at or in” (BDAG, 375).

[677] Wallace, *Greek Grammar*, 696–97.

[678] *Westminster Confession of Faith*, XVII, section 1.

comes to the unnatural branches of the Gentile church. He addresses the unnatural branches as a whole (corporately) and not necessarily each individual unnatural branch.[679] Those Gentiles whose outward profession or merely identify in some way with the church will be made manifest when their lack of faith or perseverance of faith indicates that they are not a true branch (Calvin, 430; Godet, 251; Moo, 2nd, 724, n. 747).[680]

Biblical Theological Comments

Romans 11:16–22 is a historical illustration of the sinful pride of man when the Lord pours out His grace in salvation on a group of people. The choice of God to pour out His grace and salvation on the nation of Israel was all centered on the Messiah Jesus. When the Father sent Jesus most of the people did not accept Him but crucified Him which became a colossal tragedy for the nation of Israel. Paul seems to use the Gentiles as a foil to destroy the Jewish arguments of ethnic superiority (Runge, 195). However, Paul also sees the sinful pride of the Gentiles as he makes his argument with the olive tree illustration for when the natural branches (Israel) are broken off because of their unbelief the unnatural branches (Gentiles) are grafted by God's grace into the blessings of the olive tree. However, the temptation of the Gentiles is to boast in this gracious privilege which came by faith through the provision of God in the Abrahamic promises–the "root" (v. 18). Instead of boasting in God's beautiful grace they are endanger of proudful boasting. Thus, Paul warns them to fear! The concept of fear in the OT wisdom literature is rich and prominent in the biblical theology of the OT. If one wanted to describe a godly man especially in the OT one of these phrases would be, he fears God. However, in the context of Rom 11:20–22, this fear is directed to the failure of persevering in faith which would indicate a lack of a true saving faith (1 Cor 15:2; Tit 1:15–16; Col 1:22-23) which will end in eternal judgment. Thus, the goodness of God's salvation and the severity of His judgment are displayed as a lesson of God's wisdom polemic[681] in His drama of salvation history that magnifies His glory!

Application and Devotional Implications

The principle we may draw from this passage is: if you take God's blessings for granted and turn away from Him in unbelief, God will remove that nation or individual from His blessings. This principle has application to a nation and to individuals (for Israel 2 Chron 7:14; 12:1–12; for the nations Jer 18:7–10). God has showered abundant blessings both physically and spiritually upon the USA for over 200 years. It may be that our country has received more

---

[679] It is interesting that Paul addresses the Gentile unnatural branch in Rom 11:17–24 in the singular second person, except one time (in first person singular, v. 19). See Seifrid, 672.

[680] Some think that Paul is arguing phenomenologically here. The Gentiles that fall away and never come back in their lifetime were not really grafted into the tree. They just appeared to be. Others believe the cutting off the Gentile Christians in unbelief need not be final. They can be grafted back in again and be saved. Finally, some believe in the hypothetical view (see Schreiner and Caneday, *The Race Before Us*, *passim*). This view states that a believer who stops believing will be lost forever, but a true believer could not ever do this (Moo, *NIVAC Romans*, 375).

[681] For a definition and discussion on the concept of a wisdom polemic see "The Wisdom Polemic in Romans 9-11" at the introduction section of the commentary.

blessings than any other nation since the judgment of the natural branches (Israel corporately). At least we could say this seems to be the case in the last 100 years or so. The reason for God's blessing is that we stood by faith. Yet, in the blessing and prosperity of our nation it is easy to become high minded and lose sight of the source of God's blessing and focus on the accomplishment of man and the prosperity that comes from it. Could it be that God's axe has been set to the grindstone and He is ready to cut us off from His blessings? If there ever was a time to sound the alarm and wake up from our slumbering and unbelief, it is now! The real possibility of God's judgment is a sobering thought. Therefore, we should take heed to Paul's warning and admonishment to fear. This godly fear should stimulate us to continue in God's goodness and be salt and light in our community and country. This godly fear would direct men and women to faith so that the privilege we have as individuals and a country will not be cut off in judgment. Paul's warning is very sobering: "Behold then the goodness and the severity of God."

Selected Bibliography

Arndt, William, Frederick W. Danker, and Walter Bauer, *A Greek-English Lexicon of the New Testament and Other Early Christian Literature*, 3rd ed. electronic version (Chicago: University of Chicago Press, 2000).

Baxter, A. G. and J. A. Ziesler, "Paul and Arboriculture: Romans 11:17–24," JSNT 24 (1985): 25–32.

Blass, Friedrich, Albert Debrunner, and Robert Walter Funk, *A Greek Grammar of the New Testament and Other Early Christian Literature* (Chicago: University of Chicago Press, 1961).

Bultmann, Rudolf, *TDNT* (Grand Rapids: Eerdmans, 1964). 3:653.

Campbell, William, *Paul and the Creation of Christian Identity* (London: T & T Clark, A Continuum Imprint, 2008).

Delling, Gerhard, *TDNT*, ed. Gerhard Kittel, Geoffrey W. Bromiley, and Gerhard Friedrich, vol. 1 (Grand Rapids, MI: Eerdmans, 1964–), 484–486.

Esler, Philip F. "Ancient Oleiculture and Ethnic Differentiation: The Meaning of the Olive-Tree Image in Romans 11," JSNT 26 (2003): 103–124.

Gordon, Benjamin D. "On the Sanctity of Mixtures and Branches: Two Halakic Sayings in Romans 11:16–24," JBL 135 (2016): 355–68.

Hafemann, Scott. "The Salvation of Israel in Romans 11:25–32: A Response to Krister Stendahl." *Ex Auditu* 4 (1988): 38–58.

Johnson, S. Lewis, Jr. "Romans 11:11-24, Parable of the Olive Tree," Sermon at Believers Chapel, Dallas, Texas, 2008, p. 5.

Köster, Helmut, *TDNT*, ed. Gerhard Kittel, Geoffrey W. Bromiley, and Gerhard Friedrich, vol. (Grand Rapids, MI: Eerdmans, 1964–), 107.

Liddel, Henry George et al., *GEL* (Oxford: Clarendon Press, 1996).

Michaelis, Wihlem, *TDNT*, ed. Gerhard Kittel, Geoffrey W. Bromiley, and Gerhard Friedrich, vol. 6 (Grand Rapids, MI: Eerdmans, 1964–), 161–63.

Nanos, Mark D. "'Broken Branches': A Pauline Metaphor Gone Awry?" in *Between Gospel and Election*, ed. Florian Wilk and J. Ross Wagner with assistance of Frank Schleritt,

Wissenschaftliche Untersuchungen zum Neuen Testament, 25 (Tübingen: Mohr Siebeck, 2010), 339–76.

Robertson, A. T. *A Grammar of the Greek New Testament in the Light of Historical Research* (Logos Bible Software, 2006).

Metzger, Bruce M. *A Textual Commentary on the Greek New Testament.* 2nd ed. (Stuttgart: Deutsche Bibelgesellschaft, 1994).

Schreiner, Thomas R. and Ardel B. Caneday, *The Race Before Us: A Biblical Theology of Perseverance & Assurance* (Downers Grove: IVP, 2001).

Swanson, Reuben, ed. *New Testament Greek Manuscripts: Romans* (Wheaton: Tyndale House and Pasadena: William Carey International University Press, 2001).

Vlach, Michael J. "A Non-Typical Future–Mass–Conversion View," in *Three Views on Israel and the Church: Perspectives on Romans 9–11*, eds. Jared Compton and Andrew D. Naselli (Grand Rapids: Kregel, 2018), 21–73.

Wallace, Daniel B. *Greek Grammar Beyond the Basic: An Exegetical Syntax of the New Testament* (Grand Rapids: Zondervan, 1996).

Werner Stenger, "βαστάζω," *EDNT* (Edinburg: T & T Clark, 1991), 1:208–209.

Weiss, Konrad, *TDNT*, ed. Gerhard Kittel, Geoffrey W. Bromiley, and Gerhard Friedrich, vol. 9 (Grand Rapids, MI: Eerdmans, 1964–), 488.

Westminster Confession of Faith, (Oak Harbor, WA: Logos Research, 1996), XVII, section 1

Zuck, Roy. "Theology of the Wisdom Books and Song of Songs," *Biblical Theology of the OT*, eds. Roy B. Zuck and Darrell L. Bock (Chicago: Moody Press, 1991).

Romans 11:23–27

Introduction

The singular "you" in 11:22–24 continue to represent "Gentiles" as a group and the "they" represent Israel as a group. Secondly, Paul continues with his olive tree illustration and the salvific blessing that is connected with being grafted into the olive tree. Then in v. 25 the plural "you" represent the brothers and sisters in the Roman church who he is addressing. Paul explains further his thoughts of Israel's hardening in v. 7 as a partial hardening (v. 25) and how the "fullness of the Gentiles" fits with the blessing of "all Israel will be saved" in v. 26. He finishes his point with references from Isa 59:20–21 and 27:9 (and possible other OT allusions) in vv. 26–27.

Outline

E. A Wisdom Polemic: God's Merciful Plan for Israel and Gentiles (11:11-33)
   1. Israel's hardening and the Gentiles Inclusion (11:11-15)
   2. A Warning against Gentile Believers (11:16-22)
   3. The Salvation Mystery of the Natural Branches–Israel (11:23-27)

Original Text

11.23 κἀκεῖνοι δέ, ἐὰν μὴ ἐπιμένωσι[a] τῇ ἀπιστίᾳ, ἐγκεντρισθήσονται· δυνατὸς γάρ ἐστιν ὁ θεὸς
πάλιν ἐγκεντρίσαι αὐτούς. 24 εἰ γὰρ σὺ ἐκ τῆς κατὰ φύσιν ἐξεκόπης ἀγριελαίου καὶ παρὰ φύσιν
ἐνεκεντρίσθης εἰς καλλιέλαιον, πόσῳ μᾶλλον οὗτοι οἱ κατὰ φύσιν ἐγκεντρισθήσονται τῇ ἰδίᾳ
ἐλαίᾳ. 25 Οὐ γὰρ θέλω ὑμᾶς ἀγνοεῖν, ἀδελφοί, τὸ μυστήριον τοῦτο, ἵνα μὴ ἦτε[b] ἑαυτοῖς φρόνιμοι,
ὅτι πώρωσις ἀπὸ μέρους τῷ Ἰσραὴλ γέγονεν ἄχρι οὗ τὸ πλήρωμα τῶν ἐθνῶν εἰσέλθῃ, 26 καὶ
οὕτως πᾶς Ἰσραὴλ σωθήσεται· καθὼς γέγραπται· Ἥξει ἐκ Σιὼν ὁ ῥυόμενος, ἀποστρέψει
ἀσεβείας ἀπὸ Ἰακώβ. 27 καὶ αὕτη αὐτοῖς ἡ παρ' ἐμοῦ διαθήκη, ὅταν ἀφέλωμαι τὰς ἁμαρτίας
αὐτῶν.

Textual Notes

[a] **11:23 ἐπιμένωσι(ν)** is supported by NA28, UBS5, SBLGNT, WH, ℵ* B D* Ψ 365 1739 1881. **ἐπιμείνωσι(ν)** L 049 056 1 6 33 69 88 104 131 209 226 323 326 330 440 517 489 614 618 796 910 927 945 999 1175 1241 1245 1270 1319 1352 1424 1448 1505 1506 1573 1611 1646 1734 1738 1827 1874 1891 1982 2147 2344 2400 2412 2495 2815. **ἐπιμείνωσει** is found in C. **ἐπιμίνωσιν** is found in A. All but possibly C are reflecting a 3rd person plural aorist subjective.
[b] **11:25 ἦτε + ἐν** is supported by WH B A* 630 1506 1852 2200. **ἦτε + παρ'** is supported by NA28 [παρ' in brackets], UBS5 [παρ' in brackets], ℵ C D L 049 056 1 33 69 81 104 131 205 209 226 256 263 323 326 365 436 440 459 460 517 547 614 618 796 910 927 945 999 1175

1241 1242 1243 1270 1319 1352 1448 1505 1573 1611 1734 1738 1837 1854 1881 1891 1912 1962 1982 2127 2400 2412 2464 2815. **ἦτε** is supported by SBLGNT, P[46] F G Ψ 6 1506 1739. (UBS5, 533; NA28, 505; and Swanson, *NT Greek Mss. Rom*, 181). The committee of the UBS text decided to put the παρ' in brackets and rated it "C" which indicates that the committee had a difficulty coming to a conclusion which variant should be in the text (Metzger, 465). The reason why a scribe may have inserted παρ' or ἐν is because it helps to explain the difficulty in understanding the prepositional phrase (Schriener, 2nd, 607).[682] Some would also contend that *παρά* was introduced by assimilation to Rom 12:16 (Meyer, 2.198; Sanday and Headlam, 334; Cranfield, 574; Godet, 410). Thus, it is possible that a scribe added the prepositions, and the simple dative is probably the best possibility (Cranfield, 574; Jewett, 694; Schriener, 2nd, 607; Moo, 2nd, 727, n. 759). For a good summary of the choices, see Longnecker, 871.

Translation

23 And they also, if they do not persist in their lack of faith, will be grafted in; for God is able to
graft them in again. **24** For if you were cut off from what is a wild olive tree which by nature *you belong*, and were grafted into a cultivated olive tree which you by nature did not belong, how much
more these who are the natural *branches* will be grafted into one's own olive tree? **25** For I do not
want you to be ignorant, brothers, about this mystery, in order that you might not be wise in your own estimation: that a hardening has come partially on Israel until the full number of the Gentiles
has come in. **26** And in this way all Israel will be saved, just as it is written: The deliverer will come from Zion; he will turn away ungodliness from Jacob. **27** And this is my covenant with them,
when I take away their sins.

Commentary

11:23 κἀκεῖνοι δέ, ἐὰν μὴ ἐπιμένωσι[a] τῇ ἀπιστίᾳ, ἐγκεντρισθήσονται· δυνατὸς γάρ ἐστιν ὁ θεὸς πάλιν ἐγκεντρίσαι αὐτούς. "And they also, if they do not persist in their lack of faith, will be grafted in. For God is able to graft them in again." Paul begins with the connective κἀκεῖνοι δέ ("that they also")[683] and shifts his thoughts back to the natural branches (Israelites). Paul demonstrates that he is not so much following cultured horticulture for regrafting original branches back into the same olive tree for this is not the ideal protocol or actually practiced. However, the illustration fits the theology and the promise of God to Israel. We see an interesting continuum and contrast. To the Gentiles, Paul states that they will be cut off if they do not continue in the faith while Israel is promised that God will graft them back in again if they do not continue in unbelief (Murray, 2:89).

The particles ἐὰν μὴ with the subjective ἐπιμένωσι is a 3rd class conditional clause expressing some uncertainty about what is likely to happen.[684] There is no uncertainty that God will graft Israel back, but there is some question about some Israelites that may continue in their unbelief demonstrating they are not part of the tree (see comments on vv. 21–22). This future

---

[682] Godet, 253; Sanday and Headlam, 334 and Dunn, 676 prefer ἐν ἑαυτοῖς.

[683] It is formed from καὶ ἐκεῖνος and then δέ (BDAG, 500). Sanday and Headlam, 330 translate this conjunction, "yes, and they too." Jewett, 692, n. 260 translates it "but they also."

[684] Wallace, *Greek Grammar*, 696–97 and Middendorf, 1106.

engrafting is future from Paul's day (ἐγκεντρισθήσονται, "will be grafted in")[685] and the time is generally expressed in 11:25–26. Paul confidently declares in v. 23 that God is able to graft (δυνατὸς γάρ ἐστιν ὁ θεὸς πάλιν) Israel back into the blessing of God which was promised to Abraham and to his descendance. The Lord's sovereign grace through the power of the Spirit will work in the heart of future Israel to cause them to want to turn to Him (Zech 12:10). This same power is now working in the lives of Gentiles to graft them into the blessings of the olive tree (Jewett, 692). Cranfield (570–71) seems to be right that Paul expresses this thought in v. 23 to guard against the possibility of the Gentile Christians from assuming that Israel cut off from the olive tree could not be grafted back into the favor of the olive tree. In other words, he forcefully rejects that Israel has been replaced by the Church. God's omnipotence (δυνατὸς γάρ ἐστιν ὁ θεὸς πάλιν) will in His timing graft Israel back into the blessing of the olive tree.

11:24 εἰ γὰρ σὺ ἐκ τῆς κατὰ φύσιν ἐξεκόπης ἀγριελαίου καὶ παρὰ φύσιν ἐνεκεντρίσθης εἰς καλλιέλαιον, πόσῳ μᾶλλον οὗτοι οἱ κατὰ φύσιν ἐγκεντρισθήσονται τῇ ἰδίᾳ ἐλαίᾳ. "For if you were cut off from what is a wild olive tree which by nature *you belong*, and were grafted into a cultivated olive tree which you by nature did not belong, how much more these who are the natural *branches* will be grafted into one's own olive tree?" Paul summarizes his thoughts in vv. 17–23 using again the olive tree illustration. Therefore, he uses the connective phrase εἰ γὰρ ("for if"; see note on v. 15) and uses a lesser to a greater argument. However, the first part of v. 24 is sequentially difficult to understand. The subject σὺ ("you," 2nd person singular) in an emphatic position is further identified with the 2nd person aorist passive verb ἐξεκόπης ("were cut off") which has four Greek words (prepositional phrase) between them. The preposition ἐκ ("from") and the genitive singular article τῆς ("the") are connected with the singular genitive noun ἀγριελαίου ("wild olive tree") which has three Greek words in between them. Between τῆς (the article) and … ἀγριελαίου is the prepositional phrase κατὰ φύσιν ("by nature") and the verb ἐξεκόπης ("were cut off"). However, the verb ἐξεκόπης is between the noun ἀγριελαίου ("wild olive tree") and the prepositional phrase κατὰ φύσιν ("by nature") which modifies the noun (ἀγριελαίου – "wild olive tree"). All of these Greek constructions are grammatically allowable but not something that is usual and especially all these combinations in one part of a sentence. Many translations (NASB, AV, NRSV) take κατὰ φύσιν ("by nature") as referring to ἀγριελαίου ("wild olive tree") stressing the nature of the wild branch from the wild olive tree. This phraseology would be stressing a tautology, a wild olive tree is wild by nature. This view is possibly what Paul is stressing, but Cranfield (571) may be right that the κατὰ φύσιν does not refer to what kind of tree or the nature of the tree, but it refers to the way the cut-off branch belongs to the tree (Moo, 2nd, 725, n. 753). Cranfield, 571 states it this way: "the Gentile Christian has been cut out of the wild olive tree, which is the tree to which by nature he belongs." The κατὰ φύσιν/παρὰ φύσιν contrast seems not to focus upon the unnatural process of engrafting as much as the starling fact that a different kind of olive branch can be successfully engrafted (Dunn, 666). Thus, the wild olive branch (believing Gentile) is cut off from its tree and grafted into the cultivated olive tree. By nature, the wild olive branch is different from the cultivated tree and branches, but both engrafted branches benefit from the root of the cultivate olive tree. However, the wild olive branch does not become Israel or the new Israel but

---

685 The divine passive ἐγκεντρισθήσονται and man's responsibility not to continue in unbelief is reflection of the divine/human clash expressed in Rom 9 (Jewett, 692).

participates in the redemptive promises of the new covenant.[686] Furthermore, the unbelieving natural branch (Israelite) if they come to believe will be grafted back into the blessing of their own cultivated olive tree. Paul's argument here is a lesser to greater argument (*a minore ad maius*). If the lesser is true–God grafting the wild olive branches (believing Gentiles) into the cultivated olive tree–how much more will He graft the natural branches (believing Israelites) back into their own tree![687] This verse is the second time Paul states the timing of the engrafting of the natural branches will happen in the future from his day (vv. 23, 24).

Whether one is an Israelite or Gentile everyone stands condemned under sin's power (Rom 3:9–12) and Paul instructs us in Rom 9 that only by God's grace can an individual be saved. Thus, whether a Gentile or Israelite the engrafting into the cultivated olive tree is through their trust in Jesus Christ as their Lord and Savior (Rom 10:9–10; 11:11-15). However, when a natural olive branch has been cut off because of unbelief, they still retain their identity to the chosen nation of Israel, but in unbelief. Paul has skillfully used an olive tree illustration to teach some important theology about the Lord's plan for Israel and believing Gentiles. It is not enough to be part of the natural tree that can trace their physical roots to the holy root (v. 16) for the unbelieving natural branches were cut off. However, the future regrafting of the believing natural branch is much easier to understand than the engrafting of the wild olive branch of the believing Gentiles (Moo (2nd, 726). However, this truth about the Gentile believers was summarize for Abraham in the latter part of Gen 12:3.

11:25 Οὐ γὰρ θέλω ὑμᾶς ἀγνοεῖν, ἀδελφοί, τὸ μυστήριον τοῦτο, ἵνα μὴ ἦτε ἑαυτοῖς φρόνιμοι, ὅτι πώρωσις ἀπὸ μέρους τῷ Ἰσραὴλ γέγονεν ἄχρι οὗ τὸ πλήρωμα τῶν ἐθνῶν εἰσέλθῃ. "For I do not want you to be ignorant, brothers, about this mystery, in order that you, might not be wise in your own estimation: that a hardening has come partially on Israel until the full number of the Gentiles has come in." Paul began his argument in vv. 11–32 with the question whether Israel had stumbled to the extent that they will irretrievably be rejected. Israel indeed has fallen and has rejected their God by rejecting Jesus Christ. However, Israel's rejection of God is not final or total. In the sovereign unfolding of God's salvation-history, Gentiles and Israelites in the church take center stage. In the future, Israel will again be grafted back into the promises and blessing of their Lord (11:12, 15). Paul has used an olive tree illustration to explain His plan concerning Israel and Gentile believers in vv. 16–24. In verses 25–32 we come to the climax of Paul's argument not just for 11:11–32 but also for Rom 9–11 (Moo, 2nd, 728). In this section we see the clash between Israel's rebellious unbelief and the irrevocable promises of God to Israel as He unfolds His sovereign plan in salvation-history.

The conjunction γὰρ ("for") explains further this climatic section that has been building in Rom 9–11 and specifically 9:11–24 (Moo, 2nd, 729; Dunn, 677; Cranfield, 573). Paul specifically addresses the ἀδελφοί which literally means "brothers," however the context indicates he is addressing the Roman congregation which would include brothers and sisters in the Lord.[688] Thus, a contemporary translation today would be "brothers and sisters." Paul wants to communicate the following truth because he does not want them to be "uninformed or

---

[686] Vlach, "A Non-Typological Future-Mass-Conversion View," 70–73; Campbell, *Paul and the Creation of Christian Identity*, 121–39.

[687] This cultivated olive tree (καλλιέλαιον) is contrasted with the wild olive tree as early as Aristotle, *Plants* 1.6.40 (820b). See BDAG, 504.

[688] BDAG, 18 indicates that this word is used to address members (male and female) in the Christian community.

ignorant"[689] (ἀγνοεῖν) concerning τὸ μυστήριον τοῦτο ("this mystery"). The word "mystery"[690] in Scripture "usually refers to an event of the end times that has already been determined by God – and so, in that sense, exists already in heaven – but which is first revealed to the apocalyptic seer for the comfort and encouragement . . . [Usually it is] associated with Christ's coming and the preaching of the gospel"[691] The word also may reveal revelation of the church age and events at the end of this age when Jesus Christ comes again. The mystery that Paul addresses in Romans 11 is the sequence by which all Israel will be saved: (1) hardening of the majority of Israel; (2) Gentiles would enjoy the blessings of salvation during this hardening; and (3) when the Gentile salvation is fulfilled then Israel would experience the blessings of salvation.[692] Thus, in the present age, Israel is experiencing quantitative hardening (certain number of Israelites, cf. Rom 11:7), and a temporal hardening (certain period of time, cf. Rom 11:25). The context of Romans 11 confirms that Israel would be rejuvenated: (1) the contrast between "their stumbling" and "their defeat" with "their full inclusion" in verse 12; (2) the contrast between "their rejection" with "their acceptance" in verse 15; and (3) the contrast between "some of the branches were broken off" (v. 17) with the natural branches being "grafted back into their own olive tree" (v. 24). When the full number of the Gentiles is brought to salvation, then "all Israel will be saved." The "fullness of Israel" (11:12) is paralleled by the phrase "fullness of the Gentiles" (11:25), which is taken as quantitative (Cranfield, 558; Godet, 401; Jewett, 677; Murray, 2:79; Sanday, and Headlam, 322).[693]

The purpose clause (ἵνα "in order that") warns the church not to have an unwise estimation concerning this mystery involving a partial hardening of Israel. This admonishment most likely looks back to Paul's thoughts concerning Gentile Christians in vv. 17–21. The 3rd person dative reflexive ἑαυτοῖς is used for the 2nd person ("yourselves") intended meaning.[694] The ὅτι clause ("that...") gives the result of the admonishment.[695] Israel as a nation received a

---

689 BDAG, 12. Paul uses Οὐ γὰρ θέλω ὑμᾶς ἀγνοεῖν ("For I do not want you to be ignorant") as an introduction to stress the importance of the information that follows: Rom 1:13; 1 Cor 10:1; 12:1; 2 Cor. 1:8; 1 Thess 4:13 (Schreiner, 2nd, 594; Meyer, 229).

690 See Paul's use: Rom 11:25; 16:25; 1 Cor. 2:1(?), 7; 4:1; 13:2; 14:2; 15:51; Eph. 1:9; 3:3, 4, 9; 5:32; 6:19; Col. 1:26, 27; 2:2; 4:3; 2 Thess. 2:7; 1 Tim. 3:9, 16. Longenecker, 895, n. 49 leads us in the right direction when he states that Paul's use of mystery has a Semitic background in the Jewish Scripture and not a Hellenistic mystery cult background. See Dunn, 678–79; Fitzmyer, 621 and Byrne, 354.

691 Moo, 2nd, 729 paraphrases Wilcken's summary (*Der Brief des Paulus an die Römer*, 2:253). See Dunn, 677–79 on the background of the term "mystery." Bell, *The Irrevocable Call of God*, 256–57 believes that Paul's mystery did not come from some vision or apocalyptic revelation but rather through the study of Scripture (see also Hofius, "'All Israel Will Be Saved,'" 38; Cranfield, 574). Moo, 2nd, 730 is likely correct that Paul's understanding of this mystery went beyond his OT study to direct revelation as well. Vlach, "A Non-Typological Future-Mass-Conversion View," 49 gives a comprehensive definition of mystery in the NT: "(1) hidden meanings found in symbols (Rev 1:20; 17:5, 7), (2) a completely new truth not found in previous Scripture (1 Cor 15:51), or (3) an earlier truth in the OT that is now coming to fruition with Jesus (Eph 6:19)." Rom 11:25 mystery seems to fit best with the third view (Meyer, 230). Beale and Gladd, *Hidden but Now Revealed*, 20 accept the basic definition of "divine wisdom that was previously 'hidden' but has now been 'revealed.'" However, they sharpen the definition with these two basic simultaneous definitions: (1) "God's wisdom has finally been disclosed, but nevertheless (2) his wisdom remains generally incomprehensible to nonbelievers."

692 Longenecker, 895–96 adds two others from 11:26b–27: (1) Deliverer will come from Zion turning Israel from ungodliness; and (2) God's covenantal promise of taking away Israel's sins will take place.

693 Sullivan, *The Isaianic NE in Rom 9–11*, 361–62.

694 Zerwick and Grosvenor, *A Grammatical Analysis of the Greek New Testament*, 485. The translation is literally "before yourselves" which may be smoothed out to be translated as "in your own estimation."

695 Some conclude the ὅτι clause at the end of v. 25, but many connect v. 26 with the clause. See comments on v. 26.

hardening (πώρωσις)[696] from God that is "partial" (ἀπὸ μέρους)[697] because it will end at the time of the "fullness of the Gentiles." The hardening is not a degree of hardening of every Israelite but partial in the sense that not all Israelites were hardened (11:7, 17). Murray, 2:92 says "the hardening of Israel is partial not total, temporary not final, 'in part' indicating the former, 'until the fulness of the Gentiles be come in' the latter." The verb γέγονεν ("has come") is probably an intensive perfect[698] emphasizing the present state of Israel's hardening from a past action from God when they rejected and crucified their Messiah Jesus. Paul states the harden of Israel will last ἄχρι οὗ τὸ πλήρωμα τῶν ἐθνῶν εἰσέλθῃ ("until the fullness of the Gentiles comes in"). Some scholars believe the hardening of Israel will last right up to the last day. Thus, the lifting of the hardening ends at the final judgment–terminative sense (Calvin, 436; Lenski, 713–23).[699] Others indicate the Greek construction here indicates that the reversal of the condition of Israel (i.e. hardening) will happen when the fullness of the Gentiles comes in (Moo, 2nd, 733). The debate is over the Greek ἄχρι clause at the end of v. 25. The preposition/conjunction ἄχρι is used 48 times (49 if you count Mk 16:8 in some manuscripts) in the NT.[700] The Greek construction in the last part of Rom 11:25 is ἄχρι with the genitive singular relative pronoun (οὗ, masculine here in v. 25) used in conjunction with an aorist subjective verb that follows in this construction (ἄχρι οὗ τὸ πλήρωμα τῶν ἐθνῶν εἰσέλθῃ). There are 8 other constructions in the NT with this combination (Luke 1:20; 21:24; Acts 7:18; 1 Cor 11:26; 15:25; Gal 3:19; Heb 3:13; Rev 2:25). If one broadens the search to include aorist indicatives and not just aorist subjunctives then three more verses may be added (Acts 1:2; Luke 17:27 = Matt 24:38).[701] All eight of the texts that use the aorist subjunctive support a reversal of the condition in the context and one out of the three of the aorist indicatives supported the reversal of the conditions in the context (Luke 17:27 and Matt 24:38 are the two that support a terminative sense). Furthermore, 27 out of 38 uses of temporal use of ἄχρι support the reversal of the conditions in the context. Thus, this evidence strongly supports the understanding that the hardening of Israel will be lifted when the τὸ

---

[696] BDAG, 900 translates it "insensibility (=a closed mind)."

[697] BDAG, 633 translates it "a partial" or "in part" hardening. The Greek phrase ἀ ὸ μέρους may be taken at least three ways: adjectival, modifying Ἰσραήλ—"hardening has come on part of Israel" (Barrett, 206; Jewett, 700), or adverbial modifying γέγονεν—"a hardening has come partially on Israel" (Godet, 253–54; Meyer, 230; Moo, 2nd, 732 n. 783) or possibly πώρωσις—"a partial hardening has come on Israel" (Dunn, 679; Thielman, 546). The adverbial alternative is most likely for ἀπὸ μέρους is used adverbially in its four other Pauline occurrences (Rom. 15:15, 24; 2 Cor. 1:14; 2:5). However, the constructions of the other four occurrences were clearly adverbial and did not have any other grammatical option. Thus, the "partial hardening" translation may be Paul's thought. On the other hand, the difference in meaning is not significant (Moo, 2nd, 732, n. 783). The important point is that the partial hardening is not in degree but in number. Nanos, "'Callused', Not 'Hardened': Paul's Revelation of Temporary Protection Until all Israel Can Be Healed," 52–73 translates it "callus."

[698] Wallace, *Greek Grammar*, 574–75.

[699] Wright, *The Climax of the Covenant*, 249.

[700] Logos Bible Software 8.12.

[701] Ten of the 48 texts where ἄχρι is used have a spatial and not a temporal use (Acts 11:5; 13:6; 22:4; 26:22; 28:15; 2 Cor 3:14; Heb 4:12; Rev 12:11; 14:20; 18:5). Thus, 38 occurrences remain. Out of the 38, there are 27 occurrences (Moo, 2nd, 733, n. 785 lists 25) that seems to be clear enough in the context to denote a period of time which will come to an end and what follows indicate a change of circumstance from the previous period (Luke 1:20; 4:13; 21:24; Acts 1:2; 3:21; 7:18; 13:11; 20:6, 11; 22:22; 27:33; Rom 1:13; 1 Cor 11:26; 15:25; Gal 3:19; 4:2; Phil. 1:6; Heb 3:13; 6:11; Rev 2:10; 2:25, 26; 7:3; 15:8; 17:17; 20:3, 5).

πλήρωμα ("the fullness") of Gentiles has come in.[702] The context supports this understanding throughout vv. 11–24.

The τὸ πλήρωμα τῶν ἐθνῶν εἰσέλθῃ ("the fullness of the Gentiles has come in") is variously understood. The context and concept of the use of εἰσέλθῃ ("has come in") is probably referring to the eternal salvation in the eschatological kingdom (Sanday and Headlam, 335; Moo, 2nd, 733; Cranfield, 576; Murray, 2:93; Dunn, 680). The word τὸ πλήρωμα ("fullness") is discussed in Rom 11:12 and paralleled in v. 15. The debate is whether τὸ πλήρωμα is translated as qualitative ("fulfill, fulfillment, completion, fullness") which stresses the full blessing to the believing Gentiles. Or is it quantitative (Cranfield, 575; Dunn, 680) stressing the "full number" of Gentiles or the completion of the mission of the Gentiles (Rom 15:16–19; Mt 24:14). The qualitative meaning is how the Bible authors consistently use this word, but in v. 25 the meaning of τὸ πλήρωμα in combination with εἰσέλθῃ ("come in") is awkward (Moo, 2nd, 733–34). Thus, it seems best to use the same meaning and conclusion of τὸ πλήρωμα found in 11:12 which indicated a quantitative meaning. Both definitions, qualitative and quantitative, could be represented here. The qualitative denotation is brought about through the quantitative number suggested in v. 25. The translation "full number" seem to capture the thought (NRSV, NIV, NET, HCSB, LEB). This appears to satisfy the awkwardness of εἰσέλθῃ used with τὸ πλήρωμα τῶν ἐθνῶν (Moo, 2nd, 708). Jesus in Luke 21:24 speaks about the Gentiles trampling down of Jerusalem "until the times of the Gentiles be fulfilled." The "times of the Gentiles" refers to the domination of the Gentiles over Israel and Jerusalem from Nebuchadnezzar to the second coming of Christ. "The fullness of the Gentiles" (11:25) is referring to the completion of the salvation of the Gentiles and provoking Israel to jealousy. When this happens then the partial hardening of corporate ethnic Israel will be lifted. Then there will be a great ingathering of the salvation of Israelites (11:24).

11:26a καὶ οὕτως πᾶς Ἰσραὴλ σωθήσεται· καθὼς γέγραπται. "And in this way all Israel will be saved, just as it is written." This verse is a center of exegetical and theological controversies. First, there are basically four options to interpret καὶ οὕτως ("and then"). Bell gives the four possible positions: (1) temporal (or a logical sequence with a temporal sense) (Käsemann, 313; Barrett, 223); (2) consequence or conclusion; (3) manner and connect it with "as it is written" in v. 26; and (4) manner and connect it with the latter part of v. 25.[703] The first view, temporal sense, has received some incorrect criticism. Some have stated that οὕτως is rarely used in a temporal way (Fitzmyer, 623). Many follow Hofius,[704] who states that the use of οὕτως is never used in a temporal sense. However, van der Horst,[705] indicates that there are plentiful examples of the temporal usages in classical, Judeo-Greek, and early Christian literatures. Acts 7:8, 20:11 and 27:17 are given as NT examples while some would add 1 Thess 4:17. Someone may not believe 11:26 should be categorize by the temporal sense but it has been demonstrated as a possible option.[706] This view would indicate that the fullness of the Gentiles come in and then after this event all Israel will be saved. The second view, consequence/conclusion, is a rare use in

---

[702] Storms, *Kingdom Come*, 323 who takes the position of ἄχρι as terminative in 11:25 "openly acknowledged that this is not its most frequent sense." However, he believes it is probable to take a terminative view in the light of his understanding of Rom 11 from a Historical Remnant view.

[703] Bell, *Provoked to Jealousy*, 258–60; Moo, 2nd, 734–35.

[704] Hofius, "Das Evangelium und Israel," 175–202.

[705] van der Horst, "'Only then will all Israel be saved,'" 521–39. Scott, "'And Then All Israel Will Be Saved' (Rom 11:26)," 491 also agrees with Horst.

[706] However, BDAG, LSJ, and *The Brill Dictionary of Ancient Greek*, do not list this option.

the NT and is not likely the understanding of Paul.[707] The third view takes καὶ οὕτως as manner and connects it with the following phrase καθὼς γέγραπται ("just as it is written….").[708] The meaning would be "in this way Israel will be saved, that is just as it is written…" However, Paul nowhere else connects καθὼς after οὕτως except in Phil 3:17, but here the construction is not exactly the same as 11:26.[709] In Phil 3:17, the Greek construction has an article (τοὺς) before οὕτω.[710] Though Wagner accepts the third view he agrees if καθὼς is to be understood as part of the citation formula (καθὼς γέγραπται) in 11:26 then "it is certainly possible to take οὕτως with what precedes" (the last part of v. 25 which is view 4).[711] Therefore, the fourth view is preferred: "And in this way all Israel will be saved." The argument of Paul's thought in vv. 11–24 is briefly summarized in v. 25b and a conclusion in v. 26a. Lewis Johnson, Jr. states this view by taking καὶ οὕτως ("and thus") in Rom 11:26 as indicating manner and linking it with 11:25b.[712] Bell states that this would make οὕτως have a logical understanding with a temporal sense.[713] Moo agrees with this view: "While not having a temporal *meaning*, [it] has a temporal *reference*; for the manner in which all Israel is saved involves a process that unfolds in definite stages."[714] Those stages are articulated in the comments on v. 25. After all the Gentiles enter into salvation, then all Israel will be saved. The choice of Paul's verbs from a perfect (γέγονεν – "has happened") in v. 25c to an aorist subjective (εἰσέλθῃ - "has come in") in v. 25d and finally a future passive (σωθήσεται – "will be saved") in v. 26a seem to suggest a sequence in the mystery (Jewett, 701). Thus, only "some of the (natural) branches were broken off" (v. 17, unbelieving Israelites) and the remnant of believing Israelites will continue to exist until the fullness of the Gentile salvation is completed. The believing remnant of Israel in this age is not part of the spiritual hardening that has come upon Israel who have rejected Jesus as their Messiah.

Another debate or controversy is the meaning of πᾶς Ἰσραὴλ ("all Israel") in v. 26 (this term is only found here in the NT). Let's begin with the meaning of "Israel" and then consider the word "all" with it. The two major positions are: (1) ethnic Israel or (2) spiritual Israel made up of both Jews and Gentiles. The latter view has several supporters in modern times.[715]

---

[707] Hofius, "'All Israel will be Saved,'" 35; Fitzmyer, 623. Moo, 2nd, 735, n.796 states that Paul uses only 4 out of 74 occurrences of οὕτως in a clear reference of "consecutive" meaning (οὕτως Rom 1:15; οὕτως καὶ 6:11; 1 Cor 14:25; 1 Thess 4:17). 1 Thess 4:17 may be temporal but maybe better classified as both temporal sequence and means (Thielman, 547).

[708] BDAG, 742; Wagner, *Heralds of the Good News*, 279–80, n. 195.

[709] In the NT, this construction order is also found in Luke 24:24, "…and found it just exactly as…" (καὶ εὗρον οὕτως καθὼς καὶ). This verse supports the third view. See also LXX texts by Wagner (Ibid.) that support more the third view than the fourth view. Dunn, 681 believes this view is much less likely.

[710] καὶ σκοπεῖτε τοὺς οὕτω περιπατοῦντας καθὼς ἔχετε τύπον ἡμᾶς ("and observe those who walk according to the pattern you have in us" NASB).

[711] Wagner, Heralds of the Good News, 280, n. 195.

[712] Lewis Johnson, Jr., "Evidence from Romans 9–11," 214. See also Bell, *Provoked to Jealousy*, 134–36; Bell, *The Irrevocable Call of God*, 258–60; Moo, 2nd, 735; Godet, 256; Dunn, 681; Byrne, 354;

[713] Bell, *The Irrevocable Call of God*, 259. See also Jewett, 701; Schreiner, 2nd, 602; Thielman, 547; Saucy, "Does Apostle Paul Reverse the Prophetic Tradition of the Salvation of Israel and the Nations?," 67; Barrett, 203.

[714] Moo, 2nd, 735. See also Dunn, 681 and Jewett, 701.

[715] Fitzmyer, 624 cites the following church Fathers who support spiritual Israel (both Jews and Gentiles): Irenaeus, Clement of Alexandria, Theodore of Mopsuestia and Theodoret of Cyrrhus. See also Calvin, 437; Godet, 256. Scholars from the 20th century onwards include: Barth, 416; Marten H. Woudstra, "Israel and the Church: A Case for Continuity," in Continuity and Discontinuity, 235–37; Wright, *The Climax of the Covenant*, 231–67, especially 249–50; Wright, "Romans and the Theology of Paul," 56–62 and Wright, 10:689. For a good concise critique of Wright, see Vanlaningham, "An Evaluation of N. T. Wright's View of Israel in Romans 11," 179–93; as well as the critique by Das, *Solving the Romans Debate*, 235–45. In Rom 11:28, Paul describes "Israel" as an

However, the contextual support indicates that Paul has used "Israel" 11 times[716] in Romans 9–11 and each time it refers to ethnic Israel.[717] Paul introduces himself in Rom 11:1 as an Israelite from the tribe of Benjamin being a part of the remnant of the nation by God's grace (9:5–7). Couple this thought with the statement in 9:4–5 and it appears that "all Israel" does not include Gentiles, especially since Paul contrasts Israel and "the nations" throughout 11:11–32. However, there are at least three different views as to who Paul means by ethnic Israel: (1) the elect of the nation of Israel;[718] (2) the whole nation, including every single member;[719] and (3) the nation as a whole, but not necessarily including every individual member.[720] The last two positions have the greater support.[721] The best view of "all Israel" is either the 12 tribes of Israel or a selection from all twelve tribes of Israel for this usage is common in the OT and in Jewish Second Temple period.[722]

The first position that the elect remnant of Israel is the "all Israel" has difficulties also. The collective remnant down through the ages still has the function of pointing to a future time when God will deal with the whole of Israel. The promise to Elijah which Paul uses in 11:2–5 and the promise to the remnant of Paul's day is to give them the hope of a greater and full salvation of the nation in the future.[723] In Paul's thought in Rom 9–11 the disobedience of Israel is the majority. In Rom 9:4 Paul grieves over Israel; in 9:31 Israel errors in pursuing a "law of

---

enemy. If Israel is the church in v. 26, how does one explain that Israel in v. 28 now means ethnic Israel? What in the context indicates this change when the context of Romans 11 is a discussion between ethnic Israelites and Gentiles? See Das, *Solving the Romans Debate*, 237–39.

[716] Rom 9:6[2x], 27[2x], 31; 10:19, 21; 11:2, 7, 25, 26.

[717] Watson, *Paul, Judaism and the Gentiles*, 311; Schreiner, 622; Moo, 2nd, 736. Some would say Rom 9:6 (cf. Gal 6:16) refers to both Jews and Gentiles. For example, Moo, 2nd, 736 accepts this view in Gal 6:16 and Phil 3:3 but not in Rom 9–11. Childs, *The Church's Guide for Reading* Paul, 185, note 169 concludes that anyone who believes the promises to ethnic Israel in Rom 9:1–5 have been forfeited and fulfilled by the church has a serious misunderstanding. For further support for ethnic Israel, see also Fitzmyer, 624 and Murray, 2:96; Osborne, "The OT Background of Paul's 'All Israel' in Romans 11:26a," 284–87 and Scott, "'And Then All Israel Will Be Saved' (Rom 11:26)," 489–527.

[718] Berkhof, *Systematic Theology*, 699; Berkouwer, *The Return of Christ*, 949; Horne, "The Meaning of the Phrase 'And Thus All Israel Will Be Saved' (Romans 11:26)," 333–34; Hoekema, *The Bible and the Future*, 140–47; Lenski, 723–28; Hendriksen, 2:381–82; Merkle, "Romans 11 and the Future of Ethnic Israel," 709–21 and Merkle, "A Typological Non-Future-Mass-Conversion View," 161–208; Kruse, 442–44, 450–51; Sanday and Headlam, 336. For a critique of this view, see Hoehner, "Israel in Romans 9-11," 155; Johnson, "Evidence from Romans 9–11," 217–19; Cranfield, 576–77; Murray, 2:97–98; Vlach, "Response to Merkle," 209–222; Zaspel and Hamilton, Jr. "Response to Merkle," 223–234; Das, *Solving the Romans Debate*, 245–60.

[719] Meyer, 2:234–35; Bell, *Provoked to Jealousy*, 137–39; Hoehner, "Israel in Romans 9–11," 155–56; Bell, *The Irrevocable Call of God*, 261–63; Osborne, "The OT Background of Paul's 'All Israel' in Romans 11:26a," 284–93; Jewett, 702.

[720] Godet, 411; C. K. Barrett, 223–24; Murray, 2:98; Käsemann, 313; Cranfield, 577; Dunn, 681; Moo, *The* Epistle *to the Romans*, 722.

[721] Scott, "'And Then All Israel Will Be Saved' (Rom 11:26)," 500–507 categorizes the OT use of כָּל־יִשְׂרָאֵל into 4 categories: (1) all 12 tribes, or northern or southern kingdom (Israel and Judah): a) pre-Monarchic Israel; b) United Monarchy of Israel and Judah; c) unified entity in the land despite the exiles and tribulation; d) unified entity through time (diachronic usage) Deut 13:11; Mal 3:22 (MT); Dan 9:11 (p. 503); (2) representatives or selection from all 12 tribes (or tribes of the northern kingdom after the united monarchy); (3) the northern tribes; 4) Judah. He also examined the Jewish literature and states that the expression "all Israel" was not widely used in Jewish Second Temple literature (p. 514). He concludes that "the OT 'all Israel' does not denote each and every individual, but rather a collective whole or some subset of the whole" (p. 515). Fitzmyer says that the Hebrew phrase כָּל־יִשְׂרָאֵל is used 148 times in the OT and Scott, Ibid., 500 say it occurs 154 times.

[722] Ibid., 507.

[723] Das, *Solving the Romans Debate*, 250; Hafemann, "The Salvation of Israel," 49.

righteousness;" in 10:21 Israel is a "disobedient and obstinate people." Then in 11:7 Paul declares that Israel did not receive what she was seeking. He breaks this down to say the elect obtained it, but the rest were hardened. "Their transgression" (vv. 11, 12) refers to the majority and Paul has the unbelief of the majority (vv. 12, 15) in mind when salvation now is going to the Gentiles while his desire is to see just "some" Israelites come to salvation during this age. Das is correct when he says, "Paul never refers to the 'full number *of the remnant.*' Paul does not claim that *some* of those who currently reject, an elect remnant, will come to accept. He claims that *the very Israelites* who reject will come to accept."[724] In the future, the nation of Israel that is hardened will one day accept the Lord. Romans 11:28 also helps to support this view. The dual status of Israel being enemies according to the gospel and beloved because of the fathers fits ethnic Israel as a whole and not the church or the elect remnant during this age (see comments on v. 28).

There are two other positions that need to be distinguished. Some understand "all Israel" as ethnic Israel in a diachronic sense,[725] referring to the nation as it exists throughout history while others understand it in a synchronic sense,[726] referring to one moment in history, usually referring to the eschatological salvation at the end. There seem to be only three occurrences in the OT of the phrase "all Israel" that is used diachronically.[727] Moo, 2nd, 738 states "no occurrence of the phrase 'all Israel' has a clear diachronic meaning."[728] Scott concludes, "With some possible exceptions, 'all Israel' normally refers to the contemporary people of Israel, rather than to the collective manifestation of the people either in the past or in the future." To say it another way, "more than 98% of all instances of the phrase [all Israel] are synchronic."[729] Thus, the synchronic sense is preferred.[730] Israel referring to one moment in history in this text, is referring to the eschatological salvation at the end when Jesus Christ comes.

Finally, does Paul understand "all Israel" (v.26) as a corporate ethnic group referring to every Israelite at the time of salvation or only Israel as a group (corporately) but not necessarily every single Israelite at the time stated? Paul uses a future passive (σωθήσεται) to express the thought about "all Israel will be saved." Paul uses this word 5 times in Rom 9–11 and 4 of the 5 times the grammatical construction is a future passive (9:27; 10:9, 13; 11:26; [11:14 aorist subjunctive]). In these texts Paul is expressing eternal salvation in context of restoration or at least using the background of the OT text that has the context of restoration (Jewett, 702). First, in Rom 9:27 the word σωθήσεται ("will be saved") is used for the Hebrew word יָשׁוּב ("return") from Isa 10:22 which refers to the remnant returning to the land of Israel after the exile. The

---

[724] Das, Ibid., 256. See also below under the "Biblical Theology" section for more opposition to this view.

[725] Sanday and Headlam, 335–36; Otried Hofius, "'All Israel Will Be Saved'," 35–36; Bell, *Provoked to Jealousy*, 140–41; Fitzmyer, 623; Bell, *The Irrevocable Call of God*, 264–65; Merkle, "Rom 11 and the Future of Ethnic Israel, 709–21.

[726] Murray, 2:98; Cranfield, 2:577; Dunn, 681–82; Moo, 2nd, 738; Hoehner, "Israel in Romans 9–11," 156; Schreiner, *Romans*, 622; Scott, "'And Then All Israel Will Be Saved' (Rom 11:26)," 498–519.

[727] Scott, "'And Then All Israel Will Be Saved' (Rom 11:26)," 507.

[728] Ibid., 500, n. 30 for the complication for the count of כָּל־יִשְׂרָאֵל in the LXX.

[729] Das, *Solving the Romans Debate*, 257.

[730] Even Wright, *The Climax of the Covenant*, 246 acknowledges that this is the usual view. For the debate and refutation of the *Sonderweg* ("special way") which proposes two ways for salvation, one for the Gentiles and one for the Jews, see Hafemann, "The Salvation of Israel in Romans 11:25–32," 38–58; Räisänen, "Paul, God and Israel: Romans 9–11 in Recent Research," 178–206; Hvalvik, "A 'Sonderweg' for Israel," 87–107; Moo, 2nd, 740–41; Hoehner, "Israel in Romans 9–11," 157–58; Bell, *Provoked to Jealousy*, 143–45; Shum, *Paul's Use of Isaiah in Romans*, 242, n. 193; Bell, *The Irrevocable Call of God*, 267–70. See Nanos, "'Callused', Not 'Hardened'," 59, n. 18 for more of an eclectic answer.

context of the Isaianic text of Isa 10:20–27 is the promise return and restoration of Israel.[731] Second, Rom 10:9 uses the future passive σωθήσῃ ("shall be saved") to express the essential condition of salvation which involves the heart speaking out of the mouth (Deut 30:8–14). Previous context in Deuteronomy 30:1–8 discussed the restoration of Israel to the land.[732] The third text is Rom 10:13 (σωθήσεται) which is a citation from Joel 3:5a (MT/LXX; Eng 2:32). Joel 3:5b (MT/LXX; Eng 2:32b) states that salvation is in Mount Zion and in Jerusalem where survivors in Israel will be restored.[733] It should be noted that after Rom 10:13 Paul focuses on the reason that Israel has not called on the Lord for salvation (10:14–21).[734] The fourth text is Rom 11:14 (*σώσω* aorist subjunctive) where the thought of Paul goes back to Rom 10:19 (Deut 32:21). The mission to the nations by Paul, the apostle to the Gentiles, will somehow make Israel jealous during the period of the Gentles salvation which happens before the ultimate restoration of Israel. At Israel's restoration the Gentiles will rejoice with Israel in Zion (Deut 32:43; Rom 15:10).[735] Notice that Paul's mission to the Gentiles is also a driving force for the restoration of Israel. Thus, it is not surprising that Paul would use at least Isa 59:20-21 and 27:9 in Rom 11:26b-27. Again, the context is the coming of the Messiah at His second coming will save and restore Israel (Moo, 2nd, 740; Cranfield, 577; Dunn, 692).

We will investigate these OT texts in the following pages, but we need to answer fully the question who is "All Israel" of Rom 11:26a? "All Israel" is the ethnic nation of Israel corporately at the time of the second coming of Jesus Christ and likely refers to every believing Israelite that is left on earth at this coming. One of the OT texts that is closely related to Rom 11:25–27 is Zech 12–14.[736] Zech 12:1 address Israel and mentions specifically Jerusalem and Judah (12:1, 2, 4, 5, 6, 7, 9, 10, 11; 13:1; 14:2, 4, 8, 10, 11, 12, 14, 16, 17). The connective phrase that links the context of Zech 12–14 is the phrase בַּיּוֹם־הַהוּא ("in that day" Zech 12:3, 4, 6, 8a, 8b, 9, 11; 13:1, 2, 4; 14:4, 6, 8, 9, 13, 20, 21). First, we learn that the time of Israel's salvation is immediately after the judgment upon the nations (Zech 12:9–10) and closely related to Rom 11:25–27. Second, the cause of this salvation is a work of God that comes in two stages: God pouring out a spirit of grace and supplication on Israel and Israelites "look" (repenting and believing)[737] on the Lord whom they crucified (Zech 12:8–10). Third, the extent of repentance is throughout the land (Zech 12:11–13). Fourth, the result of repentance is spiritual cleansing from sin, impurity, false prophets and gods (Zech 13:1–2). Finally, about 2/3 of the nation of Israel at this time will perish and about 1/3 will be the ones that will call upon the Lord and be saved at the Lord's second coming (Zech 12:10; 13:9).[738] These events are some of the events that precede the second coming of the Lord (Zech 14). The OT passages in Rom 11:26b and 27 confirm the time of Israel's eschatological salvation.

---

[731] See this commentary on Rom 9:27–28. See also Scott, "'And Then All Israel Will Be Saved' (Rom 11:26)," 519–20 and Sullivan, *The Isaianic New Exodus in Rom 9–11*, 210–16.

[732] Scott, Ibid., 520-21 and Sullivan, Ibid., 260–67.

[733] See this commentary on Rom 10:11. Scott, Ibid., 521 and Sullivan, Ibid., 275.

[734] Scott, Ibid., 521

[735] See this commentary on Rom 10:11. Scott, Ibid.

[736] Feinberg, *God Remembers: A Study of Zechariah*, 228; Vlach, *He will Reign Forever*, 538.

[737] Unger, *Zechariah*, 217–18; Barker, "Zechariah," 683.

[738] McClain, *The Greatness of the Kingdom*, 197–98; Fruchtenbaum, *Israelology*, 546, 787; Fruchtenbaum, *The Footsteps of the Messiah*, 341, 799; Woods, *The Coming Kingdom*, 162–63; Walvoord, *The Prophecy Knowledge Handbook*, 330–312; Unger, Ibid., 234–35; Barker, "Zechariah," 683–84, 687; Klein, *Zechariah*, 369, 393.

11:26b–27 Ἥξει ἐκ Σιὼν ὁ ῥυόμενος, ἀποστρέψει ἀσεβείας ἀπὸ Ἰακώβ. [27]καὶ αὕτη αὐτοῖς ἡ παρ' ἐμοῦ διαθήκη, ὅταν ἀφέλωμαι τὰς ἁμαρτίας αὐτῶν. "The deliverer will come from Zion; he will turn away ungodliness from Jacob. 27 And this is my covenant with them, when I take away their sins." Paul supports his statement that "all Israel will be saved"[739] by quoting the conflation of at least Isaiah 59:20–21 and 27:9.[740]

Isaiah 59:20-21 & 27:9a in Romans 11:26-27

Isaiah 59:20–21 (LXX) καὶ ἥξει ἕνεκεν Σιων ὁ ῥυόμενος καὶ ἀποστρέψει ἀσεβείας ἀπὸ Ιακωβ. [21]καὶ αὕτη αὐτοῖς ἡ παρ' ἐμοῦ διαθήκη, εἶπεν κύριος· τὸ πνεῦμα τὸ ἐμόν, ὅ ἐστιν ἐπὶ σοί, καὶ τὰ ῥήματα, ἃ ἔδωκα εἰς τὸ στόμα σου, οὐ μὴ ἐκλίπῃ ἐκ τοῦ στόματός σου καὶ ἐκ τοῦ στόματος τοῦ σπέρματός σου, εἶπεν γὰρ κύριος, ἀπὸ τοῦ νῦν καὶ εἰς τὸν αἰῶνα.
Isaiah 59:20–21 (NETS)[741] And the one who delivers will come for Sion's sake,
and he will turn impiety away from Iakob. [21]And this is the covenant to them from me, said the Lord, my spirit that is upon you and my words that I have put in your mouth shall not fail out of your mouth or out of the mouth of your offspring, for the Lord has said it, from now on and forever.
Isaiah 59:20–21 (MT)

20 וּבָא לְצִיּוֹן גּוֹאֵל וּלְשָׁבֵי פֶשַׁע בְּיַעֲקֹב נְאֻם יהוה׃
21 וַאֲנִי זֹאת בְּרִיתִי אוֹתָם אָמַר יהוה רוּחִי אֲשֶׁר עָלֶיךָ וּדְבָרַי אֲשֶׁר־שַׂמְתִּי בְּפִיךָ לֹא־יָמוּשׁוּ מִפִּיךָ
וּמִפִּי זַרְעֲךָ וּמִפִּי זֶרַע זַרְעֲךָ אָמַר יהוה מֵעַתָּה וְעַד־עוֹלָם׃

Isaiah 59:20–21(NASB) A Redeemer will come to Zion, And to those who turn from transgression in Jacob," declares the LORD. [21]"As for Me, this is My covenant with them," says the LORD: "My Spirit which is upon you, and My words which I have put in your mouth shall not depart from your mouth, nor from the mouth of your offspring, nor from the mouth of your offspring's offspring," says the LORD, "from now and forever."
Isaiah 27:9 (LXX) διὰ τοῦτο ἀφαιρεθήσεται ἡ ἀνομία Ιακωβ, καὶ τοῦτό ἐστιν ἡ εὐλογία αὐτοῦ, ὅταν ἀφέλωμαι αὐτοῦ τὴν ἁμαρτίαν, ὅταν θῶσιν πάντας τοὺς λίθους τῶν βωμῶν κατακεκομμένους ὡς κονίαν λεπτήν, καὶ οὐ μὴ μείνῃ τὰ δένδρα αὐτῶν, καὶ τὰ εἴδωλα αὐτῶν ἐκκεκομμένα ὥσπερ δρυμὸς μακράν.
Isaiah 27:9 (NETS) Because of this the lawlessness of Iakob will be removed. And this is his blessing, when I remove his sin, when they make all the stones of the altars broken pieces like fine dust, and their trees will not remain, and their idols will be cut down like a forest far away.
Isaiah 27:9 (MT) לָכֵן בְּזֹאת יְכֻפַּר עֲוֹן־יַעֲקֹב וְזֶה כָּל־פְּרִי הָסִר חַטָּאתוֹ בְּשׂוּמוֹ׀ כָּל־אַבְנֵי מִזְבֵּחַ כְּאַבְנֵי־גִר מְנֻפָּצוֹת לֹא־יָקֻמוּ אֲשֵׁרִים וְחַמָּנִים׃
Isaiah 27:9 (NASB) Therefore through this Jacob's iniquity will be forgiven; And this will be the full price of the pardoning of his sin: When he makes all the altar stones like pulverized chalk stones; *When* Asherim and incense altars will not stand.
Romans 11:26b–27 Ἥξει ἐκ Σιὼν ὁ ῥυόμενος, ἀποστρέψει ἀσεβείας ἀπὸ Ἰακώβ. [27]καὶ αὕτη αὐτοῖς ἡ παρ' ἐμοῦ διαθήκη, ὅταν ἀφέλωμαι τὰς ἁμαρτίας αὐτῶν.

---

[739] Scott, "'And Then All Israel Will Be Saved' (Rom 11:26)," 519–24 demonstrates the usage of σῴζω in Rom 9–11 has the background of the Old Testament restoration.

[740] Much of the information concerning Rom 11:26b–27 is found in Sullivan, *The Isaianic New Exodus in Rom 9–11*, 2nd ed., chapter 10.

[741] New English Translation of the Septuagint.

Romans 11:26b–27 "The deliverer will come from Zion; he will turn away ungodliness from Jacob." [27]and this is my covenant with them, when I remove their sins.

For the most part, Paul quotes each text in the form that is identical with the LXX Isaiah.[742] The major textual dispute, which has brought out a series of comments, is the reading of ἕνεκεν Σιών ("for the sake of Zion") in the LXX,[743] which becomes ἐκ Σιών ("from Zion") in Romans 9:26. The MT reads לְצִיּוֹן ("to Zion").[744] Though it is not possible to know exactly how or where Paul obtained the phrase, he makes use of this phrase and quotation to accomplish his point in the argument of Romans 11.[745] Wagner has correctly argued for the following position: "Rather than focus on the Lord's victorious return *to* Zion, as does LXX Isaiah 59:20, Paul's quotation depicts the Lord's coming in person *from* a restored Zion to bring deliverance to his people who are scattered among the nations."[746] The time of this deliverance is the second coming of Jesus Christ. Paul uses three future tenses in Rom 11:26–27: "all Israel will be saved," "the Deliverer will come," and "He will turn ungodliness from Jacob" (Schreiner, 2nd, 604). In the Lord's second coming He will convert and cleanse Israel from their sins.[747] This eschatological deliverance at the second coming,[748] which uses the phrase ἐκ Σιών, is found in passages like

---

[742] For textual discussion on the quotation, see Stanley, *Paul and the Language of Scripture*, 166–71 and Wagner, *Heralds of the Good News*, 282–84, especially the footnotes.

[743] In the LXX manuscripts, ἐκ Σιών is found in the minuscules 22c–93, 564*, 407, 534, the Bohairic Copitic version and quotations by Ephiphanius, Hilary, and Jerome. Symachus and Aquila has τῇ Σιών (Ziegler, *Isaias*, 14:343; Stanley, "'The Redeemer Will Come ἐκ Σιων'," 133, note 43). For an extended discussion of the textual differences and possible Hebrew or Greek *Vorlage*, see Stanley, Ibid., 133–35, especially n. 44. Fitzmyer, 624 believes ἐκ Σιών was possibly an "influence from Ps 14:7, or perhaps it comes from a copyist's error, misreading εἰς Σιών." See also Jewett, 703–04, especially note 87 where several authors argue that Paul used a text that is not extant today. This is difficult to prove. For a critique of Berndt Schaller's position that Paul used a corrupt text, see Pinto, "The Contribution of the Isaiah Quotations to Paul's Argument in Romans 9–11," 168–69. It is possible Paul uses the minority Greek witnesses, but it is possible that he borrows or conflates this phrase from another text.

[744] The Hebrew לְ is translated in a general way ("with respect to") in the LXX use of ἕνεκεν where one would expect more of a local connotation ("to"). This article "is not the proper particle of motion or direction, though it often supplies its place as well as that of other prepositions … [it] properly denotes relation in the widest sense, and commonly equivalent to *as to, with respect to* … determined by the context" (Alexander, *Isaiah*, 2:377). Probably referring to location (HALOT, 508; BDB, 510).

[745] Seifrid, 674 states that "Paul's reading is probably theologically motivated, since his entire citation of the text is highly interpretive." Stanley, "'The Redeemer Will Come ἐκ Σιων'," 125, n. 26 thinks it may be "a reference to the place of Jesus' birth ('Zion' = Palestine or the Jewish people), his death ('Zion' = Jerusalem), or his expected return." Fitzmyer, 625 merely refers to "from Zion" as an indication of Jesus' origin (from David or more generically from the Jews) or possibly referring to Jerusalem, the place of his death and resurrection. Holland, 385 gives two possibilities: (1) he is a Jewish Messiah, but he comes to save both Jews and Gentiles or (2) Paul is stressing the source of salvation that it is not in the institution of Judah, but it comes from Zion. Understanding the phrase from its Jewish OT setting, Holland's second position appears to be a good possibility, though all these possibilities depend to some extent on accepting that Paul deliberately modified the LXX text, which cannot be established for certain. On the other hand, it is entirely plausible that Paul chose his particular reading from among existing variants.

[746] Wagner, *Heralds of the Good News*, 284.

[747] See comments on Rom 11:25–26a concerning the events of Jesus Christ's coming and Israel in Zech 12–14.

[748] For support of this view, see Jewett, 704; Scott, "'And Then All Israel Will Be Saved' (Rom 11:26)," 496–97; Kim, *God, Israel, and the Gentiles*, 138–39; Thielman, 548; Schreiner, 2nd, 603; Middendorf, 1168; Moo, 2nd, 739–40 (Moo,727-28 slightly more developed in his 2nd ed.); Lambrecht, *Pauline Studies*, 46; Hofius, "'All Israel Will Be Saved,'" 36; Dunn, 682; Käsemann, 314; Sandy and Headlam, 337; Cranfield, 578; Holland, 385, n.

Isaiah 2:3–4, Micah 4:2–3, Joel 3:16 (MT/LXX 4:16), Psalm 14:7 (MT 14:7; LXX 13:7), Psalm 53:6 (MT Ps 53:7; LXX Ps 52:7),[749] and Psalm 110:2–3 (MT 110:2–3; LXX 109:2–3). This kind of deliverance is found in the context of the quotations in the Old Testament that Paul quotes in Romans 11:26–27. Scott states that "[a]ccording to Isa 49:22; 60:4, 9; 66:20, the nations will bring the exiles as an offering to the Temple, implying not only that the nations will become devotees *before* the exiles are brought back to Jerusalem, but also that Jerusalem experiences restoration before many exiles arrive."[750]

Isaiah 27 and 59 are found in the background of the Zion traditions[751] with the warrior motif[752] in the pattern of the NE,[753] which helps to interpret the thought of Paul. Käsemann agrees that the underlying tradition is "the apocalyptic expectation of the restitution of Israel and the associated pilgrimage of the nations to Zion" (312). In Isaiah 59, the Lord bares his mighty arm of salvation by donning his warrior battle dress of righteousness, salvation, vengeance, and fury (59:16–17) and comes to judge his adversaries even to the farthest coastlands so that his name and glory may be seen throughout the earth (59:18–19). The Redeemer[754] will come to Zion for there he will rule and reign (Isa 59:20; 60:14), and from the physical city of Zion, the effects of redemption will flow out to the Jewish people and also to the nations. At this point, it is critical for understanding Paul not to miss the flow of the Isaianic context of chapters 59–60 and mistakenly take Zion in Romans 11:26b (Isa 59:20) as heavenly Zion.[755]

---

32. Others refer it to the first coming of Christ (Lenski, 729; Wright, *The Climax of the Covenant*, 250–51; Wright, "Romans and the Theology of Paul," 60–61; Kirk, "Why Does the Deliver Come ἐκ Σιὼν [Romans 11.26]?," 81–99); Das, *Paul and the Jews*, 109–11.

[749] LXX Ps 13:7 and LXX Ps 52:7 are identical.

[750] Scott, "'And Then All Israel Will Be Saved' (Rom 11:26)," 495. Scott also points out that *Psalms of Solomon* 17 states that the same process: a restoration in Jerusalem, the land, and then later the Diaspora returns with the pilgrimage of the nations (p. 496). On the role of Messiah and the regathering of the Diaspora, Scott draws attention to sources that support this point: *4 Ezra* 13:39–50; *2 Baruch* 40:2; *Targum Jeremiah* 33:13.

[751] For a summary of the Zion Tradition, see Sullivan, *The Isaianic NE in Rom 9–11*, 348–55.

[752] For a summary of the warrior motif, see Sullivan, Ibid., 352–61.

[753] For a definition of the concept of the NE, see the introduction to Romans 9–11 in this commentary or Sullivan, Ibid., 12–17.

[754] The LXX translates the Hebrew word גאל with ὁ ῥυόμενος. Stanley, "'The Redeemer Will Come ἐκ Σιων'," 137 does not believe that Paul read the term ὁ ῥυόμενος in a Christological sense. However, the Christological interpretation of this phrase is widely accepted: Dunn, *The New Perspective on Paul*, 443; Jewett, 704; Wagner, *Heralds of the Good News*, 297, n. 236; Schreiner, 619–20; Hofius, "'All Israel Will Be Saved,'" 36; Dunn, 682; Cranfield, 578; Sanday and Headlam, 337. Holland, 386, believes that Paul chose the term "deliverer" because in his paschal theology the term "Redeemer" was dropped in preference for the title "Firstborn" (see Holland, *Contours of Pauline Theology*, 207–324). This position is debatable, but Holland has some forceful arguments.

[755] Wagner, *Herald of the Good News*, 276–98; Fitzmyer, 624; Stanley, "'The Redeemer Will Come ἐκ Σιων'," 138; Hoehner, "Israel in Romans 9–11," 157 take it as physical Zion on earth (cf. Rom 9:33). Others take Zion as a heavenly Zion (cf. Gal 4:26) and not an earthly one for which the deliverer will come (Holland, 385; Seifrid, 673; Cranfield, 578; Jewett, 704; Schreiner, 2nd, 603; G. Wagner, "The Future of Israel: Reflections on Romans 9–11," 109–10). Moo, 2nd, 742–43 believes Paul is using a spatial metaphor because Israel is not located in Zion for they have rejected the deliverer, pictured as located outside of the Holy Land, and they are in a new spiritual exile. Scott states, "The restoration begins in Jerusalem and the land but is later completed when the Diaspora returns in conjunction with (and facilitated by!) the eschatological pilgrimage of the nations. In both stages, the Messiah is very much involved: restoration begins in Israel, the nations are brought in, and then 'all Israel will be saved'" ("'And Then All Israel Will Be Saved' [Rom 11:26]," 496). For Scott, there is today an "already" stage of a remnant of Israelites that are being saved and then a "not yet" stage when "all Israel" will be saved at the parousia of Christ. For a different view on this point, see Donaldson, *Paul and the Gentiles*, 187–97. Wagner,

The glory of the Lord has its effect upon the nations, for they bring their wealth and escort the dispersed Israelites back to Zion; and this return is connected to the redemption of God from Zion (Isa 60:1–5,15–22). The streaming of the nations and the dispersed from Israel all coming to the source of redemption in Zion has caused some to submit another Old Testament source in the conflation of the quotation in Romans 11:26–27. One of the primary candidates for this source is Psalm 14:7 (LXX Ps 13:7): "O that deliverance for Israel would come from Zion (ἐκ Σιών)! When the Lord restores the fortunes of his people, Jacob will rejoice; Israel will be glad."[756] If Paul draws on Psalm 14:7 in his quotation of Romans 11:26 then the conflation would also fit the underlying NE theme that is established in Deuteronomy 30:1–10.[757] Wright seems to agree when he states that the "language of covenant renewal, replete with echoes of Joel 2, Ezekiel 36, and Jeremiah 31, also sends us back to Deuteronomy 30, as expounded in [Rom] 10:6–11."[758] The Lord's covenantal promise is to restore his people back to the land and to circumcise their hearts so that they will love and obey God. The redemption will come from Zion, for the Redeemer who reigns in Zion will bring his people to the city as the nations make their pilgrimage to this place (Isa 60, 66). At this time, the Lord's covenantal promise to forgive their sins will be seen in its fullness. This forgiveness is reflected in the New covenant recorded in Jer 31:31–37. Here one sees that the Lord will put the law in their hearts, a heart that has been changed as well as the Spirit that will give them ability to obey the Lord (cf. Deut 30:1–10; Ezk 36:22–28).

The supplemental phrase from Isaiah 27:9 concerning Israel's iniquity being forgiven is set in the context of the phrase "in that day" (27:2, 12, 13), which often has an eschatological sense. At this time, Israel will repent from their idolatry and sins (27:9b) and the Lord will regather and restore his people back to the "holy mountain at Jerusalem" (27:13). Isaiah 59:16–21 stresses God's work of grace and mercy for he will initiate this undeserved redemption and forgiveness. In Isaiah 27:9–13, the responsibility of Israel to repent from their sins is more the focus as God forgives and restores the people to Zion. The victorious Warrior who brings judgment to the nations and redemption to Zion will set up his reign in Zion and restore his people to his holy mountain. Part of this restoration is the forgiveness of their sins. This motif is part of the NE theme that is summarized in the Song of Moses: "Praise his people, O you nations; for he avenges the blood of his servants, and takes vengeance on his adversaries, and makes expiation for the land of his people" (Deut 32:43).

Paul seems to conflate Isaiah 59:20–21 with 27:9 in Romans 11:26–27, for both texts have the background of the Zion traditions with the NE motifs of redemption and forgiveness of sins. The background of the Zion traditions, especially the eschatological pilgrimage of the

---

Heralds of the Good News, 293, note 227 gives a good critique of Donaldson. See also Wagner, "The Future of Israel," 105.

[756] Other sources that have been submitted because of the use of the phrase ἐκ Σιών are Isa 2:3–4/Mic 4:2–3; Joel 3:16 (MT/LXX 4:16); Ps 110:2 (109:2 LXX), Amos 1:2; Obad 1:21 (see Wagner, *Heralds of the Good News*, 285). Bruno, "The Deliverer from Zion," 123–32 supports Isa 2:3–4 as the source. Stanley, "'The Redeemer Will Come ἐκ Σιων'," 135 also mention these texts and gives an historical argument about the Jews of the Diaspora. Evans, "Paul and the Prophets: Prophetic Criticism in the Epistle to the Romans," 127 "wonder[s] if it is not a change suggested by the messianically understood Numbers 24:17: 'A star will arise from [ἐκ] Jacob, a man will arise from [ἐκ] Israel.'" This is possible but the position is difficult to substantiate in the absence of specific evidence.

[757] Scott, "'And Then All Israel Will Be Saved' (Rom 11:26)," 522–23 connects Isa 59:21 with Deut 30:11–14, but he does not connect it with the NE.

[758] Wright, "The Letter to the Romans," 692.

nations to Zion with the dispersed Israelites, provides helpful reasons to explain why Paul declares that a deliverer is sourced in Zion and comes from Zion. The NE theology supporting this quotation from Isaiah is Deuteronomy 30:1–10.[759] Wagner has succinctly summarized the point, "We have found Paul's reading of the prophet to be shaped by his larger cultural context as well as by features of the wider literary and theological contexts of Isaiah."[760] Wagner's point confirms the findings of the author of this commentary, which has attempted to establish the Dodd/Hays concept of total context in Paul's use of Isaianic texts in Romans 9–11.[761]

The illustration of the olive tree in Romans 11:17–24 gives the present generation hope that God will accomplish his promises and graft Israel back into his blessings in the future (Rom 11:23–24). In Romans 11:30–32, Paul accentuates and magnifies the mercy of God in his sovereign plan. However, the general time and certainty of the fulfilling the Lord's covenant to Israel is expressed in Romans 11:25–28.

Biblical Theological Comments

Michael Vlack is correct when he states that there is only one group of people that God used to bring the blessing to the world while in unbelief; then, God will use this group to bring a greater blessing to the world when this group believes. This group cannot be the church because the true church is not in unbelief and does not bring in a global restoration of all things. This group is not the remnant of Israel because the remnant alone does not bring in the world blessing and historically often the remnant has suffered at times with Israel as a whole has suffered. The one group that will fulfill the above first statement is the nation of Israel as a whole which at this present time is in unbelief, but one day in the future will be saved.[762]

In Rom 9, Paul states that not all ethnic Israel is Israel in a spiritual sense (9:6) and God has chosen some of the Israelites to be saved (9:11–16). In Rom 11, he states that some of ethnic Israel were chosen and become part of the remnant of salvation at this time (9:27) during the church age, but the rest were hardened (9:28–29; 11:7). Then he declares that all of ethnic Israel will be saved (11:26). These statements are not a contradiction, but an important distinction in salvation-history. James in Acts 15:13–14 says that God is taking out a people among the Gentiles to be saved (Rom 9:24–26) starting during the first century. When the full number of the Gentiles are brought into God's saving promise then God will at that time save all ethnic Israel. Paul is not arguing that all ethnic Israelites throughout history will be saved. Instead, he affirms that God will have mercy on all ethnic Israel at a point in time on a future generation of Israelites after the last number of Gentiles have believed. Schreiner (2nd, 606) states it this way: "Gentiles were elected to salvation when the Jews were expecting to be the special objects of God's favor, and the Jews will be grafted in again at a time in which gentiles will be tempted to believe that they are superior to ethnic Israel." Paul will argue in Rom 11:30–32 that this salvation-history plan by God was constructed so that God alone will be glorified in displaying His mercy upon all!

---

[759] See the discussion in Sullivan, 2nd, *The Isaianic NE in Rom 9–11*, 266–70.

[760] Wagner, *Heralds of the Good News*, 286, note 212.

[761] For a brief summary of the Dodd/Hays total context concept, see the introduction to Romans 9–11 in this commentary or Sullivan, 2nd, *The Isaianic NE in Rom 9–11*, 9, 53–54.

[762] Vlach, "A Non-Typological Future-Mass-Conversion View," 43.

The understanding of "all Israel" is important in this section. Fred Zaspel and James Hamilton, Jr. give 11 reasons why they believe that "all Israel" in Rom 11:26 does not refer to a cumulative total of ethnic Israelites (a remnant) across the centuries, but it refers to ethnic Israel as a people at a given point of time in the future.[763] First, "all Israel" in the OT overwhelmingly refers to corporate Israel that exist at a given time. Second, Israel is lost, and the remnant are those Israelites who believe. To affirm the salvation of just the remnant would leave the problem of "all Israel" unsolved. Third, there is a contrast between "some" of Israel and the remnant (11:5, 7, 14) in comparison to "all Israel" (11:26) and their "fullness" (11:12). The sum of all the remnant is still the remnant. Identifying the remnant with all Israel confuses Paul's contrast. Fourth, the remnant only interpretation misunderstands the role of the remnant which is a hope for future Israel as a whole. The concept of the remnant in Rom 11:1–10 provides the hope and fuller future plans for ethnic Israel in 11:11–32. Fifth, the contrast in 11:12 and 15 concerns corporate Israel. This thought concerning corporate Israel is still in view in vv. 23–26. Paul is not admonishing the remnant to persevere to the end, but that Israel be grafted back in "again."–a reversal of "partial hardening" to "all Israel saved." Sixth, the mystery of 11:25 involved a succession of events: Israel's failure, Gentile inclusion and then Israel's regathering. The mystery was not that the remnant would be saved–the OT spoke about this. The manner of Israel's salvation was the issue: first to Israel, then from Israel to the Gentiles and then back to Israel. Seventh, the problem of v. 25 finds its answer in v. 26. "The Israel who is partially and temporarily hardened (v. 25) is the Israel who will be saved (v. 26), whose sins will be forgiven (v. 27), and who are presently enemies of the gospel yet beloved (v. 28)" (p. 127). Eighth, the OT promises used by Paul in 11:26–27 (Isa 27:9; 59:20–21; Jer 31:31–24) explicitly express the time of national conversion of corporate Israel and not merely the remnant. Ninth, the word "Jacob" (11:26b) is used for the man Jacob, or to the whole of Israel and at times "Jacob" is distinguished from the remnant (Isa 10:21), but "Jacob as the remnant seems unprecedented" (p. 128). Tenth, what is presently pruned from the olive tree is corporate Israel and corporate Israel will be grafted back into the olive tree. Thus, corporate ethnic Israel not the remnant, remains in Paul's view to be grafted back into the blessings of the olive tree. Finally, in 11:28 Paul says, "they are enemies" ("all Israel" [v. 26a] is ethnic Israel as a whole, "Jacob" v. 26b). However, at the same time they are beloved because of the promises to the fathers which will be the future reversal of the corporate nation's unbelief.

Application and Devotional Implications

Paul does not want us to be ignorant about the mystery concerning Israel and the Gentiles. A "mystery" in Scripture is basically God's wisdom revealed to man through divine revelation. Paul has been given the privilege to explain the plan of God concerning His people, Israel. He makes the mystery known to Israel so they will be encouraged though at present a partial hardening has been placed on Israel as a whole because of their unbelief (11:7). He is especially making this mystery known to Gentiles so that they will not be prideful because they received the blessings of God (i.e. their salvation) by being grafted into the Olive tree. God also uses the salvation of Gentiles as a means to make Israel jealous to the point that some (a remnant) will trust in their Messiah in this present age (11:13–14). The mystery of God also

[763] Zaspel and Hamilton, "A Typological Future-Mass-Conversion View," 123–29,

includes that Israel as a whole will continue until the fullness of the Gentiles come in (11:25). When the full number and blessings of the Gentiles are completed then all Israel will be saved. In other words, there is coming a time when the last Gentile is saved and then the full number of Israelites will repent and believe in their Messiah Jesus. Paul calls it a "fullness" in 11:12. He calls it an "acceptance" in 11:15. At Christ's second coming, God says in Zech 12:10, "And I will pour out on the house of David and on the inhabitants of Jerusalem, the Spirit of grace and supplication so that they will look on Me whom they have pierced; and they will mourn for Him, as one mourns for an only son, and they will weep bitterly over Him like the bitter weeping of a first born." God's sovereign hand through the Holy Spirit will cause Israel to repent and they will experience the grace of forgiveness in the New Covenant expressed by the OT passages in Isaiah 59:20–21, 27:9, and Jer 31:34 that are cited in Rom 11:26–27. Whether you are an Israelite, or a Gentile the Lord offers salvation to you through faith in the saving work of Jesus Christ on the cross.

Selected Bibliography

Alexander, Joseph Addison, *Commentary on the Prophecies of Isaiah*, 2 vols. in 1 (Grand Rapids: Zondervan,1975).

Barker, Kenneth L. "Zechariah," in *Expositor Bible Commentary*, gen. ed. Frank E. Gaebelein, vol. 7 (Grand Rapids: Zondervan, 1985).

Beale, G. K. and Benjamin L. Gladd, *Hidden but Now Revealed: A Biblical Theology of Mystery* (Downers Grove: IVP, 2014).

Bell, Richard H. *Provoked to Jealousy: The Origin and Purpose of the Jealousy Motif in Romans 9–11*, Wissenshaftliche Untersuchungen zum Neuen Testament 263 (Tübingen: Mohr Siebeck, 1994).

Bell, Richard H. *The Irrevocable Call of God: An Inquiry into Paul's Theology of Israel*, Wissenshaftliche Untersuchungen zum Neuen Testament 184, (Tübingen: Mohr Siebeck, 2005).

Berkhof, Louis, *Systematic Theology* (Grand Rapids: Eerdmans, 1946).

Berkouwer, G. C. *The Return of Christ* (Grand Rapids: Eerdmans, 1972).

Brown, Francis, Samuel Rolles Driver, and Charles Augustus Briggs, *Enhanced Brown-Driver-Briggs Hebrew and English Lexicon* (Oxford: Clarendon Press, 1977), 510.

Campbell, William S. *Paul and the Creation of Christian Identity* (London: T & T Clark, A Continuum Imprint, 2008).

Childs, Brevard S. *The Church's Guide for Reading Paul: The Canonical Shaping of the Pauline Corpus* (Grand Rapids: Eerdmans, 2008).

Das, A. Andrew. *Paul and the Jews* (Peabody MA: Hendrickson, 2003).

Das, A. Andrew. *Solving the Romans Debate* (Minneapolis: Fortress Press, 2007).

Donaldson, Terence L. *Paul and the Gentiles: Remapping the Apostle's Convictional World* (Minneapolis: Fortress Press, 1997).

Dunn, J. D. G. *The New Perspective on Paul*, rev. ed. (Grand Rapids: Eerdmans, 2008).

Evans, Craig A., "Paul and the Prophets: Prophetic Criticism in the Epistle to the Romans (with special reference to Romans 9–11)," in *Romans and the People of God: Essays in Honor of Gordon D. Fee on the Occasion of His 65th Birthday*, eds. Sven K. Soderlund and N. T. Wright (Grand Rapids: Eerdmans, 1999).

Feinberg, Charles L. *God Remembers: A Study of Zechariah* (Portland: Multinomah Press, 1965).

Fruchtenbaum, Arnold G. *Israelology: The Missing Link in Systematic Theology* (Tustin, CA: Ministries Press, rev. 1994).

Fruchtenbaum, Arnold G. *The Footsteps of the Messiah: A Study of the Sequence of Prophetic Events*, rev. ed. (Trustin, CA: Ariel Ministries, 2003).

Hafemann, Scott. "The Salvation of Israel in Romans 11:25–32: A Response to Krister Stendahl." *Ex Auditu* 4 (1988): 38–58.

Hoehner, Harold W. "Israel in Romans 9-11," in *Israel, the Land and the People: An Evangelical Affirmation of God's Promises*, eds. H. Wayne House (Grand Rapids: Kregel Publications, 1998).

Hoekema, Anthony A. *The Bible and the Future* (Grand Rapids: Eerdmans, 1979).

Hofius, Otfried, "Das Evangelium und Israel," in *Paulusstudien*, Wissenschaftliche Untersuchungen zum Neuen Testament, 51 (Tübingen: Mohr Siebeck, 1989).

Hofius, Otfried, "'All Israel Will Be Saved': Divine Salvation and Israel's Deliverance in Romans 9–11," *The Princeton Seminary Bulletin*, Supplement 1, (1990): 19–39.

Holland, Tom. *Contours of Pauline Theology: A Radical New Survey of the Influence on Paul's Biblical Writings* (Fearn, Scotland: Christian Focus, 2004).

Horne, Charles M. Horne, "The Meaning of the Phrase 'And Thus All Israel Will Be Saved' (Romans 11:26)," *Journal of the Evangelical Theological Society* 21 (December 1978): 329–34.

Van der Horst, Pieter W. "'Only then will all Israel be saved': A Short Note on the Meaning of καὶ οὕτως in Romans 11:26," *Journal of Biblical Literature* 119 (2000): 521–39.

Hvalvik, Reidar, "A 'Sonderweg' for Israel: A Critical Examination of a Current Interpretation of Romans 11:25–27," *Journal for the Study of the New Testament* 38 (February 1990): 87–107.

Johnson, S. Lewis, Jr. "Evidence from Romans 9–11," in *A Case for Premillennalism: A New Consensus* (Chicago: Moody Press, 1992).

Klein, George L. *Zechariah*, vol. 21B, The New American Commentary (Nashville, TN: B & H, 2008).

Kirk, J. R. Daniel, "Why Does the Deliver Come ἐκ Σιὼν (Romans 11.26)?," *Journal for the Study of the New Testament* 33 (2010): 81–99.

Koehler, Ludwig, et al., *The Hebrew and Aramaic Lexicon of the Old Testament* (Leiden: E. J. Brill, 1994–2000).

Lambrecht, Jan, *Pauline Studies, Collected Essays,* Bibliotheca Ephemeridum Theologicarum Lovaniensium, 115 (Leuven: Peeters, 1994).

McClain, Alva J. *The Greatness of the Kingdom* (Winona Lake, IN: BMH Books, 1974).

Merkle, Ben L. "Romans 11 and the Future of Ethnic Israel," *Journal of the Evangelical Theological Society* 43 (December 2000); 707–21.

Merkle, Benjamin L. "A Typological Non-Future-Mass-Conversion View," in *Three Views on Israel and the Church: Perspectives on Romans 9–11*, eds. Jared Compton and Andrew D. Naselli (Grand Rapids: Kregel, 2018), 161–208.

Montanari, Franco, ed. Madeleine Goh and Chad Schroeder, *The Brill Dictionary of Ancient Greek* (Leiden; Boston: Brill, 2015).

Nanos, Mark D. "'Callused', Not 'Hardened': Paul's Revelation of Temporary Protection Until All Israel Can Be Healed," in *Reading Paul in Context: Explorations in Identity Formation: Essays in Honour of William S. Campbell* (London: T & T Clark, 2010).

Nanos, Mark D. "'Broken Branches': A Pauline Metaphor Gone Awry?" in *Between Gospel and Election*, ed. Florian Wilk and J. Ross Wagner with assistance of Frank Schleritt, Wissenschaftliche Untersuchungen zum Neuen Testament, 25 (Tübingen: Mohr Siebeck, 2010), 339–76.

Osborne, William L. "The OT Background of Paul's 'All Israel' in Romans 11:26a," *Asia Journal of Theology* 2 (1988): 282–93.

Pinto, Carlos Osvaldo Cordoro, "The Contribution of the Isaiah Quotations to Paul's Argument in Romans 9–11" (Ph.D. diss., Dallas Theological Seminary, 2003).

Räisänen, Heikki, "Paul, God and Israel: Romans 9–11 in Recent Research," in *The Social World of Formative Christianity and Judaism: Essays in Tribute to Howard Clark Kee* (Philadelphia: Fortress Press, 1988), 178–206.

Saucy, Robert L. "Does Apostle Paul Reverse the Prophetic Tradition of the Salvation of Israel and the Nations?," in *Building on the Foundations of Evangelical Theology: Essays in Honor of John S. Feinberg*, eds Gregg R. Allison and Stephen J. Wellum (Wheaton: Crossway, 2015).

Scott, James M. "'And Then All Israel Will Be Saved' (Rom 11:26)," in *Restoration: Old Testament, Jewish, and Christian Perspectives*, ed. James M. Scott. Supplements to the Journal for the Study of Judaism, vol. 72 (Leiden: Brill, 2001), 489–527.

Shum, Shiu-Lun, *Paul's Use of Isaiah in Romans: A Comparative Study of Paul's Letter to the Romans and the Sibylline and Qumran Sectarian Texts* (Tübingen: Mohr Siebeck, 2002).

Storms, Sam, *Kingdom Come: The Amillennial Alternative* (Fearn, Scotland: Mentor, 2013).

Stanley, Christopher D. "'The Redeemer Will Come ἐκ Σιων': Romans 11:26–27 Revisited." In *Paul and the Scriptures of Israel*. Journal for the Study of the New Testament Supplement Series, (Sheffield: JSOT Press, 1993).

Sullivan, Steven P. *The Isaianic New Exodus in Romans 9–11: A Biblical and Theological Study of Paul's Use of Isaiah in Romans* (Silverton, OR: Lampion Press, 2017).

Sullivan, Steven P. *The Isaianic New Exodus in Romans 9–11: A Biblical and Theological Study of Paul's Use of Isaiah in Romans*, 2nd ed. (Middletown, RI: Stone Tower Press, 2023).

Swanson, Reuben, ed. *New Testament Greek Manuscripts: Romans*. (Wheaton: Tyndale House and Pasadena: William Carey International University Press, 2001).

Unger, Merrill F. *Zechariah: Prophet of Messiah's Glory* (Grand Rapids: Zondervan, 1963).

Vanlaningham, Michael G. "An Evaluation of N. T. Wright's View of Israel in Romans 11," *Bibliotheca Sacra* 170 (Apr-Jun 2013): 179–93.

Vlach, Michael J. "A Non-Typological Future-Mass-Conversion View," in *Three Views on Israel and the Church: Perspectives on Romans 9–11*, eds. Jared Compton and Andrew D. Naselli (Grand Rapids: Kregel, 2018).

Vlach, Michael J. "Response to Merkle," in *Three Views on Israel and the Church: Perspectives on Romans 9–11*, eds. Jared Compton and Andrew D. Naselli (Grand Rapids: Kregel, 2018), 209–222.

Vlach, Michael J. *He will Reign Forever: A Biblical Theology of the Kingdom of God* (Silverton, OR: Lampion Press, 2017).

Wagner, Günter. "The Future of Israel: Reflections on Romans 9–11," in *Eschatology and the New Testament: Essays in Honor of George Raymond Beasley-Murray*, ed. W. Hulitt Gloer (Peabody: Hendrickson, 1988), 77–112.

Wagner, J. Ross. *Heralds of the Good News: Isaiah and Paul in Concert in the Letter to the Romans*. Supplements to Novum Testamentum, eds. M. M. Mitchell and D. P. Moessner, vol. 101 (Leiden: Brill, 2002).

Walvoord, John F. *The Prophecy Knowledge Handbook* (Wheaton: Victor Books, 1990).

Watson, Francis, *Paul, Judaism and the Gentiles: Beyond the New Perspective*, rev. and exp. ed. (Grand Rapids: Eerdmans, 2007).

Woods, Andrew M. *The Coming Kingdom* (Duluth, MN: Grace Gospel Press, 2016).

Woudstra, Marten H. "Israel and the Church: A Case for Continuity," in *Continuity and Discontinuity: Perspectives on the Relationship Between the Old and New Testaments, Essays in Honor of S. Lewis Johnson, Jr.*, ed. John S. Feinberg (Wheaton: Crossway, 1988). 221–38.

Wright, N. T. *The Climax of the Covenant: Christ and the Law in Pauline Theology*. Edinburgh: Clark, 1991.

Wright, N. T. "Romans and the Theology of Paul," in *Pauline Theology, Romans Volume III* eds. David M. Hays and E. Elizabeth Johnson (Atlanta: Society of Biblical Literature, 2002), 30–67.

Zaspel, Fred G. and James M. Hamilton, Jr. "A Typological Future-Mass-Conversion View," in *Three Views on Israel and the Church: Perspectives on Romans 9–11*, eds. Jared Compton and Andrew D. Naselli (Grand Rapids: Kregel, 2018), 97–140.

Zaspel, Fred G. and James M. Hamilton, Jr. "Response to Merkle," in *Three Views on Israel and the Church: Perspectives on Romans 9–11*, eds. Jared Compton and Andrew D. Naselli (Grand Rapids: Kregel, 2018), 223–234.

Zerwick, Max and Mary Grosvenor, *A Grammatical Analysis of the Greek New Testament*, 5th ed. (Rome: Editrice Pontificio Istituto Biblico, 1996).

Ziegler, Joseph, *Isaias*. Septuaginta: Vetus Testamentum Graecum, 3rd ed. (Göttingen: Vandenhoeck & Ruprecht, 1939, 1983).

Romans 11:28–32

Introduction

Paul's climatic declaration of Israel's salvation is stated by referring to Scripture in verses 26–27, God's promise and election in verses 28–29, and His magnificent mercy in verses 30–32. It is here that Paul resolved the seemingly irreconcilable conflict of Israel's hostility and disobedience to God and God's irrevocable promises to Israel. In this process, God will show Israel and Gentiles are in disobedient so that He may show mercy to all!

Outline

E. A Wisdom Polemic: God's Merciful Plan for Israel and Gentiles (11:11-33)
1. Israel's hardening and the Gentiles Inclusion (11:11-15)
2. A Warning against Gentile Believers (11:16-22)
3. The Mystery of Israel's Salvation (11:23-27)
4. The Mercy of God in Salvation (11:28-32)

Original Text

11.28 κατὰ μὲν τὸ εὐαγγέλιον ἐχθροὶ δι' ὑμᾶς, κατὰ δὲ τὴν ἐκλογὴν ἀγαπητοὶ διὰ τοὺς πατέρας·
29 ἀμεταμέλητα γὰρ τὰ χαρίσματα καὶ ἡ κλῆσις τοῦ θεοῦ. 30 ὥσπερ γὰρ ὑμεῖς ποτε ἠπειθήσατε τῷ
θεῷ, νῦν δὲ ἠλεήθητε τῇ τούτων ἀπειθείᾳ, 31 οὕτως καὶ οὗτοι νῦν ἠπείθησαν τῷ ὑμετέρῳ ἐλέει
ἵνα καὶ αὐτοὶ [νῦν[a]][764] ἐλεηθῶσιν· 32 συνέκλεισεν γὰρ ὁ θεὸς τοὺς[b] πάντας εἰς ἀπείθειαν ἵνα τοὺς
πάντας ἐλεήσῃ.

Textual Notes

[a] **11:31 νῦν** is supported by SBLGNT B ℵ D* 1506. NA28 and UBS5 place **[νῦν]** in the text in brackets. **No νῦν** is supported by P^{46} A Ψ $D^{1.2}$ F G L 049 056 1 6 81 104 131 205 209 226 323 326 330 424 436 440 459 460 489 517 547 614 618 796 910 927 945 999 1175 1241 1242 1243 1245 1270 1315 1352 1424 1448 1505 1611 1646 1734 1738 1739 1836 1837 1854 1874 1881 1891 1982 2125 2147 2200 2344 2400 2412 2495 2815 **𝔐. ὕστερον** is supported by 33 88 256 263 365 1319 1573 1735 1852 1912 2127. (Swanson, *NT Greek Mss*, 185; UBS5, 533). The external support for ὕστερον is the weakest of the three possibilities. It solves the problem in the text for Israel is not now receiving mercy but will in the future. However, this too makes it suspect, especially since it is not well supported externally. The support for including νῦν is the Alexandrian uncials B and ℵ and the Western text of D. On the other hand, the support for omitting the article has the early text of P^{46} and Alexandrian texts of A (also 33, 81, 104, 326, 1175, 1739), the corrector of D, and western uncials F, G and Ψ with also the manuscripts of the

[764] This νῦν is left in the text with brackets but it is quite possible that it was not in the original text.

Majority Text. The inclusion of νῦν expresses a balance in the sentence, but on the other hand this may be why a scribe added it. The decision is very difficult, but I would give a slight edge in leaving it out though I placed it in brackets in the Greek text.

[b] **11:32 τοὺς πάντας** (pl. mas acc) is supported by ℵ B A L Ψ D[1.2] 049 056 1 6 33 81 88 104 131 205 209 226 256 263 323 326 330 365 424 436 440 459 460 489 517 547 614 618 796 910 927 945 999 1175 1241 1242 1243 1245 1270 1315 1319 1352 1434 1448 1505 1506 1573 1611 1646 1734 1735 1738 1739 1825 1836 1837 1852 1854 1874 1881 1891 1912 1962 1982 2125 2127 2147 2200 2344 2400 2412 2495 2815. **τά πάντα** (pl neuter acc) is supported by P[46vid] D* (F G have **πάντα**) (Swanson, *NT Greek Mss*, 185; UBS5, 534). Some contend that this reading was probably an assimilation of Gal 3:22.[765] The meaning of the text is not affected with either case, but the reading of τοὺς πάντας has the strongest external evidence.

Translation

28 With respect to the gospel *they (Israel) are* enemies on your behalf, but with respect to election *they are* beloved because of the fathers. **29** For the gifts and the call of God are irrevocable. **30** For just as you at one time were disobedient to God but now you have received mercy because of their disobedience, **31** so also they now have disobeyed for the sake of mercy for you in order that they also might [now] receive mercy. **32** For God has shut up all to disobedience in order that he might have mercy on all.

Commentary

11:28 κατὰ μὲν τὸ εὐαγγέλιον ἐχθροὶ δι' ὑμᾶς, κατὰ δὲ τὴν ἐκλογὴν ἀγαπητοὶ διὰ τοὺς πατέρας. "With respect to the gospel *they (Israel) are* enemies on your behalf, but with respect to election *they are* beloved because of the fathers."

κατὰ μὲν	τὸ εὐαγγέλιον	ἐχθροὶ	δι'	ὑμᾶς,
κατὰ δὲ	τὴν ἐκλογὴν	ἀγαπητοὶ	διὰ	τοὺς πατέρας

With respect to the gospel	*they (Israel) are* enemies	on behalf of	you,
With respect to the election	*they (Israel) are* beloved	because of	the fathers.

The lack of connective word (an asyndeton)[766] between vv. 25–27 and 28ff is noted and suggests a slight break in Paul's thought (Moo, 2nd, 744; Cranfield, 579). The subject of the sentence, "they" in v. 28, is not in the original and must be supplied from the preceding context in v. 27 (αὐτοῖς "them"), which refers to collective noun "Jacob" (Ἰακώβ) in v. 26b–another

[765] Metzger, *A Textual Commentary on the Greek NT*, 465; Moo, 2nd, 727, n. 761; Schreiner, 2nd, 613.

[766] Blass, Debrunner, and Funk, *A Greek Grammar*, §463. See Longenecker, 901 for further thoughts. Jewett, 706 summarizes the rhetorical form of Paul this way: "Since each term in this rhetorical form is multivalent, the precise connotation intended by Paul has to be inferred from the context as well as from the internal logic of the *paromoiosis* itself."

name for ethnic Israel. This name Jacob in turn refers back to "all Israel" (πᾶς Ἰσραὴλ) in 26a.[767] In the discussion in v. 26a, "all Israel" refers to all of ethnic Israel as a whole.

The phrase with μὲν is used 179 times in the NT (BDAG, 629 says 180 times)[768] and only one other place κατὰ μὲν is found and that is in 1 Pet 4:6 (μὲν κατὰ). Furthermore, 1 Peter 4:6 is the only other place that combination of κατὰ μὲν … κατὰ δὲ is found in the same sentence in the NT. First Pet 4:6 is difficult to translate and interpret but the construction seems to be used as a contrast that correlates two points.[769] A contrast that is clearly a construction indicating both points are happening simultaneously in 11:28.[770]

The preposition κατὰ ("with respect to")[771] in v. 28 denotes a dual relationship to the gospel[772] and election of God. The unbelieving Israelite apart from God's grace are enemies of the gospel. The passive sense of ἐχθροὶ ("enemies") has the meaning of "those hated by God" (Godet, 258; Murray, 2:100; Cranfield, 580; Schreiner, 2nd, 609; Thielman, 549). However, the active sense "those who hate God (Fitzmyer, 625; Jewett, 707; Dunn, 685) seems to be the meaning for the thought is directed to the phrase "for your sake" (δι' ὑμᾶς),[773] "to view to the advantage of" Gentile believers (Cranfield, 580).[774] The first preposition διὰ ("for the sake of")[775] denotes the reason why something exists or happens and it has a forward view orientation

---

[767] Waymeyer, "The Dual Status of Israel in Romans 11:28," 61.

[768] Logos 8.13.

[769] 1 Pet 4:6, εἰς τοῦτο γὰρ καὶ νεκροῖς εὐηγγελίσθη, ἵνα κριθῶσι μὲν κατὰ ἀνθρώπους σαρκὶ ζῶσι δὲ κατὰ θεὸν πνεύματι (possible translation: "For the gospel has for this purpose been preached also to the dead that though they may be judged *on the one hand according to* (μὲν κατὰ) men in the flesh, they may live *on the other hand according to* (δὲ κατὰ) God in the Spirit." Wallace, *Greek Grammar*, 672 indicates that μὲν … δὲ ("on the one hand … on the other hand") construction expresses a correlation and in Rom 11:28, it is a correlation in a contrast. In this context, this construction forms a dual status: both "enemies" and "beloved". See further discussion on this point in the discussion on this verse.

[770] Hendriksen, 384 argues that Paul switches subject mid-verse from the Israelites who are enemies of God because of the rejection of the gospel to Israelites that are God's elect (remnant) is quite improbable (Moo, 2nd, 746). Equally improbable is the possibility (Lenski, 732–34) that Paul shifted the temporal reference by saying Israelites were now enemies, but in the future, they are beloved because of election (Moo, 2nd, 746, n. 842). If Paul wanted to convey a shift in time or subject change, then the combination of ποτε … νῦν δὲ ("once" or "formerly" … "but now") would clearly convey their point (Rom 11:30; Gal 4:8–9; Eph 5:8a; Col 1:21–22a; 3:7–8; Philem 10–11). However, instead of using these contrastive changes, Paul used a contrast that correlated the two parts (Waymeyer, "The Dual Status of Israel in Romans 11:28," 65–66).

[771] BDAG, 513.

[772] There is some discussion what Paul means here with the word τὸ εὐαγγέλιον ("the gospel"). Cranfield 579 states that the gospel is "the progress of the gospel in the world." However, most of Paul's uses of the word "gospel" refers to the content of the gospel centered around Jesus Christ and the cross (1:1, 9, 16; 2:16; 10:16; 15:16, 19, 29; 16:25).

[773] Paul uses the second person to reference Gentiles and distinguish the Israelites by using third person in Rom 11. Rom 11:19 is one exception where he uses a first person for Gentiles.

[774] Cranfield, 580, Dunn, 684, Middendorf, 1170, n. 185 are correct that parallel forms in this verse do not necessarily mean parallel meaning, especially since the διὰ clauses can have different meaning. Moo, 2nd, 745 is theologically correct that both meanings are true in Rom 9–11: "hated, hardened, and rejected" by God (9:13, 17–23; 11:7–10, 15, 25); and "disobedient, unbelieving, and stubborn" on their part (9:31–32; 10:3, 1421; 11:11, 12, 20, 23, 30–31. However, Paul's immediate context seems better fit with the active meaning.

[775] BDAG, 225. Moo, 2nd, 745, denotes the first διὰ as a "final sense." See Blass, Debrunner, and Funk, *A Greek Grammar*, §222. Emphasis is on the cause/effect or action/result. From the standpoint of the gospel and salvation in Jesus Christ, unbelieving Israel has become an enemy (the cause or the action), but this action brought the gospel and salvation to the church, especially the Gentiles (effect/result) (Beale, Brendsel, and Ross, *An Interpretive Lexicon of NT Greek*, 8, 35). However, this Israelite transgression against God and the gospel is part of God's plan to reach the Gentiles (11:11–15) – "for your sake."

(Cranfield, 580) concerning the Gentile believers. For the most part Paul seems to refer back to 11:11–15[776] and the blessing of the gospel to the Gentiles through transgression of Israel. As one reads the book of Acts often the fiercest attacks against the gospel came from unbelieving Israelites. Their rejection of the gospel and their persecution of believers manifested that they were enemies of God. On the other hand, because of the promise of the Abrahamic covenant Israel is beloved in God's sight for Romans 11 indicates that He will once again save and spiritually bless Israel. God's election (ἐκλογὴν) of Israel designates them as his beloved (ἀγαπητοὶ) (Deut 7:6–8; LXX Isa 41:8–9; 44:1–2). Paul also relates love with God's election (Rom 9:13; 25; Eph 1:4–5). Here in v. 28 the election is referring to Israel as a whole, a corporate entity (cf. 11:2) (Cranfield, 580; Murray, 2:100). All Israel is beloved of God, but their status of eternal salvation ultimately depends on God individually choosing them for salvation in this age (the remnant) and in the last days ("all Israel") (Moo, 2nd, 746). Again, the reference of "they" in v. 28b is not in the original but the nearest referent is "they" (v. 27), "Jacob" (v.26b), which in turn is referred to as "all Israel" in v. 26a. Vlack and Waymeyer are correct when they eliminate the view that Paul in v. 28 is speaking of the church because the church is not an enemy of the gospel. Secondly, Israel in this context cannot be the remnant of ethnic Israel throughout their history because the remnant is not both beloved of God and an enemy of the gospel at the same time.[777] This dual status[778] is a description of ethnic Israel that is simultaneously true until the eschatological time set by God in the future.

The second διὰ denotes purpose and has a backward orientation.[779] The Lord's gracious promise to Abraham, Isaac, and Jacob ("the fathers, 9:5; 11:28; 15:8) is the only reason why the Lord will save "all Israel" and the people of Israel will receive the promised blessings. Verse 28 is the introduction to Paul's theme of God's mercy (vv. 30b, 31b, 32b). The dual status of Israel wraps up Paul's argument concerning Israel. Israel now is at enmity with God because as a whole Israel is against the gospel. This thought is expressed broadly in Rom 9:30–10:21. The promised and positive side of irrevocable blessings is broadly expressed in 9:6b–29 and 11:1–27 (Moo, 2nd, 744). In v. 28, Paul is not referring to the election of the remnant, but the corporate election of the nation as a whole to whom God placed His grace and promises to them (cf. 9:4–5; 11:1–2) (Moo, 2nd, 746; Murray, 2:101; Cranfield, 580).

11:29 ἀμεταμέλητα γὰρ τὰ χαρίσματα καὶ ἡ κλῆσις τοῦ θεοῦ. "For the gifts and the call of God are irrevocable." Paul uses γὰρ ("for") to indicate the causal support of v. 28.[780] The τὰ χαρίσματα ("the gifts") seems to be a summary of Israel's privileges which are numerated to some degree in Rom 9:4–5 (Moo, 2nd, 747; Schreiner, 2nd, 610; Jewett, 708; Dunn, 686, 694; Murray 2:101).[781] The ἡ κλῆσις ("call") refers to at least the election by God as His beloved (v.

---

[776] See the interpretation of 11:15 as referring to Israel's rejection of God.

[777] Vlack, "A Non-Typological Future-Mass-View," 60 and Waymeyer, "The Dual Status of Israel in Romans 11:28," 62–63.

[778] Moo, 2nd, 744; Dunn, 693; Waymeyer, "The Dual Status of Israel in Romans 11:28," 63; Vlach, "A Non-Typological Future-Mass-Conversion View," 59–60.

[779] BDAG, 226; Moo, 2nd, 745; Cranfield, 580. The "fathers" are the ground for them to be "beloved" (Beale, Brendsel, and Ross, *An Interpretive Lexicon of NT Greek*, 9, 35).

[780] Waymeyer, "The Dual Status of Israel in Romans 11:28," 70. Schreiner, 2nd, 610 indicates it "functions as the ground or explanation for verse 28" (see also Jewett, 708).

[781] Calvin, 440 and Käsemann, 316 suggest that this is one idea (hendiadys) "the benefits of God's call." However, it is likely best to make it two ideas that are coupled together (Cranfield, 581).

28b), to whom He gives gifts.[782] Cranfield, 581 declares that "we may understand God's calling of Israel to be His special people, to stand in a special relation to Himself, and to fulfil a special function in history."[783] God's call did not depend upon the fathers' merits, but because He willed it so out of his holy mercy and grace. What does Paul say about God concerning these gifts? He uses a very rare word ἀμεταμέλητα which is used only one other place in the NT (2 Cor 7:10). This Greek word is also placed as the first word in the verse to give it the greatest possible emphasis (Cranfield, 582). The Greek lexicon defines it passively as "not to be regretted or without regret." Then the lexicon explains further, "Hence also irrevocable, of someth. one does not take back."[784] This thought harkens back to the 9:6 and 11:1–2, 11. This statement magnifies God's faithfulness. Paul alluded to this irrevocable faithfulness in his question in Rom 3:3–4. God's promises are connected to His character of immutability; therefore, his gifts and calling to Israel is irrevocable, even in the face of unbelief and rejection by His people. The salvation of Israel near or at the second coming of Jesus Christ will fulfill the covenantal promises to the fathers and he will graft them back into their own olive tree (Schreiner, 2nd, 610).

11:30–31 ὥσπερ γὰρ ὑμεῖς ποτε ἠπειθήσατε τῷ θεῷ, νῦν δὲ ἠλεήθητε τῇ τούτων ἀπειθείᾳ, [31] οὕτως καὶ οὗτοι νῦν ἠπείθησαν τῷ ὑμετέρῳ ἐλέει ἵνα καὶ αὐτοὶ [νῦν][785] ἐλεηθῶσιν. "For just as you at one time were disobedient to God but now you have received mercy because of their disobedience, 31 so also they now have disobeyed for the sake of mercy for you in order that they also might [now] receive mercy."

Formal Parallelisms in vv. 30–31

v. 30 ὥσπερ γὰρ ὑμεῖς ποτε ἠπειθήσατε τῷ θεῷ, νῦν δὲ ἠλεήθητε τῇ τούτων ἀπειθείᾳ,
v. 31 οὕτως καὶ οὗτοι νῦν ἠπείθησαν τῷ ὑμετέρῳ ἐλέει ἵνα καὶ αὐτοὶ [νῦν] ἐλεηθῶσιν.[786]

---

[782] See Paul's earlier argument of calling concerning the seed of Abraham which is connected to God's election (Rom 9:7, 11, 24, 25, 26) (Jewett, 708).

[783] Saucy, "Does Apostle Paul Reverse the Prophetic Tradition of the Salvation of Israel and the Nations?," 77 states that Israel was called to serve in salvation history to fulfil a special function in history as God's people (Ex 19:5–6).

[784] BDAG, 53. Schreiner, 2nd, 610 adds that ἀμεταμέλητα is a legal term and demonstrates the "unbreakable nature of God's gift and calling." For other uses outside the Bible, see Jewett, 709.

[785] This νῦν is left in the text with brackets but it is quite possible that it was not in the original text.

[786] The first view takes the phrase τῷ ὑμετέρῳ ἐλέει with ἠπείθησαν in v. 31. This first view would be translated "… they have disobeyed *for the sake of mercy for you* in order that they also might [now] receive mercy" (Moo, 2nd, 749; Schriener, 2nd, 611; Dunn, 688; Käsemann, 316; Middendorf, 1139). See also Moo, 2nd, 749 for his critique and support of the first view. This construction forms a tight and epigrammatic form with rhythmic clauses and balanced phrases (Dunn, 687). Others argue for the second view that the phrase τῷ ὑμετέρῳ ἐλέει should be taken with the verb in the phrase ἵνα καὶ αὐτοὶ [νῦν] ἐλεηθῶσιν (Murray, 2:102, n. 59; Sanday and Headlam, 338; Cranfield, 584–86; Fitzmyer, 627–28; Godet, 262; Meyer, 240). The second view's translation is "… in order that they too may now receive mercy *as a result of God's mercy to you*" (NIV). Cranfield and others give examples that they say support this syntactical construction: John 13:29; Acts 19:4; 2 Cor 2:4; Gal 2:10; Col 4:16. None of the examples by Cranfield and others have the broad context of οὕτως καὶ in combination with ἵνα καὶ which deal with a correlation (of mercy) in a contrast (disobedience) in vv. 30–31. In the 50 uses of οὕτως καὶ in the NT (Logos 8.14) it appears in combination with ἵνα καὶ (used 31 times [Logos, 8.14]) only in Rom 11:31. In the examples of Cranfield's texts only one text (Col 4:16) uses ἵνα καὶ for the others only have ἵνα. Only John 13:29 uses a dative prepositional phrase (John 13:29). Finally, the dative prepositional phrase in Rom 11:31 is five words away from the verb ἐλεηθῶσιν which it supposedly modifies (Schreiner, 2nd, 611). This point is not impossible in Greek grammar but not likely. Though the second view is possible, the parallel argument and syntax support is better reflected in the first view. See Moo, 2nd, 747 who shows the chiasm that exist between 11:30 and 31 (Dunn, 688).

v. 30a For just as you at one time were disobedient to God
v. 31a so also they now have disobeyed for the sake of mercy for you

v. 30b but now you have received mercy because of their disobedience,
v. 31b in order that they also might [now] receive mercy.

Paul continues to address specifically the Gentiles as he uses the second person plural verbs (ἠπειθήσατε, ἠλεήθητε) and pronouns (ὑμεῖς, ὑμετέρῳ) and addresses Israelites by using the third person plural verbs (ἠπείθησαν, ἐλεηθῶσιν) with a plural masculine pronoun (αὐτοὶ) and plural masculine demonstrative pronouns (τούτων, οὗτοι) in vv. 30–31. He is summarizing very briefly what he has already stated in more detail in 11:12–15. Paul's theme in this summary is the contrast between disobedient men (both Israel and Gentiles) and the mercy of God.[787] Gentiles are central in v. 30 and Israelites are central in v. 31.

The conjunction combination ὥσπερ γὰρ is used 13 times in the NT.[788] This construction is usually translated "for just as" and used in each case as a comparison. This construction ὥσπερ γὰρ in combination with νῦν δὲ in v. 30 is only found here in the NT.[789] The two possible translations of the phrase νῦν δὲ are "but now" (NASB, ESV, NRSV, NET, LEB) or "and now." Since the comparison is in the context of contrast, the translation of "but now" is preferred. The Gentiles received mercy through the result of Israel's disobedience. The phrase τῇ τούτων ἀπειθείᾳ is probably a casual dative, "because of their disobedience" (Moo, 2nd, 748, n. 850).[790] The word ποτε refers to time in a general way. The Greek lexicon BDAG, 856 defines it as "generalization of time, at some time or other of the past" ("once or formerly"). Thus, "at one time" fits well as a translation. Moo, 2nd, 748 seems to be correct that Paul is painting a broad picture of salvation history from the old era to the new one (Eph 2:12–13). Through Israel's disobedience and unbelief, God has extended his mercy in salvation to the Gentiles (cf. 15:9). God's mercy is sovereign in dispensing his salvation which Paul has detailed in 9:15–18. The Gentile's reason to receive the gospel and salvation is because of Israel's disobedience to the gospel (11:12, 15, 17) according to the mystery of 11:25.

Paul seems to be making a chiastic construction in 11:30b and 11:31a (Moo, 2nd, 748; Dunn, 688):

ἠλεήθητε τῇ τούτων ἀπειθείᾳ "You received mercy *because of their disobedience*" (dative clause v.30b)

ἠπείθησαν τῷ ὑμετέρῳ ἐλέει "They have disobeyed *for the sake of mercy for you*" (dative clause v.31a)

---

[787] God's mercy "demonstrates benevolent goodness to those in a pitiable or miserable condition, even though they do not deserve it" (MacArthur and Mayhue, *Biblical Doctrine*, 182).

[788] Logos 8.14 compiles the following: Matt 12:40; 24:27, 37; 25:14; Luk 17:24; Joh 5:21; Rom 5:19; 6:19: 11:30; 1 Cor 11:12; 15:22; Jas 2:26.

[789] The rest of the 12 verses have the following combination construction (Logos 8.14): ὥσπερ γὰρ … οὕτως (Matt 12:40; 24:27, 37; Luke 17:24; 5:21), ὥσπερ γὰρ … καὶ (Matt 25:14), ὥσπερ γὰρ … οὕτως καὶ (John 5:21, 26; Rom 5:19; 1 Cor 11:12; 15:22; Jas 2:26), ὥσπερ γὰρ … οὕτως νῦν (Rom 6:19).

[790] Wallace, *Greek Grammar*, 168; Blass, Debrunner, Funk, *A Greek Grammar*, §196; Käsemann, 316; Fitzmyer, 627. Some acknowledge the possibility of a temporal dative: "at the time of their disobedience." (N. Turner, *Syntax*, 243; Moule, *Idiom Book*, 44) or an instrumental use: "by means of their disobedience" (Cranfield, 584; Dunn, 688).

Many concluded that since we have this parallel structure then one must have parallel meaning in their dative clauses. However, v. 28 demonstrated that this is not necessarily true (Moo, 745, 749; Dunn, 688). Understanding the chiastic construction above would parallel the thought of 11:12 and 15 and give support that τῷ ὑμετέρῳ ἐλέει ("for the sake of mercy for you" v. 31a) modifies ἠπείθησαν ("they have disobeyed") that appears before it and not ἐλεηθῶσιν ("be shown mercy") at the end of v. 31.[791]

Paul states in v. 31 that they (Israel) now during this salvation history age have disobeyed God and rejected the salvation in Jesus Christ. However, this disobedience by Israel became the opportunity for Gentiles to experience the mercy of God in salvation. In turn, the mercy to the Gentiles will be used by God for the purpose (ἵνα) to again show mercy in salvation to Israel (Dunn, 688). The future salvation of Israel as a whole (corporately) has been demonstrated in 11:12, 15, 24, 25–26 and made certain in vv. 28–29. This could not be the believing remnant of Israel in the church age because they do not need God's mercy for the Gentiles to receive mercy.[792] Some commentators think that the second "now" in verse 31 has become part of the argument that Paul is not teaching about a great future conversion of Israel, but refers to the remnant of Israel believing in this age.[793] However, if the second νῦν in v. 31 is actually part of the original text then Paul is expressing imminency ("now," at any time) of this event of God's final mercy upon the nation of Israel (Moo, 2nd, 750; Schreiner, 2nd, 612; Käsemann, 316; Dunn, 687).[794] The concept of imminency does not necessarily mean that the event is guaranteed to be fulfilled in few days or years. Imminency means that nothing else has been revealed by God that needs to be done (11: 25–26) before God's mercy to the Gentile is fulfilled and God will pour out his mercy on Israel. Thus, from our viewpoint it could happen at any time though it could be a long time off. Evidently, Paul does not specifically know when the fullness of the Gentiles will be fulfilled; thus, he is not precise. On the other hand, if the second "now" in v. 31 is original then the fullness of the Gentiles is presented as imminent, at any time, and therefore ushering in the future salvation of Israel making this event also imminent (Schreiner, 2nd, 612).

11:32 συνέκλεισεν γὰρ ὁ θεὸς τοὺς πάντας εἰς ἀπείθειαν ἵνα τοὺς πάντας ἐλεήσῃ. "For God has shut up all to disobedience in order that he might have mercy on all." Verse 32 concludes Paul's argument in 9–11 which was briefly summarized in vv. 30–31. Both Israel and Gentiles were disobedient, and God displayed his mercy on both groups. The γὰρ ("for") introduces a further explanation of his conclusion (Cranfield, 586).[795] The verb συνέκλεισεν ("shut up") is the first Greek word of the sentence placing an emphasis on this action. The word may be defined as "to confine to specific limits" such as to "confine or imprison."[796] The emphasis and image of this

---

[791] See footnote under the "Formal Parallelism in vv. 30–31."

[792] Vlach, "A Non-Typological Future-Mass-Conversion View,"61.

[793] Keep in mind that the second νῦν ["now"] in v. 31 is doubtful whether it is part of the original text–see comments in the textual criticism section. If the second νῦν is not part of the original text, then their argument for Israel being the remnant in this age from this text does not have much support.

[794] Vlach, Ibid., 61–62; Stählin, *TDNT*, 4:1112, n. 43, states "Paul in R. is still expecting an imminent *parousia* (cf. 13:11) the blessing of the Jews is expected any moment now in the νῦν of transition between the comings." Cranfield, 585–86 calls it an "eschatological now" beginning with the "gospel events and extends to the Parousia as a unity."

[795] BDAG, 189.

[796] BDAG, 952. In Luke 5:6 it is used in catching fish by closing up a net. The word is also used in Gal 3:22 where Scripture "has locked everything in under the power of sin." This Lexicon expressed the meaning of the word in Rom 11:32 this way: God "has imprisoned them all in disobedience, i.e. put them under compulsion to be disobedient or given them over to disobedience." Moo, 2nd, 750, n. 864 states if Paul depended upon the LXX where

word reminds us of Rom 1:24, 26, 28 (Moo, 2nd, 750; Cranfield, 586; Jewett, 711). However, God's ultimate purpose was to magnify his infinite mercy![797]

The major interpretative problem in this verse is how to understand the combination of τοὺς πάντας … τοὺς πάντας ("all … all"). If one understands the fallen nature of every man, then the first "all" does not usually cause a problem. However, what does Paul mean by the final "all"? One serious error in the interpretation of this verse is to understand that Paul is teaching universal salvation (everyone will be saved).[798] This position disregards the previous contextual limitations where the "all" refers to Gentile and Israelite groups (Schreiner, 2nd, 613; Sanday and Headlam, 339; Murray, 2:103; Thielman, 552). Further, this view contradicts the Bible and Pauline teaching even the context of Rom 9–11 (e.g. 9:11–24). While other scholars decry that Paul expresses contradictory viewpoints in Rom 9–11 and this verse plays into their understanding.[799] Some conclude that the "all" is potentially available to everyone, but people become "self-excluded from God's salvation" if they don't believe (Alford, 2:437). This is possible, but the context and argument of Paul better fit the case that "all" should fit the context of vv. 30-31. The context of Israelites and Gentiles in a corporate sense (the people group as a whole, but not each and everyone in the group) is to what Paul is referring (Calvin, Murray, Moo, 2nd, 751). The article τοὺς ("the") with the Greek word πάντας ("all") seems to emphasize the collective or corporate aspect (Moo, 2nd, 751, n. 870). There are many times that the plural masculine accusative article τοὺς and the plural masculine accusative πάντας appear in the same sentence,[800] but there is only one other place in the NT where the plural accusative article τοὺς modifies πάντας in the same way as in Rom 11:32 and that is in 2 Cor 5:10.[801] Here in 2 Cor 5:10 the collective or corporate aspect of "all" is supported. This Pauline passage helps to support a collective or corporate interpretation of the word "all" in 11:32. Paul in v. 32 is <u>not</u> saying that all human beings in the world will be saved, but rather, first, Gentiles as a collective group were shut up in disobedience and the nation of Israel corporately (the people group as a whole, but not each and everyone in the group) might receive God's mercy. Now Gentiles corporately (the people group as a whole, but not each and everyone in the group) are receiving God's mercy while Israelites collectively (the people group as a whole, but not each and everyone in the group) are shut up to their disobedience. Finally, in the future God will again pour out his mercy on Israel (see 11:25–26).

In the light of the context of salvation history, the Lord may declare that he has shut up all in disobedience and he has demonstrated his marvelous mercy to all! This astonishing display

---

the verb is used with εἰς then it is often used of "God's act of enclosing or giving over people to their enemies (Ps 31:8) or to the plague (Ps 78:50) or death (Ps 78:62)." Jewett, 711 says it express the idea of "confining someone in something."

[797] See commentary footnote on Rom 11:30–31 for the definition of "mercy."

[798] See Dodd, 183–86 and Jewett, 708-09 as examples. On the other hand, Cranfield, 588 and Dunn, 689 argue that universalism is a possibility.

[799] Räisänen, "Paul, God and Israel: Romans 9–11 in Recent Research," 192–96. Watson, *Paul, Judaism, and the Gentiles*, rev. & exp. ed., 340–43 softens this argument and states that Paul's understanding developed and thus there is development and change in his argument in Rom 9–11. Thus, he concludes that Paul was not concerned about consistency. Moo, 2nd, 752 is correct that this so-called inconsistency in Paul's teaching in Rom 9–11 fails to give due attention to contextual and theological presuppositions and framework that enables interpreters to solve seemingly contradictions at the conceptual level.

[800] According to Logos 8.14, these perimeters are found 252 times in 104 verses.

[801] There are other places where the article in other Greek cases modifies only the word "all" (i.e. 1 Cor 9:22; Phil 2:21; Mk 14:64; 1 Cor 10:17; 2 Cor 5:14b; 4:13; etc. [BDAG, 784]).

of His character and plan should cause all to fall on our faces in awesome praise and worship. This is exactly what Paul does in his final section in vv. 33–36.

Biblical Theological Comments

Paul has skillfully articulated the concept of individual election within or alongside of the corporate election of the nation of Israel. The times that Paul lived in caused him to interweave both together but to keep them separate and distinct: the corporate election of all Israel (9:4–5; 11:1–2; 28b–29) and the individual election of both Israelites and Gentiles. Thus, not all Israelites will respond to the gospel is not at odds with the election of Israel and "all Israel" (v. 26) will be saved because the fulfillment of this statement did not require the salvation of every single Israelite throughout history (not diachronic)! Hofius insightfully states, "… membership in the people of Israel does not *eo ipso* mean membership in Israel the community of salvation, and the physical descendants of Abraham are not as such also 'children of Abraham' in the spiritual sense and therefore 'children of God' and 'heirs of the promise.'"[802] In the church age some Israelites and many Gentiles are being saved (individual election). In the future, the Lord will graft the nation of Israel back into the promised blessings of the patriarchs (represented by the roots which is the beginning of the olive tree in Rom 11) and this includes His mercy in eternal salvation. This corporate event will happen during the events of the second coming of Jesus Christ (11:12, 15, 25–26; a synchronic event). Moo, 2nd, 753 correctly states that individual election of 9:6–29 "does not revoke Israel's election, but shows that it does not have a necessary salvific significance. Within the corporate election of Israel, there is operating, Paul shows, an election of individuals. This individual election in Paul's day is being extended to Gentiles and restricted to a remnant among Israel." Thus, in God's plan at this time He has moved from the nation of Israel as his primary instrument of His plan to the church which is made-up of Gentiles and Israelites. When the church has accomplished His purpose and the fullness of the Gentiles have come in (v. 25) then again God will take up the nation of Israel to fulfill His promises and accomplish His purpose in the world (11:11–12, 15, 25–32).

From a corporate view, Israel is beloved by God because of the promises to the patriarchal fathers (v. 28b). God's gift and calling to Israel is irrevocable though at this time, it is not fulfilled (v. 29). The present disobedience of Israel will in the future be dramatically changed by God and "all Israel will be saved" by the mercy of God (vv. 26, 32). Thus, just like the Gentiles who were disobedient and now God is showing them mercy, Israel who are now in disobedience to God will be shown mercy (vv. 30–31). This grand plan by God is to demonstrate that both Israel and Gentiles are disobedient sinners and it is only the magnificent mercy of our great God that anyone is eternally saved! *Soli Deo Gloria*!

Application and Devotional Implications

In Rom 11:28–29 Paul proves that the restoration of Israel is from the gift and the calling of God. In other words, the restoration of Israel is guaranteed because of the immutable character of God! In v. 28 Paul summarizes a lot of his argument. First, from the standpoint of the gospel,

[802] Hofius, "All Israel Will Be Saved.'" 32.

Israel is an enemy because she has rejected it. Yet, their rejection was done for the sake of Gentiles–that they may be saved. Second, from the standpoint of God's choice to be a nation with His promises they are beloved. However, Israel is not blessed because of her sake but because of the fathers (Abraham, Isaac and Jacob). The Abrahamic covenant which was given to Abraham and reaffirmed to Isaac and Jacob is the basis for all the promises God gave Israel. These promises are secured to Israel, not on the ground of her merit but on the ground of God's fidelity to His Word and His magnificent mercy. What is the nature of God's security to his promises? It is found in 11:29. The only reason why God will restore the rebellious and obstinate nation is because the gifts and calling of God are irrevocable (immutable).

My beloved, we ought to take comfort in this principle of God's immutability–His promises are irrevocable! God has promised us many things in His Word. For example, He promised to save us from hell and deliver us to heaven if we place our trust in Jesus Christ's saving work on the cross. This truth is a testimony to the mercy and grace of God! But what if you sin against God? What if you rebel against Him and go your own way for a period of time? What if in a moment of weakness, you deny Him in some way like Peter did on the eve of Jesus' trial. Will He cast you aside? Will He cast you into eternal hell? No, a thousand times no! The gift of salvation and His calling to it are irrevocable. However, this truth does not give me license to go out and sin because I know God will not cast me off. No, we have the warning that a man who lives in sin may wake up to the fact that his profession of faith in salvation may be a false one! A true child of God has the security of God's promises, but he will not experience the blessing of them unless he walks in the obedience of faith by the power of the Holy Spirit.

Selected Bibliography

Arndt, William, Frederick W. Danker, and Walter Bauer, *A Greek-English Lexicon of the New Testament and Other Early Christian Literature*, 3rd ed. electronic version (Chicago: University of Chicago Press, 2000).

Beale, G. K., Daniel J. Brendsel, and William A. Ross. *An Interpretive Lexicon of New Testament Greek: Analysis of Prepositions, Adverbs, Particles, Relative Pronouns, and Conjunctions* (Grand Rapids: Zondervan, 2014).

Blass, Friedrich, Albert Debrunner, and Robert Walter Funk, *A Greek Grammar of the New Testament and Other Early Christian Literature* (Chicago: University of Chicago Press, 1961).

Hofius, Otried, "All Israel Will Be Saved': Divine Salvation and Israel's Deliverance in Romans 9–11," trans. Judith G. Volf, Princeton Seminary Bulletin, Supplementary, 1 (1990): 19–39.

MacArthur, John and Richard Mayhue, gen. eds. *Biblical Doctrine: A Systematic Summary of Bible Truth* (Wheaton: Crossway, 2017).

Metzger, Bruce M. *A Textual Commentary on the Greek New Testament*, 2nd ed. (New York: American Bible Society, 1994).

Moulton, J. H. and G. Milligan, *The Vocabulary of the Greek Testament.* 1930. Reprint (Peabody, MA: Hendrickson, 1997).

Moule, C. F. D. An Idiom-Book of New Testament Greek, 2nd ed. (Cambridge: Cambridge University Press, 1959).

Räisänen, Heikki. "Paul, God and Israel: Romans 9–11 in Recent Research." In *The Social World of Formative Christianity and Judaism: Essays in Tribute to Howard Clark Kee*, eds. Jacob Neusner et al., 178–206 (Philadelphia: Fortress Press, 1988).

Saucy, Robert L. "Does Apostle Paul Reverse the Prophetic Tradition of the Salvation of Israel and the Nations?," in *Building on the Foundations of Evangelical Theology: Essays in Honor of John S. Feinberg*, eds Gregg R. Allison and Stephen J. Wellum (Wheaton: Crossway, 2015).

Stählin, Gustav. "Νῦν (ἄρτι)," ed. Gerhard Kittel, Geoffrey W. Bromiley, and Gerhard Friedrich, *TDNT*, vol. 4 (Grand Rapids, MI: Eerdmans, 1964–68).

Swanson, Reuben, ed. *New Testament Greek Manuscripts: Romans* (Wheaton: Tyndale House and Pasadena: William Carey International University Press, 2001).

Turner, Nigel, *Syntax*, vol. 3 in *A Grammar of New Testament Greek*, James H. Moulton (Edinburgh: T & T Clark, 1963).

Vlach, Michael J. "A Non-Typological Future-Mass-Conversion View," in *Three Views on Israel and the Church: Perspectives on Romans 9–11*, eds. Jared Compton and Andrew D. Naselli (Grand Rapids: Kregel, 2018).

Wallace, Daniel B. *Greek Grammar Beyond the Basic: An Exegetical Syntax of the New Testament* (Grand Rapids: Zondervan, 1996).

Watson, Francis. *Paul, Judaism and the Gentiles: Beyond the New Perspective*. Revised and expanded edition (Grand Rapids: Eerdmans, 2007).

Waymeyer, Matt. "The Dual Status of Israel in Romans 11:28," *The Master's Seminary Journal*, 16 (Spring 2005); 57-71.

Romans 11:33–36

Introduction

Paul closes his argument in Rom 9–11 with what we may call a doxological wisdom polemic. A wisdom polemic is where God, usually through the prophets, uses the genre of wisdom to construct a disputation against the people of God because of their lack of knowledge, understanding, and rebellion against the character and plan of God. The opposition of human wisdom to God's wise plan of judgment, redemption, and restoration sets up what may be called a "wisdom polemic." This wisdom polemic was first discussed in Rom 9:20 in this commentary and can also be seen in Paul's thinking in 1 Corinthians.[803] The arrangement of the motifs and vocabulary of Romans 11:33–36 suggests that Paul composed a wisdom hymn[804] based on the Isaianic wisdom theme. From a literary standpoint, the climatic conclusion of Romans 11:33–36 is most directly connected with chapters 9–11.[805] These last four verses of chapter 11 form a triadic structure: three exclamatory statements (v. 33), three rhetorical questions (vv. 34–35), and a summary doxology in three prepositional phrases (v.36).[806] The implied answer to each rhetorical question is "no one," and the questions convey the overall truth of the vast difference between the infinite God and finite humans. A brief summary of 11:34–35 is: God is incomprehensible, has no counsellors, and is not obligated to anyone because he has not received anything from anyone to make him a debtor.[807]

Outline

E. A Wisdom Polemic: God's Merciful Plan for Israel and Gentiles (11:11-33)
   1. Israel's hardening and the Gentiles Inclusion (11:11-15)
   2. A Warning against Gentile Believers (11:16-22)
   3. The Mystery of Israel's Salvation (11:23-27)

---

[803] For a detail discuss on the wisdom polemic and 1 Corinthians, see Sullivan, *The INE in Rom 9–11*, 2nd, 121–132.

[804] Dunn, 700 and Dumbrell, 115. Moo, 2nd, 759 states that Paul probably borrows extensively from OT wisdom traditions (vv. 34–35), apocalyptic, (v. 33) and Hellenistic Jewish teachings (v. 36). Paul may have borrowed a hymn from the synagogue (Johnson, *The Function of Apocalyptic and Wisdom Traditions in Romans 9–11*, 164–73) or composed it from various traditions (Bornkamm, *Early Christian Experience*, 105–11). Johnson, *The Function of Apocalyptic and Wisdom Traditions in Romans 9–11*, 167–68 correctly rejects Hanson's (*The New Testament Interpretation,* 91) Christological view of Rom 11:34–35, viewing it as a proof text of Christ as a pre-existent Wisdom of God. However, Fitzmyer, 633 argues that Paul does not borrow from Jewish sources but composes it himself. Jewett, 714 questions Pauline composition of the doxology. Smith, *Isaiah 40-66*, 106 states that Isa 40:13 is an instructional speech on the greatness of God. This point has some parallels with the hymnic material. Concerning this point, see also Westermann, *Isaiah 40-66*, 49 and Koole, *Isaiah III: Isaiah 40-48*, 87. At present, no view clearly distinguishes itself above the others concerning the origin of the wisdom hymn.

[805] Murray, 2:104–05; Cranfield, 589; Käsemann, 318; Moo 2nd, 759; and Naselli, *From Typology to Doxology*, 25–28. *Contra* Fitzmyer *Romans*, 633 who widens the connection to chaps 1–11.

[806] Naselli, *From Typology to Doxology*, 29–38. For discussion on rhetorical questions in Isaiah, see Kuhtz, "The Form, Location and Function of Rhetorical Questions in Deutero-Isaiah," 129-42.

[807] The source of this paragraph came from Sullivan, *The INE in Rom 9–11*, 2nd, 196-98.

4. The Mercy of God in Salvation (11:28-32)
5. A Wisdom Polemic Doxology (11:33-36)

Original Text

11.33 Ὦ βάθος πλούτου καὶ σοφίας καὶ γνώσεως θεοῦ· ὡς ἀνεξεραύνητα[a] τὰ κρίματα αὐτοῦ καὶ ἀνεξιχνίαστοι αἱ ὁδοὶ αὐτοῦ. 34 Τίς γὰρ ἔγνω νοῦν κυρίου; ἢ τίς σύμβουλος αὐτοῦ ἐγένετο; 35 ἢ τίς προέδωκεν αὐτῷ, καὶ ἀνταποδοθήσεται αὐτῷ; 36 ὅτι ἐξ αὐτοῦ καὶ δι' αὐτοῦ καὶ εἰς αὐτὸν τὰ πάντα· αὐτῷ ἡ δόξα εἰς τοὺς αἰῶνας, ἀμήν.

Textual Notes

[a] **11:33 ἀνεξεραύνητα τὰ κρίματα αὐτοῦ καὶ ἀνεξιχνίαστοι** is supported by NA28, UBS5, SBLGKNT ℵ B A. **ἀνεξερεύνητα τὰ κρίματα αὐτοῦ καὶ ἀνεξειχνίαστοι** is supported by F G. **ἀνεξερεύνητα τὰ κρίματα αὐτοῦ καὶ ἀνεξιχνίαστοι** is supported by D L Ψ 049 056 and most of the other minuscules (Swanson, *NT Greek Mss*, 186). These differences do not change the understanding of the verse.

Translation

33 O the depth of the riches and of the wisdom and of the knowledge of God! How unsearchable are his judgments and inscrutable his ways! **34** For who has known the mind of the Lord? And who has been his counselor? **35** Or who has given to him in advance, and it will be given back to him? **36** For from him and through him and for him are all things. To him be the glory forever. Amen.

Commentary

11:33-36 Ὦ βάθος πλούτου καὶ σοφίας καὶ γνώσεως θεοῦ· ὡς ἀνεξεραύνητα τὰ κρίματα αὐτοῦ καὶ ἀνεξιχνίαστοι αἱ ὁδοὶ αὐτοῦ. 34 Τίς γὰρ ἔγνω νοῦν κυρίου; ἢ τίς σύμβουλος αὐτοῦ ἐγένετο; 35 ἢ τίς προέδωκεν αὐτῷ, καὶ ἀνταποδοθήσεται αὐτῷ; 36 ὅτι ἐξ αὐτοῦ καὶ δι' αὐτοῦ καὶ εἰς αὐτὸν τὰ πάντα· αὐτῷ ἡ δόξα εἰς τοὺς αἰῶνας, ἀμήν. "O the depth of the riches and of the wisdom and of the knowledge of God! How unsearchable are his judgments and inscrutable his ways! 34 For who has known the mind of the Lord? And who has been his counselor? 35 Or who has given to him in advance, and it will be given back to him? 36 For from Him and through Him and to Him are all things. To Him be the glory forever. Amen." The particle Ὦ ("O") demonstrates Paul's profound conviction and emotion concerning the wisdom polemic that God has reveal in Rom 9–11.[808] The noun βάθος ("depth") with the genitive modifier πλούτου ("riches") continues the profound heart and emotions of Paul. He is expressing the inexhaustible depth of wealth

[808] Blass, Debrunner and Funk, A Greek Grammar, §146(2). BDAG, 1101 says it is expressing that Paul is "standing amazed at."

concerning God's divine knowledge.[809] Not only of God's γνώσεως ("knowledge," Col 2:3) but also his σοφίας ("wisdom," Rev 5:12).[810] The syntactical construction of the following genitives connected by two καὶ ("and") connectives (πλούτου καὶ σοφίας καὶ γνώσεως θεοῦ) modify the noun βάθος ("depth").[811] This way Paul is emphasizing the inexhaustible and unsearchable "depth" by three descriptive adjectives. The infinite depth of God's character is being magnified (1 Cor 2:10). The last two words (σοφίας, γνώσεως) are attributes or qualities of God and are often labeled by theologians as the communicable attributes of God. Communicable attributes mean that these qualities may also be displayed as properties of human character who bear the image of God.[812] However, of course, not to the infinite degree of God. The word πλούτου is not a direct description of an attribute of God (Schreiner, 2nd, 616). Thus, some use this as an argument against making these three words separate description of βάθος ("depth"). But there is something else that unifies these words together. Some have applied the word πλούτου ("riches")[813] with the thoughts of Rom 11:12 where the word also appears twice (Moo, 2nd, 760), while others refer it to the general resources of God (1 Cor 1:21, 24; Eph 3:10). However, the context of God's wisdom polemic plan helps to define the "riches" Paul is expressing. The riches of God's wisdom polemic have been expressed in Rom 9–11 and this context helps to define riches. This definition would include the thought of 11:12 but it is more than this. Thus, the riches of God's plan fit together with the character of God as He unfolds the wisdom polemic of the ages. The "riches" is the display of God's character and plan briefly argued in Rom 11 specifically and Rom 9–11 overall. A wisdom polemic is where God, usually through the prophet, uses the genre of wisdom to construct a disputation against the people of God because of their lack of knowledge, understanding, and rebellion against the character and plan of God.[814]

The beginning of the last phrase of v. 33 is introduced with ὡς ("how") which is a less common translation. It is classified as "a relatively high point on a scale involving exclamation, *how!*"[815] The last part of v. 33 is syntactically parallel with the same meter and rhyme at the beginning and end:

adjective -	article -	subject noun -	possessive pronoun:
ἀνεξεραύνητα	τὰ	κρίματα	αὐτοῦ
ἀνεξιχνίαστοι	αἱ	ὁδοὶ	αὐτοῦ.

Paul mentions the unsearchable (ἀνεξεραύνητα)[816] judgments of God and the inscrutable (ἀνεξιχνίαστοι)[817] ways of God. Paul is stressing by these two words the human inability and

---

[809] BDAG, 162.

[810] Wilckens, Ulrich, *TDNT*, 518 gives a brief summary of wisdom and concludes that wisdom in Rom 11:33–36 is "vitally related" to Christ in salvation history."

[811] Moo, 2nd, 760, n. 897; Cranfield, 589; Käsemann, 319; Fitzmyer, 634; Jewett, 716 (see NRSV, ESV, NET). Schreiner, 2nd, 615 Murray, 2:105–06; Godet, 265 think that σοφίας and γνώσεως θεοῦ are dependent on πλούτου having a translation of "O the depth of the riches both of the wisdom and knowledge of God" (KJV, CSB, NASB, NIV). This is possible, but the way the text is written does not make this view obvious.

[812] Berkhof, *Systematic Theology*, 55.

[813] See a definition of πλούτου in the commentary under 11:12.

[814] See Sullivan, *The* INE *in Rom 9–11*, 2nd, 162, n. 1.

[815] BDAG, 1105.

[816] Ibid., 77 and *TDNT* 1:357 define it as "unfathomable or unsearchable." This word is only used here in the NT and it is not found in the LXX. Delling says, "The exact connotation of the term implies the abandonment of all attempts to solve theoretically the question of the meaning of the judgment on Israel, so that Paul describes even his own answer as an attempt for which he cannot claim absolute validity" (Ibid.).

[817] BDAG, 77 defines it as "inscrutable, incomprehensible." Used here and Eph 3:8 in the NT and three times in LXX (Job 5:9; 9:10; 34:24; also, Prayer of Manasseh 6; *1 Clem* 20.5).

inaccessibility to God's decisions and ways unfolding in the world. The word κρίματα (judgments) is used 27 times in the NT but only twice in the plural, here and in 1 Cor 6:7.[818] Moo, 2nd, 761 is probably correct that the meaning of κρίματα refers more to God's executive decision dealing with the plan of salvation history; however, it would include judicial decisions in it (Schreiner, 2nd, 617; Cranfield, 590; Sanday and Headlam, 590; Fitzmyer, 634). The word ὁδοὶ ("ways") may be used by Paul as a segway into the wisdom way in Isa 40 that he uses in v. 34.[819] Human being merely see the events of life one after the other and never in the same context how God sees them and plans them. Only when He expresses and interprets the events of history may we have the correct perspective on His plan. Even when God tells us His redemption history, it is often difficult to consistently put all the piece together satisfactorily.

God's plan includes judgments and seemingly unrighteous events that call into question the character and plan of God. Romans 9–11 is Paul's attempt to explain God's faithfulness to his covenantal plan expressed in the Old Testament, though it includes in the present age, Israel has been hardened (at least in part) and the nation as a whole is in unbelief. Here at the end of Romans 9–11, the Isaianic wisdom polemic culminates in the wisdom doxology because God is presented as executing the NE redemption plan in wonderful mercy that magnifies his wisdom and knowledge and vindicates the riches of His wise, eternal plan.[820]

In v. 34 Paul uses two rhetorical questions from the NE background of Isa 40:13, which is connect to v. 33 with a conjunction γὰρ ("for) to explain[821] his thoughts from Isaiah. He uses these two questions from Isaiah to stress that mere human beings cannot understand completely or comprehensively God's plan. However, he makes this point in a very interesting and powerful way. Let's peal back the onion and see the beauty of Paul's use of the OT context to express this NT point. It is important to remember that the conflation of Isaiah 29:16 and 45:9 in Romans 9:20 anticipates the final Isaianic quotation in Romans 11:34 (Isa 40:13), which shares the same theme of a NE wisdom polemic and forms an *inclusio*[822] thought pattern in Rom 9–11. Thus, this *inclusio* introduces and concludes the broad theme of Rom 9–11, God's NE wisdom polemic that exults His wise character and plan. The connection with the NE motif is associated first with Isaiah 40:3–5. The concept of the "way (דֶּרֶךְ) of the Lord" and the "highway (מְסִלָּה) for our God" (Isa 40:3) is to prepare for the glory of the Lord to be revealed and "all people shall see it together" (Isa 40:5). The writer of Isaiah parallels the eschatological hope and comfort that are

---

[818] Logos 8.14. Schreiner, 2nd, 615, n. 5 is correct that the two words in 11:12 are not a complete parallel for the objective genitives "world" and "Gentiles" are helpful to define the word "riches." However, the context of the wisdom polemic doxology and the *inclusio* argument with Rom 9:20 helps us to define the "riches." See Sullivan, *The INE in Rom 9–11*, 2nd, chp. 6.

[819] The most frequent cited intertestamental text that is like in some ways Paul's subject is II Baruch 14:8–9 (The Book of the Apocalypse of Baruch the son of Neriah). However, Paul is more influenced by wisdom of the OT then any evidence from the intertestmental literature. See Holland, *Contours of Pauline Theology*, 51-68. Davila, *The Provenance of the Pseudepigrapha, passim* challenged the criteria used to determine what was either Jewish or early Christian writings and has built on Robert A. Kraft's work to present a better criterion to study the Old Testament pseudepigrapha. See his summary conclusion in chapter 5 or Davila's article "The Old Testament Pseudepigrapha as Background to the New Testament," 53-57. See also de Jonge, "The Pseudepigrapha of the Old Testament and Early Christianity," 59-71. Bauckham, *The Jewish World around the New Testament*, 461-83 evaluates and qualifies Davila's view. It seems to be very difficult to obtain objective data from the pseudepigrapha except possibly broadly repeated themes that can be collaborated with other sound evidence.

[820] Sullivan, *The INE in Rom 9–11*, 2nd, 204.

[821] A casual conjunction (Wallace, *Greek Grammar*, 674).

[822] An *inclusio* is a literary device known as bracketing which creates a frame by placing similar material at the beginning and end of a sentence or section and may consist of words or a phrase, or paragraph(s) or ideas, etc. It can be used to bring out purpose or importance in the literary composition or how one part may relate to another.

stated in Isaiah 40:3–5 with the Exodus in Isaiah 11:16. Thus, the background of Isaiah 40:13 is the concept of the "way" (דֶּרֶךְ) in the INE and its connection with the wisdom of Yahweh. The "way" terminology has both a spatial and sapiential connotations and it richly conveys the background of the Exodus.[823] Therefore, the word "way" not only may refer to a physical path to return to Yahweh and Jerusalem, but the word can refer to a rejection of the idolatrous wisdom and the embracing of the wisdom and way of Yahweh. This sapiential way contributes to the INE background for Isaiah 40:13.[824]

Isaiah 40:12–14 deals with the rhetorical question concerning God's incomparable power and wisdom. In sum, God is incomparable because he is omnipotent, omniscience, all-wise, and all-understanding whether he deals with the path of justice or in the way of all things, whether the activity is in the heavens or on the earth. The argument in Isaiah 40:12–26 is a wisdom polemic taken up in a NE motif to encourage the people not to rebel but to marvel over the sovereign God and his sapiential plan. The very core of this polemic is found in Isaiah 40:13–14.[825]

Paul quotes Isaiah 40:13 in 1 Corinthians 2:16 where he takes the first and the third phrases of the OT text while using the first two phrases of Isaiah 40:13 in Romans 11:34. His purpose for quoting the Isaianic passage in 1 Corinthians 2:16 is revealed when one understands Paul's answer to the Isaianic question, "Who has known the mind of the Lord?" Paul's answer is, "But we have the mind of Christ." In the context of 1 Corinthians 2, the "mind of Christ" is God's wisdom of salvation through the crucified Christ, which was hidden but now is made known through the Holy Spirit. In the context of Isaiah 40, the "mind of the Lord" draws upon the wisdom polemic and the NE salvation context. Thus, the context of the NE wisdom motif is appropriated by Paul when he cites Isaiah 40:13 in 1 Corinthians 2:16. Likewise, when he uses Isaiah 40:13 in the wisdom doxology of Romans 11:34, the influence of the NE salvation would be strongly anticipated.[826]

The contexts of Isaiah 40:13 and Roman 11:33–36 have several parallels. In Isaiah 40, God is comforting Israel. Even though there is to be a Babylonian captivity, God's glory and presence are promised in a future restoration. God's plan has difficult and, at times, confusing complexities, which become challenging to reconcile with the glory and comfort of Isaiah 40. For example, the writer of Isaiah declares that the people of God have blind eyes, deaf ears, and

---

[823] Part of the conclusion of Lund, *Way Metaphors and Way Topics in Isaiah 40–55*, 302 is that "this double understanding of the ways of YHWH reflects something that has been prominent throughout the whole of Isaiah 40–55 . . . The analysis pointed out that one can probably establish a close connection in the Old Testament between YHWH's own ways and those ways he gives his people to walk in. This is made clear in Isaiah 40–55 by means of YHWH's way in the people's desert serving, in turn, as a way for the people out of their desert situation."

[824] These summary thoughts come from Sullivan, *The INE in Rom 9–11*, 2nd, 189–94. See especially pp. 204–07 that briefly summarizes the NE motif in Isa 40:1–11.

[825] Goldingay, *The Message of Isaiah 40–55*, 39 suggests that the two "theologically freighted expressions in v.13" open up the possibility of reading verse 13 on two levels. First, verse 13 should be read in the context of Isa 40:12–14, and secondly, in the context of its theological significance of later chapters of 40–48. For example, "a man of his counsel" may be an oblique reference and introduction to Cyrus (Isa 45:1). This point is an intriguing thought, but it seems too speculative. One could perhaps apply this theological reading in a broad and general way. For example, God's counsel would encompass the plan to use Cyrus and this event would find application from God's wise counsel and plan.

[826] This paragraph was taken from Sullivan, *The INE in Rom 9–11*, 2nd, 198. Schreiner, 636 highlights the remarkable similarities in themes in 1 Cor 2:16 and Rom 11:34. For example, human beings cannot understand the wisdom of God without the aid of the Holy Spirit. However, he misses the key concept of the NE.

dull hearts,[827] while other places the writer affirms that God removes the blindness and deafness.[828] The imagery of this removal is a helpful description of the NE redemption. Furthermore, some intriguing statements address not only the judgment of Gentiles, but also their inclusion in God's blessing.[829] In the midst of this Gentile conundrum, the question of God's righteousness and the wisdom of his plan becomes the polemic. In Romans 9–11, Paul discusses the election of a remnant to comfort Israel concerning their present condition of unbelief and reminds them of the future restoration. However, there is the mystery of God's plan that deals with the partial hardening of Israel until the fullness of the Gentile salvation comes in.

In the past, God's way was not understood. The captives of Israel in Babylon did not understand God's mind and his plan of redemption and restoration. "[S]imilarly no human being could anticipate the wisdom of God's plan by which he has arranged history to bring about the salvation of both Jews and gentiles in a most improbable way."[830] In God's plan for this age, he "has extended salvation to the uncircumcised gentiles and at the end of history will again fold in unbelieving Jews. Does the inclusion of Israel again seem incredible? It is no more incredible than the pledge to rescue Israel from the dominion of Babylon."[831] The background of Isaiah 40:13 carries with it the admonishment not to rebel against the wise plan of God but to marvel over it. The wisdom polemic as a NE motif of God's "way" is used by Paul in his doxology.[832] Wagner summarizes:

> Paul's appropriation of Isaiah 40:13 is of a piece with his use of other Isaianic texts in Romans to speak about contemporary Israel, particularly Isaiah 29:16/45:9 (Rom 9:20), Isaiah 28:16/8:14 (Rom 9:33), and Isaiah 40:21/28 (Rom 10:18, 19). In each case, the wider context in Isaiah portrays Israel challenging God's wisdom and doubting God's power and faithfulness to save them. Paul appears to have found in these Isaianic oracles an analogue to the resistance his message now faces from his contemporaries .... In his concluding doxology, the apostle takes refuge in the incomprehensible wisdom of God who has in his hands the redemption of his people Israel, and indeed of the entire world.[833]

In Rom 11:35, Paul in combination with Isaiah 40:13 also uses a quotation most likely from Job 41:11a (41:3a MT, LXX).[834] Job's questioning of God led to the rebuke of Job 38–41,

---

[827] Cf. Isa 29:9–12; 42:16–21; 44:18–20; 48:8.

[828] Cf. Isa 29:18; 32:3; 35:5; 42:7.

[829] Cf. Isa 2:2–4; 45:22; 49:22; 52:15; 55:5; 56:3–8.

[830] Schreiner, *Romans*, 2nd, 618.

[831] Ibid.

[832] The last two paragraphs were taken from Sullivan, *The INE in Rom 9–11*, 2nd, 199.

[833] Wagner, *Heralds of the Good News*, 304. Paul's quotation from Isa 40:13 is within a rich Jewish heritage where the wisdom and understanding of God is understood to be beyond human comprehension. For examples, see Ps 106:2; Jer 10:7; Sir 16:20; Wisd Sol 9:16–17; 11:21; Pss Sol 5:3, 12; 15:2; *1 Enoch* 93:11–14 (Dunn, *Romans 9–16*, 38b:700; Naselli, *From Typology to Doxology*, 99-103). However, what is innovative in Paul's citation in Rom 11:34 is the wisdom polemic in a NE motif, which reflects the sovereignty of God's ways in the context of Jews and Gentile salvation. The concept of the total context of Dodd/Hays and the wisdom polemic as part of the NE theme help to answer the concern of Robert Foster, Review of Andrew David Naselli, *From Typology to Doxology: Paul's Use of Isaiah and Job in Romans 11:34–35, Review of Biblical Literature* (http://www.bookreviews.org, Apr 2014). His main concern is the connection of Isaiah 40 and Job 41 with the Romans 11:34–35 and how to justify the typological connection.

[834] See Naselli, *From Typology to Doxology*, 63–90; and Richard J. Clifford, "Second Isaiah," in *The Anchor Bible Dictionary*, ed. David N. Freedman (New York: Doubleday, 1992), 3:497. The meaning of the "way" (דרך) of God in the context of Isa 40:13 is found in Job 23:11, 26:14, and 36:23. Dunn, 698 links Rom 11:33–36

which dealt with God's inscrutable wisdom and justice in operating his universe. Schreiner, 2nd, 619 states Paul's use of Job 41:11a (41:3a MT, LXX) this way:

> Just as Job doubted God's wisdom and ability in his suffering, so too the Roman Christians might be inclined to question God's wisdom in terms of his saving plan for world history. Job's vision of God's greatness was too circumscribed. God accomplished his plan with respect to Job in wisdom and justice, and so too his plan to save some Jews and Gentiles is wise and just. God is debtor to no one's wisdom, strength, or goodness and he has accomplished his purposes by his own initiative.

The argument of Job 41:11a (41:3a MT, LXX) supplements the wisdom polemic context that is expressed in Isaiah 40:13.[835]

Naselli summarizes the contextual parallels of Isaiah 40:13 and Job 41:3a (MT, LXX) in seven points: (1) both Job and Israel experienced God's blessing; (2) God's withdrawal of blessing, which seems to be unjust to both Job and Israel, makes restoration seem impossible; (3) they both question God's righteousness and his plan; (4) the difficulty of receiving revelation did not provide all the answers they wanted; thus, they were tempted to doubt God's wisdom – the difficulty for Israel is to understand how the Gentiles' prominent role fits into the reference with Israel; (5) they both need to repent of their flawed view of God and his plan, and trust him; (6) Job experienced and Israel will experience God's restoration and blessing in a greater degree; and (7) God's plan demonstrates his sovereign wisdom and mercy.[836] These parallels point to a typological use of Isaiah 40:13 and Job 41:11a (41:3a MT, LXX) in Romans 11:34–35.[837] God's character is highlighted as he reveals himself to Job in Job 41:11a (41:3a MT, LXX) and to Israel in Isaiah 40:13 and now is connected with Paul's revelation to the Christians in Romans 11:34–35. Paul appears to use the historical contexts and the theologies of Job and Isaiah to affirm and praise the plan of God for Israel.[838] The response that should be elicited for God's grand plan is the highest praise and admiration to the merciful sovereign God. However, Paul couches the doxology in a wisdom polemic from a NE motif, for he is aware of the historical negative response of his people to God's sovereign plan.

In sum, Paul uses three main points in his wisdom polemic doxology that may be discerned from Isaiah 40:13 and Job 41:11a (41:3a MT, LXX): (1) The incomparable God is incomprehensible (Isa 40:13a); (2) the wise God is devoid of counsellors (Isa 40:13b); and (3) the God who owns the universe is without creditors (Job 41:3a).[839] These three points should be

---

to Job, such as Job 15:8 with Rom 11:34. Jewett, 720 agrees that Job 41:3 in Rom 11:35 has a broad consensus, but the differences between the texts cause him to be cautious. Fitzmyer, 635 suggests also the possibility of Job 35:7 or 41:1 are possible sources for the quotation.

[835] The parallels of Isaiah 40 and Job 38–41 are recognized by Blenkinsopp, *Isaiah 40–55*, 190–91; Oswalt, *Isaiah Chapter 40–66*, 59; Koole, *Isaiah III: Isaiah 40–48*, 87, 93; Grogan, "Isaiah," 725; and Smith, *Isaiah 40–66*, 106.

[836] Naselli, *From Typology to Doxology*, 133, 134–35, 138 is used with the writer's modifications.

[837] Ibid., 191–96. Aageson, "Typology, Correspondence and the Application of Scripture in Romans 9–11," 51–72 argues for correspondence instead of typology.

[838] Here are some common parallels that the context and theology of Isa 40:13, Job 41:3a, and Rom 11:33–34 share: (1) God has stripped the blessings away from Israel because of their disobedience and this event seems unfair to them. This shift appears to make their restoration impossible. (2) They question God's character, especially his righteousness. (3) Each text is polemical for they doubt God's wisdom and plan. (4) God promises a restoration to blessing in such a way and degree that it will magnify God's wisdom and his sovereign plan.

[839] In v. 35, the word προέδωκεν is used only here in the NT and it means to "give in advance" (BDAG, 867; Moulton and Milligan, *The Vocabulary of the Greek Testament*, 539). In the LXX, the word is only found in 4 Kingdom 6:11 (Logos 8.14). The word ἀνταποδοθήσεται is used seven times in six verses in the NT (Lk 14:14 [2x];

placed in the background of the wisdom polemic against God's way and plan. The concept of the "way" in Isaiah 40 has spatial and sapiential connotations. Both of these connotations have been connected with the INE. God's way is a promised physical and spiritual restoration where the glory of Yahweh will be revealed, and all flesh will see it together (Isa 40:3–5). God's way is also connected with his wise plan in Isaiah 40:12–14. In the day of this Isaianic oracle, God's people needed to trust in the sovereign plan of God and not turn in disobedience to the false gods of the idols. In Romans 9–11, Paul seems to have found in these Isaianic oracles a similarity to the rebellion and unbelief that his message now faces from his contemporaries.[840]

Paul supplements the argument in Romans 11:35 with the following point: God owns everything, and he does not owe anyone anything (Job 41:3a). He knows the "path of justice" (Isa 40:14) for his "judgments are unsearchable" (Rom 11:33). God knows "the way of understanding" (Isa 40:14) for his "ways are inscrutable" (Rom 11:33). Paul ends his argument in Romans 9–11 with a breath-taking crescendo of praise to God's mercy, omniscience, wisdom, incomprehensibility, incomparability, independence, and sovereignty. Furthermore, Romans 11:34–35 places the doxology in the wisdom polemic context. Paul seeks to persuade his readers not to rebel against God's wise plan of redemption. He directs them to marvel over it by joining in full submission to this great doxology.[841]

The ὅτι ("for") in v. 36 is a soft or loosely causal[842] referring back most likely to vv.34–35.[843] An ancient interpretation found a reference to the Trinity in the three prepositional phrases (Moo, 2nd, 762; Cranfield, 592). However, this interpretation has largely been rejected (Schreiner, 2nd, 620, n. 15). Paul's view of the supremacy of God is expressed by three prepositions summing up all things: God is the source (ἐξ) all things, the means (διά) of all things, and the goal (εἰς) of all things. Paul's expression briefly, simply, and profoundly encompasses the beginning, the continual existence (determining how long something last), and the end (cf. 1 Cor 8:6; 11:12c). The One who exists from everlasting to everlasting (Ps 90:2) is the source and the cause of the creation of all things. He determines when it, he, or she exists, the characteristics of the created existence, and how long and what the ordain function the creation will perform (Eccl 3:1–11; Ps 139:16; Prov 16:4). Jewett, 722 states that this creation theology in v. 36 was typical in Hellenistic Judaism and was more missional than doctrinal; however, he also states that these prepositions express the "mystery of salvation" and not just the "doctrine of creation." Naselli prefers the language as borrowed from the Greek stoic philosophers indirectly through Hellenistic Judaism.[844] The actual wording of v. 36 is not copied from the OT; however, it is rooted in the theology of the OT. The Creator of all things executes his all-encompassing sovereign plan with all its detail which magnifies his matchless glory. Thus, Paul ends this section with the summation statement that is the chief and supreme end and purpose of all of creation: "To Him be the glory forever" (lit. "unto the ages"). Soli Deo Gloria! (1 Chron 16:29–

Rom 11:35; 12:19; 1 Thess 3:9; 2 Thess 1:6; Heb 10:30 (Logos 8.14). BDAG, 87 defines it as "practice reciprocity with respect to an obligation, repay, pay back, requite." The word is used 62 times in the LXX (Logos 8.14).

[840] Wagner, *Heralds of the Good News*, 304.

[841] Comments on v. 35 came from Sullivan, *The INE in Rom 9–11*, 2nd, 200–203.

[842] Blass, Debrunner, Funk, *A Greek Grammar*, §456(1); Robertson, *A Grammar of the Greek*, 962; BDAG, 732 (4, b).

[843] Naselli, "Paul's Use of Isaiah 40:13 and Job 41:3A in Rom 11:34–35," 54; Schreiner, 2nd, 619. Others refer it only to v. 35. Moo, 2nd, 762 refers it to vv. 33–35.

[844] Naselli, "Paul's Use of Isaiah 40:13 and Job 41:3A in Rom 11:34–35," 55–56. See further explanation in Moo, NIV Application Romans, 391; Jewett, 721–22; Dunn, 701–02; Schreiner, 2nd, 619; Cranfield, 591; Sanday and Headlam, 340–41.

31,36; Ps 19:1–6; 29:1–2; 33:9; 47:8; 90:2; 93:1–2; 115:1; 139:16; Eccl 3:1–14; Isa 40:12–28; 42:5; 43:7, 45:12; 46:9–11; 48:11). Paul ends his doxological wisdom polemic with a familiar synagogue affirmation ἀμήν ("amen," "so be it").[845] Paul is encouraging the Roman congregation to affirm the Gentile and Israelite mystery (vv. 25–26) just explained in this chapter (Jewett, 723).

In summing up the broad picture, Paul conflates Isaiah 29:16 and 45:9 in Romans 9:20 to warn his interlocutor by highlighting and intertwining the Isaianic wisdom polemic. In addition, the conflation of Isaiah 29:16 and 45:9 in Romans 9:20 anticipates the final Isaianic quotation in Romans 11:34 (Isa 40:13), which shares the same theme of a wisdom polemic. The significance of this *inclusio* is to direct the reader to Paul's overall point that is stated in the wisdom polemic doxology in Rom 11:33–36 where everyone is called to marvel over the wise God and his sovereign plan.[846]

Biblical Theological Comments[847]

Paul uses Isaiah 29:16 and 45:9 in Romans 9:20 together with Romans 11:34, which draws upon Isaiah 40:13 (and the supplement text Job 41:[3a] 11a), thereby creating an *inclusio* in the argument of Romans 9–11.[848] The first part of the *inclusio* uses the wisdom polemic in the motif of the NE to warn the readers not to rebel against God's wise plan. A wisdom polemic is where God, usually through the prophet, uses the genre of wisdom to construct a disputation against the people of God because of their lack of knowledge, understanding, and rebellion against the character and plan of God. The election of some and the hardening of others are part of a difficult plan to understand and accept. In this polemic, Paul draws upon the theological context of the Isaianic wisdom polemic in Isaiah 29:16 and Isaiah 45:9. Paul also chooses the Isaianic wisdom polemic of Isaiah 40 and the wisdom section of Job 41 because certain portions of their teachings are parallel. The wisdom polemic in the theology of the INE is the theme and context of Paul's argument. The more the reader understood the history of Israel and the theology of Isaiah in particular, the more powerful would be the force of Paul's quotations from Isaiah. Paul makes use of the wisdom polemic to express God's redemption of Jews and Gentiles, which is conveyed in the NE theme.

God's plan includes judgments and seemingly unrighteous events that call into question the character and plan of God. Romans 9–11 is Paul's attempt to explain God's faithfulness to his covenantal plan expressed in the Old Testament, though in the present age, Israel has been hardened (at least in part) and the nation as a whole is in unbelief. At the end of Romans 9–11, the Isaianic wisdom polemic culminates in the wisdom doxology because God is presented as executing the NE redemption plan in wonderful mercy that magnifies his righteous character and vindicates his eternal plan.

---

[845] See also Rom 1:25; 9:5; 15:33, and 16:24. BDAG, 53 state that it is a "strong affirmation of what is stated" and may be translated "let it be so, truly, amen." Notice Paul's explanation and instructions in 1 Cor 14:16.

[846] Sullivan, *The INE in Rom 9–11*, 2nd, 188.

[847] This section was taken from Sullivan, The INE in Rom 9–11, 2nd, 203–04.

[848] Kim, *God, Israel, and the Gentiles*, 141 and Johnson, *The Function of Apocalyptic and Wisdom Traditions in Romans 9–11*, 173 recognize an *inclusio* with Rom 9:1–5 and 11:33–36. Naselli, *From Typology to Doxology*, 25 recognizes an *inclusio* with Rom 9:5b and 11:36b. One main point that goes against this being an *inclusio* is Rom 9:1–5, which is Christological in emphasis where Rom 11:33–36 is not.

Scholars have recognized the wisdom polemic in Isaiah; however, not specifically in Isaiah 44–45 and only occasionally has it been linked to the NE. What is new is the association of the wisdom polemic and the NE as inherent to Paul's use of his chosen Isaianic quotations in Romans 9:20 and 11:34. This clarifies the significance of using the particular quotation from Isaiah in order to underline his point. Whether it is in the days of the first Exodus or a NE, God's wisdom is sufficient to bring his people to deliverance and restoration even though they themselves do not comprehend his plan.

Application and Devotional Implications

If you will stop and reflect upon all that Paul has told us about God's plan in Rom 9–11 what should be our response? What should be our response to the absolute sovereignty of God? What should be our response to the infinite wisdom and knowledge of God's eternal plan? What should be our response to the perfect judgment which God performs? We may not understand all of it or how it fits together but our response should be praise to God from the depth of our soul!

As Paul penned these words, I believe he became overwhelmed at this point with the majesty and awesomeness of God and His plan. Notice he says, "Oh the depth of the riches, of the wisdom and knowledge of God!" Have you had difficulty putting together God's sovereignty in election and man's responsibility? Have you wonder why God can raise up a Pharaoh to demonstrate the power and glory of God by hardening his heart? Do you question why God in His eternal plan decreed to allow His nation to go its own way and be hardened, but will in the future graft them back into eternal blessings? Yet, on the other hand, you did not say thank you with deep groanings of gratitude for He brought salvation to us Gentiles.

But, do we say, "Couldn't there be a better plan?" Paul answers us by saying His judgments are unsearchable, and we are not able to trace them. His ways are unfathomable or incomprehensible! Cranfield (590) writes, "God's judgments, as the judgments of the merciful God designed to further His purpose of mercy … do not conform to men's, even believing men's, preconceptions and (they) defeat our efforts to keep track of them." "… God's judgments and ways cannot be judged from a higher vantage point but are to be discerned as right only in subjection to them as the affairs and ways of God."

By God's infinite wisdom He made His plan and purpose and by His knowledge He employed the man to attain its end. If someone thinks that man had some part or influence upon God determining or carrying out His plan, Paul rebukes them by quoting Isa 40:13 and Job 41:11a in Rom 11:34–35. "For who has known the mind of the LORD, or who became His counselor? Or who has first given to Him that it might be paid back to him again?" (NASB). Paul is again exulting the sovereignty, self-sufficiency and wisdom of God. "For from Him and through Him and to Him are all things. To Him be the glory forever. Amen" (Rom 11:36 NASB). Listen to the hymn writer Alfred Mace (1944), who wrote the hymn Victory:

O lead me to the Man that died
Who all God's nature glorified;
Descending to the depth of woe;
And for us vanquished every foe.
O lead me on to Zion's hill,
To see the Lord His word fulfill;
His glorious king is sitting there;

Ruling over earth and sea and air.
There too, the eternal Three in One;
Blest Father, Spirit and the Son;
Rest undisturbed forevermore;
I wonder Worship and adore!

"Oh, the depth of the riches, of the wisdom, and knowledge of God! How unsearchable are His judgments and inscrutable his ways!" (v. 33).

Selected Bibliography

Aageson, James W. "Typology, Correspondence and the Application of Scripture in Romans 9–11." *Journal for the Study of the New Testament* 31 (September 1987): 51–72.

Arndt, William, Frederick W. Danker, and Walter Bauer, *A Greek-English Lexicon of the New Testament and Other Early Christian Literature*, 3rd ed. electronic version (Chicago: University of Chicago Press, 2000).

Blass, Friedrich, Albert Debrunner, and Robert Walter Funk, *A Greek Grammar of the New Testament and Other Early Christian Literature* (Chicago: University of Chicago Press, 1961).

Blenkinsopp, Joseph. *Isaiah 1–39: A New Translation with Introduction and Commentary*. The Anchor Bible, vol. 19 (New York: Doubleday, 2000).

Bornkamm, Günther, *Early Christian Experience* (New York: Harper & Row, 1969).

Bauckham, Richard, *The Jewish World around the New Testament* (Grand Rapids: Baker, 2010).

Davila, James R. *The Provenance of the Pseudepigrapha: Jewish, Christian, or other?*, Supplement to the Journal for the Study of Judaism (Leiden: Brill, 2005).

Davila, James R. "The Old Testament Pseudepigrapha as Background to the New Testament." *Expository Times* 117 (2005): 53–57.

De Jonge, Marinus, "The Pseudepigrapha of the Old Testament and Early Christianity," in *The New Testament and Hellenistic Judaism*, eds. P. Borgen and S. Giversn (Aarhus: Aarhus University Press, 1995), 59-71.

Delling, Gerhard, "Ἀνεξωρεύνητος," ed. Gerhard Kittel, Geoffrey W. Bromiley, and Gerhard Friedrich, *TDNT* (Grand Rapids, MI: Eerdmans, 1964).

Goldingay, John. *The Message of Isaiah 40–55: A Literary-Theological Commentary* (London. T & T Clark, 2005).

Grogan, Geoffrey W. "Isaiah." In *Expositor's Bible Commentary*, ed. Frank Gaebelein, re. ed., vol. 6, 433–863 (Grand Rapids: Zondervan, 2008).

Holland, Tom, *Contours of Pauline Theology* (Fearn, Scotland: Mentor Imprint, 2004).

Johnson, *The Function of Apocalyptic and Wisdom Traditions in Romans 9–11*. Society of Biblical Literature Dissertation Series, ed. Charles Talbert, vol. 109 (Atlanta: Scholars Press, 1989).

Kim, Johann D. *God, Israel, and the Gentiles: Rhetoric and Situation in Romans 9–11*, Society of Biblical Literature Dissertation Series (Atlanta: Society of Biblical Literature, 2000).

Koole, Ian L. *Isaiah III: Isaiah 40–48. Historical Commentary on the Old Testament*. Trans. Anthony P. Runia, eds. Cornelis Houtman, Willem S. Prinsloo, Wilfred G. E. Watson, Al Wolters, vol. 1 (Leuven: Peeters, 1997).

Koole, Ian L. Isaiah III: Isaiah 49–55. *Historical Commentary on the Old Testament*. Trans. Anthony P. Runia, eds. Cornelis Houtman, Willem S. Prinsloo, Wilfred G. E. Watson, Al Wolters, vol. 2 (Leuven: Peeters, 1998).

Kuhtz, Kenneth, "The Form, Location and Function of Rhetorical Questions in Deutero-Isaiah," in *Writings and Reading the Scroll of Isaiah: Studies of Interpretive Tradition*, Vetus Testamentum Supplement (Leiden: Brill, 1997), 129-42.

Lund, Øystein. *Way Metaphors and Way Topics in Isaiah 40–55*. Forschungen aum Alten Testament, 2. Reihe. (Tübingen: Mohr Siebeck, 2007).

Moulton, James Hope and George Milligan, *The Vocabulary of the Greek Testament* (London: Hodder and Stoughton, 1930).

Naselli, Andrew D. *From Typology to Doxology: Paul's Use of Isaiah and Job in Romans 11:34–35* (Eugene, OR: Pickwick Publication, 2012).

Naselli, Andrew D. "Paul's Use of Isaiah 40:13 and Job 41:3a (Eng 41:11a) in Romans 11:34–35" (Ph.D. diss., Trinity Evangelical Divinity School, 2010).

Oswalt, John N. *The Book of Isaiah 40–66*. New International Commentary on the Old Testament, ed. R. K. Harrison (Grand Rapids: Eerdmans, 1998).

Robertson, A. T. *A Grammar of the Greek New Testament in the Light of Historical Research*. (Logos Bible Software, 2006).

Smith, Gary. *Isaiah 40–66*. The New American Commentary. Vol. 15B (Nashville: B & H, 2009).

Sullivan, Steven P. *The Isaianic New Exodus in Romans 9–11* (Silverton: OR: Lampion Press, 2017).

Sullivan, Steven P. *The Isaianic New Exodus in Romans 9–11*, 2nd ed. (Middletown, RI: Stone Tower Press, 2023).

Wagner, J. Ross. *Heralds of the Good News: Isaiah and Paul in Concert in the Letter to the Romans*. Supplements to Novum Testamentum, eds. M. M. Mitchell and D. P. Moessner, vol. 101 (Leiden: Brill, 2002).

Wallace, Daniel B. *Greek Grammar Beyond the Basic: An Exegetical Syntax of the New Testament* (Grand Rapids: Zondervan, 1996).

Wilckens, Ulrich, "Σοφία, Σοφός, Σοφίζω," ed. Gerhard Kittel, Geoffrey W. Bromiley, and Gerhard Friedrich, *TDNT* (Grand Rapids, MI: Eerdmans, 1964–68).

BIBLIOGRAPHY

Romans Commentary Bibliography

Abasciano, Brian J. *Paul's Use of the Old Testament in Romans 9:1–9: An Intertextual and Theological Exegesis*. Library Studies of the New Testament 301. London: T & T Clark, 2005.

Abasciano, Brian J. *Paul's Use of the Old Testament in Romans 9:10-18: An Intertextual and Theological Exegesis*. Library Studies of the New Testament 317. London: T & T Clark, 2012.

Alford, Henry. *Alford's Greek Testament: An Exegetical and Critical Commentary*, vol. 2. Grand Rapids: Guardian Press, 1976.

Barrett, Charles K. *The Epistle to the Romans*. Black´s New Testament Commentaries, 2nd ed. Peabody: Hendrickson or London: Continuum, 1991.

Barth, Karl. *The Epistle to the Romans.* Translated by Edwyn C. Hoskyns. 6th ed. Oxford: Clarendon Press, 1933.

Boice, James Montgomery. *Romans: God and History Romans 9–11*. Grand Rapids: Baker, 1993.

Bruce, F. F. *Romans*, Tyndale New Testament Series. Downers Grove: InterVarsity, 1985.

Byrne, Brendan. *Romans*, Sacra Pagina Series. Vol 6. Collegeville: The Liturgical Press, 1996.

Calvin, John *Commentary on the Epistle of Paul the Apostle to the Romans*. Trans. & ed. John Owen. Bellingham, WA: Logos Bible Software, 2010.

Chrysostom, John. "Homilies of St. John Chrysostom, Archbishop of Constantinople, on the Epistle of St. Paul to the Romans," in *Saint Chrysostom: Homilies on the Acts of the Apostles and the Epistle to the Romans*, ed. Philip Schaff, trans. J. B. Morris, W. H. Simcox, and George B. Stevens, vol. 11, A Select Library of the Nicene and Post-Nicene Fathers of the Christian Church, First Series. New York: Christian Literature Company, 1889.

Cranfield, C. E. B. *A Critical and Exegetical Commentary on the Epistle to the Romans*. 2 vols. International Critical Commentary, New Series, eds. J. A. Emerton and C. E. B. Cranfield. Edinburgh: T & T Clark, 1975–79.

Dumbrell, William J. *Romans: A New Covenant Commentary*. Eugene: Wipf and Stock, 2005.

Dunn, James D. G. *Romans 9–16*. Word Biblical Commentary. Vol 38A. Dallas: Word Books, 1988.

Fitzmyer, Joseph A. *Romans: A New Translation with Introduction and Commentary*, Anchor Bible, eds. William F. Albright and David N. Freedman. Vol 33. Garden City: Doubleday, 1993.

Fruchtenbaum, Arnold G. *The Book of Romans*, Ariel's Bible Commentary. San Antonio: Ariel Ministries, 2022.

Gill, John. "Romans to Revelation," in *Gill's Commentary*, vol. 6. Grand Rapids: Baker, repr. 1980.

Haldane, Robert. *A Commentary on the Epistle to the Romans*. London: The Banner Truth Trust, 1958.

Harrison, Everett F. and Donald A. Hagner, "Romans," in *The Expositor's Bible Commentary: Romans–Galatians (Revised Edition)*, ed. Tremper Longman III & Garland, David E., vol. 11. Grand Rapids: Zondervan, 2008.

Hendriksen, William, *Exposition of Paul's Epistle to the Romans,* New Testament Commentaries. Grand Rapids: Baker, 1981.

Hodge, Charles. *A Commentary on Romans*. The Geneva Series of Commentaries. rev. ed. 1864. Reprint, London: The Banner of Truth Trust, 1972.

Holland, Tom, *Romans: The Divine Marriage, A Biblical Theological Commentary*. Eugene: Wipf and Stock, 2011.

Hultgren, Arland J. *Paul's Letter to the Romans: A Commentary*. Grand Rapids: Eerdmans, 2011.

Jewett, Robert. *Romans: A Commentary*, Hermeneia: A Critical and Historical Commentary on the Bible. Minneapolis: Fortress Press, 2007.

Johnson, S. Lewis, adapted by Mike Abendroth. *Discovering Romans: Spiritual Revival for the Soul*. Grand Rapids: Zondervan, 2014.

Käsemann, Ernest. *Commentary on Romans*, trans. and ed. G. W. Bromiley. Grand Rapids: Eerdmans, 1980.

Keck, Leander E. *Romans*, Abingdon New Testament Commentaries. Nashville: Abingdon Press, 2005.

Kruse, Colin G. *Paul's Letter to the Romans*. The Pillar New Testament Commentary. Grand Rapids: Eerdmans, 2012.

Kuss, Otto. *Der Römerbrief: Übersetzt und erklärt*. 3 vols. Regensburg: Pustet, 1957–1978.

Leenhardt, Franz J. *The Epistle to the Romans*, trans. Harold Knight. London: Lutterworth Press, 1957.

Lenski, R. C. H. *The Interpretation of St. Paul's Epistle to the Romans*. Columbus: Wartburg Press, 1945.

Liddon, H. P. *Explanatory Analysis of St. Paul's Epistle to the Romans*. Reprint Minneapolis: James and Klock, 1977.

Longenecker, Richard N. *The Epistle to the Romans*. The New International Greek Testament Commentary. Grand Rapids: Eerdmans, 2016.

Matera, Frank J. *Romans*. Paideia Commentaries on the New Testament. Grand Rapids: Baker Academic, 2010.

MacArthur, John F. *Romans*, 2 vols., MacArthur New Testament Commentary. Chicago: Moody Press, 1991.

Meyer, Heinrich August Wilhelm. *Critical and Exegetical Handbook to the Epistle to the Romans*, ed. William P. Dickson, trans. John C. Moore and Edwin Johnson, vol. 2, Critical and Exegetical Commentary on the New Testament. Edinburgh: T & T Clark, 1874.

Michel, Otto. *Der Brief an die Roemer. Meyers Kommentar*. Goettingen: Vandenhoeck und Ruprecht, 1966.

Middendorf, Michael P. *Romans 9–16*, ed. Dean O. Wenthe and Curtis P. Giese, Concordia Commentary. Saint Louis, MO: Concordia Publishing House, 2016.

Moo, Douglas J. *The Epistle to the Romans,* New International Commentary on the New Testament. Grand Rapids: Eerdmans, 1996.

Moo, Douglas J. *The Epistle to the Romans,* 2nd ed. New International Commentary on the New Testament. Grand Rapids: Eerdmans, 2018.

Moo, Douglas J. *The NIV Application Commentary: Romans*. Grand Rapids: Zondervan, 2000.

Morris, Leon. *The Epistle to the Romans*. The Pillar New Testament Commentary. Grand Rapids, MI; Eerdmans, 1988.

Mounce, Robert H. *Romans*. The New American Commentary, electronic ed. Logos Library System. Nashville: B & H, 2001, c.1995.

Murray, John. *The Epistle to the Romans*. New International Commentary on the New Testament. Vol 2. Grand Rapids: Eerdmans, 1959–65.

Nicoll, W. Robertson. "Romans," in *The Expositor's Greek Testament*, vol. 2. Repr. Grand Rapids: Eerdmans, 1976.

Piper, John. *The Justification of God: An Exegetical and Theological Study of Romans 9:1-23*. Grand Rapids: Baker Academic, 1993.

Runge, Steven E. *High Definition Commentary: Romans*. Bellingham, WA: Lexham Press, 2014.

Sanday, William and Arthur C. Headlam, *A Critical and Exegetical Commentary on the Epistle to the Romans*, 5th ed. International Critical Commentary. Edinburgh: T & T Clark, 1902.

Schlier, Heinrich. *Roemerbrief Kommentar*, Herders theologischer Kommentar, 6. Freiburg: Herder, 1977.

Schreiner, Thomas R. *Romans*, Baker Exegetical Commentary on the New Testament. Vol. 6 Grand Rapids: Baker, 1998.

Schreiner, Thomas R. *Romans*, 2nd ed. Baker Exegetical Commentary on the New Testament. Vol. 6. Grand Rapids: Baker, 2018.

Seifrid, Mark A. "Romans." In *Commentary on the New Testament Use of the Old Testament*, ed. G. K. Beale and D. A. Carson. Grand Rapids: Baker, 2007, 607–694.

Shedd, William G. T. *A Critical and Doctrinal Commentary on the Epistle of St. Paul to the Romans*. Reprint Minneapolis: Klock & Klock, 1978.

Stuhlmacher, Peter. *Paul's Letter to the Romans: A Commentary*, trans. Scott J. Hafemann. Louisville: Westminster Press and John Knox Press, 1994.

Thielman, Frank S. *Romans*, Zondervan Exegetical Commentary on the New Testament. Grand Rapids, 2018.

Wardlaw, Ralph. *Lectures on the Epistle to the Romans*, ed. J. S. Wardlaw, vol. 2. Posthumous Works of the Rev. Ralph Wardlaw, D. D. Edinburgh. London: A. Fullarton & Co., 1861.

Wilckens, Ulrich. *Der Brief an die Römer*. Evangelisch-Katholischer Kommentar zum Neuen Testament, 3 vols. Neukirchen/Vluyn: Neukirchener and Zürich: Benziger, 1978–1982.

Wright, N. T. "Romans," in *New Interpreter's Bible*, ed. Leander E. Keck. Vol. 10. Nashville: Abingdon Press, 2002.

Reference and Grammar Bibliography

Albertz, R. "פלא," in *Theological Lexicon of the Old Testament*, vol. 2. Peabody: Hendrickson, 1997.

Arndt, William, Frederick W. Danker, and Walter Bauer, *A Greek-English Lexicon of the New Testament and Other Early Christian Literature*, Chicago: University of Chicago Press, 2000.

Balz, Horst Robert and Gerhard Schneider, eds. *EDNT*, 3 vols. Grand Rapids: Eerdmans, 1990.

Bauernfeind, Otto. "τρέχω κτλ.," *TDNT*, ed. vol. 8. Grand Rapids: Eerdmans, 1972, 226–235.

Beale, G. K., Daniel J. Brendsel, and William A. Ross. *An Interpretive Lexicon of New Testament Greek: Analysis of Prepositions, Adverbs, Particles, Relative Pronouns, and Conjunctions*. Grand Rapids: Zondervan, 2014.

Behm, Johannes. "Μορφή, Μορφόω, Μόρφωσις, Μεταμορφόω," ed. Gerhard Kittel, Geoffrey W. Bromiley, and Gerhard Friedrich, *TDNT*, vol. 4. Grand Rapids, MI: Eerdmans, 1964–68.

Behm, Johannes. "Καινός, Καινότης, Ἀνακαινίξω, Ἀνακαινόω, Ἀνακαίνωσις, Ἐγκαινίζω," ed. Gerhard Kittel, Geoffrey W. Bromiley, and Gerhard Friedrich, *TDNT*, vol 3. Grand Rapids, MI: Eerdmans, 1964–68.

Behm, Johannes and Ernst Würthwein. "Νοέω, Νοῦς, Νόημα," ed. Gerhard Kittel, Geoffrey W. Bromiley, and Gerhard Friedrich, *TDNT*, vol. 4. Grand Rapids, MI: Eerdmans, 1964–68.

Bell, Richard H. "The Origin and Purpose of the Jealousy Motif in Romans 9-11 A Case Study in the Theology and Technique of Paul." D. Theo. diss., Eberhard-Karls-Universtiät zu Tübingen, 1990.

Bergmeier, R. "ὑποτάσσω." *EDNT*. Grand Rapids: Eerdmans, 1990.

Bertran, Georg. "θαῦμα, θαυμάζω, θαυμάσιος, θαυμαστός," in *TDNT*, eds. Gerhard Kittel, Geoffery W. Bromiley and Gerhard Fredrick, vol. 3. Grand Rapids: Eerdmans, 1964.

Blass, Friedrich, Albert Debrunner, and Robert Walter Funk. *A Greek Grammar of the New Testament and Other Early Christian Literature*. Chicago: University of Chicago Press, 1961.

Brueggemann, Walter. *Isaiah 40–66.* Westminster Bible Companion. eds. Patrick D. Miller and David L. Bartlett. Louisville: Westminster John Knox Press, 1998.

Bultmann, Rudolf. "Γινώσκω, Γνῶσις, Ἐπιγινώσκω, Ἐπίγνωσις, Καταγινώσκω, Ἀκατάγνωστος, Προγινώσκω, Πρόγνωσις, Συγγνώμη, Γνώμη, Γνωρίζω, Γνωστός," *TDNT*, vol. 1. Grand Rapids, MI: Eerdmans, 1964), 689–719.

Bultmann, Rudolf . "Ἔλεος, Ἐλεέω, Ἐλεήμων, Ἐλεημοσύνη, Ἀνέλεος, Ἀνελεήμων," *TDNT*, vol. 2. Grand Rapids, MI: Eerdmans, 1964, 477–487.

Bultmann, Rudolf and Hermann Wolfgang Beyer, "Εὐλογέω, Εὐλογητός, Εὐλογία, Ἐνευλογέω," ed. Gerhard Kittel, Geoffrey W. Bromiley, and Gerhard Friedrich, *TDNT*, vol. 2, Grand Rapids, MI: Eerdmans, 1964–68.

Bultmann, Rudolf. "Οἰκτίρω, Οἰκτιρμος, Οἰκτίρμων," ed. Gerhard Kittel, Geoffrey W. Bromiley, and Gerhard Friedrich, *TDNT*, vol. 2. Grand Rapids, MI: Eerdmans, 1964–68.

Burton, Ernest De Witt. *Syntax of the Moods and Tenses in New Testament Greek*, 3rd ed. Edinburg: T & T Clark, 1898.

Clines, David J. A. ed., *DCH*, 8 vols. Sheffield, England: Sheffield Academic Press; Sheffield Phoenix Press, 1993–2011.

Conrad, J. "פלא," in *TDOT*, vol. 11. Grand Rapids: Eerdmans, 2001.

Cushman, Neal D. "A Critique of Rikki E. Watts' Isaianic New Exodus in the Markan Prologue." Ph.D. diss., Baptist Bible Seminary, 2012.

Delling, Gerhard. "Ἄρτιος, Ἐξαρτίζω, Καταρτίζω, Καταρτισμός, Κατάρτισις." *TDNT*, vol. 1. Grand Rapids, MI: Eerdmans, 1964.

Delling, Gerhard. "Ἄρχω, Ἀρχή, Ἀπαρχή, Ἀρχαῖος, Ἀρχηγός, Ἄρχων," ed. Gerhard Kittel, Geoffrey W. Bromiley, and Gerhard Friedrich, *TDNT*, vol. 1. Grand Rapids, MI: Eerdmans, 1964.

Delling, Gerhard. "Υποτάσσω." *TDNT*, vol. 8. Grand Rapids: Eerdmans, 1969, 39–46.

Grundmann, Walter, "Καρτερέω, Προσκαρτερέω, Προσκαρτέρησις," ed. Gerhard Kittel, Geoffrey W. Bromiley, and Gerhard Friedrich, *TDNT*, vol. 3, Grand Rapids: Eerdmans, 1964–68.

Gorday, Peter. *Principles of Patristic Exegesis*: *Romans 9–11 in Origen, John Chrysostom, and Augustine*, Studies in the Bible and Early Christianity. New York: Edwin Mellen Press, 1983.

Hackenberg, W. "Ἐπίγνωσις." *EDNT*, vol. 2. Grand Rapids: Eerdmans, 1991, 25.

Hatch, Edwin and Henry A. Redpath. *A Concordance to the Septuagint and the Other Greek Versions of the Old Testament (Including the Apocryphal books)*. Akademische Druck- u. Verlagsanstalt, 1975.

Hauck, Friedrich, "Μένω, Ἐμ-, Παρα-, Περι-, Προσμένω, Μονή, Ὑπομένω, Ὑπομονή," ed. Gerhard Kittel, Geoffrey W. Bromiley, and Gerhard Friedrich, *TDNT*, vol. 4 (Grand Rapids: Eerdmans, 1964–68).

Henry George Liddell, Robert Scott and Stuart Jones. *A Greek-English Lexicon*. Oxford: Clarendon Press, 1996.

Herntrich, Vokmar. "Λεῖμμα, ὑπόλειμμα, καταλείπω [κατά-, περί-, διάλειμμα]," in *TDNT*, vol. 4. Grand Rapids: Eerdmans, 1967, 196–209.

Hodges, Zane C. and Arthur L. Farstad, ed. *The Greek New Testament According to the Majority Text*. Nashville: Nelson , 1982.

Holmes, Michael W. ed. *The Greek New Testament: SBL Edition*. Lexham Press: Society of Biblical Literature, 2011–2013.

Horst, Johannes, "Μακροθυμία, Μακροθυμέω, Μακρόθυμος, Μακροθύμως," in *TDNT*, vol. 4. Grand Rapids: Eerdmans, 1967, 374–387.

Jeremias, Joachim. "Λίθος, Λίθινος," ed. Gerhard Kittel, Geoffrey W. Bromiley, and Gerhard Friedrich, *TDNT*. Grand Rapids: Eerdmans, 1959, 268–280.

Johnson, E. Elizabeth. *The Function of Apocalyptic and Wisdom Traditions in Romans 9–11*. Society of Biblical Literature Dissertation Series, ed. Charles Talbert, vol. 109. Atlanta: Scholars Press, 1989.

Köster, Helmut "Τέμνω, Ἀποτομία, Ἀπότομος, Ἀποτόμως, Κατατομή, Ὀρθοτομέω,"ed. Gerhard Kittel, Geoffrey W. Bromiley, and Gerhard Friedrich. *TDNT*. Grand Rapids: Eerdmans, 1964.

Kruger, Paul A. "פלא," in *NIDOTTE*, ed. Willem A. VanGemeren, vol. 3. Grand Rapids: Zondervan, 1997, 616.

Liddell, Henry George, et al., *A Greek-English Lexicon*. Oxford: Clarendon Press, 1996.

Ludwig Koehler et al., *The Hebrew and Aramaic Lexicon of the Old Testament*. Leiden: E.J. Brill, 1994–2000.

Lo, Lung–Kwong. "Paul's Purpose in Writing Romans: The Upbuilding of a Jewish and Gentile Christian Community in Rome." Ph.D. diss., University of Durham, 1988.

Louw, Johannes P. and Eugene Albert Nida. *Greek-English Lexicon of the New Testament: Based on Semantic Domains*. New York: United Bible Societies, 1996.

Metzger, Bruce M. *A Textual Commentary on the Greek New Testament*. 2nd ed. Stuttgart: Deutsche Bibelgesellschaft, 1994.

Moule, C. F. D. An *Idiom Book of New Testament* Greek. 2nd ed. Cambridge: Cambridge University Press, 1959.

Moulton, James Hope and George Milligan, *The Vocabulary of the Greek Testament* London: Hodder and Stoughton, 1930.

Moulton and Howard. *A Grammar of New Testament Greek*. Edinburgh: T & T Clark, 1976.

Moulton, James Hope, Wilbert Francis Howard, and Nigel Turner. *A Grammar of New Testament Greek*. Vol. 3. Edinburgh: T & T Clark, 1988.

Muraoka, Takamitsu. *Hebrew/Aramaic Index to the Septuagint: Keyed to the Hatch-Redpath Concordance*. Grand Rapids: Baker, 1998.

Oepke, Albrecht. "Ἀπόλλυμι, Ἀπώλεια, Ἀπολλύων," in *TDNT*, vol. 1. Grand Rapids: Eerdmans, 1964, 394–397.

Oepke, Albrecht. "Διά," ed. Gerhard Kittel, Geoffrey W. Bromiley, and Gerhard Friedrich, *TDNT*, vol. 2. Grand Rapids: Eerdmans, 1964–68.

Robertson, A. T. *A Grammar of the Greek New Testament in the Light of Historical Research*. Logos Bible Software, 2006.

Robinson, Maurice A. and William G. Pierpont. *The New Testament in the Original Greek: Byzantine Majority Textform Greek New Testament*. Roswell, GA: The Original Word Publishers, 1995.

Sasse, Hermann. "Αἰών, Αἰώνιος," ed. Gerhard Kittel, Geoffrey W. Bromiley, and Gerhard Friedrich, *TDNT,* vol. 1. Grand Rapids: Eerdmans, 1964–68.

Schmidt, Karl L. and Matin A. Schmidt. "Πωρόω (πηρόω), Πώρωσις (πήρωσις), Σκληρύνω," *TDNT*, vol. 5. Grand Rapids: Eerdmans, 1964, 1025–1030.

Schrenk, Gottlob. "Ἄδικος, Ἀδικία, Ἀδικέω, Ἀδίκημα," *TDNT*, vol. 1. Grand Rapids: Eerdmans, 1964, 149–163.

Schrenk, Gottlob. "Βούλομαι, Βουλή, Βούλημα," *TDNT*, vol 1. Grand Rapids: Eerdmans, 1964.

Schrenk, Gottlob. "Εὐδοκέω, Εὐδοκία," ed. Gerhard Kittel, Geoffrey W. Bromiley, and Gerhard Friedrich, *TDNT*, vol. 2. Grand Rapids: Eerdmans, 1964, 738–751.

Schrenk, Gottlob. "Θέλω, Θέλημα, Θέλησις," *TDNT*, vol. 3. Grand Rapids: Eerdmans, 1965.

Schrenk, Gottlob et al. "Λέγω, Λόγιος, Λόγιον, Ἄλογος, Λογικός," ed. Gerhard Kittel, Geoffrey W. Bromiley, and Gerhard Friedrich, *TDNT*, vol. 4. Grand Rapids: Eerdmans, 1964–68.

Schweizer, Eduard. "Σῶμα, Σωματικός, Σύσσωμος," ed. Gerhard Kittel, Geoffrey W. Bromiley, and Gerhard Friedrich, *TDNT*, vol. 7. Grand Rapids: Eerdmans, 1964–68.

Shum, Shiu-Lun. *Paul's Use of Isaiah in Romans: A Comparative Study of Paul's Letter to the Romans and the Sibylline and Qumran Sectarian Texts*. Tübingen: Mohr Siebeck, 2002.

Silva, Moisés. rev.ed. "καλέω," *NIDNTTE*, 2nd ed. Vol. 2. Grand Rapids: Zondervan, 2014, 2:601–607.

Silva, Moisés, rev. ed. "συνείδησις," *NIDNTTE*, 2nd ed. Vol 4. Grand Rapids: Zondervan, 2014, 403-406.

Stählin, Gustav. "Ὀργή, Ὀργίζομαι, Ὀργίλος, Παροργίζω, Παροργισμός," in *TDNT*, vol. 5. Grand Rapids: Eerdmans, 1964, 419–447.

Strathmann, Hermann. "Λάος," *TDNT*, vol. 4. Grand Rapids: Eerdmans, 1967, 29–39.

Strathmann, Hermann. "λατρεία," *TDNT*, vol. 4. Grand Rapids: Eerdmans, 1967, 58–65.

Strathman, Hermann. "συνεπιμαρτυρέω," *TDNT*, vol 4. Grand Rapids: Eerdmans,1967, 508–510.

Swanson, Reuben, ed. *New Testament Greek Manuscripts: Romans*. Wheaton: Tyndale House and Pasadena: William Carey International University Press, 2001.

Turner, Nigel, *Syntax*, vol. 3 in *A Grammar of New Testament Greek*, James H. Moulton. Edinburgh: T & T Clark, 1963.

Wallace, Daniel B. *Greek Grammar Beyond the Basic: An Exegetical Syntax of the New Testament*. Grand Rapids: Zondervan, 1996.

Weiss, Konrad. "Χρηστός, Χρηστότης, Χρηστεύομαι, Χρηστολογία," ed. Gerhard Kittel, Geoffrey W. Bromiley, and Gerhard Friedrich. *TDNT*, vol 9. Grand Rapids: Eerdmans, 1964.

Werner Stenger, "βαστάζω," ed. Balz, Horst and Gerhard Schneider. *EDNT*, vol. 1. Edinburg: T & T Clark, 1991.

Wilckens, Ulrich and Georg Fohrer, "Σοφία, Σοφός, Σοφίζω," ed. Gerhard Kittel, Geoffrey W. Bromiley, and Gerhard Friedrich, *TDNT*. Grand Rapids: Eerdmans, 1964–68.

Wright, N. T. "The Messiah and the People of God: A Study in Pauline Theology with Particular Reference to the Argument of the Epistle to the Romans." Ph.D. diss., University of Oxford, 1980, 170.

Zerwick, Max and Mary Grosvenor, *A Grammatical Analysis of the Greek New Testament*. Rome: Biblical Institute Press, 1974.

Ziegler, Joseph. *Isaias*, Septuaginta: Vetus Testamentum Graecum, 3rd ed. Göttingen: Vandenhoeck & Ruprecht, 1939, 1983.

Articles and Essays Bibliography

Aageson, James W. "Scripture and Structure in the Development of Argument of Romans 9–11." *Catholic Biblical Quarterly* 48 (April 1986): 265–289.

Aageson, James W. "Typology, Correspondence and the Application of Scripture in Romans 9–11." *Journal for the Study of the New Testament* 31 (September 1987): 51–72.

Abasciano, Brian J. "Corporate election in Romans 9: A Reply to Thomas Schreiner." *Journal of the Evangelical Theological Society* 49 (April-June 2006): 351–371.

Anderson, Bernhard W. "Exodus in Covenant in Second Isaiah and Prophetic Tradition." In *Magnalia Dei, the Mighty Acts of God: Essays on the Bible and Archaeology in Memory of G. Ernest Wright*, eds. George Ernest Wright, Patrick D. Miller, Jr., Frank Moore Cross, and Werner E. Lemke, 339–60. New York: Doubleday, 1976.

Balentine, George L. "The Death of Jesus as the New Exodus." *Review and Expositor* 59 (January 1962): 27–41.

Battle, John A. "Paul's Use of the Old Testament in Romans 9:25–26." *Grace Theological Journal* 2 (Spring 1981): 115–29.

Baxter, A. G. and J. A. Ziesler. "Paul and Arboriculture: Romans 11:17–24," *JSNT* 24 (1985): 25–32.

Beale, Gregory K. "An Exegetical and Theological consideration of the Hardening of Pharaoh's Heart in Exodus 4–14 and Romans 9." *Trinity Journal* 5 (fall, 1984): 129–154.

Beale, Gregory K. "The Exodus Motif of YHWH as a Polemic." Th.M. thesis, Dallas Theological Seminary, 1976.

Beasley-Murray, G. R. "The Righteousness of God in the History of Israel and the Nations: Romans 9–11." *Review and Expositor* 73 (fall 1976): 437–50.

Beker, J. Christiaan. "Romans 9–11 in the Context of the Early Church," *Princeton Seminary Bulletin*. Supplementary, no. 1 (1990): 40–55.

Beker, J. Christiaan. "The Faithfulness of God and the Priority of Israel." In *Christians Among the Jews and Gentiles: Essays in Honor of Krister Stendahl on His 65th Birthday*, eds. G. W. Nickelsburg and G. W. MacRae. Philadelphia: Fortress Press, 1986.

Brindle, Wayne, A. "Prepared by Whom? Reprobation and Non-Calvinist Interpretations of Romans 9:22," *Criswell Theological Review* 12 (Spring 2015): 135–146.

Buren, Paul van. "Paul, The Church and Israel: Romans 9–11." *The Princeton Seminary Bulletin,* Supplemental issue 1 (1990): 5-18.

Burkitt, F. C. "On Romans IX 5 and Mark XIV 61." *Journal of Theological Studies* 5 (1903-1904): 451-455.

Campbell, William S. "Israel," in *Dictionary of Paul and His Letters*. Downers Grove: InterVarsity Press, 1993.

Campbell, William S. "The Freedom and Faithfulness of God in Relation to Israel, *JSNT* 13 (1981): 27–45.

Campbell, William S. "Romans III as a Key to the Structure and Thought of the Letter." In *Romans Debate*, ed. K. P. Donfried, revised and expanded edition, 251–64. Peabody, MA: Hendrickson, 1991.

Chisholm, Robert B., Jr. "Divine Hardening in the Old Testament." *Bibliotheca Sacra* 153 (October-December 1996): 410–434.

Cox, Dorian G. Coover. "The Hardening of Pharaoh's Heart in Its Literary and Cultural Contexts." *Bibliotheca Sacra* 163 (July–September 2006): 292–311.

Daube, David. *The Exodus Pattern in the Bible*. London: Faber & Faber, 1963.

Davies, W. D. "Paul and People of Israel." *New Testament Studies* 24 (October 1977): 4–39.

Donaldson, Terence L. *Paul and the Gentiles: Remapping the Apostle's Convictional World.* Minneapolis: Fortress Press, 1997.

Donfried, Karl P. "False Presuppositions in the Study of Romans." In *The Romans Debate,* ed. Karl P. Donfried, revised and expanded edition, 102–125. Peabody: Hendrickson, 1977, 1991.

Donfried, Karl P. "Introduction 1977: The Romans Debate," in *The Romans Debate,* ed. Karl P. Donfried, rev. and exp. ed. Peabody: Hendrickson, 1977, 1991, xli.

Dunn, James G. D. "The Purpose of Romans." In *Romans Debate*, ed. K. P. Donfried, revised and expanded edition, 245–50. Peabody, MA: Hendrickson, 1991.

Esler, Philip F. "Ancient Oleiculture and Ethnic Differentiation: The Meaning of the Olive-Tree Image in Romans 11," *JSNT* 26 (2003): 103–124.

Estes, Daniel J. "Wisdom and Biblical Theology." In *Dictionary of the Old Testament Wisdom, Poetry and Writings*, eds. Tremper Longman III and Peter Enns, 853-858. Downers Grove: InterVarsity Press, 2008.

Evans, Craig A. "Paul and the Prophets: Prophetic Criticism in the Epistle to the Romans (with special reference to Romans 9–11)," in *Romans and the People of God: Essays in Honor of Gordon D. Fee on the Occasion of His 65th Birthday*, eds. Sven K. Soderlund and N. T. Wright. Grand Rapids: Eerdmans, 1999.

Feinberg, John S. "God Ordains All Things," in *Predestination and Free Will: Four Views of Divine Sovereignty and Human Freedom*, eds. David Basinger and Randal Basinger. Downers Grove: InterVarsity Press, 1986, 19–43.

Fruchtenbaum, Arnold. "Israel and the Church." In *Issues in Dispensationalism*. Chicago: Moody Press, 1994, 118–120.

Gadenz, Pablo T. *Called from the Jews and from the Gentiles: Pauline Ecclesiology in Romans 9-11*. Wissenschaftliche Untersuchungen zum Neun Testament 2. Reihe, 267. Tübingen: Mohr Siebeck, 2009.

Gager, John G. *The Origins of Anti-Semitism: Attitudes toward Judaism in Pagan and Christian Antiquity*. New York: Oxford University Press, 1983.

Gaston, Lloyd, "Israel's Enemies in Pauline Theology," *New Testament Studies* 28 (1982), 400-23.

Gaston, Lloyd. "Israel's Misstep in the Eyes of Paul," in *The Romans Debate*, ed. Karl P. Donfried, rev. and exp. ed. Minneapolis: Augsburg Press, 1977, 1991, 309–26.

Getsbenberger, E. R. "The Woe Oracles of the Prophets." *Journal of Biblical Literature* 81 (1962): 249–263.

Getty, Mary Ann. "Paul and the Salvation of Israel: A Perspective on Romans 9–11." *Catholic Biblical Quarterly* 50 (July 1988): 456–89.

Gordon, Benjamin D. "On the Sanctity of Mixtures and Branches: Two Halakic Sayings in Romans 11:16–24," *JBL* 135 (2016): 355–68.

Hafemann, Scott. "The Salvation of Israel in Romans 11:25–32: A Response to Krister Stendahl." *Ex Auditu* 4 (1988): 38–58.

Hamlin, E. John. "Deutero-Isaiah's Reinterpretation of the Exodus in the Babylonian Twilight." *Proceedings: Eastern Great Lakes and Midwest Biblical Societies* 11 (1991): 75–80.

Hoehner, Harold W. "Israel in Romans 9-11," in *Israel, the Land and the People: An Evangelical Affirmation of God's Promises*, eds. H. Wayne House. Grand Rapids: Kregel Publications, 1998.

Hoffman, Yair. "A North Israelite Typological Myth and a Judean Historical Tradition: The Exodus in Hosea and Amos," *Vetus Testamentum* 39 (1989): 169–82.

Hofius, Otried, "All Israel Will Be Saved': Divine Salvation and Israel's Deliverance in Romans 9–11," trans. Judith G. Volf, *Princeton Seminary Bulletin*, Supplementary, 1 (1990): 19–39.

Hoover, Joseph, "The Wealth of God's Glory: A Response to John' Piper's 'Four Problems in Romans 9:22–23." *Stone-Campbell Journal* 12 (Spring, 2009), 47–58.

Horne, Charles M. Horne, "The Meaning of the Phrase 'And Thus All Israel Will Be Saved' (Romans 11:26)," *Journal of the Evangelical Theological Society* 21 (December 1978): 329–34.

Jervell, Jacob. "The Letter to Jerusalem." In *The Romans Debate*, ed. Karl P. Donfried, revised and expanded editions, 53–64. Peabody: Hendrickson, 1991.

Jewett, Robert. "Following the Argument of Romans." In *The Romans Debate*, ed. Karl P. Donfried, revised and expanded editions, 265–77. Peabody: Hendrickson, 1991.

Jobes, Karen H. "Jerusalem, our Mother: Metalepsis and Intertextuality in Gal. 4:21–31." *Westminster Theological Journal* 55 (1993), 299–320.

Johnson, E. Elizabeth. "Romans 9–11: The Faithfulness and Impartiality of God." In *Pauline Theology III Romans*, eds. David M. Hay and E. Elizabeth Johnson. Society of Biblical Literature Symposium Series, ed. Christopher R. Matthews, no. 23, 211–39. Atlanta: SBL, 2002.

Johnson, S. Lewis, Jr. "Evidence from Romans 9–11. In *A Case for Premillennialism: A New Consensus*, ed. Donald Campbell and Jeffery Townsend. Chicago: Moody Press, 1992, 199–223.

Johnson, S. Lewis, Jr. "Paul and 'The Israel of God': An Exegetical and Eschatological Case-Study." In *Essays in Honor of J. Dwight Pentecost*, ed. Stanley D. Toussaint and Charlie Dyer. Chicago, Moody Press, 1986, 181–195.

Johnson, S. Lewis, Jr. "Sermon Notes on Romans 9:19–33," at Believers Chapel, Dallas, Texas.

Karris, Robert J. "The Occasion of Romans: A Response to Professor Donfried." In *The Romans Debate,* ed. Karl P. Donfried, revised and expanded edition, 125–27. Peabody: Hendrickson, 1977, 1991.

Keesmaat, Sylvia C. "Exodus and the Intertextual Transformation of Tradition in Romans 8:14–30." *JSNT* 54 (1994): 29–56.

Kirk, J. R. Daniel, "Why Does the Deliver Come ἐκ Σιὼν (Romans 11.26)?," *Journal for the Study of the New Testament* 33 (2010): 81–99.

Lightfoot, J. B. *Saint Paul's Epistles to the Colossians and to Philemon*, rev. Grand Rapids: Zondervan, 1959.

Lim, Kar Yong. "Paul's Use of Temple Imagery in the Corinthian Correspondence: The Creation of Christian Identity." In *Reading Paul in Context: Explorations in Identity Formation Essays in Honour of William S. Campbell*, eds. Kathy Ehrensperger and J. Brian Tucker. Library of New Testament Studies, ed. Mark Goodacre, 428, 189–205. London: T & T Clark, 2010.

Lindblom, Johannes. *The Servant Songs in Deutero-Isaiah: A New Attempt to Solve an Old Problem*. Lunds: C. W. K. Gleerup, 1951.

MacArthur, John F. *Romans*, vol. 2, MacArthur New Testament Commentary. Chicago: Moody Press, 1991.

Marshall, I. Howard. "The Development of the Concept of Redemption in the New Testament." In *Reconciliation and Hope: New Testament Essays on Atonement and Eschatology Presented to L. L. Morris on his 60th Birthday*, ed. Robert J. Banks, 153–69. Grand Rapids: Eerdmans, 1974.

McKay, K. L. "Time and Aspect in New Testament Greek." *Novum Testamentum* 24,3 (1992): 209–228.

McKenzie, Steve. "Exodus Typology in Hosea." *Restoration Quarterly* 22 (1979): 100–108.

Meek, Wayne A. "On Trusting an Unpredictable God: A Hermeneutical Meditation on Romans 9–11." In *Faith and History*, ed. J. T. Carroll, et al., 105–24. Atlanta: Scholars, 1990.

Merkle, Ben L. "Romans 11 and the Future of Ethnic Israel," *Journal of the Evangelical Theological Society* 43 (December 2000); 709–21.

Merkle, Benjamin L. "A Typological Non-Future-Mass-Conversion View," in *Three Views on Israel and the Church: Perspectives on Romans 9–11*, eds. Jared Compton and Andrew D. Naselli. Grand Rapids: Kregel, 2018, 161–208.

Metzger, Bruce M. "The Punctuation of Rom, 9:5." In *Christ and Spirit in the New Testament: In Honour of Charles, Francis Digby Moule*, eds. B. Lindars and S. S. Smalley, 95–112. Cambridge: Cambridge Press, 1973.

Moo, Douglas J. "Israel and the Law in Romans 5–11: Interaction with the New Perspective." In *Justification and Variegated Nomism: Paradoxes of Paul*, eds. D. A. Carson, Peter T. O'Brien, and Mark A. Seifrid. Vol. 2, 185–216. Grand Rapids: Baker Academic, 2004.

Moo, Douglas J. "'Law,' 'Works of the Law,' and Legalism in Paul." *Westminster Journal* 45 (Spring, 1983), 73–100.

Moo, Douglas J. "Paul's Universalizing Hermeneutic in Romans." *The Southern Baptist Journal of Theology* 11 (Fall 2007): 62–90.

Moo, Douglas, J. "The Law of Christ as the Fulfillment of the Law of Moses: A Modified Lutheran View." In *The Law, the Gospel, and the Modern Christian Five Views*. Grand Rapids: Zondervan, 1993.

Moo, Douglas J. "The Law of Moses or the Law of Christ." In *Continuity and Discontinuity: Perspectives on the Relationship between the Old and New Testaments Essays in Honor of S. Lewis Johnson, Jr. ed. John S. Feinberg*. Wheaton: Crossway, 1988.

Moo, Douglas J. "The Theology of Romans 9–11." In *Pauline Theology Volume III Romans*, eds. David M. Hay and E. Elizabeth Johnson. Society of Biblical Literature Symposium Series. ed. Christopher R. Matthews, No. 23, 240–58. Atlanta: SBL, 2002.

Myers, Allen C. "Burnt Offering," In *The Eerdmans Bible Dictionary*. Grand Rapids, MI: Eerdmans, 1987, 176–77.

Nanos, Mark D. "'Broken Branches': A Pauline Metaphor Gone Awry?" In *Between Gospel and Election*, ed. Florian Wilk and J. Ross Wagner with assistance of Frank Schleritt, Wissenschaftliche Untersuchungen zum Neuen Testament, 25, 339–76. Tübingen: Mohr Siebeck, 2010.

Nanos, Mark D. "'Callused', Not 'Hardened': Paul's Revelation of Temporary Protection Until All Israel Can Be Healed." In *Reading Paul in Context: Explorations in Identity Formation: Essays in Honour of William S. Campbell*, 52–73. London: T & T Clark, 2010.

Noack, Bent. "Current and Backwater in the Epistle to the Romans." *Studia Theologica* 19 (1965): 155–66.

Oropeza, B. J. "Echoes of Isaiah in the Rhetoric of Paul: New Exodus, Wisdom, and the Humility of the Cross in Utopian-Apocalyptic Expectations." In *The Intertexture of Apocalyptic Discourse in the New* Testament, ed. Duane F. Watson, 87–112. Society of Biblical Literature Symposium Series, ed. Christopher R. Matthews, No. 14. Atlanta: Society of Biblical Literature, 2002.

Ortlund, Dane C. "The Insanity of Faith: Paul's Theological Use of Isaiah in Romans 9:33." *Trinity Journal* 30 (Fall 2009): 269–288.

Ortlund, Dane C. "'Zeal Without Knowledge': For What Did Paul Criticize His Fellow Jews in Romans 10:2–3?." *Westminster Theological Journal* 73 (Spring 2011): 23–37.

Osborne, William L. "The OT Background of Paul's 'All Israel' in Romans 11:26a." *Asia Journal of Theology* 2 (1988): 282–93.

Piper, Otto A. "Unchanging Promises: Exodus in the New Testament." *Interpretation* 11 (1957): 3–22.

Patrick, Dale. "Epiphanic Imagery in Second Isaiah's Portrayal of a New Exodus." *Hebrew Annual Review* 8 (1984): 125–141.

Rainey, A. F. "Sacrifice and Offerings," gen. ed. Merrill C. Tenney, *The Zondervan Pictorial Encyclopedia of the Bible*, vol. 5. Grand Rapids: Zondervan, 1980, 194–211.

Räisänen, Heikki. "Paul, God and Israel: Romans 9–11 in Recent Research." In *The Social World of Formative Christianity and Judaism: Essays in Tribute to Howard Clark Kee*, eds. Jacob Neusner et al., 178–206. Philadelphia: Fortress Press, 1988.

Rese, Martin. "Die Vozuege Israels in Roem 9,4–5 und Eph 2,12," *Theologische Zeitschrift* 31 (1975): 211–22.

Roberts, J. J. M. "Yahweh's Foundation in Zion," *Journal of Biblical Literature* 106 (1987): 27–45.

Roetzel, Calvin. "Διαθήκη in Rom 9,4." *Biblica* 51 (1970): 377-390.

Rooker, Mark F. "The Use of the Old Testament in the Book of Hosea." *Criswell Theological Review* 7 (1993): 51–66.

Saucy, Robert L. "Does the Apostle Paul Reverse the Prophetic Tradition of the Salvation of Israel and the Nations?" In *Building on the Foundations of Evangelical Theology: Essays in Honor of John S. Feinberg*, eds. Gregg R. Allison and Stephen J. Wellum. Wheaton: Crossway, 2015, 66–90.

Schreiner, Thomas R. "Does Romans 9 Teach Individual Election unto Salvation? Some Exegetical and Theological Reflections." *Journal of Evangelical Theological Society* 36 (March 1993): 25–40.

Schreiner, Thomas R. "Corporate and Individual Election in Romans 9: A Response to Brian Abasciano," *Journal of the Evangelical Theological Society* 49 (April - June 2006): 373–386.

Schreiner, Thomas R. "Israel's Failure to Attain Righteousness in Romans 9:30–10:3." *Trinity Journal* 12 (1991): 209–220.

Schreiner, Thomas R. "Paul's View of the Law in Romans 10:4–5. *Westminster theological Journal* 55 (Spring 1997): 55–113.

Schreiner, Thomas R. "Sacrifices and Offerings in the NT," gen. ed. Geoffrey W. Bromiley, *The International Standard Bible Encyclopedia*, rev. ed., vol. 4. Grand Rapids: Eerdmans, 1988, 273–77.

Scott, James M. "'And Then All Israel Will Be Saved' (Rom 11:26)." In *Restoration: Old Testament, Jewish, and Christian Perspectives*, ed. James M. Scott. Supplements to the Journal for the Study of Judaism, vol. 72 (Leiden: Brill, 2001), 489–527.

Segal, Alan F. "Paul's Experience and Romans 9-11." *Princeton Seminary Bulletin,* Supplementary no. 1 (1990): 56-70.

Seifrid, Mark A. "Paul's Approach to the Old Testament in Rom 10:6–8." *Trinity Journal* 6 (Spring 1985): 3–37.

Shields, Martin A. "Wisdom and Prophecy." In *Dictionary of the Old Testament Wisdom, Poetry and Writings*, eds. Tremper Longman III and Peter Enns, 876-84. Downers Grove: InterVarsity Press, 2008.

Snodgrass, Klyne R. "Streams of Tradition Emerging from Isaiah 40:1–5 and Their Adaptation in the New Testament." *Journal for the Study of the New Testament* 8 (1980): 24–45.

Sommer, Benjamin D. "Exegesis, Allusion and Intertextuality in the Hebrew Bible, a Response to Lyle Eslinger." *Vetus Testamentum* 46 (1996): 479–89.

Strickland, Wayne G. "The Inauguration of the Law of Christ with the Gospel of Christ: A Dispensational View." In *The Law, the Gospel, and the Modern Christian Five Views*. Grand Rapids: Zondervan, 1993.

Stuhlmacher, Peter. "The Theme of Romans." In *The Romans Debate*, ed. Karl P. Donfried, revised and expanded editions, 333–45. Peabody: Hendrickson, 1991.

Terrien, Samuel. "The Metaphor of the Rock in Biblical Theology." In *God in the Fray: A Tribute to Walter Brueggemann*. eds. T. Linafelt and T. K. Beal, 157–71. Minneapolis: Fortress Press, 1998.

Thielman, Frank. "Unexpected Mercy: Echoes of a Biblical Motif in Romans 9–11." *Scottish Journal of Theology* 47 (April-June 1994): 169–81.

Vanlaningham, Michael G. "An Evaluation of N. T. Wright's View of Israel in Romans 11." *Bibliotheca Sacra* 170 (Apr-Jun 2013): 179–93.

Vlach, Michael J. "What Does Christ as 'True Israel' Mean for the Nation Israel?: A Critique of the Non-dispensational Understanding." *The Master's Seminary Journal* 23 (Spring 2012): 43–54.

Vlach, Michael J. "Response to Merkle." In *Three Views on Israel and the Church: Perspectives on Romans 9–11*, eds. Jared Compton and Andrew D. Naselli (Grand Rapids: Kregel, 2018), 209–222.

Wagner, Günter. "The Future of Israel: Reflections on Romans 9–11." In *Eschatology and the New Testament: Essays in Honor of George Raymond Beasley-Murray*, ed. W. Hulitt Gloer. Peabody: Hendrickson, 1988, 77–112.

Wagner, J. Ross. "Identifying 'Updated' Prophecies in the Old Greek (OG) Isaiah: Isaiah 8:11–16 as a Test Case." *Journal of Biblical Literature* 126 (2007): 251–69.

Wagner, J. Ross. "The Future of Israel: Reflections on Romans 9–11." In *Eschatology and the New Testament: Essays in Honor of George Raymond Beasley-Murray*, ed. W. Hulitt Gloer. Peabody: Hendrickson, 1988.

Waldow, H. E. von. "The Message of Deutero-Isaiah." *Interpretation* 22 (1968): 259–87.

Wallace, Daniel B. "The Witness of the Spirit in Romans 8:16: Interpretation and Implications." *In Who's Afraid of the Holy Spirit?: An Investigation into the Ministry of the Spirit of God Today*, eds. M. James Sawyer and Daniel B. Wallace. Dallas: Biblical Studies Press, 2005.

Wasserbert, Günter. "Romans 9–11 and Jewish–Christian Dialogue: Prospects and Provisos." In *Reading Israel in Romans: Legitimacy and Plausibility of Divergent Interpretations,* eds. Christina Grenholm and Daniel Patte, 174–186. Harrisburg: Trinity Press International, 2000.

Watts, Rikki E. "Consolation or Confrontation? Isaiah 40–55 and the Delay of the New Exodus." *Tyndale Bulletin* 41 (May 1990): 31–59.

Waymeyer, Matt. "The Dual Status of Israel in Romans 11:28," *The Master's Seminary Journal*, 16 (Spring 2005): 57-71.

Williamson, H. G. M. "The Isaiah and the Wise." In *Wisdom in Ancient Israel*, eds. John Day, Robert P. Gordon and H. G. M. Williamson, 133–141. Cambridge: Cambridge Press, 1995.

Wilson, Lindsay. "Wisdom in Isaiah." In *Interpreting Isaiah: Issues and Approaches*, eds. David G. Firth and H. G. M. Williamson, 145–167. Downers Grove: InterVarsity Academic, 2009.

Woznicki, Christopher. "Is Prayer Redundant? Calvin and the Early Reformers on the Problem of Petitionary Prayer." *Journal of the Evangelical Theological Society* 60 (June–August 2017): 333–348.

Wright, N. T. "Romans and the Theology of Paul." In *Pauline Theology Volume III Romans*. eds. David M. Hay and E. Elizabeth Johnson. Society of Biblical Literature Symposium Series. ed. Christopher R. Matthews, No. 23, 30–67. Atlanta: Society of Biblical Literature, 2002.

Wuellner, Wilhelm. "Paul's Rhetoric of Argumentation in Romans: An Alternative to the Donfried-Karris Debate over Romans." In *The Romans Debate,* ed. Karl P. Donfried, revised and expanded edition, 128–46. Peabody: Hendrickson, 1977, 1991.

Zaspel, Fred G. and James M. Hamilton, Jr. "A Typological Future-Mass-Conversion View." In *Three Views on Israel and the Church: Perspectives on Romans 9–11*, eds. Jared Compton and Andrew D. Naselli. Grand Rapids: Kregel, 2018, 97–140.

Zaspel, Fred G. and James M. Hamilton, Jr. "Response to Merkle." In *Three Views on Israel and the Church: Perspectives on Romans 9–11*, eds. Jared Compton and Andrew D. Naselli. Grand Rapids: Kregel, 2018, 223–234.

General Books

Aune, David E. "Romans as a Logos Protreptikos." In *The Romans Debate*, ed. Karl P. Donfired. revised and expanded, 278–96. Peabody: Hendrickson, 1977, 1991.

Badenas, Robert. *Christ Is the End of the Law: Romans 10:4 in Pauline Perspective*. Sheffield: JSOT Press, 1985.

Bandstra, Andrew J. *The Law and the Elements of the World: An Exegetical Study in Aspects of Paul's Teaching*. Kampen: Kok, 1964.

Baur, Ferdinand C. *Paul, the Apostle of Jesus Christ: His Life and Work, His Epistles and His Doctrine: A Contribution to a Critical History of Primitive Christianity*, 2nd ed., trans. Eduard Zeller. London: Williams and Norgate, 1876.

Bavinck, Herman. *Reformed Dogmatics*, 4 vols. trans. John Vriend, ed. John Bolt. Grand Rapids: Baker, 2004.

Beale, Gregory K. "Colossians." In *Commentary on the New Testament Use of the Old Testament*, eds. G. K. Beale and D. A. Carson, 841–70. Grand Rapids: Baker, 2007.

Beale, Gregory K. *A New Testament Biblical Theology: The Unfolding of the Old Testament in the New*. Grand Rapids: Baker Academic, 2011.

Beale, Gregory K. *The Temple and Church's Mission: A Biblical Theology of the Dwelling Place of God*. New Studies in Biblical Theology, ed. D. A. Carson, 17. Downers Grover: InterVarsity Press, 2004.

Belli, Filippo. *Argumentation and Use of Scripture in Romans 9-11*. Roma: Gregorian & Biblical Press, 2010.

Beker, J. Christiaan. *Paul the Apostle: The Triumph of God in Life and Thought.* Philadelphia: Fortress Press, 1980.

Berkhof, Louis. *Systematic Theology*. Grand Rapids: Eerdmans, 1972.

Blenkinsopp, Joseph. *Isaiah 1–39: A New Translation with Introduction and Commentary*. The Anchor Bible, vol. 19. New York: Doubleday, 2000.

Boettner, Loraine. *The Reformed Doctrine of Predestination*. Philadelphia: Presbyterian and Reformed, 1972.

Bornkamm, Günther. *Paul*, trans. D. M. G. Stalker. London: Hodder and Stoughton, 1971.

Bornkamm, Günther. *Early Christian Experience*. New York: Harper and Row, 1969.

Brueggemann, Walter. *Hope Within History*. Atlanta: John Knox Press, 1987.

Brueggemann, Walter. *Isaiah 1–39*. Westminster Bible Companion, eds. Patrick D. Miller and David L. Bartlett. Louisville: Westminster John Knox Press, 1998.

Brunson, Andrew C. *Psalm 118 in the Gospel of John: An Intertextual Study of the New Exodus Pattern in the Theology of John*. Wissenshaftliche Untersuchungen zum Neuen Testament 2, Reihe 158. Tübingen: Mohr Siebeck, 2003.

Budge, E. A. Wallis. *The Book of the Dead: The Hierogllyphic Transcripts of the Papyrus of Ani.* New Hyde Park, NY: University Books, 1960.

Bullinger, E. W. *Figures of Speech Used in the Bible*, Explained and Illustrated. Grand Rapids: Baker reprint, 1968.

Byrne, Brendan. *'Sons of God' – 'Seed of Abraham': A Study of the Idea of the Sonship of God of All Christians in Paul Against the Jewish Background.* Rome: Biblical Institute Press, 1979.

Calvin, John. *Institutes of the Christian Religion*, 4 vols. Bellingham, WA: Logos Bible Software, 1997.

Campbell, Douglas A. *The Deliverance of God: An Apocalyptic Rereading of Justification in Paul.* Grand Rapids: Eerdmans, 2009.

Campbell, William S. *Paul and the Creation of Christian Identity*. London: T & T Clark: The Continuum Imprint, 2008.

Childs, Brevard S. *Isaiah*. Old Testament Library. Louisville: Westminster John Knox, 2001.

Childs, Brevard S. *The Church's Guide for Reading Paul: The Canonical Shaping of the Pauline Corpus*. Grand Rapids: Eerdmans, 2008.

Cheyne, T. K. *The Prophecies of Isaiah*. 5th ed. revised, in 2 vols. New York: Thomas Whitaker, 1895.

Cozart, Richard M. *The Present Triumph: An Investigation into the Significance of the Promise of the New Exodus of Israel in the Letter to the Ephesians*, WEST Theological Monograph Series. Eugene, OR: Wipf and Stock, 2013.

Dahl, Nils. *Studies in Paul*. Minneapolis: Augsburg Publishing House, 1977.

Das, A. Andrew. *Paul, the Law and the Covenant*. Peabody: Hendrickson, 2001.

Das, A. Andrew. *Solving the Romans Debate*. Minneapolis: Fortress Press, 2007.

Delitzsch, Franz. *Isaiah*. Biblical Commentary on the Old Testament. Translated by J. Martin, vol. 7, 2 vols in 1. Edinburgh: T & T Clark; New York: Scribner and Welford [distributor], 1890. Reprint, Grand Rapids: Eerdmans, 1973.

Dennis, John A. *Jesus' Death and Gathering of True Israel*. Wissenschaftliche Untersuchungen zum Neuen Testament 2. Reihe, 217. Tübingen: Mohr Siebeck, 2006.

Dunn, J. D. G. *The New Perspective on Paul*, rev. ed. Grand Rapids: Eerdmans, 2008.

Dunn, J. D. G. *The Theology of Paul the Apostle*. Grand Rapids: Eerdmans, 1998.

Dunson, Ben C. *Individual and Community in Paul's Letter to the Romans*. Wissenschaftliche Untersuchungen zum Neuen Testament, 2/332. Tübingen: Mohr Siebeck, 2012.

Durham, John. *Exodus*, Word Biblical Commentary. Dallas: Word Books, 1987.

Edwards, Jonathan. "The Decrees of God," in *Our Great and Glorious God*, sermons compiled and edited by Don Kistler. Morgan, PA: Soli Deo Gloria Publications, 2003.

Ellis, E. Earle. *Paul's Use of the Old Testament*. Grand Rapids: Eerdmans, 1957.

Ellison, Henry E. *The Mystery of Israel: An Exposition of Romans 9-11*. Milton Keynes, England: Patemoster, 1966.

Elliott, Mark A. *The Survivors of Israel: A Reconsideration of the Theology of Pre-Christian Judaism*. Grand Rapids: Eerdmans, 2000.

Fee, Gordon D., *God's Empowering Presence: The Holy Spirit in the Letters of Paul*. Peabody: Hendrickson, 1994.

Fichtner, Johannes. "Jesaja unter den Weisen." *Theologische Literaturzeitung* 74 (1949), 75–80, ed. and trans. "Isaiah Among the Wise." In *Studies in Ancient Israelite Wisdom* ed. J. L. Crenshaw, 429–38. New York: KTAV, 1976.

Fishbane, Michael. *Biblical Text and Texture*. Oxford: Oneworld Publication, 1998.

Forster, R. T. and V. P. Marston. *God's Strategy in Human* History. Wheaton: Tyndale, 1973.

Fruchtenbaum, Arnold G. *Israelology: The Missing Link in Systematic Theology*. Tustin, CA, Ariel Ministries Press, 1994.

Fruchtenbaum, Arnold G. *The Footsteps of the Messiah: A Study of the Sequence of Prophetic Events*, rev. ed. Trustin, CA: Ariel Ministries, 2003.

Fuller, Daniel P. *Gospel and Law: Contrast or Continuum?* Grand Rapids: Eerdmans, 1980.

Gager, John G. *The Origins of Anti-Semitism: Attitudes toward Judaism in Pagan and Christian Antiquity*. New York: Oxford University Press, 1983, 197–212.

Gathercole, Simon J. *Where Is Boasting? Early Jewish Soteriology and Paul's Response in Romans 1–5*. Grand Rapids: Eerdmans, 2003.

Gerstner, John H. "Augustine, Luther, Calvin, and Edwards on the Bondage of the Will." In *The Grace of God, The Bondage of the Will: Historical and Theological Perspectives on Calvinism*, ed. Thomas R. Schreiner and Bruce A. Ware, vol. 2, 279–295. Grand Rapids: Baker, 1995.

Goldingay, John. *The Message of Isaiah 40–55: A Literary-Theological Commentary*. London. T & T Clark, 2005.

Grogan, Geoffrey W. "Isaiah." In *Expositor's Bible Commentary*, ed. Frank Gaebelein, re. ed., vol. 6, 433–863. Grand Rapids: Zondervan, 2008.

Hamilton, Jr., James M. and Fred G. Zaspel. "A Typological Future-Mass-Conversion View." In *Three Views on Israel and the Church: Perspectives on Romans 9–11*, eds. Jared Compton and Andrew D. Naselli. Grand Rapids: Kregel, 2018.

Harris, James E. and Kent R. Weeks. *X-Raying the Pharaohs*. New York: Scribner's Sons, 1973.

Harris, Murray J. *Jesus as "God": Theos as a Christological Term in the New Testament*. Grand Rapids: Baker, 1992.

Hays, Richard B. *Echoes of Scripture in the Letters of Paul*. New Haven: Yale University Press, 1989.

Hays, Richard B. *The Conversion of the Imagination: Paul as Interpreter of Israel's Scripture*. Grand Rapids: Eerdmans, 2005.

Hermann, Alfred. "Das steinhartes Herz," *Jahrbuch für Antike und Christentum* 4. Munster: Aschendorffsche Verlagsbuchandlung, 1961.

Hodge, Charles. *Systematic Theology*, 3 vols. Grand Rapids: Eerdmans, repr. 1970.

Holland, Tom. *Contours of Pauline Theology: A Radical New Survey of the Influence on Paul's Biblical Writings*. Fearn, Scotland: Christian Focus, 2004.

Hornung, Erik. *The Ancient Egyptian Books of the Afterlife*. Trans. David Lorton. Ithaca and London: Cornell University Press, 1999.

Horton, Michael. *New Studies in Dogmatics: Justification*, vol. 1, eds. Michael Allen and Scott R. Swain. Grand Rapids: Zondervan, 2018.

Horton, Michael. *New Studies in Dogmatics: Justification*, vol. 2, eds. Michael Allen and Scott R. Swain. Grand Rapids: Zondervan, 2018.

Grudem, Wayne A. *Systematic Theology: An Introduction to Biblical Doctrine*. Grand Rapids: Zondervan, 2004.

Jensen, Joseph. *The Use of Tôrâ by Isaiah: His Debate with the Wisdom Tradition*. Catholic Biblical Quarterly Monograph Series 3. Washington: Catholic Biblical Association, 1973.

Jensen, Philip. "Poetry in the Bible." In *New Bible Commentary: 21st Century Edition.* Downers Grove: InterVarsity Press, 1994.

Jewett, Robert. *Paul's Anthropological Terms: A Study in their Use in Conflict Settings*. Leiden: Brill, 1971.

Johnson, Elizabeth E. "Romans 9-11: The Faithfulness and Impartiality of God." In *Pauline Theology III Romans*, Society of Biblical Literature Symposium Series. Atlanta: SBL, 2002.

Johnson, E. Elizabeth. *The Function of Apocalyptic and Wisdom Traditions in Romans 9–11*. Society of Biblical Literature Dissertation Series, ed. Charles Talbert, vol. 109. Atlanta: Scholars Press, 1989.

Johnson, S. Lewis, Jr. "Evidence from Romans 9–11." In *A Case for Premillennalism: A New Consensus*, eds. Donald K. Campbell and Jeffrey L. Townsend, 199–223. Chicago: Moody Press, 1992.

Keesmaat, Sylvia C. *Paul and His Story: (Re)Interpreting the Exodus Tradition*. Journal for the Study of the New Testament Supplement, ed. Stanley E. Porter, 181. Sheffield: Sheffield Academic Press, 1999.

Kennedy, Titus. *Unearthing the Bible*. Eugene, OR: Harvest House, 2020.

Kim, Johann D. *God, Israel, and the Gentiles: Rhetoric and Situation in Romans 9–11*. Society of Biblical Literature Dissertation Series, vol. 176. Atlanta: Society of Biblical Literature, 2000.

Klein, W. W. Klein, *The New Chosen People: A Corporate View of Election*. Grand Rapids: Zondervan, 1990.

Koch, Dietrich-Alex. *Die Schrift als Zeuge des Evangeliums: Untersuchungen zur Verwendung und zum Verständnis der Schrift bei Paulus*. Beiträge zur historischen Theologie, vol. 69. Tübingen: Mohr Siebeck, 1986.

Koole, Ian L. Isaiah III: *Isaiah 40–48. Historical Commentary on the Old Testament*. Trans. Anthony P. Runia, eds. Cornelis Houtman, Willem S. Prinsloo, Wilfred G. E. Watson, Al Wolters, vol. 1. Leuven: Peeters, 1997.

Koole, Ian L. Isaiah III: *Isaiah 49–55. Historical Commentary on the Old Testament*. Trans. Anthony P. Runia, eds. Cornelis Houtman, Willem S. Prinsloo, Wilfred G. E. Watson, Al Wolters, vol. 2. Leuven: Peeters, 1998.

Lambrecht, Jan, *Pauline Studies, Collected Essays,* Bibliotheca Ephemeridum Theologicarum Lovaniensium, 115 (Leuven: Peeters, 1994).

Lightfoot, J. B. *St. Paul's Epistle to the Philippians* (Grand Rapids: Zondervan, 1976).

Long, Gary D. *The Doctrine of Salvation*. Sterling VA: G.A.M. Printers, 1978.

Lund, Øystein. *Way Metaphors and Way Topics in Isaiah 40–55*. Forschungen aum Alten Testament, 2. Reihe. Tübingen: Mohr Siebeck, 2007.

Luz, Ulrich. *Das Geschichtsverstaendnis des Paulus*. München: C. Kaiser, 1968.

McKane, Williams. *Prophets and Wise Men*. London: SCM Press, 1965.

Meadors, Gary T. "Conscience," eds. Walter A. Elwell and Walter A. Elwell, *Evangelical Dictionary of Biblical Theology*. Grand Rapids: Baker Book House, 1996.

Meyer, Jason C. *The End of the Law: Mosaic Covenant in Pauline Theology*. NAC Studies in Bible and Theology, ed. E. Ray Clendenen. Nashville: B & H Academic, 2009.

Moo, Douglas J. "The Theology of Romans 9–11." In *Pauline Theology Volume III Romans*, eds. David M. Hay and E. Elizabeth Johnson. Society of Biblical Literature Symposium Series. ed. Christopher R. Matthews, No. 23. Atlanta: SBL, 2002, 240–258.

Morales, Rodrigo J. *The Spirit and the Restoration of Israel: New Exodus and New Creation Motifs in Galatians*. Wissenshaftliche Untersuchungen zum Neuen Testament 2. Reihe 282. Tübingen: Mohr Siebeck, 2010.

Morenz, Siegfried. *Egyptian Religion*. Trans. Ann E. Keep. Ithaca: Cornell University Press, 1973.

Morgan, Donn F. *Wisdom in the Old Testament Traditions*. Louisville: John Knox Press, 1981.

Morris, Leon. *The Apostolic Preaching of the Cross*. Grand Rapids: Eerdmans, 1955.

Munck, Johannes. *Christ and Israel: An Interpretation of Romans 9–11*. Translated by Ingeborg Nixon. Philadelphia: Fortress Press, 1967.

Naselli, Andrew D. *From Typology to Doxology: Paul's Use of Isaiah and Job in Romans 11:34–35*. Eugene, OR: Pickwick Publication, 2012.

Naselli, Andrew D. "Paul's Use of Isaiah 40:13 and Job 41:3a (Eng 41:11a) in Romans 11:34–35." Ph.D. diss., Trinity Evangelical Divinity School, 2010.

Ninow, Friedbert. *Indicators of Typology within the Old Testament: The Exodus Motif*. New York: Peter Lang Publication, 2001.

Nixon, R. E. *The Exodus in the New Testament*. Tyndale Monographs. London: Tyndale Press, 1963.

Nwachukwu, Mary Sylvia Chinyere. *Creation-Covenant Scheme and Justification by Faith: A Canonical Study of the God-Human Drama in the Pentateuch and Letter to the Romans*. Rome: Gregorian University Press, 2002.

O'Brien, Peter Thomas. *The Epistle to the Philippians: A Commentary on the Greek Text*. New International Greek Testament Commentary. Grand Rapids: Eerdmans, 1991.

Oss, Douglas A. "Paul's Use of Isaiah in Its Place in His Theology with Special Reference to Romans 9–11." Ph.D. diss., Westminster Theological Seminary, 1992.

Oswalt, John N. *The Book of Isaiah 40–66*. New International Commentary on the Old Testament, ed. R. K. Harrison. Grand Rapids: Eerdmans, 1998.

Packer, J. I. *Evangelism and the Sovereignty of God*. Downers Grove: InterVarsity, 1961.

Pao, David W. *Acts and Isaianic New Exodus*. Biblical Studies Library. Grand Rapids: Baker, 2002.

Pao, David W. and Eckhard J. Schnabel. "Luke." In *Commentary on the New Testament Use of the Old Testament*, eds. G. K. Beale and D. A. Carson, 251–414. Grand Rapids: Baker, 2007.

Pink, Arthur W. *The Attributes of God*. Swengel, PA: Reiner Publication, n.d.

Price, Randall. *The Stones Cry Out: What Archaeology Reveals about the Truth of the Bible*. Eugene, OR: Harvest House, 1997.

Price, Randall with H. Wayne House. *Zondervan Handbook of Biblical Archaeology*. Grand Rapids: Zondervan, 2017.

Räisänen, Heikki. *Paul and the Law*, 2nd ed. Eugene, OR: Wpif and Stock, 2010.

Reymond, Robert L. "A Consistent Supralapsarian Perspective on Election." In *Perspectives on Election: Five Views*, ed. Chad O. Brand, 150–194. Nashville: B & H, 2006.

Richardson, Peter. *Israel in the Apostolic Church,* Society for New Testament Studies Monograph Series, ed. Mathew Black. Cambridge: Cambridge University Press, 1969.

Robinson, John A. T. *Wrestling with Romans*. London: SCM Press, 1979.

Ryle, J. C. "A Man of One Thing," https://www.jcryle.info/2016/08/a-man-of-one-thing.html. Swanson, *NT GK Mss*., 2021.

Sanders, E. P. *Paul, the Law, and the Jewish People*. Minneapolis: Fortress Press, 1983.

Schreiner, Thomas R. *Forty Questions about Christians and Biblical Law*. Grand Rapids: Kregel, 2010.

Schreiner, Thomas R. *The Law and Its Fulfillment: A Pauline Theology of Law*. Grand Rapids: Baker, 1993.

Schreiner, Thomas R. and Ardel B. Caneday. *The Race Set Before Us: A Biblical Theology of Perseverance & Assurance*. Downers Grove: IVP, 2001.

Segal, Alan F. *Paul the Convert: The Apostolate and Apostasy of Saul the Pharisee*. New Haven: Yale University, 1990.

Shedd, William G. T. *Dogmatic Theology*, ed. Alan W. Gomes, 3rd ed. Phillipsburg: Presbyterian & Reformed Publishing, 1894, repr. 2003.

Shum, Shiu-Lun. *Paul's Use of Isaiah in Romans: A Comparative Study of Paul's Letter to the Romans and the Sibylline and Qumran Sectarian Texts*. Tübingen: Mohr Siebeck, 2002.

Silva, Moisés. *Philippians,* 2nd ed., Baker Exegetical Commentary on the New Testament. Grand Rapids, MI: Baker Academic, 2005.

Smith, Gary. *Isaiah 40–66*. The New American Commentary. Vol. 15B. Nashville: B & H, 2009.

Steele, David N. and Curtis C. Thomas. *The Five Points of Calvinism: Defined, Defended, Documented.* Philadelphia: Presbyterian and Reformed, 1975.

Stendahl, Krister. *Paul among Jews and Gentiles*. London: SCM, 1977.

Stanley, Christopher D. *Arguing with Scripture: The Rhetoric of Quotations in the Letters of Paul*. London: T & T Clark, 2004.

Stanley, Christopher D. *Paul and the Language of Scripture: Citation Technique in the Pauline Epistles and Contemporary Literature.* Society for New Testament Studies Monograph Series, ed. Richard Bauckham, vol. 74. Cambridge: Cambridge University Press, 1992.

Strauss, Mark L. *The Davidic Messiah in Luke-Acts: The Promise and Its Fulfillment in Lukan Christology*. Journal for the Study of the New Testament Supplement Series 110, ed. Stanley E. Porter. Sheffield: Sheffield Academic Press, 1995.

Sullivan, Steven P. *The Isaianic New Exodus in Romans 9–11: A Biblical and Theological Study of Paul's Use of Isaiah in Romans*. Silverton, OR, Lampion Press, 2017.

Sullivan, Steven P. *The Isaianic New Exodus in Romans 9–11: A Biblical and Theological Study of Paul's Use of Isaiah in Romans*, 2nd ed. Middleton, RI: Stone Tower Press, 2023.

Swanson, Reuben, ed. *New Testament Greek Manuscripts Romans: Variant Readings Arranged in Horizontal Lines Against Codex Vaticanus*. Wheaton: Tyndale House, 2001.

Tan, Paul Lee. *Encyclopedia of 7,700 Illustrations*. Rockville, MA: Assurance Publisher, 1979.

Thielman, Frank. *From Plight to Solution: a Jewish Framework to Understanding Paul's View of the Law in Galatians and Romans*. *Novum Testamentum,* Supplements. Leiden: Brill, 1989.

Turretin, Francis. *Institutes of Elenctic Theology*, trans. George M Giger, ed. James T. Dennison, Jr., 3 vols. Phillipsburg: P&R Publishing, 1992.

Vlach, Michael J. "A Non-Typical Future–Mass–Conversion View." In *Three Views on Israel and the Church: Perspectives on Romans 9–11*, eds. Jared Compton and Andrew D. Naselli. Grand Rapids: Kregel, 2018.

Volf, Judith M. Gundry. *Paul and Perseverance: Stay in or Fall Away*, Wissenschaftliche Untersuchungen zum Neuen Testament, no. 2 vol. 37. Tübingen: Mohr Siebeck, 1990.

Wagner, J. Ross. *Heralds of the Good News: Isaiah and Paul in Concert in the Letter to the Romans*. Supplements to Novum Testamentum, eds. M. M. Mitchell and D. P. Moessner, vol. 101. Leiden: Brill, 2002.

Wallace, Daniel B. *Greek Grammar Beyond the Basic: An Exegetical Syntax of the New Testament*. Grand Rapids: Zondervan, 1996.

Wasserberg, Günter. "Romans 9–11 and Jewish-Christian Dialogue: Prospects and Provisos." In *Reading Israel in Romans: Legitimacy and Plausibility of Divergent Interpretations,* eds. Christina Grenholm and Daniel Patte. 174–86. Romans Through History and Cultures Receptions and Critical Interpretations. Harrisburg: Trinity Press International, 2000.

Watson, Francis. *Paul, Judaism and the Gentiles: Beyond the New Perspective*. Revised and expanded edition. Grand Rapids: Eerdmans, 2007.

Watson, Francis. *Paul, Judaism and the Gentiles: A Social Approach*. Cambridge, Cambridge Press, 1989.

Watts, John D. W. *Isaiah 1–33*. Word Biblical Commentary, ed. John D. W. Watts, vol. 24. Logos 5 Electronic version. Waco: Word Books, 1985.

Weiser, Artur, *Das Buch der zwoelf kleine Propheten*, II, Altes Testament Deutsh. Göettingen: Vandenhoeck und Ruprecht, 1967.

Whedbee, J. William. *Isaiah and Wisdom*. Nashville: Abingdon Press, 1971.

Estermann, Claus. *Isaiah 40–66*. Trans. D. M. G. Stalker. Old Testament Library, eds. Peter Ackroyd, James Barr, John Bright, and G. Ernest Wright. Philadelphia: Westminster Press, 1969.

Westminister Confession of Faith. Oak Harbor, WA: Logos Research, 1996.

Wildberger, Hans. *Isaiah 28–39: A Commentary*. Continental Commentaries. Trans. Thomas H. Trapp. Minneapolis: Fortress Press, 2002.

Wiles, G. P. *Paul's Intercessory Prayers: The Significance of the Intercessory Prayer Passages in the Letters of St. Paul*. Cambridge: Cambridge University Press, 1974.

Wilk, Florian. "Between Scripture and History: Technique and Hermeneutics of Interpreting Biblical Prophets in the Septuagint of Isaiah and Letters of Paul." In *The Old Greek of Isaiah: Issues and Perspective*, eds. Arie van der Kooij and Michaël N. van der Meek. Leuven: Peeters, 2010, 189–209.

Wright, N. T. *The Climax of the Covenant: Christ and the Law in Pauline Theology*. Edinburgh: Clark, 1991.

Wright, N. T. *Paul and the Faithfulness of God*. Christian Origins and the Question of God, vol. 4. Minneapolis: Fortress Press, 2013.

Wright, N. T. "Romans and the Theology of Paul," in *Pauline Theology, Romans Volume III* eds. David M. Hays and E. Elizabeth Johnson. Atlanta: Society of Biblical Literature, 2002, 30–67.

Yonge, Charles Duke with Philo of Alexandria, *The Works of Philo: Complete and Unabridged*. Peabody, MA: Hendrickson, 1995.

Zaspel, Fred G. Zaspel and James M. Hamilton, Jr. "A Typological Future-Mass-Conversion View." In *Three Views on Israel and the Church: Perspectives on Romans 9–11*, eds. Jared Compton and Andrew D. Naselli. Grand Rapids: Kregel, 2018.

Zuck, Roy. "Theology of the Wisdom Books and Song of Songs," *Biblical Theology of the OT*, eds. Roy B. Zuck and Darrell L. Bock. Chicago: Moody Press, 1991.

Ancient Sources

Chrysostom, John, "Homilies of St. John Chrysostom, Archbishop of Constantinople, on the Epistle of St. Paul to the Romans," in *Saint Chrysostom: Homilies on the Acts of the Apostles and the Epistle to the Romans*, ed. Philip Schaff, trans. J. B. Morris, W. H. Simcox, and George B. Stevens, vol. 11, A Select Library of the Nicene and Post-Nicene Fathers of the Christian Church, First Series. New York: Christian Literature Company, 1889.

ABOUT THE AUTHOR

Dr. Steven P. Sullivan is a Distinguished Professor from the College of Biblical Studies-Houston, Texas (CBS) where he taught Bible, Theology, and Ministry skills. He was a pastor for 20 years and now retired from the faculty at CBS after 30 years on March 31, 2022. Steve holds a B.S. in Pharmacy (1973) from the University of Oklahoma. He received his Doctor of Pharmacy (2001) in Oklahoma and is a retired register pharmacist in Oklahoma and Texas. He earned a Master of Theology (1979) in historical theology and a Doctor of Ministry (2000) in pastoral ministry at Dallas Theological Seminary. Steve received a Ph.D. (2015) at the University of Wales Trinity St. David, UK in biblical and theological studies. He has done post-doctoral research at Tyndale House, Cambridge, England. He has published articles in the *Dictionary of Premillennial Theology* (Kregel, 1996), *Evangelical America: An Encyclopedia of Contemporary American Religion Culture* (ABC-CLIO, 2017), and *Scripture, Texts, and Tracings in Romans* (Lexington/Fortress Academic, 2021). He has also published his Ph.D. work with the title *The Isaianic New Exodus in Romans 9-11: A Biblical and Theological Study of Paul's Use of Isaiah in Romans* (Lampion Press, 2017 and 2nd ed. Stone Tower Press, 2023).

Dr. Sullivan was also adjunct professor (2013-2018) at the Bible Seminary in Katy, Texas. He retired to Oklahoma City where he has a teaching ministry in the community and his church and spends much of his time researching and writing. Steve and his wife, Vicki, were married in 1975 and have two grown sons and three granddaughters and two grandsons.